The
Romantic
Spirit

THE ROMANTIC SPIRIT
1990 EDITION

First printing, October 1990

ISBN 0-9610996-4-X

With many thanks to Mother and Pop,
for their help and $upport!

INTRODUCTION

The 1990 Edition of The Romantic Spirit is a
complete revision of the original "Romantic
Spirit" and the three subsequent updates that
have been published. In addition, the 1990
Edition of The Romantic Spirit contains pre-
viously unpublished information that has been
gathered throughout 1989 and 1990. In fact,
this edition contains a collection of data
that spans approximately the past 30 years of
romance.

The purpose of this bibliography is to present
a useful and usable tool for the Romance reader,
the booksellers (both new and used), and for the
collector.

Bracketed names [   ] are reported to be the real
name of the author(s).

The names in parenthises (   ) are the pseudonyms
for the author(s).

The following symbols are used to indicate the type
of subject matter in many of the entries:

<BIOG>	Biography
<CO>	Contemporary
<DNS>	Release Date Not Set
<ED>	Edwardian
<ENG>	Published in England
<GEO>	Georgian
<GOT>	Gothic
<HO>	Historical
<HF>	Historical Fantasy
<HR>	Historical Romance
<HR-REIC>	Historical Reincarnation
<IN>	Intrigue
<INSP>	Inspiration Romance
<M&B>	Mills & Boon
<MED>	Medical
<M-GOT>	Modern Gothic
<MY>	Mystery
<NF>	Non-Fiction
<P&E>	Politics & Espionage
<PROM>	Promotional
<RA>	Romantic Adventure
<RE>	Regency

\<RE-IN\>	Regency Intrigue
\<REM\>	Regency Mystery
\<RF\>	Romantic Fantasy
\<RM\>	Romantic Mystery
\<RS\>	Romantic Suspense
\<RW\>	Romantic Western
\<SAGA\>	Family Saga
\<SN\>	Supernatural
\<T-T\>	Time Travel
\<TMC\>	Title May Change
\<VIC\>	Victorian

The following symbols, @, #, $, %, ^, &, *, +, =, <, >, signify an attempt to identify the titles of books with spin-off or connecting characters.

Certain enclosed initals following a book title indicate that the book is part of a series. Also, in recent years, romance books have developed "series within series". These books, by one or more author, are listed throughout The Romantic Spirit alpha-betically by the series name. These books are also listed under the author(s) name. If "In sequence" is inserted before the title, these books should be read in the sequence listed.

Below is a key to those initials which appear next to the "series" books:

\<AAS\>	Americans Abroad Series
\<AES\>	American Explorers Series
\<AIS\>	American Indian Series
\<ATS\>	American Tribute Series
\<AWD\>	A Woman's Destiny
\<BGS\>	Birthstone Gothic Series
\<BZS\>	Berkley Zodiac Gothic
\<CCS\>	Calloway Corners Series-Harlequin SuperRomance
\<CGS\>	Cameo Gothic Series
\<CofCW\>	Cities Of The Civil War
\<CIFK\>	Christmas Is For Kids-Harlequin American
\<COAR\>	Century Of American Romance-Harlequin American
\<CMS\>	Cajun Melodies Series-Harlequin American

\<DJC\>	Diamond Jubilee Collection- Silhouette Romance
\<DTR\>	Deane Sisters Trilogy- Harlequin Intrigue
\<FWS\>	Frontier Women Saga
\<GARS\>	Golden Age Of Rome Series
\<GCT\>	Gull Cottage Trilogy- Harlequin American
\<HofFS\>	Hall Of Fame Series
\<HofCS\>	Heart Of The City Series
\<IMS\>	Immigration Sagas
\<L&L\>	Leather And Lace
\<MEQ\>	Montclair Emeralds Quartet- Harlequin Temptation
\<MOAS\>	Making Of America Series
\<MMS\>	Man Of The Month Series- Silhouette Desire
\<RMMS\>	Rocky Mountain Magic Series Harlequin American
\<RWS\>	Rivers West Series
\<TCS\>	Thirteen Colonies Series
\<WOW\>	Women Of The West
\<WWT\>	Women West Trilogy
\<WWWW\>	Women Who Won The West
\<ZGS\>	Zodiac Gothic Series

Series Abbreviations:

\<C\>	Candlelight
\<CE\>	Candlelight Ecstasy
\<CES\>	Candlelight Ecstasy Supreme
\<HQR\>	Harlequin Romance
\<HRS\>	Harlequin Reader Serivce
\<HQP\>	Harlequin Presents
\<HAR\>	Harlequin American
\<HQT\>	Harlequin Temptation
\<HI\>	Harlequin Intrigue
\<HSR\>	Harlequin SuperRomance
\<LS\>	Loveswept
\<SCAL\>	Second Chance At Love
\<R\>	Silhouette Romance
\<SD\>	Silhouette Desire
\<IM\>	Silhouette Intimate Moments
\<SSE\>	Silhouette Special Edition
\<SR\>	SuperRomance - Worldwide

An endeavor has been made to keep this bibliography as uncomplicated and readable as possible.
Publishers are not listed with each book because
(1) many books are no longer being published and
(2) many books have been published by more than one
house. To learn the status of any book, call your
local new or used book dealer.

Every effort has been made and every resource
available has been used to unsure the accuracy
of The Romantic Spirit. HOWEVER, THERE IS NO
GUARANTEE THAT ALL INFORMATION IS INCLUDED, OR
THAT DESCREPANCIES MAY NOT EXIST. I hope you find
The Romantic Spirit both informative and enjoyable.
Feel free to write and let me know. All comments
are welcome.

Lisa Miller
LAM Enterprises
P. O. Box 5571
San Antonio, TX 78230

AALLYN, Alysse
           [Melissa Clark]
Devlyn

AARON, Anna
  Sweet Dreams: <YA>
    40 Secrets

ABBEY, Anne Merton   <HR>
               [Jean Brooks]
        [Jean Brooks-Janowiak]
  Kathryn: In The Court Of Six
    Queens

ABBEY, Christina
  [John Sawyer w/ Nancy
          Buckingham Sawyer]
  Candlelight:
    157 Pattern Of Loving
    162 Time For Trusting

ABBEY, Margaret
      [Margaret Elizabeth York]
  Amber Promise
  Bridgetown Maid, The
  Brother-in-Arms
  Crowned Boar, The
  Francesca
  Girdle Of Amber
  Flight Of The Kestrel, The
  Shadow Of The Tower Series:
    Warwick Heiress   3
    Son Of York   4

ABBEY, Ruth   <GOT><RS>
            [Ruth Pattison]
  Bridge Of Tears
  Evil At Nunnery Manor
  Portrait Of Doubt
  Prisoner Of The Manor
  Shadow Between, The

ABBOTT, Alice   <GOT>
  [Kathryn Kilby Borland w/
      Helen Ross Smith Speicher]
  Goodbye Julie Scott
  Third Tower, The

ABBOTT, Jane Worth
  [Virginia Myers w/Stella Cameron]
  Harlequin SuperRomance:
    In Sequence:
  192   Faces Of A Clown
  223   Choices
  263   Yes Is Forever

ABBOTT, Jeanne   <RE>
        [Diane J. A. Monarch]
  Substitute Bridegroom, The

ABBOTT, Jennie
        [Diane J. A. Monarch]
  Turning Points: <YA>
    8 Wish For Tonight, A

ABBOTT, Rose Marie
  Candlelight:
    662 Bride Of Vengeance   <RE>

ABBOTT, Sandra
　　Castle Of Evil
　　River And The Rose, The
　　Whispering Gables

_____

_____

ABEL, Dorothy Leigh
　　Rhapsody Romance:
　　　Candy Shoppe, The
　　　Until Then
　　　Whisper Of Love, The

_____

_____

ABELS, Harriette S.
　　　　　　　[Harriette Sheffer Abels]
　　Avalon:
　　　Follow Me, Love
　　Caprice Romance:　　　　　　<YA>
　　　 9　Special Love, A
　　　18　New Love For Lisa, A
　　　44　Cupid Confusion
　　　50　First Impression
　　　62　Good Sport, A
　　　74　Lucky In Love

_____

_____

ABRAHAMSEN, Christine Elizabeth
　　　　　　　　　(Kathleen Westcott)

ABSALOM, Stacy
　　Harlequin Presents:
　　　943　Ishbel's Party
　　Harlequin Romance:
　　　2581　Knave of Hearts
　　　2671　Passion And The Pain, The
　　　2689　Dark Night Dawning

_____

_____

ACASTER, Linda
　　Harlequin Historical <Set#1>:
　　　5　Hostage Of The Heart

_____

_____

ACKWORTH, Robert
　　　　　　　[Robert Charles Ackworth]
　　　　　　　　　(Roberta Ackworth)
　　Candlelight:
　　　32　North Country Nurse

_____

_____

ACKWORTH, Roberta
　　　　　　　　[Robert Ackworth]
　　Mary Winters, Student Nurse

_____

_____

ADAIR, Dennis w/ Janet ROSENSTOCK
　　Story of Canada:　　　　　<HS>
　　　In sequence:
　　　　Kanata
　　　　Bitter Shield
　　　　Thundergate
　　　　Wildfires
　　　　Victoria (end)

_____

_____

ADAMS, Alice
　　　　　　　　[Alice Boyd Adams]
　　Beautiful Girl
　　Careless Love
　　Families And Survivors
　　Listening To Billie
　　Rich Rewards
　　To See You Again

_____

_____

ADAMS, Alicia
　　MacFadden Romance:
　　　28　Lovewinds
　　　66　Moonlit Sands
　　　76　Sweet Innocent

_____

_____

ALAN, Jane

(Lilian Chisholm)
(Anne Lorraine)
Harlequin Romance:
924　Doctor Jonathan

AIRLIE, Catherine
[Jean S. MacLeod]
Harlequin Classic:
69　Country Of The Heart
Harlequin Romance:
789　Country Of The Heart
979　Doctor Overboard
1062　One Summer's Day
1081　Nurse Jane In Teneriffe
1141　Valley Of Desire, The
1170　Red Lotus
1202　Land Of Heart's Desire
1240　Green Rushes, The
1258　Nobody's Child
1288　Last Of The Kintyres, The
1328　Wind Sighing, A
1352　Mountain Of Stars, The
1370　Ways Of Love, The
1464　Unlived Year, The

ALBANO, Peter
(Andrea Robbins)
Waves Of Glory

ALBRAND, Martha　　(Deceased)<RS>
[Mrs. Sydney J. Lamon]
After Midnight
Call From Austria, A
Day In Monte Carlo, A
Desperate Moment
Endure No Longer
Final Encore
Hunted Woman, The
Linden Affair, The
Manhatten North
Mask Of Alexander, The
Meet Me Tonight
Nightmare In Copenhagen
No Surrender
None Shall Know
Obsession Of Emmet Booth, The
Remembered Anger
Rhine Replica
Taste Of Terror, A
Wait For The Dawn
Whispering Hill
Without Orders
Zurich AZ900

AITKEN, Kate
Harlequin Romance:
768　Never A Day So Bright

AKS, Patricia　　　　　　　<YA>
Dreamboy For Katie, A
New Kind Of Love, A
Searching Heart, The
Two Worlds Of Jill, The
First Love From Silhouette:
47　Three Weeks Of Love
Two By Two Romance:
3　Change Of Heart
Wildfire:　　　　　　　　<YA>
In sequence:
Junior Prom
Senior Prom

ALBRIGHT, Elizabeth　　　<RE>
[Karen Lahey]
Noble Ambition, A

6

ALBRITTON, Carol w/Patricia MAXWELL
        (Elizabeth Trehearne)

ALCOTT, Cynthia   <RS>
Dudgeons Of Crowly Hall, The
Storm Over Windmere

ALCOTT, Julia
                [Edythe Cudlipp]
Long Lost Love, A
Adventures In Love:
   17 Island Of Love
   20 Key To Her Heart, The

ALDEN, Dion
Reckless Dreamer   <CO>

ALDEN, Elizabeth
                [Charlene Joy Galbot]
Silhouette Desire:
   225 No Sense Of Humor
Silhouette Romance:
   366 Never Say Never

ALDEN, Sue
Avalon:
   Nurse Of St. John
   Magnificent Challenge, The

ALDERTON, Therese   <RE>
                [Theresa Grazia]
Crimson Deception
Second Season

ALDRIDGE, Dawn
Magic Moments: <YA>
   9 Song For Mandy, A

ALERDING, Kathy
             [Kathleen Puyear-Alerding]
Candlelight Ecstasy:
   355 Calling The Shots
Candlelight Ecstasy Supreme:
    91 Bending The Rules
   111 With Open Arms

ALERS, Rochelle
Starlight Romance:
   Careless Whispers

ALEXANDER, Bea
First Love From Silhouette: <YA>
   44 Someone Like Jeremy Vaughn
   69 Advice And Consent
   85 In The Long Run
Silhouette Inspirations:
   10 Inlet Of The Heart

ALEXANDER, Donna
                [Donna Kimel Vitek]
MacFadden Romance:
    98 Red Roses, White Lilies
   103 Lover's Question, A
   117 No Turning Back
   128 In From The Storm

ALEXANDER, Jan   <GOT><RS>
                [Victor Jerome Banis]
Bishop's Palace, The
Blood Ruby   <BGS:#7>

7

ALEXANDER, Jan (cont.)
  Blood Moon
  Darkwater
  Devil's Dance, The
  Girl Who Never Was, The
  Glass House
  Glass Painting, The
  House Of Fools
  Haunting Of Helen Wren, The
  House At Rose Point, The
  Green Willows
  Jade Figurines, The
  Lion's Gate, The   <BZG>
  Moon Garden
  Second House
  Shadows
  Wolves Of Craywood, The
  White Jade

_____

_____

ALEXANDER, Jean
  Nurse In South America

_____

_____

ALEXANDER, Karen   <HR>
  Palaces Of Desire

_____

_____

ALEXANDER, Kate   <HR>
                   [Tilly Armstrong]
  Fields Of Battle
  Friends And Enemies
  Paths Of Peace

_____

_____

ALEXANDER, Marsha   <CO>
          [Marsha Durchin Alexander]
  All Mine To Give
  Royal Suite
  Harlequin SuperRomance:
    189 Whispers In Eden

_____

_____

ALEXANDER, Megan
                [Mildred Teague Fish]
  SuperRomance:
    17 Contract For Marriage
    95 Blossoms In The Snow
  Harlequin SuperRomance:
    230 Once A Stranger
    285 Dilemma
    377 Words Of Wisdom
    413 Silver Gifts, Golden
         Dreams

_____

_____

ALEXANDER, Serena
                   [Alice Ramirez]
  Second Chance At Love:
    8 Rapture Regained

_____

_____

ALEXANDER, Susan
  Harlequin Presents:
    499 Wedding In The Family
    719 Marriage Contract, The
    807 Temporary Husband
    1031 Winter Sunlight

_____

_____

ALEXANDER, Trisha
                       [Pat Kay]
  Silhouette Special Edition:
    640 Cinderella Girl

_____

_____

ALEXIE, Angela   <HR>
              [Angela Dunton Talias]
  Sometimes A Stranger   <CO>
  Treacherous Heart, The
  Velvet Thorn, The
  Harlequin SuperRomance:
    140 More Than Yesterday

_____

_____

8

ALGERMISSEN, Jo Ann
                    (Anna Hudson)
Harlequin American Romance:
   64 Capture The Sun
Harlequin Historical <Set#2>:
   56 Golden Bird
Silhouette Desire:
   246 Naughty But Nice
   276 Challenge The Fates
   300 Serendipity Samantha
   318 Hank's Woman
   361 Made In America
   409 Lucky Lady
   486 Butterfly
   539 Bedside Manner
   559 Sunshine
Silhouette Special Edition:
   374 Purple Diamonds
   455 Blue Emeralds
   542 Paper Stars
   607 Best Man
   655 Would You Marry Me
                    Anyway?

ALLAN, Jeanne
                    (Jeanne Allen)
Harlequin Romance:
   2845 When Love Flies By
   2875 Waiting Heart, The
   2899 Game Is Love, The
   2935 Trust In Love
   2989 One Reckless Moment
   3073 Bluebirds In The Spring

ALLAN, Margaret
   Incomers, The

ALLARDYCE, Paula   <RE>
                    [Ursula Torday]
   Carradine Affair, The
   Eliza
   Emily

ALLARDYCE, Paula (cont.)
   Gentleman Rogue
   Haunting Me
   Legacy Of Pride
   Miss Philadelphia Smith
   Moonlighters, The
   My Dear Miss Emma
   Octavia
   Paradise Row
   Rebel Lover, The
   Rogue's Lady, The   <GEO>
   Shadowed Love
   Vixen's Revenge, The
   Waiting At The Church

ALLEN, Anita   <GOT>
                    [Anita Allen Schenck]
   False Face Of Death, The
   Spell Of Ghoti, The
   Thunder Rock

ALLEN, Barbara
                    [Vivian Stuart Mann]
Harlequin Romance:
   1159 Gay Gordons, The
   1186 Someone Else's Heart

ALLEN, Barbara   <CS>
   Time Is A Lover

ALLEN, Catherine R. w/
                    Dorothea JENSEN
                    (Catherine Moorhouse)

ALLEN, Charlotte Vale   <CO>
   Acts Of Kindness
   Another Kind Of Magic
   Becoming
   Destinies
       (HB: The Marmalade Man)

9

ALLEN, Charlotte Vale (cont.)
  Dream Train
  Gentle Stranger
  Gifts Of Love
  Hidden Meanings
  Illusions
  Intimate Friends
  Julia's Sister
  Love Life
  Matters Of The Heart
  Meet Me In Time
  Memories
  Mixed Emotions
  Moments Of Meaning
  Night Magic
  Painted Lives
  Pieces Of Dreams
  Promises
  Running Away
  Sweeter Music
  Time Steps
  Times Of Triumph

ALLEN, D. H.
                (Marianne Montgomery)

ALLEN, Danice Jo
                    (Emily Dalton)

ALLEN, Elisabeth Offutt
  Hounds Of The Moon, The
  Petals From The Dogwood Tree
  Avalon:
    Skip To My Loo, My Darling

ALLEN, Elizabeth Evelyn   <HR>
  Freedom Fire
  Lady Anne, The
  Rebel
  Witch Woman
   In Sequence:
     To Fortune Born
     Bright Destiny

ALLEN, Emily Ann w/ Diana REEP
                        (Diana Reep)

ALLEN, Erika Vaughn
  Adventures In Love:
    18 Voices In The Wind

ALLEN, Hervey   <HO>
     [William Hervey Allen, Jr.]
  Anthony Adverse: In Sequence:
    Roots Of The Tree, The
    Other Bronze Boy, The
    Lonely Twin, The
  City In The Dawn Series:
    In Sequence:
      Forest And The Fort, The
      Bedford Village
      Toward The Morning

ALLEN, Jeanne
                (see Jeanne Allan)
  Harlequin Romance:
    2665 Peter's Sister

ALLEN, Laine
                [Elaine Lakso]
  Second Chance At Love:
    276 Undercover Kisses
    304 Fire Within, The
    346 Tangling With Webb
    404 Courting Trouble
    445 Friendly Persuasion

ALLEN, Mary Elizabeth
                    (Kitty Grey)

ALLEN, Sheila Rosalynd <RE>
    (Sheila O'Hallion)
The Lovers Ot Steadford
Abbey Series:
  Reluctant Ghost, The   I
  Meddlesome Ghost, The   II
  Helpful Ghost, The   III
  Passionate Ghost, The   IV

ALLENDE, Isabel   <CO>
Eva Luna
House Of The Spirits, The <CS>
Of Love And Shadows

ALLISON, Elizabeth
       [Alice Harron Orr]
Rapture Romance:
  24 Dance Of Desire

ALLISON, Heather
    [Hether MacAllister]
Harlequin Romance:
  3091 Deck The Halls

ALLISON, Moeth
     [Mollie Aghadjian]
Silhouette Imtimate Moments:
    8 Love Everlasting
   43 Russian Roulette
  102 Every Other Weekend
  111 Soft Touch

ALLISON, Penny
         [Carol Katz]
Silhouette Desire:
  20 King Of Diamonds
  65 Reckless Venture
 143 North Country Nights

ALLISON, Penny (cont.)
Silhouette Romance:
 271 Night Train To Paradise

ALLISTER, Barbara   <RE>
        [Barbara Teer]
Captivated Countess, The
Frustrated Bridegroom, The
Midnight Bride
Mischevious Matchmaker, The
Prudent Partnership, The
Temporary Husband, The

ALLYN, Ashley   <HR>
       [Susan Leslie]
Channing Hall
(Third book in the trilogy)
(See Evelyn Gray)

ALLYN, Jennifer
Love & Life:
  Forgiveness

ALLYNE, Kerry
Harlequin Presents:
  361 Bindaburra Outstation
  513 Coral Cay
  743 Legally Bound
  783 Tropical Eden
Harlequin Romance:
 2019 Summer Rainfall
 2094 Bound For Marandoo
 2184 Tuesday's Jillaroo
 2205 Wool King, The
 2248 West Of The Waminda
 2283 Plains Of Promise, The
 2323 Across The Great Divide
 2341 Sweet Harvest
 2389 Challenge, The

ALLYNE, Kerry
  2407 Reunion At Pitereeka
  2479 Mixed Feelings
  2515 Valley Of Lagoons
  2527 Spring Fever
  2593 Somewhere To Call Home
  2647 Time To Forget
  2725 Merringannee Bluff
  2737 Return To Wallaby Creek
  2761 Stranger In Town
  2809 Tullagindi Rodeo, The
  2869 Carpentaria Moon
  2929 Losing Battle
  2947 Beneath Wimmera Skies
  2990 Man Of The High Plains
  3037 Dark Memories

ALLYSON, Kym   <GOT>
          [John M. Kimbro]
Moon Shadow, The   <BZG>

ALRED, Margaret
           (Anne Saunders)

ALSOBROOK, Rosalyn   <HR>
        (see Gina Delaney)
  Desire's Gamble
  Emerald Storm
  Ecstasy's Fire
  Elusive Caress
  Runaway Bride
  Thorn Bush Blooms, The
  Wanton Bride
  Wild Western Bride
  Harlequin American Romance:
    63 Tiny Flaw, A
   103 All Or Nothing

ALSOBROOK, Rosalyn W/ Jean HAUGHT
         (Jalynn Friends)

ALTER, Eric
Valley, The   <HS>

AMANN, Marilyn Medlock
        (Amanda Stevens)

AMERICANS ABROAD SERIES (AAS>
  Crystal Rapture
          Sarah Edwards
  Passion's Tempest
          Emma Harrington
  Desert Enchantress
          Laurel Collins
  Sapphire Moon
          Peggy Cross
  Passion's Song
          Carolyn Jewel
  Ivory Temptress
          Emma Harrington
  Silken Roses
          Elane Osborne
  Rapture's Legacy
          Susan Phillips
  Twice Promised
          Nancy Knight
  Fire And Sand
          Sarah Edwards

AMERICAN EXPLORERS SERIES <AES><HO>
  1 Jed Smith: Freedom River
          Fred Lawrence
  2 Lewis & Clark: Northwest Glory
          James Raymond
  3 Jim Bridger: Mountain Man
          Laura Parker
  4 Daniel Boone: Westward Trail
          Neal Barrett, Jr.
  5 John Fremont: California Bound
          Michael Beahan

AMERICAN EXPLORERS SERIES (cont.)
6 Kit Carson: Trapper King
                     Laura Parker
7 Zebulon Pike: Pioneer Destiny
                   Richard Woodley
8 Marcus Whitman:
   Frontier Mission
                        Greg Hunt
9 Francis Parkman:
   Dakota Legend
                     Randall King
10 Escalante: Wilderness Path
                   Peter T. Blairson
11 Davy Crockett:
   Frontier Fighter
                     Lee Bishop
12 Alexander Mackenzie:
   Lone Courage
                        Guy Forve
13 John Bozeman:
   Mountain Journey
                        Greg Hunt
14 Joseph Walker:
   Frontier Sheriff
                     Fred Lawrence

_____

_____

AMERICAN INDIAN SERIES: <AIS><HO>
1 Comanche Revenge
                     Jeanne Sommers
2 Blackfoot Ambush
                   Catherine Weber
3 Crow Warriors
                    Bill Hotchkiss
4 Chippewa Daughter
                     Jane Toombs
5 Creek Rifles
                   Peter Hansen
6 Cheyenne Raiders
                  Jackson O'Reilly
7 Cherokee Mission
                    Karl Meyer
8 Apache War Cry
                   Donald Porter
9 Sioux Arrows
                   Donald Porter
10 Nez Perce Legend
                  Mick Clumpner
11 Kiowa Fires
                   Donald Porter

AMERICAN INDIAN SERIES (cont.)
12 Shoshone Thunder
   Bill Hotchkiss w/
                     Judith Shears
13 Arapaho Spirit
                     Jane Toombs
14 Pawnee Medicine
   Bill Hotchkiss w/
                     Judith Shears

_____

_____

AMERICAN TRIBUTE SERIES: <ATS>
(Oklahoma)
Silhouette Special Edition:
289 Love's Haunting Refrain
                     Ada Steward
295 This Long Winter Past
                   Jeanne Stephens
301 Right Behind The Rain
                     Elaine Camp
307 Cherokee Fire
                     Gena Dalton
313 Nobody's Fool
                     Renee Roszel
319 Misty Morning, Magic
     Nights   Ada Steward

_____

AMERSKI, Beth
                     (Beth Stanley)

AMES, Angela Taylor   <CO>
   Diane
   Eve
   Joy

_____

AMES, Jennifer
           [Jennifer Greig-Smith]
   Doctor Ted's Clinic
   Dr. Brad's Nurse
   Jilted
   Love Will Win
   Nurse's Holiday

AMES, Jennifer (cont.)
Rich Twin, Poor Twin
Avalon:
Reluctant Cinderella, The

AMES, Leslie   <GOT>
                [W. E. Daniel Ross]
Angry Wind, The
Bride Of Donnybrook
Hidden Chapel, The
Hill Of Ashes, The   <CO>
Hungry Sea, The
King's Castle
Phantom Bride, The
Wind Over The Citadel
NOTE: Orlando Joseph Rigoni also
    wrote as "Leslie Ames".

AMES, Norma   <RS>
My Path Belated
Whisper In The Forrest

AMES, Rachel
                (Sarah Gainham)

AMES, Winter   <RE>
                [Phyllis Taylor Pianka]
Second Chance At Love:
    7   Emerald Bay
    18 Bird Of Paradise

AMIEL, Joseph
Birthright
Deeds

ANASTASI, Agatha Della
Caporetto
Time For Roses, A   <HS>

ANDERS, Jeanne
Serenade/Serenata: <Insp>
    24 Language Of The Heart

ANDERS, Julia
Candlelight:
    622 Counterfeit Honeymoon <RO>

ANDERSEN, Jan
Storm Castle   <GOT>
Harlequin Romance:
    1387 House Called
            Green Bays, The
    1499 Silent Moon, The
    1532 Man In The Shadow, The
    1709 Man From Coral Bay, The
    1838 Master Of Koros
    1872 Cinnamon Hill

ANDERSEN, Linda
Passion's Price
Heartfire Romance: <HR>
    Temptation's Touch

ANDERSEN, Susan
Lovestruck:
    Shadow Dance   <RS>

ANDERSON, Ann   <RS>
Affair At Timber Lake, The
House Of Gold

ANDERSON, Blaine   <HR>
    [Blaine Aislinn Anderson]
Lovestruck:
    Destiny's Kiss
    Love's Sweet Captive

ANDERSON, Catherine
    [Adeline Catherine Anderson]
Harlequin Intrigue:
    92 Reasonable Doubt
    114 Without A Trace
    135 Switchback

ANDERSON, Gail
Harlequin SuperRomance:
    272 Orchid Moon

ANDERSON, Juanita B. w/
                Nickolea GERSTNER
    No Bed In Deseret   <HO>

ANDERSON, Ken
A Hearth Romance:
    1 Doctor's Return, The

ANDERSON, Lee
Avalon:
    Body In The Attic, The
    Deadly Errand
    Family Secrets
    Love's Tender Challenge
    Smile In The Sun

ANDERSON, Marlene J.
                    (Joan Lancaster)
ANDERSON, Robert
    After

ANDERSON, Roberta w/ Mary KUCZKIR
                    (Fern Michaels)

ANDERSON, Shirley Lord
                    (Shirley Lord)

ANDERSON, Sue Lynn   <GOT>
    Shadows Across The Bayou

ANDERSON, Susan M.   <HR>
                    (Lindsay Randall)
    Stolen Dreams

ANDERSON, Virginia
                    (Megan Ashe)

ANDERSSON, C. Dean w/
                Nina Romberg ANDERSSON
                    (Asa Drake)

ANDRAU, Marianne
Mystique:
    84 Tangled Web, A
    97 Love's Testimony
    107 Out Of The Night
    112 By Love Betrayed
    151 Emerald Pool, The
    155 Mask Of Destiny
    161 Dark Persuasion

ANDRE, Alix
Mystique:
    4 Island Of Deceit
    26 Ghosts Of Ardnamore

ANDREWS, Stephanie
  Dawn Of Love: <YA><HO>
    4 Fearless Love

ANDREWS, Susan
  Harlequin American Romance:
    206 Fair Game

ANDREWS, Windy
  Two Hearts Romance: <YA>
    Vacation Fever

ANDREZEL, Pierre   <RS>(Deceased)
  [Karen Christentzen
                Dinesen Blixen]
  Angelic Avengers, The

ANGELL, Jeanette
  Straight On Till Morning
  West With The Night
  In sequence: <Saga>
    Wings
    Flight

ANGLIN, Joyce
  Loveswept:
    373 Feeling The Flame

ANKRUM, Barbara   <HR>
  Heartfire Romance:
    Passion's Prize

ANNABELLA   <HR>
                    [Charlotte Lowe]
  Passion's Pawn
  Polreath Women, The

ANNADALE, Barbara
                      [Jean Bowden]
  Bonnet Laird's Daughter, The
  French Lady's Lover, The

ANNE-MARIEL
                      [Anne Goud]
  Embrace My Scarlet Heart   <Saga>
  One Evening I Shall Return
  Rendezvous In Peking
  Tigress Of The Evening

ANSLE, Dorothy Phoebe
                    (Laura Conway)
                      (Hebe Elsna)
             (Vicky Lancaster-Eng.)
               (Lyndon Snow-Eng.)

ANSTON, Linell
            [Linell Evanston Nemeth]
  Harlequin Regency Romance:
    26 Lady Elizabeth

ANTHONY, Diane
                    [Diane Antonio]
  Once A Lover
  Out Of A Dream
  Sweet Indulgence

ANTHONY, Evelyn   <HO>
  [Evelyn Bridget Patricia
            Stephens Ward-Thomas]
  All The Queens Men
  Anne Boleyn
  Cardinal And The Queen
  Charles The King
  House Of Vandekar, The
  Legend, The
  Rendezvous, The
  Valentina
  Victor And Albert
  In sequence:
    Clandara
    French Bride, The
  Trilogy:
    Rebel Princess
    Royal Intrigue
    Far Flies The Eagle   <GOT><RS>
  Assassin, The
  Grave Of Truth, The
  Janus Imperative, The
  Mission To Malaspiga
  Occupying Power, The
  Persian Price, The
  Place To Hide, A
  Poellenberg Inheritance, The
  Return, The
  Scarlet Thread, The
  Silver Falcon, The
  Stranger At The Gates
  Tamarind Seed, The
  Voices On The Wind
  In sequence:
    Defector, The
    Company Of Saints, The

ANTHONY, Page
          [Page & Anthony Traynor]
  To Love Forever

ANTONIO, Diane
                (Diana Anthony)
                (Diana Lyndon)

ANZELON, Robyn
  Harlequin Gothic Romance:
    Goblin Tree, The
  Mystique:
    137 Goblin Tree, The
  SuperRomance:
    49 Forever Spell, The
  Harlequin SuperRomance:
    120 Sandcastle Dreams
    198 Searching

APPLEGATE, Katherine
                (Katherine Kendall)

APPLEYARD, Susan   <HR>
  King's White Rose, The
  Sultan's Red Rose, The

ARBOR, Jane
  Harlequin Classic:
     15 Sandflower   (576)
     19 Queen's Nurse   (524)
     31 By Yet Another Door
     70 Jasmine Harvest   (780)
     83 Nurse Of All Work   (690)
     96 Lake Of Shadows   (887)
    115 No Silver Spoon   (832)
    119 Towards The Dawn   (474)
    128 Dear Intruder   (919)
    173 Golden Apple Island   (1182)
  Harlequin Premiere Edition:
      8 Flash Of Emerald
  Harlequin Romance:
    780 Jasmine Harvest
    801 Desert Nurse
    832 No Silver Spoon
    858 No Lease For Love
    887 Lake Of Shadows
    919 Dear Intruder
    950 Kingfisher Tide
   1000 Girl Named Smith, A
   1048 High Master Of Clere

ARLEN, Leslie (cont.)
  Hope And Glory
  Rage And Desire
  Fortune And Fury

_____

_____

ARLISS, Joen   <GOT><RS>
  Beloved Victim
  Nightmare's Nest
  Shadow Over Seventh Heaven

_____

_____

ARMITAGE, Aileen
                    [Aileen Quigley]
  Hawksmoor   <Epic>

_____

_____

ARMSTRONG, Carolyn T.
  Honeysuckle Love   <L&L:#6>

_____

_____

ARMSTRONG, Charlotte   (Deceased)
          [Charlotte Armstrong Lewi]
                      (Jo Valentine)
                           <GOT><RS>
  Baloon Man, The
  Better To Eat You, The
  Black-Eyed Stranger, The
  Case Of The Weird Sisters, The
  Catch-As-Catch-Can
  Chocolate Cobweb, The
  Dram Of Poison, A
  Dream Of Fair Women
  Dream Walker, The
  Friday's Child
  Gift Shop, The
  Girl With A Secret, The
  I See You
  Incident In A Corner
  Innocent Flower, The
  Lay On, MacDuff
  Lemon In The Basket
  Little Less Then Kind, A
  Mark Of The Hand, The

ARMSTRONG, Charlotte (cont.)
  Mask Of Evil
  Mischief
  One-Faced Girl, The
  Protege, The
  Seven Seats To The Moon
  Something Blue
  Trouble In Thor, The
  Turret Room, The
  Unsuspected
  Witch's House, The
  Who's Been Sitting In My Chair?

_____

ARMSTRONG, Evelyn Stewart   <HR>
  Daughter Of Valdoro
  Valdoro's Mistress
  Harlequin Historical <Set#1>:
    9 Keepsake, The

_____

ARMSTRONG, Juliet
  Harlequin Classic:
    54 Singing Flame, The
    91 I'll Never Marry   (681)
  Harlequin Romance:
    892 House Of The Swallows, The
    938 Doctor Is Indifferent, The
   1066 Nurse At Ste. Monique
   1136 Pride You Trampled, The
   1220 Isle Of The Hummingbird
   1322 Wind Through The Vineyards
   1493 Orange Blossom Island
   1585 Flowering Valley, The
   1694 Tideless Sea, The

_____

_____

ARMSTRONG, Lindsay
  Harlequin Presents:
    559 Melt A Frozen Heart
    607 Enter My Jungle
    806 Saved From Sin
    871 Finding Out

ARMSTRONG, Lindsay (cont.)
887 Love Me Not
927 An Elusive Mistress
951 Surrender, My Heart
983 Standing On The Outside
1039 Shadow Of Moonlight, The
1071 Reluctant Wife
1095 When You Leave Me
1183 Heat Of The Moment
1295 One More Night
1327 Love Affair, A
Harlequin Romance:
2443 Spitfire
2497 My Dear Innocent
2582 Perhaps Love
2653 Don't Call It Love
2785 Some Say Love
2876 Heart of The Matter, The
2893 When The Night Grows Cold
3013 Marrying Game, The

ARMSTRONG, Thomas
                    (Noreen O'Neill)

ARMSTRONG, Tilly
                    (Kate Alexander)
                    (Tania Langley)
Candlelight:
582 Joy Runs High   <RO>

ARNETT, Caroline   <RE>
        [Lois Dwight Cole Taylor]
Claudia
Melinda
Stephanie
Theodora
Coventry:
65 Christina
Coventry Classic:
Clarissa

ARNOLD, Francena
A Hearth Romance:
2 Deepening Stream, The
3 Fruit For Tomorrow
4 Light In My Window

ARNOLD, Judith
                    [Barbara Keiler]
Harlequin American Romance:
104 Come Home To Love
120 Modern Man, A
130 Flowing To The Sky
139 Jackpot
149 Special Delivery
163 Man And Wife
189 Best Friends
Keeping The Faith Trilogy:
201 Promises
205 Commitments
209 Dreams
225 Comfort And Joy
240 Twilight
255 Going Back
259 Harvest The Sun   <XTS>
281 One Whiff Of Scandal
304 Turning Tables
330 Survivors
342 Lucky Penny
362 Change Of Life
378 One Good Turn
389 Loverboy, A   <COAR>
Harlequin SuperRomance:
460 Raising The Stakes
Harlequin Temptation:
122 On Love's Trail

ARNOLD, Margot   <HR>
[Petronelle Marguerite Mary Cook]
Affairs Of State
Love Among The Allies   <CO>
Marie
Officer's Woman, The
Villa On The Palatine, The
Zadok's Treasure

ARNOUT, Susan
  Frozen Lady, The   <HS>

_____

_____

ARROYA, Santana   <HR>
      [Stephen Joseph Arroyo]
  Bright Glows The Dawn

_____

_____

ARTHUR, Elaine
  First Love From Silhouette: <YA>
  56 Romance In Store

_____

_____

ARTHUR, Katherine
                [Barbara Eriksen]
  Harlequin Romance:
  2755 Cinderella Wife
  2821 Road To Love
  2905 Forecast Of Love
  2948 Send Me No Flowers
  2971 Remember In Jamaica
  2991 Through Eyes Of Love
  3014 Loving Deceiver
  3043 Mountain Lovesong
  3061 One More Secret
  3103 To Tame A Cowboy

_____

_____

ARTHUR, Lee   <HO>
  Mer-Lion, The

_____

_____

ARTHUR, Phyllis
  Mirror Of Time
  Avalon:
    Goddess In The Home

_____

_____

ARVONEN, Helen   <GOT><RS>
  Circle Of Death
  Choice Of Angels, A
  Doorway To Death
  Garden Of Grief
  Least Of All Evils, The
  Remember With Tears
  Rickshaw Bend
  Shadow Of The Truth
  Sorrow For Angels, A
  Stranger In Her House
  Summer Of Evil, The
  Whistle At My Window
  Witches Of Brimstone Hill, The

_____

_____

ASCANI, Sparky
  The Avon Romance:
    Ransomed Heart, The

_____

ASH, Kathleen
  Second Chance At Love:
  77 Beyond Pride

_____

ASH, Melissa
                  [June E. Casey]
  Dawnstar Romance:
    Promises In The Sand

_____

_____

ASH, Pauline
  Harlequin Romance:
  833   Seaside Hospital
  916   Doctor Vannard's Patients
  970   Challenge To Nurse Honor
  1033 With Love From Dr. Lucien
  1065 Student Nurse At Swale
  1113 Bequest For Nurse Barbara
  1161 Doctor Napier's Nurse
  1249 Doctor Arnold's Ambition
  1289 Much-Loved Nurse, The

_____

_____

ASH, Rosalie
  Harlequin Romance:
    Melting Ice   HRS55

ASHBY, Juliet
  [Louise Lee Outlaw-Shallit]
  Silhouette Romance:
    162 One Man Forever
    258 Midnight Lover
    279 Dream Of Passion

ASHBY, Kay   <GOT><RS>
  Briarwood
  Climb A Dark Cliff
  Cold Chill Of Coptos
  Crown Valley
  Marcadia

ASHBY, Nora
  Gone From Breezy Hill   <Saga>

ASHCROFT, Laura   <HS>
          [Janice Carlson]
  Heart Of Fire

ASHE, Douglas   <GOT>
      [John Franklin Bardin]
  Longstreet Legacy, The

ASHE, Megan
        [Virginia Anderson]
  Rapture Romance:
    46 Mountain Man, A
    83 Lightning Touch, The

ASHE, Rosalind   <RS>
  Black Wind
  Hurricane Wake, The
  Moths
  Star-Crossed

ASHER, Inez
  Family Sins

ASHER, Miriam   <GOT>
  Nightmare In Eden

ASHFIELD, Helen   <RE>
        [Pamela Bennetts]
  Beau Barron's Lady
  Loving Highwayman, The
  Michaelmas Tree, The
  Midsummer Morning
  Regency Rogue
  Regency Jewel Series:
      Emerald
    2 Sapphire
    3 Pearl
    4 Garnet
    5 Ruby
    6 Opal
    7 Topaz
    8 Crystal

ASHFORD, Jane   <RE>
        [Jane Le Compte]
  Cachet   <CO><RS>
  First Season
  Headstrong Ward, The
  Impetuous Heiress, The
  Irresolute Rivals, The
  Marchington Scandal, The
  Meddlesome Miranda
  Mirage   <CO><RS>
  Radical Arrangement, A

ASHFORD, Jane (cont.)
Reluctant Rake, The
Repentant Rebel, The
Rivals Of Fortune
Three Graces, The
Warner Regency:
  11 Gwendeline
  19 Bluestocking
  25 Man Of Honour
  32 Rivals Of Fortune

ASHLEY, Alma   <HR>
Love's Raging Torment

ASHLEY, Faye
            (Ashley Summers)
Adam's Daughter
Blue Wildfire
Harlequin Temptation:
  167 Besieged

ASHLEY, Jacqueline
    [Jacqueline Ashley Casto]
Harlequin American Romance:
  20 Love's Revenge
  40 Hunting Season
  78 Other Half Of Love, The
  136 In The Name Of Love
  157 Spring's Awakening
  182 Long Journey Home, The
  208 Question Of Honor, A
  299 Gift, The
  316 Love Thy Neighbor
Harlequin Intrigue:
  4 Secrets Of The Heart

ASHLEY, Mellyora   <RE>
Lady In Disguise, A

ASHLEY, Rebecca   <RE>
    [Lois Arvin Walker]
Feuds And Fantasies
Lady Fair
Lady's Lament
Right Suitor, The
Suitable Arrangement, A
Candlelight:
  621 An Intriguing Innocent
  638 Season Of Surprises, A
  677 Willful Widow, A
  695 Arrogant Aristocrat, The
  707 Intrepid Encounter

ASHLEY, Sarah
Second Chance At Love:
  133 Cherished Moments

ASHLEY, Suzanne
    [Susan Cody Brown]
Silhouette Special Edition:
  556 Bittersweet Betrayal

ASHTON, Andrea   <HO>
Cleopatra's Daughter

ASHTON, Ann   <RS>
    [John M. Kimbro]
Haunted Portrait, The
Three Cries Of Terror
Candlelight: <IN>
  514 Phantom Reflection,The
Starlight Romance:
  Concession
  If Love Comes
  Lovely And The Lonely, The
  Passion Allegro
  Right Time To Love, The
  Star Eyes

ASHTON, Elizabeth
Harlequin Premiere Edition:
 13 Gilded Butterfly, The
Harlequin Presents:
 179 Sanctuary In The Desert
Harlequin Romance:
 1373 Pied Tulip, The
 1421 Parisian Adventure
 1453 Benevolent Despot, The
 1534 Cousin Mark
 1636 Flutter Of White Wings
 1659 Parade Of Peacocks, A
 1713 Alpine Rhapsody
 1741 Moorland Magic
 1762 Sigh No More
 1789 Errant Bride
 1810 Rocks Of Arachenza, The
 1835 Dark Angel
 1853 Road To The Border, The
 1869 House Of The Eagles, The
 1891 Scorched Wings
 1918 Player King, The
 1933 Miss Nobody From Nowhere
 1946 Crown Of Willow
 1972 Lady In The Limelight
 1989 My Lady Disdain
 2044 Mountain Heritage
 2076 Aegean Quest
 2093 Voyage Of Enchantment
 2116 Green Harvest
 2172 Breeze From The Bosphorus
 2179 Questing Heart, The
 2192 Golden Girl, The
 2200 Rendezvous In Venice
 2247 Willing Hostage, The
 2256 Garden Of The Gods, The
 2300 Moonlight On The Nile
 2311 Joyous Adventure, The
 2324 Reluctant Partnership
 2347 Rekindled Flame, The
 2395 Borrowed Plumes
 2401 Sicilian Summer
 2425 Silver Arrow
 2444 Rebel Against Love
 2503 White Witch
 2863 Bride On Approval

ASHTON, Fiona
Written In The Stars

_____

_____

ASHTON, Kate   <HR>
                       [Margaret Ball]
Sunset And Dawn

_____

_____

ASHTON, Katherine
                    (Katherine Talbot)

ASHTON, Laura   <HR>
Belle Marie

_____

_____

ASHTON, Mollie   <RE>
                    [Mollie Aghadjian]
Noble Imposter, The
Harlequin Historical <Set#2>:
 46 Terms Of Surrender
Harlequin Regency Romance:
 Debt Of Honor, A

_____

_____

ASHTON, Violet
          [Margery Violet Ashton]
In sequence:
 Love's Triumphant Heart
 Love's Rebellious Pleasure
In sequence:
 Swansong
 Love By Fire

_____

_____

ASQUITH, Nan
                    (Susanna Broome)
Harlequin Premiere Edition:
 14 Changing Stars, The

ASQUITH, Nan (cont.)
  Harlequin Romance:
     898 My Dream Is Yours
    1192 Certain Spring, The
    1223 Garden Of Persephone, The
    1261 With All My Heart
    1284 Only My Heart To Give
    1411 Turn The Page
    1476 Believe In Tomorrow
    1734 Girl From Rome, The
    1753 Time May Change

_____

ASTIN, Cynthia
  MacFadden Romance:
    205 Love's Wild Rose

_____

_____

ASTLEY, Juliet   <RS>
                          [Norah Lofts]
  Copsi Castle
  Fall Of Midas, The

_____

_____

ASTLEY, Thea   <HS>
              [Thea Beatrice May Astley]
  It's Raining In Mango

_____

_____

ASTON, Sharon
                     [Helen Van Slyke]
  Santa Ana Wind, The

_____

_____

ASTRAHAN, Syrie A.
           [Syrie A. Astrahan James]
  Silhouette Desire:
    262 Songbird
    334 Sky's The Limit, The

_____

_____

ATKIN, Jane
  Candlelight Ecstasy:
    404 Moment's Enchantment, A
    451 Flight Of Fancy
    468 No Way To Treat A Lady
    498 Knight Of Illusions
  Candlelight Ecstasy Supreme:
    124 Fragile Deception, A

_____

_____

ATKINS, Jane
                          (Sarah Keene)
ATKINSON, Oriana
  Golden Season, The

_____

_____

ATWOOD, Kathryn   <HR>
                        [Kathy Ptacek]
  Aurora
  Lawless Heart, The
  My Lady Rogue
  Renegade Lady
  Satan's Angel

_____

_____

AUBERT, Rosemary
                          (Lucy Snow)
  Harlequin SuperRomance:
    216 Firebrand

_____

_____

AUDRENN, Joel
  Mystique:
     93 House Of Lies
    128 Chance Encounter

_____

_____

AUEL, Jean M.
            [Jean Marie Auel]
    Earth's Children Saga: <HF><Saga>
    In sequence:
        Clan Of The Cave Bear, The
        Valley Of The Horses
        Mammoth Hunters, The
        Plains Of Passage, The

AUGUST, Elizabeth
            [Bettie Wilhite]
    Silhouette Romance:
    554 Author's Choice
    590 Truck Driving Woman
    626 Wild Horse Canyon
    668 Something So Right
    719 Nesting Instinct, The
    749 Joey's Father
    771 Ready-Made Family
    790 Man From Natchez,The<WITS>

AUMENTE, Joy
                    (Joy Darlington)
                    (Joy Gardner)

AUSTEN, Charlotte   <HR-Reic>
                    [Adele Leone]
    Love Everlasting

AUSTEN, Dee
    Dawn Of Love: <YA>
    1 Reckless Love
    6 Promise Forever

AUSTEN, Jane   <GOT><RE>
    Emma
    Mansfield Park

AUSTEN, Jane (cont.)
    Northanger Abbey
    Persuasion
    Pride & Prejudice
    Sandition
    Sense And Sensibility
    Watsons, The   w/John COATES

AUSTEN, Jillian   <HO>
    Way Of The Dragon

AUSTIN, Alex   <CO>
    Bride, The

AUSTIN, Deborah
                    (Jacqueline Marshall)

AUSTIN, Emily   <HR>
    Raven McCord

AUSTIN, Marilyn   <RS>
    Backwater Bayou
    Stolen Secrets
    Avalon:
        Dream For Tomorrow, A
        Holly Hathway,
            Physical Therapist
        Kate Conners,
            Family Therapist
    Serenade/Serenata: <Insp>
        40 Love More Precious

AUSTIN, Nancy w/ Mary KEVERN
                    (Miranda North)

27

AUSTIN, Sarah
  MacFadden Romance:
    106 Retreat To Hidden Valley

AUSTIN, Stephanie
  Love & Life:
    Only A Housewife

AVALLONE, Michael
  [Michael Angelo Avallone, Jr.]
                (Priscilla Dalton)
               (Jean-Anne Depre)
                 (Dorothea Nile)
                 (Edwina Noone)
      (see Amanda Jean Jarrett)
  (see Lee Davis Willoughby <MOAS>)

AVEY, Ruby
                   (Vicki Page)

AVON CHRISTMAS ROMANCE:
  Six Little Angels
                Betina M. Krahn
  Match Made In Heaven
                     Linda Ladd
  Christmas Melodies
                 Catherine Hart
  Candle In The Snow
              Barbara Dawson Smith
  Silent Night, Starry Night
               Katherine Sutcliffe

AWBREY, Elizabeth   <HR>
                [Elizabeth Beach]
  Reckless Angel

AYERS, Rose   <HR>
       [Lillian Bethel Greenwood]
  Street Sparrows, The

AYLESFORD, Susan
  MacFadden Romance:
    263 Twilight Of Tenderness

AYLWORTH, Susan
                   (Shannon Gale)

AYRE, Jessica
  Harlequin Romance:
    2504 Not To Be Trusted
    2599 Hard To Handle
    2641 New Discovery

AYRES, Janet
  SuperRomance:
    26 Odyssey Of Love

AYRES, Ruby M.
                [Ruby Mildred Ayres]
  Black Sheep, The
  Living Apart
  Love Changes
  Lover Who Lied, The
  One Summer
  Phantom Lover, The
  Princess Passes, The
  Road That Bends, The
  Rosemary: For Forgetting
  Thousandth Man, The
  Weekend Woman

BACHER, June Masters
 Pioneer Saga: In sequence: <Insp>
  Love Is A Gentle Stranger
  Love's Silent Song
  Diary Of A Loving Heart
  Love Leads Home
 Rhapsody Romance:
  Heart That Lingers, The
  Until There Was You
  With All My Heart

BACHMANN, Diana
 Beyond The Sunset
 Tides Of The Heart

BACON, Nancy   <CO>
 Bayou Lady   <HR>
 Love And Dreams
 Love Game, The
 Love & Life:
  Candles And Caviar
  Champagne And Roses
  Country Music
  Honeysuckle Moon
  Winter Morning

BACZEWSKI, Janice Kay Johnson
              (Kay Bartlett)
              (Janice Kay Johnson)
              (Janice Stevens)

BACZEWSKI, Janice Kay Johnson w/
     Norma Kay Tadlock JOHNSON
              (Kay Kirby)

BADE, Tom w/ Robin STEVENSON
              (Robin St. Thomas)
              (see Robin Stevenson)

BADGER, Rosemary
 Harlequin Romance:
  2617 Corporate Lady
  2629 Girl Called Andy, A
  2695 Time Of Deception, A
  2749 Matter Of Marnie, A
  2773 Shadows Of Eden
  2827 Time To Trust
  2864 Good-Time Guy, The

BADGLEY, Anne   <RS>
 Rembrandt Decision, The

BAEHR, Consuelo Saah
 Daughters   <HR>

BAEHR, Patricia
          [Patricia Goehner Baehr]
 Magic Moments: <YA>
  4 Indian Summer

BAER, Jill   <GOT>
          [Agnes Joan Sewell Gilbert]
 House Of Whispers

BAER, Judy
                    (Judy Kaye)
 Bride And Groom:
  3 Country Bride
 Everlasting Love: <Insp>
  1 Bid For My Heart
 First Love From Silhouette: <YA>
  111 Girl Inside, The

BAER, Judy (cont.)
Promise Romance: <Insp>
    29 Dakota Dream
Serenade/Serenata: <Insp>
     9 Love's Perfect Image
    18 Tender Adversary
    28 Shadows Along The Ice
Sweet Dreams: <YA>
   148 Riddles Of Love
   161 My Perfect Valentine
   167 Working At Love
Sweet Savage Sophmore Year: <YA>
     2 Spring Break

BAER, Tracy
MacFadden Romance:
    81 Love In Bloom

BAGGETT, Nancy w/ Eileen BUCKHOLTZ
                        (Amanda Lee)

BAGNARA, Elsie Poe
                        (Norah Hess)

BAGNEL, Joan
Forbidden Rites
Goatsong Rituals, The
Gone The Rainbow, Gone The Dove
Sturbridge Dynasty, The

BAGWELL, Stella
Silhouette Romance:
   469 Golden Glory
   485 Moonlight Bandit
   510 Mist On The Mountain, A
   543 Madeline's Song
   560 Outsider, The
   587 New Kid In Town, The
   621 Cactus Rose
   634 Hillbilly Heart
   657 Teach Me

BAGWELL, Stella (cont.)
   674 White Night, The
   699 No Horsing Around
   723 That Southern Touch
   748 Gentle As A Lamb

BAIER, Anna Lee
                        (Ana Leigh)

BAILEY, E. M   <RS>
                [Elizabeth Bailey]
Tiara:
Falling Place, The

BAIRD, Jacqui
Harlequin Presents:
  1079 Dark Desiring

BAIRD, Marie-Terese
Lesson In Love, A

BAKER, Allison
                [Alice Crumbaker]
Aysa

BAKER, Betty Doreen Flook
                (Elizabeth Renier)

BAKER, Christine
                (Christine West)
Circle Of Love:
    12 Love's Dream

BAKER, Darlene
                (Heather Lang)

30

BAKER, Donna
Saffron

_____

_____

BAKER, Fran
                (Cathlyn McCoy)
Loveswept:
   161 Seeing Stars
   246 Widow And The
        Wildcatter, The
   363 King Of The Mountain

_____

_____

BAKER, Fran w/ Judith NOBLE
             (Judith Baker)

BAKER, Judith
   [Fran Baker w/ Judith Noble]
   Silhouette Desire:
     5 When Last We Loved
   21 Love In The China Sea

_____

_____

BAKER, Madeline   <HR>
   First Love, Wild Love
   Forbidden Fires
   Lacey's Way
   Love Forevermore
   Love In The Wind
   Renegade Heart
   Whisper In The Wind, A   <T-T>
   In sequence:
     Reckless Heart
     Reckless Love
     Reckless Desire

_____

_____

BAKER, Maggie
   Harlequin Temptation:
   339 Man For The Night, A

_____

_____

BAKER, Marc
            (Marceil Baker)
           (Marcia Miller)

BAKER, Marceil   <GOT>
           [Marc Baker]
   Friendly Evil, A

_____

_____

BAKER, Mary Gladys Steel (Deceased)
           (Sheila Stuart)

BAKER, Oleda
   Reluctant Goddess

_____

_____

BAKER, Sarah
   MacFadden Romance:
   13 Night Bird's Song, The

_____

_____

BAKKER, Kit
   Harlequin Intrigue
   14 Sea Treasure
   Harlequin SuperRomance:
   387 Julianne's Song   <CMS>

_____

_____

BALDWIN, Cathy-Jo Ladame
           (Cathryn Ladame)
           (Cathryn Ladd)

BALDWIN, Cynthia
   MacFadden Romance:
   257 Destiny's Embrace

_____

_____

BALDWIN, Faith   (Deceased)
   [Faith Baldwin Cuthrell]
   Adams Eden
   Alimony

BALDWIN, Faith (cont.)
American Family
And New Stars Burn
Any Village
Arizona Star
Beauty
Blue Horizons
Breath Of Life
Career By Proxy
Change Of Heart
Close And Quiet Love, A
Departing Wings
Enchanted Oasis
Face Towards The Spring
Garden Oats
Give Love The Air
Golden Shoestring, The
Harvest Of Hope
Heart Has Wings, The
Heart Remembers, The
He Married A Doctor
High Road, The
Honor Bound
Hotel Hostess
Innocent Bystander
Job For Jenny, A
Judy: A Story Of Devine Corners
Letty And The Law
Lonely Man
Look Out For Liza
Love's A Puzzle
Make-Believe
Marry For Money
Medical Center
Men Are Such Fools
Moon's Our Home, The
New Girl In Town
No Bed Of Roses
No Private Heaven
Office Wife, The
One More Time
Private Duty
Rain Forest
Rehearsal For Love
Rest Of My Life With You, The
Rich Girl, Poor Girl
Search For Tomorrow
Skyscraper
Sleeping Beauty
"Something Special"
Station Wagon Set

BALDWIN, Faith (cont.)
Take What You Want
Testament Of Trust
That Man Is Mine
There Is A Season
Three Faces Of Love, The
Three Women
Thresholds
Thursday's Child
Time And The Hour
Twenty-Four Hours A Day
Velvet Hammer, The
West Wind, The
White Collar Girl
White Magic
Yesterday's Love
You Can't Escape

BALDWIN, Rebecca   <RE>
          [Helen Chappell]
Arabella And The Beast
Cassandra Knot, The
Dartwood's Daughters
Gentleman From Philadelphia, A
Lady Scandal
Matter Of Honor, A
Coventry:
    14 Matchmakers, The
    30 Peerless Theodosia
   118 Sandition Quadrille, A
   143 Season Abroad, A
   173 Very Simple Scheme, A
   201 Dollar Duchess, The

BALE, Karen A.   <HR>
Desperado Dream
Distant Thunder
Forever Passion, The
Sweet Medicine's Prophecy:
    1 Sun Dancer's Passion
    2 Little Flower's Desire
    3 Winter's Love Song
    4 Savage Fury

BALE, Karen A. (cont.)
  5 Sun Dancer's Legacy
  6 Cheyenne Surrender

BALL, John
  In The Heat Of The Night
  Miss One Thousand Spring Blossoms

BALIN, Beverly   <HO>
  King In Hell

BALL, Margaret
                     (Kate Ashton)
                     (Kathleen Fraser)
                     (Catherine Lyndell)
  Bridge To The Sky, A

BALKEY, Rita   <HR>
         [Rita Balkey Oleyar]
  Glorious Conquest
  Prince Of Passion
  Silk And Steel
  Tears Of Glory
  Heartfire Romance:
    Midnight Ecstasy
    Passion's Disguise
    Passion's Fury

BALLA, Willetta
  Bells Beneath The Sea

BALLANTINE, Belinda
  Change Of Luck, A

BALL, Barbara
  Caprice Romance: <YA>
    34 Hidden Heart, The

BALOGH, Mary   <RE>
                (see A Regency Christmas)
  An Unacceptable Offer
  An Unlikely Duchess
  Certain Magic, A
  Constant Heart, The

BALL, Donna
                     (Donna Carlisle)
                     (Rebecca Flanders)
                     (see Felicia Gallant)
  Winners: A Love Story
  Starlight Romance:
    Summer Masquerade

  Daring Masquerade
  Desire After Dark
  Double Wager, The
  First Snowdrop, The
  Gentle Conquest
  Gift Of Daisies, A
  Incurable Matchmaker, The
  Lady With A Black Umbrella
  Obedient Bride, The
  Promise Of Spring, A   &
  Red Rose

BALL, Donna w/
         Elizabeth Shannon HARPER
                     (Leigh Bristol)

  Secrets Of The Heart
  Trysting Place, The
  Ungrateful Governess, The

BALL, Doris Bell Collier
                     (Josephine Bell)

BALOGH, Mary (cont.)
In sequence:
Chance Encounter, A
Wood Nymph, The
Raine Family Trilogy:
Gilded Web, The   &
Web Of Love
Devil's Web, The

BALSER, Joan   <HR>
Passions Of The Realm

BAMFORD, Susannah
Blind Trust

BANCROFT, Iris   <HR>
[Iris Nelson Bancroft]
(Iris Brent)
(Andrea Layton)
Dawn Of Desire
Love's Burning Flame
Passionate Heart, The
Rapture's Rebel
Whispering Hope

BANCROFT, Robert
[Robert R. Kirsch]
Castilian Rose

BANGERT, Ethel   <GOT>
[Ethel Elizabeth Bangert]
Clover Hill
Thought Of Love, The
Avalon:
An Opal For Nurse Kate
Child Of The Wind
Down Under Nurse
Gold Country Nurse

BANGERT, Ethel (cont.)
Haunting Fear, The
Nurse In Spain
Nurse Of The Sacramento
Nurse Susanne's Bold Journey
Nurse Under Suspicion
Reservation Nurse
Secret Of The Peony Vase, The

BANIS, V. J.
Earth And All It Holds, The
San Antone   <HS>
This Splendid Earth

BANIS, Victor
Sword And The Rose, The

BANIS, Victor Jerome
(Jan Alexander)
(V. J. Banis)
(Victor Banis)
(Lynn Benedict)
(Elizabeth Monterey)

BANISTER, Margaret S.   (Deceased)
Burn Then, Little Lamp
Tears Are For The Living

BANKS, Barbara
Candlelight:
538 Dragonseeds   <IN>

BANNISTER, Patricia
(Gwyneth Moore)
(Patricia Veryan)

BARBER, Lenora
[Janet Wing]
Silhouette Desire:
78 Blueprint For Rapture

BARBER, Noel
Farewell To France, A   <Saga>
Other Side Of Paradise, The
Sakkara   <Saga>
Tanamera
Weeping And The Laughter, The
                                <Saga>

BARBIERI, Elaine   <HR>
Captive Ecstasy
Defiant Mistress
Ecstasy's Trail
Love's Fiery Jewel
Passion's Dawn
Sweet Torment
Tarnished Angel
Untamed Captive
Wings Of A Dove
Wishes On The Wind
In sequence:
  Amber Fire
  Amber Treasure
  Amber Passion
Harlequin SuperRomance:
177 Race For Tomorrow

BARCHILON, John
Crown Prince, The   <Saga>

BARCLAY, Alisha
Starlight Romance:
  Love's Twilight

BARCLAY, Virginia   <MED>
[Virginia McDonnell]
Mid-City Hospital Series:
In sequence:
  Emergency
  High Risk
  Trauma
  Crisis
  Double Face
  Life Support

BARDIN, John Franklin   (Deceased)
                         (Douglas Ashe)

BARKER, Becky
[Rebecca Barker]
Candlelight Supreme:
170 Captured By A Cowboy

BARKER, Berta LaVan
Avalon:
  Dangerous Waters
  Dream House For Nurse Rhonda, A
  Dr. Laurie's Conquest
  Lianne's Island Love
  Lost In A Mist
  Magic Of Happiness
  Magic Of Paris, The
  Nurse - Companion
  Nurse For Dr. Turner, A
  Thousand Happiness, A

BARKER, Megan   <RE>
[Roger Erskine Longrigg]
Black-Eyed Susan

BARKER, Pat   <HO>
Century's Daughter, The

BARKER, Shirley   (Deceased)<RS>
    [Shirley Frances Barker]
    Last Gentleman, The
    Liza Bowe
    Swear By Apollo

BARKIN, Jill
                   [Susan Johnson]
    Hot Streak

BARKLEY, Jessica
                   [Cori L. Deyoe]
    Silhouette Desire:
    556 Montana Man
    Silhouette Special Edition:
    406 Into The Sunset

BARLOW, Linda
    Fires Of Destiny   <HR>
    Leaves Of Fortune   <SAGA>
    Second Chance At Love:
    168 Beguiled
    188 Flights Of Fancy   &
    224 Bewitched
    238 Knight Of Passion
    264 By Love Possessed   &
    300 Siren's Song
    Silhouette Desire:
    379 Midnight Rambler
    Silhouette Intimate Moments:
    166 Hold Back The Night

BARNARD, Judith w/ Michael FAIN
                   (Judith Michael)

BARNES, Brian   <HO>
    Time And Chance

BARNES, Elizabeth
                   [Avery Thorne Andrew]
    Harlequin Presents:
    1328 In Spite Of Themselves
    Harlequin Romance:
    2972 No Love In Return
    3056 Now And Forever

BARNES, Joanna
    Lucy Cade   <HR>
    Pastora   <HS>
    Silverwood   <Saga>

BARNES, Margaret Campbell <HO>
    Lady On The Coin   w/Hebe ELSNA
    With All My Heart
    History Of The Tudors:
    In sequence:
        Isabel The Fair
        Passionate Brood, The
        Tudor Rose, The
        Within The Hollow Crown
        Brief Gaudy Hour
        King's Bed, The
        My Lady Of Cleves
        King's Fool
        Mary Of Carisbrooke

BARNETT, Jill   <HR>
                   [Jill Stadler]
    Heart's Haven, The
    Surrender A Dream

BARNEY, Frances
    Golden Girl
    Rivals For Robin
    Avalon:
        Lantern In The Night
        Summer Of Awakening

BAROLINI, Helen
 Love In The Middle Ages   <CO>
 Umbertina   <Saga>

BARR, Elisabeth   <GOT><HR><RE><RS>
                     [Irene Edwards]
 Castle Heritage
 Sea Treasure, The
 Song Of The Black Witch
 Storm Witch, The
 Candlelight:
  144 Opal Pendant, The   <RE>
  188 Master Of Roxton
  213 Revelry Manor
  577 Flowers Of
         Darkness, The   <RO>

BARR, Pat
              [Patricia Miriam Barr]
 Jade   <HS>
 Kenjiro

BARRACLOUGH, June   <HR>
 Heart Of The Rose, The
 Kindred Spirits
 Rook's Nest

BARRETT, Elizabeth
                  (Christine Collins)
                     (Cara McLean)
 Loveswept:
  76 Tailor-Made
 Pageant Romance:
  In Perfect Harmony
  When In Paris

BARRETT, Helen w/ Karen HITZIG
                 (Justin Channing)

BARRETT, Jean
                 [Robert Lee Rogers]
 Second Chance At Love:
  242 Fire Bird
 Silhouette Desire:
  574 Hot On Her Trail
  617 Heat

BARRETT, Karen Lawton
 Meteor Kismet:
  20 Cheated Hearts

BARRETT, Martha Barron   <HO>
 God's Country

BARRETT, Mary Ellin
 American Beauty
 An Accident Of Love
 Castle Ugly   <RS>

BARRETT, Maye   <GOT><RE>
                      [Max Barrett]
 Crystal Palace, The
 Lady Of Stantonwyck, The
 Thorn In The Rose, The
 Threat Of Love, The

BARRETT, Jr., Neal
                 (see Rebecca Drury)
 Daniel Boone: Westward
  Trail   <AES:#4>

37

BARRETT, William E.   (Deceased)
        [William Edmund Barrett]
  Edge Of Things, The
  Empty Shrine, The
  Fools Of Time, The
  Glory Tent, The
  Lady Of The Lotus
  Left Hand Of God, The
  Red Lacquered Gate
  Shadows Of The Images, The
  Shape Of Illusion, The
  Sudden Strangers, The
  Wine And The Music, The
  To The Last Man
  Woman In The House, A

BARRICKLOW, Patti B.
        (Patricia Burroughs)

BARRIE, Monica
        [David M. Wind]
  Alana   <HR>
  By Invitation Only
  Queen Of Knights   <HF>
  Silhouette Intimate Moments:
    6 Island Heritage
   20 Gentle Winds, The
         (sequel to Tapestry #24)
   46 Crystal Blue Desire
   62 Breed Apart, A
   82 Distant Worlds
  Silhouette Special Edition:
   94 Cry Mercy, Cry Love
  221 Silken Threads
  243 Lovegames
  267 Perfect Vision, A
  279 Ashes Of The Past
  302 Special Delivery
  330 Emerald Love,
         Sapphire Dreams
  364 Executives, The
  Tapestry: <HR>
   24 Gentle Fury
   49 Turquoise Sky
   60 Silver Moon

BARRIE, Susan
        [Ida Pollock]
  Harlequin Classic:
    6 So Dear To My Heart (572)
   14 Dear Tiberius   (580)
   23 Heart Specialist   (587)
   41 Four Roads To
         Windrush   (687)
   78 Gates Of Dawn   (792)
  123 Moon At The Full   (904)
  147 Castle Thunderbird   (997)
  174 Accidental Bride   (1189)
  Harlequin Petite:
    2 Air Ticket
  Harlequin Romance:
  765 Case Of Heart Trouble, A
  779 Mistress Of Brown Furrows
  792 Gates Of Dawn
  831 Hotel At Treloan
  904 Moon At The Full
  926 Mountain Magic
  967 Wings Of The Morning, The
  997 Castle Thunderbird
 1020 No Just Cause
 1043 Marry A Stranger
 1078 Royal Purple
 1099 Carpet Of Dreams
 1128 Quiet Heart, The
 1168 Rose In The Bud
 1189 Accidental Bride
 1221 Master Of Melincourt
 1259 Wild Sonata
 1311 Marriage Wheel, The
 1359 Return To Tremarth
 1428 Night Of The
         Singing Birds
 1526 Bride In Waiting
 2240 Victoria And The
         Nightingale

BARROLL, Clare   <HR>
  Iron Crown, The   <HS>
  Season Of The Heart
  Shadow Man, The

BARRON, Ann/Ann Forman<GOT><HR><RS>
                    (Annabel Erwin)
Banner Bold And Beautiful
Bride Of Menace
Dark Vengeance
Firebrand
Gentle Kiss Of Death
Proud Glory
Serpent In The Shadows
Spin A Dark Web
Strange Legacy
Windswept

BARRON, Elizabeth   <RE>
        [Susan Bowden Twaddle]
An Amicable Arrangement
Elusive Countess, The
Miss Drayton's Crusade
Vicount's Wager, The

BARRY, Andrea
        [Hania "Annette" Bartle]
Silhouette Romance:
    194 African Enchantment

BARRY, Iris   <RS>(Deceased)
Darkness At Mantia, The
House Of Deadly Night, The
Nurse Dawn's Discovery

BARRY, Jane
            [Jane Powell Barry]
Grand Illusions
Shadow Of Eagles, A
Time In The Sun, A

BARRY, Loretta   <RS>
Sudden Silence

BARRY, Lucy
            [Lucy Brown Barry]
Stagestruck Secretary

BART, Peter
Destinies
        w/Dennel Bart PETITCLERC
Thy Kingdom Come

BARTEL, Constance
Woman Like That, A

BARTELL, Linda Lang   <HR>
Caressa
The Avon Romance:
    Brittany
    Marisa
    In sequence:
    Brianna
    Alyssa

BARTHOLOMEW, Barbara
Ann And Jay   <YA>
Magic Moments: <YA>
     2 Someone New
     5 Love Like This, A
    12 Lucky At Love
Silhouette Inspirations:
     4 Something Special
    20 Promise Once Made, A
    28 For Every Season

BARTHOLOMEW, Barbara (cont.)
  Silhouette Romance:
    428 Man Of Character, A
    457 Romantic And The
         Realist, The

_____

_____

BARTHOLOMEW, Dale
  MacFadden Romance:
    69 Starlight Rendezvous

_____

_____

BARTLE, Hania "Annette"
                  (Andrea Barry)

BARTLETT, Jean Anne   <GOT>
             [Jean Anne Lustberg]
  Valago Crest
  Willow Grove
  Torment Of Aaron Burr Series:
    In sequence:
      Angelica
      Theodosia
      Eliza

_____

_____

BARTLETT, Kathleen
           [Lauran Bosworth Paine]
  Deception Of The Heart
  Lovers In Autumn

_____

_____

BARTLETT, Kay
           [Janice Kay Johnson Baczewski]
  Silhouette Intimate Moments:
    254 Shiver Of Rain, A
    275 Family Ties

_____

_____

BARTLETT, Lynn/Lynn M.   <HR>
              [Lynn M. Bartlett]
  Silhouette Intimate Moments:
    290 Price Of Glory, The
    362 Twilight Prince, The

BARTLETT, Lynn (cont.)
  Courtly Love
  Defy The Eagle
  Promise Me Love

_____

_____

BARTLETT, Stephanie   <HR>
  Highland Jade

_____

_____

BARTON, Beverly
                  [Beverly Beaver]
  Silhouette Desire:
    580 Yankee Lover
    621 Lucky In Love

_____

_____

BARZMAN, Ben w/ Norma BARZMAN
  Rich Dreams

_____

_____

BASILE, Gloria Vitanza   <RS>
                  (Michaela Morgan)
  Appassionato   <HO>
  House Of Lions
  Global 2000 Trilogy:
    Eye Of The Eagle
    Jackal Helix, The
    Sting Of The Scorpion, The
  Manipulators Trilogy: <CO>
    In sequence:
      Manipulators, The
      Born To Power
      Giants In The Shadow

_____

_____

BASSETT, Sara Ware
  Adrift
  Beacon, The
  Beyond The Breakers
  Cross Currents
  Echoes Of The Tide
  Girl In The Blue Pinafore

40

BASSETT, Sara Ware (cont.)
Head Winds
Heart's Haven
Sea Magic
Silver Moon Cottage
South Cove Summer
To Each His Dream
Whispering Pine, The
White Sail, The
Within The Harbor

BASTIEN, Dorothy
Wildfire: <YA>
    I Want To Be Me

BATES, Baldwin   <HO>
Sultan's Warrior, The

BATES, Jenny
                        [Maura Seger]
Second Chance At Love:
    175 Dazzled
To Have And To Hold:
    5 Gilded Spring

BATTLE, Lois
Habit Of The Blood, A
Past Is Another Country, The
Season Of Change
Southern Women   <Saga>
War Brides
Yesterday's Music

BATTLES, Edith   <GOT>
                   [Roxy Edith Battles]
Secret Of Castle Drai

BATTYE, Gladys
                        (Margaret Lynn)

BAUER, Marsha
Heartfire Romance: <HR>
    Treasured Embrace
    Sweet Conquest

BAUER, Pamela
                   [Pamela Muelbauer]
Harlequin SuperRomance:
    236 Halfway To Heaven
    288 His And Hers
    330 Walking On Sunshine
    378 Honey Trap, The
    406 Memories

BAUGHMAN, Dorothy   <GOT>
Avalon:
    Ghost Of Aronov Point
    Icy Terror
    Secret Of Montoya Mission

BAULING, Jayne
Harlequin Presents:
    247 Walk In The Shadows
    505 Wait For The Storm
    663 Valentine's Day
    775 Rage To Possess
    863 Matching Pair
    879 Thai Triangle
    911 To Fill A Silence
    928 Abode Of Princes
   1007 Dangerous Passion, A
   1239 Roses All The Way

BAUMAN, Carolyn   <GOT>
  Secret Of Haverly House, The
  _____

  _____

BAUMAN, Lauren
  Harlequin SuperRomance:
    354 Seasons
    447 Prism Love
  _____

  _____

BAUMANN, Margaret
                  (Marguerite Lees)
  Harlequin Romance:
    778 Case In The Alps, A
    827 Sheila Of Children's Ward
    842 Nurse Barby's Secret Love
    947 Woman Alone, A
   1366 Design For Loving
   1962 Debt Of Honour
  _____

  _____

BAUMGARDNER, Cathie Linz
                    (Cathie Linz)

BAUMGARTEN, Sylvia
                    (Ena Halliday)
                  (Louisa Rawlings)

BAWDEN, Nina   <GOT>
      [Nina Mary Mabey Kark]
  Afternoon Of A Good Woman
  Anna Apparent
  Birds On The Trees, The
  Devil By The Sea
  Familiar Passions
  Grain Of Truth, The
  Little Love, A Little Learning, A
  Solitary Child, The
  Tortoise By Candlelight
  Under The Skin
  Walking Naked
  Woman Of My Age
  _____

  _____

BAXTER, Mary Lynn
  Silhouette Classic:
    20 Tears Of Yesterday <SE31>
  Silhouette Desire:
    24 Shared Moments
   527 Added Delight
   542 Winter Heat
   571 Slow Burn
  Silhouette Imtimate Moments:
    19 Another Kind Of Love
    52 Memories That Linger
    74 Everything But Time
   117 Handful Of Heaven, A
   130 Price Above Rubies
   156 When We Touch
   197 Fool's Music   &
   217 Moonbeams Aplenty   &
   272 Knight Sparks
   296 Wish Giver
  Silhouette Special Edition:
     9 All Our Tomorrows
    31 Tears Of Yesterday
    96 Autumn Awakening
   360 Between The Raindrops
  _____

  _____

BAYER, William
  Punish Me With Kisses
  Raptor
  Tangier
  Visions Of Isabelle
  _____

  _____

BAYNER, Rose
  First Love From Sihouette: <YA>
    80 Endless Summer
   125 Summer Of My Independence
   142 Wilder Special, The
   149 Off The Hook
   164 On The Loose
  _____

  _____

BEACH, Elizabeth Aubrey
    (Elizabeth Awbrey)
    (Elizabeth Stuart)

BEACH, Neva
Candlelight Ecstasy:
  414 To The Highest Bidder

BEAHAN, Michael
    [Michael Shnayerson]
John Fremont: California
    Bound   <AES:#5>

BEAN, Amelia   <HO>
    [Myrtle Amelia Bean]
Fancher Train, The

BEAR, Joan E.
    (Elizabeth Mayhew)

BEARDSLEY, Charles
    [Charles Noel Beardsley]
(see Lee Davis Willoughby <MOAS>)
Apartment, The
Center, The
Eyes Of Love, The
Marina Tower
Motel
Office Affair, The
Passion Seekers
Resort, The

BEATY, Betty
Harlequin Romance:
  790 South To The Sun
  824 Amber Five
 1004 Path Of The Moonfish, The
 1155 Miss Miranda's Walk
 1941 Love And The Kentish Maid

BEATY, Betty (cont.)
 2004 Head Of Chancery
 2069 Fly Away, Love
 2166 Master At Arms

BEATY, Betty w/ David BEATY   <HO>
Wings Of The Morning

BEAUCHAMP, Margary
MacFadden Romance:
   6 Way Of Love, The
  62 Touch Of Love, A
  73 Inherit The Dream
  77 Garden Of Light, The

BEAUDRY, Antoinette   <HR>
Desert Of Desire
Jungle Of Desire
River Of Desire
Strands Of Desire
Tropic Of Desire

BEAUFORT, Jane
            [Ida Pollock]
Harlequin Romance:
 1149 Nightingale In The
        Sycamore, A
 1181 Dangerous Love

BEAUMAN, Sally
         (Vanessa James)
Dark Angel   <SAGA>
Destiny   <CS>

BEAUMONT, Anne
                    (Rosina Pyatt)
Harlequin Presents:
1231 That Special Touch
Harlequin Romance:
3049 Another Time, Another Love

BEAUMONT, Helen   (Deceased)
                    (Jill Eckersley)
                    (Denise Emery)
                    (Jill Sanderson)
                    (Anna Stanton)
Sapphire Romance: <ENG>
  Whisper To The Waves

BEAUMONT, Lisa   <HR>
  Flames Of Tournay
  Fires Of Rapture

BEAUMONT, Marie
[Judith Linsley w/ Ellen Rienstra]
Harlequin SuperRomance:
  391 Catherine's song   <CMS>

BEAVER, Beverly
                    (Beverly Barton)

BECHKO, Peggy
  SuperRomance:
    47 Dark Side Of Love

BECK, Pamela w/ Patti MASSMAN <CO>
  Fling
  Rich Men, Single Women

BECKFORD, Grania
  Touch The Fire

BECKMAN, Delores
  Young Love: <YA>
    Who Loves Sam Grant?

BECKMAN, Patti
[Charles and/or
  Patricia E. Kennelly Boeckman]
First Love From Silhouette: <YA>
    3 Please Let Me In
Silhouette Inspirations:
    8 With The Dawn
Silhouette Romance:
    8 Captive Heart
   37 Beachcomber, The
   54 Louisiana Lady
   72 Angry Lover
   96 Love's Treacherous Journey
  124 Spotlight To Fame
  154 Daring Encounter
  179 Mermaid's Touch
  227 Forbidden Affair
  273 Time For Us
  348 On Stage
  571 Someday My Love
Silhouette Special Edition:
   13 Bitter Victory
   61 Tender Deception
   85 Enchanted Surrender
  109 Thunder At Dawn
  169 Storm Over The Everglades
  212 Nashville Blues
  226 Movie, The
  270 Odds Against Tomorrow
  278 Dateline: Washington
  321 Summer's Storm
  370 Danger In His Arms

BECKWITH, Lillian
           [Lillian Comber]
  Proper Woman, A

BECNEL, Rexanne   <HR>
  My Gallant Enemy

BEDFORD, Debbi
      [Deborah Lynn Pigg Bedford]
  Harlequin SuperRomance:
    154 Touch The Sky
    239 Distant Promise, A
    333 Passages
    384 To Weave Tomorrow

BEECH, Jane
  Harlequin Romance:
    1215 Soft Is The Music

BEECHAM, Jahnna
  Sweet Dreams: <YA>
    125 Parade Of Hearts
    130 Dance With Me
    139 Right Combination, The
    143 Crazy For You
    149 Practice Makes Perfect

BEHAN, Brian   <HR>
  Kathleen

BEISHIR, Norma
  Angels At Midnight   <CO>
  Time For Legends, A

BELL, Anthea   <RE>
  Floral Companion, The
  London Season, A

BELL, Betsy
  Avalon:
    Nurse Carrie's Island
    Nurse In The Wilderness

BELL, Donna   <RE>
  Scandalous Miss, The
  All's Fair

BELL, Georgianna   <HR>
  Passionate Jade

BELL, Josephine   <GOT>
      [Doris Bell Collier Ball]
  Hole In The Ground, A
  Stranger On A Cliff

BELL, Marguerite
  Masquerade:
    3 Rose For Danger, A
    8 Devil's Daughter, The

BELL, Sallie Lee
  A Hearth Romance:
    5 Barrier, The
    6 By Strange Paths
    7 Last Surrender, The
    8 Long Search, The   <MY>
    9 Romance Along The Bayou
   10 Scar, The
   11 Substitute, The

45

BELL, Sallie Lee (cont.)
12 Through Golden Meadows
13 Until The Daybreak
21 Light From The Hill

BELLAMANN, Henry   <RS>
King's Row
Richest Woman In Town
Victoria Grandolet

BELLAMY, Jean   <GOT><RS>
Ghost Of Coquina Key
Mistress Of Ghosthaven
Prisoner Of Ingecliff, The

BELLE, Pamela   <HR>
In sequence:
Wintercombe
Herald Of Joy
Heron Family Saga: In sequence:
Moon In The Water, The
Chains Of Fate, The
Alethea
Lodestar, The

BELMONT, Kate/Kathryn
[Mary Jo Territo]
That Certain Smile   <CO>
Silhouette Intimate Moments:
40 Time To Sing, A
Silhouette Special Edition:
72 Night Music
112 From The Beginning
173 From The Flames

BELVEDERE, Lee
[Valerie Merle Spanner Grayland]
Farewell To A Valley
Avalon:
Fringe Of Heaven
Return To Moon Bay
Smiling House, The
Thunder Beach
Candlelight:
124 Meet A Dark Stranger

BENEDICT, Barbara
Golden Dreams
Golden Tomorrows   <HR>
Lovestorm
Catch Of The Season

BENEDICT, Lynn   <GOT><RS>
[Victor Jerome Banis]
Bloodstone
Family Affair, A
Fatal Flowers, The
Lucifer Cult, The
Moonfire
Twisted Tree, The
Whisper Of Heather

BENET, Deborah
[Deborah Elaine Camp]
Rapture Romance:
13 Sweet Passion's Song
23 Midnight Eyes
44 Winter Flame
64 Wrangler's Lady
76 Riptide
94 Dream To Share, A

BENJAMIN, Linda   <HR>
    [Linda Hender Wallerich]
    Beloved Outlaw
    Ecstasy's Fury
    Midnight Chase
    Midnight Desire
    Passion's Gamble
    Texas Wildcat
    Wild For Love

BENJAMIN, Nikki
    [Barbara Vosbein]
    Silhouette Special Edition:
    539 Emily's House
    Silhouette Intimate Moments:
    359 Man To Believe In, A

BENNETT, Barbara
    Beggar's Virtue, The
    Rough Music, A
    So Wild A Love
    Serenade/Serenata: <Insp>
    15 Forever Eden

BENNETT, Christine
    [William Arthur Neubauer]
    Sharon Contemporary Teens:
    Girl Of Black Island
    Gloria's Ghost
    Wind In The Sage

BENNETT, Connie
    [Constance Bennett]
    Harlequin SuperRomance:
    293 Share My Tomorrows
    327 Thinking Of You
    364 When I See Your Face
    373 Changes In The Wind
    416 Playing By The Rules
    436 Believe In Me

BENNETT, Constance   <HR>
    (Connie Bennett)
    Morning Sky
    In sequence:
    Pirate's Vixen, The
    Pirate's Pleasure

BENNETT, Corintha   <RE>
    [Carolyn Wheat]
    Jemima Dancer

BENNETT, Elizabeth Deare
    Gower Court Manor
    Regatta Summer

BENNETT, Emma
    [Emma Frances Merritt]
    Candlelight Ecstasy:
    120 That Certain Summer
    135 By Passion Bound
    139 River Enchantment
    167 Beneath The Willow Tree
    228 Loving Brand
    257 With Each Passing Hour
    274 With All My Heart
    285 Passionate Ultimatum
    329 Loving Persuasion

BENNETT, Janice   <RE>
    [Eileen Witton]
    Forever In Time   <T-REG>
    Timely Affair, A   <T-REG>
    Midnight Masque
    In sequence:
    An Eligible Bride
    Tempting Miss, A
    In sequence:
    Tangled Web
    An Intriguing Desire

BENNETT, Janice N.   <GOT><RS>
  Castle On The River, The<CGS:#13>
  Haunted, The
  House Of Athena
  Pioneers, The

_____

_____

BENNETT, Laura w/
          Jean HARVEY & Tina MacKENZIE
                    (Justine Harlow)

BENNETT, Rebecca
                    [Ruby Frankel]
  Candlelight:
  691 Merry Chase, A   <RE>

_____

_____

BENNETTS, Pamela
                    (Helen Ashfield)
                    (Margaret James)
  Death Of The Red King
  Don Pedro's Captain
  Masquerade:
  23 Dear Lover England

_____

_____

BENSEN, Donald Ronald
                    (Julia Thatcher)

BENSON, Anne
                    [Ann Mikita Kolaczyk]
  Escape To Love   <RE>
  Love's Gentle Smile
  Tangled Web, The

_____

_____

BENSON, E.F./Edward F.   <GOT><HO>
  Raven's Brood
  Secret Loves
  Make Way For Lucia: In sequence:
    Queen Lucia
    Lucia In London
    Miss Mapp
    Mapp And Lucia

BENSON, E.F. (cont.)
  Worshipful Lucia, The
  Trouble For Lucia
  Male Impersonators, The

_____

BENSON, Nella/Nella J.   <HR><RE>
                    [Nella Jane Benson]
  Amaranth
  Lady's Maid, The
  Reckless Wager, The
  Touch Of Fire, The

_____

BENTLEY, Barbara   <HR>
                    [Barbara Bentley Diamond]
  Mistress Nancy

_____

_____

BENTLEY, Jayne
                    [Jayne Ann Krentz]
  MacFadden Romance:
  192 Moment Past Midnight, A
  224 Turning Towards Home
  240 Turning Towards Home
         (reprint)
  249 Maiden Of The Morning
  Other Mac Fadden's:
    Sabrina's Scheme
    Hired Husband

_____

_____

BENTLEY, Phyllis   (Deceased)<GOT>
                    [Phyllis Eleanor Bentley]
  House Of Moreys, The

_____

_____

BENTON, Darla
                    [JoAnn Leslie]
  Candlelight:
  684 Splendor By The Sea   <RO>

_____

_____

BENTON, Elsie
MacFadden Romance:
  101 Prisoners Of Paradise

BERCOVICI, Alfred
     (Alberta Simpson Carter)
Falmont Claimants, The
House Of Bondage

BENZONI, Juliette   <HO>
    [Juliette Andree
      Marguerite Benzoni]
Devil's Necklace, The
Eagle And The Nightengale, The
Lure Of The Falcon, The
Marianne
Marianne & The Crown Of Fire
Marianne & The Lords Of The East
Marianne & The Masked Prince
Marianne & The Privateer
Marianne & The Rebels
Catherine And Arnaud Series: <HR>
  In sequence:
    Belle Catherine
    Catherine, Royal Mistress
    Catherine's Quest
    Catherine And Arnaud
    Catherine's Time For Love
    Snare For Catherine, A

BERENCSI, Susan
Starlight Romance:
  Innocent Surrender
  Wildwoods And Wishes

BERENSON, Laurien
          (Laurien Blair)
First Love From Silhouette: <YA>
  208 Double Dare
Harlequin American Romance:
  210 Winner Take All
Harlequin Temptation:
  255 Lucky In Love
  310 Talisman
Loveswept:
  109 Come As You Are

BERCKMAN, Evelyn   <RS>
    [Evelyn Domenica Berckman]
Beckoning Dream, The
Case In Nullity
Evil Of Time, The
Finger To Her Lips
Fourth Man On The Rope
Heir Of Starvelings, The
Hidden Malice, A
Hovering Darkness, The
Journey's End
Lament For Four Brides
Stake In The Game, The
Stalemate
Strange Bedfellows, The
Victorian Album, The
Voice Of Air, The
Wait, Just You Wait

BERESFORD, Elisabeth
Island Of Shadows
Love Remembered
Roses Around The Door
Thunder Of Her Heart
Candlelight:
  252 Tropical Affair, A   <RO>
  259 Echoes Of Love   <RO>

BERGEN, Fran
    [Frances deTalavera Berger]
Silhouette Desire:
  191 Capitol Affair
Silhouette Special Edition:
  29 Yearning Of Angels

49

BERKLEY ZODIAC GOTHIC (cont.)
Night Of The Scorpion
                    Saliee O'Brien
Star Fire Prophecy, The
Brides Of Saturn, The
Music Of Aquarius, The
Cry Of Neptune, The
                    Anne-Marie Bretonne

BERLAND, Nancy
                    (Nancy Landon)

BERLIN, Ellin
            [Ellin Mackay Berlin]
Best Of Families, The
Lace Curtain
Land I Have Chosen
Silver Platter

BERMAN, Arnold M.
                    (Anne-Marie Bretonne)

BERNADETTE, Ann
        [Karen Ray w/ D. H. Gazdak]
Echoes Of The Heart

BERNARD, Dorothy Ann
                [Dorothy Weller]
Candlelight Ecstasy:
    53 Question Of Trust, A
   104 Speak Softly To My Soul
   190 Destiny's Touch
   275 Just Call My Name
   309 Delicate Dimensions
   351 So Dear To My Heart

BERNARD, Thelma Rene
Blue Marsh
Moonshadow Mansion   <GOT>
Winds Of Wakefield

BERNHARD, Virginia   <HR>
The Avon Romance:
    Durable Fire, The

BERT, Claudette
Mystique:
   117 Touch Of Terror, A

BETTERIDGE, Anne
            [Margaret E. Newman Potter]
    1 Spring In Morocco
    2 Truth Game, The
    3 Portuguese Affair, A
    4 Single To New York
    5 Girl Outside, The
    6 Little Bit Of Luck, A
    7 Sirocco
    8 Chains Of Love, The

BETZ, Ingrid
                    (Monica Martin)

BEVAN, Gloria
Harlequin Romance:
  1309 Hills Of Maketu, The
  1400 Distant Trap, The
  1459 Beyond The Ranges
  1510 Make Way For Tomorrow
  1576 It Began In Te Rangi
  1608 Vineyard In A Valley
  1682 Frost And The Fire, The
  1730 Flame In Fiji
  1809 Connelly's Castle

BEVAN, Gloria (cont.)
  1860 High-Country Wife
  1923 Always A Rainbow
  2008 Dolphin Bay
  2073 Bachelor Territory
  2149 Plantation Moon
  2224 Fringe Of Heaven
  2278 Kowhai Country
  2377 Half A World Away
  2426 Master Of Mahia
  2455 Emerald Cave
  2563 Rouseabout Girl, The
  2618 Greek Island Magic
  2713 Southern Sunshine
  2851 Golden Bay
        Pacific Paradise   HRS45

BEVARLY, Elizabeth
  Silhouette Special Edition:
  557 Destinations South
  590 Close Range
  639 Donovan's Chance

BEVERLEY, Jane
  Sapphire Romance: <ENG>
    Journey To Destiny

BEVERLEY, Jo   <RE>
      (see A Regency Valentine)
  Lord Wraybourne's Betrothed   &
  Stanforth Secrets, The   &
  Stolen Bride, The   &

BEYEA, Basil   <HO>
  In sequence:
    Golden Mistress, The
    Notorious Eliza

BIANCHI, Jacqui   (Deceased)
                        (Teresa Denys)

BIANCHIN, Helen
  Harlequin Premiere Edition:
    4 Willing Heart, The
  Harlequin Presents:
  271 Vines In Splendor, The
  289 Stormy Possession
  409 Devil In Command
  415 Edge Of Spring
  457 Savage Touch, The
  527 Wildfire Encounter
  695 Yesterday's Shadow
  720 Savage Pagan
  744 Sweet Tempest
  751 Dark Tyrant
  839 Bitter Encore
  975 Dark Enchantment
  1111 An Awakening Desire
  1240 Touch The Flame
  Harlequin Romance:
  2010 Bewildered Haven
  2084 Avenging Angel
  2175 Hills Of Home, The
  2378 Master Of Uluru

BICKMORE, Barbara
  East Of The Sun   <MED><Saga>
  Moon Below, The

BIDWELL, J. S.
                    (Colleen Christie)

BIDWELL, Marjory Elizabeth Sarah
                    (Elizabeth Ford)
                    (Mary Ann Gibbs)

BIEBER, Janet
          [Janet Lynn Parker Bieber]
  Loveswept:
  250 Let's Do It Again
  Silhouette Desire:
  470 Montana's Treasure

BIEBER, Janet (cont.)
533 Seeing Is Believing

BIEBER, Janet w/ Joyce THIES
[Janet Lynn Parker Bieber w/
Joyce Ann Scott Thies]
(Janet Joyce)
(Jenna Lee Joyce)

BIERCE, Jane
Harlequin American Romance:
15 Building Passion
Silhouette Romance:
594 Finishing Touch
697 Dearly Beloved

BILLINGS, Susan V.   <CO>
Sarah's Awakening

BILLS, Sharon w/ Robert BILLS
(Sarah Edwards)

BINCHY, Maeve
Echoes
Firefly Summer
Light A Penny Candle   <Saga>
Silver Wedding   <CO>

BINGHAM, Charlotte
To Hear A Nightingale   <Saga>

BINGHAM, Lisa   <HR>
Silken Dreams
The Avon Romance:
Tender Conquest

BIONDI, Diane Reidy Guest
(Diane Guest)

BIRD, Beverly
[Beverly Helland]
Comes The Rain
Silhouette Desire:
190 Best Reasons, The
209 Fool's Gold
227 All The Marbles
411 To Love A Stranger
Silhouette Intimate Moments:
3 Emeralds In The Dark
23 Fires Of Winter, The
139 Ride The Wind
172 Solitary Man, A

BIRD, Patricia
[Patricia Amy Bird]
Avalon:
Acapulco Passage
Blueprint For Love
Crystal Heart
Golden Dream
In The Shadow Of Yesterday
Island Paradise
Once Upon A Dream
Shamrock In The Sun
Shipboard Kisses
Staged For Death
Sunshine Lost

BIRD, Sarah
[Sarah McCabe Bird]
Boyfriend School, The
Do Evil Cheerfully

BIRD, Sarah McCabe
(Sarah Bird)
(Tory Cates)

53

BIRMINHAM, Sony
  The Avon Romance:
    Spitfire

_____

_____

BIRMINGHAM, Stephen
  Auerbach Will, The   <Saga>
  LeBaron Secret, The
  Our Crowd
  Shades Of Fortune

_____

_____

BIRTHSTONE GOTHIC SERIES <BGS>
  1 Ghost And The Garnet, The
                        Marilyn Ross
  2 Amethyst Tears, The
                        Marilyn Ross
  3 Stone Of Blood
                     Juanita Coulsen
  4 Dark Diamond
                        Diana Tower
  5 Shadow Over Emerald Castle
                        Marilyn Ross
  6 Moonstone Spirit, The
                        Jean DeWeese
  7 Blood Ruby
                        Jan Alexander
  8 Carnelian Cat, The
                        Jean DeWeese
  9 Gleam Of Sapphire, A
                        Diana Tower
  10 Opal Legacy
                        Fortune Kent
  11 Topaz For My Fair Lady, A
                        Jane Toombs
  12 Turquoise Talisman
                        Sharon Wagner

_____

_____

BISHOP, Carly
                   [Cheryl McGongie]
  Harlequin Dreamscape Romance:
    Prince Of Dreams

_____

_____

BISHOP, Cassandra
                     [Robin Latham]
  Silhouette Desire:
    129 Madison Avenue Marriage
    203 Outsmarted
  Silhouette Romance:
    335 Free Spirit
    387 Wish Upon A Star

_____

_____

BISHOP, Claudia
                     [Jane Feather]
  Second Chance At Love:
    186 Irresistible You
    231 Kiss Me Once Again
    235 It Had To Be You
  To Have And To Hold:
    26 That Champagne Feeling
    36 Where The Heart Is

_____

_____

BISHOP, Lee
  Davy Crockett: Frontier Fighter
                         <AES:#11>

_____

_____

BISHOP, Leslie w/ Pat C. OAKSON
                    (Robin Tolivar)

BISHOP, Mary   <GOT>
  Chill Winds Of Ravenhall, The
  Hunter's Hill
  Killraven
  Land's End
  Widow's Walk

_____

_____

BISHOP, Natalie
                      [Nancy Bush]
  Silhouette Special Edition:
    178 Saturday's Child
    198 Lover Or Deceiver

BISHOP, Natalie (cont.)
     198 Lover Or Deceiver
     231 Stolen Thunder
     245 Trial By Fire
     280 String Of Pearls
     300 Diamond In The Sky
     329 Silver Thaw
     352 Just A Kiss Away
     401 Summertime Blues   &
     472 Imaginary Lover   &
     545 Prince And The Pauper, The
     596 Dear Diary
     651 Downright Dangerous

BISHOP, Sandra
  Heartfire Romance:
    Beloved Savage

BISHOP, Sheila   <GOT><HO><RE><RS>
  Bath Assembly
  Desperate Decision
  Durable Fire, The
  Favorite Sister, The
  Goldsmith's Row
  House With Two Faces, The
  London Season, A
  Lucasta
  No Hint Of Scandal
  Onlooker, The
  Penelope Devereux
  Phantom Garden, The
  Quick Brown Fox, The
  Rosalba
  Rules Of Marriage, The
  Second Husband, The
  Speaking Likeness, The
  Sweet Nightingale
  That Night At The Villa
  Well-Matched Pair, A
  Wilderness Walk, The
  Coventry: <RE>
     101 Honora Clare
     137 Consequences

BISKIN, Sally
  Second Time Around

BISSELL, Elaine   <CO>
                     (Whitney Faulkner)
  As Time Goes By
  Empire
  Family Fortunes   <Saga>

BITKER, Marjorie A.
  Different Flame, A
  Gold Of The Evening

BITTNER, F. Rosanne   <HR>
  Ecstasy's Chains
  Embers Of The Heart   #
  Heart's Surrender
  Lawless Love
  Montana Woman   #
  Prairie Embrace
  Rapture's Gold
  Sioux Splendor
  Sweet Mountain Magic
  Lovestruck:
    This Time Forever   <Saga>
  Savage Destiny Saga: In sequence:
    Sweet Prairie Passion
    Ride The Free Wind
    River Of Love
    Embrace The Wild Land
    Climb The Highest Mountain
    Meet The New Dawn
  Blue Hawk Trilogy:
    Savage Horizons
    Frontier Fires
    Destiny's Dawn
  The Bride Series: In sequence:
    Tennessee Bride
    Texas Bride
    Oregon Bride
  In sequence:
    Arizona Bride
    Arizona Ecstasy

BLACK, Cheryl
  Heartfire Romance: <HR>
    Comanche Caress
    Comanche Love Song

_____

_____

BLACK, Hermina/Hermina A.   <RS>
  Bitter Fruit
  Calling Doctor Cardross
  Danger In Montparnasse
  Strange Enchantment
  Sweet Pilgrimage
  World Of Love, A
  Adventures In Love:
    1 Dangerous Masquerade
    2 Bitter Honey
   13 Who Is Lucinda?
   14 Lordship Of Love, The
  In England:
    Bitter Honey
    Cinderella In Sunlight
    Dance On My Dreams
    Doctor In Shadow
    East Of The Sun
    Girl From Van Leydens, The
    House In Harley Street, The
    In Pursuit Of Perilla
    Invisible Flame, The
    Jennifer Harlow, M.D.
    Let Love Go By
    Lonely Heart, The
    Loren Ruston, S.R.N.
    Love For Francesca
    Moon Over Morocco
    Nurse On The Case, The
    Private Patient
    Romance For Romany
    Shadows Of Roses
    Sister Alison
    Stardust For Dreams
    Strange Enchantment
    Strangers Can Love

_____

_____

BLACK, Irene Loyd   <RE>
  Husband For The Countess, A

_____

_____

BLACK, Jackie
        [Jacqueline Ashley Casto]
  Wayfaring Stranger   <RS>
  Candlelight Ecstasy:
    39 Winter Winds
    92 Crimson Morning
   152 Autumn Fires
   170 Promises In The Night
   187 Time For Love, A
   339 Romantic Roulette
   389 Catch Of The Season, The
   448 Island Of Illusions
   510 Vixen's Kiss, The
   527 Charlie's Chance
  Candlelight Ecstasy Supreme:
    16 Payment In Full
    28 Fascination
    56 For All Time
    61 From This Day Forward
    85 Little Bit Of Warmth, A
  Candlelight Supreme:
   157 Dark Paradise

_____

_____

BLACK, Laura   <HR><RS>
  Albany
  Falls Of Gard, The
  Glendraco
  Ravenburn
  Strathgallant
  Wild Cat

_____

_____

BLACK, Veronica   <RS>
           [Maureen Peters]
  Dangerous Inheritance
  Fair Kilmeny
  Footfall In The Mist
  Master Of Malcarew
  Moonflete
  Portrait Of Sarah

BLACK, Veronica (cont.)
Wayward Madonna, The

BLACK, William   (Deceased)
        [William Joseph Black]
In sequence: <HR>
  Bella
  Bella's Blessings

BLACKBURN, Barbara
[Evelyn Barbara Blackburn Leader]
City Of Forever

BLACKBURN, Claire
        [Linda C. Jacobs]
Return Engagement
Avalon:
  Heart On Ice
  Rainbow For Clari
  Teacher For My Heart

BLACKER, Irwin   <HO>
        [Irwin Robert Blacker]
Taos

BLACKMAN, Lynne   <HR>
        [Lynne Sabin Blackman]
Fiery Obsession

BLACKMON, Laura
Marina

BLACKMORE, Jane   <GOT><RS>
And Then There Was Georgia
Angel's Tear
Beloved Stranger
Beware The Night
Bitter Honey
Bitter Love
Bridge Of Strange Music, The
Broomstick In The Hall
City Of Forever
Closing Door, The
Cresselly Inheritance, The
Dangerous Love
Dark Between The Stars, The
Deed Of Innocence
Deep Pool, The
Flight Into Love
Hawkridge
It Couldn't Happen To Me
It Happened To Susan
Joanna
Lonely House, The
Man Of Power
Miranda
Missing Hour, The
My Sister Erica
Night Of The Bonfire
Night Of The Stranger
Of Wind And Fire
Other Mother, The
Other Room, The
Perilous Waters
Ravenden
Raw Summer
Room In The Tower, The
Square Of Many Colours, The
Stephanie (Return To Love)
Tears In Paradise
That Night
Three Letters To Pan
Trap For Lovers, A
Velvet Trap, The
Woman On Her Own, A
Candlelight:
  524 Tears In Paradise   <IN>
  646 Perilous Waters   <RO>

BLACKSTOCK, Charity   <RS>
                    [Ursula Torday]
  Daughter, The
  Dewey Death
  Encounter, The
  English Wife, The
  Foggy, Foggy Dew
  Ghost Town
  House Possessed, A
  Jungle, The
  Knock At Midnight, The
  Lemmings, The
  Lonely Stranger, The
  Monkey On A Chain
  People In Glass Houses
  Shirt Front, The
  Widow, The

_____

_____

BLACKTREE, Barbara
                  [Barbara Coultry]
  Rapture Romance:
    99 Ariel's Song

_____

_____

BLACKWELL, Judith
               [Judy Blackwell Myers]
  Crosswinds Keepsake:
    35 Just Like Jessica

_____

_____

BLACKWOOD, Stephanie   <GOT>
                   [Sigmund Miller]
  Lamontane

_____

_____

BLAIR, Alison   <YA>
                   [Janice Boies]
  No Contest

_____

_____

BLAIR, Alma
  Avalon:
    Web Of Danger
    Unwitting Witness, The
    Dark Side Of Paradise, The

_____

_____

BLAIR, Christina   <GOT>
  Crystal Destiny

_____

_____

BLAIR, Cynthia
  All Our Secrets
  Crazy In Love   <YA>
  Forever Rainbows
  Just Married   <CO>
  Lover's Choice
  Once There Was A Fat Girl
  Summer House
  Three Of Us, The
  Love & Life:
    Battle Scars
    Beautiful Dreamer
    Commitment

_____

BLAIR, Jennifer
                 [Adeline McElfresh]
  Candlelight:
    46   Assignment In The Islands
    58   Skye Manor
    93   Danger At Olduvai
    152 Evil Island   <MY>
    167 Kanesbrake
    182 Dangerous Assignment
    195 Long Shadow, The
    215 Safe Harbor
    218 To Last A Lifetime

_____

_____

BLAIR, Joan
  Harlequin Romance:
    811 Way To The Wedding, The
    907 Two For The Doctor

_____

_____

BLAIR, Kathryn
                (Rosalind Brett)
                (Celine Conway)
Harlequin Classic:
  26 Golden Rose, The   (650)
  44 House At Tegwani, The(717)
  51 Fair Invader, The   (M&B)
  99 Sweet Deceiver   (893)
 121 Mayenga Farm   (941)
 130 Barbary Moon   (972)
 139 Primrose Bride, The   (988)
 156 Dangerous Kind Of
        Love, The   (878)
 164 Tulip Tree, The   (1059)
 175 No Other Haven   (1012)
Harlequin Romance:
 766 Enchanting Island, The
 785 Surgeon's Marriage, The
 805 Love This Enemy
 823 Dear Adversary
 843 Summer At Barbazon, A
 861 Bewildered Heart
 878 Dangerous Kind Of Love,The
 893 Sweet Deceiver
 920 Man At Mulera, The
 941 Mayenga Farm
 954 Doctor Westland
 972 Barbary Moon
 988 Primrose Bride, The
1012 No Other Haven
1038 Battle Of Love
1059 Tulip Tree, The
1083 Dearest Enemy
1107 They Met In Zanzibar
1148 Flowering Wilderness

BLAIR, Kathryn
[Mary Kathryn Scamehorn
          w/ Karen Blair Parker]
Harlequin American Romance:
 285 Home Is The Sailor
 328 Dancing In The Aisles

BLAIR, Laurien
               [Laurien Berenson]
Silhouette Desire:
 105 Sweet Temptation
 130 Between The Covers
 210 That Special Magic
 243 Taken By Storm

BLAIR, Leona
Morning Into Night
Privilege
World Of Difference, A   <Saga>
In sequence:
  Woman's Place, A
  With This Ring

BLAIR, Shannon
Sweet Dreams: <YA>
  69 Call Me Beautiful
  79 Star Struck
  88 Wrong Kind Of Boy

BLAIRSON, Peter T.
Escalante:
  Wilderness Path   <AES:#10>

BLAKE, Andrea
                   (Anne Weale)
Harlequin Classic:
  58 September In Paris (HR755)
 108 Now And Always   (HR864)
 126 Whisper Of Doubt   (HR944)
 134 Night Of
        The Hurricane   (HR974)

BLAKE, Antonio
    [Mildred Havill Juskevice]
  Candlelight:
    635 Lasting Love   <RO>

BLAKE, Jennifer   <HR>
    [Patricia Maxwell]
  Bride Of A Stranger
    (Original by Patricia Maxwell)
  Dark Masquerade
    (Original by Patricia Maxwell)
  Embrace And Conquer
  Fierce Eden
  Golden Fancy
  Louisiana Dawn
  Love And Smoke   <CO>
  Love's Wild Desire
  Midnight Waltz
  Night Of The Candle
    (Original by Patricia Maxwell)
  Perfume Of Paradise
  Prisoner Of Desire
  Southern Rapture
  Spanish Serenade
  Storm And The Splendor, The
  Surrender In Moonlight
  Sweet Piracy
    (Original by Patricia Maxwell)
  Tender Betrayal
  In sequence:
    Royal Seduction
    Royal Passion

BLAKE, Jillian
  Silhouette Intimate Moments:
    27 Diana's Folly
    67 East Side, West Side
  Silhouette Special Edition:
    256 Water Dancer
    299 Heartstroke
    323 Sullivan vs. Sullivan
    399 Vision To Share, A

BLAKE, Karen
  Coventry:
    116 Question Of Honor, A

BLAKE, Katherine   <GOT>
    [Dorothy Blake Walter]
  Night Stands At The Door

BLAKE, Laurel
    [Elaine Fowler Palencia]
  Second Chance At Love:
    66 Stormy Passage
    154 Stranger In Paradise
    202 Into The Whirlwind

BLAKE, Monica
              [Marie Muir]
  Hidden Heritage

BLAKE, Stephanie   <HR>
    [Jacques Bain Pearl]
  Blaze Of Passion
  Bride Of The Wind
  Callie Knight
  Devil In My Heart, The
  Fires Of The Heart
  Glorious Passion, A
  Scarlett Kisses
  Secret Sins
  So Wicked My Desire
  Texas Lily
  This World Is Mine
  Unholy Desires
  Wicked Is My Flesh
  In sequence:
    Flowers Of Fire
    Daughter Of Destiny

BLAKE, Susan
  First Kiss: <YA>
    1 Head Over Heels
  Sweet Dreams: <YA>
    60 Summer Breezes
    84 Last Word, The
    150 Summer Secrets
    162 Trading Hearts
  Sweet Dreams Special:
    2 Change Of Heart, A

BLAKE, Vanessa   <GOT>
                        [May Brown]
  Blood Emerald
  Bride Of Misfortune
  Dark Guardian
  Master Of Evrington
  Pentallion
  Queen's Consent, The

BLAKE, Veronica
  Heartfire Romance: <HR>
    Apache Tigress
    Desperado Desire
    Savage Dreams
    Texas Rose

BLAKELEE, Alexandra
                   [Alexandra Hine]
  Circle Of Love:
    14 Botticelliman, The

BLAKELY, Melissa
                    [Lilla Brennan]
  Candlelight:
    231 Hold Me Forever   <RO>

BLANCHET, Lise
  Mystique:
    82 Shadow Of Evil

BLANFORD, Virginia
                      (Sarah Crewe)

BLANSHARD, Audrey   <HO><RE>
  Chelbeck Charger, The
  Frensham Inheritance, The
  Granborough's Filly
  Lucetta
  Shy Young Denbury, The
  Virginian At Venncombe, A
  Coventry:
    17 Lydeard Beauty, The
    33 Fearns Of Audley Stree,The
    60 Sir Ranulf And The Runaway
    87 An Affair Of Dishonour
    120 Catherine

BLAYNE, Diana
                [Susan Spaeth Kyle]
  Denim And Lace
  Candlelight Ecstasy:
    94 Waiting Game, A
    113 Loving Arrangement, A
    138 White Sand, Wild Sea
    184 Dark Surrender
  Candlelight Ecstasy Supreme:
    49 Color Love Blue
    110 Tangled Destinies

BLAYNE, Sara   <RE>
  Duel Of The Heart
  Passion's Lady
  Heartfire Romance: <HR>
    Sea Witch
    Sweet Abandon

BLAYNEY, Mary
  Silhouette Desire:
    448 True Colors
  Silhouette Romance:
    688 Father Christmas

BLEVINS, Winfred
  Powder River   <RWS:#4>
  Yellowstone, The   <RWS:#1>

BLICKLE, Katrinka   <GOT><RS>
  [Katrinka Blickle Pellecchia]
  Dark Beginnings
  Heart Of The Harbour
  North Sea Mistress
  Verity

BLISHEN, Edward
              (see Leon Garfield)

BLIXEN, Karen Christentze Dinesen
              (Pierre Andrezel)

BLOCK, Barbara
  Sweet Savage Sophomore Year: <YA>
    3 Uptown Love

BLOCK, Paul
  Salomon Family: <HS>
    In sequence:
      San Francisco
      The Deceit

BLOCKINGER, Betty
    [Peggy O'More Blocklinger]
  Escape From Love
  Lady Lookout Of Phantom Peak

BLOCKINGER, Betty (cont.)
  Legacy Of Love, A
  Love To Lean On, A

BLOCKINGER, Peggy O'More
              (Betty Blockinger)
              (Jeanne Bowman)
              (Peggy O'More)
BLOOM, Jill
  Harlequin Intrigue:
    57 Playing With Fire
  Harlequin Temptation:
    37 Two Of A Kind
    105 Sky's The Limit, The

BLOOM, Ursula   <HR>
              (Sheila Burns)
              (Mary Essex)
              (Sara Sloane)
  Bitter Sweet
  Born For Love
  Change Of Heart, A
  Fire And The Rose, The
  Forever Autumn
  Great Tomorrow, The
  Gypsy Flame
  Honor's Price
  King's Wife, The
  Love Is But A Dream
  Love: Old And New
  Magnificent Courtesan, The
  Mirage Of Love
  Mirage On The Horizon
  Mistress To The King
  Passionate Heart, The
  Passion's Pilgrim
  Prelude To Yesterday
  Queen's Affair, The
  Secret Lover, The
  Sunday Love
  Sweet Spring Of April
  Tomorrow Never Comes
  When Doctors Love
  Yesterday's Tomorrow

BLOSS, Janet Adele
Sweet Dreams: <YA>
   156 Two Boys Too Many

BLUE, Rose
Caprice Romance: <YA>
   70 Heart To Heart

BLUNDELL, Judy
                (Kathleen Garvey-YA)
                (Jude O'Neill)

BLYTH, Juliet   <RE>
                [Stella Riley]
   Lucifer's Champion
   Parfait Knight, The

BLYTH, Myrna
   Cousin Suzanne
   For Better And For Worse

BLYTHE, Leonora   <RE>
                [Leonora Burton]
   Felicia
   Lady Tara
   Coventry:
     6 Helene
    44 Miranda
   134 Carolina
   156 Sally

BLYTHE, Megan
                [Michalann Perry]
   Heartfire Romance: <HR>
   Satin Chains

BOAST, Philip
   London's Child   <Saga>

BOATNER, Patricia
   All Our Tomorrows

BOATRIGHT, Lori   <YA>
   Out Of Bounds

BOCKOVEN, Georgia
   SuperRomance:
    82 Restless Tide
   Harlequin SuperRomance:
   102 After The Lightning
   138 Little By Little
   179 Today, Tomorrow, Always
   222 Long Road Home, The
   246 Love Songs   &
   Harlequin Temptation:
    14 Tracings On A Window
    57 Gift Of Wild Flowers, A
    94 Week From Friday, A
   161 Tomorrow's Love Song &

BODE, Margo   <HR>
   Jasmine Splendor

BODEEN, Dewitt   <GOT>
   13 Castle Walk

63

BODINE, Sherrill w/ Elaine SIMA
                    (Lynn Leslie)
                    (Leslie Lynn)

BOECKMAN, Patricia Ellen Kennelly
        and/or Charles BOECKMAN
                    (Patti Beckman)

BOESE, Dawn C.
                    (Dawn Carroll)

BOGUE, Lucile
        [Lucile Maxfield Bogue]
    Salt Lake

_____

_____

BOIES, Jan/Janice
                    (Alison Blair-YA)
                    (Anne Hunter Lowell)
    Caprice Romance: <YA>
     71 Learning To Love
    First Kiss: <YA>
      5 Right Boy, Wrong Girl
    Sweet Dreams: <YA>
    114 Just The Way You Are
    124 More Than Friends
    138 Heart And Soul
    158 Crossed Signals
    164 Playing To Win
    174 Love On Strike

_____

_____

BOLANDER, Judith
    Harlequin SuperRomance:
    246 Best Of Yesterday, The

_____

_____

BOLDT, Lana McGraw
    Fionna's Will   <Saga>
    Flower Of The Pacific   <Saga>

_____

_____

BOLES, Paul Darcy
    Glory Day
    Limner, The
    Loving Letty
    Mississippi Run, The

_____

_____

BOLTON, Muriel Roy   (Deceased)<HR>
    Golden Porcupine

_____

_____

BOLT, Maxine
    Avalon:
      Memories Of Moonwind
      Silver Swan, The
      Dream To Build On, A
      Hard Hats And Roses

_____

BOND, Evelyn   <GOT><RS>
                    [Morris Hershman]
    Beloved Traitor
    Bride Of Terror
    Clouded Mirror, The
    Crimson Candle, The
    Dark Sonata
    Devil's Footprints, The
    Doomway
    Evil In The House
    Girl From Nowhere, The
    Hornet's Nest
    Imperial Blue
    Lady In Darkness
    Heart's Intrigue, The   <RE>
    Lady Of Storm House
    Heritage Of Fear
    House Of Distant Voices
    House Of Shadows
    Raven's Eye
    Ventian Secret, The
    Waiting Eyes, The   <ZGS>
    Widow In White

_____

_____

BOND, Rebecca
[Rebecca Czuleger]
Harlequin American Romance:
92   In Passion's Defense
109 Bed And Board
172 Open Channels
Harlequin Intrigue:
31   Matthias Ring, The

BONDS, Parris Afton
[Parris Afton Wilkes Bonds]
(see Silhouette Summer Sizzlers)
Blue Bayou
Blue Moon
Deep Purple
Dust Devil
Flash Of The Firefly, The
Lavender Blue
Love Tide
Mood Indigo
Savage Enchantment
Snow And Ice
Star Dust
Sweet Golden Sun
Silhouette Classic:
5   Wind Song   <IM5>
Silhouette Intimate Moments:
5   Wind Song
41   Widow Woman
77   Spinster's Song
     In sequence:
113   Midsummer Midnight
153   Man For Hire
189   Wanted Woman
218   Renegade Man
241   That McKenna Woman
253   That Malcolm Girl (Sub-
       scription Only)
       That Mescalero Man (Never
       Published)
Silhouette Romance:
70   Made For Each Other
526 Run To Me

BONHAM, Barbara   <GOT><HR>
[Barbara Lee Thomas Bonham]
(See Sara North)
Bittersweet
Dance Of Desire
Dark Side Of Passion, The
Diagnosis: Love
Green Willow
Passion's Price
Proud Passion
Sweet And Bitter Fancy
Avalon:
    Army Nurse
    Nina Stewart, R.N.

BONNER, Rachael
Silhouette Inspirations:
32   Impatient Blossom, The

BONNER, Terry Nelsen   <HO>
Australia/New South Wales Series:
1   Rum Colony
2   First Families
3   Free Woman, The
         [Laura Castoro]
4   Pioneers, The
         [Mollie Gregory]
5   Outback, The
6   Wildings, The
7   Diggers
         [Steve Krauzer]
8   Seekers
9   The Defiant
         [Sheila Raeschild]
10   Unvanquished
         [Marc Olden]

BOOHER, Dianna   <CO>
[Dianna Daniels Booher]
Last Caress, The

BOOTH, Rosemary Frances
               (Frances Murray)

BOOTON, Kage   <GOT>
     [Catherine Kage Booton]
  Place Of Shadows
  Toy, The
  Troubled House, The

BORG, Sven-Hugo   <HO>
  Ride The Wild Sea

BORIS, Martin
  Woodbridge 1946

BORIS, Robert
         (see Edward Hannibal)

BORLAND, Kathryn Kilby w/
      Helen Ross Smith SPEICHER
             (Alice Abbott)

BOSLER, Coleen Quinn
           (Coleen Quinn)

BOSNA, Valeria
           (Valeria King)
         (Sarah Montrose)

BOSSE, Malcolm
  In sequence: <Saga>
    Warlord, The
    Fire In Heaven

BOSTOCK, William   <HO>
  I, Cleopatra
  Lovemakers
  Way We Are, The

BOSTWICK, Angela
           (Angela Wells)

BOSWELL, Barbara
          (Betsy Osborne)
  Loveswept:
   53 Little Consequences   &
   78 Sensuous Perception   ^
   95 Darling Obstacles
  117 Landslide Victory   @
  142 Trouble In Triplicate
  158 Always, Amber   ^
  160 Bedside Manners   &
  164 Whatever It Takes
  183 Tangles
  194 Not A Marrying Man   @
  207 Playing Hard To Get   #
  236 Sharing Secrets   #
  242 Intimate Details   #
  261 Baby, Baby   &
  272 And Tara, Too   #
  313 Ms. Fortune's Man
  334 Simply Irresistible   %
  359 One Step From Paradise %
      Last Brady, The   #
  Loveswept Golden Classic:
  Darling Obstacles   <LS95>
  Silhouette Desire:
  558 Rule Breaker   <MMS>
  583 Another Whirlwind
      Courtship
  609 Bridal Price, The

BOULET, Ada
            (Ada John)

BOURGEOUS, Camille
          (Robin Carol)

BOURNE, Caroline   <HR>
  In sequence:
  Allegheny Ecstsy
  Allegheny Captive

BOURNE, Caroline (cont.)
  Falcon's Lady
  On Rapture's Wing
  Wild Southern Rose
  In sequence:
    Texas Conquest
    Texas Fire

BOURNE, Caroline w/ Debbie HANCOCK
                    (Elizabeth Leigh)

BOURNE, Hester   <RS>
                    [Molly Troke]
  Haunted Island
  In The Event Of My Death   <GOT>
  Red Raincoat, The
  Scent Of Roses, A
  Spanish House, The

BOURNE, Joanna Watkins   <RE>
  Her Ladyship's Companion

BOWDEN, Jean
                (Barbara Annandale)
                (Belinda Dell)

BOWDEN, Susan
        [Susan Bowden Twaddle]
  Redcliffe Family Trilogy:
    In The Shadow Of The Crown
    Divided Heart, The

BOWDLER, Lucy
  Avalon:
    Janis Hall Nurse Instructor
    Nurse Sandra's Choice

BOWE, Kate
                [Mary Ann Taylor]
  SuperRomance:
    28 Love's Glittering Web
  Harlequin SuperRomance:
    117 Horizons

BOWEN, Alice/Alyce
  Candlelight Ecstasy:
    463 Dangerous Encounter
    501 Intimate Persuasion
  SuperRomance:
    32 Dangerous Promise

BOWEN, Charlene
  Avalon:
    Change Of Heart
    Wandering Heart, The
    To Catch A Rainbow
    Reach For A Star
    Summer's Love Dream, A

BOWEN, Judith
                [Judy E. Corser]
  Silhouette Romance:
    732 That Man Next Door

BOWEN, Marjorie   <HO><RS>
            [Gabrielle Margaret Long]
  Boundless Waters
  Dark Rosaleen
  Dickon
  Glen O'Weeping
  House Of Sorrows
  Lyndly Waters
  Pale Rose
  Poisoners, The
  Queen's Caprice, The
  Soldier From Virginia
  Violante

67

BOWERS, Mary Curtis
Avalon:
    Best Nurse In Missouri
    Loves Of Nurse Rachael, The
    Nurse Becky's New World
    Nurse Carrie's Roses
    Nurse Charly's New Love
    Nurse Heather's Choice
    Nurse In Australia
    Nurse In Peru
    Nurse Jamie's Surprise
    Nurse Jill's Perfect Man
    Nurse Karen's Masquerade
    Nurse Sarah's Confusion

_____

_____

BOWERS, Terry
Avalon:
    Dance Of Love

_____

_____

BOWERSOCK, Melissa
    Love's Savage Destiny
    Love's Savage Embrace

_____

_____

BOWES, Florence   <GOT>
    Web Of Solitude
    Starlight Romance:
        Beauchamp
        Interlude In Venice
        Macorvan Curse, The

_____

_____

BOWMAN, Jeanne
            [Peggy O'More Blocklinger]
    City Hospital Nurse
    Conflict For Nurse Elsa
    Door To Door Nurse
    Doomed To Hate
    Empty House, The
    From Molly With Love

BOWMAN, Jeanne (cont.)
    Girl In The Mirror
    Happiness Habit, The
    Lady Mayor
    Leave Love Alone
    Letter From Annette
    Love Campaign, The
    Love Took Second Place
    Lovelorn Lady
    Man Too Many, A
    Measure Of Love, A
    Medicare Nurse
    Nurse A La Mode
    Nurse Betrayed
    Nurse On Polka Dot Island
    Nurse On Pondre Island
    Off-Camera Love
    Penny For Love, A
    Ready For Love
    Recess For The Teacher
    Small Town Nurse
    Strange Impersonation
    Touch Of Laughter
    Trust In Love
    Why Not Try Love?
    Sharon Contemporary Teens: <YA>
        Secret Of The Forest
    Starlight Romance:
        Lakeville Lady
        That Girl

_____

_____

BOYARD, Alexis
    Savage Embrace

_____

_____

BOYD, Esther
                    [Edmond A. D. Boyd]
    Candlelight:
        552 Omen For Love   <RO>
        583 Precious Pirate   <RO>
        624 Bali Breezes   <RO>

_____

_____

68

BOYLE, Ann
    [Ann Peters Boyle]
    (Audrey Brent)
    (Ann Bryan)
Moon Shadows
To Find A Unicorn
Avalon:
  Beyond The Wall
  Dark Mountain
  One Golden Earring
  Rim Of Forever
  Snowy Hills Of Innocence, The
  Sundown Girl
  Veil Of Sand
  Well Of Three Echoes, The
Candlelight:
  80 Stormy Slopes
Caprice Romance: <YA>
  33 Never Say Never
MacFadden Romance:
  108 Desert Song

BOYNTON, Judy
Candlelight:
  544 Guardian Of Innocence <IN>

BRACALE, Carla
First Kiss: <YA>
  3 Falling For You
  6 Fair-Weather Love
Sweet Dreams: <YA>
  163 My Dream Guy
  168 Dream Date

BRADER, Norma
Candlelight Ecstasy:
  244 Settling The Score

BRADFORD, Barbara w/ Sally SIDDON
    (Sally Bradford)
    (Barbara Siddon)

BRADFORD, Barbara Taylor
Act Of Will   <Saga>
Triumph Of Lydia Cave, The
Voice Of The Heart   <CO>
Women In His Life, The
Emma Harte Trilogy:
  Woman Of Substance, A
  Hold The Dream
  To Be The Best

BRADFORD, Laura
    [Paul B. Paalborg]
Players

BRADFORD, Lily
Second Chance At Love:
  11 Moonfire Melody
  17 Heart Of The Glen

BRADFORD, Mary Ellen   <YA>
Make Your Dreams Come True:
  1 Angie's Choice
  7 Language Of Love

BRADFORD, Sally
[Sally Siddon w/ Barbara Bradford]
Harlequin Temptation:
  263 When Fortune Smiles
Harlequin SuperRomance:
  281 Arrangement, The
  365 Spring Thaw

BRADFORD, Sarah
  Blood Of The Borgias, The   <HS>

_____

_____

BRADLEY, Kate
              [Kathleen Bryant]
  Silhouette Intimate Moments:
  231 Ancient Secrets
  346 Sheep's Clothing

_____

_____

BRADLEY, Marion Zimmer   <GOT>
  Castle Terror
  Drums Of Darkness - Leo   <ZGS>
  Firebrand, The   <HF>
  Mists Of Avalon, The   <HF>
  Souvenir Of Monique

_____

_____

BRADLEY, Muriel
          [Muriel Demens Bradley]
  Flowers In Winter   <CO>
  Sudden Summer, The   <CO>
  In sequence: <HR>
    Tanya
    Destiny's Star
  Heartfire Romance: <HR>
    Ecstasy's Wings
  Silhouette Intimate Moments:
    28 Waltz In Scarlet
    66 Island Man

_____

_____

BRADSHAW, Gillian
        [Gillian Marucha Bradshaw]
  Hawk Of May
  Kingdom Of Summer
  Arthurian Trilogy: <HO>
    Beekeeper's Daughter
    Beacon At Alexandria, The
    Imperial Purple

_____

_____

BRADSTREET, Valerie   <RE>
            [Mary Linn Roby]
  Fortune Wheel, The
  Ivory Fan, The

_____

_____

BRADY, Brett
  First Love From Silhouette: <YA>
  49 One Of A Kind

_____

_____

BRAGG, Melvyn   <HR>
  Maid Of Buttermere, The

_____

_____

BRAMSCH, Joan
  Loveswept:
    41 Sophisticated Mountain Gal
    64 Kiss To Make It Better, A
    81 Light Side, The
    88 At Nightfall
   119 Stallion Man, The
   200 With No Reservations

_____

_____

BRAMWELL, Charlotte   <GOT>
            [John M. Kimbro]
  Brother Sinister
  Cousin To Terror
  Stepmother's House

_____

_____

BRAND, Christianna   <RE>
      [Mary Christianna Milne Lewis]
  Brides Of Aberdar, The
  Court Of Foxes
  Starrbelow

_____

_____

BRAND, Debra
(Suzanne Rand)

BRAND, Irene
  Love Is The Key   <Insp>
  Promise Romance: <Insp>
    3 Change Of Heart, A
   24 Mighty Flame, A
  Serenade/Saga: <HR><Insp>
   33 Where Morning Dawns

_____

_____

BRAND, Susan   <RS>
  [Susan Bonthron Roper]
  Shadows On The Tor

_____

_____

BRANDEWYNE, Rebecca   <HR>
  [Mary Rebecca Wadsworth Brandewyne]
  And Gold Was Ours
  Desire In Disguise
  Forever My Love
  Heartland
  Love, Cherish Me
  No Gentle Love
  Outlaw Hearts, The   <Saga>
  Rose Of Rapture
  Chronicles Of Tintagel: <RF>
    Passion Moon Rising
  Highclyff Trilogy: <GOT>
    Upon A Moon-Dark Moor
    Across A Starlit Sea

_____

_____

BRANDON, Alicia
  [Stella Cameron w/ Linda Rice]
  Harlequin American Romance:
   121 Love Beyond Question
  Harlequin Intrigue:
    40 Full Circle

_____

_____

BRANDON, Beatrice   <RS>
  [Robert W. Krepps]
  Cliffs Of Night, The
  Court Of Silver Shadows, The

_____

_____

BRANDON, JoAnna
  [Olivia Longoria Harper w/
            Kenneth M. Harper]
  Candlelight Ecstasy:
    66 Devil's Playground, The
   112 Sing To Me Of Love
   237 Love, Bid Me Welcome
   332 Just A Kiss Away
   401 Lingering Laughter
   488 Never Give In
  Candlelight Ecstasy Supreme:
    59 All The Right Moves
   114 World In His Arms, The
  Candlelight Supreme:
   133 Suspicion And Desire

_____

_____

BRANDON, Joyce   <HR>
  After Eden
  Story Order:
    Lady And The Lawman, The
    Lady And The Outlaw, The

_____

_____

BRANDT, Cate
  Heartfire Romance: <HR>
    Colorado Jewel
    Silken Chains

_____

_____

BRANDT, Jane Lewis   <HR>
  Firebrand
  La Chingada

_____

_____

BRANSFORD, Carolyn
Partners

_____

_____

BRANTON, Danielle
Catch A Rising Star
Great Lover, The

_____

_____

BRAUER, Deana
     (Dana Daniels)
     (Dena Rhee)
Silhouette Romance:
 599 Simply Sam

_____

_____

BRAUN, Matthew   <HR>
Kincaids, The
Lords Of The Land
This Loving Promise

_____

_____

BRAUNSTEIN, Binnie Syril
     (Binnie Syril)

BRAWLEY, Ernest
Selena
Rap, The

_____

_____

BRAY, Sandra
Mystique:
 129 Strange Destiny

_____

_____

BRECK, Vivian
   [Vivian Gurney Breckenfeld]
Maggie

_____

_____

BREGMAN, Sandra
Reach For The Dream
Morning Star

_____

_____

BREMER, JoAnne
Candlelight Ecstasy:
 222 Seductive Illusion
 254 An Expert's Advice
 441 Knockout
Candlelight Ecstasy Supreme:
 69 Flirting With Danger
 106 To Love A Thief
Harlequin SuperRomance:
 302 It's All In The Game

_____

BREMER, JoAnne w/ Carol I. WAGNER
     (Joellyn Carroll)

BRENDAN, Mary   <RE>
Beloved Avenger
Gentleman's Mistress, A

_____

BRENNAN, Alice <GOT><RS>
An Acre Of Love
Brooding House, The
Candace
Castle Mirage
Consequences Of Love
Devil Take All
Devil's Dreamer, The
Fear No Evil
Ghost At Stagmere
Haunted, The
Litany Of Evil
Never To Die
Nurse's Dormitory
Romances Of Young Dr. Masters,The
Sleep Well, Christine
Thirty Days Hath July
To Kill A Witch

_____

_____

BRENNAN, Elizabeth
Girl Called Debbie, A

BRENNAN, Jan
Dream Of Destiny
Greythorn Woman, The

BRENNAN, Lilla
                    (Melissa Blakely)

BRENNER, Marie
Going Hollywood
Intimate Distance
Tell Me Everything

BRENNERT, Alan
Kindred Spirits

BRENT, Audrey
                    [Ann Boyle]
Silhouette Romance:
  63 Snowflakes In The Sun

BRENT, Casey
MacFadden Romance:
  119 Rosa Del Rio
  213 Moonflower

BRENT, Iris
                    [Iris Bancroft]
My Love Is Free
Swinger's Diary

BRENT, Joanna
Few Days In Weasel Creek, A

BRENT, Madeleine   <RS>
Capricorn Stone, The
Golden Urchin
Heritage Of Shadows, A
Long Masquerade, The
Merlin's Keep
Moonraker's Bride
Stormswift
Stranger At Wildings
Tregaron's Daughter

BRESLOW, Susan
Gift Of Love, A

BRETON, Anne-Marie   <HO>
To Flee From Eagles

BRETONNE, Anne-Marie   <GOT>
                    [Arnold M. Berman]
Cry Of Neptune, The   <BZG>
Dark Talisman
Gallows Stand In Salem, A

BRETT, Barbara
Between Two Eternities
Love After Hours
Promises To Keep   w/Hy BRETT

BRETT, Brady
First Love From Silhouette: <YA>
  49 One Of A Kind

73

BRETT, Katheryn
                    [Peg Robarchek]
Silhouette Intimate Moments:
  195 Genuine Article, The

BRETT, Rosalind
                     [Kathryn Blair]
Harlequin Classic:
   32 Stormy Haven   (656)
   43 Towards The Sun   (693)
   59 Winds In The
        Wilderness   (773)
   68 Quiet Holiday   (740)
   76 Portrait Of Susan   (783)
  153 Hotel Mirador   (989)
  160 Cottage In Spain, A   (952)
Harlequin Presents:
   43 They Came To Valeira
   55 Love This Stranger
   71 And No Regrets
Harlequin Romance:
  760 Fair Horizon
  773 Winds In The Wilderness
  783 Portrait Of Susan
  800 Sweet Waters
  815 Young Tracy
  839 Tangle In Sunshine
  856 Too Young To Marry
  869 Reluctant Guest, The
  877 Dangerous Waters
  908 Elizabeth Browne,
        Children's Nurse
  952 Cottage In Spain, A
  989 Hotel Mirador
 1101 Girl At White Drift, The
 1131 Bolambo Affair, The
 1176 Winds Of Enchantment
 1319 Brittle Bondage

BRETTON, Barbara
  Fire's Lady   <HR>
  Midnight Lover   <HR>
  Harlequin American Romance:
    3 Love Changes

BRETTON, Barbara (cont.)
   49 Sweetest of Debts, The
   91 No Safe Place
  138 Edge Of Forever, The
  161 Promises In The Night
  175 Shooting Star
  193 Playing For Time   &
  211 Second Harmony
  230 Nobody's Baby
  251 Honeymoon Hotel   &
  274 Fine Madness, A   &
  305 Mother Knows Best   <GCT>
  322 Mrs. Scrooge   <CIFK>
  355 All We Know Of Heaven
  365 Sentimental Journey <COAR>
  369 Stranger In Paradise<COAR>
Harlequin Intrigue:
   18 Starfire

BREW, Cathleen   <HR>
  Innocent Revenge

BREWSTER, Martha   <HR>
  On Wings Of Song
  Sweet Enemy

BRIAN, Marilyn
                     [Jillian Dagg]
  To Have And To Hold:
   19 Passion's Glow

BRICKNER, Richard P.
              [Richard Pilpel Brickner]
  Tickets   <CO>

BRIDE, Nadja
          [Josephine Nobisso]
  Torch:
    Hide And Seek

BRIDGE, Ann   <RS>
  [Mary Dolling Sanders O'Malley]
  Enchanter's Nightshade
  Episode At Toledo, The
  Four-Part Setting
  Frontier Passage
  Ginger Griffin, The
  Illyrian Spring
  Malady At Madiera
  Moments Of Knowing
  Nightshade
  Peking Picnic
  Place To Stand, A
  Singing Waters
  Julia Probyn Story:
    Emergency In The Pyrenees
    Dangerous Islands, The
    Lighthearted Quest, The
    Numbered Account, The
    Portuguese Escape, The
    Julia In Ireland

BRIDGE, Susan
            (Elisabeth Carey)

BRIER, Margaret
  MacFadden Romance:
    206   Enchanted Evening

BRIGGS, Victor   <HR>
  In sequence:
    Sacred Ground, The
    Reap The Harvest

BRIGHT, Elizabeth   <HR>
          [Robert Liston]
  Destiny's Thunder
  Lasting Splendor, A
  Virginians, The
  Morgan-Kingston Family:
    In Sequence:
    Reap The Wild Harvest
    Passion's Heirs
    Desire's Legacy
    Heritage Of Passion, A

BRIGHT, Laurey
          [Daphne de Jong]
  Silhouette Classic:
    14   Deep Waters   <SE62>
    30   When Morning Comes <SE143>
  Silhouette Romance:
    107   Tears Of Morning
    125   Sweet Vengeance
    356   Long Way From Home
    525   Rainbow Way, The
    568   Jacinth
  Silhouette Special Edition:
    62   Deep Waters
    143   When Morning Comes
    213   Fetters Of The Past
    516   Sudden Sunlight, A
    564   Games Of Chance
    586   Guilty Passion, A

BRINDLEY, Louise
  Forever Violets
  Forever Roses
  In The Shadow Of The Brontes
  Wild Thorn Summer   <RE>

BRINGLE, Mary   <CO>
  [Mary Hanford Brannum Bringle]
          (Kathleen Morris)
  Open Heart

BRINK, Carol   <RS>
       [Carol Ryrie Brink]
   Bellini Look, The
   Snow In The River

BRINK, Inga
   A Dark Desire Romance: <RS>
     Tropic Of Terror

BRISCO, Patty   <GOT><RS>
   [Patricia Matthews w/
            Clayton Matthews]
   Crystal Window, The
   Horror At Gull House
   House Of Candles
   Mist Of Evil
   Avalon:
     Merry's Treasure

BRISKIN, Jacqueline
   Afterlove
   California Generation
   Dreams Are Not Enough   <Saga>
   Everything And More   <Saga>
   Naked Heart, The
   Onyx, The
   Paloverde
   Rich Friends
   Too Much Too Soon

BRISTOL, Joanna
   Evie's Fortune In Paris
   Evie's Roman Fortune
   Fortunes Of Evie

BRISTOL, Leigh   <HR>
   [Donna Ball w/
         Elizabeth Shannon Harper]
   Hearts Of Fire
   Sunswept
   Twice Blessed
   Fielding Trilogy:
     Scarlet Sunrise
     Amber Skies
     Silver Twilight

BRISTOW, Gwen   (Deceased)<HR>
   Calico Palace
   Celia Garth
   Jubilee Trail
   Ninth Guest, The   w/Bruce MANNING
   Tomorrow Is Forever
   Plantation Trilogy:
     Deep Summer
     Handsome Road, The
     This Side Of Glory

BRISTOWE, Anthony   <RS>(Deceased)
         [Anthony Lynn Bristowe]
   Tunnel, The

BRITT, Katrina
   Harlequin Premiere Edition:
     15 Girl Called Tegi, A
     25 Man At Keywest, The
   Harlequin Presents:
    207 Girl In Blue
   Harlequin Romance:
   1300 Kiss In A Gondola, A
   1393 Healer Of Hearts
   1490 Fabulous Island, The
   1525 Unknown Quest, The
   1626 Spray Of Edelweiss, A
   1679 Gentle Flame, The
   1703 Reluctant Voyager
   1727 Strange Bewilderment
   1760 Guarded Gates, The
   1793 King Of Spades, The

BRITT, Katrina (cont.)
1866   Greater Happiness, The
1892   House Called Sakura, The
1906   Take Back Your Love
1969   Spanish Grandee, The
2017   Emerald Garden, The
2039   If Today Be Sweet
2070   Villa Faustino, The
2121   Faithful Heart, The
2143   Silver Tree, The
2171   Enchanted Woods, The
2212   Open Not The Door
2238   Hills Beyond, The
2269   Midnight Sun, The
2305   Man On The Peak, The
2343   Flowers For My Love
2371   Island For Dreams
2397   Wrong Man, The
2449   Hotel Jacarandas

BROADRICK, Annette (cont.)
433   With All My Heart
464   Touch Of Spring, A
499   Irresistible   <MMS>
552   Loving Spirit, A   <MMS>@
577   Candlelight For Two   @
Silhouette Romance:
329   Circumstantial Evidence
359   Provocative Peril
412   Sound Of Summer
442   Unheavenly Angel
501   Strange Enchantment
533   Mystery Lover
544   That's What
        Friends Are For   %
609   Come Be My Love   %
676   Love Remembered, A
742   Married

BRITTON, Kate   <GOT>
Avalon:
   Nightmare At Lilybrook

BROCATO, Kathryn
        [Katherine King Brocato]
Meteor Kismet:
   8   Storm Warning

BRITTON, Vickie & Loretta JACKSON
Avalon:
   Path Of The Jaguar
   Nightmare In Morocco

BROCHER, Maggi   <CO>
   American Beauty
   Cheerleaders
   Partings

BROADRICK, Annette
(see Silhouette Christmas Stories)
Silhouette Desire:
   185   Hunter's Prey
   219   Bachelor Father
   242   Hawk's Flight
   272   Deceptions
   283   Choices
   314   Heat Of The Night
   336   Made In Heaven
   360   Return To Yesterday   &
   367   Adam's Story   &
   414   Momentary Marriage

BROCK, Rose   <GOT>
                  [Joseph Hansen]
   Tarn House

BRODEEN, Melody
MacFadden Romance:
   186   Portrait Of Yesterday
   219   Wishing Stone, The

BRONSON, Maureen
  [Maureen Woodcock w/
              Antoinette Bronson]
  Harlequin Historical <Set#2>:
  32 Delta Pearl
  Harlequin SuperRomance:
    478 New Promises

BRONTE, Charlotte
  Emma
  Jane Eyre
  Professor, The
  Shirley
  Villette

BRONTE, Emily   <GOT>
  Wuthering Heights

BRONTE, Louisa   <HR>
  [Janet Louise Roberts]
  Her Demon Lover
  Lord Satan
  American Dynasty Series:
    In sequence:
      Vallette Heritage, The
      Van Rhyne Heritage, The
      Gunther Heritage, The
      Clifton Heritage, The
      Landau Heritage, The
      This Shining Splendor
  Greystone Tavern Series:
    In sequence:
      Greystone Tavern
      Gathering At Greystone
      Freedom Trail To Greystone
      Casino Greystone
      Moonlight At Greystone
      Greystone Heritage

BROOKE, Alice
  Silhouette Romance:
  242 No Gurarantees
  320 Harbor Lights

BROOKE, Allison
  My Turn To Love
  Tomorrow Will Be Mine

BROOKE, Laura
  Fallen Roses

BROOKES, Beth
                   [Eileen Nauman]
  Second Chance At Love:
   36 Hold Fast Til Morning
   53 Untamed Desire
  131 On Wings Of Passion
  183 Torrid Nights
  358 Where Enchantment Lies

BROOKINS, Dana
  My Secret Love

BROOKS, Anne/Anne Tedlock
                      (Deceased)
                    (Ann Carter)
  Centennial Summer
  Once Upon A Cruise
  One More Camilia
  Point Virtue   <HR>
  With A Heart Full Of Love
  Sharon Romance:
    Evergreen Girl

79

BROOKS, Betty
Heartfire Romance: <HR>
   Apache Captive
   Warrior's Embrace
   Wild Texas Magnolia
Indian Quartet:
   Savage Flame
   Passion's Angel
   Passion's Siren
   Apache Sunset

BROOKS, Caroline   <RE>
   An Old Scandal
   Marchman's Lady
   Regency Rose
   Runaway Princess, The
   Sea Change, A

BROOKS, Janice Young   <HR>
   Cinnamon Wharf
   Circling Years, The   <CS>
   Crown Sable
   Forbidden Fires
   Glory
   Guests Of The Emperor
   In Love's Own Time
   Our Lives, Our Fortunes
   Season Of Desire
   Seventrees
   Still The Mighty Waters

BROOKS, Janice Young w/
       Jean BROOKS-JANOWIAK
         (Valerie Vayle)

BROOKS, Jean
       [Jean Brooks-Janowiak]
       (Anne Merton Abbey)
       (Valerie Vayle)

BROOKS, Kandi
         [Kandius Brooks]
Silhouette Special Edition:
  471   Real World, The

BROOKS, Kandius
         (Kandi Brooks)
         (Brooke Sinclair)

BROOKS, Laura   <GOT>
   Old Evil House, The   <CGS:#16>

BROOKS, Madeleine
MacFadden Romance:
  19   Fiesta La Masquerade

BROOME, Susannah
         [Nancy Pattison]
   Amulet Of Fortune, The
   Pearl Pagoda, The

BROUDE, Craig Howard
         (Melissa Hepburne)
         (Lisa Lenore)

BROUSE, Barbara
         (Araby Scott)
         (Abra Taylor)

BROWN, A. L.
         (Dana Warren Smith)

BROWN, Dee   <HO>
   Conspiracy Of Knaves

BROWN, Diana   <RE>
   Come Be My Love
   Blue Dragon, The   <HO>
   Debt Of Honour, A
   Emerald Necklace, The
   Hand Of A Woman, The   <HR>
   St. Martin's Summer
   Sandalwood Fan, The

BROWN, Elizabeth
   A Hearth Romance:
     14 Candle Of The Wicked, The

BROWN, Erin J.   <GOT>
   Terrors At Penharris Manor, The

BROWN, Fern/Fern G.   <YA>
   Our Love
   Rodeo Love

BROWN, Gayle Rogers
                (Gayle Rogers)

BROWN, J.P.S.   <HO>
   Arizona Saga:
    1 Blooded Stock, The

BROWN, Joan Winmill
   Rhapsody Romance:
     Another Love
     If Love Be Ours
     Love's Tender Voyage

BROWN, Kitt
           [Aola Vandergriff]
   Allyssa Deane   <FWS:#5>

BROWN, Kitt
   Kentucky Spitfire -
     Caitlyn McGregor   <FWS:#1>
   Texas Wildflower -
     Lauren Kane   <FWS:#3>

BROWN, Lois Ann w/ Nancy JACKSON
                 (Ann Dabney)

BROWN, Lois Ann w/ Barbara LEVY
                (Jessica Eliot)

BROWN, Marion Marsh
   Prairie Teacher
   Candlelight:
     23 Nurse Abroad, A

BROWN, Mary
   Playing The Jack   <HR>

BROWN, May
                 (Vanessa Blake)

BROWN, Rosellen
   Tender Mercies

BROWN, Sandra
         [Sandra Lynn Cox Brown]
                (Laura Jordan)
                (Rachel Ryan)
            (Erin St. Claire)
   Best Kept Secrets
   Mirror Image
   Slow Heat In Heaven
   Doubleday Loveswept Trilogy:
     Texas! Lucky
     Texas! Chase
     Texas! Sage
   In sequence: <HR>
     Sunset Embrace
     Another Dawn

BROWN, S..dra (cont.)
Harlequin American Romance:
  1 Tomorrow's Promise
Loveswept:
    1 Heaven's Price
  22 Breakfast In Bed   &
  51 Send No Flowers   &
  66 In A Class By Itself
  79 Thursday's Child
 115 Riley In The Morning
 136 Rana Look, The
 154 22 Indigo Place
 185 Sunny Chandler's Return
 197 Demon Rumm
 217 Fanta C   @
 229 Tidings Of Great Joy
 252 Adam's Fall   @
 263 Hawk O'Toole's Hostage
 300 Long Time Coming
 336 Temperature's Rising
 366 Whole New Light, A
Loveswept Golden Classic:
  In A Class By Itself   <LS66>
Loveswept Silver Signature
Edition:
  Send No Flowers   <LS51>
Second Chance At Love:
 106 Relentless Desire
 137 Temptation's Kiss
 164 Tempest In Eden

BROWN, Susan Cody
           (Suzanne Ashley)

BROWN, Virginia   <HR>
    [Virginia Brown Bianchi]
    (Virginia Lynn)
Desert Dreams
Heaven Sent
Legacy Of Shadows
Moonflower
Savage Awakening
Wild Heart
Wildfire
The Avon Romance:
  Defy The Thunder
  Storm Of Passion

BROWN, Virginia w/ Melinda Jane
  HARRISON   (Emma Harrington)

BROWN, Wenzell
  Dark Drums
  Possess And Conquer

_____

_____

BROWNE, Lizbie   <RE>
  Golden Dolly

_____

_____

BROWNING, Amanda
Harlequin Presents:
 1055 Perfect Strangers
 1329 Web Of Deceit
Harlequin Romance:
 3031 Asking Price, The

_____

_____

BROWNING, Diana
        [Florence Hershman]
  All The Golden Tomorrows <Saga>

_____

_____

BROWNING, Dixie
  [Dixie Stevens Burrus Browning]
          (Zoe Dozier)
(see Silhouette Christmas Stories)
Silhouette Classic:
  12 Finders, Keepers <SE50>
Silhouette Desire:
  68 Shadow Of Yesterday
  91 Image Of Love
 111 Hawk And The Honey, The
 121 Late Rising Moon
 169 Stormwatch   &
 188 Tender Barbarian, The
 212 Matchmaker's Moon
 234 Bird In The Hand, A
 264 In The Palm Of Her Hand
 324 Winter Woman, A
 337 There Once Was A Lover

BROWNING, Dixie (cont.)
403 Fate Takes A Holiday
427 Along Came Jones
474 Thin Ice
517 Beginner' Luck   <MMS>
541 Ships In The Night
588 Twice In A Blue Moon <MMS>
637 Just Say Yes
Sihouette Romance:
  12 Unreasonable Summer
  38 Tumbled Wall
  53 Chance Tomorrow
  73 Wren Of Paradise
  93 East Of Today
 113 Winter Blossom
 142 Renegade Player   &
 164 Island On The Hill
 172 Logic Of The Heart
 191 Loving Rescue
 203 Secret Valentine, A
 221 Practical Dreamer
 275 Visible Heart
 292 Journey To Quiet Waters
 305 Love Thing, The
 323 First Things Last
 381 Something For Herself
 460 Reluctant Dreamer
 527 Matter Of Timing, A
 747 Homing Instinct, The
Silhouette Special Edition:
  50 Finders Keepers
 110 Reach Out To Cherish
 181 Just Desserts
 205 Time And Tide
 228 By Any Other Name
 314 Security Man, The
 414 Belonging

BROWNING, Dixie w/ Mary WILLIAMS
(Bronwyn Williams)

BROWNING, Pamela
(Pam Ketter)
(Melanie Rowe)
Harlequin American Romance:
 101 Cherished Beginnings

BROWNING, Pamela (cont.)
 116 Handyman Special
 123 Through Eyes Of Love   &
 131 Interior Designs
 140 Ever Since Eve
 150 Forever Is A Long Time &
 170 To Touch The Stars
 181 Flutterby Princess, The
 194 Ice Crystals
 227 Kisses In The Rain
 Heartland Trilogy:
 237 Simple Gifts
 241 Fly Away
 245 Harvest Home
 287 Feathers In The Wind
 297 Until Spring
 354 Humble Pie
 384 Man Worth Loving, A
Harlequin Romance:
2659 Touch Of Gold

BROWNLEIGH, Eleanora   <HR>
[Rhoda Cohen]
Heirloom
Keepsake
Memento
Remembrances
Secrets
Woman Of The Century, A

BROWNLEY, Margaret
(Kate Damon)

BROWNLIE, Noreen
(Jamisan Whitney)
Harlequin American Romance:
 188 Matter Of Time, A
Silhouette Desire:
 436 Savannah Lee
 468 'Tis The Season
 513 Race The Wind

BRUCKER, Meredith Babeaux
[Meredith Lindley Babeaux Brucker]
(Meredith Kingston)
(Meredith Lindley)
Candlelight:
234 One Love Forever   <RO>
264 Close To The Stars   <RO>

BRUFF, Nancy   <HR>
[Nancy Bruff Gardner]
Cider From Eden
Country Club, The
Desire On The Dunes

BRUNDY, Clyde M.   <HR>
Call Up The Morning
Grasslands
High Empire

BRUYERE, Toni Marsh
Harlequin Regency Romance:
Man About Town

BRYAN, Ann
[Ann Boyle]
First Love From Silhouette: <YA>
16 Someone To Love

BRYAN, Deborah
[Deborah Bryson]
Harlequin Intrigue:
64 Deathtrap

BRYAN, Eileen
[Ruth Alana Smith]
Candlelight Ecstasy:
155 Loving Adversaries
193 Memory And Desire
473 Sweet Tempest
Candlelight Ecstasy Supreme:
14 Crossfire
25 Against All Odds
48 Run For The Roses

BRYANT, Kathleen
(Kate Bradley)

BRYANT, LaRee
Sweet Texas Fury
Heartfire Romance: <HR>
Arizona Captive
Arizona Vixen
Forbidden Paradise
Texas Glory
Texas Rogue

BRYANT, Lynne Marie
Loveswept:
309 Calypso's Cowboy

BRYCE, Felicia
Avalon:
Government Nurse
Love Finds A Way
Portia In Distress
Winter Love, A

BRYER, Judith E. w/ Arnie HELLER
(Eve O'Brian)

BRYER, Judy
(Brenna Drummond)
(Allison Lawrence)

84

BRYSON, Deborah
                              (Deborah Bryan)

BRYSON, Deborah w/ Joyce PORTER
                              (Deborah Joyce)

BUCHAN, Elizabeth   <HR>
  Daughters Of The Storm

BUCHAN, Kate
  Harlequin Historical <Set#1>:
    11 Buccaneer Bride
  Masquerade:
    38 Black Fox
    54 Satan's Mountain
    76 Flame Stone, The

BUCHAN, Stuart
                              (Pamela Foxe)
                              (Becky Stuart-YA)
  Mandate Of Heaven, The   <HS>
  Crosswinds: <YA>
    6   All Our Yesterdays
    22 Love And Lucy Bloom
  Roots Of Love Series: <CO><YA>
    1   Tender Beginnings
    2   Restless Nights
    3   Forbidden Longings
    4   Bitter Promises
    5   Flames From The Ashes

BUCHANAN, Laura
                              [Florence King]
  Barbarian Princess, The

BUCHEISTER, Patt
                              (Patt Parrish)
  Loveswept:
    130 Night And Day

BUCHEISTER, Patt (cont.)
    180 Dragon Slayer, The
    202 Touch The Stars   &
    227 Two Roads   &
    251 Luck Of The Irish, The
    266 Flynn's Fate
    292 Time Out
    311 Near The Edge
    333 Fire And Ice
    352 Elusive Gypsy
    375 Once Burned, Twice As Hot
    400 Rogue, The
    415 Relentless
    432 Tropical Heat

BUCK, Barbara D.   <HR>
  Enchanted Heart, The

BUCK, Carole
                              [Carol E. Buckland]
  Second Chance At Love:
    219 Encore
    246 Intruder's Kiss
    261 At Long Last Love
    269 Love Play
    289 Fallen Angel
    317 Mr. October
    334 Swann's Song
    350 Happily Ever After
    359 Cody's Honor
    410 Chasing Rainbows
    424 All That Jazz
    436 Rainbow's End
    448 Real Thing, The
    459 Simply Magic
    465 Love And Laughter
  Silhouette Desire:
    565 Time Enough For Love
    614 Paradise Remembered
  Silhouette Romance:
    752 Make- Believe Marriage

BUCK, Gayle   <RE>
        (see A Regency Christmas)
Demon Rake, The
Hearts Betrayed
Honor Besieged
Lord John's Lady
Love's Masquerade
Righteous Rakehell, The
Waltzing Widow, The
Willowswood Match

BUCK, Pearl S.   (Deceased)
        [Pearl Sydenstricker Buck]
All Under Heaven
Angry Wife, The
Bridge For Passing, A
Come, My Beloved
Command The Morning
Death In The Castle
Dragon Seed
Exile, The
Goddess Abides, The
God's Men
Hidden Flower, The
Imperial Woman
Kinfolk
Letter From Peking
Living Reed, The
Long Love, The
Mandala
Mother, The
Mrs. Stoner And The Sea
New Year, The
Pavilion Of Women
Peony
Portrait Of A Marriage
Promise
Rainbow, The
Three Daughters Of Madame Liang
Time Is Noon, The
Townsman, The
Voices In The House
House Of Earth Trilogy:
    Good Earth, The
    Sons
    House Divided, A

BUCKHOLDER, Marta
                (Marta Lloyd)

BUCKHOLTZ, Eileen w/ Nancy BAGGETT
                (Amanda Lee)

BUCKHOLTZ, Eileen w/ Ruth GLICK
                (Amanda Lee)
                (Rebecca York)

BUCKHOLTZ, Eileen w/ Ruth GLICK,
Louise TITCHENER and Carolyn MALES
                (Alyssa Howard)
                        .

BUCKINGHAM, Callie
Avalon:
    Nurse At Orchard Hill

BUCKINGHAM, Nancy   <GOT><RS>
        [John Sawyer w/ Nancy Sawyer]
Call Of Glengarron
Cloud Over Malverton
Dark Summer, The
Hour Before Moonrise, The
House Called Edenhythe, The
Jade Dragon, The
Legend Of Baverstock Manor, The
Return To Vienna
Storm In The Mountains
Valley Of The Ravens, The
Vienna Summer
Candlelight:
    192 Quest For Alexis

BUCKLAND, Carol E.
                (Carole Buck)

BUCKLEY, Priscilla   <RS>
Turia

BUCKVAR, Felice   <CO>
    [Felice Spitz Buckvar]
All The Way
Happily Ever After
Ten Miles High

_____

_____

BUDD, Carol   <RS>
    [Carol Pellegrini Budd]
White Lies
Scarlet Scandals

_____

_____

BUDLONG, Ware Torrey
                       (Lee Crosby)
                     (Judith Ware)
                    (Joan Winslow)

BUDLONG, Ware Torrey w/ Frank SMITH
                   (Jennifer Hale)

BUECHTING, Linda
                    (Kelly Adams)
                   (Kelly Jamison)

BULK, Nancy Harwood
                      (Dee Holmes)

BULL, Molly
Serenade/Serenata: <Insp>
    36 For Always

_____

_____

BULLARD, Ann Elizabeth
                    (Casey Stuart)

BULLARD, Anne
Meteor Kismet:
    15 Matter Of Time, A

_____

_____

BULLEN, Fiona
To Catch The Sun

_____

_____

BULLINGER, Maureen
                  (Samantha Quinn)

BULOCK, Lynn
Avalon:
    My Funny Valentine
    Tallie's Song
    Promise Of Summer, The
    Roses For Caroline
    Leave Yesterday Behind

_____

_____

BURAK, Linda w/ Joan ZEIG
                 (Alicia Meadowes)

BURCHELL, Mary   (Deceased)
                        [Ida Cook]
Harlequin Classic:
     3 On The Air   (521)
    13 Paris--And My Love   (565)
    20 Over The
          Blue Mountains   (533)
    28 Choose The One
          You'll Marry   (546)
    38 Across The Counter   (603)
    47 Dear Sir   (605)
    55 Love Him Or Leave Him(616)
    72 Inherit My Heart   (782)
    88 Wedding Dress, The   (813)
   106 Away Went Love   (837)
   118 Then Come Kiss Me   (422)
   127 For Ever And Ever   (461)
   136 Love Is My Reason   (494)
   145 Stolen Heart   (686)
   154 House Of Conflict   (712)
   163 Dear Trustee   (478)
   176 And Falsely
          Pledge My Love   (895)
Harlequin Presents:
    67 Accompanied By His Wife
    75 Dare I Be Happy?
    83 Yet Love Remains
    99 Love Made The Choice
   111 Such Is Love
   123 Little Sister
   155 Nobody Asked Me
Harlequin Romance:
   782 Inherit My Heart
   813 Wedding Dress, The

BURCHELL, Mary (cont.)
```
 837  Away Went Love
 844  Meet Me Again
 871  Yours To Command
 895  And Falsely Pledge My Love
 915  Strange Quest Of Nurse
        Anne, The
 956  Take Me With You
 980  Song Begins, A              &
1003  Heart Cannot Forget, The
1029  Choose Which You Will
1052  Meant For Each Other
1075  Cinderella After Midnight
1100  Broken Wing, The           &
1117  Dearly Beloved
1138  Loving Is Giving
1165  Ward Of Lucifer
1187  Sweet Adventure
1214  Marshall Family, The
1244  When Love Is Blind         &
1270  Though Worlds Apart
1298  Missing From Home
1330  Home For Joy, A
1354  When Love's Beginning
1382  To Journey Together
1405  Curtain Rises, The         &
1431  Other Linding Girl, The
1455  Girl With A Challenge
1474  My Sister Celia
1508  Child Of Music             &
1543  But Not For Me
1567  Do Not Go, My Love
1587  Music Of The Heart         &
1632  One Man's Heart
1655  It's Rumoured In The
        Village
1704  Except My Love
1733  Call And I'll Come
1767  Unbidden Melody            &
1792  Pay Me Tomorrow
1811  Strangers May Marry
1834  Song Cycle                 &
1871  Brave In Heart, The
1890  Tell Me My Fortune
1919  Just A Nice Girl
1936  Remembered Serenade        &
1947  Girl In The Blue Dress,The
1964  Under The Stars Of Paris
2043  Elusive Harmony
2061  Honey
```

BURCHELL, Mary (cont.)
```
2290  Bargain Wife
2359  Nightingales
2379  Yours With Love
2528  Masquerade With Music
2707  On Wings Of Song           &
```

BURFORD, Lolah
  Alyx
  Edward, Edward
  MacLyon
  Seacage: A Romance For Another
    Time, In Three Voices
  Vision Of Stephen, The
  Vice Avenged: A Moral Tale

BURGER, Pixie   \<HR\>
  Woman Of Two Continents, A \<Saga\>

BURGESS, Joanna   \<RE\>
                (Carolyn Fireside)
  Kissing Lesson, The

BURGESS, Joanne Harris
                (Joanna Harris)

BURGESS, Mallory   \<HR\>
                [Mary Sandra Hingston]
  Jerico's Daughter
  Ride The Savage Sea
  The Avon Romance:
    Wild Land, Wild Love
  Tudor Series:
    Pasion Rose
    Passion Fire
    Passion Star
  NOTE: Also "Passion Song" by
        Catherine FitzGerald

BURGHLEY, Rose
                  [Ida Pollock]
Harlequin Classic:
  24 And Be Thy Love   (617)
 143 Garden Of Don Jose (928)
 177 Highland Mist   (1079)
Harlequin Romance:
 928 Garden Of Don Jose, The
 960 Man Of Destiny
1023 Sweet Surrender, The
1051 Bride Of Alaine
1079 Highland Mist
1102 Quality Of Magic, A
1245 Bay Of Moonlight, The
1386 Alpine Doctor, The

BURKE, Diana   <RE><VIC>
[Sue Burrell w/ Michaela Karni]
Candlelight:
 626 Heart Of The Matter, The
 681 Impoverished Heiress, The

BURKE, James Wakefield   <HO>
Blazing Dawn, The

BURKE, John Frederick
            (Jonathan Burke)
             (Owen Burke)

BURKE, Jonathan   <RS>
[John Frederick Burke]
Goodbye, Gillian

BURKE, Owen
         [John Frederick Burke]
Figurehead, The   <Saga>

BURKE, Rosalind
Love Has Many Seasons
Wonder Of Love, The

BURKHARDT, Mary
Heartfire Romance: <HR>
  Forbidden Hearts

BURKHOLZ, Herbert
Snow Gods, The

BURMAN, Margaret
Sweet Dreams: <YA>
 16 How Do You Say Goodbye?
 45 Dream Prom

BURN, Helen Jean
Savannah   <Saga>

BURNES, Caroline
           [Carolyn Haines]
Harlequin Intrigue:
  In sequence:
   86 Deadly Breed, A
  100 Measure Of Deceit
  115 Phantom Filly

BURNES, Caroline (cont.)
134 Fear Familiar
154 Jaguar's Eye, The

BURNETT, Ruth
Avalon:
April Games
Beautiful Medic, The
Captain's Nurse, The
Dr. Galen's Dilemma
Lord Of The Island
Love Star
Nurse And The Talisman, The
Nurse Maggie's Dream
Nurse Of Mount Juliet
Picolata Treasure, The
Secret Of Thundermyer
House, The
Sweetest Treasure, The
Telltale Kiss, The
To Love A Mermaid
Topaz Promise, The
When Lily Smiles

BURNS, Carol w/ Deborah JONES
(Samantha Holder)

BURNS, Patricia   <HR>
Stacey's Flyer

BURNS, Sheila
[Ursula Bloom]
Acting Sister
Flying Nurse, The
Nurse On Wings
Nurse Who Shocked The
Matron, The
Sister Loving Heart

BURRELL, Sue w/ Michaela KARNI
(Diana Burke)

BURROUGHS, Patricia
[Patti B. Barricklow]
Heartfire Romance:
What Wild Ecstasy
Loveswept:
421 Some Enchanted Season
Silhouette Desire:
447 Razzmatazz
490 Beguiled Again

BURROWS, Marjorie
The Avon Romance:
Winter Hearts, The

BURT, Katharine Newlin   <RS>
Branding Iron, The
Close Pursuit
Hidden Creek
Lady In The Tower
Lost Isobel
Rapture Beyond
Red Lady, The
Ree
Snow-Blind
Strong Citadel
Tall Ladder, The
This Woman And This Man
Adventures In Love:
15 Very Tender Love, A

BURTON, Katherine
Harlequin SuperRomance:
292 Sweet Summer Heat
346 Tess   <CCS>

BURTON, Kristin w/ Susan B. OSSANA
(Susanna Christie)

BURTON, Leonora
(Leonora Blythe)

BURTON, Philip
You My Brother

BUSH, Nancy   <HR>
(Natalie Bishop)
Danner Family:
  Lady Sundown
  Danner's Lady
First Love From Silhouette: <YA>
  32 Dare To Love
  78 Bittersweet Sixteen

BURTON, Rebecca
(Rebecca Winters)
By Love Divided
Loving Season, The

BUSHYHEAD, Anne
(Nicole Jordan)

BUTLER, Beverly   <HR>
[Beverly Kathleen Butler]
Magnolia Plantation

BUSBEE, James Jr.
(see Jonathan Scofield)

BUSBEE, Shirlee   <HR>
[Shirlee Elaine Egan Busbee]
Deceive Not My Heart
Gypsy Lady
Lady Vixen
Midnight Masquerade
Spanish Rose, The
Tiger Lily, The
While Passion Sleeps

BUTLER, David   <HO>
Disraeli:
  A Portrait Of A Romantic
Edward The Seventh
Lillie
Lusitania
Royal Victorians
Edward The King: In sequence:
  Prince Of Hearts
  Monarch Among Men

BUTLER, Gwendoline   <GOT><RS>
[Gwendoline Williams Butler]
(Jennie Melville)
Meadowsweet
Olivia
Red Staircase, The
Sarsen Place
Vesey Inheritance, The

BUSH, Christine
Avalon:
  Nurse At Deer Hollow
  Nurse At Eagles Watch
  Season Of Fear   <GOT>

BUSH, Kim Ostrom
(Kimberleigh Caitlin)
(Kimberly Cates)

BUTLER, Jean Rouverol
(Jean Rouverol)

BUTLER, Mary A.   <RE>
  Genuine Article, The

_____

_____

BUTLER, Mary/Mary E.   <REM>
  Gallant Heiress, The
  Harlequin Regency:
    Deception So Agreeable

_____

_____

BUTLER, Rae   <HR>
             [Raymond Ragan Butler]
  Arabesque

_____

_____

BUTLER, Richard
  Against The Wind

_____

_____

BUTLER, Robert Olen
  Alley's Of Eden, The

_____

_____

BUTLER, Rose
  MacFadden Romance:
    78 Gaelic Heirs, The

_____

_____

BUTTERWORTH, Emma Macalik
  As The Waltz Was Ending   <YA>

_____

_____

BUTTERWORTH, William Edmund III
                    (Eden Hughes)
                    (Allison Mitchell)

BUXTON, Anne
                    (Anne Maybury)
                    (Katherine Troy)

BYERS, Cordia   <HR>
  Calista
  Heather
  Lady Fortune
  Love Storm
  Nicole La Belle
  Pirate Royale
  Ryan's Gold
  Star Of The West, A
  In sequence:
    Silk And Steel
    Desire and Deceive

_____

_____

BYFIELD, Sue
  Harlequin Romance:
    2529 To Be Or Not To Be

_____

_____

BYINGTON, Kaa
                    (Sybil Le Grand)
                    (Octavia Street)

BYRD, Elizabeth   <HO>
  Famished Land, The
  Flowers Of The Forrest, The
  Ghosts In My Life, The
  I'll Get By
  Immortal Queen
  Lady Of Monkton
  Long Enchantment, The
  Maid Of Honour
  Rest Without Peace
  Search For Maggie Hare, The
  Strange And Seeing Time, A

_____

_____

BYRNE, Beverly   <HR>
   Come Sunrise
   Jemma
   Jason's People   <Saga>
   Matter Of Time, A
   Morgan Women, The   <Saga>
   Womens's Rites
   Griffin Saga: In sequence:
      Outcast, The
      Adventurer, The
      Fiery Splendor

_____

_____

CABOT, Isobel
Answer With Love
Road To Love
Summer's Love, A
Avalon:
    Come Summer, Come Love
    Enchanted Carousel
    Love Finds Dr. Shelly
    Missing Witness
    Nurse Lauren's Challenge
    Nurse Mara's Fear
    Share Of Danger
    Summer Of Discovery
Candlelight:
    24 Nurse Janice Calling
    67 Nurse Audrey's Mission
   148 Lost Inheritance (Love
        Finds Nurse Joanne) <MY>

CADE, Robin
          [Christopher Nicole]
Fear Dealers, The

CADELL, Elizabeth
    [Violet Elizabeth Cadell]
Any Two Can Play
Around The Rugged Rock
Brimstone In The Garden
Canary Yellow
Come Be My Guest
Corner Shop, The
Crystal Clear
Cuckoo In Spring, The
Deck With Flowers
Empty Nest, The   <RS>
Enter Mrs. Belchamber
Fledgling, The
Fox From His Lair, The
Friendly Air, The

CADDEL, Elizabeth (cont.)
Game In Diamonds
Gay Pursuit
Golden Collar, The
Home For The Wedding
Honey For Tea
I Love A Lass
Iris In Winter
Last Straw For Harriet
Letter To My Love   <ENG>
Lion In The Way, A
Marrying Kind, The
Mixed Marriage   <ENG>
Money To Burn
Mrs. Westerby Changes Course
Out Of The Rain
Parson's House
Past Tense For Love, The
Remains To Be Seen   <RS>
Return Match
Royal Summons
Shadows On The Water   <RS>
Singing Heart, The
Stratton Story, The   <ENG>
Sun In The Morning
Toy Sword, The
Waiting Game, The   <GOT>
Yellow Brick Road, The
Wayne Family Trilogy:
    Lark Shall Sing, A
    Blue Sky Of Spring, The
    Six Impossible Things

CADWALLADER, Sharon
Sweet Dreams: <YA>
   119 Star-Crossed Love

CAILLE, Julie   <RE>
Scandalous Marquis, The
Change Of Heart

CAILLOU, Alan <HO>
　　　　　　　　[Alan Lyle-Smythe]
Joshua's People　　　　　<Saga>
Prophetess, The
Woman Of Quality, A　　　<HR>

CAIMI, Gina
Lovestruck:
　Betrayals
Silhouette Desire:
　125　Passionate Awakening
　174　Wilder Enchantment, A
　218　Hearts Are Wild
　270　Unfinished Rhapsody
　308　Branded
　338　Forbidden Fantasies

CAIN, Ellen Jacob
　　　　　　　　(Ellen James)

CAINE, Jeffrey
Heathcliff　　　　　　　<HR>

CAINE, Leslie
Silhouette Romance:
　10　Bridge Of Love

CAINE, Michael
In sequence:
　Creole Surgeon
　Worship The Wind

CAINE, Rebecca
　　　　　　　　[Margery Hilton]
Harlequin Presents:
　84　That Summer Of Surrender
　107　Pagan Heart

CAINE, Rebecca (cont.)
Harlequin Romance:
　2045　Child Of Tahiti

CAIRD, Janet　　　　　<GOT><RS>
In A Glass Darkly
Murder Remote
Murder Scholastic
Perturbing Spirit
Umbrella-Maker's Daughter, The
Adventures In Love:
　3　Loch, The
　19　Shrouded Way, The

CAITLIN, Kimberleigh　　　<HR>
　　　　　　　　[Kim Ostrom Bush]
Nightwylde
Sky Of Ashes, Sea Of Flames

CAJIO, Linda
Loveswept:
　145　All Is Fair
　177　Hard Habit To Break
　201　Rescuing Diana
　224　Double Dealing
　247　Silk On The Skin
　268　Strickly Business
　298　At First Sight
　Kitteridge Women:
　337　　Desperate Measures
　367　　Unforgettable
　403　　Just One Look
　　　　Knights In White Satin

CAJUN MELODIES SERIES <CMS>
Harlequin SuperRomance:
　387　Julianne's Song
　　　　　　　　Kit Bakker
　391　Catherine's Song
　　　　　　　　Marie Beaumont

CAJUN MELODIES SERIES (cont.)
397 Jessica's Song
Virginia Nielsen

CALDE, Mark   <HO>
Conquest

CALDWELL, Betty   <GOT>
Vanderleigh Legacy, The

CALDWELL, Celeste   <GOT>
Thirteen Towers

CALDWELL, Claire
First Love From Silhouette: <YA>
90 Surf's Up For Laney

CALDWELL, Grace
MacFadden Romance:
9 Winds Of Paradise, The
18 Stranger And The Sea, The

CALDWELL, Margaret
Born To The Sun

CALDWELL, Taylor   (Deceased)
[Taylor Caldwell Prestie]
Answer As A Man
Arm And The Darkness, The
Balance Wheel, The
Bright Flows The River
Captains and The Kings

CALDWELL, Taylor (cont.)
Ceremony Of The Innocent
Dear And Glorious Physician
Devil's Advocate, The
Dialogues With The Devil
Dynasty Of Death
Eagles Gather, The
Earth Is The Lord's, The
Final Hour, The
Glory And The Lightning
Grandmother And The Priests
Great Lion Of God
I, Judas   w/Jess STEARN
Late Clara Beame, The
Let Love Come Last
Listener, The
Maggie, Her Marriage
Melissa
Never Victorious, Never Defeated
No One Hears But Him
On Growing Up Tough
Pillar Of Iron, A
Prologue To Love
Romance Of Atlantis w/Jess STEARN
Sound Of Thunder
Strong City, The
Tender Victory
Testimony Of Two Men
There Was A Time
Turnbulls, The
This Side Of Innocence
Time No Longer
To Look And Pass
Wide House, The
Your Sins And Mine

CALDWELL-WILSON, Marolyn
Judy Sullivan Books:
Flight Into Danger
Whirlwind   <RS>

CALIF, Lee   <GOT>
Shadow Mansion

CALLAHAN, Elizabeth
MacFadden Romance:
  10 Night Of The Tempest

CALLENDER, Joan
Harlequin Romance:
  873 Nurse Julie Of Ward Three

CALLOWAY CORNERS SERIES <CCS>
Harlequin SuperRomance:
  338 Mariah   Sandra Canfield
  342 Jo   Tracy Hughes
  346 Tess   Katherine Burton
  350 Eden   Penny Richards

CALLOWAY, Jo
             [Jo Homan Calloway]
Ashes Of Honor   <HR>
Special Sparrow
Candlelight:
  615 To Seize The Rainbow <RO>
Candlelight Ecstasy:
  82 To Catch The Wild Wind
  97 Dance The Skies
 109 Where The River Bends
 121 Dawn's Promise
 150 One Of A Kind
 164 Illusive Lover
 188 Windsong
 220 Classic Love, A
 238 Heartbeats
 273 Scattered Roses
 282 To Remember Love
 376 Southern Fire
 387 Through The Eyes Of Love
 437 Escape To Paradise
Candlelight Ecstasy Supreme:
  6 Time Of A Winter Love
 24 Somewhere In The Stars
 41 Touched By Fire
 70 All The Days To Come

CALLOWAY, Jo (cont.)
Finding Mr. Right:
  Mirrors Of Love

CALVIN, Henry   <RS>
It's Different Abroad

CAMBARDS, Michelle
Mystique:
  48 Guilty Of Love
  63 Trial By Love

CAMEO GOTHIC SERIES <CGS>:
  1 Golden Fig, The
               Nancy T. Smith
  2 Fear Among The Shadows
               Louise Hoffman
  3 Shadow Of A Cat
               Poppy Nottingham
  4 Stones Of Strendleigh, The
               Geraldine Killoran
  5 Yesterday's Evil
               Lydia Benson Clarke
  6 Flames Over The Castle
               Diana LaPoint
  7 Tapestry Of Terror
               Marianne Ruuth
  8 Without A Grave
               Poppy Nottingham
  9 Devil's Due, The
               Lanora Miller
 10 Fire On The Cliffs
               Chris Waynar
 11 Rievaulx Abbey
               Norma Davison
 12 Picture Of Death, A
               Diana LaPoint
 13 Castle On The River, The
               Janice N. Bennett
 14 To Dream Of Evil
               Louise Hoffman

CAMEO GOTHIC SERIES (cont.)
15 Darkness At Bromley Hall
                    Marybeth Morgan
16 Old Evil House, The
                    Laura Brooks
17 Findlay's Landing
                    Margaret Chittenden
18 Bright Sun, Dark Moon
                    Frances P. Statham
19 Web Of Days   Helen Orr
20 Girl In The Shadows
                    Zoa Sherbourne
21 Masquerade Of Evil
                    Eva Zumwalt
22 Buried Remembrance
                    Naomi Smith
23 Willough Haven
                    Geraldine Killoran
24 Unforgiven, The
                    Maynah Lewis
25 Winterscape
                    Anastasia Cleaver
26 Deathbed Of Roses
                    Michaeljohn

_____

_____

CAMERON, Barbara
            [Barbara Cameron Smith]
Candlelight Ecstasy:
   63 Metal Mistress, The
   124 An Affair To Remember
Harlequin Temptation:
   66 Star Ride
Silhouette Desire:
   158 Rapture Of The Deep

_____

_____

CAMERON, Blair
   [Mary Kathryn Scamehorn
            w/ Karen Blair Parker]
Candlelight Ecstasy:
   410 Sweet-Time Loving
   528 What Every Woman Wants
Candlelight Ecstasy Supreme:
   62 Boss Lady
   78 Bright Flame, Distant Star
   98 Million-Dollar Lover
Candlelight Supreme:
   131 Man For Amy, A

CAMERON, Blair (cont.)
   150 Night Of His Life, The

_____

_____

CAMERON, Caryn
                    [Karen Harper]
Harlequin Historical <Set#2>:
   11 Dawn's Early Light
   27 Silver Swords
   39 Liberty's Lady   +
   49 Freedom Flame   +
   61 Braden's Bride
   70 Wild Lily

_____

_____

CAMERON, Claire
Adventures In Love:
   21 Amethyst Summer

_____

CAMERON, D. Y.
Cornish Serenade

_____

CAMERON, Eleanor Elford   <GOT><RS>
House On The Beach
Spider Stone, The

_____

CAMERON, Julie   <GOT>
                    [Lou Cameron]
Darklings, The
Devil In The Pines
Kitten Down A Well

_____

_____

CAMERON, Kate   <HR>
                    [Beverly McGlamry]
As If They Were Gods

_____

_____

CAMERON, Kate   <GOT>
   [Elizabeth Lorinda duBreuil]
Kiss Me, Kill Me
Holderly Hall Series:
   Legend Of Holderly Hall   1
   Shadows Of The Past   2
   Voices In The Fog   3
   Deadly Nightshade   4
   Music From The Past
Whispering Hill Series:
   Evil At Whispering Hills   1
   Curse Of Whispering Hill, The 2
   Shadows On The Moon   3
   Legacy Of Terror   4
   Awakening Dream, The   5
   Echoes Of Evil   6

CAMERON, Kay
                [Virginia Coffman]
Scarlet Ribbons: <HR>
   Passion's Rebel

CAMERON, Kenneth M.   <HO>
Father Of Fires, The
Sky Woman

CAMERON, Lou   <HO>
                (Julie Cameron)
         (Mary Louise Manning)
         (see Jonathan Scofield)
(see Lee Davis Willoughby <MOAS>)
(see Lee Davis Willoughby <WWWW>)
Wilderness Seekers, The <MOAS:#1>

CAMERON, Meg
Dawn Of Love: <YA>
   3 Savage Spirit

CAMERON, Miranda   <RE>
                    [Mary Kahn]
   Dissolute Duke, The
   Lord Cleary's Revenge
   Meddlesome Heiress, The
   Reluctant Abigail, The
   Scandalous Bargain, A
   Undaunted Bride, The

CAMERON, Peta
Harlequin Romance:
   868 This Starry Stranger

CAMERON, Stella
Harlequin American Romance:
   153 Shadows
   195 No Stranger   &
   226 Second To None   &
   243 Party Of Two, A
   268 Message, The
   306 Friends
   360 Risks
Harlequin Intrigue:
    50 All That Sparkles
    83 Some Die Telling
   107 Death In The House, A
   123 Late Gentleman, The
Harlequin SuperRomance:
   185 Moontide
   340 Once And For Always
   448 One Summer
   451 One Winter

CAMERON, Stella w/ Virginia MYERS
                (Jane Worth Abbott)

CAMERON, Stella w/ Linda RICE
                (Alicia Brandon)

CAMP, Candace Pauline
                (Lisa Gregory)
                (Kristin James)
                (Sharon Stephens)

CAMP, Debbie
                [Deborah Elaine Camp]
Gateway To The Heart

CAMP, Debby
                [Deborah Elaine Camp]
Facade
Tandem

CAMP, Deborah   <HR>
                [Deborah Elaine Camp]
Belle Starr
The Avon Romance:
  Black-Eyed Susan
  Blazing Embers
  Fallen Angel
  Primrose

CAMP, Deborah Elaine
                    (Deborah Benet)
                    (Debbie Camp)
                    (Debby Camp)
                    (Deborah Camp)
                    (Delayne Camp)
                    (Elaine Camp)
              .   (Delaine Tucker)
                    (Elaine Tucker)

CAMP, Delayne
                [Deborah Elaine Camp]
Harlequin Temptation:
  289 Newsworthy Affair, A

CAMP, Elaine
                [Deborah Elaine Camp]
Silhouette Desire:
  207 Love Letters
  251 Hook, Line And Sinker
  298 Destiny's Daughter
  398 Weathering The Storm
  419 Second Mr. Sullivan, The

CAMP,Elaine (cont.)
Silhouette Romance:
  99 To Have, To Hold
  173 Devil's Bargain
  270 This Tender Truce
Silhouette Special Edition:
  113 For Love Or Money
  159 In A Pirate's Arms
  263 Just Another Pretty Face
  285 Vein Of Gold
  301 Right Behind The Rain<ATS>
  316 After Dark

CAMPBELL, Bethany
                [Sally McCluskey]
Harlequin Intrigue:
  65 Pros And Cons
  116 Roses Of Constant, The
  151 Dead Opposites
Harlequin Romance:
  2726 After The Stars Fall
  2779 Only A Woman
  2803 Thousand Roses, A
  2815 Sea Promises
  2852 Long Way Home, The
  2877 Heartland
  2911 Flirtation River
  2949 Diamond Trap, The
  3000 Lost Moon Flower, The
  3019 Snow Garden, The
  3045 Heart Of The Sun, The
  3062 Dancing Sky
  3079 Ends Of The Earth, The
  3109 Every Woman's Dream

CAMPBELL, Caroline   <RE>
                [Leslie A. Safford]
Love Masque

CAMPBELL, Diana   <RE>
Breath Of Scandal, A
Counterfeit Countess, The

CAMPBELL, Diana (cont.)
  Earl's Invention, The
  Family Affairs
  Kissing Cousins
  Late Lord Latimer, The
  Lord Margrave's Deception
  Marriage Of Inconvenience, A
  Payment In Kind
  Reluctant Cyprian, The

CAMPBELL, Drusilla   <HR>
  Autumntide
  Dream Of Fire, A
  Frost And The Flame, The
  Men Like Gods
  Reunion   <CO>
  Hopewell Saga: In sequence:
    Broken Promises
    Silent Dreams
    Stolen Passions
    Tomorrow's Journey

CAMPBELL, Hope
                    (True Summers)

CAMPBELL, Jane
                    [Jane Edwards]
  Candlelight:
    64 Believe No Evil

CAMPBELL, Joanna
                    [JoAnn Simon]
  Sweet Dreams: <YA>
    8 Thoroughbred, The
    22 Secret Identity
    52 Love Notes

CAMPBELL, Lainey
  First Love From Silhouette: <YA>
    206 Wish Too Soon, A

CAMPBELL, Margaret   <RS>
                    [Gabrielle Margaret Long]
  Blanche Fury
  Spectral Bride, The
  Spider In The Cup, The

CAMPBELL, Patricia
  Cedarhaven

CAMPBELL, Phyllis
  Avalon:
    Come Home, My Heart

CAMPBELL, Wanza J.   <HR>
  Runaway Rapture

CANADAY, Lee
                    [Louise Lee Outlaw-Shallit]
  Candlelight:
    254 Victim Of Love   <RO>

CANADEO, Anne
                    (Anne Cavaliere)
                    (Alyssa Douglas)

CANARY, Brenda Brown
  Home To The Mountain

CANAVAN, Jean
  Shadow Of The Flame
  Tapestry: <HR>
     64 Midwinter's Night
     84 Highland Tryst

CANDLISH, Jasmine
  [Jasmine Rosemary
              Cresswell Candlish]
              (Jasmine Craig)
              (Jasmine Cresswell)

CANFIELD, Miriam   <GOT>
              [Dorothy Fletcher]
  Tuscany Madonna, The

CANFIELD, Sandra
                   (Karen Keast)
  Harlequin SuperRomance:
     213 Cherish This Moment
     252 Voices On The Wind
     278 Night Into Day
     338 Mariah   <CCS>
     419 Tigers By Night

CANFIELD, Sandra w/ Penny RICHARDS
                   (Sandi Shane)

CANHAM, Marsha   <HR>
  Wind And The Sea, The
  The Avon Romance:
     Bound By The Heart
     China Rose
  In sequence:
     Pride Of Lions, The
     Blood Of Roses, The

CANNAM, Helen
  High And Lonely Road, A

CANNON, Helen
  Better Place I Know, A
  Season's Change
  Where The Truth Lies

CANON, Mary   <HR>
  Wild Rose
  O'Hara Dynasty: In sequence:
     Defiant, The
     Survivors, The
     Renegades, The
     Exiled, The
  Harlequin Temptation:
     38 How The Game Is Played

CANTOR, Eli
  Love Letters   <CO>

CAPRON, Jean F.
  Avalon:
     Puzzle From The Past
     Just Good Friends
  First Love From Silhouette: <YA>
     218 Days Of Loving
  Sweet Dreams: <YA>
     78 Never Say No To Love

CARBONI, Susan G.
                   (Susan Gordon)

CARD, Orson Scott
  Saints   (Epic)

CARDEW, Penelope
  Love As Large As The Land, A
  Sheer Cliffs Of Love, The
  Shifting Winds Of Love, The

102

CARDIFF, Sara <RS>
Bonapart Kiss, The
Fool's Apple
Inner Steps, The
Severing Line, The
Speaking Stones, The

CAREY, Elisabeth
[Susan Bridge]
Coventry:
102 Twist Of Chance <GEO>
165 Marriage By Bequest <GEO>
204 Debt Of Honour

CAREW, Jean <RS>
Believe In Me
Doctor Lochinvar
First Girl
Look Back, My Love
Love Is Enough
Marrying Kind, The
"New" Veda Vail, The
Nurse's Masquerade
Run, Nurse, Run
Society Nurse
Swing From A Star
Terror At Bramble Tor
Yours, With Love
Sharon Romance:
Cara's Masquerade
Sharon Contemporary Teens:
Stage Struck

CAREY, Suzanne
[Verna Carey]
Silhouette Desire:
4 Kiss And Tell
69 Passion's Portrait
92 Mountain Memory
126 Leave Me Never
176 Counterparts
206 Angel In His Arms
268 Confess To Apollo
310 Love Medicine
368 Any Pirate In A Storm
Silhouette Intimate Moments:
330 Never Say Goodbye
Silhouette Romance:
633 Most Convenient
Marriage, A
682 Run, Isabella
736 Virgin Territory
777 Baby Contract

CAREW, Jocelyn <HR>
[Jacquelyn Aeby]
Crown Of Passion
Follow The Shadows
Golden Sovereigns, The
Pavilion Of Passion

CAREY-BRODEUR, Diane L. w/
Gregory E. BRODEUR
(Diane Carey)
(Lydia Gregory)

CARFAX, Catherine <RS>
Locked Tower, The

CAREY, Diane
[Diane L. Carey-Brodeur w/
Gregory E. Brodeur]
After The Torchlight <GOT>
Harem
Sudden Storm
Under The Wild Moon

CARL, Lillian Stewart
Housefull Of Visions, A <RS>

CARLES, Riva
              [Irving A. Greenfield]
  Thrall Of Love

CARLETON, Cathleen
              [Kaye Wilson Klem]
  Ride From The Night

CARLETON, Marjorie   <GOT>
  Demarest Inheritance, The
Shadows On The Hill
  Vanished

CARLISLE, Amanda   <HS>
  Southland

CARLISLE, Donna
              [Donna Ball]
  Silhouette Desire:
   417 Under Cover
   476 Man Around The House, A
   530 Interlude
   555 Matchmaker, Matchmaker

CARLISLE, Sarah   <RE>
  Widow Aubrey
  Coventry:
   20 Cleopatra's Carpet
   36 Mille Cecie
   67 Daphne
  108 Penny Wise
  132 Kit And Kitty

CARLOCK, Lynn
  First Love From Silhouette: <YA>
  176 Daughter Of The Moon

CARLOW, Joyce
  Bylines
  Emerald's Hope
  Glory Years, The
  Succession   <Saga>

CARLSON, Janice
              (Laura Ashcroft)
              (Ashland Price)

CARLSON, Nancy
  Loveswept:
   10 Hard Drivin' Man

CARLSON, Nola
  Caprice Romance: <YA>
    8 Three's A Crowd
   26 New Face In The Mirror, A
   41 Spring Dreams
   63 Sixteenth Summer

CARLTON, Lori
              (Lori Leigh)

CARMICHAEL, Carol   <HS>
  Dynasty Of Desire

CARMICHAEL, Emily   <HR>
             [Emily Krokosz]
  Autumnfire
  Devil's Darling, The
  Surrender
  Touch Of Fire   <Saga>
  Visions Of The Heart

CARNEGIE, Sacha
Guardian, The
Scarlet Banners Of Love

CARNELL, Lois.
Harlequin American Romance:
28 Beyond The
Flight Of Birds

CARNELL, Lois C.
House That Lived Again,The

CARNELL, Lois Christian
(Lois Carnell)
(Lois C. Carnell)
Avalon:
Summer Magic At Summerset
Love Rides The Wind

CARNEY, Daniel
Macau   <CO>
Under A Raging Sky   <Saga>

CAROL, Robin   <RS>
[Camille Bourgeois]
Ancestor, The
Gypsy's Curse   <CO>

CAROTHERS, Annabel   <HS>
Kilcaraig

CARPENTER, Amanda
Harlequin Presents:
703 Wall, The
735 Great Escape, The
759 Raging Passion

CARPENTER, Ann (cont.)
919 Waking Up
991 Rose-Coloured Love
1047 Reckless
1127 Gift Of Happiness, The
1175 Caprice
Harlequin Romance:
2605 Deeper Dimension, A
2648 Damaged Trust, A

CARPENTER, Brooke
MacFadden Romance:
68 Prelude To Love

CARPENTER, Cyndy   <HR>
Rapture's Heaven

CARR, Eleni
[Helen C. Maragakis]
First Love From Silhouette: <YA>
11 It's My Turn
Harlequin SuperRomance:
245 Forever Bond, The
289 More Than Ever
313 Till There Was You
372 Matter Of Time, A
Silhouette Romance:
168 Moonlight And Memories
Silhouette Special Edition:
16 Mayan Moon
130 Play It Again

CARR, Jess   <HO>
Falls Of Rabbor, The
Frost Of Summer, The
Midas Touch, The
Millie And Cleve
Moonshiners, The
Saint Of The Wilderness, The

CARR, Jess (cont.)
Second Oldest Profession, The
Star Rising, A

_____

_____

CARR, John Dickson   <GOT>
Bride Of Newgate, The

_____

_____

CARR, Josephine
Crosswinds: <YA>
  26 My Beautiful Fat Friend

_____

CARR, Karyn
Serenade/Serenata:
  26 Journey Toward Tomorrow

_____

CARR, Madeleine   <HR>
Island Of Promise

_____

_____

CARR, Nicole
Make Your Dreams Come True: <YA>
   3 Worthy Opponents
   6 Holiday Of Love

_____

_____

CARR, Philippa
          [Eleanor Burford Hibbert]
Cornwall Saga:
In sequence:
  Miracle At St. Brunos, The
  Lion Triumphant, The
  Witch From The Sea, The
  Saraband For Two Sisters
  Lament For A Lost Lover
  Love Child, The
  Song Of The Siren, The
  Will You Love Me In September
  Adultress, The

CARR, Philippa (cont.)
  Knave Of Hearts
  Voices In A Haunted Room
  Return Of The Gypsy, The
  Midsummer's Eve
  Pool Of St. Branok, The
  Changeling, The
  Black Swan, The

_____

_____

CARR, Robyn   <HR>
  Bellerose Bargain, The
  Blue Falcon, The
  Braeswood Tapestry, The
  By Right Of Arms
  Chelynne
  Everlasting Covenant, The
  Rogue's Lady
  Tempted
  Troubadour's Romance, The
  Women's Own
  Silhouette Special Edition:
    517 Informed Risk

_____

_____

CARR, Sherry
                [Sydney Ann Clary]
  Second Chance At Love:
    116 Let Passion Soar

_____

_____

CARRAS, Helen
                [Helen C. Maragakis]
  Candlelight Ecstasy:
    396 Passion's Rogue

_____

_____

CARRO, Patricia
                (Patricia Markham)
  Silhouette Intimate Moments:
    234 Deja Vu

_____

_____

CARROL, Kathleen
[Kathleen Creighton Modrovich]
Harlequin American Romance:
151 Angel's Walk

CARROL, Shana   <HR>
[Frank Schaefer w/ Kerry Newcomb]
Paxton Women Saga:
(Numbers indicate 'Story Order')
1 Raven
4 Yellow Rose
5 Paxton Pride
3 Live For Love
2 Rebels In Love

CARROLL, Abby
Two By Two Romance: <YA>
2 Jed & Jessie

CARROLL, Dawn
                    [Dawn C. Boese]
Harlequin Temptation:
268 Code Name: Casanova

CARROLL, Enid
MacFadden Romance:
Blue Sea Interlude

CARROLL, Joellyn
[JoAnne Bremer w/ Carol I. Wagner]
Candlelight Ecstasy:
131 Run Before The Wind
159 Flight Of Splendor, A

CARROLL, Joy
                    (Heather Hill)
Glitter Girl   <CO>
Moth, The
Prides Court
Proud Blood
Soul's End

CARROLL, Lorraine
Silhouette Special Edition:
646 Lead With Your Heart

CARROLL, Malissa
[Carol I. Wagner w/
              Marian F. Scharf]
Candlelight Ecstasy:
281 Match Made In Heaven

CARROLL, Marisa
[Carol I. Wagner w/
              Mariam F. Scharf]
Harlequin American Romance:
127 Natural Attraction
160 Jenna's Choice
190 Tomorrow's Vintage
256 Come Home To Me
286 Ties That Bind
Harlequin SuperRomance:
268 Remembered Magic
318 Gathering Place
     McKendrick Family Series:
418 Rescue From Yesterday
426 Refuge From Today
437 Return To Tomorrow

CARROLL, Mary
                    [Annette Sanford]
Silhouette Romance:
2 Shadow And Sun
45 Too Swift The Morning
75 Divide The Wind

CASEY, John
An American Romance

CASEY, June w/ Joan TRIGLIA
(June Triglia)

CASEY, June E.
[June E. Triglia Casey]
(Melissa Ash)
(Casey Douglas)
(Constance Ravenlock)
(June Trevor)
Torch:
Mountain Of Desire

CASEY, Sara
Two By Two Romance: <YA>
1   Cassie & Chris

CASPARY, Vera
Bachelor In Paradise
Bedelia
Dreamers, The
Evvie
Laura
Secret Of Elizabeth, The

CASS, Zoe   <GOT><RS>
Island Of The Seven Hills
Silver Leopard

CASSELMAN, Lucy
Thanos Island
Candlelight:
591 Forbidden Blessing   <RO>

CASSIDY, Becka
[Beverly Vines-Haines]
First Love From Silhouette: <YA>
40 Lucky Star

CASSIDY, Kris
Meteor Kismet:
12 Born To Be Wild

CASSINI, Igor
Pay The Price   <HS>

CASSITY, Joan   <HR>
The Avon Romance:
Now & Again

CASTELL, Megan
[Jeanne Williams]
Queen Of A Lonely Country

                                      •
CASTLE, Brenda
(Georgina Ferrand)
Harvest Of Happiness
Whispers Of Fear

CASTLE, Helen
Emergency Ward Nurse
Ivy Anders, Night Nurse

CASTLE, Jayne
[Jayne Ann Krentz]
Double Dealing
Trading Secrets   <RS>

111

CATLIN, Barbara
       [Barbara Catlin Craven]
Silhouette Special Edition:
  488 Smoky's Bandit
  519 Mr. Right*
  * see "Prisoner Of Love" SE303
     by Maranda Catlin

CATLIN, Maranda
  [Martha Rand Hix w/
        Barbara Catlin Craven]
Silhouette Special Edition:
  303 Prisoner Of Love*
  * see "Mr. Right" SE519
     by Barbara Catlin

CATO, Nancy   <HR>
All The Rivers Run
Brown Sugar
Chindera   <Saga>
Forefathers   <Saga>
Heart Of The Continent   <HS>

CAUDELL, Marian
Sweet Dreams: <YA>
  99 One Boy Too Many
 112 Listen To Your Heart

CAUVIN, Patrick
Blind Love
Little Romance, A
Two Of A Kind

CAVA, Roberta
Avalon:
  That Something Special

CAVALIERE, Anne
           [Anne Canadeo]
Silhouette Desire:
  328 Perfect Timing
  512 Squeeze Play

CAVANAGH, Helen
First Love From Silhouette: <YA>
  132 Candy Papers, The
Wildfire: <YA>
  Angel
  Just A Summer Girl
  Kiss And Tell
  Place For Me, A
  Second Best
  Superflirt

CAVANAUGH, Arthur   <HR>
Rosemoore

CAVANAUGH, Sara
Tiara:
  Woman In Space, A

CAVANDISH, Faith   <RS>
Silent Portrait

CAVANNA, Betty   <YA>
       (Elizabeth Harrison)
Storm In The Heart

CENTURY OF AMERICAN ROMANCE <COAR>
Harlequin American Romance:
  345 American Pie   (1895)
          Margaret St. George

CHADWICK, Joseph
          (Janet Conroy)
       (JoAnne Creighton)

CHALLANS, Mary
         (Mary Renault)

CHALLONER, Robert   \<HR\>
Jamaica Passage

<hr>

<hr>

CHAMBERLAIN, Diane   \<CO\>
Lovers And Strangers
Private Relations

<hr>

<hr>

CHAMBERS, Ginger
  [Virginia Anne Smith Chambers]
Candlelight:
  648 Kindred Spirit, The   \<RO\>
Candlelight Ecstasy:
   40 Call It Love
   83 Fire Of The Soul, A
  102 Sweet Persuasion
Candlelight Ecstasy Supreme:
   18 Heart Divided, A
   43 Harbor Of Dreams
  100 Too Close For Comfort
  123 Cupid's Dilemma
Harlequin American Romance:
   32 Game Of Hearts
   71 Passion's Prey
  107 In Love's Shadow
  169 When Heart's Collide
  238 Firefly In The Night
  254 Call My Name Softly
  288 Passages Of Gold
  335 Nightshade

<hr>

<hr>

CHAMPLIN, Caroline Llewellyn
    (Caroline Llewellyn)

CHANCE, Lisbeth   \<RS\>
       (Leigh Daniels)
Baja Run
Judy Sullivan Books:
  Cutting Edge

<hr>

<hr>

CHANCE, Sara
      [Sydney Ann Clary]
Silhouette Desire:
   46 Her Golden Eyes
   83 Home At Last
  107 This Wildfire Magic
  183 Touch Of Passion, A
  244 Look Beyond Tomorrow
  357 Where The Wandering Ends
  388 Double Solitaire
  406 Shadow Watch
  430 To Tame The Wind
  New Orleans Trilogy:
  467 Southern Comfort
  485 Woman In The Shadows
  500 Eye Of The Storm
  524 With A Little Spice
Silhouette Intimate Moments:
  299 Fire In The Night

<hr>

<hr>

CHANDLER, Bryn
Behind The Badge   \<CO\>
Love & Life:
  Ambition

<hr>

<hr>

CHANDLER, Laurel
       [Nancy Holder]
Rapture Romance:
   15 Treasures Of Love
   30 Heart's Victory
   59 Boundless Love
   85 Shades Of Moonlight

<hr>

<hr>

CHANDOS, Faye
   [Irene Maude Mossop Swatridge]
                 (Jan Tempest)
  Harlequin Romance:
   796 Hibiscus House

CHANG, Diana
  Eye To Eye
  Gift Of Love, The
  Perfect Love, A

CHANNING, Justin   <HR>
  [Karen Hitzig w/ Helen Barrett]
  Carolina Woman
  Southern Blood   <Saga>

CHAO, Evelina
  Gates Of Grace   <Saga>

CHAPEL, Ashley
  MacFadden Romance:
   155 Kiss Of Satin, A
   164 Sweet Savage

CHAPLIN, Patrice
  Unforgotten, The   <M-GOT>

CHAPMAN, Hester W.   <RS>
  Limmerston Hall

CHAPMAN, Laura
  Change Of Heart, A
  Multiple Choice

CHAPMAN, Margaret
  Harlequin Romance:
   2125 Gift Of Love, The
   2157 Night Of No Moon

CHAPMAN, Renate   <GOT>
  Avalon:
    Dark Moon
    Evil In Waiting
    Haunted Heart
    House Of Shadows
    Lost Legacy, The
    Love's Secret Plan
    Milmorra House
    Mystic Island
    Watcher
    Waters Dark/Deep

CHAPMAN, Vera   <HR>
  Blaedud The Birdman
  Green Knight, The
  King Authur's Daughter
  King's Damosel, The
  Wife Of Bath, The

CHAPPELEAR, Laurie
               (Laurie Grant)

CHAPPELL, Helen
           (Rebecca Baldwin)
  Acts Of Love
  All Things In Their Season
  Passions

CHAPPELL, Mollie   <RE>
  Caroline
  Lesson In Loving, A
  Loving Heart, The
  Coventry:
    3 Romantic Widow, The <VIC>
   98 Serena

CHARBONNEAU, Louis
  From A Dark Place   <RS>

CHARLES, Anita
             [Ida Pollock]
  Harlequin Romance:
  1030 Black Benedicts, The
  1056 One Coin In The Fountain
  1238 White Rose Of Love
  1278 King Of The Castle, The

CHARLES, Esme
  Love Is A Stranger

CHARLES, Iona   <GOT>
  [Carolyn Nichols w/
          Stanlee Miller Coy]
  Cassia Great House
  Draw A Dark Circle
  Grenencourt
  Reluctant Lady Darden, The
  When Only The Bougainvillea
    Blooms

CHARLES, Maggi
    [Margaret Hudson Koehler]
  Silhouette Intimate Moments:
   90 Love's Other Language

CHARLES, Maggi (cont.)
  Silhouette Romance:
  134 Magic Crescendo
  Silhouette Special Edition:
   23 Love's Golden Shadow
   45 Love's Tender Trial
  158 Mirror Image, The
  258 That Special Sunday
  269 Autumn Reckoning
  305 Focus On Love
  336 Yesterday's Tomorrow
  362 Shadow On The Sun
  381 Star Seeker, The
  429 Army Daughter
  459 Different Drummer, A
  479 It Must Be Magic   &
  497 Diamond Moods   &
  520 Man Of Mystery, A
  546 Snow Image, The
  575 Love Expert, The
  599 Strickly For Hire
  647 Shadows On The Sand

CHARLES, Marie
    [Marie Rydzynski Ferrarella]
  Second Chance At Love:
   65 Smoldering Embers
  107 Scenes From The Heart
  145 Claimed By Rapture

CHARLES, Theresa   <GOT><RS>
  [Charles John Swatridge w/
    Irene Maude Mossop Swatridge]
  Burning Beacon, The
  Dark Legacy
  Fairer Than She
  House On The Rocks
  Lady In The Mist
  Return To Terror
  Shrouded Tower, The

CHARLTON, Ann
  Harlequin Presents:
   857 An Irresistible Force
   912 Titan's Woman
   967 Deception Trap, The
  1008 Street Song
  1319 Love Spin
  Harlequin Romance:
  2660 Place Of Wild Honey, A
  2684 No Last Song
  2701 Winter Sun, Summer Rain
  2762 Driftwood Dragon, The
  2977 Ransomed Heart

CHARLTON, Josephine
          [Josephine C. Hauber]
  Candlelight Ecstasy Supreme:
    64 Behind The Scenes
  Silhouette Desire:
   135 Table For Two

CHARLTON, Madeline
  Harlequin Romance:
  1686 Alpenrose
  2055 Sense Of Words, A

CHARPENTIER, Lydia   <GOT>
  Magician's Daughter, The

CHASE, Anya Seton
                      (Anya Seton)

CHASE, Carolyn   <HR>
  (publisher's pseudonym for
           writers in this series)
  Thirteen Colonies Series:
    1 Georga:
       Renegade Hearts
    2 South Carolina:
       Scoundrel's Caress

CHASE, Carolyn (cont.)
    3 Massachusetts:
       Smuggler's Embrace, The
    4 New York:
       Frontier Rouge
              [Trana M. Simmons]
    5 Maryland:
       Rebel's Kiss
              [Marilyn Cunningham]

CHASE, Elaine Raco
  Candlelight:
   567 Rules Of The Game   <RO>
  Candlelight Ecstasy:
    19 Tender Yearnings
    43 Dream Come True, A
    56 Double Occupancy
    72 Designing Woman
   100 No Easy Way Out
   162 Video Vixen
   226 Special Delivery
   499 Dare The Devil
  Finding Mr. Right:
   Best-Laid Plans
  Romantic Mystery Series:
   Dangerous Places
   Dark Corners
   Rough Edges
  Silhouette Desire:
   104 Calculated Risk
   138 Lady Be Bad

CHASE, Loretta/Loretta Lynda   <RE>
                  [Loretta Chekani]
  Devil's Delilah, The   &
  Knaves' Wager
  Viscount Vagabond   &
  Sandalwood Princess
  In sequence:
   Isabella
   English Witch, The

CHASE, Marian
Silhouette Romance:
267 Share The Dream

CHASE-RIBOUD, Barbara   <HO>
From Memphis And Peking
Sally Hemmings
Valide, A Novel Of The Harem

CHASTAIN, Sandra
Sweetwater   <HR>
Loveswept:
235 Too Hot To Handle   &
262 For Love Of Lacey   &
277 Showdown At Lizard Rock   @
320 Silver Bullet Affair, The
344 Joker's Wild   @
374 Penthouse Suite
391 Adam's Outlaw
410 Run Wild With Me
     Danny's Girl

CHATER, Elizabeth   <RE>
                        (Lisa Moore)
Duke's Dilemma, The
Earl And The Emigree, The
Emerald Love
Kings's Doll, The
Lady Dearborn's Debut
Marriage Mart, The
Miss Cayley's Unicorn
Place For Alfreda, A
Reformed Rake, The
  (sequel to Coventry #191)
Runaway Debutante, The
Time To Love, A
Coventry:
  26 Elsingham Portrait, The
  43 Gamester, The
  95 Milady Hot At Hand
 114 Lord Randal's Tiger

CHATER, Elizabeth (cont.)
139 Random Gentleman, The
146 Gallant Lady
164 Season For The Heart, A
167 Angela
176 Milord's Liegewoman
191 Delicate Situation, A<GEO>

CHATFIELD, Susan
        [Susan Chatfield Fasshaurer]
Candlelight Ecstasy:
   6 Leaves Of Fire,
        Flame Of Love
  47 Dawning Of Desire
MacFadden Romance:
  88 Bride Of The Lion
Sapphire Romance: <ENG>
  Love Bargain, The
Torch:
  Hunter's Pride
Torchlite:
  Banyon's Daughter

CHATTERTON, Louise
First Love From Silhouette: <YA>
  92 Just The Right Age

CHEATHAM, Lillian
Portrait Of Emma   <GOT>
Secret Of Saramount, The   <VIC>
Candlelight:
 549 Runaway Heiress, The   <RE>
Candlelight Ecstasy:
   4 Shadowed Reunion, The
Coventry:
  91 Saxon Inheritance, The
Harlequin Presents:
 808 Lady With A Past
 888 Winter Heart, The
Harlequin Romance:
2683 Island Of Dolphins

CHEEVER, Susan   <CO>
  Handsome Man, A

_____

_____

CHEKANI, Loretta
                    (Loretta Chase)
                    (Loretta Lynda Chase)
CHENEY, Sally
  Harlequin Historical <Set#2>:
    36 Games Of Hearts

_____

_____

CHENIER, Blanche   <RE>
  Coming Of Peace, The
  Regency Row
  Return Of The Swallows
  Summer Masquerade
  Coventry:
    25 Lady Of Fortune, A
    42 Love In Exile
    77 Defiant Heart, The
  Harlequin Regency Romance:
    19 Lucinda
    37 Wayward Heiress, The

_____

_____

CHESNEY, Marion   <RE>
        [Marion Chesney Gibbons]
  Annabelle
  At The Sign Of
    The Golden Pineapple
  Duke's Diamonds
  Education Of Miss Patterson, The
  Flirt, The
  French Affair, The
  Henrietta
  Lady Lucy's Lover
  Lessons In Love
  Milady In Love
  Miss Flona's Fancy
  Original Miss Honeyford, The
  Paper Princess, The
  Penelope

CHESNEY, Marion (cont.)
  Perfect Gentleman
  Poor Relation, The
  Pretty Polly
  Savage Marquess, The
  Scandalous Lady Wright, The
  Sweet Masquerade
  Those Endearing Young Charms
  To Dream Of Love
  Viscount's Revenge, The
  In sequence:
    Westerby Inheritance, The
    Westerby Sisters, The
  A House For The Season Series:
    In sequence:
      Miser Of Mayfair, The
      Plain Jane
      Wicked Godmother, The
      Rake's Progress
      Adventuress, The
      Rainbird's Revenge
  The School For Manners Series:
    Tribble Sisters:
      In sequence:
        Refining Felicity
        Perfecting Fiona
        Enlightening Delilah
        Finessing Clarissa
        Animating Maria
        Marrying Harriet
  The Six Armitage Sisters:
    In sequence:
      Minerva
      Taming Of Annabelle, The
      Deirdre And Desire
      Daphne
      Diana The Huntress
      Frederica In Fashion
  The Travelling Matchmaker:
    Emily Goes To Exeter
  The Waverly Women:
    In sequence:
      First Rebellion, The
      Silken Bonds
      Love Match, The
  Coventry:
        Love And Lady Lovelace
    15 Regency Gold

CHESNEY, Marion (cont.)
49 Ladys Margery's Intrigue
83 Constant Companion, The
106 Quadrille
145 My Lord's, My Ladies,
And Marjorie
163 Ghost And Lady Alice, The

CHILD, Judith w/ Lisa NEHER
(Juli Greene)

CHILDRESS, Susan
[Susan Wiggs]
Embrace The Day   <HS>

CHESNUTT, Linda w/ Georgia PIERCE
(Lindsey Hanks)

CHESTER, Deborah   <HR><RE>
French Slippers
Heart's Desire
Love So Wild, A
Royal Intrigue
Sign Of The Owl, The
Candlelight:
712 Royal Image   <RE>
Harlequin Historical <Set:#2>:
22 Captured Hearts

CHESTER, Sarah   <HR>
[Marion Chesney Gibbons]
Dancing On The Wind

CHETWYND-HYNES, J.
And Love Survived   <T-T>

CHEYNEY, Jeanne
Secret Of Giltham Hall, The
First Love From Silhouette: <YA>
127 Patch Of Black Satin, A
Serenade/Saga: <HR><Insp>
26 Conviction Of Charlotte
Grey, The

CHIMENTI, Francesca   <GOT><RS>
Night Falls Too Soon
Psychiatrist's Nurse
Silent Room, The
Web Of Allyngrood, The
Candlelight:
508 Web Of Deception, The <IN>

CHIN, Charla w/ Jane KIDDER
(Charlotte Simms)

CHIN, Sandra
Lady In Blue

CHISHOLM, Gloria
Andrea   <YA><Insp>

CHISHOLM, Lilian
[Jane Alan]
Harlequin Romance:
851 Song For Tomorrow, A
866 Hearts Go Singing
889 Friend Of The Family, A

CHISHOLM, Mary MacKeller
Clown In The Windmill, The

CHITTENDEN, Margaret   <GOT>
     [Margaret Rosalind
      Barrass Chittenden]
     (Rosalind Carson)
Beyond The Rainbow   <CO>
Face In The Mirror, The
Findlay's Landing   <CGS:#17>
Forever Love   <RS>
House Of The Twilight Moon
Other Child, The
Song Of Dark Water
Harlequin Dreamscape Romance:
   This Time Forever
Harlequin SuperRomance:
   366 Until October
   444 Scent Of Magic, The

_____

_____

CHOATE, Gwen
          (See Kristin Michaels)

CHOATE, Jane McBride
   Avalon:
      Badge Of Love

_____

_____

CHRISTENBERRY, Judith
     [Judith Russell Christenberry]
               (Judith Stafford)
Moonlight Charade

_____

_____

CHRISTENBERRY, Judy
   Notorious Widow, The   <RE>
   Meteor Kismet:
      5 Little Inconvenience, A

_____

_____

CHRISTIAN, Catherine
   Pendragon, The

_____

_____

CHRISTIAN, Jill
               [Noreen Dilcock]
   Harlequin Classic:
      74 Tender Bond, The
   Harlequin Romance:
      1651 Scent Of Lemons, A

_____

_____

CHRISTIANSEN, Ruth
   False Rainbow

_____

_____

CHRISTIE, Colleen
               [J. S. Bidwell]
   Silhouette Romance:
      558 Kiss Is Still A Kiss, A

_____

_____

CHRISTIE, Michelle
               [Gerry O'Hara]
   MacFadden Romance:
      149 Triston's Lair
      199 Forever Love
      241 King Of The Castle

_____

_____

CHRISTIE, Susanna
   [Susan B. Ossana w/
               Kristin Burton]
   Silhouette Intimate Moments:
      143 Find Of A Lifetime, The
      186 Eden's Temptation
      203 Close Encounter

_____

_____

CHRISTMAS IS FOR KIDS <CIFK>
   Harlequin American Romance:
      321 Carol Christmas, A
                      Muriel Jensen
      322 Mrs Scrooge
                      Barbara Bretton

CITIES OF THE CIVIL WAR (cont.)
New Orleans   Miriam Pace
New Orleans #2:
   Delta Desire   Miriam Pace
Savannah   John T. Foster
Vicksburg   John T. Foster

CLAGUE, Maryhelen   <HR>
                            (Ashley Snow)
Cole's Landing   <Saga>
Moment Of The Rose
So Wondrous Free
Rest Here, My Heart
Sandenny
Scarlet Town
In sequence:
   Beyond The Shining River
   Beside The Still Waters

CLAIR, Daphne
                         [Daphne de Jong]
Harlequin Presents
   355   Darling Deceiver
   367   Something Less Than Love
   385   Wilder Shore, A
   458   Dark Remembrance
   481   Promise To Pay
   506   Loving Trap, The
   679   Ruling Passion, A
   687   Marriage Under Fire
   711   Take Hold Of Tomorrow
   881   Dark Dream
   1056 No Escape
   1096 No Winner
   1271 Wayward Bride, The
Harlequin Romance:
   2197 Streak Of Gold, A
   2292 Sleeping Fire, The
   2329 Jasmine Bride, The
   2420 Never Count Tomorrow
   2516 Pacific Pretence

CLAIRE, Eva
                         [Claire DeLong]
Silhouette Special Edition:
   149   Appalachian Summer
   240   Star Attraction

CLAIRE, Evelyn
Starlight Romance:
   No More Heartache
   Perscription For Love
   Storm Remembered

CLAIRMONT, Claire
                        [Robert Marshall]
Dark Desire Romance: <RS>
   Cruel And Loving Touch, A

CLAPP, Patricia   <GOT>
Jane-Emily

CLARE, Cathryn
                          [Cathy Stanton]
Silhouette Desire:
   399   To The Highest Bidder
   508   Blind Justice
   550   Lock, Stock And Barrell
   591   Five By Ten

CLARE, Jane
                          [Dinah Shields]
Silhouette Intimate Moments:
   26   Old Love, New Love
Silhouette Special Edition:
   70   Traces Of Dreams

CLARE, Kalindi
  First Love From Silhouette: <YA>
  192 First Impressions

CLARK, Jean   <HR>
  Marriage Bed, The
  Untie The Winds

CLARE, Samantha
  Circle Of Love:
   15 Heron's Keep

CLARE, Shannon
                  [Linda Harrel]
  Queen's Rival, The   <HR>
  SuperRomance:
   43 Sweet Temptation
   78 Snow Bride
  Harlequin SuperRomance:
   113 Wake The Moon

CLARK, Amanda
  [Janet O'Daniel w/ Amy Midgley]
  Harlequin Romance:
  3007 Blueprint For Love
  3104 City Girl, Country Girl
  Serenade/Serenata: <Insp>
   27 Flower Of The Sea

CLARK, Eleanor
  Baldur's Gate

CLARK, Gail   <RE>
                 (Maggie MacKeever)
                   (Grace South)
  Dulcie Bligh
  Cotillion Regency:
   1 Baroness Of Bow Street, The
   8 Right Honourable Viscount, The
  11 Bachelor's Fare

CLARK, Kathy
  Candlelight Ecstasy:
   306 Another Sunny Day
   356 Private Affair, A
   378 Golden Days
   419 Hint Of Splendor, A
   469 Passion And Possession
   494 Destiny's Lady
   518 Carousel Of Love
  Harlequin American Romance:
   224 Sweet Anticipation
   282 Kissed By An Angel   &
   333 Sight Unseen   <RMM>
   348 Phantom Angel   &
   366 Angel Of Mercy   &
   383 Starting Over
  Pageant Romance:
   No Satisfaction

CLARK, Louise
                   (Roslyn MacDonald)
CLARK, Marianne
                   [Marianne Willman]
  Rapture Romance:
   33 Apache Tears
   88 Here There Be Dragons

CLARK, Melissa
                   (Alysse Aallyn)
CLARK, Norma Lee   <RE>
  Daring Duchess, The
  Emily
  Hester
  Impulsive Miss Pymbroke, The
  Infamous Rake, The
  Kitty Quinn   <HR>

CLARK, Norma Lee (cont.)
    Lady Jane
    Mallory
    Marriage Mart, The
    Miss Holland's Betrothal
    Perfect Match, The
    Pippa
    Sophia And Augusta
    Coventry:
        5   Megan
        28 Fanny
        56 Zandra
        183 Tynedale Daughters, The

CLARK, Roberta   <HR>
    Mari's Caress

CLARK, Sabina
                    [Marianne Willman]
    Second Chance At Love:
        6   An Artful Lady

CLARK, Sandra
    Harlequin Presents:
        514 Wolf Man, The
        968 Too Dangerous To Love
    Harlequin Romance:
        2533 Moonlight Enough
        2569 Stormy Weather
        2780 Fool To Say Yes, A

CLARKE, Brenda
    [Brenda Margaret Lilian Clarke]
                    (Brenda Honeyman)
    Far Morning, The
    Lofty Banners, The

CLARKE, Janet Kotselas   <CO>
                    (Jane Christopher)
                    (JoAnna Kenyon)
                    (Nell Kincaid)
    Small Town

CLARKE, Lydia Benson   <GOT>
                        [Eloise Meaker]
    Demon Cat
    Seance For Susan
    Yesterday's Evil   <CGS:#5>

CLARKE, Marion   <RS>
                        [Marion C. Schultz]
    Master Of Brendan's Isle, The

CLARKE, Pippa
    Harlequin Presents:
        944 Puppet Master, The
        1009 Dancing In The Dark

CLARY, Sydney Ann
                        (Sherry Carr)
                        (Sara Chance)
    Duchess And The Devil, The   <RE>
    Candlelight Supreme:
        145 Undercover Affair
    Harlequin Regency Romance:
        13   Misfit Match

CLAUDIA, Susan   <GOT><RS>
    Madness At The Castle
    Master Of Foxhollow
    Mrs. Barthelme's Madness
    Other Brother, The
    Searching Specter, The
    Silent Voice, A

CLAUSSE, Suzanne
  Mystique:
     22 Haunting Image, The
     64 Requiem For A Murder
     69 Death's Dark Deceit
     85 Brides Ransom
     91 Motive For Revenge
     99 Fly South To Danger
    105 Edge Of Violence
    153 Bittersweet

CLAY, Rita
              [Rita Clay Estrada]
  Silhouette Desire:
      3 Wise Folly   &
     32 Yesterday's Dreams
     45 Experiment In Love
     82 Summer Song
    120 Recapture The Love   &
  Silhouette Romance:
     97 Wanderer's Dream
    182 Sweet Eternity

CLAYTON, Donna
              [Donna Fasano]
  Silhouette Romance:
    720 Mountain Laurel

CLEARY, Gwen
  Dream's Desire
  Heartfire Romance: <HR>
    Ectasy's Masquerade
    Passionate Possession
    Victoria's Ecstasy

CLEAVER, Anastasia   <GOT><RS>
              (Natasha Peters)
  Summerstorm
  Winterscape   <CGS:#25>

CLEAVES, Margaret Major
      [Margaret Ann Major Cleaves]
                     (Ann Major)
  Candlelight:
    603 Midnight Surrender   <RE>

CLEEVE, Brian   <HR>
  Escape From Prague
  For Love Of Crannagh Castle
  Hester
  Judith
  Kate
  Sara
  Tread Softly In This Place
  Triumph Of O'Rourke
  You Must Never Go Back

CLEMENCE, Ruth
  Witchery Island   <M&B>
  Harlequin Romance:
   1063 Man From Rhodesia, The
   1195 Spread Your Wings
   1418 Cure With Kindness, A
   1619 Happy With Either
   1697 Healing In The Hills
   1814 Time To Love, A
   1985 Wife Made To Measure
   2158 Man With A Mission

CLEMENS-FOX, Carol
                     (Alicia Fox)

CLEMENT, Claire
  Promises For Tomorrow

CLEMENT, Ernest C.
                 (Candace Connell)

127

CLEMENTS, Abigail   <RS>
  Christabel's Room
  Highland Fire
  Mistress Of The Moor
  Sea-Harrower, The

CLERMONT, Shana   <HO>
                    [Dean McElwain]
  Memphis   <CofCWS>
  Natchez   <CofCWS>

CLEWS, Roy   <HO>
  Drums Of War, The
  King's Bounty, The
  Valiant And The Damned,The <Saga>

CLIFFORD, Kay
  Harlequin Romance:
    2468 No Time For Love
    2505 Temporary Affair, A
    2611 Man Of Gold
    2642 Duke Wore Jeans, The
    2881 Dream Of Love
    2912 Recipe For Love

CLOETE, Stuart   (Deceased)<HO>
  Congo Song
  Fiercest Heart, The
  Hill Of Doves, The
  How Young They Died
  Mask, The
  Rags Of Glory
  Turning Wheels, The
  Victorian Son
  Watch For The Dawn

CLOSS, Hannah   <HO>
  Tristan

CLOSS, Hannah (cont.)
  Tarn Trilogy:
    Silent Tarn, The
    Deep Are The Valleys
    High Are The Mountains

CLOUD, Patricia   <HR>
              [Pat Wallace Strother]
  This Willing Passion

CLUMPNER, Mick
  Nez Perce Legend   <AIS:#10>

COATE, Evelyn
  Candlelight Ecstasy:
    342 Wanted, Man To Love

COATES, John
                    (see Jane Austen)

COATES, May
  Harlequin Romance:
    1357 Ripples In The Lake
    1677 Stranger At The Door

COBURN, Jean Ann
  Torch:
    Brief Encounter

COCKCROFT, Ann
  Silhouette Romance:
    294 Beloved Pirate
  Tapestry: <HR>
    45 Pirate's Promise
    67 River Jewel

COCKRELL, Barbara
          (Katrina Hamilton)
          (Barbara Hargis)

CODDINGTON, Lynn
          (Allison Hayes)

COFFARO, Katherine
  [Katherine Coffaro Kovacs]
Harlequin American Romance:
  44 Logical Passion, A
  70 No Other Love
  81 Sunward Journey
Harlequin American Romance
Premiere Edition:
  Gently Into Night

———————————————————

COFFER, Helene Lewis
Silhouette Inspirations:
  17 Turn, My Beloved

———————————————————

COFFEY, Marie Butler   <CO>
Four Women

———————————————————

COFFMAN, Elaine   <HR>
  [Elaine Gunter Coffman]
Escape Not My Love
If My Love Could Hold You
My Enemy, My Love

———————————————————

COFFMAN, Virginia   <GOT><RS>
  [Virginia Edith Coffman]
          (Kay Cameron)
          (Victor Cross)
     (Virginia C. Deuvaul)
          (Jeanne Duval)
        (Diana Saunders)
        (Ann Stanfield)
Affair At Alkali
Alpine Coach, The

COFFMAN, Virginia (cont.)
Beach House, The
Black Heather
Call Of The Flesh
Candidate's Wife, The
Careen
Castle At Witches' Coven
Castle Barra
Chinese Door, The
Cliffs Of Dread, The
Curse Of The Island Pool
Dark Desire
Dark Palazzo, The
Dark Winds
Demon Tower, The
Devil Vicar, The
Enemy Of Love
Evil At Queen's Priory, The
Fatal Touch, The
Few Fiends To Tea, A
Fire Dawn
Garden Of Shadows
Haunted Place, A
High Terrace, The
Hounds Of Hell, The
House At Sandelwood, The
House On The Moat, The
Hyde Place
Ice Forest, The
Isle Of Darkness
Isle Of The Undead
Jeweled Darkness, The
Legacy Of Fear (Fear Of Heights)
Looking Glass, The
Lucifer Cove Series: In sequence:
  Devil's Mistress, The
  Priestess Of The Damned
  Devil's Virgin, The
  Masque Of Satan
  Chalet Diabolique
  From Satan With Love
Marsanne
Masque By Candlelight
Masque By Gaslight
Masque Of Satan
Master Of Blue Mire, The
Mist At Darkness, The
Mistress Devon

COFFMAN, Virginia (cont.)
  Night At Sea Abbey
  Of Love And Intrigue
  Orchid Tree, The
  Pacific Cavalcade
  Rest In Silence
  Richest Girl In The World, The
  Shadow Box, The
  Stalking Terror, The
  Strange Secrets
  Survivor Of Darkness
  Veronique
  Villa Fountains, The
  In sequence: <Saga>
    Dynasty Of Dreams
      (HB: The Lombard Calvacade)
    Dynasty Of Desire
      (HB: The Lombard Heiress)
  In sequence:
    Gaynor Woman, The
    Dinah Faire
  In sequence:
    Moura
    Beckoning From Moura
    Dark Beyond Moura
    Vicar Of Moura, The Devil
    Beyond Moura
  Vampyre Of Moura, The

_____

COGHLAN, Peggie w/ Hugh C. RAE
              (Jessica Stirling)

COHEN, Barbara
  Two Hearts Romance: <YA>
    Lover's Games

_____

_____

COHEN, Rhoda
              (Eleanora Brownleigh)
              (Diana Loy)

COHEN, Sandee
  All We Know Of Heaven

_____

_____

COHEN, Sharleen Cooper   <CO>
  Day After Tomorrow, The
  Ladies Of Beverly Hills, The
  Love, Sex And Money
  Martial Affairs
  Regina's Song

_____

_____

COHEN, Sharron
  Harlequin Presents:
  1015 High Country
  Harlequin Romance:
  2839 Odd Man Out

_____

_____

COHEN, Susan
              (Elizabeth St. Clair)

COKER, Elizabeth Boatwright   <HR>
  Blood Red Roses
  Daughter Of Strangers
  Grasshopper King, The
  India Allan
  La Belle

_____

_____

COLBY, Lydia   <GOT>
  Touch Of Evil, The

_____

_____

COLDSMITH, Don   <HO>
  Smoky Hill, The   <RWS:#2>
  Spanish Bit Saga:
    1 Trail Of The Spanish Bit
    2 Elk-Dog Heritage, The
    3 Follow The Wind
    4 Buffalo Medicine
    5 Man Of The Shadows
    6 Daughter Of The Eagle
    7 Moon Of Thunder
    8 Sacred Hills, The
    9 Pale Star
   10 River Of Swans

COLEMAN, Clara   <RS>
   Nightmare In July
   Scent Of Sandalwood, A

   _____

   _____

COLEMAN, Clayton W.   <GOT>
   Timbalier

   _____

   _____

COLEMAN, Lonnie   <HO>
   Adam's Way
   Clara
   Escape The Thunder
   Golden Vanity, The
   King
   Orphan Jim
   Sam
   Sound Of Spanish Voices, The
   Southern Lady, The
   Time Moving West
   Trilogy:
      Beulah Land
      Look Away, Beulah Land
      Legacy Of Beulah Land, The

   _____

   _____

COLEMAN, Patricia   <RE>
   Daring Deceptions

   _____

   _____

COLEMAN, Terry
   Southern Cross   <HS>

   _____

   _____

COLETTE
   Gigi
   Juliede Carneilhan
   Other One, The
   Ripening Seed, The
   Tender Shoot, The
   Vagabond, The
   In sequence:
      Cheri

COLETTE (cont.)
   Last Of Cheri
   Shackle, The
   Claudine At School
   Claudine And Annie
   Claudine In Paris
   Claudine Married

   _____

   _____

COLLETT, Dorothy
   Avalon:
      Troubled Kisses

   _____

   _____

COLLIER, Leona   <RS>
   Change Of Heart
   Ghostly Bridegroom, The
   London Belle   <RE>

   _____

   _____

COLLIN, Marion
                  [Marion Cripps Collin]
   Harlequin Romance:
      860   Nurse At The Top
      913   Doctors Three
      1169 Doctor's Delusion, The

   _____

   _____

COLLINS, Christine
                  [Elizabeth Barrett]
   Candlelight Ecstasy:
      532   Man's Fancy, A

   _____

   _____

COLLINS, Colette
   Rhapsody Romance:
      Promise Me Forever

   _____

   _____

COLLINS, Kathryn
   SuperRomance:
      97   Wings Of Night, The

COLLINS, Kathryn (cont.)
Harlequin SuperRomance:
156 Windy Fire
207 Dreams Gather

COLLINS, Laurel   <HR>
        [Linda Catherine Wiatr]
Dark Surrender
Desert Enchantress   <AAS>
Silver Eyes   <WOW:#2>

COLLINS, Marion Smith
                        (Marion Smith)
Sparrow Falls, A
Harlequin Temptation:
    5 By Mutual Consent
   22 By Any Other Name
   35 This Thing Called Love
   49 On The Safe Side
   63 This Time, This Moment
   86 Without A Hitch
  114 For Love Or Money
  211 Foxy Lady
Loveswept:
  134 Out Of The Clear Blue
Silhouette Intimate Moments:
  179 Another Chance
  252 Better Than Ever
  320 Catch Of The Day
Silhouette Romance:
  773 Home To Stay

COLLINS, Susanna
                        [Sue Ellen Gross]
Second Chance At Love:
    1 Flamenco Nights
   14 Hard To Handle
   19 Destiny's Spell
   62 On Wings Of Magic
   94 Breathless Dawn
  134 Parisan Nights
  172 Wrapped In Rainbows
  201 Brief Enchantment

COLLINS, Toni
Silhouette Romance:
  664 Ms. Maxwell & Son

COLLINS, Wilkie   <GOT>
Lady Of Glenwith Grange, The
Moonstone, The
Woman In White, The
Yellow Mask, The

COLLINSON, Marie
MacFadden Romance:
    4 Dawn Of Love
   99 Still Of The Night, The

COLMAN, Hila   <YA>
Not For Love
Triangle Of Love

COLT, Zandra
                        [Florence Stevenson]
Second Chance At Love:
   40 Cactus Rose
   92 Splendid Savage

COLTER, Cara
Silhouette Romance:
  491 Dare To Dream

COMBER, Lillian
                        (Lillian Beckwith)

COMBS, Becky
Loveswept:
   23 Taking Savannah

133

COMBS, Susan
  Meteor Kismet:
    23 Perfect Match, A

COMER, Ralph   <GOT>
  To Dream Of Evil (Mirror Of
    Dionysos)

COMFORT, Iris   <GOT>
  Echoes Of Evil
  Starlight Romance:
    Shadow Masque

COMICI, Luciano
  Heart Is No Stranger, The

COMINS, Ethel M.
  Her Father's Daughter
  Avalon:
    Love's Impossible Dream
    Love's Tangled Web
    Moon Goddess, The
    Mystery Island
    Under A Dancing Star

COMPTON, Anne
  Harvest Of Dreams
  Warrior Wives

COMPTON, Katherine
  The Avon Romance:
    Eden's Angel

CONANT, Constance   <HR>
  Star Trilogy:
    Southern Star
    Falling Star
    Star Of The West

CONARAIN, Alice "Nina"
                    (Elizabeth Hoy)

CONAWAY, James/J.C.
                    (Leila Lyons)
                  (Vanessa Valcour)
  Angel Possessed   <GOT>
  New Orleans Series: <HR>
    1 River Of Time, The
    2 Pale Moon Rising A

CONFORD, Ellen   <YA>
  Dear Lovey Hart, I Am Desperate
  Hail, Hail Camp Timberwood
  You Can Never Tell

CONKLIN, Barbara
  Sweet Dreams: <YA>
      1 P. S., I Love You   &
     13 Summer Jenny Fell In Love
     23 Falling In Love Again   &
     36 Summer Dreams
     67 I Believe In You
     72 Goodbye Forever
     96 First, Last And Always
    141 Winter Dreams

CONLEE, Jaelyn
                    [Fayrene Preston]
  Second Chance At Love:
     71 Satin And Steel   *
  * see "Emerald Sunshine" LS284
        by Fayrene Preston

CONLEY, Karen
Passion's Firebird
_____

_____

CONLIN, Christine   <CO>
Love Is Where You Find It
_____

_____

CONN, Phoebe   <HR>
          [Phoebe Conn Ingwalson]
Arizona Angel
Beyond The Stars   <RF>
By Love Enslaved   <Saga>
Captive Heart
Ecstasy's Paradise
Emerald Fire
Hearts Of Gold
Loving Fury
No Sweeter Ecstasy
Savage Fire
Savage Storm
Tender Savage
In sequence:
   Love's Elusive Flame
   Starlit Ecstasy
_____

_____

CONNELL, Candace   <GOT>
              [Ernest C. Clement]
Ellena
House At Parson's Landing, The
Red Turrets Of Orne, The
Candlelight:
   551 Dark Legacy   <IN>
_____

_____

CONNOLLY, Vivian   <RS>
                  (Susanna Rosse)
Fires Of Ballymorris, The
Five Ports To Danger
Prometheus Trap, The
South Coast Of Danger
Velvet Prison, The

CONNOLLY, Vivian (cont.)
Coventry:
   68 Counterfeit Bride, The
  140 Cecilia
SuperRomance:
   63 Love In Exile
To Have And To Hold:
   10 I Know My Love
   21 Moonlight And Magnolias
   30 Promises To Keep
   49 Sweet Country Music
_____

_____

CONRAD, Constance
                   [Ruby Frankel]
Silhouette Desire:
   27 On Wings Of Night
_____

_____

CONRAD, Helen
              [Helen Manak Conrad]
                     (Jena Hunt)
                    (Raye Morgan)
Silver Linings
Candlelight Ecstasy:
  386 Stroke Of Genius, A
  413 Something Wild And Free
  440 At His Command
  470 Wild Temptation
  495 Tender Fury
  517 Wife For A Night
Dawnstar Romance:
   Heart Of Gold
Harlequin Romance:
 2731 Tears Of Gold
Harlequin SuperRomance:
  322 Desperado
Harlequin Temptation:
    3 Everlasting
  118 Diamond In The Rough
Loveswept:
    8 Temptation's Sting
   68 Undercover Affair
Pageant Romance:
   Chasing Dreams
_____

_____

135

CONRAD, Jean
Serenade/Saga: <HR><Insp>
22 Applegate Landing
47 Golden Gates

_____

_____

CONRAD, Pamela
Amanda

_____

_____

CONRAN, Shirley <CO>
Savages
In sequence:
Lace
Lace II

_____

_____

CONROY, Janet <GOT>
[Joseph Chadwick]
Harlan Legacy, The

_____

_____

CONSTANT, Jan
Masquerade:
47 Rebel And The Redcoat, The
86 Mackenzie's Woman

_____

_____

CONVERSE, Jane
[Adela Maritano]
Accused Nurse
Alias Miss Saunders, R. N.
Art Colony Nurse
Back Stage Nurse
Beth Lloyd, Surgical Nurse
Cinderalla Nurse
Condemned Nurse
Crusading Nurse

CONVERSE, Jane (cont.)
Dr. Holland's Nurse
Emergency Nurse
Expedition Nurse
Heartbreak Nurse
Hostage Nurse
Ice Show Nurse
Jet Set Nurse
Masquerade Nurse
No Claim On Love
Nurse Against The Town
Nurse Forrester's Secret
Nurse In Acapulco
Nurse In Charge
Nurse In Crisis
Nurse In Danger
Nurse In Hollywood
Nurse In Las Vegas
Nurse In London
Nurse In Panic
Nurse In Rome
Nurse In Turmoil
Nurse On The Riviera
Nurse On Trial
Obstetrical Nurse
Party Nurse, The
Penthouse Nurse
Pleasure Cruise Nurse
Recruiting Nurse
Second Chance Nurse
Settlement-House Nurse
Society Nurse
Surf Safari Nurse
Terry Allen, Nurse In Love
Thrill Show Nurse
Undercover Nurse
Young Nurses
Candlelight:
614 Flight For Dreamers, A<RO>
Silhouette Romance:
129 Moonlit Path
Silhouette Special Edition:
5 Paradise Postponed
40 Heartstorm
64 Mist Of Blossoms
117 Coral Sea, The

_____

_____

CONWAY, Celine
[Kathryn Blair]
Ships Surgeon   <M&B>
Harlequin Classic:
    45 Rustle Of Bamboo,The (620)
    50 Tall Pines, The   (736)
    85 Full Tide   (807)
   104 Blue Caribbean, The (863)
   113 At The Villa Massina (885)
   150 My Dear Cousin   (934)
   157 Perchance To Marry   (996)
   165 Return Of Simon, The (911)
Harlequin Romance:
   754 Rancher Needs A Wife, The
   807 Full Tide
   826 Doctor's Assistant
   863 Blue Caribbean, The
   885 At The Villa Massina
   911 Return Of Simon, The
   934 My Dear Cousin
   965 Came A Stranger
   996 Perchance To Marry
  1019 Flower Of The Morning
  1046 Three Women

CONWAY, Jean
MacFadden Romance:
   188 Softer Than Moonlight

CONWAY, Laura   <GOT><RS>
            [Dorothy Phoebe Ansle]
Abbot's House, The
Cast A Long Shadow
Dark Dream
Dark Symmetry
Don't Shut Me Out
Francesca
Heiress Apparent
House Called Pleasance, A
Link In The Chain, A
Moment Of Truth
Night Of The Party, The
Strange Visitor

CONWAY, Laura (cont.)
Take Heed Of Loving Me
Too Well Beloved
Undying Past, The
Unforgotten, The

CONWAY, Theresa   <HR>
      [Theresa Ann Whitcomb Conway]
Crimson Glory
Gabrielle
Honor Bound
Paloma
Passion For Glory, A
Seeds Of Destiny
Silver Clouds, Golden Dreams
Wine Of Paradise
Tapestry: <HR>
    12 Love Chase

COOGAN, Beatrice   <HR>
Flower Of The Storm, The (The
    Big Wind)

COOK, Arlene
Rhapsody Romance:
    One True Love

COOK, Bonna Lee DuBois
                 (Bonna Lee DuBois)

COOK, Deridre
                    (Dorothy Cork)

COOK, Eugenia   <GOT>
Forbidden Tower, The

COOK, Ida   (Deceased)
                     (Mary Burchell)

COOK, Jacquelyn
  Serenade/Saga   <HR><Insp>
    17 River Between, The
    31 Wind Along The River

_____

_____

COOK, Petronelle
  [Petronelle Marguerite Mary Cook]
                      (Margot Arnold)

COOK, Sally
  Harlequin Presents:
    1223 Deep Harbour
    1287 Belonging
    1320 Hijacked Heart
  Harlequin Romance:
    Takeover Bid   HRS25

_____

_____

COOK, Susan
  MacFadden Romance:
    15 Home For Summer

_____

_____

COOK, W.   <HR>
                       [Will Cook]
  Sabrina Kane

_____

_____

COOKE, John Byrne
  Snowblind Moon, The   <Saga>

_____

_____

COOKSON, Catherine
          [Catherine McMullen Cookson]
               (Catherine Marchant)
                  (Katie McMullen)
  Bailey Chronicles, The
  Bannaman Legacy, The
  Black Candle, The   <Saga>

COOKSON, Catherine (cont.)
  Black Velvet Gown, The
  Blind Miller, The
  Cinder Path, The
  Color-Blind
  Dwelling Place, The
  Fanny McBride
  Feathers In The Fire
  Fenwick Houses
  Fifteen Streets, The
  Gambling Man, The
  Garment, The
  Girl, The
  Glass Virgin, The
  Hannah Massey
  Harrogate Secret, The
  Husband, The
  Invisible Cord, The
  Invitation, The
  Joe & The Gladiator
  Kate Hannigan
  Katie Mulholland
  Lanky Jones
  Long Corridor, The
  Maggie Rowan
  Man Who Cried, The
  Matty Doolin
  Menagerie, The
  Our John Willie
  Our Kate <Biog>
  Parson's Daughter, The
  Pure As The Lily
  Rooney
  Round Tower, The
  Slinky Jane
  Slow Awakening, The
  Spaniards Gift, The
  Thorman Inheritance, The
  Tide Of Life, The
  Unbaited Trap, The
  Trilogy:
    Tilly
    Tilly Wed
    Tilly Alone
  Mallen Trilogy:
    Mallen Streak, The
    Mallen Girl, The
    Mallen Lot, The

COOKSON, Catherine (cont.)
  Mary Ann Series:
    Grand Man, A
    Lord And Mary Ann, The
    Devil And Mary Ann, The
    Love And Mary Ann
    Life And Mary Ann
    Marriage And Mary Ann
    Mary Ann And Bill
    Mary Ann's Angels

COOLEY, Leland Frederick   <HR>
  Art Colony, The
  California   <HS>
  Dancer, The
  God's High Table
  Richest Poor Folks, The
  Run For Home, The

COOMBS, Ann   <HR>
                              [Nina Pykare]
  Fire Within, The

COOMBS, Nina
                              [Nina Pykare]
  Rapture Romance:
      1 Love So Fearful
      6 Passion's Domain
     32 Forbidden Joy
     56 Sun Spark
    103 Before It's Too Late

COONEY, Caroline/Caroline B.
  I'm Not Your Other Half
  Last Dance
  Chrystal Falls: <YA>
      3 Bad And The Beautiful, The
      4 Morning After, The
  First Love From Silhouette: <YA>
     25 Personal Touch, The

COONEY, Caroline (cont.)
  Follow Your Heart Romance: <YA>
      2 Boys, Boys, Boys
      3 Stage Set For Love, A
      4 Sun, Sea, And Boys
      7 Racing To Love
      9 Suntanned Days
  Wildfire: <YA>
    An April Love Story
    He Loves Me Not
    Nancy And Nick

COONEY, Linda A.
  Couples: <YA>
      1 Change Of Hearts
      2 Fire And Ice
      3 Alone, Together
  Moonstone Novels: <YA><RS>
      1 Deadly Design
      4 Fatal Secrets

COOPER, Ann
  Harlequin Premiere Edition:
      2 Lion's Den, The
     16 Kragen's Heir
     26 MacLean's Woman
  Harlequin Presents:
    295 Battle With Desire
  Harlequin Romance:
   2383 Fool's Paradise
   2630 Maelstrom

COOPER, Barbara/Barbara A.   <HR>
  Savage Passion, The
  Winds Of Passion
  Harlequin Historical <Set#1>:
      7 Fortune's Kiss

COOPER, Jeffrey   <YA>
  Bonnie's Blues
  Finny In Love

COOPER, Jilly   <CO>
  Bella
  Emily
  Harriet
  Imogene
  Octavia
  Players
  Prudence
  Riders

COOPER, Lynna   <GOT>
                     [Gardner Fox]
  An Offer Of Marriage
  Brittany Stones, The
  Folly Hall
  Forgotten Love
  From Paris With Love
  Hearts In The Highlands
  Her Hearts Desire
  Hour Of The Harp, The
  Inherit My Heart
  Moon Chapel
  Portrait Of Love
  Stark Island
  Substitute Bride
  Adventures In Love:
     6 My Treasure, My Love
     9 Hired Wife, The
    10 An Offer Of Marriage
    11 Substitute Bride
    22 Stars Cry Love
    29 Deep Water, Deep Love

COOPER, M. E.
                     [Eileen Hehl]
  Couples: <YA>
     4 Made For Each Other
     5 Moving To Fast

COOPER, M. E. (cont.)
     6 Crazy Love
     7 Sworn Enemies
     8 Making Promises
     9 Broken Hearts.
    10 Secrets
    11 More Than Friends
    12 Bad Love
    13 Changing Partners
    14 Picture Perfect
    15 Coming On Strong
    16 Sweethearts
    17 Dance With Me
    18 Kiss And Run
    19 Show Some Emotion
    20 No Contest
    21 Teacher's Pet
    22 Slow Dancing
    24 Something New
    25 Love Exchange
    26 Head Over Heels
    27 Sweet And Sour
    28 Lovestruck
    29 Take Me Back
    30 Falling For You
    31 Prom Date
    32 Playing Dirty
    33 Mean To Me
    34 Don't Get Close
    35 Break Away
    36 Hold Me Tight
  Couples Special Edition: <YA>
    Be Mine!
    Beach Party!
    Sealed With A Kiss!
    Summer Heat

COOPER, Parley/Parley J.
                   <GOT><HO><RS>
                   (Jack Mayfield)
  Dark Desires
  Devil Child, The
  Golden Fever
  Grand Deception
  Inheritance, The
  Marianne's Kingdom

COOPER, Parley (cont.)
Moonblood
My Lady Evil
Restaurant: A Novel
San Francisco   <HofCS>
Shuddering Fair One, The

COPELAND, Frances
          (Fran Fisher)

COPELAND, Lori
Fool Me Once
Tale Of Love
Claxton Brothers Trilogy: <HR>
Avenging Angel
Passion's Captive
Sweet Talkin' Stranger
Candlelight Ecstasy:
134 Playing For Keeps
181 Tempting Stranger, A
217 All Or Nothing
239 Out Of Control   &
267 Winning Combination, The
294 Rainbow's End   &
320 Forever After
350 Spitfire
406 Love Of Our Own, A
429 Hot On His Trail
444 When Lightning Strikes
462 Out Of This World
479 Tug Of War
497 Passion's Folly
516 Up For Grabs
Candlelight Ecstasy Supreme:
39 Two Of A King
52 Only The Best
76 High Voltage
89 More Than She
     Bargained For
Harlequin American Romance:
261 Trouble With Thorny, The
336 Tall Cotton
Loveswept:
387 Darling Deceiver
440 Tis The Season
     Squeeze Play

COPELAND, Lori (cont.)
Pageant Romance:
Dancy's Woman

COPPULA, Susan   <HR>
   [Susan Carrol Coppula]
    (Susan Carroll)
    (Serena Richards)
In sequence:
Winterbourne
Shades Of Winter

CORBETT, Elizabeth
Continuing City, The
Distant Princess, The
Hamilton Terrace
Hidden Island
Hotel Belvedere
In Miss Armstrong's Room
Kimball Collection, The
Nice Long Evening, A
Paige Girls, The
Sunday At Six
Three Lives Of Sharon Spence
Wainwright Inheritance, The

CORBETT, Paula
Silhouette Desire:
156 Maid In Boston

CORBIN, DeLinda
   [DeLinda Maxwell Corbin]
Pageant Romance:
Auction Affair

CORBY, Jane   <GOT><RS>
As Deadly Does
Fall Darkness, Fall

CORBY, Jane (cont.)
  Farewell To The Castle
  Focus On Love
  Nightmare Legacy
  Nurse Of Greenmeadow
  Nurse's Alibi
  Nurse With The Red-Gold Hair
  Peril At Stone Hall
  Riverwood
  Shadow And The Fear, The
  Traveling Nurse
  Wings Of Desire
  Candlelight:
      7 Girl In The Tower
     27 Staff Nurse
  Sharon Romance:
      House Next Door, The
  Starlight Romance:
      Love's Refrain

CORCORAN, Barbara   <YA>
  Ask For Love
      You Get Rice Pudding
  Beloved Enemy
  By The Silvery Moon
  Call Of The Heart
  Child Of The Morning
  Love Is Not Enough
  Making It
  May I Cross Your Golden River
  Song For Two Voices
  Moonstone Novels: <RS>
      2 Shadowed Path, The
      6 When Darkness Falls
  Trilogy:
      Abigail
      Abbie In Love
      Husband For Gail, A

CORCORAN, Dorothy w/ Mary Ann
SLOJKOWSKI
                  (DeAnn Patrick)

CORDELL, Melissa   <GOT>
  Bond Of Evil
  Shades Of Peril

CORES, Lucy   <HR><RE>
              [Lucy Michaella Cores]
  Destiny's Passion
  Fatal Passion
  Katya
  Mermaid Summer

COREY, Gayle
              [Elaine Hauptman]
  Harlequin Temptation:
     200 Top Marks

COREY, Nina   <GOT>
  Age Of Aquarius, The

COREY, Ryanne
  Silhouette Desire:
     615 Valentine Street
              Hustle, The

CORIOLA
  Mystique:
      61 Intrigue In Morocco
      73 Stranger At Midnight
     134 Echoes Of Innocence
     148 Cruel Betrayal

CORK, Dorothy
              [Deridre Cook]
  Harlequin Premiere Edition:
      6 Kurranulla Round, The

COOK, Dorothy (cont.)
  Harlequin Romance:
    1511 Where Black Swans Fly
    1549 Night For Possums, A
    1644 Wayaway
    1668 Summer Mountain
    1692 Butterfly Montane
    1714 Spirit Of The Sun
    1757 Girl At Saltbush Flat, The
    1784 Red Plains Of Jounima, The
    1812 Promise To Keep, A
    1876 Gate Of The Golden Gazelle
    1894 Quicksilver Summer
    1927 Wandalilli Princess
    1966 Red Diamond
    1978 Eye Of The Sun, The
    2057 Dreamtime At Big Sky
    2115 Breakers On The Beach
    2139 Outback Rainbow
    2199 Thousand Miles Away, A
    2242 Forget And Forgive
    2253 Heart Of The Whirlwind
    2259 Island Of Escape
    2288 Walkabout Wife
    2372 Outback Runaway
    2390 Barefoot Bride
  Silhouette Romance:
     77 Secret Marriage
    103 By Honour Bound
    148 Reluctant Deceiver
    188 No More Regrets
    219 Island Spell
    238 Outback Dreaming
    286 Man From The Past, The
    304 Chosen Wife
    365 Wildest Dreams
    397 With Marriage In Mind

_____

_____

CORNBERG, Catherine Gaskin
                    (Catherine Gaskin)

CORNELIUS, Kay
  Serenade/Saga: <HR><Insp>
    21 Love's Gentle Journey

_____

_____

CORNETT, Nina
  Candlelight:
    137 Alaskan Summer

_____

_____

CORNWELL, Bernard
  Redcoat   <HO>

_____

_____

CORREN, Grace   <GOT><RS>
                    [Robert Hoskins]
  Attic Child, The
  Dark Island
  Dark Threshold
  Darkest Room, The
  Evil In The Family
  House Of Counted Hatreds
  Mansion Of Deadly Dreams
  Place On Dark Island, A

_____

_____

CORRIE, Jane
  Harlequin Romance:
    1956 Impossible Boss, The
    2020 Rainbow For Megan
    2038 Sinclair Territory
    2053 Green Paddocks
    2072 Bahamian Pirate, The
    2087 Dangerous Alliance
    2098 Rimmer's Way
    2159 Rafferty's Legacy
    2167 Patterson's Island
    2194 Texan Rancher, The
    2209 Peacock's Walk
    2257 Island Bride, The
    2285 Caribbean Cocktail
    2313 Spanish Uncle, The
    2335 Tasmanian Tangle
    2365 Station Boss, The
    2384 Island Fiesta
    2413 Pirate's Lair
    2431 Bride For Sale
    2521 Ross's Girl

CORRIE, Jane (cont.)
2551 Man With Two Faces
2743 Cartier's Strike
Bond Of Fate HRS7
Muldoon Territory HRS39

CORSER, Judy E.
(Judith Bowen)

CORSON, Martha
(Anne Lacey)
(see Kristin Michaels)

CORY, Diane <HR>
Token Of Jewels, A
High Society

COSCARELLI, Kate <CO>
Fame And Fortune
Living Color
Perfect Order
Pretty Women

COSGROVE, Rachel
[Rachel Cosgrove Payes]
Linda's Gifts
Designs For Love
Candlelight:
19 Candystripers, The

COSTAIN, Thomas B. <HO>
Below The Salt
Black Rose, The
Conquerors, The
Darkness And The Dawn, The
For My Great Folly
Last Love, The
Moneyman, The
Ride With Me
Son Of A Hundred Kings
Silver Chalice, The

COSTAIN, Thomas (cont.)
Tontine, The
History Of The Plantagenets:
In sequence:
Conquering Family, The
Magnificent Century, The
Three Edwards, The
Last Plantagenets, The

COTT, Christine Hella
SuperRomance:
22 Midnight Magic
30 Tender Wilderness, A
50 Dangerous Delight
98 Perfume And Lace
Harlequin SuperRomance:
144 Riches To Hold
168 Season Magic
178 Strawberry Kiss
220 Cinnamon Hearts

COUGHLIN, Patricia
[Patricia Madden Coughlin]
(Liz Grady)
(see Silhouete Summer Sizzlers)
Wild Paradise <CO>
Harlequin Temptation:
83 Message For Jesse
Silhouette Special Edition:
438 Shady Lady
485 Bargain, The
523 Some Like It Hot
602 Spirit Is Willing, The

COUGHLIN, Patricia Madden
(Patricia Coughlin)
(Liz Grady)

COUGHLIN, William J.
Her Father's Daughter

COULDERY, Vivienne
Coventry:
  100 Swans Of Brhyadr

COULSON, Juanita   <GOT><RS>
             [Juanita Ruth Coulson]
Dark Priestess
Death God's Citadel, The
Door Into Terror
Fear Stalks The Bayou   <ZGS>
Fire Of The Andes
Secret Of Seven Oaks
Stone Of Blood   <BGS:#3>
Web Of Wizardy, The

COULTER, Catherine   <HR><RE>
             [Jean Coulter Pogony]
False Pretenses   <CO><RM>
Impulse   <CO><RM>
Regency's:
  An Honorable Offer
  An Intimate Deception
  Autumn Countess, The
  Generous Earl, The
  Lord Deverill's Heir
  Lord Harry's Folly
  Rebel Bride, The
In sequence:
  Sweet Surrender
  San Francisco Trilogy:
    Midnight Star
    Wild Star
    Jade Star
In sequence:
  Chandra
  Medieval Trilogy:
    Fire Song
    Earth Song
    Secret Song
In sequence:
  Devil's Embrace
  Devil's Daughter
Magic Trilogy:
  Midsummer Magic
  Calypso Magic
  Moonspun Magic

COULTER, Catherine (cont.)
Night Trilogy:
  Night Fire
  Night Shadow
  Night Storm
Silhouette Intimate Moments:
  In sequence:
  121   Aftershocks
  190   Afterglow
Silhouette Special Edition:
  331 Aristocrat, The

COULTER, Stephen
Chateau, The

COULTRY, Barbara
             (Barbara Blacktree)

COURCELLES, Sandra
             (Samantha Day)

COURT, Katherine   <GOT><RS>
             [Elizabeth K. Schrempp]
But Don't Go Alone
Whisper, Whisper
Candlelight:
  601 Mask Of Love, The   <RO>

COURTER, Gay
Midwife
River Of Dreams   <Saga>

COURTNEY, Caroline   <RE>
  1 Duchess In Disguise
  2 Wager For Love, A
  3 Love Unmasked
  4 Guardian Of The Heart
  5 Dangerous Engagement
  6 Fortunes Of Love, The

COY, Stanlee Miller
                    (Cissie Miller)

COY, Stanlee Miller w/ Carolyn
NICHOLS
                    (Iona Charles)

CRACO, Catherine
Lovestruck:
  By Invitation Only

CRAIG, Dolores
                    [Miriam Lynch]
  Scalpel Of Honor

CRAIG, Georgia
                    [Peggy Dern]
  Alaska Love
  Girl Outside, The
  Heart Remembers, The
  Her Plantation Home
  No Part Of Marriage
  Nurse At Guale Farms
  Nurse Comes Home, A
  Nurse With Wings
  Perry Kimbro, R. N.
  Piney Wood's Nurse, The
  Society Nurse
  This, Too, Is Love
  Too Young To Marry
  Sharon Romance:
    Come Home Holly Lowman
  Sharon Contemporary Teens:
    Junior Prom Girl

CRAIG, Jasmine   <HR>
                    [Jasmine Candlish]
  Devil's Envoy, The
  Empire Of The Heart
  Second Chance At Love:
    29 Tender Triumph
    46 Runaway Love

CRAIG, Jasmine (cont.)
    80 Stormy Reunion
   118 Imprisoned Heart
   170 Refuge In His Arms
   187 Surprised By Love
   243 Dear Adam
   274 Master Touch
   318 One Step To Paradise
   396 For Love Of Christy
   446 Knave Of Hearts
  To Have And To Hold:
    32 Under Cover Of Night

CRAIG, M. S.
                    [Mary Francis Craig]
  Chicagoans: Dust To
    Diamonds   <Saga>

CRAIG, Mary
                    [Mary Francis Craig]
  Blessings
  Candle For The Dragon, A
  Mistress Of Lost River
Shadows Of The Past
  Were He A Stranger

CRAIG, Mary Francis
                    (M. S. Craig)
                    (Mary Craig)
                    (Mary S. Craig)
                    (Mary Shura Craig)
                    (Alexis Hill)
                    (Mary Francis Shura)

CRAIG, Mary S.   <HR>
                    [Mary Francis Craig]
  Dark Paradise   <Saga>

CRAIG, Mary Shura   <HR>
        [Mary Francis Craig]
Fortune's Destiny   <Saga>
Lyon's Pride
Pirate's Landing   <Saga>

―――――――――――――――――――――――――

CRAIG, Rianna
        [Sharron & Rick Harrington]
Harlequin American Romance:
    56 Love Match
Harlequin Intrigue:
    39 On Executive Orders

―――――――――――――――――――――――――

CRAIG, Vera
        [Donald Sydney Rowland]
Candlelight:
    84 Glen Hall
   126 Now And Forever
   130 Land Of Enchantment
   131 Love Barrier, The
   133 Path Of Peril

―――――――――――――――――――――――――

CRAMPTON, Helen
        [Marion Chesney Gibbons]
Marriage A'la Mode
Cotillion Regency:
    2 Marquis Takes A Bride, The
   10 Highland Countess, The

―――――――――――――――――――――――――

CRANDALL, Elizabeth   <GOT>
White Violets

―――――――――――――――――――――――――

CRANE, Leah
        [Jean Hager]
SuperRomance:
    66 Dark Ecstasy

―――――――――――――――――――――――――

CRANE, Marion
Sweet Dreams: <YA>
    87 Programmed For Love

―――――――――――――――――――――――――

CRANE, Teresa
Hawthorne Heritage, The   <HS>
Molly

―――――――――――――――――――――――――

CRANMER, Kathryn
Harlequin Romance:
  2517 Passionate Enemies
  2620 Pas de Deux
  2719 Wrecker's Bride
  2767 Secret Lover

―――――――――――――――――――――――――

CRAVEN, Barbara Catlin
                (Barbara Catlin)

CRAVEN, Barbara Catlin w/ Martha
Rand HIX
                (Maranda Catlin)

CRAVEN, Sara
Harlequin Presents:
   191 Strange Adventure
   195 Gift For A Lion, A
   199 Wild Melody
   215 Temple Of The Moon
   235 Place Of Storms, A
   243 Past All Forgetting
   251 Devil At Archangel, The
   255 Dragon's Lair
   291 High Tide At Midnight
   307 Moth To The Flame
   325 Solitaire
   331 Flame Of Diablo
   368 Fugitive Wife
   398 Shadow Of Desire
   411 Moon Of Aphrodite
   440 Summer Of The Raven
   459 Witching Hour
   487 Dark Summer Dawn

CRECY, Jeanne (cont.)
My Face Beneath The Stone
Night Hunters, The
Winter Keeper, The

CREEKMORE, Donna   <RS>
Silver Shroud, The
Candlelight:
528 Coachman's Daughter, The
706 Difficult Miss Livingston,The

CREEL, Catherine   <HR>
Breathless Passion
Captive Flame
Cimarron Bride
Golden Obsession
Nevada Captive
Rapture's Rogue
Scoundrel's Bride
Surrender To Desire
Texas Bride
Texas Flame
Texas Spitfire
Texas Torment
Yankee And The Belle, The

CREESE, Bethea
Dream Comes True
Harlequin Romance:
859 Irish Rose
1413 Family Face, The

CREFELD, Donna   <HO>
From This Land

CREIGHTON, JoAnne   <GOT>
[Joseph Chadwick]
Dark Side Of Paradise, The
Harlan Legacy, The
House Of Fury
Inn Of Evil
Mask Of Evil, The

CREIGHTON, Kathleen
[Kathleen Creighton Modrovich]
(see Silhouette Christmas Stories)
Loveswept:
139 Delilah's Weakness
163 Still Waters
208 Katie's Hero
239 Prince And The Patriot,The
279 Winter's Daughter
299 Sorcerer's Keeper, The
Silhouette Classic:
15 Demon Lover   <IM84>
Silhouette Desire:
584 Heart Mender, The
Silhouette Intimate Moments:
84 Demon Lover
157 Double Dealings
196 Gypsy Dancer
216 In Defense Of Love   &
240 Rogue's Valley
289 Tiger Dawn
322 Love And Other Surprises &

CRENSHAW, Nadine
Edin's Embrace
Heartfire Romance: <HR>
Captive Melody
Mountain Mistress

CRESSWELL, Jasmine
        [Jasmine Candlish]
Forgotten Marriage   <Eng>
Princess, The
Rossiter Arrangement, The
Substitute Bride, The
Coventry:
 188 Damewood Legacy, The <VIC>
 199 Lord Carrisford's Mistress
      Reluctant Viscountess, The
Harlequin Historical <Set#1>:
   6 Moreton Scandal, The
Harlequin Intrigue:
  51 Undercover
  77 Chase The Past
 105 Free Fall
 124 Charades   <DTR>
Harlequin Presents:
 913 Hunter's Prey
Harlequin Regency Romance:
 Traitor's Heir
Masquerade:
  41 Abducted Heiress, The
  62 Tarrisbroke Hall
  88 Blackwood Bride, The
Silhouette Desire:
 113 Mixed Doubles

CREWE, Sarah
        [Virginia Blanford]
Second Chance At Love:
 135 Golden Illusions
 195 Night Flame
 233 Seaflame
 281 Windflame

CREWS, Ethel Maxam
                    (Mia Maxam)

CRICHTON, Robert
 Camerons, The   <CS>
 Secret Of Santa Vittoria

CRISTY, Ann
        [Helen Mittermeyer]
Second Chance At Love:
  49 From The Torrid Past
  60 Torn Asunder
 103 Enthralled
 166 No Gentle Possession
 223 Mystique
To Have And To Hold:
   3 Tread Softly
  24 Homecoming

CRISWELL, Millie
 Heartfire Romance:
 Brazen Virginia Bride

CRITCHLEY, Lynne
 Heavenly Romance: <YA>
 Dream Of Spring

CROCKETT, Christina
        [Linda Crockett Gray]
SuperRomance:
  55 To Touch A Dream
Harlequin SuperRomance:
 103 Moment Of Magic, A
 146 Song Of The Seabird
 171 Windward Passage

CROFT, Jesse Taylor
 Trainmasters Series: <HS>
 Trainmasters, The
 Railroad War, The

CROISSANT, Kay w/ Catherine DEES
                (Catherine Kay)
                (Kate McKenzie)

CROMPTON, Anne
                           (Anne Eliot)
  Untamed, The
  Warrior Wives   <HR>
  Woman's Place, A

CROMWELL, Elsie
                          [Elsie Lee]
  Governess, The
  Ivorstone Manor   <RS>

CRONE, Alla   <HR>
  East Lies The Sun
  Legacy Of Amber
  North Of The Moon
  Winds Over Manchuria

CRONIN, A. J.   (Deceased)
  Shannon's Way
  Three Loves

CROOK, Beverly Courtney   <YA>
  Fair Annie Of Old Mule Hollow

CROSBY, Lee   <GOT><RS>
              [Ware Torrey Budlong]
  Bridge House
  Doors To Death

CROSE, Susan
                   (Lisa Jackson)
             (Michelle Mathews)
  Loveswept:
  264 Brass Ring, The

CROSS, Caitlin
                [Doranna Berger]
  Silhouette Special Edition:
  272 High Risk
  341 Catch The Wind
  380 Shadow Of Doubt
  413 Natural Woman, A

CROSS, Charlene   <HR>
  Heart So Innocent, A
  Masque Of Enchantment

CROSS, Judi
  First Love From Silhouette: <YA>
  231 Something To Treasure

CROSS, Melinda
  Harlequin Presents:
  847 Lion Of Darkness
  889 Very Private Love, A
  914 What's Right
  959 Call Of Home, The
  1224 One Hour Of Magic
  1247 King Of The Mountain
  1312 Defiant Dream, A

CROSS, Peggy   <HR>
  Sapphire Moon   <AAS>

CROSS, Victor   <GOT>
             [Virginia Coffman]
  Blood Sport

CROW, Donna Fletcher
               (Donna Fletcher)
  Serenade/Serenata: <Insp>
    11 Greengold Autumn
    17 Desires Of Your Heart, The
    38 Love Unmerited

CROWCROFT, Jane   <GOT>
           [Peter Crowcroft]
  Of Love Incarnate
  Witch Love

CROWE, Cecily   <GOT><RS>
  Abbeygate
  Bloodrose House
  Miss Spring
  Northwater
  Talisman, The
  Tower Of Kilraven, The
  Twice-Born, The

CROWE, Evelyn A.
  Harlequin SuperRomance:
    In sequence:
    112   Summer Ballad
    160   Charade
    186   Moments Of Madness
    233   Final Payment
    262   Twice Shy
    294   Wild Wind, A
    362   Word Of Honor

CRUMBAKER, Alice
            (Allison Baker)

CRUZ, Joan Carroll
  Desires Of Thy Heart

CSIDA, Joseph
  In sequence: <HS>
    Remember This House
    This Place Of Honor
  Steeles Saga: <HS>
    In sequence:
    Magic Ground, The
    Unknown Shores, The

CUDLIPP, Edith
             (Julia Alcott)
       (Bettina Montgomery)
          (Nicole Norman)
         (Maureen Norris)
        (Rinalda Roberts)

CUEVAS, Judith
  Heartfire Romance: <HR>
    Starlit Surrender

CULP, John H.   <HO>
  Born Of The Sun
  Bright Feathers
  Oh, Valley Green
  Restless Land, The
  Timothy Baines
  Treasure Of The Chisos, The
  Whistle In The Wind

CULVER, Carol
             (Carol Grace)

CULVER, Colleen
         (Colleen Faulkner)

CUMBERLAND, Patricia
  Harlequin Romance:
  1417 Doctor In India

CUMMINGS, Barbara
Crosswinds Keepsakes: <YA>
  22 Playing Games

CUMMINGS, Monette   <RE><RE-I>
                [Mona A. Cummings]
Beauty's Daughter, The
Don't Wager On Love
Guardian Devil
Husband For Holly, A
Lady Sheila's Groom
Royal Conspiracy
Scandalous Widow, The
Scarlet Lady
See No Love

CUMMINS, Mary
                    (Susan Taylor)
Forbidden Love
Song Of Autumn
Harlequin Romance:
  1350 Above Rubies
  1404 Diamonds On The Lake
  1435 Scarlet Sunset
  1482 Monkey Puzzle, The
  1568 Sea Tangle
  1612 Mistress Of Elvan Hall
  1652 Pearl For Love, A

CUNLIFFE, Corinna   <RE>
                [Corinna Wildman]
Hand Of Fortune
Play Of Hearts
Unsuitable Chaperone, The

CUNNINGHAM, Cathy   <GOT><RS>
                [Chet Cunningham]
Curse Of Valkyrie House
Demons Of Highpoint House, The

CUNNINGHAM, Chet   <HR>
              (Cathy Cunningham)
              (See Farris Fletcher)
Beloved Rebel
Bloody Gold
Cheyenne Payoff
Devil's Gold
Die Of Gold
Frisco Lady, The
Gold And The Glory, The
Gold Wagon, The
Patriots, The
Power And The Prize, The
Rainbow Saga
Seeds Of Rebellion
This Splendid Land

CUNNINGHAM, Jan
              (Chelsey Forrest)

CUNNINGHAM, Madelyn   <HR>
Monique

CUNNINGHAM, Marilyn
              (see Carolyn Chase)
Bride And Groom:
  2 Just Family And Friends
Candlelight Ecstasy:
  435 Thrill Of His Kiss, The
  485 Under The Northern Lights
  515 Forbidden Passion
Silhouette Intimate Moments:
  334 Someone To Turn To
  355 Enchanted Circle

CURLING, Audrey   <HR><RE>
Caste For Comedy
Echoing Silence, The
Enthusiast In Love
Heart Denied, A
Quarter Of The Moon, A
Sapphire And The Pearl, The

CURRIE, Ann Brooke   <HR>
  Natalya

CURRIE, Katy
                    [Susan Spaeth Kyle]
  Silhouette Inspirations:
    5 Blind Promises

CURRY, Elissa
                        [Nancy Martin]
  Fair Kate   <HR>
  Second Chance At Love:
    174 Trial By Desire
    178 Winter Wildfire
    193 Lady With A Past
    213 Black Lace And Pearls
    227 Dating Game
    247 Lady Be Good
    263 Gentleman At Heart
    287 Sophisticated Lady
    324 Fortune's Choice
  To Have And To Hold:
    18 Playing For Keeps
    23 Kiss Me Cait

CURTIS, Jean
  Harlequin Romance:
    1204 This Was Love
    1285 Out Of A Dream

CURTIS, Mary/Mary H.
                    [Mary Haskell Curtis]
                        (Mary Haskell)
  Kisses For Kate   <YA>
  Silhouette Special Edition:
    424 Love Lyrics
    526 Cliffhanger

CURTIS, Mary Haskell
                        (Mary Curtis)
                        (Mary H. Curtis)
                        (Mary Haskell)

CURTIS, Peter
                        [Norah Lofts]
  Devil's Own, The
  No Question Of Murder

CURTIS, Richard Hale   <HO>
  (publishers pseudonym for
            writers in this series):
  Skymasters Series:
    1 To Soar With Eagles
                        [Tad Richards]
    2 Seekers Of The Sky
                        [Robert Kail]
    3 After The Hawk
                        [Ian McMahan]
    4 Barnstormers, The
                        [Richard Deming]
    5 Birds Of War
                        [John Toombs]
    6 Wind Nor Rain Nor Dark Of
       Night
                        [Robert Kail]
    7 Aviatrix, The
                        [Dan Streib]
    8 Every Man An Eagle
                        [Len Levinson]
    9 Through Clouds Of Flame

   10 Cry Of The Condor

CURTIS, Stefanie
  Sweet Dreams: <YA>
    118 Heart To Heart
    126 Here's My Heart
    140 Love Detour
    157 Mr. Perfect

CURTIS, Susannah   <GOT>
                     [Helen Upshall]
  Monk's Retreat

CURTIS, Tom and Sharon
  [Thomas Dale Curtis w/
       Sharon Lee Blakslee Curtis]
                     (Robin James)
                     (Laura London)
  Keepsake (SCAL #58 and THH #1)
  Sunshine And Shadows
  Loveswept:
    25 Lightning That Lingers

CURTISS, Ursula   <RS>
  Birthday Gift, The
  Danger: Hospital Zone
  Face Of The Tiger, The
  In Cold Pursuit
  Iron Cobweb, The
  Menace Within, The
  Out Of The Darkness
  Second Sickle, The
  So Dies The Dreamer
  Stairway, The
  Voice Out Of Darkness
  Wasp, The

CURZON, Lucia   <RE>
                 [Florence Stevenson]
  Second Chance At Love:
    3   Chadbourne Luck, The
    33 An Adverse Alliance
    57 Morning Bride
    87 Queen Of Hearts
    123 Dashing Guardian, The

CUSHING, Enid
  Coventry:
    90 Maid-At-Arms
    (see Andre NORTON)

CUST, Barbara
  Web Of Intrigue
  Harlequin Romance:
    1588 Leaping Flame, The
    1982 Scent Of The Maquis

CUTHRELL, Faith Baldwin
                    (Faith Baldwin)

CZULEGER, Rebecca
                    (Rebecca Bond)
                    (Rebecca Forster)

156

DABNEY, Ann
[Lois Ann Brown w/ Nancy Jackson]
Candlelight:
242 Life Time To Love, A <RO>

DAGG, Jillian
(Marilyn Brian)
(Jillian Fayre)
(Faye Wildman)

DAHEIM, Mary   <HR>
Destiny's Pawn
Love's Pirate
Passion's Triumph
Pride's Captive
Harlequin Historical <Set#2>:
54 King's Ransom

DAHLIN, Betty
Avalon:
Lesson In Love
Listen To The Roses
Roman Butterfly

DAILEY, Janet
[Janet Ann Haradon Dailey]
Best Way To Lose (SSE#132)
Fiesta San Antonio (HP# 192)
For Bitter Or Worse (HP# 267)
For The Love Of God (SR# 118)
Foxfire Light (SSE# 36)
Glory Game, The
Great Alone, The   <Saga>
Heiress
Hostage Bride, The (SR# 82)

DAILEY, Janet (cont.)
Ivory Cane, The (HR# 219)
Lancaster Men, The (SR#106)
Leftover Love (SSE# 150)
Masquerade
Master Fiddler (HP# 252)
Mistletoe And Holly (SR# 195)
Nightway
No Quarter Asked (HP# 124)
Pride Of Hannah Wade, The
Ride The Thunder
Rivals
Rogue, The
Second Time, The (SR# 177)
Seperate Cabins (SR# 213)
Silver Wings, Santiago Blue
Something Extra (HP# 248)
Sweet Promise (HP# 308)
Terms Of Surrender (SSE# 1)
Touch The Wind
Western Man (SR# 231)
Wildcatter's Woman (SR# 153)
Calder Series:
This Calder Range
Stands A Calder Man
This Calder Sky
Calder Born, Calder Bred
Harlequin Presents/
Janet Dailey Americana
NOTE: Some of the following books
were reprinted under the
"Americana" name. The number
and State name denotes that
book's order in the series.
124 No Quarter Asked
131 Boss Man From Ogallala
(27 Nebraska)
139 Savage Land
(43 Texas)
147 Fire And Ice
(5 California)
151 Land Of Enchantment
(31 New Mexico)
159 Homeplace, The
(15 Iowa)
167 After The Storm
(6 Colorado)
171 Dangerous Masquerade
(1 Alabama)

DAILEY, Janet (cont.)
180 Night Of The Cotillion
       (10 Georgia)
183 Valley Of TheVapours
       (4 Arkansas)
192 Fiesta San Antonio
200 Show Me
       (25 Missouri)
203 Blue Grass King
       (17 Kentucky)
208 Lyon's Share, A
       (13 Illinois)
211 Widow And The Wastrel, The
       (35 Ohio)
219 Ivory Cane, The
223 Indy Man, The
       (14 Indiana)
227 Darling Jenny
       (50 Wyoming)
231 Reilly's Woman
       (28 Nevada)
236 To Tell The Truth
       (37 Oregon)
239 Sonora Sundown
       (3 Arizona)
248 Something Extra
252 Master Fiddler, The
256 Beware Of The Stranger
       (32 New York)
259 Giant Of Mesabi
       (23 Minnesota)
264 Matchmakers, The
       (8 Deleware)
267 For Bitter Or Worse
272 Green Mountain Man
       (45 Vermont)
275 Six White Horses
       (36 Oklahoma)
279 Summer Mahogany
       (19 Maine)
284 Bride Of The Delta Queen
       (18 Louisana)
292 Tidewater Lover
       (46 Virginia)
302 Low Country Lair
       (40 South Carolina)
308 Sweet Promise
313 For Mike's Sake
       (47 Washington)

DAILEY, Janet (cont.)
319 Sentimental Journey
       (42 Tennessee)
326 Land Called Deseret, A
       (44 Utah)
332 Kona Winds
       (11 Hawaii)
338 That Boston Man
       (21 Massachusetts)
343 Bed Of Grass
       (20 Maryland)
349 Thawing Of Mara, The
       (38 Pennsylvania)
356 Mating Season, The
       (16 Kansas)
363 Lord Of The High Lonesome
       (34 North Dakota)
369 Southern Nights
       (9 Florida)
373 Enemy In Camp
       (22 Michigan)
386 Difficult Decision
       (7 Connecticut)
391 Heart Of Stone
       (29 New Hampshire)
399 One Of The Boys
       (30 New Jersey)
416 Wild And Wonderful
       (48 West Virginia)
421 Tradition Of Pride, A
       (24 Mississippi)
427 Travelling Kind, The
       (12 Idaho)
Silhouette Romance:
82 Hostage Bride, The
106 Lancaster Men, The
118 For The Love Of God
153 Wildcatter's Woman
177 Second Time, The
195 Mistletoe And Holly
213 Separate Cabins
231 Western Man
Silhouette Special Edition:
1 Terms Of Surrender
36 Foxfire Light
132 Best Way To Lose, The
150 Leftover Love

158

DALEY, Margaret
    [Margaret Kathleen Ripy Daley]
                (Kathleen Daley)
                    (Kit Daley)
                  (Patti Moore)
                (Margaret Ripy)
DALLAS, Georgia
    This Band Of Gold   <Insp>

_____

DALLAS-DAMIS, Althena G.
    In sequence:
        Island Of The Winds
        Windswept

_____

_____

DALLMAYR, Ilse
                    (Heidi Strasser)
DALLY, Emma
    Passage Of Seasons   <Saga>

_____

DALTON, Claire
    Second Life Of Cecily Pride, The

_____

_____

DALTON, Elyse
    Mirror Of The Heart

_____

_____

DALTON, Emily
                    [Danice Jo Allen]
    Harlequin Regency Romance:
        31 Country Chit, The
        44 An Infamous Sea Bath

_____

_____

DALTON, Gena
                    [Genell Dellin]
    Silhouette Special Edition:
        69   Sorrel Sunset
        147 April Encounter
        201 Wild Passions
        307 Cherokee Fire   <ATS>

_____

DALTON, Jackie
                    [Jackie Troutman]
    Dark Lullaby   <RS>
    Avalon:
        Forbidden Treasure

_____

DALTON, Jenifer   <HR>
                    [David M. Wind]
    Run On The Wind
    Whispers Of Destiny

_____

DALTON, Margot
    Harlequin SuperRomance:
        401 Under Prairie Skies
        425 Sagebrush and Sunshine   &
        431 Magic And Moonbeams   &
        457 Ask Me Anything
        475 Golden Lion

_____

DALTON, Pat
    Second Chance At Love:
        368 Twice In A Lifetime
        406 Conspiracy Of Hearts
        433 Close Scrutiny
        472 Close To Sunrise
    Starlight Romance:
        Winds Of Destiny

_____

DALTON, Priscilla   <GOT><RS>
                    [Michael Avallone]
Darkening Willows, The
Ninety Gramercy Park
Silent, Silken Shadows, The

DANA, Erin
                        [Nancy Elliott]
Candlelight Supreme:
   139 Footprints In The Sand
   182 For The Love Of Jade

DALY, Saralyn
In The Web
Love's Joy, Love's Pain

DALZELL, Helen
Harlequin Premiere Edition:
   27 In Search Of Mary Ann
Harlequin Romance:
   2570 Not The Marrying Kind

DANA, Rose
                      [W. E. Daniel Ross]
Arctic Nurse
Bermuda Nurse
Construction Camp Nurse
Department Store Nurse
Down East Nurse
Network Nurse
Night Club Nurse
Nurse In Jeopardy
Operation Room Nurse

DAMIO, Ward
                    (see Rebecca Drury)
(see Lee Davis Willoughby <MOAS>)

DAMON, Kate
                    [Margaret Brownley]
Trilogy: <HS>
   Napa

DAMON, Lee
                       [Jane H. Look]
Again The Magic
Harlequin SuperRomance:
   135 Summer Sunrise
Second Chance At Love:
   120 Laugh With Me, Love
           With Me
To Have And To Hold:
   16 Lady Laughing Eyes

DANBURY, Iris
Harlequin Petite:
   1 Illyrian Summer
Harlequin Romance:
   1137 Doctor At Drumlochan
   1178 Rendezvous In Lisbon
   1211 Bride Of Kylsaig
   1257 Doctor At Villa Ronda
   1301 Hotel By The Loch
   1331 Hotel Belvedere
   1372 Isle Of Pomegranates
   1398 Feast Of The Candles
   1439 Serenade At Santa Rosa
   1461 Island Of Mermaids
   1485 Chateau Of Pines
   1519 Summer Comes To Albarosa
   1558 Legend Of Roscano
   1620 Jacaranda Island
   1671 Mandolins Of Montori
   1771 Silver Stallion, The
   1804 Fires Of Torretta, The
   1837 Amethyst Meadows, The
   1873 Pavement Of Pearl, A
   2011 Windmill Of Kalakos, The
   2042 Scented Island, The
   2122 Painted Palace, The

DANCER, Lacey
Meteor Kismet:
   7 Silent Enchantment

DANE, Eve
           [Elizabeth Darrell]
Lion By The Mane, A
Shadows In The Fire
Vaaldorp Diamond, The

DANELLA, Utta
           [Franz Schneekluth Verlag]
Those Von Tallien Women

DANIEL, Elaine
Circle Of Love:
   5 Cinderella Season

DANIEL, Megan   <RE>
           [Donna Meyer]
Amelia
American Bride, The
Miss Pennington's Choice
Queen Of Hearts, The
Reluctant Suitor, The
Sensible Courtship, The
Unlikely Rivals, The

DANIELS, Carol   <HR>
           [Carol Viens]
Valley Of Dreams

DANIELS, Dana
           [Deana Brauer]
Second Chance At Love:
  230 For Love Or Money
  302 Unspoken Longings
  385 Hint Of Scandal, A
  439 Lady Eve, The

DANIELS, Dorothy   <GOT><HR><RS>
          (Danielle Dorsett)
          (Angela Gray)
        (Cynthia Kavanaugh)
          (Helaine Ross)
         (Suzanne Somers)
        (Geraldine Thayer)
     (Helen Gray Weston)
Affair In Hong Kong
Affair In Marakesh
Apollo Fountain, The
Attic Rope, The
Beaumont Tradition, The
Bell, The
Blackthorn
Blue Devil Suite
Bridal Black
Caldwell Shadow, The
Candle In The Sun
Carson Inheritance, The
Castle Morvant
Child Of Darkness
Circle Of Guilt
Cliffside Castle
Conover's Folly
Cormac Legend, The
Cruise Ship Nurse
Curse Of Mallory Hall, The
Dance In The Darkness
Danger Mansion
Darkhaven
Dark Heritage
Dark Island
Dark Stage, The
Dark Villa
Diablo Manor
Duet
Duncan Dynasty, The

DANIELS, Dorothy (cont.)
In sequence: <HR>
    Sisters Of Valcour
    For Love Of Valcour
    Crisis At Valcour

DANIELS, Faye   <HR>
    Ashes To Empire

DANIELS, Joleen
                [Gayle Malone Schimek]
    Silhouette Special Edition:
    507 Reckoning, The
    645 Against All Odds

DANIELS, Jordana
    Afterglow   <CO>

DANIELS, Judith
                [Judy Pelfrey]
    Silhouette Special Edition:
    389 Sun Always Rises, The

DANIELS, Kayla
                [Karin Hofland]
    Silhouette Special Edition:
    474 Spitting Image
    578 Father Knows Best
    654 Hot Prospect

DANIELS, Kristy   <CO>
    [Kristy Montee w/ Daniel Norman]
    Dancer, The
    Hot Type

DANIELS, Laura
    McFadden Romance:
    24 Dream And The Dance, The

DANIELS, Leigh
                [Lisbeth Chance]
    Harlequin Intrigue:
    106 On The Run

DANIELS, Melonie   <HR>
    River Queen, The

DANIELS, Norman
    Wyndward: In sequence:
    Wyndward Passion
    Wyndward Fury
    Wyndward Peril
    Wyndward Glory
    Forever Wyndward

DANIELS, Rebecca
    Silhouette Intimate Moments:
    369 L.A. Heat

DANIELS, Rhett
                [Judy Pelfrey]
    Silhouette Special Edition:
    184 Overtures Of The Heart

DANIELS, Val
                [Alfie Thompson]
    Harlequin Romance:
    3092 Silver Bells

DANIELS, Velma S. w/
                    Peggy E. KING
  Serenade/Serenata: <INSP>
    6 Fountain Of Love

_____

_____

DANIELS-HENDERSON, Beth
                    (Beth Henderson)

DANIELSON, Peter
  Children Of The Lion: <HS>
    1 Children Of The Lion
    2 Shepherd Kings, The
    3 Vengeance Of The Lion
    4 Lion In Egypt, The
    5 Golden Pharoah, The
    6 Lord Of The Nile
    7 Prophecy, The
    8 Sword Of Glory
    9 Deliverer, The
   10 Exodus, The
   11 Sea Peoples, The
   12 Promised Land, The

_____

_____

DANLEY, Marguerite
  Love's Portrait

_____

_____

DANN, Victoria
                    (Victoria Glenn)

DANO, Linda
                  (see Felicia Gallant)

DANTON, Pierre
  In sequence: <HS>
    No River So Wide
    Mississippi Nights

_____

_____

DANTON, Rebecca   <GOT><HR><RE>
                  [Janet Louise Roberts]
  Amethyst Love   <RE>
  Fire Opals
  Ship Of Hate
  Sign Of The Golden Goose
  White Fire
  Coventry:
   21 Highland Brooch, The
   75 Ruby Heart, The
  177 French Jade
  Coventry Classic:
    Star Sapphire

_____

_____

D'AOUST, Susan Saxton
  Long Shadows   <HS>

_____

_____

DAOUST, Pamela
                  (Katharine Kincaid)

DARBY, Catherine   <GOT><HO><RS>
                   [Maureen Peters]
  Dream Of Fair Serpents, A
  The Falcon Saga:
    1 Falcon For A Witch, A
    2 King's Falcon, The
    3 Fortune For A Falcon
    4 Season Of The Falcon
    5 Falcon Royal
    6 Falcon Tree, The
    7 Falcon And The Moon, The
    8 Falcon Rising
    9 Falcon Sunset
   10 Seed Of The Falcon
   11 Falcon's Claw
   12 Falcon To The Lure
  The Moon Chalice Quest:
    1 Whisper Down The Moon
    2 Frost On The Moon
    3 Flaunting Moon, The
    4 Sing Me A Moon
    5 Cobweb Across The Moon
    6 Moon In Pisces

_____

_____

DARBY, Emma
  Conflict Of Women, A
  Into The Arena

DARBY, Joanna
                              (Joanna Marks)

DARCY, Clare   <RE>
  Allegra
  Caroline And Julia
  Cressida
  Elyza
  Eugenia
  Gwendolen
  Lady Pamela
  Letty
  Regina
  Rolande
  Victoire
  Trilogy:
    Cecily
    Georgina
    Lydia

DARCY, Emma
  Harlequin Presents:
  648   Twisting Shadows
  680   Tangle Of Torment
  823   Don't Play Games
  840   Fantasy
  864   Song Of A Wren
  882   Point Of Impact
  903   Man In The Park
  921   World Apart, A
  935   Impossible Dream, The
  960   Woman Of Honour
  984   Don't Ask Me Now
  999   Unpredictable Man, The
  1020 Wrong Mirror, The
  1033 One That Got Away, The
  1048 Strike At The Heart
  1080 Positive Approach, The
  1103 Mistress Of Pillatoro
  1151 Always Love
  1177 Priceless Love, A
  1199 Aloha Bride, The

DARCY, Emma (cont.)
  1232 Falcon's Mistress, The
  1272 Power And The Passion, The
  1288 Ultimate Choice, The
  1335 To Strong To Deny
  Harlequin Romance:
  2900 Blind Date
  2941 Whirlpool Of Passion
  3085 Pattern Of Deceit

DARCY, Lilian
  Harlequin Romance:
    Flying Doctor   HRS27

D'ARCY, Pamela   <HR><RE>
                        [Mary Linn Roby]
  Angel In The House
  Heritage Of The Heart
  Heritage Of Strangers, A
  Hired Heart, The
  Magic Moment

DARE, Jessica   <CO>
                         [Joann Leslie]
  Harvest Of Dreams
  Rhapsody

DARLING, Joan
                         [Doris Stuart]
  Second Chance At Love:
    314   Man Around The House
    402   Carolina Moon
  To Have And To Hold:
    45   Tyler's Folly

DARLINGTON, Joy
                  [Joy Aumente]
   Fast Friends
   Those Van Der Meer Women

DARWIN, Jeanette
               [Candace Schuler]
   Rapture Romance:
     87 Cherished Account, A

DARNELL, Berde
   Heartfire Romance: <HR>
    Passion's Whisper

D'ASTOR, Jean
   Mystique:
    16 Sea Gull, The
    23 Tower Of Mallcombe
    75 Coast Of Fear, The
    98 Fatal Choice

DARRELL, Elizabeth   <HO>
                (Eve Dane)
               (Edna Dawes)
             (Eleanor Drew)
          (Emma Drummond)
   Beyond All Frontiers
   Gathering Wolves, The
   Jade Alliance, The
   In sequence: <HS>
    At The Going Down Of The Sun
    And In The Morning

DAVENAT, Colette   <HR>
   Deborah
   Deborah & The Many Faces Of Love
   Deborah And The Siege Of Paris

DAVENPORT, Francine   <RS>
   Secret Of The Bayou, The

DARRINGTON, Paula
           (Paula Williams)

DARTEY, Leo
   Mystique:
    46 Stranger Threatens, A
    50 Midnight Visitor
    66 Return To Foxdale

DAVENPORT, Kathryn
   Heartfire Romance: <HR>
    Nevada Loving
    Pirate's Mistress

DARTY, Peggy   <GOT><HR><Isnp>
   Wailing Winds Of Juneau Abbey,The
   Widowed Bride Of Ravenoaks, The
   Serenade/Saga:
    20 Kincaid Of Cripple Creek
    29 Cimarron Sunset
   Serenade/Serenata:
    8 Mountain To Stand Strong,A

DAVENPORT, Kathryn w/ Evelyn
   ROGERS   (Keller Graves)

DAVENPORT, Marcia
   Constant Image, The
   East Side, West Side
   My Brother's Keeper
   Of Lena Geyer
   Valley Of Decision, The

DAVESON, Mons
    [Mons Violet Henson Daveson]
    Harlequin Romance:
    1415 House In The Foothills,The
    1456 This Too I'll Remember
    2461 Land Of Tomorrow
    2534 My Lord Kasseem
    2575 MacKenzie Country
    2756 Girl Of Mystery
          Promise Me   HRS 1
          Out Of The Blue   HRS19
          No Gentle Encounters   HRS53
          Paradise Island   HRS59

DAVIDS, Marilyn
                    [David M. Wind]
    Rapture Romance:
    50 Love So Fresh, A

DAVIDSON, Andrea
                    [Susan L. Lowe]
    Harlequin American Romance:
    16   Music In The Night
    21   Untamed Possession
    45   Treasures Of The Heart
    122 An Unexpected Gift
    324 Best Gift Of All,The<CIFK>
    371 Light On Willow Lane, The
    Harlequin American Romance:
    Premiere Edition:
      Golden Cage, The
    Harlequin Intrigue:
    25 Siren's Lure, A
    41 Out From The Shadows

DAVIDSON, Diane   <HO>
    Feversham

DAVIES, Dianna
    Songs Of Love

DAVIES, Frances
                    [Leone Lewensohn]
    Harlequin Temptation:
    185 Lady Is A Champ, The
    228 P. S. I Love You
    338 Ben & Liz & Tony & Ross
    Second Chance At Love:
    146 Taste For Loving, A
    192 Love Thy Neighbor
    239 Mysterious East
      In sequence:
    296   Fortune's Darling
    363   Fortune's Hunter

DAVIES, Gordon Winthrop
                    (Melissa Davies)

DAVIES, Gwynneth   <GOT><RS>
                    [William Delligan]
    Portrait Of Susan, The
    Terror At Deercliff House, The

DAVIES, Iris
                    (Iris Gower)

DAVIES, Joyce
    First Love From Silhouette: <YA>
    177 Day In September, A

DAVIES, Melissa   <GOT>
                    [Gordon Winthrop Davies]
    Face Of Chalk, The

DAVIS, Berrie   <GOT>
  Fourth Day Of Fear, The
  Trevena's Daughter
  Candlelight:
    576 Dark Paradise   <RO>

DAVIS, Catherine
                  (see Mildred Davis)

DAVIS, Deborah
  Harlequin Romance:
    2917 Healing Effect, The

DAVIS, Diane Wicker
                  (Delaney Devers)
  The Avon Romance:
    Call Back The Dawn   <HR>
    Passion's Honor
    In sequence:
      Heart Of The Raven
      Heart Of The Falcon

DAVIS, Elinor
  Harlequin Romance:
    1222 Dark Confessor

DAVIS, Elizabeth   <GOT>
                  [Lou Ellen Davis]
  My Soul To Keep

DAVIS, Genevieve   <HR>
  Children Of Passion
  Fancy
  Passion In The Blood

DAVIS, George
  Coming Home
  Love, Black Love

DAVIS, Gwen   <CO>
  Marriage
  R.O.M.A.N.C.E.

DAVIS, Joyce Ellen   <RS>
  Moonlight And Murder

DAVIS, Julia
  Love's Treasure Trove
  Never Say Die

DAVIS, Julie
                  (Juliana Davison)
  Gathering Passion, The
  Melissa
  Right To Die
  Story Of No, The

DAVIS, Justine
  Silhouette Intimate Moments
    371 Hunter's Way

DAVIS, Kathryn
  Memories And Ashes   <RS>
  Child Of Awe
  The Dakotas Series: <HS>
    In sequence:
      At The Wind's Edge
      Endless Sky, The

169

DAVIS, Kathryn Lynn
   Too Deep For Tears

DAVIS, Leslie
       [Leslie Davis Guccione]
   Moonstone Novels: <YA><RS>
    5 Something Out There
   Velvet Glove: <RS>
    16 Touch Of Scandal, A
    19 Splintered Moon, The

DAVIS, Lou Ellen
             (Elizabeth Davis)

DAVIS, M. H.   <HO>
   Winter Serpent, The

DAVIS, Madeline
             (Madeline Garry)

DAVIS, Maggie
   Diamonds And Pearls
   Eagles
   Hustle, Sweet Love
   Miami Midnight
   Wild Midnight   <RS>
   In sequence: <CO>
    Satin Doll
    Satin Dreams
   Harlequin Temptation:
    272 Dreamboat

DAVIS, Mary Johnson w/
           Deborah JORDAN
         (Rosemary Jordan)

DAVIS, Melanie   <HR>
       [Claudette Williams]
   Wild Dawn Fever

DAVIS, Mildred   <GOT>
   Lucifer Land   w/ Catherine DAVIS
   Room Upstairs, The
   Scorpion
   Sound Of Insects, The
   Tell Them What's-Her-Name Called
   Third Half, The
   Three Minutes To Midnight
   Walk Into Yesterday

DAVIS, Suzannah
   Candlelight Ecstasy:
    430 Prisoner Of Passion
    465 Not For Any Price
    513 Deceptions And Desire
    523 Flight Of Desire
   Harlequin SuperRomance:
    359 Airwaves
    455 Evening Star
   Judy Sullivan Books:
    No Bed Of Roses   <CO>
   The Avon Romance:
    Devil's Deception
    Devil's Moon
    Outlaw Heart
    Untamed Glory

DAVIS, Wendi
           [Nancy Holder]
   First Love From Silhouette: <YA>
    21 Teach Me To Love
    46 Sealed With A Kiss

DAVISON, Jean   <RS>
  Devil's Horseman, The
  Dreaming Witness
  Golden Torrent, The
  Candlelight:
    500 Golden Lure, The   <IN>

DAVISON, Juliana   <HR>
                  [Julie Davis]
  Golden Locket
  Warner Regency:
    13 Pink Phaeton, The
    16 Velvet Ribbons
    18 Petals Of The Rose
    29 Countess By Contract

DAVISON, Norma   <GOT>
  Rievaulx Abbey   <CGS:#11>

DAWES, Edna
                  [Elizabeth Darrell]
  Dearest Tiger
  Fly With My Love
  Hidden Heart Of Fire
  Pink Snow

DAWKINS, Louisa
  Natives And Strangers

DAWSON, Cleo   <HO>
  She Came To The Valley

DAWSON, Elizabeth
  Harlequin Romance:
    1878 Isle Of Dreams
    2306 Bending Reed, The

DAWSON, Helena
  Harlequin Romance:
    3008 Heart Of Marble

DAWSON, Saranne
                  [Saranne Hoover]
  Greenfire   <FR>
  Candlelight Ecstasy:
    436 Days Of Desire
    533 Private Intentions
  Harlequin American Romance:
    180 Intimate Strangers
    222 Summer's Witness
    364 Talent For Love, A

DAY, Dianne
  Obsidian   <GOT>
  Stone House, The

DAY, Jocelyn
                  [Lorena McCourtney]
  Second Chance At Love:
         Tender Conquest   <Prom>
    5   Glitter Girl
    52   Steele Heart, The
    82   Tarnished Rainbow
    128 Marrying Kind, The
    150 Island Fires
    196 Sometimes A Lady

DAY, Lucinda
  [Marie Flasschoen w/
              Mirian Scheirman]
  Circle Of Love:
    3 Gates Of The Sun
   23 Aloha, My Love

DAY, Samantha
            [Sandra Courcelles]
  Harlequin Romance:
  2672 Turn Of The Tide, The
  2840 For Karin's Sake
  2923 There Must Be Love
  3015 Under A Summer Sun

DAYTON, Lily
            [Linda Hampton]
  Candlelight Ecstasy Supreme:
   63 Caught In The Middle

DEAN, Dinah
            [Marjory May]
  Harlequin Historical <Set#1>:
    3 Country Cousins, The
  Harlequin Regency Romance:
      Country Gentleman, The
    7 Cockermouth Mail, The
  Masquerade:
   24 Flight From The Eagle
   45 Ice King, The
   81 Eagle's Fate, The

DEAN, Karen Strickler   <YA>
  Mariana
  In sequence:
    Maggie Adams, Dancer

DEAN, Karen Strickler (cont.)
    Between
    Stay On Your Toes,
    Maggie Adams!

DEAN, Nell Marr
      [Nell Marr Dean Ratzlaff]
  Circus Nurse
  Fashions For Carol
  Society Doctor
  Time For Strength, A
  Trials Of Dr. Carol, The
  Avalon:
    Courage To Suffer
    Nurse In Paradise Isle
    Romance On Capri
    Terror Over Bluehaven
  Candlelight:
   70 Nurse Kelly's Crusade

DEAN, Rena
  Harlequin American Romance:
  319 Public Secret

De ANDREA, William L.
  (see Lee Davis Willoughby <MOAS>)

DEANE, Leslie   <CO>
  Girl With The Golden Hair, The

DEANE, Sonia
  Betrayal Of Doctor Vane, The<M&B>
  Aston Hall:
  107 Doctors In Love

DEANE TRILOGY <DTR>
Harlequin Intrigue:
  120 Treasure Hunt
                    Leona Karr
  122 Hide And Seek
                    Cassie Miles
  124 Charades
                Jasmine Cresswell

DEBERRY, Virginia w/ Donna GRANT
                  (Marie Joyce)

DeBETS, Julie
              (Maura McGiveny)

de BILIO, Beth
Candlelight:
  506 Widow's Escort, The <IN>

De BLASIS, Celeste   <HR><RS>
  Night Child, The
  Proud Breed, The   <HS>
  Suffer A Sea Change
  Tiger's Woman, The
  Falconer Family Trilogy: <HS>
  Wild Swan
  Swan's Chance
  Season Of Swans, A

De BOER, Marjorie   <HR><RE>
      [Marjorie Rockwell De Boer]
  Crown Of Desire
  Unwelcome Suitor, The
  Whitbourne Legacy, The
  American Regency Romance:
  Beloved Adversary
  Duet For My Lady, A

DeBORDE, Sherry
  Spring Will Come

DeCOTO, Jean
  SuperRomance:
    29 Heart's Awakening
  Harlequin SuperRomance:
    145 Delta Nights

de COVARRUBIAS, Barbara Faith
            (Barbara Faith)

DEE, D. J.
  Avalon:
  Nurse Mickey's Crisis

DEE, Sherry
          [Sheryl Flournoy]
  Silhouette Desire:
    8 Make No Promises
    63 Share Your Tomorrows

DEEM, James
  Crosswinds: <YA>
    30 Frog Eyes Loves Pig

DEES, Catherine w/ Kay CROISSANT
            (Catherine Kay)
            (Kate McKenzie)

DEFORGES, Regine
  Blue Bicycle, The

de FORREST, Betty   <GOT>
    Snows Of Yesterday, The
    _____

    _____

de GALE, Anne
    Heartlines: <YA>
    5   Island Encounter
    _____

    _____

De GAMEZ, Tana
    Like A River Of Lions
    Yoke And The Star, The
    _____

    _____

De GUISE, Elizabeth
                    [Elizabeth Hunter]
    Masquerade:
    4   Puritan Wife
    _____

    _____

DEITERLE, Robin   <HR>
    Winds Of Fire
    _____

    _____

de JARNETTE, Harriette   <HR>
    Golden Threshold, The
    The Plantation Trilogy:
        Passion Stone, The
        Follow The North Star
        Still Grows The Stars
    _____

    _____

De JAY SCOTT, Marianne   <GOT>
    Van Dyne Collection, The
    _____

    _____

de JONG, Daphne
                    (Laurey Bright)
                    (Daphne Clair)
                    (Claire Lorel)

de JOURLET, Marie
                    [Paul H. Little]
    Windhaven Plantation Saga: <HO>
    In sequence:
        Windhaven Plantation
        Storm Over Windhaven
        Legacy Of Windhaven
        Return To Windhaven
        Windhaven's Peril
        Trials Of Windhaven
        Defenders Of Windhaven
        Windhaven's Crisis
        Windhaven's Bounty
        Windhaven's Triumph
        Windhaven's Fury
        Windhaven's Destiny
        Windhaven's Hope
        Windhaven's Glory
    _____

    _____

de KERPELY, Theresa
    Arabesque
    Fugue
    _____

    _____

DELANEY DYNASTY
    This Fierce Splendor (prequel)
                    Iris Johansen
    The Untamed Years:
    In sequence:
        Golden Flames
        Velvet Lightning
                    Kay Hooper
    In sequence:
        Wild Silver
        Satin Ice
                    Iris Johansen
    In sequence:
        Copper Fire
        Silken Thunder
                    Fayrene Preston
    The Shanrock Trinity:
    Rafe, The Maverick (LS#167)
                    Kay Hooper
    York, The Renegade (LS#168)
                    Iris Johansen
    Burke, The Kingpin (LS#169)
                    Fayrene Preston

DELANEY DYNASTY (cont.)
The Delaneys Of Killaroo:
Adelaide, The Enchantress
Kay Hooper
Matilda, The Adventuress
Iris Johansen
Sydney, The Temptress
Fayrene Preston

DELANEY, Gina   <HR>
Australian Romance Series:
Wild Flame
Patricia Rae Walls
Wild Splendor
Patricia Rae Walls
Wild Fury
Patricia Rae Walls w/
Rosalyn Alsobrook
Wild Destiny
Rosalyn Alsobrook

DELANEY, Laurence
Blood Red Wine   <Saga>
Sea Ranch   <RS>

---

de la ROCHE, Mazo   (Deceased)<HR>
(listed by publishing date)
Jalna
Whiteoaks Of Jalna
Finch's Fortune
Master Of Jalna, The
Young Renny
Whiteoak Harvest
Whiteoak Heritage
Wakefield's Course
Building Of Jalna, The
Return To Jalna
Mary Wakefield (A Jalna Book)
Renny's Daughter
Whiteoak Brothers, The (Jalna)

de la ROCHE, Mazo (cont.)
Variable Winds At Jalna
Centenary At Jalna
Morning At Jalna

DELATOUR, Elise
MacFadden Romance:
5   Ivory Princess, The
59 Enchanted Land, The

DELATUSH, Edith
[Edith Grieshammer Delatush]
(Edith de Paul)
(Alyssa Morgan)
(Edith St. George)
Candlelight Ecstasy:
333 When Midnight Comes
371 Hand In Hand
395 Cape Cod Affair, The
425 Tonight You're Mine
467 Burning Nights
511 Best Revenge, The

De LAUER, Marjel
In sequence: <HS>
Traders, The
Where Rivers Run Gold

DELAUNEY, Rachel   <HR>
Fleur

DELDERFIELD, R. F.   <HS>(Deceased)
[Ronald Frederick Delderfield]
All Over The Town
Charlie Come Home
Mr. Sermon
Return Journey

DELDERFIELD, R. F. (cont.)
  Stop At A Winner
  To Serve Them All My Days
  Avenue Series: In sequence:
    Dreaming Suburb, The
    Avenue Goes To War, The
  Horseman Riding By Trilogy:
    Long Summer Day
    Post Of Honor
    Green Gauntlet, The
  Series: In sequence:
    Diana
    Unjust Skies, The
  Swann Saga: In sequence:
    God Is An Englishman
    Theirs Was The Kingdom
    Give Us This Day
  Historicals:
    Farewell The Tranquil Mind
    Seven Men Of Gascony
    Too Few For Drums

DELINSKY, Barbara (cont.)
   65 Secret Of The Stone
   79 Chances Are
   87 First Things First
   98 Straight From The Heart
  116 First, Best And Only
    Matchmaker Series:
  130   Real Thing, The
  144   Twelve Across
  150   Single Rose, A
  164 Cardinal Rules
  173 Heatwave
  199 T.L.C.
  218 Fulfillment   <MEQ>
  249 Through My Eyes
  280 Montana Man
  297 Having Faith
    Crosslyn Rise:
  317   Dream, The
  321   Dream Unfolds, The
  325   Dream Comes True, The

de LEON, Ana Lisa
              [Celina Rios Mullan]
  Harlequin American Romance:
   61 Kiss Goodnight and
         Say Good-bye

DELL, Belinda
                    [Jean Bowden]
  Harlequin Romance:
  1162 Island Of Love
  1193 Hospital In Kashmir
  1371 Dancing On My Heart
  1407 Next Stop Gretna
  1475 Vermilion Gateway, The
  1623 Flowers For The Festival
  1749 Lovely Is The Rose
  1797 Darling Pirate, The
  1846 Lake Of Silver

DELINSKY, Barbara
  [Barbara Ruth Greenburg Delinsky]
              (Billie Douglass)
              (Bonnie Drake)
  Commitments
  Heart Of The Night
  Facets
  Fingerprints   <RS>
  Twilight Whispers
  Within Reach
  Harlequin Intrigue:
   34 Threats And Promises
  Harlequin Temptation:
      Jasmine Sorcery   <PROM>
    4 Special Something, A
   17 Bronze Mystique
   41 Forever Instinct, The

DELLAMERE, Wanda
  SuperRomance:
   24 Call Of The Heart

DELLIGAN, William
                  (Gwynneth Davies)
                  (Ellen Orford)

DELLIN, Genell
  [Billie Genell Smith Dellin]
          (Gena Dalton)
  First Love From Silhouette: <YA>
    12 In My Sister's Shadow
    42 Promises To Come
  The Avon Romance:
    Cherokee Dawn

DELMONICO, Andrea   <GOT><RS>
  Chateau Chaumond
  Eyrie Of An Eagle

DELMORE, Diana   <RE>
                    [Lois S. Nollett]
  Anthea
  Cassandra
  Dorinda
  Leonie
  Melissande

DeLONG, Claire
  [Claire Ann Evans DeLong]
              (Eva Claire)
              (Claire Evans)

DELUTRY, Jean
  Mystique:
    135 Victim Of Love

De LYN, Nicole
                    [Eve Woodland]
  MacFadden Romance:
    180 Cherished Memory
    187 Let This Be Love
    216 Roses Of The Dawn
    244 Enchantment
    248 Fire And Ice

DeLYONNE, Susan
              [Sue Ellen Gross]
  6 Days, 5 Nights

DEMAINE, Christy   <RS>
  Master Of Revenge, A

DeMARIA, Robert   <HR>
  Empress, The
  Passion For Power, A
  Stone Of Destiny
  In sequence: <Saga>
    Sons
    Brothers

DEMETROPOULOS, Nicholas
              (Jean Evans)
              (Marianne Evans)

DEMING, Richard
          (see Richard Hale Curtis)
    (see Lee Davis Willoughby <MOAS>)

DeMOSS, Marguerite   <RS>
  Scarlet Storm, The

DENBY, Edwin   <GOT>
  Looking At The Dance
  Scream In A Cave

DENGLER, Sandy
  Serenade/Saga: <HR><Insp>
    1 Summer Snow
    5 Song Of The Nereids
   12 Winterspring

177

DENGLER, Sandy (cont.)
    27 Opal Fire
    30 This Rolling Land

_____

_____

DENHAM, Mary Orr
                            (Mary Orr)

DENIS, Charlotte
    King's Wench

_____

_____

DENNIS, Roberta
    Silhouette Desire:
    60 Between The Lines

_____

_____

DENNISTON, Elinore
                            (Rae Foley)

DENNORE, Roberta
                        (Rochel DeNorre)

DENNY, Lesley
    Listening Sky, The

_____

_____

DENNY, Roz
    [June Hayden w/ Judy Simpson]
    Harlequin Romance:
    3032 Red Hot Pepper

_____

_____

DeNORRE, Rochel
                    [Roberta Dennore]
    An Innocent Heart
    Golden Love, A
    Love So Proud, A
    Rebel In Love
    Woman Of New Orleans, A   <AWD>

_____

_____

DENT, Roxanne   <HR>
                     (Melissa Masters)
    Ashes Of Tamar, The
    Barbary Bride
    Bitter Harvest
    Island Of Fear   <GOT>
    Sweetwater Saga
    White Fog, The

_____

_____

DENTON, Kate
    [Carolyn Hake w/ Jeanie Lambright]
    Harlequin Romance:
    2870 Winner Take All
    2966 Business Arrangement, A
    3057 Home Safe

_____

_____

DENYS, Teresa   <HR>
                     [Jacqui Bianchi]
    Flesh & The Devil, The
    Silver Devil, The

_____

_____

DEOBOLD, Sue   <HR>
    Militant Heart, The
    Savage Splendor

_____

_____

de PAUL, Edith
                      [Edith Delatush]
    Candlelight:
    672 Viscount's Witch, The <RE>

_____

_____

de PRE, Jean-Anne   <GOT><RS>
                    [Michael Avallone]
    Aquarius My Evil
    Die, Jessica, Die
    Sound Of Dying Roses, A
    Third Woman
    Warlock's Woman

_____

_____

DERINGER, Jane Flower
Avalon:
  Opalescent Moon, The

DERN, Peggy   (Deceased)
  [Erolie Pearl Gaddis Dern]
            (Georgia Craig)
            (Peggy Gaddis)
            (Gail Jordan)
            (Perry Lindsay)
Country Nurse
Doctor's Wife, The
Florida Nurse
Karen
Love Trap
Nurse At Burford's Landing
Nurse In The Tropics
Nurse Called Hope
Nurse With A Dream
Nurse's Dilemma
Orchids For A Nurse
Season For Love, The
Second Chance
Trusting Heart, The
Understand, My Love
Harlequin Classic:
  172 Nora Was A Nurse   (362)

DERRICK, Neil w/ Edward FIELD
            (Bruce Elliott)

De ST. JEOR, Owanna
Judy Sullivan Books:
  Bad Timing   <RS>

DESCHAMPS, Fanny   <HO>
  King's Garden, The

De SECARY, Jean
Mystique:
  17 Portrait Of Love
  108 Twist Of Fate

DeSHA, Sandra
            (Sandra Donovan)

DESMAREST, Marie-Anne
  Torrents

DESMOND, Hilary
  Linton Park Series:
    1 Anne
    2 Charlotte

DEUVAUL, Virginia C.
            [Virginia Coffman]
  Masque By Gaslight   <ENG>

DEVERAUX, Jude   <HR>
            [Jude Gilliam White]
  Black Lyon, The
  Casa Grande
  Enchanted Land, The
  Knight In Shining Armor, A   #
  Maiden, The
    (prequel to "The Princess")
  Mountain Laurel   #
  Wishes   @#
  Montgomery Brothers Saga:
    In sequence:
      Velvet Promise, The
      Highland Velvet
      Velvet Song
      Velvet Angel

179

DEVERAUX, Jude   <HR>
  Montgomery's In America Quartet #
    Story Order:
      1 The Raider
      2 The Temptress   @
      3 The Awakening
      4 The Princess
  Tapestry: <HR>
      15 Sweetbriar   &
  The James River Trilogy:
    Counterfeit Lady
    Lost Lady
    River Lady   &
  The Twins: In sequence:
    Twin Of Ice   @
    Twin Of Fire
  Trilogy, The Falcon Saga:
    Taming, The
    Conquest, The

_____

_____

de VERE, Jane   <ENG><HO>
                       [Julia Watson]
  Scarlet Women, The

_____

_____

DEVERS, Delaney
             [Diane Wicker Davis]
  Second Chance At Love:
      284 Lucky's Woman
      337 Smiles Of A Summer Night
      388 Places In The Heart
  To Have And To Hold:
      40 Heart Victorious, A

_____

_____

de VINCENT, Eleanora   <GOT><HR>
  Dark Dream Of Love
  Tower Park

_____

_____

DEVINE, Thea
  Montana Mistress
  Heartfire Romance: <HR>
    Ecstasy's Hostage
    Reckless Desire
    Relentless Passion
    Shameless Desire
    Shameless Ecstasy

_____

DE VITA, Sharon
  Silhouette Romance:
      475 Heavenly Match
      498 Lady And The Legend
      545 Kane And Mabel
      573 Baby Makes Three
      593 Sherlock's Home   &
      610 Italian Knights   &
      693 Sweet Adeline

_____

_____

DEVOE, Lily   <CO>
  For Love Of A Stranger
  Made In Heaven

_____

DEVON, Anne   <RE>
                  [Marian Pope Rettke]
  Second Chance At Love:
      39 Widow Of Bath, The
      69 Rogue's Lady, The
      105 Defiant Mistress

_____

DEVON, Georgina   <RE>
                  [Alison J. Hentges]
  Lady Of The Night

_____

_____

DEVON, Lynn   <RS>
  Jade

_____

_____

DEVON, Marian   <HR><RE>
             [Marian Pope Rettke]
  Escapade
  Fortunes Of The Heart
  Heather And The Blade, The
  Lady Harriet Takes Charge
  M'Lady Rides For A Fall
  Miss Armstead Wears Black Gloves
  Miss Osborne Misbehaves
  Miss Romney Flies Too High
  Question Of Class, A
  Scandal Broth
  Scoundrel's Daughter, The
  Sir Sham

_____

_____

DEVON, Nicola
  House Of Illusion

_____

_____

DEVORE, Mary w/ Joan DORNBUSCH
                 (Madelyn Dohrn)

DEWAR, Sandra
  Silhouette Special Edition:
    405 Conquer The Memories

_____

_____

DeWEESE, Jean   <GOT>
             [Eugene DeWeese]
  Beholden To None
  Carnelian Cat, The   <BGS:#8>
  Cave Of The Moaning Wind <ZGS>
  Doll With The Opal Eyes
  Hour Of The Cat
  Moonstone Spirit, The   <BGS:#6>
  Nightmare In Pewter

DeWEESE, Jean (cont.)
  Reimann Curse, The
  Web Of Guilt   <ZGS>
  Starlight Romance:
    Backhoe Gothic, The

_____

_____

De WINTERS, Danielle
                 [Keith Timson]
  Passionate Rebel

_____

_____

DEYOE, Cori L.
                 (Jessica Barkley)

de ZAVALA, Marisa
             [Celina Rios Mullan]
  Candlelight Ecstasy:
    27 Golden Fire, Silver Ice

_____

_____

DIAL, Joan   <HR>
          [Joan Mavis Rogers Dial]
               (Katherine Kent)
               (Katherine Sinclair)
               (Amanda York)
  Deadly Lady
  Echoes Of War
  Lovers & Warriors
  Roses In Winter
  Susanna
  Untamed   <HS>

_____

_____

DIAMOND, Barbara Bentley
                 (Barbara Bentley)

DIAMOND, Graham
                 (Rochelle Leslie)

DIAMOND, Jacqueline   <RE>
                  [Jackie D. Hyman]
Day-Dreaming Lady, The
Forgetful Lady, The
Lady In Disguise
Lady Of Letters, A
Song For A Lady
Harlequin American Romance:
   79 Dream Never Dies, The
  196 An Unexpected Man
  218 Unlikely Partners
  239 Cinderella Dare, The
  270 Capers And Rainbows
  279 Ghost Of A Chance, A
  315 Flight Of Magic
  351 By Leaps And Bounds
Harlequin Regency Romance:
   14 Lady's Point Of View, A

_____

_____

DIAMOND JUBILEE COLLECTION   <DJC>
Silhouette Romance:
   Wild Lady (SR90)   Ann Major
   Circumstantal Evidence (SR329)
                    Annette Broadrick
   Island On The Hill   (SR164)
                     Dixie Browning

_____

_____

DIAMOND, Petra
                  [Judith Sachs]
Second Chance At Love:
  275 Night Of A Thousand Stars
  327 Play It Again, Sam
To Have And To Hold:
   31 Confidentially Yours

_____

_____

DIAMOND, Rebecca
First Love From Silhouette: <YA>
   15 Summer Romance

_____

_____

DIAMOND, Suzanne
All She Wants

_____

_____

Di BENEDETTO, Theresa   <HR>
Silver Mist
Wildflower

_____

_____

DICKENS, Monica   <GOT>
Room Upstairs, The

_____

_____

DICKERSON, Marilyn
Lord Hap

_____

_____

DIDION, Joan
Democracy
Miami

_____

_____

DI DONATO, Georgia   <HO>
Woman Of Justice

_____

_____

Di FRANCESCO, Phyllis w/ Nira
   HERRMANN   (Phyllis Herrmann)

DI FRANCO, Anthony
Ardent Spring   <Saga>
Streets Of Paradise, The

_____

_____

DILCOCK, Noreen
     (Jill Christian)
     (Norrey Ford)

DILLON, Catherine   <RS>
 Beloved Captive
 Constantine Cay
 White Fires Burning
 White Khan, The

<hr>
<hr>

DILLON, Eilis   <HR>
 Across The Bitter Sea
 Blood Relations
 Wild Geese

<hr>
<hr>

DILLON, Patricia   <HR>
    [R. Patricia Dillon]
 Love Alone

<hr>
<hr>

DIMICK, Cherylle Lindsey
     (Dawn Lindsey)

DINESEN, Isak
     (Pierre Andrezel)

DINGLEY, Sally Garrett
     (Sally Garrett)

DINGWELL, Joyce
     (Kate Starr)
 Harlequin Classic:
  16 Wednesday's Children (626)
  57 If Love You Hold
  87 Girl At Snowy River (808)
 103 Tender Conquest (854)
 112 Third In The House (894)
 Harlequin Premiere Edition:
  28 Man Like Brady, A
 Harlequin Romance:
 761 House In The Timberwoods

DINGWELL, Joyce (cont.)
 808 Girl At Snowy River, The
 854 Tender Conquest
 894 Third In The House, The
 917 Timber Man, The
 964 Project Sweetheart
 999 Greenfingers Farm
 1069 Man From The Valley, The
 1124 New Zealander, The
 1160 Boomerang Girl, The
 1179 Will You Surrender
 1229 Taste For Love, A
 1251 Venice Affair
 1296 Wind And The Spray, The
 1320 Spanish Lace
 1342 Feel Of Silk, The
 1365 Hotel Southerly
 1378 No Females Wanted
 1401 One String For Her Bow
 1426 Guardian Nurse
 1452 I And My Heart
 1492 Drummer And The Song, The
 1517 Crown Of Flowers
 1541 Clove Orange
 1566 September Street
 1589 Nickel Wife
 1615 Thousand Candles, A
 1633 Red Ginger Blossom
 1657 Wife Of Sim
 1688 Pool Of Pink Lilies, The
 1738 Mutual Look, The
 1772 Sister Pussycat
 1808 There Were Three Princes
 1826 Habit Of Love, The
 1856 Cattlemen, The
 1867 Flamingo Flying South
 1887 Love And Lucy Brown
 1910 Cane Music
 1932 Kissing Gate, The
 1952 Corporation Boss
 1961 Deep In The Forest
 1981 New Broom, The
 1998 Road Boss, The
 2047 Inland Paradise
 2123 Drift Of Jasmine, A
 2164 Year Of The Dragon
 2189 Remember September
 2216 All The Days Of Summer
 2225 Boss's Daughter, The

DIXON, Rhonda
  Judy Sullivan Books:
    Corrie's Cat Ring
    Man Around The House   <CO>

DOBKIN, Kaye
                    [Kathy Dobkin]
  Desire & Dreams
  Promise Me Tomorrow
  Turning Points: <YA>
    3 Valentine For Betsy, A

DOBNER, Maeva Park   <GOT><RS>
  Gingerbread House, The
  Heather
  High Walk To Wandlemere
  Sea Wind
  Woman In The Maze, The

DOBRAVOLSKY, Barbara
  Love's Forbidden Flame

DOBSON, Margaret
  Jane Bailey Series: <RM>
    Touchstone
    Primrose
    Soothsayer
    Nightcap
  Candlelight Ecstasy:
    145 Cactus Rose
    173 Restless Wind
    211 Tender Journey
    300 Stand Still The Moment
  Candlelight Ecstasy Supreme:
    30 Eventide

DODDINGTON, Paula
  Innocence Of Love, The
  Reasonable Doubt

DODGE, Alice M.
  Captain's Brigade, The
  Avalon:
    Dare To Dream
    Girl In Exile
  Candlelight:
    83 Girl Of The Far Country

DODSON, Sam   <HR>
  Dance Of Love, The
  I, Victoria
  Majorca
  Sausalito

DODSON, Susan
  Crosswinds: <YA>
    10 Eye Of The Storm, The

DOHRN, Madelyn
    [Joan Dornbusch w/ Mary Devore]
  Silhouette Romance:
    523 Best Defense, The
  Silhouette Special Edition:
    501 Labor Of Love
    616 Two For The Price Of One
    633 One For One

DOIG, Ivan   <HO>
  Dancing At The Rascal Fair

DOLAN, Charlotte   <RE>
  Subsitute Bridegroom, The

DOLAN, E. V.
  Time For Us, A   <CO>

DOMENICA
  Mystique:
   101 Island Of Fear

DOMINIQUE, Meg
               [Annette Sanford]
  Harlequin Romance:
  2774 Sand Castles
  Harlequin Temptation:
    2 When Stars Fall Down
   27 Rebel Heart
   43 Yes, With Love
   71 As Love Would Have It

DOMNING, Joan J.
  Loveswept:
   12 Hunter's Payne
   13 Tiger Lady
   19 Pfarr Lake Affair
   39 Kirsten's Inheritance
   54 Gypsy And The
        Yachtsman, The
   63 Lahti's Apple

DONAHUE, Marilyn Cram   <GOT><RS>
  Crooked Gate, The
  House At Sutter's Sands, The
  Pearl Is In The Oyster, The
  Piece Of Me Is Missing, A
  Sutter's Sands

DONALD, Robyn
  Harlequin Presents:
   232 Bride At Whangatapu
   260 Dilemma In Paradise
   285 Summer At Awakopu
   303 Wife In Exchange
   320 Shadow Of The Past
   441 Interloper, The
   500 Dark Abyss, The
   567 Mansion For My Love
   623 Guarded Heart, The
   631 Return To Yesterday
   649 An Old Passion
   665 Gates Of Rangitatau, The
   696 Durable Fire, A
   904 An Unbreakable Bond
   936 Long Journey Back
   952 Captives Of The Past
   976 Willing Surrender, A
  1040 Country Of The Heart
  1064 Late Loving, A
  1104 Smoke In The Wind
  1128 Sweetest Trap, The
  1233 Love's Reward
  1263 Bitter Homecoming, A
  1303 No Guarantees
  1343 Matter Of Will, A
  Harlequin Romance:
  2391 Bay Of Stars
  2437 Iceberg

DONALD, Vivian   <RS>
        [Charles R. MacKinnon]
        (see Charles Stuart)
  Cathy's Choice
  Elizabeth In Love
  For Love Or Money
  Happy Isle, The
  Julie's Girl
  Lady Ambassador, The
  Laird And The Lady, The
  Love On Location
  Love Royal*
  Roots Of Love, The
  Royal Scot, The

DONALDSON, Nancy
  Promise Romance   <Insp>
    30 Almost Like Old Friends

DONARICO, Elnora
  Avalon:
    Nurse Jessica's Cruise
    Nurse Vicky's Love

DONER, Mary Frances
  Darker Star, The
  Return A Stranger
  Wind And The Fog, The
  Avalon:
    Not By Appointment
    Thine Is The Power

DONICH, Catherine Lee w/
        Linda Sherwood WOLTHAUSEN
        (Catherine Leigh)

DONNE, John
  Love Poems Of John Donne

DONNELLY, Frances
  Shake Down The Stars

DONNELLY, Jane
  Harlequin Premiere Edition:
    17 So Long A Winter
  Harlequin Romance:
    1227 Man Apart, A
    1332 Don't Walk Alone
    1376 Shadows From The Sea
    1432 Take The Far Dream
    1462 Man In The Next Room, The
    1483 Never Turn Back
    1548 Halfway To The Stars

DONNELLY, Jane
    1592 Mill In The Meadow, The
    1660 Stranger Came, A
    1681 Long Shadow, The
    1723 Rocks Under Shining Water
    1859 Man Outside, The
    1882 Ride Out The Storm
    1929 Collision Course
    1993 Dark Pursuer
    2027 Silver Cage, The
    2064 Intruder, The
    2090 Dear Caliban
    2124 Four Weeks In Winter
    2150 Touched By Fire
    2187 Black Hunter, The
    2195 Love For A Stranger
    2217 Spell Of The Seven Stones
    2255 Forest Of The Night
    2270 Behind A Closed Door
    2293 Savage Sanctuary, A
    2325 Man To Match, A
    2373 No Way Out
    2408 When Lightning Strikes
    2456 Flash Point
    2510 Diamond Cut Diamond
    2552 Call Up The Storm
    2576 Face The Tiger
    2635 Fierce Encounter, A
    2649 Moon Lady
    2654 Frozen Heart, The
    2702 Ring Of Crystal
    2738 To Cage A Whirlwind
    2810 Ride A Wild Horse
    2871 Force Field
    2906 No Place To Run
    2954 Fetters Of Gold
    3033 When We're Alone
          Devil's Flower, The HRS78
  Other:
    Don't Look Back

DONNER, Katherine
  MacFadden Romance:
    121 Eternal Tides, The
    125 Safe In My Heart
    135 Counterfeit Kisses
    178 Campaign For Love
    233 Silver Twilight

187

DONOVAN, Sandra
                [Sandra DeSha]
   Heartfire Romance: <HR>
      Deception's Fire
      Rapture's Reward

DORE, Christy
                [Jim Plagakis]
   Torchlite:
      Passionate Awakening

DORIEN, Ray   <GOT>
   House Of Dread, The
   Noonday Nurse

DORNBUSCH, Joan w/ Mary DEVORE
                (Madelyn Dohrn)

DORR, Roberta Kells   <HR>
   Bathsheba
   David And Bathsheba
   Shulmit

DORS, Alexandra
             [Dorothy McKittrick]
   Silhouette Romance:
      368 Come In From The Cold

DORSET, Ruth
                [W. E. Daniel Ross]
   Behind Hospital Walls
   Front Office Nurse
   Head Nurse
   Hotel Nurse
   Surgical Nurse
   Nurse Takes A Chance, The

DORSETT, Daniella   <GOT>
                [Dorothy Daniels]
   Dueling Oaks, The

DORSEY, Christine   <HR>
   Traitor's Embrace
   Wild Virginia Nights
   Meteor Kismet:
      11 By The Book

DORSEY, Christine w/ Anne ELLIOTT
                (Christine Elliott)

DORTH, Cassandra   <HR>
   In Passion's Tempest

DOUGLAS, Alyssa
                [Anne Canadeo]
   Pageant Romance:
      Paradise Days, Paradise Nights
      Sweet Temptation

DOUGLAS, Ben   <GOT>
   Challenge At Castle Gap

DOUGLAS, Carole Nelson   <HR>
      [Carole Frances Nelson Douglas]
   Amberleigh
   Exclusive, The   <CO>
   Fair Wind, Fiery Star
   Heir Of Rengarth
   Lady Rogue

DOUGLAS, Carole Nelson (cont.)
In sequence: <RF>
  Probe
  Counterprobe
Sword And Circlet Trilogy: <SF>
  Keepers Of Edavant
  Six Of Swords
  Seven Of Swords
The Las Vegas Quartet:
  Crystal Days
  Crystal Nights
Love & Life:
  Bestman, The
  Her Own Person
  In Her Prime
Loveswept:
  92 Azure Days,
     Quicksilver Nights

DOUGLAS, Diana
  Nurse Deceived
  Nurse In Disaster
  Nurse In Spain
  Nurse Lambert's Conflict
  Nurse On Location
  Resort Nurse
  Sea Nurse
  Ski Lodge Nurse
  Surfing Nurse
  Surgical Nurse

DOUGLAS, Elizabeth   <HR>
                   [Bettie Marie Wilhite]
  An Exquisite Deception

DOUGLAS, Casey
                   [June E. Casey]
  SuperRomance:
    25 Infidel Of Love
    56 Proud Surrender
    75 Dance-Away Lover
  Harlequin SuperRomance:
    107 Edge Of Illusion
    131 Taste Of A Dream
    194 Kentucky Woman
    271 Season Of Enchantment

DOUGLAS, Gail
  Loveswept:
    283 On Wings Of Flame
    302 Flirting With Danger
    327 Lost In The Wild
    The Dreamweavers Quartet:
    355   Swashbuckling Lady
    361   Gambling Lady
    379   Sophisticated Lady
    385   Bewitching Lady
    422 It Had To Be You
         Banned In Boston

DOUGLAS, Diana
  Apollo Nurse
  Caribbean Nurse
  Casino Nurse
  Doctor In Shadow
  Dude Ranch Nurse
  Duty Nurse
  Fledgling Nurses, The
  Hocky Star Nurse
  Mystery Nurse
  New Orleans Nurse
  Nurse Chadwick's Sorrow

DOUGLAS, Gloria
                   [Gloria Upper]
  Harlequin Temptation:
    88 Winning Hearts

DOUGLAS, Kate   <HR>
  Pirate's Wild Paradise
  The Avon Romance:
    Captive Of The Heart

DOUGLAS, Kathryn   <HR>
          [Kathryn Ewing]
Amelia
Vivian Of Cavendish Square <Saga>
Cavendish Chronicles, The <Saga>
     Includes:
        Cavendish Square
        Cavendish Pride
        Cavendish Way, The

DOUGLAS, LaLette
               (Lafayette Hammett)

DOUGLAS, Lloyd C.   <HR>
Disputed Passage
Dr. Hudson's Secret Journal
Forgive Us Our Trespasses
Green Light
Magnificent Obsession
Robe, The
White Banners

DOUGLAS, Monica
Harlequin Romance:
1706 Shadow Of The Past

DOUGLAS, Sheila
Harlequin Premiere Edition:
    7 Beloved Surgeon
   18 Surgery By The Sea
Harlequin Romance:
 1729 Young Doctor, The
 1897 Westhampton Royal
 2015 Sherringdon Hall
 2097 Reluctant Neighbor, The
 2336 Return To Lanmore
 2392 Girl Between, The
 2518 Uncertain Heart, The

DOUGLASS, Amanda Hart   <HR>
Christabel
Charlotte
Heavens Blaze Forth, The
Kathleen
McCormack's Mountain
Pirate's Mistress, The
Sugar Hill

DOUGLASS, Billie
               [Barbara Delinsky]
Silhouette Desire:
   38 Sweet Serenity
   56 Flip Side Of Yesterday
   74 Beyond Fantasy
Silhouette Intimate Moments:
   80 Variation On A Theme
Silhouette Special Edition:
    6 Search For A New Dawn
   32 Time To Love, A
   58 Knightly Love
   80 Fast Courting
  123 An Irresistible Impulse
  133 Carpenter's Lady, The

DOUGLASS, Jessica   <HR>
          [Linda Hender Wallerich]
Snowfire

DOUGLASS, Thea Coy   <HR>
Royal Poinciana

DOVER, Mary Frances
Return A Stranger

DOWDELL, Dorothy <CO><GOT><HR><RS>
    (see Amanda McAllister)
Border Nurse
Glory Land
Golden Flame
Hawk Over Hollyhedge Manor
Highflying Woman
House In Munich, The
Seafaring Woman   <HS>
Tahoe
Wildcatter Woman
Woman's Empire, A   <Saga>
Candlelight:
    30 Arctic Nurse
    85 Allerton Rose, The
   100 Strange Rapture
   634 Hibiscus Lagoon   <RO>
   678 Impossible Dream, The <RO>

DOWLING, Shirley
Love Needs No Reasons   <CO>

DOWNES, Kathleen
                    [Deidre K. Downes]
Loveswept:
    49 Man Next Door, The
    93 Practice Makes Perfect
   151 Char's Webb
   211 Evenings In Paris

DOWNIE, Jill   <HR>
Angel In Babylon
Dark Laisons
Mistress Of Moon Hill
Raven In The Glass, The
Turn Of The Century

DOYLE, Amanda
Harlequin Romance:
  1036 Outback Man, The

DOYLE, Amanda (cont.)
  1085 Change For Clancy, A
  1116 Play The Tune Softly
  1190 Shadow And The Sun, The
  1239 This Wish I Have
  1308 Mist In Glen Torran, A
  1351 Girl For Gillgong, The
  1448 Year At Yattabilla, The
  1486 Post At Gundooee, The
  1527 Dilemma At Dulloora
  1562 Kookaburra Dawn
  1630 Escape To Koolonga
  1960 Return To Tuckarimba

DOYLE, Barbara
Candlelight:
   519 Search For Yesterday   <RO>
   559 Midnight Embrace, The   <RO>
   703 My Lady's Deception   <RE>
Velvet Glove: <RS>
     9 Hunted Heart, The

DOYLE, Emily
                    [Betty L. Henrichs]
Silhouette Special Edition:
    95 Matter Of Trust, A

DOZIER, Zoe
                    [Dixie Browning]
Avalon:
    Home Again, My Love
    Warm Side Of The Island

DRAKE, Asa
    [C. Dean Andersson w/
            Nina Romberg Andersson]
Crimson Kisses
Lair Of Ancient Dreams, The

DRAKE, Bonnie
                    [Barbara Delinsky]
Candlelight Ecstasy:
    3 Passionate Touch, The
    9 Surrender By Moonlight
   18 Sweet Ember
   32 Sensuous Burgundy
   42 Ardent Protector, The
   70 Whispered Promise
   85 Lilac Awakening
  101 Amber Enchantment
  114 Lover From The Sea
  132 Silver Fox, The
  146 Passion And Illusion
  186 Gemstone
  219 Moment To Moment

_____

_____

DRAKE, Connie
                    [Connie Scotts Fedderson]
Heartfire Romance: <HR>
    Angel's Fire

_____

_____

DRAKE, David
Strangers And Lovers

_____

_____

DRAKE, Shannon   <HR>
              [Heather Graham Pozzessere]
Blue Heaven, Black Night
Emerald Embrace
Lie Down In Roses
Ondine
Princess Of Fire
Tomorrow The Glory   <Saga>

_____

_____

DRAYTON, Mary
All Our Secrets

_____

_____

DRESSLER, Gladys M.
                    (Gladys McGorian)
DREW, Eleanor
                    [Elizabeth Darrell]
    Burn All Your Bridges

_____

_____

DREW, Patricia   <GOT><RS>
                    [Lloyd S. Haye]
Deep In A Dark Country
Who Is Melody?

_____

_____

DREYER, Eileen
                    (Kathleen Korbel)
DRUETT, Joan   <HR>
    Abigail

_____

_____

DRUMMOND, Brenna
                    [Judy Bryer]
Silhouette Special Edition:
   42 Proud Vintage

_____

_____

DRUMMOND, Emma   <HR>
                    [Elizabeth Darrell]
Beyond All Frontiers
Bridge Of A Hundred Dragons, The
Burning Land, The
Captive Freedom, A
Dragon Of Destiny
Forget The Glory
Scarlet Shadows

_____

_____

DRUMMOND, June   <RS><RS>
Bluestocking, The
Farewell Party

_____

_____

DRUMMOND, William   <GOT>
  Gaslight

_____

_____

DRUON, Maurice
  Ardent Infidels, The
  Matter Of Time, A

_____

DRURY, Rebecca   <HO>
(publisher's pseudonym for
    writers in this series)
Women At War Series:
  1 Mourning And Triumph
           [Greg Hunt]
  2 Freedom's Journey
           [Barry Myers]
  3 Ships Aflame
           [Barry Myers]
  4 Sunday's Courage
           [Barry Myers]
  5 Wives And Widows
           [Greg Hunt]
  6 Blue Glory
           [Jane Toombs]
  7 Tears And Laughter
           [Ernest A. Tremblay II]
  8 Sisters Of Battle
           [Robert Thompson]
  9 Savage Beauty
           [Jane Toombs]
 10 Splendid Victory
           [Greg Hunt]
 11 Darkness At Dawn
           [Will Holt]
 12 Courage At Sea
           [Ward Damio]
 13 Valient Wings
           [Neal Barrett, Jr.]
 14 Distant Thunder
 15 Desert Battle
           [Hugh Zachry]
 16 Bitter Victory
           [Hugh Zachry]
 17 Inchon Diary
           [Adrien Lloyd]
 18 Mission To Darkness
           [Greg Hunt]

_____

_____

DRYMON, Kathleen   <HR>
        (Kathleen McCall)
  Destiny's Splendor
  Gentle Savage
  Kimberly's Kiss
  Tender Passions
  Texas Blossom
  Savage Dawn
  Velvet Savage
  Wild Desires

_____

_____

DuBARRY, Michele   <HR>
  Loves Of Angela Carlyle:
  1 Into Passion's Dawn
  2 Across Captive Seas
  3 Toward Love's Horizon

_____

_____

DuBAY, Sandra   <HR>
  Burn On, Sweet Fire
  By Love Beguiled
  Claverleigh Curse, The   <GOT>
  Crimson Conquest
  In Passion's Shadow
  Mistress Of The Sun King
  Quicksilver
  Scarlet Surrender
  Tempest
  Where Passion Dwells
  Whispers Of Passion
  Wilder Shores Of Love
  In sequence:
    Flame Of Fidelity
    Fidelity's Flight

_____

_____

duBOIS,
  Listener, The

_____

_____

DuBOIS, Claudie
MacFadden Romance:
40 Ivory Sands

DuBOIS, Bonna Lee
       [Bonna Lee DuBois Cook]
Judy Sullivan Books: <RS>
Long Ago Love

DuBOIS, Jill   <HO>
Angel's Wing
Reap The Bitter Wind

DUBOIS, Sally
       [Lynn Vincentnathan]
Candlelight Ecstasy:
13 Marriage Season, The

duBOIS, Theodora   <GOT>
Devil And Destiny, The
Face Of Hate, The
Footsteps, The

duBREUIL, Elizabeth Lorinda
             (Deceased)
           (Kate Cameron)
        (Lorinda duBreuil)
         (Lorinda Hagen)
     (Margaret Maitland)

duBREUIL, Lorinda   <GOT>
   [Elizabeth Lorinda duBreuil]
Evil, Evil
Legend Of Molly Moor, The
Nightmare Baby   <SN>
Secret, The

DUBUS, Elizabeth/Elizabeth Nell
Marguerite Tanner   <CO>
Twilight Of The Dawn
Cajun Trilogy: <Saga>
  Cajun
  Where Love Rules
  To Love And To Dream

DUCKETT, Madelaine G.
        (Madelaine Gibson)

DUCOTY, Lyn
Harlequin Temptation:
33 Pocketful Of Dreams, A

DUFFIELD, Anne
       [Anne Tate Duffield]
Come Back, Miranda
Dusty Dawn
Fiametta
Forever Tomorrow
Golden Summer, The
Grand Duchess, The
Harbor Lights
Tomorrow Is Theirs

DUKE, Elizabeth
Harlequin Romance:
2833 Softly Flits A Shadow
     Windarra Stud   HRS23
3034 Island Deception
3110 Fair Trial

DUKORE, Jesse
Sweet Dreams: <YA>
29 Never Love A Cowboy
44 Long Distance Love

duMAURIER, Angela   <GOT>
  Treveryan

---

duMAURIER, Daphne   (Deceased)
                            <GOT><RS>
  Castle Dor w/Arthur QUILLER-COUCH
  Come Wind, Come Weather
  Don't Look Now
  Echoes From The Macabre
  Flight Of The Falcon, The
  Frenchman's Creek
  Glass Blowers, The
  Golden Lads
  House On The Strand, The
  Hungry Hill
  I'll Never Be Young Again
  Jamaica Inn
  King's General, The
  Loving Spirit, The
  Mary Anne
  My Cousin Rachel
  Parasites, The
  Progress Of Julius, The
  Rebecca
  Rule Britannia
  Scapegoat, The

DUNAWAY, Diane   <HR>
  Desert Hostage
  Candlelight Ecstasy:
    158 Desire And Conquer

DUNAWAY, Patricia
  Promise Romance: <Insp>
     1 Irish Lace
     7 Lessons In Love
    16 Distant Call, A
    27 No Limits On Love

DUNAWAY, Patti
                    (Poppy Nottingham)
  Surrender By The Sea

DUNBAR, Inga
  Harlequin Historical <Set#1>:
     1 Rose Royale

DUNBAR, Jean
  Harlequin Romance;
    1358 Home To White Wings
    1468 Yesterday, Today,
             And Tomorrow
    1537 Summer Nights, The
    1606 Quiet Veld, The

DUNCAN, Carol
                    [Carol S. Duncan]
  Silhouette Intimate Moments:
    270 Stranger On The Shore

DUNCAN, Judith
                    [Judith Mulholland]
  SuperRomance:
     51 Tender Rhapsody
     77 Hold Back The Dawn
  Harlequin SuperRomance:
    114 Reach The Splendor
    143 When Morning Comes
    196 Into The Light
    251 All That Matters
    291 Beginnings
    407 Streets Of Fire

DUNN, Carola   <RE>
          (see A Regency Valentine)
Angel
Black Sheep's Daughter, The   @
Byron's Child   <T-T>
Gabrielle's Gamble
     (HB: The Man In The Green Coat)
Lady In The Briars   @
Lavender Lady
Lord Iverbrook's Heir
Man In The Green Coat, The
Miser's Sister, The
Miss Hartwell's Dilemma   &
Polly And The Prince   <DNS>@
Smugglers' Summer
Two Corinthians   &
Harlequin Regency Romance:
     25 Susceptible Gentleman, A
     39 Poor Relation, A
     52 Lord For Miss Larkin, A
Warner Regency:
     30 Toblethorpe Manor

_____

DUNN, Christine w/ Eileen McMAHON
Desire

_____

DUNNE, Mary Jo
  First Love From Silhouette: <YA>
     61 Here Comes Kary

_____

DUNNE, Mary Collins
  Avalon:
     Enchanted Summer
     Cruise Of The Coral Queen
     Nurse Of The Crystalline Valley
     Nurse Of The Midnight Sun
     Nurse Of The Vineyards
     Return To Timberlake
     Secret Of Cliffsedge, The
     Standby Nurse

_____

_____

DUNNETT, Dorothy
  House Of Niccolo Series: <HS>
     In sequence:
        Niccolo Rising
        Spring Of The Ram, The
        Race Of Scorpions
  Lymond Chronicles: <HS>
     In sequence:
        Game Of Kings, The
        Queen's Play
        Disorderly Knights, The
        Pawn In Frankincense
        Ringed Castle, The
        Checkmate

_____

_____

du PONT, Diane   <HR>
  Emerald Embrace, The
  French Passion, The

_____

DUPONT, Ellen
                        (Ivy St. David)

DuPRE, Gabrielle   <HR>
  [Dianne M. Kleinschmidt w/
                   Sandra Smith-Ware]
  Ariane: Beloved Captive
  Forget Me Not

_____

_____

DUPREY, Richard
  Silver Wings

_____

_____

DUQUETTE, Anne Marie
  Harlequin Romance:
     2918 An Unlikely Combination
     3080 Unlikely Places

_____

_____

DURAN, Betty
                        (Ruth Jean Dale)

196

DWORMAN, Brenda Joyce
      (Brenda Joyce)

DWYER, Deanna   <GOT><RS>
 Children Of The Storm
 Dark Of Summer, The
 Demon Child, The
 Legacy Of Terror

DWYER-JOYCE, Alice   <RS>
 Cry The Soft Rain
 Diamond Cage, The
 Glass Heiress, The
 Gibbet Fen
 Gingerbread House, The
 Glitter--Dust, The
 House Of Jackdaws, The
 Lachlan's Woman
 Master Of Jethart, The
 Moonlit Way, The
 Penny Box, The
 Rainbow Glass, The
 Reach For The Shadows
 Storm Of Wrath, The
 Strolling Players, The
 Swiftest Eagle, The
 Unwinding Corner, The

DYER, Lois Faye
 Meteor Kismet:
  4 Winter Fire
  21 That James Boy

DYMOKE, Juliet   <HO>
 The Plantagenets:
  Pride Of Kings, The
  Royal Griffin, The

DYMOKE, Juliet (cont.)
 Lady Of The Garter
 Lion Of Mortimer, The
 Lord Of Greenwich, The
 Sun In Splendour, The

DYNE, Michael   <HO>
 Glitter And The Gold, The

DYNE, Michael w/ Ethel FRANK
      (Evelyn Hanna)

EADE, Charles w/ Ursula BLOOM
                    (Lozania Prole)

EADY, Carol Maxwell
  Her Royal Destiny   <HR>

EAGLE, Kathleen
  (see Silhouette Christmas Stories)
  Harlequin Historical <Set#2>:
     2 Private Treaty
    30 Medicine Woman
    50 Heaven And Earth
  Now And Forever:
     6 Heat Lightning
  Silhouette Classic:
    26 Someday Soon   <SE204>
  Silhouette Intimate Moments:
   148 For Old Times' Sake
   242 More Than A Miracle   &
   257 But That Was Yesterday
   284 Paintbox Morning   &
  Silhouette Special Edition:
   204 Someday Soon
   274 Class Act, A
   304 Georgia Nights
   359 Something Worth Keeping
   396 Carved In Stone
   437 Candles In The Night   &
   576 'Til There Was You

EARLEY, Fran
                      [Bob Whearley]
  Harlequin Intrigue:
    52 Candidate For Murder
    69 Ransom In Jade
    76 Moving Target
    79 Setup
    98 Hot Pursuit

EARLY, Tom
  Texas Saga:
    Sons Of Texas
    Raiders, The
    Rebels, The

EASTVALE, Margaret
  As The Sparks Fly   <RE>
  Danger In The Wind
  Masquerade:
    72 Change Of Heart

EATOCK, Marjorie   <GOT>
  Haunted Heirloom
  Ivory Tower, The
  Too Many Candles
  Candlelight:
   585 Wedding Journey, The   <RO>
  Candlelight Ecstasy:
    34 Stolen Holiday
  Judy Sullivan Books:
    See No Evil

EATON, Evelyn   <HO>
        [Evelyn Sybil Mary Eaton]
  Give Me Your Golden Hand
  Go Ask The River
  Love Is Recognition   <Poems>
  King Is A Witch, The
  Quietly My Captain Waits
  Restless Are The Sails

EATON, Laura
  Second Chance At Love:
   181 Rushing Tide

EBEL, Suzanne
 Dear Kate
 Family Feeling, The
 Girl By The Sea
 Most Auspicious Star, A
 Name In Lights, A
 To Seek A Star

EBERHARDT, Alfred F.
            (see Franklin M. Proud)

EBERHARDT, Anna
                   (Tiffany White)

EBERT, Alan w/ Janice ROTCHSTEIN
 The Tiernan Saga:
  In sequence:
   Traditions
   Long Way Home, The

EBISCH, Glen
 Crosswinds: <YA>
    2 Lou Dunlop: Private Eye
    4 Cliffhanger
   11 Shock Effect
   18 Angel In The Snow
 First Love From Silhouette: <YA>
  219 Behind The Mask

ECKERSLEY, Jill
                 [Helen Beaumont]
 Little Loving, A

ECKERT, Allan W.   <HO>
 Court-Martial Of Daniel Boone
 Crossbreed, The
 Dreaming Tree, The
 Great Auk, The

ECKERT, Allan W. (cont.)
 Hab Theory, The
 Savage Journey
 Song Of The Wild
 Narratives Of America:
    1 Frontiersman, The
    2 Wilderness Empire
    3 Conquerors, The
    4 Wilderness War
    5 Gateway To Empire
    6 Twilight Of Empire

ECKERT, Roberta   <RE>
 Duke's Gambit, The
 Heir To Vengeance
 Lady Angel
 My Lady Adventress

ECKSTEIN, Ernst   <HO>
 Nero: Butcher Of Rome   <GARS>

EDELMAN, Maurice   <HR>
 Disraeli: In Love
 Disraeli Rising

EDEN, Dorothy   <GOT><RS>
                    (Mary Paradise)
 American Heiress, The
 An Afternoon Walk
 An Important Family
 Bride By Candlelight
 Bridge Of Fear
 Brooding Lake
 Cat's Prey
 Crow Hollow
 Darkwater
 Daughters Of Ardmore Hall
 Deadly Travelers, The
 Death Is A Red Rose

EDEN, Dorothy (cont.)
  House On Hay Hill, The
  Lady Of Mallow
  Lamb To The Slaughter
  Laughing Ghost, The
  Listen To Danger
  Melbury Square
  Millionaire's Daughter, The
  Never Call It Loving
  Night Of The Letter, The
  Pretty Ones, The
  Ravenscroft
  Salamanca Drum, The
  Shadow Wife, The
  Siege In The Sun
  Sleep In The Woods
  Speak To Me Of Love
  Stonehaven
  Storrington Papers, The
  Time Of The Dragon, The
  Vines Of Yarrabee, The
  Voice Of The Dolls, The
  Waiting For Willa
  Whistle For The Crows
  Winterwood
  Yellow Is For Fear
    And Other Stories
  Writing as Mary Paradise:
    Face of An Angel
    Marriage Chest,The
    Shadow Of A Witch

_____

_____

EDEN, Frances J. S.
  Love Gift, The
  Ninth Life, The

_____

_____

EDEN, Laura
                  [Claire Harrison]
  Silhouette Romance:
    105 Mistaken Identity
    210 Flight Of Fancy
  Silhouette Special Edition:
    44 Summer Magic

_____

_____

EDER, George Jackson
                  (Jackson Reed)

EDGAR, Josephine
                  [Mary Mussi]
  Bright Young Things
  Dancer's Daughter, The
  Dark Tower, The
  Devil's Innocents, The
  Lady Of Wildersley, The
  Margaret Normanby   <HR>
  My Sister Sophie
  Stranger At The Gate, The
  Time Of Dreaming
  In sequence:
    Duchess
    Countess

_____

_____

EDGEWORTH, Ann
  Barriers Of Love
  Masquerade:
    39 Runaway Maid
    59 Devil's Angel, The

_____

_____

EDGHILL, Rosemary   <RE>
  Ill-Bred Bride, The
  Turkish Delight
  Two Of A Kind

_____

_____

EDMONDS, Janet
  Turn Of The Dice
  Harlequin Historical <Set#1>:
    4 Count Sergei's Pride

_____

_____

EDMONDS, Walter D.
  Young Ames

_____

_____

EDWARD, Elaine   <GOT><RS>
   [Marie Elaine Edward]
  Amberleigh
  Lenore
  Terror Manor

EDWARDS, Adrienne
  [Anne Kolaczyk w/ Ed Kolaczyk]
  Second Chance At Love:
   338 Destiny's Darling
   369 Creature Comforts
   397 Whistling Dixie
   449 Some Kind Of Wonderful
  To Have And To Hold:
   29 Honorable Intentions

EDWARDS, Andrea
  [Anne Kolaczyk w/ Ed Kolaczyk]
  All Too Soon
  Corporate Affair
  Silhouette Intimate Moments:
   291 Above Suspicion
  Silhouette Special Edition:
   363 Rose In Bloom
   428 Say It With Flowers
   490 Ghost Of A Chance
   550 Violets Are Blue
   591 Places In The Heart
   618 Make Room For Daddy
  The Avon Romance:
  Now Comes The Spring

EDWARDS, Anne   <GOT><HO>
  Child Of Night
  Haunted Summer
  Hesitant Heart, The
  Miklos Alexandrovitch Is Missing

EDWARDS, Anne (cont.)
  Shadow Of A Lion
  Survivors, The

EDWARDS, Cassie   <HR>
  Beloved Embrace
  Desire's Blossom
  Eden's Promise
  Elusive Ecstasy
  Enchanted Enemy
  Eugenia's Embrace
  Forbidden Embrace
  Island Rapture   <CO>
  Love's Legacy   <GOT>
  Passion's Fire
  Passion's Web
  Portrait Of Desire
  Rapture's Rendezvous
  Roses After Rain
  Secrets Of My Heart
  Silken Rapture
  When Passion Calls
  Chippewa Series: &
  In sequence:
   Savage Obsession
   Savage Innocence
   Savage Heart
   Savage Torment
   Savage Paradise
  Savage Series:
   In sequence:
   Savage Surrender   (Ojibway)
   Savage Eden   (Miami)
   Savage Splendor (Chippawa)&
   Savage Whispers   (Kiowa)
   Savage Bliss   (Suquamish)
   Savage Dream   (Navaho)
  Harlequin Historical <Set#2>:
   5 Passion In The Wind
   17 Gentle Passion, A
   42 Passion's Embrace

EDWARDS, Emily Ruth
Harlequin Romance:
  2791 Hunter's Snare

EDWARDS, Estelle
             [Mollie Gregory]
Rapture Romance:
  21 Moonslide
  47 Knave Of Hearts, The

EDWARDS, Irene
          (Elisabeth Barr)

EDWARDS, Jane
          (Jane Campbell)
Affair Of The Albatross
Avalon:
  Houseboat Mystery
  Susannah Is Missing!
  Hesitant Heart, The
  Terror By Design
  Dangerous Odyssey
Candlelight:
  127 Island Interlude
Harlequin Temptation:
  90 Listen With Your Heart

EDWARDS, Jaroldeen
Mountains Of Eden, The   <Saga>
Wildflower

EDWARDS, Judi
Silhouette Special Edition:
  470 Perfect Ten, The

EDWARDS, Kathryn
Torch:
  Broken Promises

EDWARDS, Kathryn (cont.)
Torchlite:
  Surrender Of Wills

EDWARDS, Pamela
Inherit The Storm   <Saga>

EDWARDS, Patricia
         [Patricia Watters]
Harlequin SuperRomance:
  446 Sweet Promised Land

EDWARDS, Paula
Silhouette Romance:
  23 Bewitching Grace

EDWARDS, Rachelle   <HR><RE>
An Unequal Match
Captain's Lady, The
Dangerous Dandy
Devil's Bride
Hasty Marriage, A
Highwayman And The Lady, The
Lady Of Quality
Lord Trenton's Proposal
Love Finds A Way
Lucifer's Lady
Marylebone Park
Miranda's Folly
Rake's Revenge, The
Ransome Inheritance, The
Reckless Masquerade
Regency Masquerade
Runaway Bride
Scoundrel's Daughter, The
Silken Net, The
Sweet Hoyden
Thief Of Hearts, The

203

EDWARDS, Rachelle (cont.)
  Coventry:
     16 Wager For Love
     51 Lord Heathbury's Revenge
     71 Debt Of Love
    104 Merchant's Daughter, The
    115 Outrageous Lady
           Caroline, The
    133 Smithfield Bargain, The
    149 Fortune's Child
    186 Marriage Bargain, The <RE>

EDWARDS, Samuel   <HO>
                   [Noel B. Gerson]
  Caves Of Guernica, The
  Daughter Of Gascony   <HofFS>
  Divine Mistress
  Exploiters, The
  King's Messenger, The   <HofFS>
  Naked Maja, The
  Queen's Husband, The   <HofFS>
  Scimitar, The

EDWARDS, Sarah   <HR>
             [Sharon w/ Robert Bills]
  Crystal Rapture   <AAS>
  Fire And Sand   <AAS>

EGERTON, Denise
  Reckless Lady

EIRES, Anita
  Heartlines: <YA>
     1 Summer Awakening

EIRLS, Sandra Lynn
  Rainbow Gypsy, The   <CO>

EKERT-ROTHOLZ, Alice
  Checkpoint Orinoco
  Sydney Circle, The

ELEGANT, Robert
            [Robert Sampson Elegant]
  Dynasty   <HS>
  From A Far Land
  Manchu   <HS>
  Mandarin   <HS>

ELGIN, Mary   <GOT>
                   [Walter Stewart]
  Wood And The Trees, The
  In sequence:
    Man From The Mist, A
    Highland Masquerade

ELIOT, Anne   <GOT><RS>
                   [Anne Crompton]
  Dark Beneath The Pines, The
  Incident At Villa Rahmana
  Return To Aylforth
  Shadows Waiting
  Stranger At Pembroke

ELIOT, Carolyn
  Starlight Romance:
    Disobedient Heart

ELIOT, Jessica
[Lois Ann Brown w/ Barbara Levy]
Candlelight:
    516 Rendezvous In Athens   <RO>
    550 Home To The Highlands   <IN>
    689 Vintage Year, A   <RO>

ELLIOT, Douglass   <HO>
American Patriot Series:
  In sequence:
    New Breed, The
    Great Deception, The
    Bold Destiny

ELIOT, Winslow
                (Ellie Winslow)
"ELIZABETH"
Elizabeth And Her German Garden
Enchanted April, The
Father
Jasmine Farm, The
Love
Mr. Skeffington
Princess Priscilla's Fortnight
Solitary Summer, The
Vera

ELKINS, Charlotte
                (Emily Spenser)

ELLERBECK, Rosemary
[Rosemary Anne
            L'Estrange Ellerbeck]
            (Anna L'Estrange)
            (Nicola Thorne)
            (Katherine Yorke)

ELLINGSON, Marnie   <RE>
Dolly Blanchard's Fortune
Wicked Marquis, The
Candlelight:
    572 Double Folly   <RE>
    579 Unwilling Bride   <RE>
    588 Jessica Windom   <RE>
    702 Mistress Of Langfort
         Court, The   <RE>

ELLIOT, Lucy
                [Nancy A. Greenman]
                (see HQ Christmas Stories)
Harlequin Historical <Set#2>:
    8   Shared Passions
    24 Frontiers Of The Heart
    44 Summer's Promise
    64 Contraband Desire

ELLIOT, Rachel
Harlequin Presents:
    1207 Journey Back To Love
Harlequin Romance:
    2978 Song Of Love

ELLIOTT, Anne w/ Christine DORSEY
                (Christine Elliott)

ELLIOTT, Bruce
    [Edward Field w/Neil Derrick]
Village

ELLIOTT, Christine
[Christine Dorsey w/ Anne Elliott]
Captain's Conquest, The

205

ELLIS, Janine
Harlequin Romance:
2330 Rough Justice

_____

_____

ELLIS, Julie   <GOT><HR>
[Julie M. Ellis]
(Susan Marino)
(Susan Marvin)
(Susan Richard)
Daughter's Promise, A   <Saga>
East Wind
Eden
Eulalie
Evil At Hillcrest
Girl In White
Glorious Morning
Hampton Heritage, The
Hampton Women, The
Jeweled Dagger, The
Kara
Long Dark Night Of The Soul
Loyalties
Magnolias, The
Maison Jennie
Only Sin, The
Rendezevous In Vienna
Rich Is Best
Savage Oaks
Velvet Jungle, The
Walk A Tightrope
Walk Into Darkness
Wexford
Where Running Waters Meet

_____

_____

ELLIS, Kathy
Where The Wilderness Ends

_____

_____

ELLIS, Leigh
[Anne Rudeen w/ Louisa Rudeen]
Green Lady   <GOT>
Tessa Of Destiny

_____

_____

ELLIS, Louise
Harlequin Romance:
1225 Nurse Camden's Cavalier
1345 Three Nurses
1369 Rona Came To Rothmere
1394 Nurse Sandra's
       Second Summer
1473 Silent Heart

_____

_____

ELLIS, Patricia
[Valerie Mangrum]
Silhouette Romance:
684 Sweet Protector

_____

_____

ELLISON, Marjorie
(Marjorie Norrell)

ELLISON, Suzanne
[Suzanne Pierson Ellison]
Harlequin Intrigue:
46 Nowhere To Run
Harlequin SuperRomance:
165 Wings Of Gold
258 Pinecones And Orchids
283 For All The Right Reasons
308 Words Unspoken
315 Fair Play
369 Candle In The Window
393 With Open Arms
The Living West Trilogy:
420   Heart Of The West
423   Soul Of The West
427   Spirit Of The West
452   Size Of Trust, The

_____

ELLISON, Suzanne Pierson
(Suzanne Ellison)
Serenade/Saga: <HR><Insp>
32 Sycamore Settlement
Serenade/Serenata: <Insp>
25 One More River

_____

_____

ELMBLAD, Mary   <CO>
    All Manner of Riches
    Little Company

- - - - - - - - - - - - - - - - - -

- - - - - - - - - - - - - - - - - -

ELSNA, Hebe   <HR><RE>
    (see Margaret Campbell Barnes)
    Brimming Cup, The
    China Princess, The
    Gallant Lady
    Heir Of Garlands, The
    Love Match, The
    Queen's Ward, The
    Saxon's Folly
    Wise Virgin, The

- - - - - - - - - - - - - - - - - -

- - - - - - - - - - - - - - - - - -

ELVER, Rose
    Harlequin Premiere Edition:
     19 Lark Ascending
    Harlequin Presents:
     245 Golden Apples
    Harlequin Romance:
     1949 Shining Wanderer
     2054 Fire Mountain
     2244 Tiger Sky

- - - - - - - - - - - - - - - - - -

- - - - - - - - - - - - - - - - - -

ELWARD, James
                    (Rebecca James)
                    (Hillary Waugh)
                (see Helen Van Slyke)
    Ask For Nothing More   <CO>

- - - - - - - - - - - - - - - - - -

- - - - - - - - - - - - - - - - - -

ELWOOD, Muriel   <HR>
    Bigamous Duchess, The
    Deeper The Heritage
    Heritage Of The River

- - - - - - - - - - - - - - - - - -

- - - - - - - - - - - - - - - - - -

EMERICK, Lucille   <GOT>
    Web Of Evil
    You'll Hang, My Love
                    w/ Francis SWANN

- - - - - - - - - - - - - - - - - -

- - - - - - - - - - - - - - - - - -

EMERSON, Janet
    Turning Points: <YA>
     12 Only You

- - - - - - - - - - - - - - - - - -

- - - - - - - - - - - - - - - - - -

EMERSON, Kathy Lynn
                    (Kaitlyn Gorton)

EMERSON, Mark
    Two-By-Two Romance: <YA>
     14 Looking At You

- - - - - - - - - - - - - - - - - -

- - - - - - - - - - - - - - - - - -

EMERY, Denise
                    [Helen Beaumont]
    Sapphire Romance:
     Bells Of Utrecht
     Sunrise In Hong Kong

- - - - - - - - - - - - - - - - - -

- - - - - - - - - - - - - - - - - -

EMM, Catherine
                    [Kay McMahon]
    Heartfire Romance: <HR>
     Forbidden Magic

- - - - - - - - - - - - - - - - - -

- - - - - - - - - - - - - - - - - -

ENDERLE, Judith
    (see Stephanie Gordon Tessler w/
              Judith Enderle)
    Caprice Romance: <YA>
     10 Someone For Sara
     11 Cheer Me On
     14 SWAK Sealed With A Kiss
     17 Programmed For Love
     30 When Wishes Come True
     39 Sing A Song Of Love

ERICKSON, Lynn (cont.)
  Woman Of San Francisco, A   <AWD>
  Harlequin Intrigue:
    42 Arena Of Fear
  Harlequin SuperRomance:
    132 Snowbird
    157 Faces Of Dawn, The
    184 Chance Worth Taking, A
    199 Stormswept
    231 Dangerous Sentiment, A
    255 Tangled Dreams
    276 Perfect Gem, A
    298 Fool's Gold
    320 Firecloud
    347 Shadow On The Sun
    370 In From The Cold
    404 West Of The Sun
    439 Northern Light, The
  Tapestry Romance: <HR>
    High Country Pride

  _____

  _____

ERICKSON, Roger
  Maggie And David

  _____

  _____

ERIKSEN, Barbara
                    (Katherine Arthur)

ERLBACH, Arlene
  Crosswinds: <YA>
    1 Does Your Nose Get In The
       Way, Too?
    5 Guys, Dating And Other
       Disasters
    20 Dropout Blues

  _____

  _____

ERNEST, Francine
  MacFadden Romance:
    182 Love's Magic Moment

  _____

  _____

ERNEST, Jeanette
                    [Judy Wells Martin]
  Rapture Romance:
    3 Lover's Lair
    12 Dear Doubter

  _____

  _____

ERSKINE, Andra
                    [Judy Wells Martin]
  Rapture Romance:
    84 Priority Affair

  _____

  _____

ERSKINE, Barbara
  Kingdom Of Shadows   <T-T>
  Lady Of Hay

  _____

  _____

ERSKINE, Helen
                    [Helen Santori]
  First Love From Silhouette: <YA>
    6 Kate, Herself
    17 Golden Girl
  Silhouette Romance:
    140 Fortunes Of Love

  _____

  _____

ERSKINE, Margaret   <GOT><RS>
              [Margaret Wetherby Williams]
  Besides The Wench Is Dead
  Brood Of Folly
  Caravan Of Night
  Case Of Mary Fielding, The
  Case With Three Husbands, A
  Dead By Now
  Don't Look Behind You
  Ewe Lamb, The
  Family At Tammerton, The
  Give Up The Ghost
  Graveyard Plot, A
  Harriet Farewell
  House In Hook Street, The
  No. 9 Belmont Square

ERSKINE, Margaret (cont.)
Old Mrs. Ommanney Is Dead
Painted Mask, The
Silver Ladies, The
Sleep No More
Voice Of Murder, The
Voice Of The House, The

ERWIN, Annabel
[Ann Forman Barron]
Aurielle
Liliane

ESLER, Anthony   <HR>
Babylon
Blade Of Castlemayne, The
For Love Of A Pirate
Forbidden City
Hellbane
Lord Libertine

ESMOND, Harriet   <RS>
Darsham's Tower
Eye Stones, The
Florian Signet, The

ESPEY, John w/
            Carolyn SEE and Lisa SEE
            (Monica Highland)

ESSENMACHER, Eugenia Riley
            (Eugenia Riley)

ESSEX, Marianna
[Joan Van Nuys]
Rapture Romance:
   41 Torrent Of Love
   92 Love Came Courting

ESSEX, Mary
[Ursula Bloom]
Assistant Matron
Dare-Devil Doctor
Romantic Theatre Sister
Sympathetic Surgeon, The

ESSIG, Terry
[Terry Parent Essig]
Silhouette Romance:
   552 House Calls
   662 Wedding March, The
   725 Fearless Father

ESTEY, Norbert
All My Sins

ESTRADA, Rita Clay
                        (Rita Clay)
                        (Tira Lacy)
Harlequin Temptation:
   In sequence:
   48   Will And The Way, The
   72   Woman's Choice, A
   100 Something To Treasure
   136 Best Things In Life, The
   166 Ivory Key, The
   188 Little Magic, A
   220 Trust   <MEQ>
   265 Second To None
   313 To Buy A Groom

EVANICK, Marcia
Loveswept:
   322 Perfect Morning
   404 Indescribably Delicious
   427 Satin Sheets And
            Strawberries

EVANOVICH, Janet
                              (Steffie Hall)
  Loveswept:
    254 Grand Finale, The
    289 Thanksgiving
    303 Manhunt
    343 Ivan Takes A Wife
    362 Back To The Bedroom
    392 Smitten
    422 Wife For Hire

EVANS, Cicely Louise   <GOT>
  Nemesis Wife
  Saint Game, The

EVANS, Claire
                            [Claire DeLong]
  Second Chance At Love:
    22 Led Into Sunlight
    64 Apollo's Dream
   115 Come Winter's End

EVANS, Elaine   <GOT><RS>
  Black Autumn
  Dark And Deadly Love, A
  Shadowland
  Wintershade

EVANS, Jean
                    [Nicholas Demetropoulos]
  Harlequin Romance:
      Design For Love   HRS29

EVANS, Laurel
                           [Ellen Wilson]
  Silhouette Desire:
   144 Business After Hours
   167 Timeless Rituals
   200 Permanent Arrangement, A

EVANS, Laurel (cont.)
   248 Moonlight Serenade
   278 Designing Heart
   401 Built To Last

EVANS, Marianne
                    [Nicholas Demetropoulos]
  Splendid Passion, A

EVANS, Patricia Gardner
  Harlequin Historical <Set#2>:
    14 Silver Noose
  Silhouette Intimate Moments:
   151 Flashpoint
     Trilogy:
   228   Whatever It Takes   &
   243   Summer Of The Wolf   &

EVENS, Lori
  Avalon:
    Autumn Kisses

EVERETT, Gail
                        [Mary Arlene Hale]
  Journey For A Nurse
  My Favorite Nurse
  Search For Love
  Candlelight:
   154 Designs On Love
   207 Teach Me To Love
   211 Love Is The Winner
   219 Way To The Heart, The
   223 When Summer Ends
   224 Love's Surprise

EVERITT, Marjorie
  Avalon:
    Danger At Demon's Cove

EVERITT, Marjorie (cont.)
    Touch Of Honey, A
    River Of Stars

EWING, Kathryn
                (Kathryn Douglas)

EWING, Tess
                [Virginia K. Smiley]
    Second Chance At Love:
    48 Starburst

EYERLY, Jeannette   <YA>
    More Than A Summer Love

EYRE, Annette
                [Anne Worboys]
    Give Me Your Love
    Magnolia Room, The
    Venetian Inheritance

EYRE, Katherine Wigmore   <GOT><RS>
    Chinese Box
    Mistress Of Fear
    Monk's Court
    Sandalwood Fan, The

EYRE, Marie   <GOT><RS>
    Absence, The
    Blackgable Inn
    Bury Me Not At Sea
    Eyrie Of The Fox
    Girl In The Tiffany Dress, The
    Omen, The
    Presence, The
    Return To Gravesend

FABER, Doris
  Mystique:
    28 Journey Into Danger
    139 Quest For Love

FABIAN Erika
  Harlequin SuperRomance:
    116 Sky Riders

FABIAN, Ruth   <GOT>
                    [Aileen Quigley]
  Scent Of Violets, A

FAGYAS, Maria
                  [M. Bushe-Fedete]
  Court Of Honor
  Dance Of The Assassins
  Devil's Lieutenant

FAID, Mary
  Aston Hall:
    108 No Stars So Bright

FAIN, Michael w/ Judith BARNARD
                    (Judith Michael)

FAIRBAIRN, Ann
  Five Smooth Stones
  That Man Cartwright

FAIRBAIRNS, Zoe
  Stand We At Last   <HS>

FAIRCHILDE, Sarah   <RE>
  Dance Of Desire

FAIRE, Zabrina   <RE>
                  [Florence Stevenson]
  Warner Regency:
    2 Lady Blue
    6 Midnight Match, The
    7 Romany Rebel, The
    8 Enchanting Jenny
    12 Wicked Cousin, The
    17 Athena's Airs
    21 Bold Pursuit
    23 Pretty Kitty
    28 Tiffany's True Love
    31 Pretender To Love

FAIRFAX, Ann   <RE>
              [Marion Chesney Gibbons]
  Annabelle
  Henrietta
  My Dear Duchess
  Penelope

FAIRFAX, Gwen
                    [Mary Jo Territo]
  Candlelight Ecstasy:
    213 Lover In Disguise

FAIRFAX, Kate   <HR>
                        [Irene Ord]
  Sweet Fire

FALLON, Frederic   <HO>
  White Queen, The

FARLAND, Kathryn   <RE>
       [Kathryn Fladland]
  Miss Monica Marries

FARNES, Eleanor
  Harlequin Classic:
    81 Golden Peaks, The   (806)
    86 Song Of Summer   (722)
    92 Change Of Heart, A (753)
   131 Magic Symphony   (998)
   138 Happy Enterprise, The(487)
   149 Dream And The Dancer (912)
   158 House By The Lake,The(942)
  Harlequin Romance:
   753 Doctor Max
   806 Golden Peaks, The
   912 Dream And The Dancer, The
   942 House By The Lake, The
   975 Sister Of The Housemaster
   998 Magic Symphony
  1064 Mistress Of The House
  1087 Home For Jocelyn, A
  1109 Fortunes Of
       Springfield, The
  1142 Secret Heiress
  1171 Wings Of Memory, The
  1207 Young Intruder, The
  1246 Constant Heart, The
  1280 Flight Of The Swan, The
  1335 Red Cliffs, The
  1458 Enchanted Island, The
  1497 Doctor's Circle, The
  1584 Castle In Spain, A
  1639 Valley Of The Eagles, The
  1662 Serpent In Eden, A
  1765 Splendid Legacy, The
  1787 Runaway Visitors, The
  Masquerade:
    10 Rose And The Thorn, The

FARNSWORTH, Mona   <GOT>
  Castle That Whispered, The
  Companion Of Evil
  Cross For Tomorrow, A
  Dark Wood
  Evil That Waited, The
  Footsteps That Follow
  Great Stone Heart
  House Of Whispering Death, The
  Menace Of Marble Hill, The
  Starcrossed Road
  Three Sisters Of No End House

FARR, Caroline   <GOT><RS>
  Brecon Castle
  Castle In Canada, A
  Castle In Spain, A
  Castle Of Terror
  Castle On The Loch
  Castle On The Rhine
  Chateau Of Wolves
  Dark Citadel
  Dark Mansion
  Granite Folly
  Heiress Of Corsair Keep
  Heiress Of Fear
  House Of Dark Illusions
  House Of Destiny
  House Of Landsdown, The
  House Of Secrets
  House Of Tombs
  House Of Treachery
  House Of Valhalla
  House On The Cliffs, The
  Island Of Evil
  Mansion Malevolent
  Mansion Of Evil
  Mansion Of Menace
  Mansion Of Peril
  Ravensnest
  Room Of Secrets
  Scream In The Storm, The
  Secret At Ravenswood
  Secret Of Castle Ferrara, The
  Secret Of The Chateau, The
  Sinister House

FARR, Caroline (cont.)
So Near And Yet...
Terror Of Duncan Island
Towers Of Fear, The
Witch's Hammer

FARRANT, Sarah <GOT>
Lady Of Chantry Glades
Lady Of Monkswood Manor
Lady Of Drawbridge Court
Lady Of Rogan's Tower
Lady Of Winston Park
Reluctant Paragon, The
Sweet Jael
Tavern Wench
Touch Of Terror, A

FARRAR, Frederick W. <HO>
Agrippina: Empress Of
Depravity <GARS>

FARRAR, Helen Graham <GOT>
How Evil The Word
Web Begun

FARRELL, David
(F. E. Smith)

FARRELL, Marjorie <RE>
Miss Ware's Refusal

FARRINGTON, Renee
Golden Care
Silver Sound
Candlelight:
115 No Secret So Close

FARRINGTON, Robert <HO>
Balboa
Killing Of Richard Three
Traitors Of Bosworth, The
Tudor Agent

FARSON, Daniel
Swansdowne <Saga>

FASANO, Donna
(Donna Clayton)

FASSHAUER, Susan Chatfield
(Susan Chatfield)

FAST, Howard <HO>
[Howard Melvin Fast]
Agrippa's Daughter
April Morning
Call Of Fife And Drum, The*
*One volume containing:
Conceived In Liberty
The Proud And The Free
The Unvanquished
Citizen Tom Paine
Conceived In Liberty
General Zapped An Angel, The
Golden Fire
Hessian, The
Last Frontier, The
Max
Pledge, The
Proud And The Free, The
Spartacus
Unvanquished, The
The Lavette Saga: In sequence:
Immigrants, The
Second Generation, The
Establishment, The
Legacy, The
Immigrants Daughter, The
Dinner Party, The

FAUL, Anne
  Before The Summer Rain   <Saga>

FAULKNER, Anne Irvin
                    (Nancy Faulkner)

FAULKNER, Colleen
                [Colleen Culver]
  Heartfire Romance: <HR>
    Forbidden Caress
    Passion's Savage Moon
    Raging Desire
    Snowfire
    Temptation's Tender Kiss
    Traitor's Caress

FAULKNER, Florence
  Avalon:
    Challenge For Two, A
    Clue To Romance
    House Of Hostile Women
    Season Of Deception
    Three Little Words

FAULKNER, Nancy   <HR>
                [Anne Irvin Faulkner]
  Jade Box, The
  Savannah
  Summer Of The Fire Ship, The

FAULKNER, Whitney
                [Elaine Bissell]
  The American Dream: <HR>
    In sequence:
      Emily's Destiny
      Jane's Promise
      Kathryn's Quest
      Sara's Stand

FAURE, Jean
                [Mary I. Kilchenstein]
  Second Chance At Love:
    240 Bed Of Roses
    357 Long Road Home

FAVAGE, Paula w/ D. J. HERDA
  Winda Of Kabul, The

FAVOR, Erika
                [Lee Ann Tobin]
  Silhouette Romance:
    678 Mountain Home

FAVORS, Jean M.
                (Elizabeth Morris)

FAYE, Shirley
  Meteor Kismet:
    16 Face To Face

FAYET, Claudette
  Mystique:
    127 Spider's Eye, The
    149 Beyond Desire

FAYRE, Jillian
                [Jillian Dagg]
  Serenade Romance:
    Whispers Of The Heart

FEATHER, Jane   <RE>
                (Claudia Bishop)
  Love's Charade
  Smuggler's Lady
  Heartfire Romance: <HR>
    Beloved Enemy

218

FEATHER, Jane (cont.)
  Reckless Seduction
  The Avon Romance:
    Bold Destiny
    Chase The Dawn
    Heart's Folly
    Reckless Angel
    Silver Nights
    Brazen Whispers

FECHER, Constance
                    [Constance Heaven]
  Lion Of Trevarrock
  Lovely Wanton (Player Queen)
  Night Of The Wolf
  Player Queen
  Tudor Trilogy:
    Queen's Delight
  Traitor's Son
    King's Legacy

FEDDERSON, Connie Scotts
                    (Connie Drake)
                    (Carol Finch)
                    (Gina Robins)

FEELY, T. J.
  Embrace Tomorrow

FEHR, Richard w/ William MULVEY
                    (Sharon Steele)

FEIBLEMAN, Peter S.
  Charlie Boy
  Columbus Tree, The

FEIFER, George
  Girl From Petrovka
  Moscow Farewell

FEIFFER, Judy   <YA>
  Lovecrazy

FEINBERG, Bea   (Deceased)
                    (Cynthia Freeman)

FELBER, Edith
                    (Edith Layton)

FELDHAKE, Susan C.
  Rhapsody Romance:
    Reflection Of Love
  Serenade/Saga: <HR><Insp>
     7 In Love's Own Time
    10 Love Beyond Surrender
  Serenade/Serenata: <Insp>
     2 Love's Sweet Promise
     3 For Love alone

FELDMAN, Ellen "Bette"
                    (Amanda Russell)
                    (Elizabeth Villars)

FELDMAN, Fred   <HO>
  Jed Smith: Freedom River <AES:#1>

FELDMAN, Gilda w/ Leslie RUGG
                    (Louisa Gillette)

FELLDIN, Jeanne   <HR>
  Lovestruck:
    Boundless Love

FELLOWS, Catherine   <RE>
  Entanglement
  Leonora
  Love Match, The
  Marriage Masque, The
  Vanessa

FENTON, Ann   <GOT>
  Dark Cedars

FERGUSON, James B.   <CO>
  Fortunes

FENTON, Edward
  Anne Of The Thousand Days
  Double Darkness, The
  She Waits

FERGUSON, Janet
  Sister Of Musgrave Ward   <M&B>

FENWICK, Elizabeth   <GOT>
  Disturbance On Berry Hill

FERGUSON, Jo Ann
  At The Rainbow's End
  Nothing Wagered
  Under The Outlaw Moon
  The Foxbridge Legacy: <HS>
    Sybil
    Rebecca
    Mariel

FENWICK, Patricia
  Harlequin Classic:
    166 Wish On A Star   (1133)
  Harlequin Romance:
    841 Truant Heart
   1133 Wish On A Star
   1253 Dream Come True

FERGUSON, Margaret   <GOT>
  Sign Of The Ram, The

FERBER, Edna
  American Beauty
  Cimarron
  Fanny Herself
  Great Son
  Giant
  Ice Palace
  One Basket - Vol I
  One Basket - Vol II
  Peculiar Treasure, A
  Saratoga Trunk
  Show Boat
  So Big

FERGUSSON-HANNAY, Doris
                 (Doris Leslie)

FERM, Betty   <GOT>
  Eventide
  False Idols
  Vengeance Of Valdone, The

FERNALD, Abby
  MacFadden Romance:
    52 Destiny's Pawn

FERGUSON, Anne
  Crosswinds Keepsake: <YA>
    28 Getting It Together

FERRAND, Georgina   <GOT><RS>
                 (Brenda Castle)
  Dangerous Inheritance
  Encounter In Athens
  Heart's Own Sweet Music, The
  House Of Glass

FERRAND, Georgina (cont.)
  Moonmist - Taurus   <ZGS>
  Springtime Of Joy
  Thickening Light, The

FERRELL, Olivia (cont.)
  768 Summer Fancy
  Silhouette Special Edition:
  48 Love Has Its Reasons

FERRARELLA, Marie
  [Marie Rydzynski Ferrarella]
                (Marie Charles)
                (Marie Michael)
                (Marie Nicole)
  Harlequin American Romance:
  145 Pocketful Of Rainbows
  Silhouette Romance:
  588 Gift, The
  613 Five-Alarm Affair
  632 Heart To Heart
  686 Mother For Hire
  730 Borrowed Baby
  744 Her Special Angel
  766 Undoing Of Justin Starbuck
  Silhouette Special Edition:
  597 It Happened One Night
  652 Girl's Best Friend, A

FERRIS, Gina
                [Gina Wilkins]
  Silhouette Special Edition:
  496 Healing Sympathy
  549 Lady Beware

FERRIS, Rose Marie
                [Rose Marie Ogden Ferris]
                (Valerie Ferris)
                (Robin Francis)
                (Michelle Roland)
  Candlelight Ecstasy:
  30 Promises To Keep
  37 After The Fire
  89 Wild And Tender Magic
  207 Bristol's Law
  434 Dare To Love Again
  477 To Tame A Man
  514 Cleo's Treasure

FERRARI, Ivy
  Harlequin Romance:
  803 Model Nurse
  874 Nurse At Ryeminster
  1025 Surgery In The Hills
  1090 Nurse Kate At Fallowfield
  1266 Where No Stars Shine
  1312 Peppercorn Harvest
  1494 Valley Of Illusion, The
  1523 House Of Clouds
  1560 Windy Night, Rainy Morrow
  Other:
  Sister At Ryeminster   <M&B>

FERRIS, Valerie
                [Rose Marie Ferris]
  Candlelight Ecstasy:
  14 Heart's Awakening, The

FIANDT, Mary K.
  Willow Cabin

FERRELL, Olivia
  Silhouette Romance:
  330 Crystal Angel

FIEDLER, Jean   <RS>
  Atone With Evil

FIELD, Dawn Stewart   <HO>
  Luise

FIELD, Della
  Vietnam Nurse

FIELD, Edward w/ Neil DERRICK
                  (Bruce Elliott)

FIELD, Karen
  Harlequin SuperRomance:
    244 Time Will Tell
    331 Just Say The Word
    450 Time For Rainbows, A

FIELD, Penelope   <GOT>
                 [Dorothy Giberson]
  Someone Is Watching

FIELD, Rachel
  All This And Heaven Too
  And Now Tomorrow

FIELD, Sandra
               [Jill MacLean]
  Harlequin Presents:
    568 Walk By My Side
    639 An Attraction Of Opposites
    681 Mistake In Identity, A
    768 Change Of Heart, A
    799 Out Of Wedlock
    824 World Of Difference, A
    905 One In A Million
    977 An Ideal Match
  1034 Single Combat
  1120 Love In A Mist

FIELD, Sandra (cont.)
  1159 Chase A Rainbow
  1178 Right Man, The
  1242 Ring Of Gold
  1280 Goodbye Forever
  1336 Love At First Sight
  Harlequin Romance:
  1870 To Trust My Love
  2398 Winds Of Winter, The
  2457 Storms Of Spring, The
  2480 Sight Of A Stranger
  2577 Tides Of Summer, The

FIELDING, Joy
  Other Woman, The

FIELDING, Kate
  To Jessica, With Love

FIELDS, Terri
  Caprice Romance: <YA>
    82 1-800-Love
  Sweet Dreams: <YA>
    70 Special Someone
  102 Hearts Don't Lie
  117 Other Me, The
  129 Vote For Love, A
  Wildfire: <YA>
    Recipe For Romance

FILICHIA, Peter
  Two By Two Romance: <YA>
    8 Falling In Love

FILLINGHAM, Jan
  Lover's Landscape

FINLEY, Glenna (cont.)
    38   Diamonds For My Love
    39   Secret Of Love

FINNEY, Shan
    Sweet Dreams: <YA>
    135 Geared For Romance
    147 Trust In Love

FINNIGAN, Karen   <HR>
    Fires Of Midnight

FIOROTTO, Christine Sparks
                          (Lucy Gordon)

FIRESIDE, Carolyn
                      [Joanna Burgess]
    Anything But Love
    Goodbye Again   <CO>
    In The Grasp

FIRTH, Susanna
    Harlequin Presents:
    624 Master Of Shadows
    Harlequin Romance:
    2307 Dark Encounter
    2344 Prince Of Darkness
    2493 Overlord, The
    2564 Lions Walk Alone

FISCHER, Dorothy
    First Love From Silhouette: <YA>
    126 Between The Lines

FISH, Mildred Teague
                    (Megan Alexander)

FISHER, Alan   <HO>
    Three Passions Of Countess
    Natalya

FISHER, Fran
                    [Frances Copeland]
    First Love From Silhouette: <YA>
    50   Stay, Sweet Love

FISHER, Gene Louis
                    (Gene Lancour)
                    (Jeanne Lancour)

FISHER, Lois I.
    Sweet Dreams: <YA>
    30   Little White Lies
    54   I Can't Forget You

FITZGERALD, Amber   <RE>
                    [Nancy T. Smith]
    Starlight Romance:
    Reluctant Lover
    Suspicious Heart, The

FITZGERALD, Arlene J.   <GOT><RS>
    Blackthorn
    Devil's Gate, The
    Double Duty Nurse
    House Of Tragedy
    Northwest Nurse
    Numbers For Lovers
    Pamela's Palace

FITZGERALD, Catherine
         [Mary Sandra Hingston]
The Avon Romance:
   Passion Song
   (Last Book in Tudor Series-
         see Mallory Burgess)

FITZGERALD, Ellen   <RE>
         [Florence Stevenson]
         (see A Regency Christmas)
An Unwelcomed Alliance
Dangerous Dr. Langhorne, The
Forgotten Marriage, The
Gambler's Bride, The
Heirs Of Bellair, The
Irish Heiress, The
Julia's Portion
Lessons In Love
Lord Caliban
Marriage By Decree
Novel Alliance, A
Player Knight, The
Rogue's Bride
Romany Summer
Streak Of Luck, A
Venetian Masquerade

FITZGERALD, Julia   <HR>
                      (Deceased)
                   [Julia Watson]
Beyond Ecstasy
Desert Queen
Devil In My Arms
Fallen Woman   <ENG>
Firebird
Jeweled Serpent, The
Princess And The Pagan, The
Salamanda
Scarlet Woman
Silken Captive
Taboo
Venus Rising

FITZGERALD, Julia (cont.)
   Astromance Series:
      Castle Of The Enchantress
      Daughter Of The Gods
      Flame Of The East
      Kiss For Aphrodite, A
      Pasodoble
      Jade Moon
      Glade Of Jewels
      Temple Of Butterflies
      Devil In My Arms
   In sequence:
      Royal Slave
      Slave Lady
   Habsburg Series: <ENG>
      Changeling Queen
      Emperor's Daughter
      Habsburg Inheritance
      Pearl Of Habsburg
      Snow Queen

FITZGERALD, Maeve
                   [Maura Seger]
   Once And Forever   <ENG>

FITZGERALD, Nancy   <HR><RS>
   Grover Square
   Mayfair
   St. John's Wood
   Coventry:
      73   Chelsea

FITZGERALD, Rosemary
   This Splendid Peril

FITZGERALD, Sara
   Silhouette Desire:
      166 Affairs Of State

FITZGERALD, Valerie
Zemindar   <HS>

_____

_____

FITZPATRICK, Janie/Janine
                        [James Fritzhand]
Dreamwalker, The
Serena

_____

_____

FLADLAND, Kathryn
                        (Kathryn Farland)

FLANAGAN, Mary
Trust

_____

_____

FLANAGAN, Thomas   <HO>
Tenants Of Time, The
Year Of The French, The

_____

_____

FLANDERS, Rebecca
                        [Donna Ball]
                (see Felicia Gallant)
Obsessions   <CO>
Harlequin American Romance:
    Afterglow <PROM>
    Twice In A Lifetime <PROM>
    6 Matter Of Trust, A
   24 Best Of Friends
   41 Suddenly Love
   51 Gilded Heart
   58 Second Sight
   66 Desert Fire
   74 Third Time, The
   83 Daydreams
   89 Sometimes It's Forever
  100 Open Hands
  105 Rainbows And Unicorns
  118 Uncertain Images
  128 Last Frontier, The
  141 Straight Game, The

FLANDERS, Rebecca (cont.)
  155 Minor Miracles
  167 After The Storm
  183 Painted Sunsets
  257 Search The Heavens   <YTS>
  357 Sensation, The   <COAR>
Harlequin Dreamscape Romance:
  Earthbound
Harlequin Intrigue:
    1 Key, The
    8 Silver Threads
   13 Easy Access
Harlequin Presents:
  632 Morning Song
  666 Falkone's Promise
Harlequin SuperRomance:
  180 Growing Season, The
Harlequin Romance:
 2623 Modern Girl, A

_____

_____

FLASSCHOEN, Marie
Velvet Glove: <RS>
   12 Fires At Midnight

_____

_____

FLASSCHOEN, Marie w/ Marian
  SCHEIRMAN   (Lucinda Day)

FLEETWOOD, Frances
Concordia
Concordia Errant

_____

_____

FLEISCHER, Leonore
Ice Castles
Lipstick
Making Love
Running
Rose, The

_____

_____

FLEMING, Caroline
    (see Anne Mather)

FLEMING, Danielle
    [Nancy Morse]
Satin Swan Romance:
 Prince's Passion

FLEMING, Jane   <GOT>
    [Steve Smith]
Hawthorn Wood

FLEMING, Kate w/ Nancy MORGAN
    (Jenny McGuire)

FLEMING, Lee
    (Ginny Haymond)

FLEMING, Thomas   <HR>
    [Thomas James Fleming]
Dreams Of Glory
Good Sheperd, The
Liberty Tavern
Lovers In Exile
Officer's Wives, The   <CO>
Passionate Girl, A
Promises To Keep
Rulers Of The City
Sandbox Tree
Spoils Of War, The   <HS>
Time And Tide

FLEMING, Victoria
With Eyes Of Love   <CO>

FLETCHER, Aaron   <HO><HR>
   (see Farris Fletcher)
   (see Lee Davis Willoughby <MOAS>)
Card Game, The

FLETCHER, Aaron (cont.)
Cowboy
Dangerous Desire
Flame Of Chandrapore, The
Frontier Fires
Labyrinth
Love's Gentle Agony
Mountain Breed, The <MOAS:#2>
Treasure Of The Lost City
In sequence:
 Outback
 Outback II
New Zealanders Series:
 In sequence:
  Castaway, The
  Founders, The

FLETCHER, Donna
   [Donna Fletcher Crow]
Heartfire Romance:
 San Francisco Surrender

FLETCHER, Dorothy <GOT><RS>
   (Miriam Canfield)
Always, My Love   <CO>
Beyond Recall
Brand Inheritance, The
Caresses
Farewell To Vienna
Horizons
House Of Hate
Late Contessa, The
Meeting In Madrid
Music Master, The
New Yorker Nurse
Shadow And Sunlight
Shadow Over Long Island
Shadows On The Water
Still Waters
Whispers

FLETCHER, Farris   <HO>
  (publishers pseudonym for
        writers in this series)
  The Texans:
    1 Rawhide Country
              [Aaron Fletcher]
    2 Remember The Alamo
              [Chet Cunningham]
    3 Yellow Rose
              [H. Edwards Hunsburger]
    4 Lone Star Legacy
              [Aaron Fletcher]

_____

_____

FLETCHER, Inglis   <HO>
  Cormorant's Brood
  Queen's Gift
  Red Jasmine
  Rogue's Harbor
  Scotswoman, The
  White Leopard
  Wicked Lady
  Wind In The Forest, The
  The Albemarle/Carolina Series:
    In sequence:
      Roanoke Hundred
      Bennetts Welcome
      Men Of Albemarle
      Lusty Winds For Carolina
      Raleigh's Eden
      Toil Of The Brave

_____

_____

FLETCHER, Margaret
  Circle Of Love:
    20 Tempestuous Affair, The

_____

_____

FLETCHER, Mary
              [Mary Mann Fletcher]
  Devil's Instrument, The
  Doctor Is A Lady, The

_____

_____

FLETCHER, Mary Mann   <GOT><RS>
                     (Mary Fletcher)
  Danger-Nurse At Work
  Devil's Dress, The
  House Called Whispering
        Winds, The
  Scorpion Of Chateau Laverria, The
  Candlelight:
    53 Nurse Julie

_____

_____

FLETCHER, Susan
  Crosswinds: <YA>
    19 Haunting Possibility, The

_____

_____

FLETCHER, Violet
  MacFadden Romance:
    26 Dare To Love
    115 Island Tempest

_____

_____

FLEURY, Jacqueline   <RE>
              [Pauline A. Kjellberg]
  Cinderella Bride, The

_____

_____

FLINDT, Dawn
              [Vella Munn]
  Silhouette Special Edition:
    448 Power Within, The
    617 Prairie Cry

_____

_____

FLIXTON, Katharine   <RE>
  Glengarrick's Heir
  Lytton Abby

_____

_____

FLOOD, Charles Bracelen   <RS>
   Distant Drum
   Love Is A Bridge
   Monmouth
   Tell Me, Stranger

FLOREN, Lee
                (Grace Lang)
            (Marguerite Nelson)

FLORES, Frances
   [Frances de Talavera Berger]
   Candlelight Ecstasy:
    15 Desperate Longings
    61 Love's Wine

FLORES, Janis
                (Risa Kirk)
   Above Reproach
   Bittersweet
   Cynara
   Divided Loyalties
   Hawkshead
   High Dominion   <CO>
   Loving Ties   <CO>
   Running In Place
   Candlelight:
    510 Peregrine House <IN>

FLOREY, Kitty Burns
   Duet

FLOURNOY, Sheryl
   [Sheryl Diane Hines Flournoy]
              (Sherry Dee)
   Reckless Desire
   Silhouette Desire:
    371 Jason's Touch

FLOURNOY, Sheryl (cont.)
   Tapestry: <HR>
       Flames Of Passion
    33 Destiny's Embrace

FLOURNOY, Valerie
   Starlight Romance:
    Until Summer End's

FLYNN, Charlotte
   Moonstone Novels: <RS><YA>
    3 Dangerous Beat

FLYNN, Christine
   Silhouette Desire:
    254 When Snow Meets Fire
    296 Myth And The Magic, The
    352 Place To Belong, A
    377 Meet Me At Midnight
   Silhouette Romance:
    435 Stolen Promise
    623 Courtney's Conspiracy
   Silhouette Special Edition:
    254 Remember The Dream
    465 Silence The Shadows
    566 Renegade
    612 Walk Upon The Wind
    657 Out Of The Mist

FLYNN, Rose
   Avalon:
    Quicksilver Love

FLYNN, Veronica
           [Jacqueline Lyons]
   Candlelight Ecstasy:
    421 Race The Wind

FLYNN, Veronica (cont.)
MacFadden Romance:
141 Between Two Loves
195 Impossible Love
251 Spun Of Gold
260 Never A Stranger

FOGELIN, Marla B.   <CO>
Vow, The
Who Do You Love

FOLEY, June
Young Love: <YA>
Love By Any Other Name

FOLEY, Rae   <GOT><RS>
[Elinore Denniston]
An Ape In Velvet
Back Door To Death
Barclay Place, The
Brownstone House, The
Calculated Risk, A
Call It Accident
Curtain Call
Dangerous To Me
Dark Hill, The
Dark Intent
Death Do Us Part
Fatal Lady
Fear Of A Stranger
First Mrs. Winston, The
Girl From Nowhere, The
Girl Who Had Everything, The
Hundredth Door, The
Last Gamble, The
Malice Domestic
Man In The Shadow, The
Nightmare Honeymoon
Nightmare House
No Hiding Place
No Tears For The Dead

FOLEY, Rae (cont.)
Ominous Star
Other Woman, The
Peacock Is A Bird Of Prey, The
Put Out The Light
Reckless Lady
Repent At Leisure
Run For Your Life
Scared To Death
Shelton Conspiracy, The
Sleep Without Morning
Slippery Step, The
Suffer A Witch
This Woman Wanted
Trust A Woman
Velvet Web, The
Wake The Sleeping Wolf
Where Helen Lies
Where Is Mary Bostwick?
Wild Night

FONTAINE, Rebecca
Vintage Years, The

FOOTE, Victoria
Tapestry: <HR>
21 Snow Princess

FORBES, Cabot L.
The Bradford Saga: <HS>
In sequence:
No. 14 Washington Place
Two West 57th Street
Seven Fifty Park Avenue

FORBES, Deloris
(Stanton Forbes)

FORBES, Elaine
MacFadden Romance:
  29 Silver Lining
  31 Golden Dreams
  34 Promise Of Spring
  41 Call Of The Jaguar
  43 Voice Of The Jungle
  49 Kiss Of Summer, The
  54 Where My Heart Soars
  64 Before The Dawn
 111 Down River

FORBES, Stanton   <GOT><RS>
                  [Deloris Forbes]
Go To Thy Deathbed
If Two Of Them Are Dead
Melody Of Terror
Some Poisoned By Their Wives
Terror Touches Me
Welcome, My Dear, To Belfrey
  House

FORD, Daniel
Now Comes Theodora

FORD, Elaine
Missed Connections

FORD, Elizabeth   <GOT>
[Marjory Elizabeth Sarah Bidwell]
Dangerous Holiday

FORD, Hilary   <RS>
                  [Samuel Youd]
Bride For Bedivere, A
Castle Malindine
Sarnia

FORD, Jessie
        [Jessie Huggins Osborne]
Different Breed, A
Burning Woman, The   <HR>
Love, Remember Me   <Saga>
Love & Life Romance:
  Searching

FORD, Lila
Second Chance At Love:
  21 Mayan Enchantment

FORD, Marcia
Linda's Champion Cocker
Avalon:
  Sycamores, The

FORD, Mary Forker
Along Came A Stranger
Shadow Of Danger
Shadow Of Murder
Terror In Technicolor
Avalon:
  Roswell Heritage
Candlelight:
  165 Harvest Of Years

FORD, Norrey
                  [Noreen Dilcock]
Harlequin Romance:
  1115 Romantic Heart, The
  1139 House Of My Enemy, The
  1172 Let Love Abide
  1248 Where Love Is
  1818 One Hot Summer
  1842 Call To The Castle
  1983 Love Goddess, The
  2117 Fountain Of Love, The

FORD, Rachel
Harlequin Presents:
1160 Shadowed Love, A
1304 Love's Fugitive
1337 Web Of Desire
Harlequin Romance:
2913 Clouded Paradise
      Bring Back Yesterday HRS21
      Heirs To Loving   HRS38
      Beloved Witch   HRS69

FOREST, Regan
Harlequin Dreamscape Romance:
  Moonspell
Harlequin Intrigue:
   24 One Step Ahead
   48 Heart Of The Wolf
   84 Walking Shadow, A
  117 Secrets Of Tyrone
Harlequin Temptation:
   80 Answering Tide, The
   95 Star-Crossed
  123 Desert Rain
  152 Wherever Love Leads
  176 Wanted Man, A
  216 When Tomorrow Comes
  226 Heaven Sent
  311 Hidden Messages

FORREST, Chelsey
                    [Jan Cunningham]
Silhouette Romance:
  272 An Artist's Touch

FORREST, Pamela K.
  Heartfire Romance: <HR>
    Autumn Ecstasy

FORREST, Wilma   <GOT><RS>
  Anne Of Destiny House
  Last Hope House
  Shadow Mansion

FORRESTER, Marian   <HR>
  Farewell To Thee

FORSTER, Logan   <HR>
  Anger In The Wind

FORSTER, Rebecca
                   [Rebecca Czuleger]
  Delicate Matter, A

FORSTER, Suzanne
  Loveswept:
    314 Wild Honey
    384 Wild Child
    414 Devil and Ms. Moody, The
         Lord Of Lightning
  Silhouette Desire:
    215 Undercover Agent
    273 Hot Properties
    327 Man At Ivy Bridge, The
    446 Island Heat
  Silhouette Romance:
    519 Mr. Lonelyhearts
    627 Passions Of Kate
         Madigan, The

FORSYTH, Travis
  Sweet Seduction   <ED>

FORSYTHE, Melissa
Harlequin Romance:
2750 Perfect Choice, The
3035 Queen Of Hearts

FORVE, Guy
[Guy Cimbalo]
Alexander MacKenzie -
Lone Courage   <AES:#12>

FOSTER, Iris   <GOT>
Crimson Moon, The
Deadly Sea, Deadly Sand
Moorwood Legacy, The
Nightshade
Sabbath Quest, The

FOSTER, Jeanne
[Jeanne Williams]
Missouri Flame -
Deborah Leigh   <FWS:#2>
Wyoming Glory -
Eden Richards   <FWS:#4>

FOSTER, John T.   <HO>
Savannah   <CofCWS>
Vicksburg   <CofCWS>

FOSTER, Pauline w/ Lawrence FOSTER
(Jessica Logan)

FOSTER, Stephanie
Sweet Dreams: <YA>
58 Rhythm Of Love
66 Love Times Two
75 First Summer Love
Sweet Dreams Special: <YA>
6 Chance To Love, A

FOWLER, Peggy w/ Dennis FOWLER
(Lauren Fox)

FOWLES, John
[J. R. Fowles]
Aristos, The
Collector, The
Daniel Martin
Ebony Tower, The
French Lieutenant's Woman, The
Islands
Magus, The
Shipwreck
Tree, The

FOWLKES, Mary
Harlequin Romance:
2677 To Tame A Proud Lady

FOX, Alicia
[Carol Clemens-Fox]
Harlequin Temptation:
151 Legal Tender

FOX, Caroline
Sea Spell

FOX, Gardner   <HR>
[Gardner Francis Fox]
(Lynna Cooper)
Savage Passage

FOX, Lauren
[Penny Fowler w/ Dennis Fowler]
Second Chance At Love:
177 Sparring Partners
197 Country Pleasures

FOX, Lauren (cont.)
  248 Clash Of Wills, A
  266 Passion's Dance
  282 Storm And Starlight

FOX, Mary Virginia
  First Love From Silhouette: <YA>
  234 Treasure Of The Hills

FOX, Susan
  Harlequin Romance:
  2763 Vows Of The Heart
  2930 Black Sheep, The
  2983 Not Part Of The Bargain

FOXALL, Raymond
  Brandy For The Parson
  Dark Forest, The
  Little Ferret, The
  Silver Goblet, The
  Highwayman: In sequence:
    Society Of The Dispossessed
    Amorous Rogue, The
    Noble Pirate, The

FOXE, Jason
  Hampton Classic, The

FOXE, Pamela
                [Stuart Buchan]
  Silhouette Special Edition:
  216 Your Cheating Heart

FOXX, Rosalind
  [June Haydon w/ Judith Simpson]
  Flame Against The Wind
  Surrender By Moonlight
  Winds Of Fury, Winds Of Fire
  Coventry:
  194 Reluctant Ward

FRANCIS, Clare
          (Clare Frances Holmes)
              (Francis Holmes)
  Night Sky
  Wolf Winter   <RS>

FRANCIS, Dorothy
      [Dorothy Brenner Francis]
          (Ellen Goforth)
             (Pat Louis)
  Avalon:
  Blue Ribbon For Marni, A
  Keys To Love
  Legacy Of Merton Manor, The
  Nurse At Playland Park
  Nurse At Spirit Lake
  Nurse In The caribbean
  Nurse Of The Keys
  Nurse On Assignment
  Nurse Under Fire
  Studio Affair
  Crosswinds Keepsakes: <YA>
    1 Right Kind Of Girl, The
    7 Vonnie And Monique
  16 Special Girl (reprint)
  First Love From Silhouette: <YA>
    1 New Boy In Town
    8 Special Girl
  20 Say Please!
  27 Secret Place, A
  41 Just Friends
  82 Kiss Me, Kit
  120 Magic Circle, The
  135 Bid For Romance
  171 Write On!
  185 Stop, Thief!
  213 Follow Your Heart

FRANCIS, Emily
Harlequin Romance:
2757 Aegean Enchantment

FRANCIS, Marina
Harlequin Romance:
2887 Love's Perjury

FRANCIS, Robin
        [Rose Marie Ferris]
Harlequin American Romance:
 38 Memories Of Love
 88 Season Of Dreams, A
253 Taking A Chance
295 Shocking Ms. Pilgrim, The
301 Charmed Circle   <GCT>
Harlequin Intrigue:
A Spaulding And Darien Mystery:
147 Button, Button
159 Double Dare

FRANCIS, Sara
Harlequin Romance:
2624 Kate's Way
2673 California Dreaming

FRANCIS, Sharon
        [Maureen Crane Wartski]
Second Chance At Love:
 42 Garden Of Silvery Delights
161 Earthly Splendor
212 Silken Longing
228 Vintage Moment
Silhouette Romance:
769 Winter Heat

FRANCO, Marjorie
Love In A Different Key   <YA>

FRANK, Ethel w/ Michael DYNE
                (Evelyn Hanna)
FRANK, Jr., Harriet   <CO>
Special Effects

FRANK, Kate
MacFadden Romance:
147 Winter Palace
154 Dare Tomorrow
167 Mediterranean Blue
170 Cinnabar Sky
226 Price Of Love, The

FRANKEL, Emily
Splintered Heart, The

FRANKEL, Ruby
                (Rebecca Bennett)
                (Constance Conrad)
                (Lillian Marsh)

FRANKLIN, Edwina
                [Arlene Marks]
Harlequin Intrigue:
148 No Pain, No Gaine

FRANKLIN, Janet
Silhouette Desire:
585 Free To Dream
Silhouette Romance:
691 Makeshift Marriage
Silhouette Special Edition:
491 Right Mistake, The

FRANKLIN, Madeleine L'Engle
(Madeleine L'Engle)

FRANTZ, Carol
If Not For Love

FRASER, Alison
Harlequin Presents:
697 Princess
721 Price Of Freedom, The
745 Coming Home
865 Man Worth Knowing, A
1135 Lifetime And Beyond, A

FRASER, Anthea   <GOT>
(Vanessa Graham)
Breath Of Brimstone
Home Through The Dark
Island Of Waiting
Laura Possessed
Whistlers Lane

FRASER, Antonio   <HO>
Cromwell
King James Sixth And First
Love Letters: An Anthology
Mary Queen Of Scots
Wild Island, The

FRASER, Christine Marion
Rhanna At War   <HR>

FRASER, Jane
[Rosamunde Pilcher]
Bridge Of Corvie
Dear Tom
Harlequin Classic:
135 Young Bar   (958)

FRASER, Jane (cont.)
Harlequin Romance:
814 Long Way From Home, A
848 Keeper's House, The
958 Young Bar
1232 Day Like Spring, A

FRASER, Kathleen   <HR>
[Margaret Ball]
Highland Flame
Love's Redemption
Love's Tender Promise
My Brazen Heart
Passage To Paradise

FRASER, Sylvia   <HO>
Emperor's Virgin, The

FRAZER, Diane
An American Nurse In London
An American Nurse In Paris
An American Nurse In Vienna
Confidential Nurse
Date With Danger
Dilemma Of Geraldine Addams, The
First Year Nurse
I, Theresa, Registered Nurse
Nurse And The
Spying Stranger, The
Nurse Lily And Mr. X
Nurse Turner Runs Away
Nurse With A Past
Special Case For Peggy Bruce, A
Starring Syzanne Carteret, R.N.

FRAZIER, Pamela   <RE>
[Florence Stevenson]
Benevolent Bride, The
Daring Deception, A
Delicate Dilemma, A

FRAZIER, Pamela (cont.)
Gallant Governess, The
Virtuous Mistress, The
Willful Widow, The

_____

_____

FREDA, Dorothy M.
Love The Second Time Around

_____

_____

FREDE, Richard
Coming Out Party
Interns, The
Pilots, The

_____

_____

FREDERICK, Kate   <GOT>
Black Wind Of Penrose Island, The
Midnight Heiress
Periwinkle Brooch, The

_____

_____

FREDERICK, Thea
                [Barbara Keiler]
Second Chance At Love:
204 Beloved Adversary

_____

_____

FREDERICKS, Harriet   <GOT>
Dream Hunter, The

_____

_____

FREDMAN, John
Wolf Of Masada, The   <HS>

_____

_____

FREED, Lynn
Heart Change   <CO>

_____

_____

FREED, Mary Kay
                (Mary Kay Simmons)

FREEDMAN, Benedict w/ Nancy
FREEDMAN   <YA>
Mrs. Mike

_____

_____

FREEDMAN, Nancy
Immortals, The   <Saga>

_____

_____

FREEMAN, Cynthia   (Deceased)
                  [Bea Feinberg]
Always And Forever
Catch The Gentle Dawn
Come Pour The Wine
Days Of Winter, The
Fairytales
Illusions Of Love   <CO>
Last Princess, The
No Time For Tears
Portraits
Seasons Of The Heart
World Full Of Strangers, A <Saga>

_____

_____

FREEMAN, Joy   <RE>
Last Frost Affair, The
Suitable Match, A

_____

_____

FREETHY, Barbara
                (Kristina Logan)

FREMANTLE, Anne
                (Lady Caroline Lamb)

FRENCH, Ashley
                (see Denise Robins)

FRENCH, Janine
[Roni Finklestein w/
Antonio Van-Loon]
Starlight Romance:
Candidate For Love
Rhapsody
Waldingfield

_____

_____

FRENCH, Judith E.
The Avon Romance: <HR>
Bold Surrender
By Love Alone
Lovestorm
Scarlet Ribbons
Starfire
Tender Fortune
Windsong
Indian Moon Trilogy:
Moon Feather

_____

FRENCH, Michael   <CO>
Abingdon's
Rhythms

_____

FREY, Ruby Frazier
Red Morning

_____

FREYTAG, Josephine   <HO>
Amber Palace

_____

FRIEDLANDER, Beverly
So Gentle, So Fierce

_____

_____

FRIENDS, Jalynn   <HR>
[Rosalyn Alsobrook w/Jean Haught]
Texas Rapture

_____

_____

FRITCH, Elizabeth   <HR>
Sweet Silver Moon
Tides Of Rapture
Wild, Sweet Madness
Civil War Saga: In sequence:
Richmond: The Flame
Richmond: The Fire
Richmond: The Embers
Richmond: The Sparks
Richmond: The Blaze
California Trilogy:
Passion's Trail
Golden Fires
Heart Divided, A

_____

_____

FRITZGERALD, Nancy
Grover Square
Mayfair

_____

_____

FROHMAN, Elsa
(Eleanor Frost)

FRONTIER WOMEN SAGA <FWS>   <HO>
1 Kentucky Spitfire -
Caitlyn McGregor
Kitt Brown
2 Missouri Flame -
Deborah Leigh
Jeanne Foster
3 Texas Wildflower -
Laurian Kane
Kitt Brown

FRONTIER WOMEN SAGA (cont.)
    4 Wyoming Glory -
        Eden Richards
                        Jeanne Foster
    5 Alyssa Deane
                        Kitt Brown

FROST, Eleanor
                    [Elsa Frohman]
    Rapture Romance:
    53 Elusive Paradise
    68 Public Affair, A

FRUCHEY, Deborah   <RE>
            [Deborah Lynn Fruchey]
    Unwilling Heiress, The

FRY, Barbara
    Case For Gretchen, The
    Queen Betsy

FUCHS, Lucy   <GOT>
    Avalon:
        Dangerous Splendor
        Pictures Of Fear
        Shadow Of The Walls
        Wild Winds Of Mayaland

FULFORD, Paula
    Silhouette Desire:
    54 If Ever You Need Me
    Silhouette Romance:
    20 Island Destiny

FULLBROOK, Gladys
                [Patricia Hutchinson]
    Harlequin Romance:
    771   Nurse Prue In Ceylon
    899   Magic Moment, The
    1018 Hospital In The Tropics
    1082 Army Nurse In Cyprus
    1321 Thread Of Gold
    1346 House Called Kangaroo, A
    1412 Journey Of Enchantment
    Other:
        Apple Island   <M&B>

FULLER, Kathleen
            [Theodore Mark Gottfried]
    Riverview Series/Stockwell Saga:
        In sequence:
            Bitter Legacy
            Lion's Share, The
            Pride Of Place
            Fortune's Heirs

FURSTENBERG-FORBES, Lyn
    The Hanover Saga: In sequence:
        Hanover Heritage
        Spoils Of Hanover, The

FYFE, Sheila
    Avalon:
        Appointment With Love

FYODOROVA, Victoria w/
                    Haskel FRANKEL
    Admiral's Daughter, The

GAAN, Margaret
  Trilogy: In sequence:
    Red Barbarian
    White Poppy

GABHART, Ann/Ann H.   <HR>
  Forbidden Yearning, A
  Heart Divided, A
  Only In Sunshine
  Crosswinds: <YA>
    8 Gifting, The
   13 Kindred Spirit, A
  First Love From Silhouette: <YA>
   161 Chance Hero, A
   217 Look Of Eagles, The

GABRIEL, Ann   <HR>
  South Texas

GABRIEL, Mary
  Harlequin Romance:
   2703 Never Kiss A Stranger

GABRIEL, Tonya
  Emerald Sea

GADDIS, Margaret P.   <GOT>
  No Fire Can Warm Me

GADDIS, Peggy
                      [Peggy Dern]
  April Heart
  Beloved Intruder
  Betsy Moran, RN
  Big City Nurse
  Caribbean Melody
  Carolina Love Song
  Challenges For Nurse Genie
  Changing Heart, The
  Clinic Nurse
  Come Into My Heart
  Doctor Merry's Husband
  Doctor Sara
  Emergency Nurse
  Enchanted Spring
  Everglades Nurse
  Frost In April
  Girl Next Door, The
  Grass Roots Nurse
  Guest In Paradise, A
  Heiress Nurse
  Hill-Top Nurse
  Homesick Heart, The
  House Of Sinners
  Intruders In Eden
  Joyous Hills, The
  Lady Doctor
  Listening Heart, The
  Little Love, A
  Leota Foreman, R. N.
  Love At Second Sight
  Love Is Enough
  Love's Bitter Memories
  Love's Tropical Paradise
  Loving You Always
  Lulie
  Luxury Nurse
  Miss Doc
  Moonlight Meeting, A
  Mountain Melody
  Mountain Nurse
  No Price On Love
  Nora Was A Nurse
  Nurse And The Pirate, The
  Nurse And The Star, The
  Nurse Angela
  Nurse At Spanish Cay

GADDIS, Peggy (cont.)
Nurse At Sundown
Nurse At The Cedars
Nurse Called Happy, A
Nurse Christine
Nurse For Apple Valley, A
Nurse Hilary, Research
  Nurse   w/ Florence STUART
Nurse In Flight
Nurse's Choice
Persistent Suitor, The
Reaching Our For Love
Rehearsal For A Wedding
Return To Love
River's Edge
Second Chance At Love
Secret Honeymoon
Shadows On The Moon
Strange Shadows Of Love
Student Nurse
Three Faces Of Love
To Be Safe In His Arms
Two Games Of Love
Wedding Song
Where Love Is
Harlequin Classic:
  178 City Nurse   (405)
        Doctor Sara   (544)
Sharon Romance:
  Desired Damnations

GADSDEN, Angela
Dawnstar Romance:
  Cinderella Charade

GAEDDERT, LouAnn
Ever After
Perfect Strangers
Promise Romance: <Insp>
  26 Tuesday's Child

GAFFNEY, Patricia   <HR>
Fortune's Lady
Sweet Treason
Thief Of Hearts

GAGE, Elizabeth
MacFadden Romance:
  20 Broken Pride
  56 Strange Emotion

GAGE, Elsie   <RE>
Your Obedient Servant
Cotillion Regency:
  7 Regency Belles

GAILLARD, Robert
Marie, Island In Revolt
Marie, Mistress Of The Islands
Marie, The Captain's Mistress

GAINES, Diana
Dangerous Climate
Knife And The Needle, The
Mary In Anger
Nantucket Woman

GAINHAM, Sarah   <RS>
          [Rachel Ames]
Cold Dark Night
Hapsburg Twilight
Maculan's Daughter
Night Falls On The City
Place In The Country, A
Private Worlds
Takeover Bid
To The Opera Ball

GAIR, Diana
  Harlequin Romance:
    2519 Highlands Rapture
    2530 Jungle Antagonist

GALE, Adela   <GOT><RS>
                    [Adela Maritano]
  Angel Among Witches
  Goddess Of Terror
  Harvest Of Terror

GALE, Shannon
                    [Susan Aylworth]
  Silhouette Romance:
    702 Beneath Sierra Skies

GALIARDI, Spring
                    (Spring Hermann)

GALLAGHER, P. B.   <CO>
  Long Night, The

GALLAGHER, Patricia   <HR>
  All For Love
  Answer To Heaven
  Echoes And Embers
  Fires Of Brimstone, The
  Mystic Rose
  Perfect Love, A
  Shadows Of Passion
  Shannon
  Sons And The Daughters, The <CO>
  Summer Of Sighs
  Thicket, The
  In sequence:
    Castles In The Air
    No Greater Love
    On Wings Of Dreams

GALLAGHER, Rita   <HR>
  Passion Star
  In sequence:
    Shadows On The Wind
    Shadowed Destiny

GALLANT, Felicia w/Rebecca FLANDERS
           [Linda Dano w/ Donna Ball]
  Dreamweaver

GALLANT, Gladys   <RS>
  Living Image

GALLANT, Jennie   <RE>
                    [Joan Smith]
  Black Diamond, The
  Coventry:
    19 Lady Hathaway's
          House Party
    37 Moonless Night, The
    66 Minuet
    89 Olivia
    179 Friends And Lovers

GALLOWAY, Kara
  Harlequin Temptation:
    322 Sleight Of Heart

GALLOWAY, Laura
                    [Dorothy Ann Hillman]
  Heartfire Romance: <HR>
    Forbidden Delight

GALT, Serena
Silhouette Desire:
149 Double Game

GAMBINO, Richard
Bread And Roses <Saga>

GAMBLE, M. L.
[Marsha L. Nuccio]
Harlequin Intrigue:
110 Stranger Than Fiction
146 Diamond Of Deceit
153 When Murder Calls

GAMEL, Nona
Candlelight Ecstasy:
265 Love's Secret Garden
362 Tomorrow And Always

GANN, Ernest K. <HO>
[Ernest Kellogg Gann]
Antagonists
Band Of Brothers
Benjamin Lawless
Blaze Of Noon
Encounter, The
Fate Is The Hunter
Fiddler's Green
Gentlemen Of Adventure <Saga>
High And The Mighty
In The Company Of Eagles
Of Good And Evil
Soldiers Of Fortune
Song Of The Sirens
Trouble With Lazy Ethel
Twilight For The Gods
In sequence:
Masada
Triumph, The

GARAZIANI, Antoine
(see Pierre Sabbagh)

GARBO, Norman <CO>
Artist, The
To Love Again

GARCIA, Nancy
(Kate O'Donnell)

GARDNER, Donald <RS>
Flight Of The Bat

GARDNER, Joy
[Joy Aumente]
Tapestry: <HR>
Fortune's Bride

GARDNER, Maria
(Jillian Hunter)

GARDNER, Marjorie H.
Avalon:
Forbidden Reunion
Heart Song
Question Of Loving, A

GARDNER, Nancy/Nancy B.
[Nancy Bruff Gardner]
(Nancy Bruff)
Mist Maiden
Fig Tree

GARDNER, Toni <HR>
[Toni Brooks Gardner]
Rapture's Rainbow

244

GARFIELD, Leon
  Book Lovers
  Golden Shadow   w/ Edward BLISHEN
  Night Of The Comet, The
  Pleasure Garden, The
  Prisoners Of September, The
  Sound Of Coaches, The

GARLAND, Blanche
                          [Ruth Lesko]
  Starlight Romance:
    Castles In The Sky

GARLAND, Margaret
  Caprice Romance: <YA>
    4 Terri's Dream
    56 Winter Break
  Heavenly Romance: <YA>
    Just Between Us
    With All My Heart

GARLAND, Nicholas
  Buy Back The Dawn
  Crime Of Innocence, A   <CO>

GARLAND, Sherry   <YA>
                          [Lynn Lawrence]
  Where The Cherry Trees Bloom

GARLOCK, Dorothy   <HR>
  [Dorothy Johanna Phillips Garlock]
                    (Dorothy Glenn)
                    (Dorothy Phillips)
                    (Johanna Phillips)
  Annie Lash   &@
  Forever Victoria
  Glorious Dawn

GARLOCK, Dorothy (cont.)
  Love And Cherish
  Midnight Blue
  Nightrose
  Searching Hearts, The
  This Loving Land
  Wild, Sweet Wilderness   &
  Colorado Trilogy:
    Restless Wind
    Wayward Wind   @
    Wind Of Promise
  Wabash River Trilogy:
    Lonesome River
    Dream River
    River Of Tomorrow
  Loveswept:
    6 Love For All Time, A
    33 Planting Season, The

GARNAR, Pauline
  Harlequin Romance:
    1325 No Sooner Loved
    1444 Fond Deceiver

GARNER, Phyllia A. Whitney
                    (Phyllis A. Whitney)

GARRATT, Marie   <GOT><RS>
  Dangerous Enchantment
  Festival Of Darkness

GARRATT, Mary A.   <HO>
  Duchess Of Asherwood, The

GARRETT, George   <HO>
  Death Of The Fox
  Magic Striptease, The
  Succession, The

245

GARRETT, Sally
    [Sally Garrett Dingley]
SuperRomance:
  In sequence:
  90   Until Forever   &
Harlequin SuperRomance:
  Sequence continued:
  139   Mountain Skies
  173   Northern Fires
  201   Twin Bridges
  225   Until Now
  Rainbow Hills Series:
  243   Weaver Of Dreams
  275   Visions
  309   Promises To Keep
  344   Desert Star   &
  473   Wednesday's People

GARRETT, Sibylle
Silhouette Intimate Moments:
  184   September Rainbow   &
  211   Surrender To A Stranger
  271   Rebel's Return   &
  301   Sullivan's Challenge

GARRISON, Joan
    [William Arthur Neubauer]
Blue Herons
Castle On The Lake, The
Come Walk With Love
Dream Seeker, The
Illusion Of Love
Love's Sweet Confusion
Loving Heart, The
More Than A Woman Could Want
Questing Heart, The
Run, Heart, Run
Snatch A Dream
This Remembered Glory
Ticket To Romance
Treasured Dreams Of Love
Walks Of Dreams, The
When The Moon Laughs

GARRISON, Zoe
Golden Triple Time   <CO>

GARROD, Rene J.
Heartfire Romance: <HR>
  Colorado Caress
  Ecstasy's Bride
  Passion's Endless Tide
  Silken Caress
  Temptation's Wild Embrace
  Wild Conquest
The Avon Romance:
  Wild Rose, The

GARRY, Madeline
    [Madeline Davis]
Candlelight Ecstasy:
  483   Mysterious Stranger

GARTNER, Chloe   <HR>
Anne Bonny
Daughter Of The Desert
Highland Mistress (Mistress Of
  The Highlands)
Image And The Dream, The
Still Falls The Rain
Woman From The Glen, The

GARVEY, Kathleen
    [Judy Blundell]
First Love From Sihouette: <YA>
  170   Video Fever

GARVICE, Charles   (Deceased)
              (Caroline Hart)
            (Carolyn G. Hart)

GARWOOD, Julie   <HR>
Bride, The

246

GARWOOD, Julie (cont.)
Gift, The   @
Guardian Angel   @&
Honor's Splendour
Lion's Lady, The   &
Tapestry: <HR>
  74 Gentle Warrior
  89 Rebellious Desire
Wildfire: <YA>
  Girl Named Summer, A

GASKIN, Catherine   <RS>
  [Catherine Gaskin Cornberg]
Ambassador's Women, The   <Saga>
Blake's Reach
Charmed Circle, The
Corporation Wife
Edge Of Glass
Falcon For A Queen, A
Family Affairs
File On Devlin, The
Fiona
I Know My Love
Lynmara Legacy,The
Promises
Property Of A Gentleman, The
Sara Dane
Summer Of The Spanish Woman, The
Tilsit Inheritance, The
In sequence:
  From The Bitter Land
  Scattered Seed

GASPAROTTI, Elizabeth
    (Elizabeth Seifert)

GATES, Natalie   <GOT>
Decoy In Diamonds

GAUCH, Patricia Lee   <YA>
Green Of Me, The

GAULT, Cinda
Harlequin SuperRomance:
  296 Past Convictions

GAVER, Jessica
MacFadden Romance:
  126 Love Can Sing

GAVER, Jessyca Russell
Golden Dozen, The
How Deep The Cup
Round Trip To Nowhere
Shadow Of A Love

GAVIN, Catherine   <HO>
Black Milestone, The
Cactus And The Crown, The
Clyde Valley
Devil In Harbour
Fortress
Give Me The Daggers
House Of War, The
Hostile Shore, The
How Sleep The Brave
Madeleine
Moon Into Blood, The
Mountain Of Light, The
Snow Mountain, The
Sunset Dream, The
Traitor's Gate

GAY, Valerie   <GOT>
Spy At The Gate, A

GAYET, Caroline
Mystique:
  5 High Wind In Brittany
  11 Winter At Blackfont

GAYET, Caroline (cont.)
    15 By Love Forgotten
    18 Rendezvous In Tripoli
    30 Heart's Ransom
    37 Prisoner Of Lemnos
    77 To Stalk A Killer
    104 Dark Suspicion
    123 Mirror Of Darkness
    138 Passionate Stranger

_____

_____

GAYLE, Carol
    Summer To Decide, A

_____

GAYLE, Emma
    Masquerade:
    48 Cousin Caroline
    67 Frenchman's Harvest

_____

_____

GAYLE, Margaret
                    [Gail Hamilton]
    SuperRomance:
    52 Precious Interlude
    Harlequin SuperRomance:
    118 To Catch The Wind
    169 One In A Million

_____

_____

GAYLE, Pamela
    Vallamont

_____

_____

GAYLE, Susan
                    [Gayle Kasper]
    Harlequin Temptation:
    307 Temperature's Rising

_____

_____

GAYNOR, Anne   <HR>
    Fate's Passion
    Rebel Rapture

_____

_____

GAZDAK, D. H. w/ Karen RAY
                    (Ann Bernadette)

GEACH, Christine
                    (Anne Lowing)
                    (Christine Wilson)

GEE, Evelyn
                [D. Evelyn Hoyle Gee]
                (Constance O'Banyon)

GEE, Evelyn w/ Emma MERRITT
                    (Micah Leigh)

GELLES, Sandi
    Candlelight Ecstasy Supreme:
    44 Secrets And Desire

_____

GELLIS, Roberta   <HR>
    [Roberta Leah Jacobs Gellis]
                    (Priscilla Hamilton)
    Dragon And The Rose, The
    Masques Of Gold
    Rope Dancer, The
    Sing Witch, Sing Death
    Heiress Series: In sequence:
        English Heiress, The
        Cornish Heiress, The
        Kent Heiress, The
        Fortune's Bride
        Woman's Estate, A
    In sequence:
        Tapestry Of Dreams, A
        Fires Of Winter
    In sequence:
        Bond Of Blood
        Knight's Honor
        Sword And The Swan, The

248

GELLIS, Roberta (cont.)
  Roselynde Chronicles:
    In sequence:
      Roselynde
      Alinor
      Joanna
      Gilliane
      Rhiannon
      Sybelle
  Royal Dynasty Series:
    In sequence:
      Siren Song
      Winter Song
      Fire Song
      Silver Mirror, A

GELMAN, Jan
  Follow Your Heart Romance: <YA>
    1   Summer In The Sun
    5   Faraway Loves
    6   Take A Chance On Love
    8   Lots Of Boys
    10 Seven-Boy Vacation

GELSTHORPE, Annie L.
  Timber Town Nurse
  Avalon:
    Danger For Dr. Kerry
    Nurse Andrea Takes A Flier
    Wings For Nurse Karen
  Candlelight:
    42   Doctor Lesley's Triumph
    151 Secret Challenge, The

GENTRY, Georgina   <HR>
                      [Lynne Murphy]
  Panorama Of The Old West Series:
    In sequence:
      Heartfire Romance:
        Cheyenne Captive
        Cheyenne Princess

GENTRY, Georgina (cont.)
  Zebra Hologram:
    Comanche Cowboy
    Bandit's Embrace
    Nevada Nights
    Cheyenne Caress
    Quicksilver Passion

GENTRY, Jane
                      [Jane Malcolm]
  Silhouette Desire:
    400 Lightning Strikes Twice
    449 Taste Of Honey, A

GENTRY, Peter   <HR>
                    [Frank Schaefer w/
                       Kerry Newcomb]
  King Of The Golden Gate
  Matanza
  Rafe
  Titus Gamble

GEORGE, Catherine
  Harlequin Presents:
    640   Gilded Cage
    698   Imperfect Chaperone
    722   Devil Within
    800   Prodigal Sister
    858   Innocent Pawn
    873   Silent Crescendo
    992   Marriage Bed, The
    1016 Love Lies Sleeping
    1065 Touch Me In The Morning
    1152 Villain Of The Piece
    1148 True Paradise
    1225 Loveknot
    1255 Ever Since Eden
    1321 Come Back To Me
  Harlequin Romance:
    2535 Reluctant Paragon
    2571 Dream Of Midsummer
    2720 Desirable Property

GEORGE, Catherine (cont.)
2822 Folly Of Loving, The
2924 Man Of Iron
2942 This Time Round
3081 Consolation Prize

GEORGE, Mary
                    (Elizabeth Thornton)

GEORGE, Rebecca   <HR>
Call Home The Heart
Daphne
Wild Desire, A
Tapestry: <HR>
   82 Tender Longing

GERACHIS, Elly   <HR>
Evil Masquerade

GERARD, Jane
Jet Stewardess

GERBER, Merrill Joan   <YA>
I'm Kissing As Fast As I Can
Crosswinds: <YA>
   17 Even Pretty Girls Cry
       At Night

GERBER, Ruth
Candlelight:
   633 Marriagable Asset , A <RE>

GERGICH, Millie Grey
                    (Millie Grey)

GERMANY, Jo
                    (Josie King)
Bride For A Tiger
City Of Golden Cages
Cry Of The Rabble
Devil's Child

GERRITSEN, Tess
                    [Terry Gerritsen]
Adventure's Mistress
Masquerade For Love
Harlequin Intrigue:
   78 Call After Midnight
   136 Under The Knife

GERSON, Corrine   <CO>
Choices
Tread Softly

GERSON, Noel B.   <HO>
                    [Noel Bertram Gerson]
                    (Samuel Edwards)
                    (Paul Lewis)
                    (Dana Fuller Ross)
                    (Carter A. Vaughan)
All That Glitters
Anthem, The
Because I Loved Him: The Life
   And Loves Of Lillie Langtry
Clear For Action
Conqueror's Wife, The   <HofFS>
Cumberland Rifles, The   <HofFS>
Daughter Of Eve   <HofFS>
Emperor's Lady, The   <HofFS>
Forest Lord, The   <HofFS>
Golden Ghetto, The
Golden Lyre, The   <HofFS>
Highwayman, The   <HofFS>
I'll Storm Hell
Island In The Wind
Jefferson Square
Liner

GERSON, Noel B. (cont.)
  Mohawk Ladder, The   <HofFS>
  Neptune
  Savage Cavalier   <HofFS>
  Scimitar, The   <HofFS>
  Smugglers, The
  Special Agent
  Sunday Heroes, The
  That Egyptian Woman   <HofFS>
  Trojan, The
  Velvet Glove, The

_____

_____

GEUMLEK, Lois
  House In The Fog
  Avalon:
    Stranger In Town, A

_____

GIBBONS, Harry S.   <HO>
          [Harry Scott Gibbons]
  Tall Woman, The

_____

GIBBONS, Marion Chesney
                (Marion Chesney)
                (Helen Crampton)
                 (Ann Fairfax)
                (Jennie Tremaine)

GIBBS, Katherine   <HR>
  Travelin' Woman

_____

_____

GIBBS, Mary Ann   <HR><RE><RS>
  [Marjory Elizabeth Sarah Bidwell]
  Admiral's Lady, The
  Amateur Governess, The
  Apothecary's Daughter, The
  Glass Palace, The
  Guardian, The
  Horatia
  House Of Ravensbourne, The

GIBBS, Mary Ann (cont.)
  Jubilee For A Rough Diamond
  Lady In Berkshire, A
  Moon In A Bucket, The
  Most Romantic City, A
  Parcel Of Land, A
  Polly Kettle
  Romantic Frenchman, The
  Sea Urchins, The
  Sugar Mouse, The
  Tempestuous Petticoat, The
  Year Of The Pageant, The
  Young Lady Of Fashion, A
  Young Lady With Red Hair
  Coventry:
     2 Tulip Tree, The
    88 Dinah
   129 Renegade Girl
   198 Kitty

_____

GIBBS, Nora
                (Dallas Romaine)

GIBERSON, Dorothy
                (Penelope Field)

GIBESON, Jacqueline
                (Sabina Grant)
                (Jacqueline La Tourrette)

GIBSON, Hannah   <GOT>
  Maze Of Dark Desires

_____

_____

GIBSON, Madelaine   <RE>
          [Frances G. Duckett]
  Rake's Reward
  Vicious Viscount, The

_____

_____

GIBSON, Marsha   <HR>
  Passion's Treasure

_____

_____

GIBSON, Rosemary
Harlequin Romance:
    Adoring Slave   HRS70

_____

_____

GIDDINGS, Lauren   <RE>
        [Nancy Gideon]
Bartered Bride
Sweet Tempest

_____

_____

GIDEON, Nancy
        (Lauren Giddinss)
        (Dana Ransom)

GIDEON, Robin
        [K. D. Severson]
Heartfire Romance: <HR>
   Ecstasy's Princess
   Outlaw Ecstasy
   Passion's Tender Embrace
   Shadow Passion

_____

_____

GILBERT, Agnes Joan Sewell
        (Jill Baer)

GILBERT, Anna   <RS>
      [Marguerite Lazarus]
Family Likeness, A
Flowers For Lilian
Images Of Rose
Leavetaking, The
Look Of Innocence, The
Long Shadow, The
Miss Bede
Remembering Louise
Walk In The Wood, A

_____

_____

GILBERT, Brynn   <HR>
Love's Bold Embrace

_____

_____

GILBERT, Jacqueline
Harlequin Premiere Edition:
  10 Autumn In Bangkok
Harlequin Presents:
 160 Dear Villian   &
 600 House Called Bellevigne, A
 801 Capricorn Man
 929 Poppy Girl
1073 Sweet Pretence
Harlequin Romance:
2102 Every Wise Man   @&
2214 Country Cousin
2308 Scorpio Summer   @&
2492 Trodden Paths, The   &
2631 Chequered Silence, The

_____

_____

GILBERT, Kate
Second Chance At Love:
 391 Moonshine And Madness
 418 Cupid's Campaign

_____

_____

GILBERT, Nan
     [Mildred Greiger Gilbertson]
Knight Came Riding, A

_____

_____

GILBERT, Peggy
Avalon:
   Time To Dance, A

_____

_____

GILBERTSON, Mildred Greiger
        (Nan Gilbert)

GILCHRIST, Elizabeth
Second Chances   <CO>

_____

GILCRIST, Rupert
Dragonard Saga:
   Dragonard

GILCRIST, Rupert (cont.)
  Dragonard Blood
  Dragonard Rising
  Master Of Dragonard Hill, The
  Siege Of Dragonard Hill
  Guns Of Dragonard

GILES, Elizabeth   \<GOT>
  As Darker Grows The Night
  Children Of The Griffin

GILES, Janet Holt   \<HO>
  Damned Engineers
  Enduring Hills, The
  Forty Acres And No Mule
  Harbin's Ridge   w/Henry GILES
  Kinta Years, The
  Miss Willie
  Plum Thicket, The
  Shady Grove
  Six-Horse Hitch
  Tara's Healing
  Wellspring
  American Frontier Series:
    In sequence:
      Kentuckians, The
      Johnny Osage
      Savanna
      Run Me A River
      Believers, The
      Great Adventure, The
      Voyage To Santa Fe
      Land Beyond
        The Mountains, The
      Hannah Fowler

GILES, Katherine
  Share Of Earth And Glory, A

GILES, Raymond   \<HO>
  Dark Master
  Rogue Black
  Warm December, A
  Sabrehill Plantation Series:
    In sequence:
      Sabrehill
      Slaves Of Sabrehill
      Rebels Of Sabrehill
      Storm Over Sabrehill
      Hellcat Of Sabrehill

GILGE, Jeanette
  Serenade/Saga: \<HR>\<Insp>
   2 Call Her Blessed
  11 All The Days After Sunday

GILL, Ann
  Nurse On Call

GILL, Judy
  Other Side Of The Hill, The
  Doubleday Loveswept:
    Bad Billy Culver
  Loveswept:
  228 Head Over Heels
  270 Pockets Full Of Joy
  282 Renegade
  294 Hennessey's Heaven
  307 Light Another Candle
  335 Mermaid
  339 Scent Of Roses, A
  377 Golden Swan
  389 Stargazer
  406 Desperado
  424 Dream Man   &
  436 Moonlight Man   &

GILLEN, Cathy
    [Cathy Gillen Thacker]
Serenade Romance:
  Island Of Desire

GILLEN, Lucy
    (Rebecca Stratton)
Harlequin Premiere Edition:
  5 Storm Eagle, The
Harlequin Romance:
 1383 Wife For Andrew, A
 1408 Silver Fishes, The
 1425 Good Morning, Doctor
      Houston
 1450 Heir To Glen Ghyll
 1481 Nurse Helen
 1507 Marriage By Request
 1533 Girl At Smuggler's
      Rest, The
 1553 Doctor Toby
 1579 Winter At Cray
 1604 That Man Next Door
 1627 My Beautiful Heathen
 1649 Sweet Kate
 1669 Time Remembered, A
 1683 Dangerous Stranger
 1711 Summer Season
 1736 Enchanted Ring, The
 1754 Pretty Witch, The
 1782 Painted Wings
 1806 Pengelly Jade, The
 1822 Runaway Bride, The
 1847 Changing Years, The
 1861 Stairway To
      Enchantment, The
 1877 Means To An End
 1895 Glen Of Sighs
 1908 Touch Of Honey, A
 1928 Gentle Tyrant
 1930 Web Of Silver
 1958 All The Long Summer
 1979 Handful Of Stars, A
 1995 Hungry Tide, The
 2012 Return To Deepwater
 2026 House Of Kingdom, The
 2092 Master Of Ben Ross
 2134 Heron's Point

GILLEN, Lucy (cont.)
 2178 Back Of Beyond
 2319 Hepburn's Quay

GILLENWATER, Sharon   <HR>
  Heather Moon
  Highland Whispers
  Unwilling Heart

GILLESPIE, Jane
  Brightsea
  (sequel to "Sense & Sensibility"*)
  Ladysmead
    (sequel to "Mansfield Park"*)
  Teverton Hall
    (sequel to "Pride & Prejudice"*)
            * All by Jane Austen

GILLETTE, Louisa
    [Gilda Feldman w/ Leslie Rugg]
  Long Way Home, A
  Tapestry: <HR>
  53 Glorious Treasure
  76 River Of Rapture
  91 Pas de Deux

GILLMAN, Olga
  Harlequin Romance:
  857 Quiet Spot, The

GILMER, Ann
    [W. E. Daniel Ross]
  "Girl In Love"
  Glamour Girl
  Kate Wilder, R.N.
  Nurse Crane - Emergency

GILMER, Ann (cont.)
Nurse In The Tropics
Nurse On Call
Traveling With Sara
Avalon:
  Celebrity Nurse
  Love In The Sun
  Nurse At Breakwater Hotel
  Skyscraper Nurse
Candlelight:
  44 Surgeon's Nurse

GILMER, Donna
Eye Of The Wind

GILMORE, Cecile
Avalon:
  Hold Me Fast
  Lesser Love, The
  Web Of Honey
  Wedding Is Destiny
Candlelight:
  87 Never Another Love

GILMORE, Marjorie
Fast Tracks

GILMOUR, Ann
          [Ann Boyce McNaught]
Harlequin Romance:
  1121 Team Doctor

GILMOUR, Barbara
Harlequin Romance:
  1154 You Can't Stay Here

GILPIN, Joanna
          [Joanna McGauran]
Harlequin Temptation:
  163 First Mates
  239 Simple "I Do", A
  330 Chance It

GILZEAN, Elizabeth
[Elizabeth Houghton
          Blanchet Gilzean]
          (Elizabeth Houghton)
          (Mary Hunton)
Arctic Nurse   <M&B>
Harlequin Classic:
  29 Children's Hospital (571)
  63 Kate Of Outpatients (649)
  71 Doctor Mark Temple   (685)
Harlequin Romance:
  1001 No Place For Surgeons
  1026 Doctor In Corsica

GIMBEL, Joan
Judy Sullivan Book:
  Surrender Mountain

GINNES, Judith S.
          (Paige Mitchell)

GIRION, Barbara
Going Places: <YA>
  1 Prescription For Success
  2 Front Page Exclusive
  3 Portfolio To Fame:
       Cameron's Story
  4 Prime Time Attraction
Two Hearts Romance: <YA>
  In The Middle Of A Rainbow

GLENN, Elizabeth
              [Martha Gregory]
Harlequin American Romance:
  14 Dark Star Of Love
  36 Taste Of Love
Harlequin Temptation:
 124 Homing Instinct, The
 175 Where Memories Begin
 195 More Than Words
 224 First A Friend
 238 Gone Fishin'
SuperRomance:
  67 What Love Endures

GLENN, Victoria
              [Victoria Dann]
Silhouette Romance:
 321 Not Meant For Love
 362 Heart Of Glass
 386 Mermaid
 396 Matthews Affair, The
 455 Man By The Fire
 508 One Of The Family
 534 Winter Heart, The
 585 Moon In The Water
 628 Tender Tyrant, The
 652 Enchanted Summer, The
 718 Second Time Lucky

GLICK, Ruth
              (Amanda Lee)
Harlequin SuperRomance:
 382 Closer We Get, The

GLICK, Ruth w/ Eileen BUCKHOLTZ
              (Amanda Lee)
              (Rebecca York)

GLICK, Ruth w/ Eileen BUCKHOLTZ,
  Carolyn MALES & Louise TITCHENER
              (Alyssa Howard)

GLICK, Ruth w/ Louise TITCHENER
              (Alexis Hill)
           (Alexis Hill Jordan)
             (Tess Marlowe)

GLOVER, Judith
  Imagination Of The Heart, The

GLUYAS, Constance   <HR>(Deceased)
      [Constance Harris Gluyas]
  Born To Be King
  Brandy Kane   <CO>
  Bridge To Yesterday
  Brief Is The Glory
  Flame Of The South
  House On Twyford Street, The
  Lord Sin
  Madam Tudor
  My Lord Foxe
  Passionate Savage, The
  Vantable Hall
  Woman Of Fury
  In sequence:
    King's Brat, The
    My Lady Benbrook
  In sequence:
    Savage Eden
    Rogue's Mistress

GOBINEAU, Marceline
  Story Of Stephanie: In sequence:
    Passions Of Spring, The
    Snows Of Sebastopol, The
    Emperor's Agent, The
    All For My Love

GODDEN, Rumer
  Breath Of Air, A
  Peacock Spring, The

GODWIN, Elizabeth
Passion And The Rage, The

GOFF, Jacqueline
(Jenna Ryan)

GOFORTH, Ellen
[Dorothy Francis]
Silhouette Romance:
5   Path Of Desire
144 New Dawn, A

GOLD, Herbert
True Love   <CO>

GOLDEN AGE OF ROME SERIES <GARS>
Octavia: Prisoner Of Passion
                    Wilhelm Walloth
Nero: Butcher Of Rome
                    Ernst Eckstein
Pearl Maiden, The
                    H. Rider Haggard
Sejanus: Secret Ruler Of Rome
                    John W. Graham
Agrippina: Empress Of Depravity
                    Frederick W. Farrar

GOLDENBAUM, Sally
(see Adrienne Staff)
Loveswept:
206 Dream To Cling To, A
233 Baron, The
Silhouette Desire:
423 Honeymoon Hotel
460 Chantilly Lace
520 Once In Love With Jessie
557 Passionate Accountant, The
603 Fresh Start, A

GOLDENBAUM, Sally w/ Adrienne STAFF
(Natalie Stone)

GOLDIE, Patricia
Under Southern Stars   <Saga>

GOLDING, Morton J.
(Patricia Morton)

GOLDREICH, Gloria   <HO>
Mothers
This Burning Harvest
This Promised Land
West To Eden
In sequence: <HS>
Leah's Journey
Leah's Children

GOLDRICK, Emma
Harlequin Presents:
688   And Blow Your House Down
791   Miss Mary's Husband
825   Night Bells Blooming
841   Rent-A-Bride, Ltd.
866   Daughter Of The Sea
890   Over-Mountain Man, The
953   Hidden Treasures
1035 If Love Be Blind
1087 My Brother's Keeper
1208 Madeleine's Marriage
1281 Heart As Big As Texas, A
Harlequin Romance:
2661 Road, The   &
2739 Trouble With Bridges, The
2846 Tempered By Fire   &
2858 King Of The Hill
2889 Temporary Paragon
2943 To Tame A Tycoon
2967 Latimore Bride, The   &
2984 Pilgrim's Promise
3111 Girl He Left Behind, The

259

GOLON, SergeAnne   `<HR>`
  In sequence:
    Angelique
    Angelique And The King
    Angelique And The Sultan
    Angelique In Revolt
    Angelique In Love
    Countess Angelique, The
    Temptation Of Angelique, The
    Angelique And The Demon
    Angelique And The Ghosts

GOOD, Susanna   `<HR>`
  Burning Secrets

GOODING, Kathleen
  Belfriere

GOODMAN, Irene w/ Alex KAMAROFF
                 (Diana Morgan)

GOODMAN, Jo   `<HR>`
  Midnight Princess   &
  Passion's Sweet Revenge   &
  Scarlet Lies
  Violet Fire
  In sequence:
    Passion's Bride
    Velvet Night
  McClellan Family Trilogy:
    Crystal Passion
    Seaswept Abandon
    Tempting Torment

GOODMAN, Liza
  Harlequin Romance:
    Eagle's Revenge   HRS28

GOODMAN, Ruth
               (Megan McKinney)

GOODWIN, Hope
                 (Linda Lee)
  Avalon:
    Acts Of Love
    Storm Over Edgecliff
  Caprice Romance:
    78 Dream For Julie, A
  Starlight Romance:
    Shadows Over Paradise

GOODWIN, Suzanne
  Cousins
  Lovers

GORAN, Lester   `<HS>`
  Heritage Series:
    In sequence:
      This New Land
      Covenant With Tomorrow

GORDON, Angela
  Fate Of The Lovers
  Game Called Love, A
  Love Has Many Faces
  Love In Her Life
  Love Is A Tempest
  Love Of Damocles, The
  Not Too Soon For Love
  Not Without Love
  Stranger In The Shadows

GORDON, Barbara
  Defects Of The Heart   `<CO>`

GORDON, Deborah Brooke Hannes
                    (Brooke Hastings)

GORDON, Diana   <RS>
                    [Lucilla Andrews]
Few Days In Endel, A

_____

_____

GORDON, Ethel/Ethel E.
Freebody Heiress, The
French Husband, The
Candlelight:
  630 Chaperone, The   <RO>
  663 Freer's Cove   <RO>

_____

_____

GORDON, Jane   <RS>
                    [Elsie Lee]
Mistress Of Mount Fair
Season Of Evil

_____

_____

GORDON, Jeffie Ross
[Stephanie Gordon Tessler W/
            Judith Ross Enderle]
Crosswinds Keepsake: <YA>
  18 Nobody Knows Me
First Love From Silhouette: <YA>
  198 Touch Of Genius, A
  216 Journal Of Emily Rose, The
  221 Touch Of Magic, A
Sunfire Romance: <HR><YA>
       Jacquelyn
  26 Nora

_____

_____

GORDON, Katharine
Peacock Quartet:
  Emerald Peacock, The
  In The Shadow Of The Peacock
  Peacock Ring, The
  Peacock In Jeopardy

_____

_____

GORDON, Lucy
[Christine Sparks Fiorotto]
Silhouette Desire:
  164 Take All Myself
  179 Judgement Of Paris, The
  245 Coldhearted Man, A
  317 My Only Love, My Only Hate
  333 Fragile Beauty, A
  363 Just Good Friends
  380 Eagle's Prey
  416 For Love Alone
  493 Vengeance Is Mine   <MMS>
  544 Convicted Of Love
  627 Sicilian, The
Silhouette Romance:
  306 Carrister Pride, The
  353 Island Of Dreams
  390 Virtue And Vice
  420 Once Upon A Time
  503 Pearl Beyond Price, A
  524 Golden Boy
  596 Night Of Passion, A
  611 Woman Of Spirit, A
  639 True Marriage, A
  754 Song Of The Lorelei
Silhouette Special Edition:
  148 Legacy Of Fire
  185 Enchantment In Venice
  547 Bought Woman

_____

_____

GORDON, Martha Starr
                    (Martha Starr)

GORDON, Ruth
Shady Lady

_____

_____

GORDON, Susan   <RE>
                    [Susan G. Carboni]
Match Of The Season

_____

_____

GORDON, Victoria
Harlequin Presents:
  689 Blind Man's Buff
Harlequin Romance:
 2427 Sugar Dragon, The
 2433 Wolf At The Door
 2438 Everywhere Man, The
 2458 Dream House
 2469 Always The Boss
 2531 Dinner At Wyatt's
 2540 Battle Of Wills
 2690 Stag At Bay
 2714 Bushranger's Mountain
 2727 Cyclone Season
 2775 Age Of Consent
 2854 Forest Fever
 3025 Arafura Pirate
 3098 Love Thy Neighbour

GORDON, Yvonne
Moment Of Magic
Aston Hall:
  102 Escape To Ecstasy

GORING, Anne   <RS>
Morwenna

GORMAN, Beth
        [Lauran Bosworth Paine]
Lanterns Of The Night
Love Has A Double
Love Is A Stranger
Aston Hall:
  120 Gentle Lover

GORMAN, Susan
Sweet Dreams: <YA>
  145 This Time For Real
  155 Game Of Love, The

GORMLEY, Gerard
Doll, The

GORTON, Kaitlyn
        [Kathy Lynn Emerson]
Silhouette Intimate Moments:
  307 Cloud Castles

GOTTFRIED, Theodore Mark
        (Kathleen Fuller)
        (Katherine Tobias)

GOUD, Anne
        (Anne-Mariel)

GOUDGE, Eileen
Garden Of Lies   <CO>
Seniors: <YA>
   1 Too Much, Too Soon
   2 Smart Enough To Know
   3 Winner All The Way
   4 Afraid To Love
   5 Before It's Too Late
   6 To Hot To Handle
   7 Hands Off, He's Mine
   8 Forbidden Kisses
   9 Touch Of Ginger, A
  10 Presenting Superhunk
  11 Bad Girl
  12 Don't Say Goodbye
  13 Kiss And Make Up
  14 Looking For Love
  15 Sweet Talk
  16 Heart For Sale
  17 Life Of The Party
  18 Night After Night
  19 Treat Me Right
  20 Against The Rules
Super Seniors: <YA>
   1 Old Enough
   2 Hawaiian Christmas
   3 Something Borrowed,
      Something Blue

GOUDGE, Eileen (cont.)
    4 Deep-Sea Summer
Swept Away: <YA>
    1 Gone With The Wish
    3 Love On The Range
    5 Spell Bound
    6 Once Upon A Kiss

GOULD, Lois
    Final Analysis
    La Presidenta
    Necessary Objects
    Sea-Change, A
    Such Good Friends

GOUDGE, Elizabeth   (Deceased)
    Bird In The Tree, The
    Blue Hills, The
    Book Of Faith, A
    Castle On The Hill, The
    Child From The Sea, The
    City Of Bells, A
    Dean's Watch, The
    Gentian Hill
    Golden Skylark, The
    Green Dolphin Street
    Heart Of The Family, The
    Island Magic
    Joy Of The Snow, The
    Middle Window, The
    Pedlar's Pack, A
    Pilgrim's Inn
    Rosemary Tree, The
    Scent Of Water, The
    Sister Of The Angels, The
    Smoky-House
    Ten Gifts
    Towers In The Mist
    Valley Of Song, The
    Well Of The Star, The
    White Witch, The

GOWANS, Elizabeth
    Heart Of The High Country <Saga>

GOWAR, Antonia
    Cashing In   <CO>

GOWER, Iris   <HR>
                         (Iris Davies)
    Beloved Captive
    Welsh Mining Town Series:
        Black Gold
        Copper Kingdom
        Fiddler's Ferry
        Morgan's Women
        Proud Mary
        Spinners' Wharf

GRABEKLIS, Lita
    Destiny's Darling

GRABENDIKE, Barbara
    San Francisco Nurse

GOULART, Ronald Joseph
                    (Jillian Kearny)

GOULD, Judith
    Dazzle   <CS>
    Love Makers   <CS>
    Sins   <CO>

GRABIEN, Deborah   <HR>
    Fire Queen

263

GRACE, Alicia   <GOT><RS>
          [Irving A. Greenfield]
Clovecrest
Enchanted Circle
Hawksbill Manor
Head Of Medusa, The
Hour Of Evil (The Head Of Medusa)
House At Swansea
House Of The Darkest Death
Mass Of A Dead Witch
Terrified Heart, The (The
  Terrified Target)
Wharf Sinister

GRACE, Anita   <GOT>
         [Irving A. Greenfield]
Dunsan House

GRACE, Carol
               [Carol Culver]
Silhouette Romance:
  690 Room For Nanny
  751 Taste Of Heaven, A

GRADY, Liz
      [Patricia Madden Coughlin]
Second Chance At Love:
  198 Too Close For Comfort
  210 Touch Of Moonlight
  232 Hearts At Risk
  260 Heart Of Gold
  283 Heart Of The Hunter
  310 Lovers And Pretenders
  335 Stolen Kisses
  361 Dark Splendor
  401 Reclaim The Dream

GRAHAM, Brenda Knight
  Serenade/Saga: <Insp>
  4 Juliana Of Clover Hill

GRAHAM, Elizabeth
               [E. Schattner]
Harlequin Presents:
  392 Dangerous Tide
  403 Thief Of Copper Canyon
  446 Madrona Island
  493 Passionate Imposter
  543 Stormy Vigil
  583 Vision Of Love
  617 Highland Gathering
Harlequin Romance:
  2062 Girl From Finlay's River
  2088 Shores Of Eden, The
  2126 Fraser's Bride
  2170 Heart Of The Eagle
  2190 Mason's Ridge
  2223 New Man At Cedar Hills
  2237 Return To Silver Creek
  2263 Man From Down Under
  2320 Devil On Horseback
  2326 Come Next Spring
  2374 Jacintha Point
  2708 Passion's Vine
  2715 Big Sur

GRAHAM, Elizabeth
             (Laura Parrish)

GRAHAM, Gwethalyn
Earth And High Heaven

GRAHAM, Heather   <HR>
    [Heather Graham Pozzessere]
Devil's Mistress
Every Time I Love You   <HR-REIC>

GRAHAM, Heather (cont.)
   In sequence:
      Golden Surrender
      Viking's Woman, The
      North American Woman Series: <HR>
      In sequence:
         Sweet SavageEden
         Pirate's Pleasure
         Love Not a Rebel
   Candlelight Ecstasy:
      117 When Next We Love
      125 Tender Taming
      154 Season For Love, A
      177 Quiet Walks The Tiger
      214 Tender Deception
      241 Hours To Cherish
      271 Serena's Magic
      335 Hold Close The Memory
      359 Sensuous Angel
      452 Maverick And The Lady, The
      476 Eden's Spell
      512 Siren From The Sea
   Candlelight Ecstasy Supreme:
      1   Tempestuous Eden
      10   Night, Sea And Stars
      17   Red Midnight
      37   Arabian Nights
      67   Queen Of Hearts
      94   An Angel's Share
      108 Dante's Daughter
      127 Handful Of Dreams
   Candlelight Supreme:
      159 Liar's Moon

GRAHAM, John W.   <HO>
   Sejanus:
      Secret Ruler Of Rome   <GARS>

GRAHAM, Leslie
   First Love From Silhouette: <YA>
      55   Love On The Run
      91   Rx For Love

GRAHAM, Lou   <HR>
   Fanny G.
      Seventh Sister, The

GRAHAM, Lynne
   Harlequin Presents:
      1167 Veranchetti Marriage, The
      1313 An Arabian Courtship
   Harlequin Romance:
      Bittersweet Passion HRS15

GRAHAM, Marteen   <HR>
   Ariane

GRAHAM, Marteen Dee
   Silver Sundown

GRAHAM, Olivia
   McFadden Romance:
      36   Twilight Interlude

GRAHAM, Vanessa
                        [Anthea Fraser]
   Second Time Around   <ENG>

GRAHAM, Winston   <HO>
                  [Winston Mawdsley Graham]
   Cordelia
   Fortune Is A Woman
   Grove Of Eagles
   Japanese Girl
   Marnie
   Merciless Ladies, The
   Night Journey
   Take My Life
   Woman In The Mirror

GRAHAM, Winston (cont.)
Poldark Saga: <HS>
  Ross Poldark
  Demelza
  Jeremy Poldark
  Warleggan
  Black Moon, The
  Four Swans, The
  Angry Tide, The
  Stranger From The Sea, The
  Miller's Dance, The
  Loving Cup, The

GRAMES, Selwyn Anne   <HR>
Royal Savage

GRAMM, Nancy
Silhouette Desire:
  339 Then Came Love
  422 About Last Night...
  479 High Jinx

GRANBECK, Marilyn   <HR>
    [Marilyn Ruth Podest Granbeck]
Celia
Elena
Fifth Jade Of Heaven, The
Lorielle
Maura
Winds Of Desire

GRAND, Natalie
                    (Susanna Hart)

GRANDOWER, Elissa   <GOT>
          [Hillary Baldwin Waugh]
Blackbourne Hall
Seaview Manor

GRANDOWER, Elissa (cont.)
Secret Room Of Morgate House, The
Summer At Raven's Roost, The

GRANDVILLE, Louise
                       [Dan Streib]
MacFadden Romance:
  42 Winter Wish
  55 Autumn Morning
  63 Castles In The Sky

GRANGE, Peter   <HO>
              [Christopher Nicole]
Devil's Emissary, The
Golden Goddess, The
King Creole
Tumult At The Gate, The

GRANGER, George
                 (Georgia Granger)
         (see Amanda Jean Jarrett)
          (see Jonathan Scofield)

GRANGER, Georgia   <HO>
               [George Granger]
Wild And The
  Wayward, The   <MOAS:#8>

GRANGER, Katherine
            [Mary Fanning Sederquest]
Second Chance At Love:
   89 Man's Persuasion, A
  206 Wanton Ways
  301 Man Of Her Dreams
  341 Place In The Sun, A
  380 Sweet Disorder, A
Silhouette Desire:
  392 Ruffled Feathers
  410 Unwedded Bliss

GRANT, Sara (cont.)
    619 Kerandraon Legacy
    709 Child Called Mathew, A

GRANT, Tracy w/ Joan GRANT
                    (Anthea Malcolm)

GRANT, Vanessa
                    [Vanessa Oltmann]
    Harlequin Presents:
    895 Storm
      In sequence:
    1088   Jenny's Turn
    1112   Stray Lady
    1179 Take Over Man
    1209 Stranded Heart
    1234 Awakening Dreams
    1264 Wild Passage
    1289 Taking Chances
    1322 So Much For Dreams
    Harlequin Romance:
    2888 Chauvinist, The

GRANTLEY, Samantha
    All That Glisters
    Natural Life, The

GRAVE, Andrew   <GOT>
    Golden Deed, The

GRAVES, Keller
[Kathryn Davenport w/Evelyn Rogers]
    Heartfire Romance: <HR>
      Brazen Embrace
      Desire's Fury
      Lawman's Lady
      Rapture's Gamble
      Velvet Vixen

GRAVES, Tricia
    Rapture Romance:
      38 Heart On Trial

GRAY, Adrian
    Doctor's Desires
    Doctor's Women
    Young Doctors, The

GRAY, Alicia
    Enchanted Circle

GRAY, Alison
                    [Alma Moser]
    Dawnstar Romance:
      Porter's Designs

GRAY, Andrea
    Fair Wind For Love, A

GRAY, Angela   <GOT><RS>
                    [Dorothy Daniels]
    Ashes Of Falconwyck, The
    Blackwell's Ghost
    Island Of Fear
    Lattimore Arch, The
    Love Of The Lion, The
    Nightmare At Riverview
    Ravenswood Hall
    Stranger In The Dark, A
    Warlock's Daughter, The
    Watcher In The Dark, The

GRAY, Brenna
Seasoned To Taste

GRAY, Janet
[Sybil Russell]
Second Chance At Love:
298 Hearts Are Wild

GRAY, Caroline
[F. Beerman]
Victoria's Walk
White Rani

GRAY, Francine du Plessix   <CO>
Lovers and Tyrants
October Blood
World Without End

GRAY, Ginna
[Virginia Gray]
(see Silhouette Christmas Stories)
Silhouette Classic:
28 Golden Illusion   <SE171>
Silhouette Romance:
285 Gentling, The   &
311 Perfect Match, The
338 Heart Of The Hurricane
352 Images
374 First Love, Last Love
417 Courtship Of Dani, The
Silhouette Special Edition:
In sequence:
171   Golden Illusion
320   Sweet Promise
265 Hearts Yearning, The
373 Cristen's Choice
In sequence:
416   Fools Rush In
468   Where Angels Fear
528   If There Be Love   &
661   Once In A Lifetime

GRAY, Harriet
(see Denise Robins)

GRAY, Janice
Harlequin Romance:
1167 Dear Barbarian
1230 Crown Of Content
1275 Shake Out The Stars
1707 Garden Of The Sun
1744 Winter Loving
1852 Star Light, Star Bright
1886 Take All My Loves
1911 Stormy Harvest
1931 Lullaby Of Leaves
2014 Moonglade
2029 Kiss For Apollo, A
2089 Green For A Season
2294 Heart Of The Scorpion

GRAY, Juliet
Crystal Cage, The
Midsummer Magic

GRAY, Kerrie
[Kathryn Graybeal]
Silhouette Romance:
666 Love Is A Gypsy

GRAY, Linda Crockett
(Christina Crockett)

GRAY, Marcy
[Lori Gray]
Silhouette Desire:
477 Pirate At Heart, A

GRAY, Marcy (cont.)
Silhouette Romance:
704 So Easy To Love
792 Be My Wife

GRAY, Mayo Loiseau
Savage Season, The

GRAY, Patsy
Caprice Romance: <YA>
13 Don't Forget To Write

GRAY, Valerie   <RE>
By Honour Bound   &
Spy At The Gate, A   &

GRAY, Vanessa   <RE>
[Jacquelyn Aeby]
Accessible Aunt, The
Best-Laid Plans
Duke's Messenger, The
Dutiful Daughter, The
Errant Bridegroom, The
Innocent Deceiver, The
Lady Of Property, A
Lady's Revenge, The
Lonely Earl, The
Lost Legacy, The
Masked Heiress, The
Orphan's Disguise, The
Reckless Gambler, The
Reckless Orphan, The
Unruly Bride, The
Wayward Governess, The
Wicked Guardian, The

GRAY, Virginia
(Ginna Gray)

GRAYBEAL, Kathryn
(Kerrie Gray)

GRAYLAND, Valerie Merle Spanner
(Lee Belvedere)
(Valerie SuBond)

GRAYSON, Elizabeth   <GOT>
By Demons Possessed
Macabre Manor
Token Of Evil, A

GRAZIA, Theresa
(Therese Alderton)
(Alberta Sinclair)
American Regency Romance:
Capital Match
English Bride, The

GRECO, Margaret
Jenny's Choice (Fool's Gold)

GREELEY, Andrew M.
Angel Fire   <RF>
Love Song   <RM>
Rites Of Spring   <RM>
St. Valentine's Night

GREEN, Billie
(see Silhouette Summer Sizzlers)
Loveswept:
7   Tryst With Mr. Lincoln, A
16   Very Reluctant Knight, A
26   Once In A Blue Moon
38   Temporary Angel
43   To See The Daisies..First
65   Last Hero, The
75   Count From Wisconsin, The
87   Dreams Of Joe
108 Tough Act To Follow, A

GREEN, Billie (cont.)
  129 Mrs. Gallagher
        And The Ne'er Do Well
  155 Glory Bound
  182 Makin' Whoopee
  215 Loving Jenny
  329 Waiting For Lila
  372 Bad For Each Other
  431 Sweet And Wilde
Loveswept Golden Classic:
  Temporary Angel   <LS38>
Loveswept Silver Signature Ed.
  Once In A Blue Moon   <LS26>
Now And Forever:
    1 Always Amy
Silhouette Special Edition:
  297 Jesse's Girl
  346 Special Man, A
  379 Voyage Of The Nightingale
  415 Time After Time

GREEN, Edith Pinero   <HR>
In sequence:
  Providence
  Destiny's Daughters

GREEN, Elaine
MacFadden Romance:
  89 Moon Over Marrekesh

GREEN, Grace
                  (Grace Reid)
Harlequin Presents:
  1323 Tender Betrayal

GREEN, Sharon
Harlequin Intrigue:
  152 Haunted House

GREENAWAY, Gladys
  Coffee In The Morning
  Devil In The Wind
  Feather Your Nest

GREENBERG, Jan
                (Jill Gregory)

GREENBERG, Joanne   <HO>
             (Hannah Green)
  In This Sign
  King's Persons, The
  Monday Voices
  Rites Of Passage
  Season Of Delight, A

GREENE, Jennifer
              [Alison Hart]
From Silhouette Books:
  Birds Bees And Babies:
    Riley's Baby
Silhouette Desire:
  263 Body And Soul
  293 Foolish Pleasure
  326 Madam's Room
  350 Dear Reader
  366 Minx
  385 Lady Be Good
  421 Love Potion
  439 Castle Keep, The
  463 Lady Of The Island
  481 Night Of The Hunter <MMS>
  498 Dancing In The Dark
  553 Heat Wave
  600 Slow Dance   <MMS>
  619 Night Light
Silhouette Intimate Moments:
  221 Secrets
  305 Devil's Night
  345 Broken Blossom

GREENE, Juli
    [Judith Child w/ Lisa Neher]
    Silhouette Romance:
    499 Beneath A Summer Moon

GREENE, Julia   <HR>
    Untamed Heart

GREENE, Maria
    Lovers' Knot   <RE>
    The Avon romance: <HR>
      Desperate Deception
      Forever Love
      Lady Midnight
      Reckless Splendor
      Winter's Flame

GREENE, Sylvia W.   <CO>
    Longings

GREENE, Yvonne
    Sweet Dreams: <YA>
      5 Little Sister
      9 Cover Girl
    91 Love Hunt, The

GREENFIELD, Irving A.   <HO>
             (Riva Carles)
             (Alicia Grace)
             (Anita Grace)
             (Gail St. John)
    Carey Guns, The
    Flame On The Wind, A
    Glow Of Morning, The
    Love Scent
    No Better World
    Play Of Darkness
    Pleasure Hunters, The

GREENFIELD, Irving A. (cont.)
    Stars Will Judge, The
    Succubus
    Tagget   w/ Don FINE
    To Savor The Past

GREENHAW, Lois   <CO>
    Backward Glances

GREENLAW, Patricia   <HO>
    Colorado Woman

GREENLEA, Denice   <RE>
             [Denice Pipkin]
    Ardent Suitor, The
    Birchwood Hall
    Fortune Seeker, The   <VIC>
    Coventry:
     50 Masquer, The
   154 Friend Of The Family, A
   197 Distant Relations

GREENLEAF, Jeanne M.
    Judy Sullivan Books:
      Above All, Love   <CO>

GREENMAN, Nancy A.
               (Lucy Elliot)

GREENWOOD, Leigh
            [Harold Lowry]
    Heartfire Romance: <HR>
      Captain's Caress, The
      Seductive Wager
      Wicked Wyoming Nights
      Wyoming Wildfire

GREENWOOD, Lillian Bethel
                    (Rose Ayers)

GREER, Francesca
                [Frankie-Lee Janas]
  Bright Dawn
  First Fire
  Second Sunrise, The

_____

_____

GREGG, Jess   <GOT>
  Other Elizabeth, The

_____

_____

GREGG, Margo
  Meteor Kismet:
    9 Prodigal Lover

_____

_____

GREGG, Meredith   <RE>
  Love From Elizabeth

_____

_____

GREGOR, Carol
  Harlequin Presents:
    1074 Marry In Haste
    1129 Trusting Heart, The
    1338 Bitter Secret
  Harlequin Romance:
    2732 Lord Of The Air
          When Winter Ends   HRS43

_____

_____

GREGORY, Diana
  Sweet Dreams: <YA>
    74 Don't Forget Me
    90 Two's A Crowd
    98 Love Is In The Air
   103 Cross My Heart
   128 One Boy At A Time
  Turning Points: <YA>
     5 Forget Me Not

_____

_____

GREGORY, Janet
  Inherit The Sea

_____

_____

GREGORY, Jill   <HR>
                [Jan Greenberg]
  Lone Star Lady
  Looking Glass Years
  Moonlight Obsession
  Promise Me The Dawn
  Reckless Rapture
  To Distant Shores
  In sequence:
    Wayward Heart, The
    My True And Tender Love

_____

_____

GREGORY, Kay
  Harlequin Presents:
    1191 No Way To Say Goodbye
  Harlequin Romance:
    2919 Star For A Ring, A
    3016 Perfect Beast, A
    3058 Impulsive Butterfly
    3082 Amber And Amethyst

_____

_____

GREGORY, Lisa   <HR>
                [Candace Pauline Camp]
  Analise
  Before The Dawn
  Bitterleaf
  Bonds Of Love
  Crystal Heart
  Light And Shadow
  Seasons   <CO>
  Solitaire   <CO>
  In sequence:
    Rainbow Season, The
    Rainbow Promise, The

_____

_____

GREGORY, Lydia
   [D. L. Carey w/ G. E. Brodeur]
   Candlelight Esctasy:
   103 Unwilling Echantress

GREGORY, Martha
                (Elizabeth Glenn)

GREGORY, Mollie   <CO>
          (Estelle Edwards)
     (see Terry Nelsen Bonner)
Equal To Princes
Triplets

GREGORY, Philippa
   Lacey Family Trilogy: <GOT><Saga>
     Wideacre
     Favored Child, The
     Meridon

GREGORY, Veronica
         [Victoria Shakarjian]
   The Avon Romance:
     Heart's Possession

GREIG, Maysie   <GOT>
      [Maysie Greig Murray]
   Catch Up To Love
   Dark Carnival
   Doctor And The Dancer, The
   Doctor On Wings
   Every Woman's Man
   Golden Garden, The
   Hello, Anna
   Love Is A Gambler
   Man Of Her Dreams, The
   Man To Protect You, A
   Married Quarters
   Never The Same

GREIG, Maysie (cont.)
   New Moon Through A Window
   Odds On Love
   One Who Kisses, The
   Pretty One, The
   Retreat From Love
   Reluctant Millionaire
   Rich Man, Poor Girl
   Screen Lover
   Ships's Doctor
   Two Of Us, The
   Unmarried Couple
   Whispers In The Sun
   Candlelight:
     123 Girl In Jeopardy

GREIG-SMITH, Jennifer
            (Jennifer Ames)
            (Maysie Greig)

GRENFELL, Julian
   Margot   <CO>

GRESHAM, Elizabeth   <GOT><RS>
   Daughter Of Darkness
   Lucifer Was Tall
   Pawn In Jeopardy
   Poisoner's Base
   Puzzle In Paisley
   Puzzle In Parchment
   Puzzle In Parquet
   Puzzle In Patchwork
   Puzzle In Pewter
   Puzzle In Porcelain

GREY, Belinda
   Masquerade:
     20 Passionate Puritan, The
     29 Loom Of Love
     35 Sweet Wind Of Morning
     44 Moon Of Laughing Flame
     58 Meeting At Scutari

GREY, Belinda (cont.)
   75 Glen Of Frost
   79 Daughter Of Isis

GREY, Charlotte
   Fancy Free
   Coventry:
   193 Golden Butterfly   <GEO>

GREY, Evelyn   <GOT>
                    [Susan Leslie]
   Trilogy:
   Camberleigh
   Mayfair
   (see Ashley Allyn for third
                book in trilogy)

GREY, Georgina   <RE>
                 [Mary Linn Roby]
   Hesitant Heir, The
   Turn Of The Cards
   Coventry:
    23 Franklin's Folly
    39 Both Sides Of The Coin
    57 Last Cotillion, The
    76 Fashion's Frown
   103 Reluctant Rivals, The
   122 Bartered Bridegroom, The
   144 Queen's Quadrille, The
   157 Belle Of Brighton, The
   162 Silver Shilling, The <GEO>
   172 Lingering Laughter
   192 London Ladies, The

GREY, Kitty   <RE>
              [Mary Elizabeth Allen]
       (see A Regency Valentine)
   Current Confusion

GREY, Millie
              [Millie Grey Gergich]
   Loveswept:
   104 Suspicion
   144 Wild Blue Yonder

GREY, Samantha
              [Deborah Perkins]
   Silhouette Romance:
   708 Mark Of Zorro, The

GREY, Shirley
   Masquerade:
    21 Crescent Moon, The

GREY, Zane   <RW>
   Betty Zane

GRICE, Julia
              [Julia Haughey Grice]
   Cry For The Demon   <SN>
   Daughters Of The Flame
   Emerald Fire
   Lovefire
   Passion Star
   Satin Embraces
   Wild Roses
   Scarlet Ribbons: <HR>
      Enchanted Nights
      Kimberly Flame
      Season Of Desire
   Tapestry: <HR>
      87 Fiery Hearts

GRIEG, Sylvia   <HR>
   Escape Me Never
   Midnight Gold

GRIERSON, Linden
Harlequin Romance:
1791 Trees Of Tarrentall, The
1820 Rising River

GRIEVESON, Mildred
(Caroline Fleming)
(Anne Mather)

GRIFFIN, Anne J.   <GOT>
[Arthur J. Griffin]
Ocean Of Fear, The
Spirit Of Brynmaster Oaks, The

GRIFFIN, Jocelyn
[Laura Sparrow]
Harlequin Romance:
2543 White Wave, The   <PROM>
Silhouette Intimate Moments:
168 Fire Signs
Silhouette Special Edition:
195 Hostages To Fortune
SuperRomance:
8 Beloved Intruder
69 Battle With Desire

GRIFFITH, Kathryn Meyer
Heart Of The Rose, The

GRIFFITH, Patricia Browning
Tennessee Blue

GRIMES, Frances Hurley
First Love From Silhouette: <YA>
84 Sunny Side Up
141 I Love You More Than
Chocolate

GRIMES, Frances Hurley (cont.)
Sweet Dreams: <YA>
154 Love Lines
Sweet Savage Sophomore Year: <YA>
1 Kiss And Tell

GRIMSTEAD, Hettie
(Marsha Manning)
Fires Of Spring
Island Affair
Kiss Of The Sun, A
Portrait Of Paula
Roses For Breakfast
September's Girl
Tender Vine, The
Tuesday's Child
Winter Rose, The
Harlequin Romance:
1403 Whisper To The Stars

GRISANTI, Mary Lee
(Perdita Shepherd)

GRISSOM, Fay   <GOT>
Portrait In Jigsaw

GRONAU, Mary Ellen   <HR>
McMahon Saga: In sequence:
Passionate Warriors
Gentle Conqueror

GROSECLOSE, Elgin
Olympia

GROSS, Joel
1407 Broadway   <CO>
Four Sisters
Home Of The Brave
Maura's Dream

276

GROSS, Joel (cont.)
This Year In Jerusalem
In sequence:
    Lives Of Rachel, The
    Books Of Rachel, The

GROSS, Sue
                [Susan Ellen Gross]
Candlelight Ecstasy:
  348 Steal A Rainbow
Candlelight Supreme:
  153 Jewel Of India, The

GROSS, Susan Ellen
                    (Sue Ellen Cole)
                    (Susanna Collins)
                    (Susan deLyonne)
                    (Sue Gross)
Midnight Fury, The

GROVE, Joan
Candlelight Ecstasy:
  277 One In A Million
  337 Diamond In The Rough
  375 Token Of Love
  432 Room For Two
  478 Scoundrel's Kiss, The
  492 Tropical Heat
  519 Captain's Seduction, The

GROVE, Martin A.
Visions   <CO>

GRUNDMAN, Donna
                [Donna A. Round Grundman]
Days To Remember
Distant Eden, A

GUCCIONE, Leslie Davis
                    (Leslie Davis)
Silhouette Desire:
  279 Before The Wind
  The Branigans:
  311 Bittersweet Harvest
  353 Still Waters
  376 Something In Common
  523 Branigan's Touch   <MMS>
  554 Private Practice

GUEST, Diane
                [Diane Reidy Guest Biondi]
Twilight's Burning

GUILD, Nicholas   <HO>
Tiglath Ashur Trilogy:
  Assyrian, The
  Blood Star, The

GULL COTTAGE TRILOGY: <GCT>
Harlequin American Romance:
  301 Charmed Circle
                    Robin Francis
  305 Mother Knows Best
                    Barbara Bretton
  309 Saving Grace
                    Anne McAllister

GUNDY, Elizabeth
Bliss
Cat On A Leash
Naked In A Public Place

GUNN, Betty Rose
Avalon:
  Nurse Whitney's Paradise

GUNTHER, H. G.
  Desert Doctor, The
  Dr. Erica Werner
  Private Hell, A
  Ravishing Doctor, The
  Summer With Danica

GUNTRUM, Suzanne Simmons
                    (Suzanne Simmons)
                    (Suzanne Simms)
  Harlequin American Romance:
    353 Golden Raintree, The<COAR>
  Harlequin Temptation:
    133 Christmas In April
    169 Genuine Article, The
    202 Made In Heaven

GUSS, Linda
                    (Natalie Grant)

GUY, Rosa
  Trilogy: <YA>
    Friends, The
    Rudy
    Edith Jackson

HAAF, Beverly T.   <RS>
                    (Beverly Terry)
  Crystal Pawns, The

HAAF, Beverly Terry   <HR>
  Lovestruck:
    Chantning, The

HAAS, Ben   <HO>
  Chandler Heritage, The   <HS>
  Daisy Canfield
  Foragers, The
  House Of Christina, The
  Last Valley, The
  Look Away, Look Away

HAASE, John
  Big Red
  San Francisco

HABERSHAM, Elizabeth   <GOT>
[Shannon Harper w/Madeleine Porter]
  Island Of Deceit

HACSI, Jacqueline
    [Jacqueline Hope Bassler Hacsi]
                    (Jacqueline Hope)
                    (Jacqueline Louis)
  Candlelight:
    244 Love's Own Dream
    511 Winter's Loving Touch <RO>
    599 East Of Paradise   <RO>

HACSI, Jacqueline (cont.)
    640 Paradise Isle   <RO>
    658 Too Rich For Her Pride<RO>

HADARY, Simone
  Second Chance At Love:
    59 Embraced By Destiny
    108 Spring Fever

HADAS, Pamela
  Passion Of Lilith

HADLEY, Liza
  Harlequin Romance:
    Welcome The Sunrise HRS41

HAGAN, Chet
  The Dewey Annals: <HO>
    Bon Marche

HAGAN, Patricia   <HR>
            [Mary Patricia Hagan]
            (Patricia Hagan Howell)
  Dark Journey Home   <RS>
  Golden Roses
  Invitation To The Wedding
  Love's Wine
  Passion's Fury
  Winds Of Terror   <RS>
  In sequence:
    Souls Aflame
    This Savage Heart
  The Coltrane Family Saga:
    In sequence:
      Love And War
      Raging Hearts, The
      Love And Glory

279

HAGAN, Patricia (cont.)
    Love And Fury
    Love And Splendor
    Love And Dreams
    Love And Honor
    Love And Triumph

HAGAR, Judith
            [Judith Polley]
    Measure Of Love, The
    Wind Of Change, The
    Judy Sullivan Books:
      Shadow Of The Eagle   <HR>
    England:
      Dangerous Deception
      Don't Run From Love
      Journey Into Love
      Man For Melanie
      Master Of Karatangi
      To Touch The Stars

HAGEN, Lorinda   <HR>
    [Elizabeth Lorinda duBreuil]
    Amy Jean
    Banners Of Desire
    Bold Blades Flashing
    Corrie
    Destiny And Desire
    In Love And War
    In The Eye Of The Law
    Lacey
    Letitia
    Mistress Of Glory
    Sister Of The Queen
    Somebody's Daughter,
      Somebody's Wife
    Summer Of '32
    Sweet Sinner

HAGER, Alice Rogers
    Washington Secretary

HAGER, Jean
       [Wilma Jean Luna Hager]
           (Leah Crane)
          (Marlaine Kyle)
        (Jeanne Stephens)
     (see Amanda McAllister)
        (see Sara North)
    Grandfather Medicine, The <MY>
    Secret Of Riverside Farm, The<YA>
    Whispering House, The   <YA>
    Candlelight:
     636 Portrait Of Love   <RO>
     652 Captured By Love   <RO>
    Candlelight Ecstasy:
     31 Web Of Desire
     258 Promise Of Spring
     354 Secret Intentions
     449 Passionate Solution, The
    Judy Sullivan Books:
      Terror In The Sunlight   <RS>
    Starlight Romance:
      Yellow-Flower Moon
    Velvet Glove: <RS>
     4 Dangerous Enchantment

HAGGARD, H. Rider   <HO>
    Pearl Maiden, The   <GARS>

HAGMAN, Bette   <RS>
    Death Beads

HAHN, Mona Lynn Lowery
            (Lynn Lowery)

HAILEY, Elizabeth Forsythe
    Life Sentences
    Woman Of Independent Means, A

HAILEY, Johanna <HR>
  [Marcia Yvonne Howl w/
                 Sharon Jarvis]
  Trilogy:
    Enchanted Paradise
    Crystal Paradise
    Beloved Paradise

HAINES, Carolyn
                 (Caroline Burnes)

HAINES, Pamela
  Diamond Waterfall, The
  Golden Lion, The   <Saga>
  Kissing Gate, The

HAKE, Carolyn w/ Jeanie LAMBRIGHT
                 (Kate Denton)

HALE, Antoinette
         [Antoinette Stockenberg]
  Candlelight Ecstasy:
  233 Trouble In Paradise
  Candlelight Ecstasy Supreme:
  93   Island Of Desire

HALE, Arlene
                 [Mary Arlene Hale]
                 (Tracy Adams)
                 (Gail Everette)
                 (Lynn Williams)
  Camp Nurse
  Chicago Nurse
  Community Nurse
  Crossroads For Nurse Cathy
  Disaster Area Nurse
  Disobedient Nurse, The
  Doctor's Daughter, The
  Dr. Barry's Nurse

HALE, Arlene (cont.)
  Dude Ranch Nurse
  Emergency Call
  Emergency For Nurse Selena
  Fires Of Passion, The
  Frightened Nurse
  Gateway To Love
  Glimpse Of Paradise
  Goodbye To Yesterday
  Heart Remembers, The
  Home To The Valley
  House On Crow's Nest Island
  In Love's Own Fashion
  Island Of Mystery
  Journey For A Nurse
  Lady Is A Nurse, The
  Lake Resort Nurse
  Leave It To Nurse Kathy
  Legacy Of Love
  Lover's Reunion
  Love's Destiny
  Mountain Nurse
  My Favorite Nurse
  New Nurse At Crestview
  Nurse From Mulberry Square, The
  Nurse From The Shadows
  Nurse Jan's Troubled Love
  Nurse Jean's Strange Case
  Nurse Julia's Tangled Loves
  Nurse Lora's Love
  Nurse Marcie's Island
  Nurse Nicole's Decision
  Nurse On Leave
  Nurse On The Beach
  Nurse On The Run
  Nurse Sue's Romance
  Nurse's New Love, A
  Nurse's Strange Romance, The
  One More Bridge To Cross
  Other Side Of The World, The
  Partners In Love
  Promise Of Tomorrow
  Runaway Heart, The
  School Nurse
  Season Of Love, The
  Stormy Sea Of Love, A
  Symptoms Of Love
  Time For Us, A
  University Nurse
  Vote For Love, A

HALEY, Jocelyn
                    [Jill MacLean]
  Dream Of Darkness
  SuperRomance:
    11 Love Wild And Free
    31 Winds Of Desire
    54 Serenade For A Lost Love
  In sequence:
    88   Cry Of The Falcon
  Harlequin SuperRomance:
    Sequence continued:
    122   Shadows In The Sun
    217 Time To Love, A
    254 Drive The Night Away

HALFORD, Laura
                    [Laura Sparrow]
  The Avon Romance:
    Seaswept

HALL, Bennie C.
  Come Be My Love (Southern Cousin)
  Golden Glow Of Love, The (Golden
    Glow)

  Make-Believe Rainbow
  No Escape From Love
  Out Of Step With Love (The
    Handmade Halo)
  Redheaded Nurse
  When Hearts Remember
  You Can't Hide Love (April In
    Arcadia)
  Sharon Romance:
    Coronation For Cinderella

HALL, Carolyn
                    (Carole Halston)

HALL, Douglas Kent   <HR>
  Master Of Oakwindsor, The

HALL, Gillian
  Stages   <CO>
  This Shining Promise   <HR>

HALL, Gimone   <GOT><HR>
  Blue Taper, The
  Devil's Walk
  Ecstasy's Empire
  Fury's Sun, Passion's Moon
  Hide My Savage Heart
  Jasmine Veil, The
  Juliet Room, The
  Kiss Flower, The
  Rapture's Mistress
  Rules Of The Heart   <Saga>
  Silver Strand, The
  Witch's Suckling

HALL, Libby
                    [Olivia M. Hall]
  Harlequin American Romance:
    373 Hearts At Risk   <COAR>
  Harlequin Temptation:
    189 Perfect Woman, The

HALL, Olivia M.
                    (Libby Hall)
                    (Laurie Page)

HALL, Steffie
                    [Janet Evanovich]
  Second Chance At Love
    409 Hero At Large
    456 Foul Play
    466 Full House

HALL, Stephanie   <GOT>
                    [William J. Smith
  Whispers In The Dustr
  Witch Of Murry Hill, The

HALLDORSON, Phyllis
  [Phyllis Taylor Halldorson]
  Silhouette Inspirations;
    3   Honor Bright
    13 Homecoming, The
    22 None So Blind
  Silhouette Romance:
    31 Temporary Bride
    79 To Start Again
    247 Mountain Melody
    282 If I Ever Loved YOU
    367 Design For Two Hearts
    395 Forgotten Loe
    456 An Honest Love
    515 To Choose A Wife
    566 Return To Raindance   &
    584 Raindance Autumn   &
    653 Ageless Passion,
        Timeless Love
    689 Dream Again Of Love
    760 Only Nanny
        Knows For Sure
    791 Lady Diamond
  Silhouette Special Edition:
    290 My Heart's Undoing
    368 Showgirl And The Professor
    430 Cross My Heart
    510 Ask Not Of Me, Love
    621 All We Know Of Heaven

HALLIDAY, Ena
  [Sylvia Baumgarten]
  Tapestry: <HR>
    Trilogy:
        Marielle
    10 Lysette
    19 Delphine

HALLIN, Emily
  [Emily Watson Hallin]
  (Elaine Harper)
  Crosswinds Keepsakes: <YA>
    21 Wanted: Tony Roston
    33 Dark Horse, A
    39 Queen Bee

HALL OF FAME SERIES <HofFS>   <HO>
  Scimitar, The
                    Noel B. Gerson
  Emperor's Lady, The
                    Noel B. Gerson
  Daughter Of Eve
                    Noel B. Gerson
  Highwayman, The
                    Noel B. Gerson
  River Devils, The
                    Carter A. Vaughan
  Dragon Cove
                    Carter A. Vaughan
  Queen's Husband, The
                    Samuel Edwards
  Cumberland Rifles, The
                    Noel B. Gerson
  Savage Gentleman
                    Noel B. Gerson
  Branded Bride
                    Carter A. Vaughan
  Charlatan, The
                    Carter A. Vaughan
  Gentle Fury, The
                    Paul Lewis
  Mohawk Ladder, The
                    Noel B. Gerson
  Seneca Hostage, The
                    Carter A. Vaughan
  Roanoke Warrior
                    Carter A. Vaughan
  Wilderness, The
                    Carter A. Vaughan
  Scoundrel's Brigade
                    Carter A. Vaughan
  Fortress Fury
                    Carter A. Vaughan

HAMILTON, Celeste (cont.)
Silhouette Special Edition:
418 Torn Asunder
447 Silent Partner
503 Fine Spring Rain, A
532 Face Value
620 No Place To Hide

HAMILTON, Clare   <GOT>
Seadrift House

HAMILTON, Daphne
SuperRomance:
48 Prelude To Paradise

HAMILTON, Diana
Harlequin Presents:
993 Song In A Strange Land
1248 Secure Marriage, A
1305 Betrayal Of Love
Harlequin Romance:
2865 Impulsive Attraction
2959 Painted Lady
2979 Wild Side, The
Dark Charade   HRS11

HAMILTON, Gail
(Margaret Gayle)
Harlequin SuperRomance:
260 What Comes Naturally
Harlequin Temptation:
135 Spring Thaw

HAMILTON, Julia   <ENG><HO>
[Julia Watson]
Anne Of Cleves
Katherine Of Aragon
Last Of The Tudors

HAMILTON, Julia (cont.)
Son Of York

HAMILTON, Katrina   <HR>
[Barbara Cockrell]
Moonlight Masquerade

HAMILTON, Lucy
[Julia A. Rhyne]
Silhouette Classic:
8 Woman's Place, A   <SE18>
Silhouette Intimate Moments:
126 Agent Provateur
Dodd Memorial Hospital:
In sequence:
229 Under Suspicion
237 After Midnight
245 Heartbeats
278 Real Thing, The
331 Emma's War
Silhouette Special Edition:
18 Woman's Place, A
92 All's Fair
172 Shooting Star
206 Bitter With The Sweet, The
337 An Unexpected Pleasure

HAMILTON, Patrick   <RS>
Gaslight
Hanover Square

HAMILTON, Paula
Candlelight Ecstasy:
231 Kiss And Tell
302 Laughter's Way
367 Perfect Illusions
392 Love War, The
420 Doctor's Orders

HAMILTON, Paula (cont.)
  Candlelight Ecstasy Supreme:
    66 Lovestruck
  Candlelight Supreme:
    146 Wanderer's Promise, The
  Silhouette Special Edition:
    340 Dream Lover
    382 In The Name Of Love
    400 Man Behind The Badge, The

HAMILTON, Priscilla
                    [Roberta Gellis]
  Love Token, The

HAMILTON, Stephen G. w/ Melinda
  HOBAUGH-HAMILTON
                    (Linda Vail)
                    (Linda Stevens)

HAMILTON, Tampson
  Paris In The Fall

HAMILTON, Tamsin
  Gypsy From Cadiz, The

HAMILTON, Violet   <RE>
  Hidden Heart, The
  Scandalous Portrait
  Sweet Pretender
  In sequence:
    An Officer's Alliance
    False Promises

HAMILTON, Virginia   <YA>
  Little Love, A

HAMLETT, Christina
  Enchanter, The

HAMLIN, Dallas
                    [Dallas Schulze]
  Candlelight Ecstasy:
    260 Desperate Yearning
  Candlelight Ecstasy Supreme:
    82 Another Eden
  Candlelight Supreme:
    135 Surrender To A Stranger
    162 Prisoner In His Arms

HAMMETT, Lafayette
                    [LaLette Douglas]
  Captain's Doxy, The

HAMMILL, Grandin
  Woman Of Destiny, A   <CO>

HAMMOND, Diana
  Sweet Lies   <CO>

HAMMOND, Mary Ann
                    [Mary Ann Slojkowski]
  Tapestry: <HR>
    40 Land Of Gold

HAMMOND, Rosemary
  Harlequin Presents:
    802 Habit Of Loving, The
    859 Malibu Music
    896 Loser Take All
    985 All My Tomorrows
    1017 Castles In The Air
    1136 One Stolen Moment

HAMMOND, Rosemary (cont.)
  1296 My Destiny
Harlequin Romance:
  2601 Full Circle
  2655 Two Dozen Red Roses
  2674 Scent Of Hibiscus, The
  2817 Plain Jane
  2968 Model For Love
  3026 Game Plan
  3051 Face Value

HAMPSON, Anne
                        (Jane Wilby)
Harlequin Presents:
    1 Gates Of Steel
    2 Master Of Moonrock
   10 Waves Of Fire
   13 Kiss From Satan, A
   16 Wings Of Night
   19 South Of Mandraki
   22 Hawk And The Dove, The
   25 By Fountains Wild
   28 Dark Avenger
   31 Blue Hills Of Sintra
   34 Stormy The Way
   37 An Eagle Swooped
   40 Wife For A Penny
   44 Petals Drifting
   47 When Clouds Part
   51 Hunter Of The East
   56 After Sundown
   59 Beloved Rake
   63 Stars Over Sarawak
   72 Way Of A Tyrant, The
   79 Black Eagle, The
   87 Fetters Of Hate
   95 Dark Hills Rising
  108 Pride And Power
  115 Fair Island, The
  125 Dear Plutocrat
  132 Enchanted Dawn
  143 Man To Be Feared, A
  152 Autumn Twilight
  168 Dangerous Friendship
  181 Isle At The Rainbow's End
  187 Hills Of Kalamata
  196 Follow A Shadow

HAMPSON, Anne (cont.)
  209 Song Of The Waves
  293 Moon Dragon
  463 Bride For A Night
  470 Beloved Vagabond
  476 Bitter Harvest
  483 Rose From Lucifer, A
  494 Windward Crest
  507 South Of Capricorn
  515 Unwanted Bride
  535 Chateau In The Palms
Harlequin Romance:
  1349 Eternal Summer
  1388 Unwary Heart
  1420 Precious Waif
  1442 Autocrat Of Melhurst, The
  1467 Beyond The Sweet Waters
  1491 When The Bough Breaks
  1522 Love Hath An Island
  1551 Stars Of Spring
  1570 Heaven Is High
  1595 Gold Is The Sunrise
  1622 There Came A Tyrant
  1646 Isle Of The Rainbows
  1672 Rebel Bride, The
  1678 Plantation Boss, The
  2082 Call Of The Outback
  2099 Boss Of Bali Creek
  2119 Moon Without Stars
  2130 Isle Of Desire
  2138 Sweet Is The Web
  2160 Shadow Between, The
  2163 Fly Beyond The Sunset
  2182 Under Moonglow
  2186 Call Of The Veld
  2215 Leaf In The Storm
  2230 Harbour Of Love
  2233 To Tame A Vixen
  2246 For Love Of A Pagan
  2266 South Of The Moon
  2272 Where The South Wind Blows
  2353 Temple Of The Dawn
Silhouette Romance:
    1 Payment In Full
    4 Stormy Masquerade
   16 Second Tomorrow
   27 Dawn Steals Softly, The
   28 Man Of The Outback
   40 Where Eagles Nest

HANCOCK, Lucy Agnes
   Nurse Barlow (292)
   Nurse In White (496)
   Nurse's Aid (356)
   Nurses Are People (339)
   Pat Whitney, R. N. (347)
   Resident Nurse (333)
   Shorn Lamb, The (397)
   Staff Nurse (332)
   Village Doctor (344)

HANCOCK, Sybil   <GOT>
   Mosshaven

HANDY, Toni
   Play Begins, The

HANKS, Lindsey   <HR>
   [Georgia Pierce w/ Linda Chesnutt]
   The Avon Romance:
     Midnight Deception
     Savage Surrender
   Heartfire Romance:

     Outlaw Lover

HANLEY, Elizabeth
   Flame And The Fire
   Guilty As Charged
   Ms. President
   Surrogate, The

HANLON, Emily
   Petersburg   <HS>

HANNA, Evelyn
   [Michael Dyne w/ Ethel Frank]
   Blaze Of Glory, (Blackberry
     Winter)
   Stolen Splendor
   Woman Against The World, A

HANNIBAL, Edward
   Better Days
   Blood Feud   w/Robert BORIS
   Dancing Man
   Chocolate Days, Popsicle Weeks
   Liberty Square Station
   Trace Of Red, A

HANNON, Irene
   Promise Romance: <Insp>
     13 In Name Only
     18 Portrait Of Love

HANSEN, Anne
              (Anne Peters)

HANSEN, Caryl
   First Love From Silhouette: <YA>
     105 One For The Road
     186 Small Wonder

HANSEN, Jeanne E.
   Heartfire Romance: <HR>
     Deception's Embrace
     Love's Wild Frontier
     Midnight Enchantment
     Shameless Dawn

HANSEN, Joseph
              (Rose Brock)

HANSEN, Kim/Kim E.   <HR>
  Rebecca McGregor
  Untamed Desire

HANSEN, Peggy M.
                (Margaret Westhaven)

HANSEN, Peter
                [David Moltke-Hansen]
  Creek Rifles   <AIS:#5>

HANSON, Mary
  Candlelight:
    609 Wicklow Castle   <RO>

HANSON, Mary Catherine
  Starlight Romance:
    Captured Hearts

HARA, Monique   <GOT>
                [Madge Harrah]
  Mirror Of Darkness
  Mists Of Milwood, The
  Shadow Of The Cat

HARBRINGER, April
  MacFadden Romance:
    191 Fool's Gold

HARDCASTLE, Catherine
                [Phyllis Thatcher]
  MacFadden Romance:
    25 In The Arms Of a Stranger

HARDING, Christina
  McFadden Romance
    35 Flight Of The Fury
    35 Yesterday's Promise
    80 Follow The Sun
    95 Say You Don't Remember

HARDING, Nancy
  Silver Land, The
  Windchild

HARDTER, Frances
                (Frances Williams)

HARDWICK, Elizabeth   <HR>
  Widow's Fire

HARDWICK, Mollie   <HR><RE>
  Atkinson Heritage, The
  Beauty's Daughter
  Blood Royal   <HO>
  Charlie Is My Darling
  Dutchess Of Duke Street, The
  Lovers Meeting
  Merrymaid, The
  Monday's Child
  Sarah's Story
  Shakespeare Girl, The
  Thomas And Sarah
  Willowwood
  Upstairs Downstairs Series:
    World Of Upstairs Downstairs
    War To End Wars, The
    Years Of Change

HARDY, Antoinette
                [Antoinette Stockenberg]
  Silhouette Special Edition:
    191 Fit To Be Loved

HARDY, Laura
                    [Sheila Holland]
Silhouette Romance:
   76 Burning Memories
  101 Playing With Fire
  130 Dream Master
  184 Dark Fantasy
  309 Men Are Dangerous
Silhouette Special Edition:
   25 Tears And Red Roses

HARDY, Ronald
                    [Ronald Harold Hardy]
Rivers Of Darkness   <Saga>

HARGIS, Barbara   <HR>
                    [Barbara Cockrell]
The Avon Romance:
   Heart Song

HARGRAVE, Leonie
Clara Reeve

HARING, Firth
Greek Revival
Three Women

HARKER, Herbert
Goldenrod
Turn Again Home

HARKNESS, Judith   <RE>
Admiral's Daughter, The
Contrary Cousins
Determined Bachelor, the
Lady Charlotte's Ruse
Montague Scandal, The

HARLEQUIN HISTORICAL
  CHRISTMAS STORIES-1989
  Tumbleweed Christmas
                    Kristin James
  Cinderella Christmas, A
                    Lucy Elliot
  Home For Christmas
                    Heather Graham Pozzessere

HARLEQUIN HISTORICAL
  CHRISTMAS STORIES-1990
  In From The Cold
                    Nora Roberts
  Miracle Of The Heart
                    Patricia Potter
  Christmas At Bitter Creek
                    Ruth Langan

HARLOWE, Justine

  [Jean Harvey w/Tina MacKenzie
                    w/Laura Bennett]
  Jealousies   <CO>
  Memory And Desire   <Saga>

HARMON, Margaret   <GOT>
Mistress Of Corey's Landing, The

HARPER, Elaine
                    [Emily Hallin]
Crosswinds Keepsake: <YA>
    4 Love At First Sight
    8 Be My Valentine
   12 Mystery Kiss, The
   15 Bird Of Paradise, The
   19 No Easy Answers
First Love From Silhouette: <YA>
    9 Love At First Sight
   18 We Belong Together
   39 Be My Valentine
   53 Light Of My Life

HARPER, Elaine (cont.)
65 Mystery Kiss, The
73 Short Stop For Romance
89 Bunny Hug
101 Fireworks
117 Turkey Trot
121 Christmas Date
129 Ghost Of Gamma Rho, The
137 Lover's Lake
145 Janine
153 Phantom Skateboard, The
169 Orinoco Adventure
181 Homecoming
197 Coral Island

HARPER, Karen   <HR>
                    (Caryn Cameron)
Eden's Gate
Firelands, The
Island Ecstasy
Midnight Mirage
One Fervent Fire
Passion's Reign
Rapture's Crown
Sweet Passion's Pain
Tame The Wind

HARPER, Madeline
[Shannon Harper w/ Madeline Porter]
Love Dance
Harlequin Temptation:
32 Every Intimate Detail
106 After The Rain
165 Ultimate Seduction, The
210 Keepsakes
271 This Time Forever
326 Jade Affair, The

HARPER, Olivia Longoria
                    (Jolene Adams)

HARPER, Olivia w/ Ken HARPER
[Olivia Longoria Harper w/
                    Kenneth M. Harper]
                    (JoAnna Brandon)
Loveswept:
52 Casey's Cavalier
214 Knight To Remember, A

HARPER, Richard   <HO>
Dragonhead Deal, the
Peacemaker, The

HARPER, Shannon w/ Donna BALL
[Elizabeth Shannon Harper w/
                    Donna Ball]
                    (Leigh Bristol)

HARPER, Shannon w/ Madeline PORTER
[Elizabeth Shannon Harper w/
    Madeline Habersham King Porter]
                    (Elizabeth Habersham)
                    (Madeline Harper)
                    (Anna James)

HARRAH, Madge
                    (Monique Hara)
Serenade/Serenata: <Insp>
16 Call Of The Dove

HARREL, Linda
                    (Shannon Clare)
Harlequin Romance:
2337 Sea Lightning
2459 Artic Enemy

HARRELL, Anne   <RS>
[Carla Amalia Neggers Jewel]
Betrayals
Minstrel's Fire

293

HARRELL, Janice
Crosswinds: <YA>
    28 Stu's Song
Crosswinds Keepsake: <YA>
     2 Starring Susy
     9 They're Rioting In Room 32
    11 Love And Pizza To Go
    23 B. J. On Her Own
    29 Masqerade
    34 Dear Dr. Heartbreak
    36 Your Daily Horoscope
    38 So Long, Senior Year
First Love From Silhouette: <YA>
    67 Puppy Love
    95 Heavens To Bitsy
   128 Secrets In The Garden
   134 Killebrew's Daughter
   159 Sugar 'N Spice
   165 Blue Skies And Lollipops
   187 Birds Of A Feather
   205 With Love From Rome
   224 Castles In Spain
   229 Risky Business, A
Two By Two Romance: <YA>
     5 One Special Summer
    13 Secret Hearts

_____

_____

HARRINGTON, Emma   <HR>
[Virginia Brown w/
         Melinda Jane Harrison]
Blue Fire   <WOW:#1>
Ivory Temptress   <AAS>
Passion's Tempest   <AAS>
Prairie Paradise
American Regency Romance:
   Fair Exchange
   Love's Gambit
   Heart's In Disguise

_____

_____

HARRINGTON, Kathleen
The Avon Romance:
   Cherish The Dream

_____

_____

HARRINGTON, Sharron w/
             Rick HARRINGTON
             (Rianna Craig)

HARRINGTON, William   <RS>
English Lady, The
Search For Elizabeth Brandt, The

_____

_____

HARRIS, Andrea   <RS>
                    [Irma Walker]
An Irish Affair
Byzantine Encounter
Scream Away, A
Windfall

_____

_____

HARRIS, Joanna   <RE>
            [Joanne Harris Burgess]
Worldly Innocent

_____

_____

HARRIS, June   <GOT>
Cursed Heiress, The

_____

_____

HARRIS, Kate
Avalon:
   While The Heart Dreams

_____

_____

HARRIS, Kathleen
Nurse On The Run
Candlelight:
    16 Nurse On Holiday

_____

_____

HARRIS, Lane
          [Monica Harris]
  Devil's Love, The

HARRIS, Louise
  Harlequin Romance:
    2685 Love's Good Fortune

HARRIS, Marilyn   <HR>
  Bledding Sorrow
  Conjurers, The
  Hatter Fox
  Last Great Love, The
  Warrick
  Eden Saga: In sequence:
    This Other Eden
    Prince Of Eden, The
    Eden Passion, The
    Women Of Eden, The
    Eden Rising
    American Eden
    Eden And Honor

HARRIS, Melinda
          [Melinda Snodgrass]
  Second Chance At Love:
    44 Crescendo
    98 Wind's Embrace, The
   152 Once More With Feeling

HARRIS, Monica
    •   (Lane Harris)

HARRIS, Norma
  Firefly   <CO>
  Sons Of Ada Stone, the

HARRIS, Rosemary   <GOT><RS>
  All My Enemies
  Double Snare
  King's White Elephant, The
  Nor Evil Dreams
  Wicked Pack Of Cards, A

HARRIS, Ruth   <CO>
  Decades
  Fun City Girls
  Husbands And Lovers
  Love And Money
  Modern Women
  Rich And The Beautiful

HARRIS, Vivian   <RE>
          [Vivian H. Tichenor]
  Candlelight:
    611 Worthy Charade, A

HARRISON, Barbara   <MED>
  City Hospital
  Cold Night's Death, A
  Gorlin Clinic, The
  Impulse
  Off Center
  Pagans
  Passion's Price   <HR>
  Rhinelander Center
  Rhinelander Pavillion
  Society Princess
  This Cherished Dream   <Saga>

HARRISON, Claire
  [Ellen "Claire" Wisoff Harrison]
            (Laura Eden)
  Fifth Diamond, The
  Somebody's Baby
  Harlequin Presents:
    671 Prophecy Of Desire

HARRISON, Claire (cont.)
```
705  Dance While You Can        &
727  Leading Man
736  Once A Lover
753  An Independent Woman
760  Dragon's Point
769  One Last Dance             &
906  Diplomatic Affair
930  Love Is A Distant Shore
1018 Fantasy Unlimited
```

HARRISON, Elizabeth   <MED>
                        [Betty Cavanna]
Accident Call
Ambulance Call
Emergency Call
Surgeon's Call

HARRISON, Janis
Starlight Romance:
  Bittersweet Storm
Tiara:
  Flame In The Wind, A

HARRISON, Melinda Jane w/
                Virgina BROWN
              (Emma Harrington)

HARRISON, Sarah   <HR>
An Imperfect Lady   <Saga>
In sequence:
  Flowers Of The Field, The
  Flower That's Free, A

HARRISON, Sue
Mother Earth, Father Sky

HARROD-EAGLES, Cynthia
Morland Dynasty: <HS>
  1 Founding, The
  2 Dark Rose, The
  3 Distant Wood, The
  4 Crystal Crown, The
  5 Black Pearl, The
  6 Long Shadow, The

HARROLD, Elyeen
Safari To Love

HARROWE, Fiona   <HR>
                  [Florence Hurd]
Bittersweet Afternoons   <CO>
Bridge Of Fire
Dark Obsession
Forbidden Wine
Fountains Of Glory
Honor's Fury
Love's Scarlet Banner
In sequence:
  Passion's Child
  Pride's Folly
Love & Life:
  Separate Ways

HART, Alison
           [Jill Alison Hart Culby]
                  (Jeanne Grant)
                (Jennifer Greene)
                (Jessica Massey)

HART, Caroline   <RS>
                [Charles Garvice]
Flee From The Past

HART, Carolyn G.
[Charles Garvice]
Brave Hearts   <CO>
Escape From Paris
Harlequin Gothic Romance:
Devereaux Legacy, The

HART, Joan Mary
Silhouette Romance:
631 Stranger At The Wedding
Silhouette Special Edition:
440 More Than A Mistress

HART, Carrie
[Carolyn Joyner]
Harlequin Temptation:
252 Hard-Headed Woman

HART, Mallory Dorn   <HR>
Defy The Sun
Jasmine On The Wind

HART, Catherine   <HR>
[Diane Tidd]
(see Avon Christmas Romance)
Night Flame
Satin And Steel
Sweet Fury
In sequence:
  Forever Gold
  Fallen Angel
In sequence:
  Silken Savage
  Summer Storm
In sequence:
  Fire And Ice
  Ashes And Ecstasy

HART, Nicole
[Rosina F. Rue]
Crosswinds Keepsake: <YA>
13 Robin's Reward
First Love From Silhouette: <YA>
94 Lead On Love
114 Courting Trouble
193 Road To Romance
Hart Mystery Series:
201 Mayhem And Magic
209 Rachel's Resistance

HART, Francis
Topaz

HART, Shirley
[Shirley Larson]
Candlelight Ecstasy:
78 Fatal Attraction, A
107 Brand Of Passion
116 Caught In The Rain
123 Wild Rhapsody
144 Surrender To The Night
161 Dangerous Haven, A
183 Night To Remember, A
208 Play To Win
290 Balance Of Power
Candlelight Ecstasy Supreme:
26 Suspicion And Seduction
50 On Any Terms

HART, Jean
Avalon:
Kate Daniels, TV Star

HART, Susannah
               [Natalie Grand]
  Silhouette Desire:
    72 Nobody's Baby
   186 Legend In His Own Time, A

HART, Virginia
           [Virginia Lee Hart]
  Harlequin Romance:
  2811 Sweet Pretender
  2882 Night Of The Spring Moon
  2980 Without Rainbows

HART, Virginia Lee
           (Virginia Hart)
  So Wild A Rose
  Where Glory Waits
  Where Passion Waits

HARTE, Marjorie   <RS>
          [Marjorie McEvoy]
  Closing Web, The
  No Eden For A Nurse
  Strange Journey

HARTE, Samantha   <HR>
  Angel
  Hurricane Sweep   <Saga>
  Kiss Of Gold
  SummerSea
  Sweet Whispers
  Timber Hill
  Vanity Blade
  Avalon:
    Snows Of Craggmoor, The <GOT>

HARTER, Evelyn
  Bosom Of The Family

HARTMAN, Lorie w/ Jan HARTMAN
          (Susannah Lawrence)

HARVEY, Adell
  Promise Romance: <Insp>
   12 Rainbow Of Promise

HARVEY, Jean w/ Tina MacKENZIE w/
  Laura BENNETT   (Justine Harlowe)

HARVEY, Judy
  Harlequin American Romance:
   23 In Loving Regret

HARVEY, Marianne
           [Mary Williams]
  Wild One, The
  Trevarvas: In sequence:
    Dark Horseman, The
    Proud Hunter, The

HARVEY, Samantha
  Harlequin Romance:
  2481 Driftwood Beach, The
  2522 Distant Man, The
  2541 Boy With Kite
  2764 Amaryllis Dreaming
       Tomorrow's Lover   HRS13

HASKELL, Leigh   <RE>
          [Leigh Shaheen]
  Paragon Bride, The
  Vengefull Viscount, The

HASKELL, Mary
[Mary Haskell Curtis]
Second Chance At Love:
124 Song For A Lifetime
144 Reach For Tomorrow
176 Crazy In Love
203 Heaven On Earth
254 Stardust Melody
272 Bit Of Daring, A
313 Blithe Spirit
353 Whispers From The Past
To Have And To Hold:
8 Hold Fast 'Til Dawn
17 All That Glitters
37 Anniversary Waltz

HASTINGS, Brooke
[Deborah Brooke Hannes Gordon]
(see Silhouette Christmas Stories)
Harlequin Historical:
25 So Sweet A Sin
Silhouette Classic:
2 Intimate Strangers   <SE2>
Silhouette Intimate Moments:
37 Interested Parties
64 Reasonable Doubts
Silhouette Romance:
13 Playing For Keeps
26 Innocent Fire
44 Desert Fire
67 Island Conquest
102 Winner Take All
528 Too Close For Comfort
Silhouette Special Edition:
2 Intimate Strangers
21 Rough Diamond
49 Matter Of Time, A
79 An Act Of Love
156 Tell Me No Lies
250 Hard To Handle
294 As Time Goes By
312 Forward Pass
349 Double Jeopardy
385 Forbidden Fruit
439 Catch A Falling Star
486 Both Sides Now

HASTINGS, Brooke (cont.)
571 Reluctant Mistress
630 Seduction

HASTINGS, Charlotte
(Charlotte Wisely)

HASTINGS, Julia   <HR>
Island Ecstasy

HASTINGS, Phyllis   <GOT>
Conservatory, The
Field Of The Forty Footsteps
House Of The Twelve Caesars
Rapture
Hastingford Trilogy: <HS>
All Earth To Love
Day Of The Dancing Sun
Gates Of Morning, The

HATCHER, Leslie
Tiara:
Magic At Sunset

HATCHER, Robin Lee   <HR>
(Robin Leigh)
Dream Tide
Gemfire
Passion's Gamble
Pirate's Lady
Promised Sunrise   <WWT>
Thorn Of Love
Wager, The
The Spring Haven Saga:
In sequence:
Stormy Surrender
Heart's Landing
Heart Storm

299

HATHAWAY, Jan
        [William Arthur Neubauer]
    Coming Of Eagles, The
    Junior Nurse
    Robynn's Way
    Treasure Of The Redwoods
    Sharon Contemporary Teens:
        Bright Morning
        Key Of Gold, The

HATTON, Pamela
    Harlequin Presents:
    1226 Remember Tomorrow

HAUBER, Josephine C.
                (Josephine Charlton)

HAUGHT, Jean   <HR>
    Bride Of The Rolling Plains
    Ecstasy's Treasure
    Flaming Ecstasy
    Forever Fancy
    Island Temptress
    Oklahoma Kiss
    Prisoner Of Passion
    Texas Temptress
    Wild Abandon

HAUGHT, Jean w/ Rosalyn ALSOBROOK
                (Jalynn Friends)

HAUPTMAN, Elaine
                (Gayle Corey)

HAVEN, Diana
    Candlelight:
    659 Menus For Romance

HAVILAND, Diana   <HR>
                [Florence Hershman]
    Defy The Storm
    Fortune's Daughter
    Love's Promised Land
    Moreland Legacy, The
    Passionate Pretender, The
    Proud Surrender

HAVILAND, Meg   <RS>
                [Helen Ketcham]
    Mistress Of Wynds

HAWKES, Sarah
                (Sarah Eagle)
                (Sally Falcon)
    Harlequin Temptation:
    264 An Unmarried Man

HAWKINS, Laura
    First Love From Silhouette: <YA>
    58 Double Exposure
    Silhouette Inspirations:
    26 Precious Moments

HAWLEY, S.R.
    Avalon:
        Deadly Secrets

HAWTHORNE, Alaina
                [Alaina W. Richardson]
    Silhouette Romance:
    672 Out Of The Blue

300

HAWTHORNE, Violet   <GOT>
   [Christopher Rainone]
   Sweet Deadly Passion

HAY, Heather   <HR>
   Heritage

HAY, Suzanne   <HR>
   Savage Destiny
   Whispers In The Wind

HAYCRAFT, Molly Costain   <HR>
   Countess Carrots
   King's Daughters, The
   Lady Royal, The
   My Lord Brother The Lion Heart
   Reluctant Queen, The
   Too Near The Throne

HAYDON, June w/ Judith SIMPSON
             (Roz Denny)
         (Rosalind Foxx)
           (Sara Logan)

HAYDON, June w/ Pat RUTHERFORD
          (Tavia Hayford]

HAYE, Jan
           (Juliet Shore)
           (Anne Vinton)
   Harlequin Romance:
   758 Helping Doctor Medway
   897 Nurse Hilary's
         Holiday Task
   977 Doctor's Difficult
         Daughter, The

HAYE, Lloyd S.
          (Patricia Drew)

HAYES, Allison
        [Lynn Coddington]
   The Avon Romance:
   Spellbound

HAYES, Leal   <RS>
   Challoners Of Bristol, The
   Dark Legend
   Harlequin House

HAYES, R. E.   <GOT>
   Nightmare Island
   Nurse In Istanbul

HAYES, Ralph/Ralph E.   <HO>
   Big Fall,The
   By Passion Possessed
   Charleston   <CofCWS>
   Dark Water
   Dragon's Fire
   Drought!
   Eastern Shore
   Forbidden Splendor
   Golden Passion
   Hostage Of Hell, The
   King's Ransom
   Love's Dark Conquest
   Name Is O'Brien, The
   Promised Land
   San Patricios
   Savage Dawn
   Sheryl
   Treasure Of Rio Verde, The
   Vengeance Is Mine
   Candlelight:
   1 Ellen Matthews,
       Mission Nurse

HAYFORD, Taria
   [June Haydon w/ Pat Rutherford]
   Serenade:
     Trail Of Love

HAYLE, Felicity
   Harlequin Romance:
     995 Nurse Ronnie's Vocation
    1217 Promise Is For Keeping, A
    1337 Campbells Are Coming, The

HAYMOND, Ginny
               [Lee Fleming]
   Love & Life:
     Someone Special

HAYNES, Barbara
   First Love From Silhouette: <YA>
     35 People Like Us
    116 Wishful Thinking

HAYNES, Velma   <RS>
   Tiara:
     Questing Heart, The

HAYNESWORTH, Susan
      [Susan Emrick Robertson]
   Silhouette Romance:
    606 O'Daniel's Pride

HAYS, Lee
             (Sarah Nichols)

HAYWORTH, Evelyne   <GOT><RS>
              [Evan Heyman]
   Evil At Bayou Laforche, The
   Haggard's Manor
   Candlelight:
    534 Ghost Of Ludlow Fair <IN>

HAZARD, Barbara   <RE>
          (Lillian Lincoln)
   Calico Countess, The
   Cloisonne Locket, The
   Dangerous Deceits
   Disobedient Daughter, The
   Emerald Duchess, The
   Enchanting Stranger, The
   Guarded Heart, The
   Lady Lochinvar
   Mad Masquerade
   Queen Bee, The
   Surfeit Of Suitors, A
   Rake's Protegee, The
   Royal Snuff Box, The
   In sequence:
     Singular Miss Carrington, The
     Dreadful Duke, The
     Turnabout Twins, The
   In sequence: <HR>
     Call Back The Dream
     Heart Remembers, The
   Coventry:
     31 Kathleen
     58 Beth
     82 Dangerous Lady
    109 Tangled Web, The
    152 Caroline
    166 Covington Inheritance, The
    184 Dangerous Deceits

HAZZARD, Shirley   <CO>
   Bay Of Noon, The
   Cliffs Of Fall
   Evening Of The Holiday, The

HAZZARD, Shirley (cont.)
  People In Glass Houses
  Transit Of Venus, The

HEAD, Ann   <GOT>
                    [Ann Head Morse]
  Always In August
  Everybody Adored Cara
  Fair With Rain

HEALY, Catherine
  Harlequin SuperRomance:
  111 Private Corners
  150 Perfect Timing

HEALY, Christine T. w/ Susan
  McGovern YANSICK   (Erin Yorke)

HEALY, Letitia
  Silhouette Romance:
   24 Summer Storm

HEART OF THE CITY SERIES
                      <HOFCS><HO>
  Dallas   Clayton Matthews
  New Orleans   Clayton Matthews
  Honolulu   Arthur Moore
  Las Vegas   Arthur Moore w/
                  Clayton Matthews
  Miami   Arthur Moore
  San Francisco   Parley J. Cooper

HEATH, Monica   <GOT><HR><RS>
  Calderwood
  Castlereagh
  Chateau Of Shadows
  Clancumara's Keep

HEATH, Monica (cont.)
  Clerycastle
  Duncraig
  Dunleary
  Falconlough
  Hawkshadow
  House Of The Strange Women
  Legend Of Blackhurst, The
  Legend Of Crownpoint, The
  Marshwood
  Mistress Of Ravenstone
  Raneslough
  Return To Clerycastle
  Secret Citadel, The
  Secret Of The Vineyard, The
  Secrets Can Be Fatal
  Unwilling Heiress, The
  Woman In Black

HEATH, Sandra   <RE>
                    [Sandra Wilson]
  Absent Wife, The
  An Impossible Confession
  Change Of Fortune, A
  Christmas Courtship, A
  Commercial Enterprise, A
  Courting Of Jenny Bright, The
  Fashion's Lady
  Lady Jane's Ribbons
  Makeshift Marriage, The
  Mally
  Mannerby's Lady
  Matter Of Duty, A
  My Lady Domino
  Opera Dancer, The
  Perfect Likeness, A
  Pilfered Plume, The
  Rakehell's Widow
  Scandalous Publication, A
  Second Lady Southvale, The
  Sherborne Sapphires, The
  Smuggler's Daughter, The
  Unwilling Heiress, The
  Wrong Miss Richmond, The

HEATH, Sharon
Jungle Nurse
Nurse At Castle Island
Nurse At Cliff End
Nurse At Moorcroft Manor
Nurse At Shadow Manor
Nurse Elaine
  And The Sapphire Star
Sunshine Nurse, The
Vacation For Nurse Dean, A

HEATON, Dorothy
Far-Away Homestead, A
Gratefully Yours
Summer's Madness, A
To Cherish My Beloved

HEAVEN, Constance   <GOT><RS>
  [Constance Fecher Heaven]
    (Constance Fecher)
    (Christina Merlin)
Astrov Inheritance, The
Astrov Legacy, The
Castle Of Doves   <HR>
Castle Of Eagles
Craven Legacy, The
Daughter Of Marignac   <Saga>
Fires Of Glenlochy, The
Heir To Kuragin
House Of Kuragin, The
Night Of The Wolf, The
Place Of Stones, A
Queen And The Gypsy, The
Queen's Favorite
Raging Fire, The
Wildcliffe Bird, The
In sequence:
  Lord Of Ravensley
  Ravensley Touch, The

HEBSON, Ann
Lattimer Legend, The

HECKART, Eleanor
Muscavado

HECKLER, Jonellen
            [Jonellen Beth Heckler]
Safe-Keeping   <CO>

HEDBERG, Nancy
Hear Me With Your Heart

HEDLEY, Catherine
MacFadden Romance:
  208 Seven Days, Seven Nights

HEERMANN, Lydia
Serenade/Serenata: <INSP>
  4 Love's Late Spring

HEGGAN, Christine
Cannes

HEHL, Eileen
                   (M. E. Cooper)
Lilac Mansion   <GOT>
Out Of Love   <YA>
Sweet Dreams: <YA>
  95 Strings Attached
  110 Playing Games
  133 Playing The Field
Wildfire: <YA>
  Out Of Bounds

HELAND, Victoria   <RE>
   [Victoria J. Richardson Heland]
                (Josephine Janes)
   Artful Cousin, The
   Mayfair Wager

HENAGHAN, Rosalie (cont.)
   2572 Man From Ti Kouka, The
   2621 For Ever And A Day
   2751 Safe Harbour
   3027 Spell Of The Mountains

HELEY, Veronica
   Coventry:
   97   Tarrant Rose, The   <GEO>
   185 Kate

HENDERSON, Beth   <RS>
         [Beth Henderson-Daniels]
   Nikrova's Passion

HELLAND, Beverly
                (Beverly Bird)

HELLER, Arnie w/ Judith E. BRYER
                (Eve O'Brian)

HELLMAN, Aviva   <CO>
   Somebody Please Love Me

HENDERSON, L. W.
   Kingdom, The

HENDERSON, Nancy
            [Nancy Henderson Ryan]
   Threshold

HELY, Sara   <RS>
   Legend Of The Green Man, The
   Sign Of The Serpent, The   <GOT>

HEMMINGS, Lauren
   MacFadden Romance:
   189 Flower Of Desire
   207 (reprint) Flower Of Desire

HENDRICKSON, Emily   <RE>
         [Doris Emily Hendrickson]
   Colonial Upstart, The
   Country Miss, A
   Double Deceit
   Gallant Lord Ives, The
   Hidden Inheritance
   Lady Sara's Scheme
   Miss Wyndham's Escapade   &
   Queen Of May   &

HENAGHAN, Rosalie
   Harlequin Romance:
   1422 Sophisticated Urchin, The
   2462 Copper's Girl

HENDRON, Grace Muirhead
   Change Of Heart, A
   Candlelight:
   17   Nurse In Alaska

HENKE, Courtney
Loveswept:
  340 Chameleon   &
  368 Dragon's Revenge, The
  394 Jinx   &

_____

_____

HENKE, Shirl   <HR>
  [Shirl Henke w/ Carol Reynard]
Capture The Sun
In sequence:
  Golden Lady
  Love Unwilling
Gone To Texas Trilogy:
  Cactus Flower
  Moon Flower
  Night Flower

_____

_____

HENLEY, Virginia   <HR>
Falcon And The Flower, The
Hawk And The Dove, The
Irish Gypsy, The
Pirate And The Pagan, The
Raven And The Rose, The
The Avon Romance:
  Bold Conquest
  Wild Hearts

_____

_____

HENRICHS, Betty L.
                 (Emily Doyle)
              (Amanda Kent)
Candlelight:
  701 Convenient Bride, The <RE>
Candlelight Ecstasy:
  349 Scarlet Memories
  502 Casanova's Downfall
Candlelight Ecstasy Supreme:
   46 Behind Every Good Woman
  102 Fire In Paradise
Candlelight Supreme:
  148 Roman Fantasy
Finding Mr. Right:
  More Than Friends

HENRICHS, Betty L. (cont.)
Velvet Glove: <RS>
    3 Love's Suspect

_____

_____

HENRY, Anne
             [Judith Henry Wall]
Harlequin American Romance:
   76 Cherokee Summer
   90 Glory Run, The
  114 Storm Within, The
  135 Tough Act To Follow, A
  171 I love You, Jonathan Sky
  212 Mixed Match, A
  252 Colonel For Jenny, A
  292 Robbing The Cradle
  347 Beloved Dreamer

_____

HENRY, Elizabeth
Second Chance At Love:
  277 Man Trouble

_____

_____

HENTGES, Alison J.
             (Georgina Devon)

HEPBURNE, Melissa
         [Craig Howard Broude]
Passion's Sweet Sacrifice
Passion's Wicked Torment
In sequence:
  Passion's Proud Captive
  Passion's Blazing Triumph

_____

_____

HEPLER, D.L.
Avalon:
  Kiss For The Captain, The

_____

_____

HERBERT, Julia
Masquerade:
  2 Runaways, The
  5 Fortune-Hunter, The
  15 Prisoner Of The Harem
  33 Bond-Woman

HERBERT, Kathleen   <HR>
Bride Of The Spear
In sequence:
  Queen Of The Lightning
  Ghost In The Sunlight, The

HERBERT, Nan   <RS>
Shadow Over Heldon Hall

HERBRAND, Jan   <GOT>
                    [Janice Herbrand]
Altheimer Inheritance, The
Dangerous House, The
Lost Heritage

HERMAN, J. B.
Where The Heart Is

HERMANN, Nancy   <HR>
                    (Jessica Jeffries)
                    (Samantha Scott)
Of Simple Dreams

HERMANN, Spring   <CO>
                    [Spring Galiardi]
Taking Chances

HERRICK, Ann
Crosswinds Keepsake: <YA>
  24 Practice Makes Perfect

HERRING, Linda
Serenade/Serenata: <Insp>
  7 Morning Song
  14 Windsong

HERRINGTON, Terri
                    (Tracy Hughes)
Candlelight Ecstasy:
  438 Secret Stirring, A
  464 Head Over Heels
  489 Stolen Moments
  500 Ticket To A Fantasy
Candlelight Supreme:
  136 Tender Betrayer
Silhouette Romance:
  318 Blue Fire
  416 Lovers' Reunion
  509 Tangled Triumphs
  561 Wife Wanted

HERRMANN, Phyllis   <HR>
[Nira Herrmann w/
            Phyllis Di Francesco]
Lovestruck:
  Hidden Fire
Meteor Kismet:
  14 Two For One

HERRON, Shaun   <GOT>
Aladale
Bird In Last Year's Nest, The
Ruling Passion, The
Through The dark And Hairy Woods
Whore-Mother, The

HERSHAN, Stella K.   <HR>
  Naked Angel

_____

_____

HERSHMAN, Florence
                    (Diana Browning)
                    (Diana Haviland)

HERSHMAN, Morris
                    (Evelyn Bond)
                    (Ian Kavanaugh)
                    (Sara Roffman)
                    (Janet Templeton)
                    (Lionel Webb)
                    (Jessica Wilcox)

HERTER, Lori
                    [Loretta M. Herter]
  Candlelight:
    574 No Time For Love   <RO>
    669 Too Close For Comfort <RO>
  Candlelight Ecstasy:
    118 To Have And To Hold
    212 All Our Tomorrows
    365 Temptress Touch, The
  Candlelight Ecstasy Supreme:
    27 Private Screenings
  Now And Forever:
    Seventh Heaven
  Silhouette Romance:
    344 Loving Deception

_____

_____

HESS, Janice
                    (Janice Carter)

HESS, Joan
  Crosswinds:
    16 Red Rover, Red Rover
  First Love From Silhouette: <YA>
    233 Future Tense

_____

_____

HESS, Norah
                    [Elsie Poe Bagnara]
  Caleb's Bride
  Devil In Spurs
  Elisha's Woman
  Forever The Flame
  Hunter's Moon
  Marna
  Wildfire

_____

_____

HEWITT, Elizabeth   <RE>
                    [Mary Jeanne Abbott]
                    [Mary Jeanne E. Hewitt]
  Airs And Graces
  An Innocent Deception
  Broken Vows
  Captain Black
  Fortune Hunter, The
  Ice Maiden, The
  Lasting Attachment, A
  Marriage By Consent
  Private Understanding, A
  Sporting Proposition, A
  Worth Inheritance, The

_____

_____

HEYER, Georgette   (Deceased)
                         <HO><RE>
                    [Georgette Rougier]
  April Lady
  Arabella
  Barren Corn
  Bath Tangle
  Beauvallet
  Black Moth, The
  Black Sheep
  Charity Girl
  Civil Contract, A
  Conqueror, The
  Convenient Marriage, The
  Corinthian, The
  Cotillion
  Cousin Kate
  False Colours
  Faro's Daughter

HIGGINS, Joyce
  Silhouette Romance:
    547 Dreams Are Forever

_____

HIGGINS, Margaret   <GOT>
  Changeling, The
  Doctor For The Dead, A
  Unholy Sanctuary
  Witch Alone, The

_____

HIGH, Monique Raphel   <HO>
  Between Two Worlds
  Eleventh Hour, The
  Encore
  Four Winds Of Heaven, The <HS>
  Keeper Of The Walls, The
  Thy Father's House   <HS>

_____

HIGHET, Helen   (Deceased)
                        (Helen MacInnes)

HIGHLAND, Monica   <HR>
  [Carolyn See and Lisa See w/
                        John Espey]
  Lotus Land   <HS>
  110 Shanghai Road

_____

_____

HIGHMORE, Jane
  Big City Nurse

_____

_____

HILL, Alexis
                  [Mary Francis Craig]
  In sequence:
    Passion's Slave
    Untamed Heart, The

_____

_____

HILL, Alexis
  [Ruth Glick w/ Louise Titchener]
  Candlelight Ecstasy:
    115 In The Arms Of Love

_____

HILL, Deborah
  Trilogy:
    This Is The House
    House Of Kingsley Merrick, The
    Kingsland

_____

HILL, Elizabeth Ann   <GOT>
  Hidden Spring, The

_____

_____

HILL, Ernestine
  Sable Night, The

_____

HILL, Fiona
                  [Ellen Jane Pall]
  Autumn Rose, The
  Country Gentleman, The
  Love Child, The
  Love In A Major Key
  Practical Heart, The
  Stanbroke Girls, The
  Sweet's Folly
  Trellised Lane, The
  Wedding Portrait, The

_____

HILL, Grace Livingston (Deceased)
    1 Where Two Ways Met
    2 Bright Arrows
    3 Girl To Come Home To, A
    4 Amorelle
    5 Kerry
    6 All Through The Night
    7 Best Man, The

311

HILL, John
Griffin Loves Phoenix
Heartbeeps
Long Sleep, The

HILL, Kaye   <CO>
Glitter Game, The

HILL, Lorna
Aston Hall:
109 Scent Of Rosemary

HILL, Meredith
Crystal Falls Series: <YA>
1 Wrong Side Of Love, The
5 Loss Of Innocence, A
6 Forbidden Love

HILL, Moira
James Sisters, The

HILL, Pamela   <GOT><RS>
Bride Of Ae
Daneclere
Devil Of Aske, The   <GOT-S>
Fire Opal
Green Salamander, The
Heatherton Heritage, The
House Of Cray, The
Malvie Inheritance, The
My Lady Glamis
Norah
Place Of Ravens, A
Strangers Forest
Sutburys, The
Tsar's Woman, The   <HO>

HILL, Pamela (cont.)
Whitton's Folly

HILL, Ruth Livingston
A Hearth Romance:
16 This Side Of Tomorrow

HILLARY, Anne   <RE>
[Anne Mikita Kolaczyk]
Candlelight:
505 Bartered Bride, The
578 Mismatched Lovers, The
661 Compromised Love
701 Diamonds And The
Arrogant Rake

HILLER, Catherine
17 Morton Street

HILLER, Flora
[Florence Hurd]
Love's Fiery Dagger

HILLIARD, Jan   <GOT><RS>
Dove Cottage
Jameson Girls, The
Miranda
Morgan's Castle
Salt Box, The
View Of The Town, A

HILLIARD Nerina
Harlequin Classic:
107 House Of Adriano,The (840)
159 Scars Shall Fade,The (927)

HINE, Alexandra
　　　　　(Alexandra Blakelee)

HINER, F. Philip
　Only For Today

HINES, Charlotte
　　　　　[Judith McWilliams]
　Second Chance At Love:
　　93　Earl's Fancy, The　　　<RE>
　160　Tender Trap
　255　Heaven To Kiss
　To Have And To Hold:
　　38　Sweet Nothings

HINES, Jeanne　　　　　　<GOT>
　　　　　[Jeanne McNeill Hines]
　　　　　(Rosamond Royal)
　　　　　(Valerie Sherwood)
　Bride Of Terror
　Keys To Queens Court, The
　Legend Of Witchwynd, The
　Scarecrow House
　Slashed Portrait, The
　Talons Of The Hawk
　Third Wife, The
　Tidehawks

HINGER, Charlotte
　Come Spring　　　　　　　<HS>

HINGSTON, Mary Sandra
　　　　　(Mallory Burgess)
　　　　　(Catherine FitzGerald)

HINKEMEYER, Michael Thomas
　　　　　(Jan Lara)
　　　　　(Vanessa Royall)

HINSDALE, Harriet　　　　<HR>
　Award, The　　　　　　　<CO>
　Be My Love
　Confederate Grey: Traveller

HINZ, Diana Whitney
　　　　　(Diana Whitney)

HITCHENS, Delores
　Abductor
　Bank With The Bamboo Door, The
　Baxter Letters, The
　In A House Unknown
　Man Who Cried All The Way Home

HITT, James　　　　　　　<HR>
　Tennessee Smith

HITZIG, Karen w/ Helen BARRETT
　　　　　(Justin Channing)

HIX, Martha
　　　　　[Martha Rand Hix]
　Heartfire Romance:　　　<HR>
　　Magnolia Nights
　　Wild Texas Rose
　Silhouette Romance:
　　779　Texas Tycoon
　Silhouette Special Edition:
　　344　Every Moment Counts

HIX, Martha Rand w/ Barbara Catlin
　CRAVEN　　　　　(Maranda Catlin)

HOAG, Tami
　Doubleday Loveswept: Magic
　Loveswept:
　　253　Trouble With J. J., The　#
　　276　McKnight In Shining Armor

HOFF, B. J.
    Serenade/Saga: <HR><Insp>
    27 To Love And To Honor

HOFFMAN, Alice
    Angel Landing   <CO>
    White Horses

HOFFMAN, Louise   <GOT><RS>
    Fear Among The Shadows <CGS:#2>
    Passing Stranger
    To Dream Of Evil   <CGS:#14>
    Candlelight:
        92 House Of Intrigue

HOFLAND, Karin
                        (Kayla Daniels)

HOH, Diane
    Chrystal Falls: <YA>
        7 Night To Forget, A
    Wildfire: <YA>
        Brian's Girl
        Loving That O'Conner Boy

HOHENBERG, John
    Parisian Girl, The   <RS>

HOHL, Joan
    [Joan Marie Reitenauer Hohl]
                        (Amii Lorin)
                        (Paula Roberts)
    (see Silhouette Summer Sizzlers)
    Second Chance At Love:
        Window Trilogy:
        450 Window On Yesterday
        454 Window On Today

HOHL, Joan (cont.)
    458 Window On Tomorrow
    Silhouette Classic:
        25 Moments Harsh,
                Moments Gentle   <IM54>
        36 Thorne's Way   <SE54>
    Silhouette Desire:
        247 Much Needed Holiday, A
        Sharp Family Trilogy:
        294 Texas Gold   @%
        312 California Copper
        330 Nevada Silver   &
        354 Lady Ice   @#<
        372 One Tough Hombre   %#
        390 Falcon's Flight   &
        475 Gentleman Insists,The<MMS>
        540 Christmas Stranger
        612 Handsome Devil   <MMS>
    Silhouette Intimate Moments:
        25 Moments Harsh,
                Moments Gentle   <IM54>
    Silhouette Romance:
        334 Taste For Rich Things, A >
        358 Someone Waiting
        376 Scent Of Lilacs, The   >
    Silhouette Special Edition:
        54 Thorne's Way   *
        444 Forever Spring   <
        537 Thorne's Wife   *

HOLBROOK, Cindy   <RE>
                [Cindy Jo Holbrook]
    Lady Megan's Masquerade
    Suitable Connection, A

HOLDEN, Genevieve   <RS>
    Something's Happened To Kate
    Velvet Target, The

HOLDEN, Joanne   <GOT>
                [Willo Davis Roberts]
    Dangerous Legacy
    Nurse At The Castle

HOLDEN, Joanne (cont.)
Nurse At The Castle
Nurse Gina
Queen's Grant Inheritance, The
Village Nurse
Where The Heart Is

HOLDEN, Monique
[Lisa Holden]
Silhouette Special Edition:
342 Tuckerville Revival

HOLDEN, Ursula   <CO>
Fallen Angels: Turnstiles
Fallen Angels: Endless Race
Fallen Angels: String Horses

HOLDER, Nancy
[Nancy L. Jones Holder]
(Laurel Chandler)
(Wendi Davis-<YA>)
(Nancy L. Jones)
Rough Cut
Loveswept:
30   Winner Take All
47   Greatest Show On Earth   &
77   Finders Keepers
103 Out Of This World
118 His Fair Lady   &
147 Once In Love With Amy
173 Emerald Fire

HOLDER, Samantha   <RE>
[Carol Burns w/ Deborah Jones]
Miss Rowland's Resolve
Scandal In Bath
Temporary Wife

HOLDING, Vera w/ John CHRISTY
Sharon Contemporary Teens:
Love Has Silent Wings

HOLDSWORTH, Diana
Silhouette Intimate Moments:
122 Shining Moment
171 Gold In The Stone

HOLLAND, Cecelia   <HO>
Antichrist
Belt Of Gold
City of God
Death Of Attila, The
Earl, The
Firedarake, The
Great Maria
Home Ground
Kings In Winter, The
Lords Of Vaumartin, The
Pillar Of The Sky
Rak'ossy
Sea Beggars, The
Two Ravens
Until The Sun Falls

HOLLAND, Isabelle   <GOT><RS>
Cecily
Counterpoint
Darcourt
deMaury Papers, The
Grenelle
Island, The
Jenny Kiss'd Me   <YA>
Kilgaren
Lost Madonna, The
Lover Scorned, A
Man Without A Face, The
Marchington Inheritance, The
Moncrieff
Perdita
Tower Abbey

318

HOLLAND, Isabelle (cont.)
Trelawny
In sequence: <YA>
  Summer Of My First Love
  After The First Love

_____

_____

HOLLAND, Lillie   <GOT>
Eighteenth Summer, The

_____

_____

HOLLAND, Margot
Masquerade:
  70 Lady Of Starlight
  90 Black Marquis

_____

_____

HOLLAND, Petra
Harlequin SuperRomance:
  462 Starlit Tomorrow

_____

_____

HOLLAND, Sarah
Harlequin Presents:
  516 Too Hot To Handle
  536 Tomorrow Began Yesterday
  552 Devil's Mistress, The
  576 Deadly Angel
  601 Fever Pitch
  1192 Heat Is On, The
Harlequin Romance:
  2705 Bluebeard's Bride

_____

_____

HOLLAND, Sheila   <GOT><HR><RE>
            [Sheila Coates Holland]
                    (Laura Hardy)
                  (Charlotte Lamb)
               (Sheila Lancaster)
                 (Victoria Woolf)
Dancing Hill
Folly By Candlelight
Love's Bright Flame

HOLLAND, Sheila (cont.)
Maiden Castle   <GEO>
Masque, The
Merchant's Daughter, The
Miss Charlotte's Fancy
Notorious Gentleman, The
Shadows At Dawn
Shadows On The Bay
Sophie
Secrets   <Saga>
  (includes "Secrets To Keep")
Secrets To Keep

_____

_____

HOLLAND, Suellen
Mountain Whipporwill   <YA>

_____

_____

HOLLIDAY, Delores
            [Delores Holliday Vile]
Greystone Shadows
Harlequin Gothic Romance:
  Blue House, The
  Seventh Gate, The
Mystique:
  140 Seventh Gate, The

_____

_____

HOLLIDAY, Judith A.
Starlight Romance:
  Hesitant Heart, The

_____

_____

HOLLINS, Mary
Cold Blows The Winds
Sacrifice, The

_____

_____

HOLLIS, Erica
SuperRomance:
  37 Passion's Triumph

_____

_____

HOLLOWAY, Ann
Golden Locket, The
Her Dream Come True

HOLLOWAY, Teresa
Campaign For Pam, A
Girl In Studio B, The
Government Girl
Nurse Farley's Decision
Nurse For The Fishermen
Nurse Karen's Secret
Nurse On Dark Island, The
Nurse Paige's Triumph
Nurse To Remember
Nurse Transplanted
River Nurse
Roses For Paula
Tomorrow's Nurse
Unwilling Witness, The

HOLLOWAY, Tess
[Teri Shapiro Kovack]
Candlelight Ecstasy:
105 Touch Of Heaven, A

HOLLYOCK, Dulcie
Harlequin Gothic Romance:
An Innocent Madness
Double Masquerade

HOLM, Stef Ann   <HR>
Firefly
Silver Desires

HOLMES, Clare Frances   <RE>
[Clare Francis]
Trafalgar Rose, The

HOLMES, Deborah Aydt
Family Ties   <Saga>

HOLMES, Dee
[Nancy Harwood Bulk]
Silhouette Intimate Moments:
327 Black Horse Island
Silhouete Special Edition:
660 Return Of Slade Garner

HOLMES, Francis
[Clare Francis]
Eagle's Pawn, The

HOLMES, Marjorie   <YA>
Young Love:
Cherry Blossom Princess
Follow Your Dream
Saturday Night
Senior Trip
Sunday Morning

HOLMES, Mary Mayer   <HR>
Irish Bride, The
White Raven, The
Wind-Rose, The
Lovestruck:
Savage Tides

HOLMGREN, Virginia/ Virginia C.
Kathy Herself
Wish On A Mountain
Candlelight:
33 Nurse Kilmer's Vow

HOLT, Helen
  Aston Hall:
    114 One Love Lost

HOLT, Victoria   <GOT><RS>
              [Eleanor Burford Hibbert]
  Bride Of Pendorric
  Captive, The
  Curse Of The Kings, The
  Demon Lover, The
  Devil On Horseback, The
  House Of A Thousand Lanterns, The
  India Fan, The
  Judas Kiss
  King Of The Castle, The
  Kirkland Revels
  Landower Legacy, The
  Legend Of The Seventh Virgin
  Lord Of The Far Island
  Mask Of The Enchantress, The
  Menfreya In The Morning
  Mistress Of Mellyn, The
  My Enemy The Queen
  On The Night Of The Seventh Moon
  Queen's Confession, The
  Pride Of The Peacock, The
  Road To Paradise Island, The
  Secret For A Nightingale
  Secret Woman, The
  Shadow Of The Lynx, The
  Shivering Sands, The
  Silk Vendetta, The
  Snare Of Serpents
  Spring Of The Tiger, The
  Time Of The Hunter's Moon, The

HOLT, Will
                    (see Rebecca Drury)

HOLTON, Frances
  Avalon:
    Caverns Of Danger
    Home From Hawaii

HOLTON, Frances (cont.)
    New Life, New Love

HONEYMAN, Brenda   <HO>
              [Brenda Clarke]
  Roses, Red And White
  Shadow Of The Tower Series:
    Warrior King, The
    Rose In Spring, The
    Warwick Heiress, The
    Son Of York
    Richmond And Elizabeth

HONG, Jane Fay w/ Evelyn Marie
  PAVLIK   (Adora Sheridan)

HONIG, Donald   <RS>
  Illusions
  Judgment Night
  Marching Home
  Love Thief, The

HOOPER, Kay
              [Glenda Kay Hooper]
                    (Kay Robbins)
  Summer Of The Unicorn   <RF>
  Candlelight:
    665 Lady Thief   <RE>
  Candlelight Ecstasy:
    77 Mask Of Passion
    90 Breathless Surrender
    153 On Wings Of Magic
  The Delaney Dynasty:
    The Untamed Years:
    In sequence:
      Golden Flames
      Velvet Lightning
  The Delaneys Of Killaroo:
    Adelaide, The Enchantress
  The Shamrock Trinity:
    Rafe, The Maverick   (LS167)

HOOPER, Kay (cont.)
Doubleday Loveswept:
    Once Upon A Time...
        Star-Crossed Lovers
Loveswept:
    32 C. J.'s Fate
    46 Something Different
    62 Pepper's Way   &
    71 If There Be Dragons   &
    83 Illegal Possession
    128 Rebel Waltz
    149 Time After Time   #
    167 Rafe, The Maverick
    189 In Serena's Web   *
"Hagan Strikes Again" series: *
    193 Raven On The Wing
    219 Rafferty's Wife
    225 Zach's Law   #
    231 Fall Of Lucas Kendrick
    237 Unmasking Kelsey
    256 Outlaw Derek
    286 Shades Of Gray

    296 Captain's Paradise
    312 It Takes A Thief
    321 Aces High
        Once Upon A Time...
    348 Golden Threads
    360 Glass Shoe, The
    390 What Dreams May Come
    408 Through The
            Looking Glass
    426 Lady And The Lion, The
Loveswept Exclusive:
    Larger Than Life
Loveswept Golden Classic:
    C. J.'s Fate   <LS32>
Silhouette Intimate Moments:
    297 Enemy Mine

_____

HOOPER, Mary
Heartlines: <YA>
    4 Friends And Rivals
    6 Follow That Dream

_____

_____

HOOVER, Mab Graff
    Serenade/Serenata: <Insp>
    5   In Comes Love
    34 New Love, A

_____

_____

HOOVER, Saranne
                        (Saranne Dawson)
                        (Pamela Lind)
    A Fantasy Romance:
        Greenfire

_____

_____

HOPE, Daphne
    Harlequin Romance:
        Look At My Heart   HRS12

_____

HOPE, Jacqueline
                    [Jacqueline Hacsi]
    Silhouette Romance:
    145 Love Captive

_____

HOPE, Margaret
                    [Alanna Knight]
    Masquerade:
    16 Queen's Captain, The
    30 Hostage Most Royal
    42 Shadow Queen, The

_____

HOPLEY, George
                    [Cornell Woolrich]
    Night Has A Thousand Eyes, The

_____

HORLER, Sydney   <GOT>
    Curse Of Doone, The
    Vampire   <SN>

_____

HORNER, Lance
                [Kenric Lance Horner]
  The Falconhurst Series:
  1 Mistress Of Falconhurst
  3 Falconhurst Fancy
                w/ Kyle ONSTOTT
  4 Flight To Falconhurst
  9 Mustee, The
  13 Heir To Falconhurst
  Black Sun, The   w/Kyle ONSTOTT
  Golden Stud
  Mahound, The
  Rogue Roman
  Street Of The Sun, The
  (see MANDINGO/FALCONHURST series)
  (see Ashley CARTER & Kyle ONSTOTT)

HORSMAN, Jennifer   <HR>
  Crimson Rapture
  Forever And A Lifetime
  Magic Embrace
  Passion Flower
  Passion's Joy

HORTON, Marian   <RE>
        [Marian Lorraine Horton]
                (Marian Lorraine)
  Mischievous Spinster

HORTON, Naomi
                [Susan Naomi Horton]
  Silhouette Desire:
  162 Dream Builder
  236 River Of Dreams
  269 Split Images
  302 Star Light, Star Bright
  320 Lady Liberty
  365 No Walls Between Us
  386 Pure Chemistry
  435 Crossfire
  487 Dangerous Kind Of Man<MMS>
  518 Ideal Man, The

HORTON, Naomi (cont.)
  596 Cat's Play
  630 McAllister's Lady   <MMS>
  Silhouette Intimate Moments:
  323 Strangers No More
  343 In Safekeeping
  Silhouette Romance:
  342 Risk Factor

HORTON, Patricia Campbell
  Royal Mistress
  Tender Fire

HOSKINS, Robert
                        (Grace Corren)
                     (Susan Jennifer)
HOSNANI, Justine
  Mark Of The Lilies

HOTCHKISS, Bill   <HO>
  Crow Warriors   <AIS:#3>
  Dance Of The Coyote
  Fire Woman
  Mountain Lamb
  People Of The Sacred Oak
  Spirit Mountain

HOTCHKISS, Bill w/ Judith SHEARS
  Pawnee Medicine   <AIS:#14>
  Shoshone Thunder   <AIS:#12>

HOUGHTON, Elizabeth
                [Elizabeth Gilzean]
  Harlequin Classic:
    8 Doctor Sara Come Home
  Harlequin Romance:
  835 Part-Time Angel

HOUGHTON, Elizabeth (cont.)
1010 Doctor Of Research
1074 New Surgeon At St.
        Lucian's
1153 Return Of Sister
        Barnett, The
1209 Stubborn Dr. Stephen, The

HOUSEMAN, Phyllis
[Phyllis Houseman
                w/ Jack Houseman]
Pageant Romance:
    Verdict Is Love, The

HOUSTON, David
Paradise
Shadows On The Moon

HOUSTON, Henrietta
[Prudence Jane Bingham Lichte]
Second Chance At Love:
75 An Improper Betrothment <RE>

HOUSTON, James
Ghost Fox
Spirit Wrestler
White Dawn: An Eskimo Saga

HOUSTON, Margaret Bell   <GOT>
Bride's Island
Yonder

HOWARD, Alyssa
[Eileen Buckholtz, Ruth Glick,
Louise Titchener & Carolyn Males]
Silhouette Desire:
100   Southern Persuasion
Silhouette Romance:
186   Love Is Elected

HOWARD, Audrey
Ambitions   <HS>

HOWARD, Donald M.
                        (Andrea St. John)

HOWARD, Eleanor
            [Eleanor Parker Hodgson]
Fortune's Choice
Tapestry: <HR>
    Cloak Of Fate

HOWARD, Guy
A Hearth Romance:
    17   Give Me Thy Vineyard

HOWARD, Jessica   <HR>
[Monroe Schere w/ Jean K. Schere]
Prairie Flame
Savage Embrace
Traitor's Bride

HOWARD, Joy
SuperRomance:
    60   Stormy Paradise

HOWARD, Julia
                    [Patricia Camden]
Candlelight Ecstasy:
   165 Passionate Venture, A
   194 Lasting Image, A
   247 Working It Out

HOWARD, Katharine
Jeanne
Ventures

HOWARD, Linda
                    [Linda Howington]
Lady Of The West   <HR>
Silhouette Christmas Stories-1987
   Bluebird Winter   &
Silhouette Classic:
    4 An Independent Wife (SE46)
   21 Against The Rules   (IM22)
Silhouette Intimate Moments:
   22 Against The Rules
   92 Tears Of The Renegade
  129 Midnight Rainbow   @
  177 Diamond Bay   @
  201 Heartbreaker   @
  281 Mackenzie's Mountain
  349 Duncan's Bride
Silhouette Special Edition:
   22 All That Glitters
   46 An Independent Wife
  177 Come Lie With Me
  230 Sarah's Child   &
  260 Cutting Edge, The
  327 Almost Forever   &
  452 White Lies   @

HOWARD, Lynnette Desley
             (Lynde Howard-ENG)
             (Lynsey Stevens)

HOWARD, Lynde
             [Lynnette Desley Howard]
All I Ever Wanted   <ENG>

HOWARD, Mary   <RS>
                    [Mary Mussi]
Anna Heritage
Clouded Moon, The
Cottager's Daughter, The
Crystal Villa, The
Devil In My Heart
Family Orchestra
Far Blue Horizons
First Star
Fool's Haven
For Love Or Money   <CO>
Gay Is Life
Intruder, The
Mist On The Hills
Promise Of Delight
Return To Love
Sixpence In Her Shoe
Strangers In Love
There Will I Follow
Unchartered Romance
Wise Forget, The
Young Lady, The

HOWARD, Stephanie
Harlequin Presents:
  1098 Reluctant Prisoner
  1130 Dark Lucifer
  1168 Highland Turmoil
  1273 Bride For A Price
  1307 Kiss Of The Falcon
Harlequin Romance:
  3093 Master Of Glen Crannach
  3112 An Impossible Passion

HOWARD, Veronica
Candlelight:
   657 Rebel In Love   <RE>

HOWARTH, Jean Stubbs
  In sequence:
    By Our Beginnings
    An Imperfect Job

HOWATCH, Susan   <GOT><RS>
  April's Grave
  Call In The Night
  Cashelmara   <Saga>
  Dark Shore, The
  Devil On Lammas Night, The
  Penmarric   <Saga>
  Shrouded Walls, The
  Waiting Sands, The
  Wheel Of Fortune, The   <Saga>
  In sequence: <CS>
    Rich Are Different, The
    Sins Of The Fathers

HOWE, Doris Kathleen
             (Mary Munro)

HOWE, Fanny   <RS>
  Blue Hills
  Bronte Wilde
  Eggs
  First Marriage
  Forty Whacks
  Holy Smoke
  Legacy Of Lanshore

HOWE, Margaret
  Calling Dr. Merryman
  Debutante Nurse
  Girl In The White Cap, The

HOWE, Susanna   <HR>
             (Bree Thomas)
  Fever Moon
  Masquerade

HOWE, Susanna (cont.)
  Snow Flame

HOWELL, Dorothy
             (Kit Prate)

HOWELL, Hannah D.   <HR>
           (Sarah Dustin)
  Amber Flame
  Compromised Hearts
  Elfking's Lady
  Promised Passion
  Thunder At Twilight   <WWT>

HOWELL, Jean   <CO>
  To Love A Stranger

HOWELL, Jessica
  First Love From Silhouette: <YA>
    37 Love Note

HOWELL, Patricia Hagan   <GOT><RS>
        [Mary Patricia Hagan]
  Dark Journey Home
  Winds Of Terror

HOWINGTON, Linda
            (Linda Howard)

HOWL, Marcia Yvonne
            (Pauline York)

HOWL, Marcia Yvonne w/ Sharon
  JARVIS   (Johanna Hailey)

HOY, Charlotte w/ Linda Varner
  PALMER   (Jessica St. James)
          (Scotney St. James)

HOY, Elizabeth
    [Alice 'Nina' Conarain]
Harlequin Classic:
  1 Do Something
      Dangerous   (501)
  10 When You Have
      Found Me   (526)
  21 City Of Dreams   (542)
  37 Dear Fugitive   (573)
 120 Homeward The Heart (925)
 129 Who Loves Believes (959)
 140 My Heart Has Wings (483)
 161 To Win A Paradise (532)
Harlequin Romance:
 903 So Loved And So Far
 925 Homeward The Heart
 959 Who Loves Believes
 992 Snare The Wild Heart
1031 Flowering Desert
1104 Faithless One, The
1132 Dark Horse, Dark Rider
1226 Honeymoon Holiday
1286 Be More Than Dreams
1368 Music I Heard With You
1397 If Love Were Wise
1520 Into A Golden Land
1538 It Happened In Paris
1605 Immortal Flower
1695 That Island Summer
1769 Girl In Green
      Valley, The
1825 Shadows On The Sand
1885 Proud Citadel
1901 Blue Jacaranda, The

HOYLE, Coral   <RE>
    [Coral Hoyle Titus]
Harlequin Regency Romance:
  4 Midsummer Masque
 15 Virgin's Heart, The
 29 Merry Go-Round, A

HRIMAK, Denise w/ Pat MATHEWS
          (Denise Mathews)

HUBBARD, Charlotte
  Heartfire Romance: <HR>
    Colorado Captive

HUBBARD, Richard   <GOT><RS>
  Daughter Of Despair
  Silence, The

HUDSON, Anna
      [JoAnn Algermissen]
  Candlelight Ecstasy:
 156 Kiss The Tears Away
 197 Design For Desire
 240 Taking A Chance
 269 Take My Hand
 286 Prize Catch, A
 305 Fire And Ice
 310 Honeymoon
 345 Whole Lot Of Woman, A
 374 Glittering Promises
 400 Jeweled Skies,
      Shimmering Sands
 439 Tears Of Love
 454 Perfect Match, The
 474 Rebel Love
 491 Fun And Games
 520 Sweet Talkin' Lover
 530 Denim And Silk
  Candlelight Ecstasy Supreme:
  13 Body And Soul

HUDSON, Harriett L.
      [Leigh Shaheen]
  In Search Of Love

HUDSON, Jan
      [Janece Oliver Hudson]
  Loveswept:
 293 Water Witch
 319 Right Moves, The
 380 Always Friday

HUDSON, Jan (cont.)
397 Step Into My Parlor
443 Deeper And Deeper

HUDSON, Janece Oliver
                    (Jan Hudson)
                    (Jan Oliver)

HUDSON, Meg
        [Margaret Hudson Koehler]
Harlequin American Romance:
    25 To Love A Stranger
SuperRomance:
     9 Sweet Dawn Of Desire
    36 Love's Sound In Silence
    53 Return To Rapture
    64 Though Hearts Resist
    70 Charm For Adonis, A
    79 Two Worlds, One Love
    94 Beloved Stranger
Harlequin SuperRomance:
   106 Rising Road, The
   126 Now In September
   141 Champagne Promises
   174 Gift From The Sea, A
   188 More Than A Memory
   234 Forever Promise, The
   250 Way To Remember, A
   274 Chance Meeting
   295 Day Before Dawn, The
   357 Until April
   465 Leftover Girl, The

HUFF, Afton Patricia   <GOT>
Key To Hawthorn Heath, The

HUFF, Tom E.   <GOT>(Deceased)
                      (Edwina Marlow)
                      (Beatrice Parker)
                      (Katherine St. Clair)
                      (Jennifer Wilde)
Marabelle

HUFF, Tom E. (cont.)
Meet A Dark Stranger
Susanna Beware
Whisper In The Darkness

HUFFORD, Susan   <GOT><RS>
                        (Samantha Hughes)
Cove's End
Delicate Deceit, A
Devil's Sonata, The
Going All The Way
Melody Of Malice
Midnight Sailing
Satan's Sunset
Skin Deep
Trial Of Innocence

HUGHES, Cally
                    [Lass Small]
Second Chance At Love:
   112 Lasting Treasure, A
   140 Innocent Seduction
   173 Cupid's Revenge
To Have And To Hold:
    15 Whatever It Takes
    25 Treasure To Share, A
           (sequel to SCAL #112)
    33 Never Too Late

HUGHES, Charlotte
Loveswept:
   159 Too Many Husbands
   220 Straight-Shootin' Lady
   241 Travelin' Man
   297 Sweet Misery
   345 Tigress
   365 Scoundrel
   409 Private Eyes
   433 Restless Nights
       Louisiana Lovin'

HUGHES, Eden   <HS>
            [William E. Butterworth]
Selkirks, The
Wiltons, The

HUGHES, Megan w/ Frank ORBACH
Givers & Takers

HUGHES, Rose
Stranger In Paradise

HUGHES, Samantha
            [Susan Hufford]
Candlelight Ecstasy:
    122 Silent Wonder, A
    179 Desert Splendor
    299 Shenandoah Summer
    346 Taste Of Heaven, A
Candlelight Ecstasy Supreme:
    11   Politics Of Passion
    29   Diamonds In The Sky

HUGHES, Tracy
            [Terri Herrington]
Harlequin American Romance:
    381 Honorbound   <COAR>
Harlequin Romance:
    2744 Quiet Lightning
    2792 Impressions
Harlequin SuperRomance:
    304 Above The Clouds
    342 Jo   <CCS>
    381 Emerald Windows
    399 White Lies And Alibis

HUGHESDON, Beverley
Song Of Songs   <HS>

HULL, Beverly Wilcox
Candlelight Ecstasy:
    384 Whisper Away, A
Candlelight Ecstasy Supreme:
    105 Spanish Moon

HULME, Ann
Harlequin Historical <Set#1>:
    10   Garden of The Azure Dragon
Harlequin Regency Romance:
    8   Unexpected American, The
    40   Scandalous Bargain, A
    53   False Fortune
Masquerade:
    26   Poor Relation, A
    83   Summer Heiress

HUMPHREY, Aileen   <HR>
Golden Swan, Thje

HUMPHREYS, Martha
First Love From Silhouette: <YA>
    102 Side By Side
    178 Broken Bow, A

HUMPHRIES, Adelaide
Clinic Nurse
Mission Nurse
Navy Nurse
Night Call
Nurse Barclay's Dilemma
Nurse Had A Secret, The
Nurse In A Nightmare

HUMPHRIES, Adelaide (cont.)
Nurse In Flight
Nurse Landon's Challenge
Nurse Laurie's Cruise
Nurse On Horseback, A
Orchids For A Nurse
Park Avenue Nurse
Test For Nurse Barbi, A
Avalon:
   Danger For Nurse Vivian
   Miracle For Nurse Louisa
Candlelight:
   13 Chesapeake Doctor
   25 Nurse Makes Headlines, The
   28 Feather In Her Cap, A
   41 Doctor Of The Keys
   57 Love Has No Logic

HUNSBURGER, H. Edwards
         (see Farris Fletcher)

HUNT, Charlotte   <GOT><RS>
             [Doris Marjorie Hodges]
Chambered Tomb, The
Cup Of Thanatos, The
Gemini Revenged
Gilded Sarcophagus, The
Touch Of Myrrh, A
Tremayne's Wife
Wreath For Jenny's Grave, A
The Casebook Of Dr. Holton:
   Lotus Vellum, The
   Thirteenth Treasure, The

HUNT, Edward
Denise
Fire In My Blood

HUNT, Greg   <HO>
             (see Rebecca Drury)
   (see Lee Davis Willoughby <MOAS>)
John Bozeman: <AES:#13>
   Mountian Journey

HUNT, Greg (cont.)
Marcus Whitman: <AES:#8>
   Frontier Mission

HUNT, Jena
                     [Helen Conrad]
Second Chance At Love:
   55 Sweet Victory
   78 Sweeter Than Wine
   127 Jade Tide
   147 Proud Possession
   470 Traces Of Indigo

HUNT, Mary Vincent
Laura's Island (Cast A Green
   Shadow)

HUNT, Rosamund
Doctor's Daughters, The
Gilded Towers
Nurse Martin's Secret
Starlit Road, The
Understanding Heart, The
Candlelight:
   10 Settlement Nurse
   22 Night Nurse
   37 Emergency Nurse

HUNTER, Damion   <HO>
Roman Saga:
   1 Centurions, The
   2 Barbarian Princess
   3 Emperor's Games, The

HUNTER, Diane   <HR>
Winds Of Destiny

HUNTER, Elizabeth
    [Elizabeth Mary Teresa Hunter]
                    (Isobel Chace)
                (Elizabeth deGuise)
Harlequin Classic:
    167 Spiced With Cloves (1071)
Harlequin Romance:
    1071 Spiced With Cloves
    1758 Crescent Moon, The
    1780 Tower Of The Winds, The
    1807 Tree Of Idleness, The
    1844 Beads Of Nemesis, The
    1888 Bonds Of Matrimony, The
    1912 Spanish Inheritance, The
    1926 Voice In The Thunder, The
    1940 Sycamore Song, The
    2032 Bride Price, The
    2048 Realms Of Gold, The
    2120 Pride Of Madeira
Silhouette Romance:
    18 Lion's Shadow, The
    51 Bride Of The Sun
    65 Touch Of Magic, A
    91 Written In The Stars
    137 One More Time
    167 Silver Nutmeg, A
    198 London Pride
    218 Fountains Of Paradise
    240 Shared Destiny
    257 Tower Of Strength, A
    268 Kiss Of The Rising Sun
    278 Time To Wed, A
    290 Rain On The Wind
    298 Song Of Surrender
    310 Loving Relations
    322 Pathway To Heaven
    360 Legend Of The Sun
    385 Eye Of The Wind
    438 Painted Vail, The
    577 Tides Of Love, The

HUNTER, Evan
    Blackboard Jungle, The
    Buddwing
    Chisholms, The:
        A Novel Of The West

HUNTER, Evan (cont.)
    Come Winter
    Every Little Crook And Nanny
    Horse's Head
    Last Summer
    Matter Of Conviction, A
    Mothers & Daughters
    Nobody Knew Where They Were
    Second Ending
    Sons
    Strangers When We Meet
    Streets Of Gold
    Walk Proud

HUNTER, James H.
    A Hearth Romance:
        18 Mystery of Mar Saba, The

HUNTER, Jillian
                    [Maria Gardner]
    The Avon Romance:
        Heart Of The Storm
        Shadows Of Splendor

HUNTER, Joan
                    [Jeanne Yarde]
    Cavalier's Woman, The
    Lord Of Kestle Mount
    Roxanna
    Under The Raging Moon

HUNTER, Julia
    MacFadden Romance:
        181 Yesterday's Shadow
        200 Kisses In The Rain
        225 Last Rose Of Summer, The
        230 Just Before Nightfall
        230 Forgotten Garden

HUNTER, Julia (cont.)
    255 Just Before Nightfall
        (reprint)

_____

_____

HUNTER, Margaret   <HR>
                    [Ronald Singer]
Love's Secret Journey

_____

_____

HUNTER, Terry
Caprice Romance: <YA>
    31 Heartbreaker
Turning Points: <YA>
    6 Keep Tomorrow For Me

_____

_____

HUNTER, Valancy
                    [Eloise Meaker]
Devil's Double
Namesake, The
Rebel Heart, The

_____

_____

HUNTON, Mary
            [Elizabeth Gilzean]
Harlequin Romance:
1041 Nurse Averil's Ward

_____

_____

HURD, Florence   <GOT>
            [Florence Schnitzer Hurd]
                    (Fiona Harrowe)
                    (Flora Hiller)
China Silk   <CO>
Curse Of The Moors
Dreamtime, The   <CO>
Gorgons Head
House Of Shadows
House On Russian Hill, The
House On Trevor Street, The
Legacy
Love's Fiery Dagger

HURD, Florence (cont.)
Moorsend Manor
Nightmare At Mountain Aerie
Night Wind At Northriding
Possessed, The
Rommany
Seance For The Dead
Secret Of Awen Castle, The
Secret Of Canfield House
Secret Of Hayworth Hall, The
Shadows Of The Heart
Storm House
Terror Of Seacliff Pines
Voyage Of The Secret Duchess, The
Wade House
Witch's Pond

_____

_____

HURLEY, Ann
                    [Ann Salerno]
Silhouette Desire:
    181 Chasing The Rainbow
    233 Year Of The Poet
    288 Catching A Comet
    321 Fair Breeze, A
Silhouette Romance:
    408 Highest Tower, The
Silhouette Special Edition:
    98 Touch Of Greatness
    167 Hearts In Exile

_____

_____

HURST, Fannie   (Deceased)
Anatomy Of me
Anitra's Dance
Back Street
Family!
God Must Be Sad
Humoresque
Imitation Of Life
Lonely Parade, The

_____

_____

HURST, Heather Smith
Candlelight:
  145 Dark Is My Destiny

HUSTED, Darrell   <RE>
Country Girl, A
Miss Cordelia Harling
Coventry:
   70 Courting
   92 Chastity's Prize
  158 Visitor From Vienna
Starlight Romance:
  Stage Daughter

HUTCHINSON, Bobby
Harlequin American Romance:
  147 Wherever You Go
  173 Welcome The Morning
  223 Follow A Wild Heart
  290 Home To The Cowboy
Harlequin SuperRomance:
  166 Sheltering Bridges
  229 Meeting Place
  253 Draw Down The Moon
  284 Northern Knights   &
  337 Patch Of Earth, A   &
  376 Remember Me
· 443 Journey's End
Harlequin Temptation:
  285 Strictly Business

HUTTON, Ann
           [Audrey Grace Hutton]
Passport To Peril

HUTTON, Audrey Grace
      [Audrey Grace Wilson Hutton]
               (Ann Hutton)
          (Barbara Whitnell)

HUXLEY, Donna
Harlequin Presents:
  754 Intimate
  776 Number One
  792 Stranger To Love, A

HYATT, Betty Hale   <HR><RE>
Anna's Story
Fandora's Story
Jade Pagoda, The
Linnet's Story
Vesper Bells, The
Candlelight:
    2 Ivy Halls
   97 Heiress Of Wainscote   <RE>
  106 Friary's Dor   <RE>
  112 Chantilly   <RE>
  118 Scarlet Hills   <RE>
  141 Castle Of Kudara, The <RE>
  143 Mistress Of Priory
         Manor, The   <RE>
  186 Golden Falcon, The
  196 Portrait Of Errin
  208 Brigand's Bride, The
  210 Gallant Spy, The
  214 Pandora's Box
  229 Love's Untold Secret
  257 Chevalier's Lady, The
Other Candlelight:
  Villa San Gabriel
Starlight Romance:
  Jade Pagoda, The
  Sapphire Lotus, The
  Shalimar Pavillion, The

HYATT, Jeramie
Ex, The   <CO>

HYDE, Cynthia   <GOT>
House Of Sinister Shadows, The

HYLTON, Sara
  Caprice
  Crimson, Falcon, The
  Desert Splendor
  Hills Are Eternal, The
  Jacintha
  My Sister Clare   <HR>
  Talisman Of Set, The
  Tomorrow's Rainbow
  Whispering Glade   <HR>

_____

HYMAN, Jackie D.   <RE>
  [Jacquelyn Diamond Hyman Wilson]
              (Jacqueline Diamond)
                 (Jacqueline Jade)
                (Jacqueline Topaz)
  Lady In Disguise
  Song For A Lady

_____

HYNNES, Lucetta L.
            (Caroline Light)

IBBOTSON, Eva
   Countess Below Stairs, A
   Madensky Square
   Magic Flutes

IHLE, Sharon J.
               (Sharon MacIver)

IMBODEN, Durant
               (Cheryl Durant)

IMMIGRATION SAGAS: <IMS>   <HO>
   Africans, The
              Betty Winston
   Chinese, The
              John Robinson
   French, The
        W. Maureen Miller
   Irish, The
         Doris Flood Ladd
   Italians, The
          E. A. Tremblay
   Jews, The
         Sharon Steeber
   Poles, The
         Susan Richard
   Russians, The
         Judith Shears
   Scots, The
          Jane Toombs

INGRAM, Grace   <RS>
   Gilded Spurs
   Red Adam's Lady

INGRAM, Nancy
   Impromptu

INGWALSON, Phoebe Conn
            (Phoebe Conn)

INNES, Evan
   America 2040 Series: <Saga>
     America 2040
     Golden World, The
     City In The Mist

INNES, Jean
         [Jean Saunders]
   Circle Of Love:
     6 Ashton's Folly
    19 Wishing Stone, The
    28 Enchanted Island
    32 Scent Of Jasmine
   Heartfire Romance: <HR>
     Buccaneer's Bride
   Dawnstar Romance:
     Silver Lady
   Torch:
     Captive Heart

IRELAND, Jane
        [Jacqueline Potter]
   Second Chance At Love:
    169 Silver Enchantment
   To Have And To Hold:
    48 Love Notes

IRISH, Lola   <HR>
   Colonial Trilogy:
     And The Wild Birds Sing
     Place Of The Swans, The

IRISH, Rosalind
Call Me Gemini
Girl From Tralee, The
Linda Premise, The
Love In An Unlikely Place
Millicent Parrish: A Debut

ISRAEL, Charles/Charles E. <HR>
Dark Victory
Hostages
Shadows On A Wall
Who Was Then The Gentleman?

IRVING, Luella
Avalon:
Nurse Patsy's Last Chance

IVES, Averil
Harlequin Classic
141 Master Of Hearts (1047)
Harlequin Romance:
872 Haven Of The Heart
984 Island In The Dawn
1047 Master Of Hearts

IRWIN, Margaret (Deceased)<HO>
Bloodstock
Bride, The: Story Of Louise
And Montrose
Elizabeth And The Prince Of Spain
Elizabeth, Captive Princess
Gay Galliard, The: Love Story
Of Mary Queen Of Scots
Proud Servant, The
Royal Flush: The Story Of Minette
Stranger Prince, The
Young Bess

IVES, Ruth
Congo Nurse
Love's Tender Rebels
Navy Nurse

IVES, Viveca
Fox And His Vixen, The

IRWIN, Marianne
                (Sara Grant)

IRWIN, Sarita
Simplicity Of Love, The

ISAACS, Susan <CO>
Almost Paradise
Close Relations
Compromising Positions
Shining Through

336

JACKSON, Angela w/ Sandra JACKSON
                              (Lia Sanders)

JACKSON, Betty
  Candlelight Ecstasy Supreme:
     8 Handle With Care
    51 Horizon's Gift

_____

_____

JACKSON, Eileen   <RE><RS>
                [Eileen V. Jackson]
                        (Helen May)
  Autumn Lace
  Castle In The Rock
  Lord Rivington's Lady
  Secret Bluestocking
  Servant Of Quality
  Wicked Corinthian, The
  Coventry:
   131 Dance For A Lady

_____

_____

JACKSON, Helen Hunt
  Ramona

_____

_____

JACKSON, Lee
  Eagle And The Serpent, The

_____

_____

JACKSON, Lisa
                    [Susan Crose]
  Silhouette Intimate Moments:
    39 Dark Side Of The Moon
    79 Gypsy Wind
   158 Mystic
  Silhouette Romance:
   717 His Bride To Be

JACKSON, Lisa (cont.)
  Silhouette Special Edition:
   118 Twist Of Fate, A
   180 Shadow Of Time, The
   194 Tears Of Pride
   215 Pirate's Gold
   233 Dangerous Precedent, A
   244 Innocent By Association
   264 Midnight Sun
   282 Devil's Gambit
   296 Zachary's Law
   315 Yesterday's Lies
   358 One Man's Love
   376 Renegade Son
   394 Snowbound
   419 Summer Rain
   467 Hurricane Force
   495 In Honor's Shadow
   525 Aftermath   &
   569 Tender Trap   &
   611 With No Regrets
   636 Double Exposure
   653 Mystery Man

_____

_____

JACKSON, Loretta
                (see Vickie Britton)

JACKSON, Nancy w/ Lois Anne BROWN
                        (Ann Dabney)

JACKSON, O. T.   <RS>
  Aftermath
  Dark Love, Dark Magic

_____

_____

JACKSON, Sandra w/ Angela JACKSON
                        (Lia Sanders)

JACKSON, Shirley   <RS>
  Birds Nest, The
  Come Along With Me
  Hangsaman
  Haunting Of Hill House, The
  Lottery, The
  Road Through The Wall, The
  Sundial, The

JACKSON, Shirley (cont.)
We Have Always Lived In A Castle

JACOB, Naomi
Founder Of The House, The
Four Generations
Collantz Saga:
"That Wild Lie..."
Young Emmanuel
Gollantz, London, Paris, Milan
Private Gollantz
Gollantz And Partners

JACOBS, Helen Hull
Savage Sally, The

JACOBS, Linda C.
(Claire Blackburn)

JACOBS, Lynn
Harlequin Romance:
3020 Folly to Love

JACQUES, Aleece   <HR>
Dance With The Devil

JADE, Jacqueline
[Jackie Hyman]
Silhouette Desire:
316 Lucky Star, A

JAFFE, Susanne
Club Tropicale
Cruise Ship, M. D.
Models, The
New Adventures Of The Models, The
Promises And Lies   <CO>

JAGGER, Brenda   (Deceased)
Days Of Grace
Distant Choices
Song Twice Over, A
Winter's Child, A
A Family Saga:
Verity
Barforth Women, The
An Independent Woman

JAHN, Michael
Kingsley's Empire
Kingsley's Fortune
(see Lee Davis Willoughby <MOAS>)

JAHODA, Gloria   <HR>
House Of Bickley, The

JAKES, John   <HR>
(Jay Scotland)
(see Gil Kane)
California Gold
I, Barbarian
King's Crusader
Man From Cannae, The
Veils Of Salome
The Kent Family Cronicles   <HS>
In sequence:
Bastard, The
Rebels, The
Seekers, The
Furies, The

JAMES, B. J. (cont)
529 Shiloh's Story   <MMS>&
595 Winter Morning

JAMES, Barbara   <GOT><RS>
Beauty That Must Die
Bright Deadly Summer

JAMES, Christine
Masquerade:
65 Unwilling Betrothal

JAMES, Dana
Harlequin Romance:
2632 Desert Flower
2841 Marati Legacy, The
2872 Eagle And The Sun, The
2926 Tarik's Mountain
2973 Snowfire
2992 Pool Of Dreaming
3068 Love's Ransom
      Heart Of Glass   HRS 5
      Rough Waters   HRS31
      Dark Moon Rising   HRS63

JAMES, Deana   <HR>
                      [Mona Sizer]
Angel's Caress   &
Captive Angel   &
Crimson Obsession
Hot December   <CO>
Lovefire
Love Stone
Love Spell
Masque Of Sapphire
   (see also Emma Merritt)
Wild Texas Heart

JAMES, Deanna (cont.)
In sequence:
   Texas Storm
   Texas Tempest
   Texas Star

JAMES, Donald   <HO>
Once A Gentleman

JAMES, Elizabeth   <CO>
Secrets

JAMES, Ellen
                 [Ellen Jacob Cain]
Harlequin Romance:
3052 Home For Love
3069 Turquoise Heart, The

JAMES, Janice
Lady Of Repute, A

JAMES, Josephine
An Affair Of The Heart
Assignment In Alaska
Peace Corps Nurse
Private Nurse
Senior Nurse

JAMES, Kristin
              [Candace Pauline Camp]
         (see HQ Christmas Stories)
Heartwood
The Sky Series: &
   Golden Sky, The

340

JAMES, Kristen (cont.)
 Sapphire Sky, The
 Summer Sky, The
 Harlequin Historical <Set#2>:
  1 Satan's Angel
  43 Gentleman, The
     (see also Dorothy Glenn)
  57 Yankee, The
 Harlequin Temptation:
  62 Wedding Gift, A
 Silhouette Classic:
  1 Dreams Of Evening   (IM1)
  27 Morning Star   (IM45)
 Silhouette Intimate Moments:
  1   Dreams Of Evening
  17 Amber Sky, The   &
  45 Morning Star
  69 Secret Fires
  89 Worlds Apart
  125 Cutter's Lady
  136 Very Special Favor, A

JAMES, Leigh Franklin
                 [Paul H. Little]
 Saga Of The Southwest: <HS>
  In sequence:
   Hawk And The Dove, The
   Wings Of The Hawk
   Revenge Of The Hawk
   Flight Of The Hawk
   Night Of the Hawk
   Cry Of The Hawk
   Quest Of The Hawk
   Shadow Of The Hawk

JAMES, Livia
 Emerald Land, The

JAMES, Margaret
                 [Pamela Bennetts]
 Marrionette
 Voice In The Darkness, A

JAMES, Margaret (cont.)
 Candlelight:
  518 Haunting Of Sara
      Lessingham, The   <IN>
  545 Ring The Bell Softly   <IN>

JAMES, Melanie
 Love Forever   <CO>

JAMES, Rebecca   <GOT><HO>
                   [James Elward]
 House Is Dark, The
 Storm's End
 Tomorrow Is Mine

JAMES, Robin
            [Sharon and Tom Curtis]
 To Have And To Hold:
  1 Testimony, The
 Second Chance At Love:
  58 Golden Touch, The

JAMES, Sally   <RE>
                   [Joyce Wilson]
 Coventry:
  64 Clandestine Affair, The
  86 Petronella's Waterloo
  107 Heir To Rowanlea

JAMES, Sandra
              [Sandra Kleinschmit]
 Harlequin SuperRomance:
  205 Family Affair, A
  249 Belonging
  277 Stronger By Far
  306 Guardian Angel

JAMESON, Claudia (cont.)
  891 Man In Room 12, The
  922 One Dream Only
  945 Adam's Law
  969 To Speak Of Love
Harlequin Romance:
  2523 Lesson In Love
  2565 Melting Heart, The
  2578 Never Say Never
  2594 Yours...Faithfully
  2691 Time To Grow, A
  2842 Immune To Love
  2857 Man Of Contrasts, A
  2878 An Engagement
        Is Announced
  2936 Playing Safe
  3001 Unconditional Love
  3046 That Certain Yearning
  3099 Second Loving, A

JAMESON, Storm   <HO>
  Decline Of Merry England, The
  Speaking Of Stendhal
  In sequence: <HS>
    Lovely Ship, The
    Voyage Home, The
    Richer Dust, A
    Captain's Wife, The
    That Was Yesterday
    Company Parade
    Love In Winter

JAMISON, Amelia   <GOT>
                  [Sally M. Singer]
  Lairds Of Turriff Hall, The

JAMISON, Kelly
                  [Linda Buechting]
  Silhouette Desire:
    579 Echoes From The Heart
    626 Hearts In Hiding

JAMISON, Susan Rau
                        (Susan Ross)

JANAS, Frankie Lee
    [Frances Leroy Griggs Janas]
                    (Francesca Greer)
                    (Sailee O'Brien)

JANES, Josephine
                    [Victoria Heland]
  Second Chance At Love:
    117 London Frolic   <RE>

JANEWAY, Elizabeth
  Daisy Kenyon
  Walsh Girls, The

JANEWAY, Harriett
  This Passionate Land

JANIFER, Lawrence M.   <GOT>
  Woman Without A Name, The

JANSEN, Laura Mae   <GOT>
  Bride Of The Shadows

JANTZ, Carolyn
  Harlequin Romance:
    2793 Separate Lives

JARDIN, Rex   <GOT>
  Devil's Mansion, The

JARMAN, Rosemary Hawley   <HO>
  Courts Of Illusion, The
  Crispins Day: The Glory Of
    Agincourt
  Crown And Candlelight
  Crown Of Glory
  In sequence:
    We Speak No Treason, Book One
    We Speak No Treason, Book Two

JARNOW, Jill
  Sweet Dreams: <YA>
    80   Shot At Love, A
    108 One Of The Boys
    142 Lifeguard Summer

JARRETT, Amanda Jean   <HO>
  (publishers pseudonym for
           writers in this series)
  Southerners Series:
    Weep No More, My Lady
    This Traitor Moon
           [Robert Derek Steeley]
    Where My Love Lies Dreaming
           [George Granger]
    Passion And The Fury, The
           [James Scafidel]
    Red Roses Forever
           [Michael Avallone]

JARRETT, Bella
                    (Belle Thorne)
  Love Will Remember
  Candlelight:
    262 Aloha, Love   <RO>

JARRETT, Roxanne
                    [Herma Werner]
  Silhouette Romance:
    175 In Name Only

JARROW, Gail
  Caprice Romance: <YA>
    75   That Special Someone

JARVIS, Sharon w/ Marcia Yvonne
  HOWL   (Johanna Hailey)

JASON, Stuart
  Black Emperor
  Black Love
  Delta Stud
  Royal Master

JASON, Veronica
                    [Velda Johnston]
  Never Call It Love
  So Wild A Heart
  Wild Winds Of Love

JAUNIERE, Claudette
  Mystique:
    3   Proper Age For Love
    9   The Law Of Love
    14   The Whims Of Fate
    39   Lost Honeymoon
    53   Conspiracy To Kill
    72   Passage To Jamaica
    122 Heart's Revenge
    143 Heart Of Deception
    154 Captive Heart
    160 Marry Into Danger
    164 Journey Of Fear

JAY, Amanda Moor
                              (Laura Kinsale)

JAY, Willa   <GOT>
                     [William Johnston]
  Fear In Borzano, A

JEAL, Tim   <HR>
  Livingston
  Marriage Of Convenience, A
  Somewhere Beyond Reproach
  Until The Colors Fade   <HS>

JEFFREY, Elizabeth
  Harlequin Premiere Edition:
   30 Jordan's Castle
  Harlequin Romance:
  2271 Shadow Of Celia

JEFFRIES, Jessica
                        [Nancy Hermann]
  Harlequin American Romance:
   22 All In The Game
  SuperRomance:
   71 Certain Sunrise, A
  Harlequin SuperRomance:
  136 Memories To Share
  176 Quiet Comes The Night

JEFFRIES, Julia   <RE>
                        [Lynda Ward]
  Chadwick Ring, The
  Clergyman's Daughter, The

JEKEL, Pamela
                        [P. L. Jekel]
  Columbia   <Saga>

JEKEL, Pamela (cont.)
  Last Of The California Girls <CO>
  Sea Star   <HR>

JENKINS, Elizabeth   <HO>
  Dr. Gully's Story
  Elizabeth And Leicester
  Henry Fielding
  Princes In The Tower, The

JENKINS, Kate
                  [Linda Jenkins-Nutting]
  Harlequin Temptation:
  182 On The Wild Side
  227 Suddenly, Sunshine
  269 Reluctant Bachelor, The

JENKINS, Priscilla
  Amaryllis

JENKINS, Sara Lucille
                              (Joan Sargent)

JENKINS-NUTTING, Linda
                              (Kate Jenkins)

JENNER, Suzanne
  [Gretchen Johnson w/ Sally Netzel]
  Judy Sullivan Book:
    Midsummer   <RS>

JENNIFER, Susan   <GOT>
                       [Robert Hoskins]
  Country Of The Kind
  House Of Counted Hatreds, The

JENNINGS, John   <HR>
    Call The New World
    Gentleman Ranker
    Next To Valcour
    Pepper Tree, The
    Raider, The
    Rogue's Yarn
    Salem Frigate, The
    Sea Eagles, The
    Shadow And The Glory, The
    Shadows In The Dusk
    Strange Brigade, The

JENNINGS, Sara
                [Maura Seger]
    Candlelight Ecstasy:
    202 Reach For The Stars
    256 Game Plan
    287 Love Not The Enemy
    314 Star-Crossed

JENSEN, Dorthea w/ Catherine R.
    ALLEN   (Catherine Moorhouse)

JENSEN, Kathryn
    Select Circles

JENSEN, Margaret Mary
    Avalon:
        Seaside Kisses
    Crosswinds: <YA>
        29 House With The Iron
                Door, The

JENSEN, Muriel
    Harlequin American Romance:
    73   Winter's Bounty
    119 Lovers Never Lose
    176 Mallory Touch, The
    200 Fantasies And Memories

JENSEN, Muriel (cont.)
    219 Love And Lavender
    244 Duck Shack Agreement, The
    267 Strings
    283 Side By Side
    321 Carol Christmas, A <CIFK>
    339 Everything
    358 Wild Iris, A
    392 Miracle, The
    Harlequin SuperRomance:
    422 To Trust A Hero
    468 Love Shadows

JENSEN, Ruby/Ruby Jean   <GOT>
    Dark Angel
    Child Of Satan House
    Girl Who Didn't Die, The
    House That Samuel Built, The
    Room Without A Key
    Satan's Sister
    Seventh All Hallow's Eve
    Candlelight:
    159 House At River's Bend

JERINA, Carol
    Brighter Than Gold   &
    Embrace An Angel
    Flirting With Disaster
    Tropic Gold
    Romantic Mystery Series:
        Tall, Dark Alibi, The
        Sweet Jeopardy
    Tapestry: <HR>
    39   Lady Raine   &
    46   Gallagher's Lady   &
    66   Fox Hunt   &

JERROLD, Pamela
                [Pamela Ronning]
    Silhouette Special Edition:
    609 Other Mother, The

JESKE, Colleen
                    (Colleen Shannon)

JESSUP, Kathryn   <MED>
  Karen Evans, M. D.: Shock Trauma
  Karen Evans, M. D.: Woman Surgeon
  Karen Evans, M. D.:
                  Space Medicine
  Karen Evans, M. D.: Transplant
          [Anne w/ Ed Kolaczyk]
  _____

  _____

JEWEL, Carla Amalia Neggers
                    (Amalia James)
                    (Carla Neggers)
                    (Carla A. Neggers)

JEWEL, Carolyn   <HR>
  Passion's Song   <AAS>
  _____

  _____

JOCELYN, Archie   <HR>
  Hooded Falcon, The
  _____

  _____

JOEL, Cynthia
  Everlasting Love: <Insp>
    3 Joyous Season, The
  _____

  _____

JOERDEN, Marga   <GOT>
  Stranger No More
  _____

  _____

JOHANSEN, Iris
  Forever Dream, The
  Wind Dancer Trilogy:
    Wind Dancer, The
    Storm Winds, The
    Reap The Winds

JOHANSEN, Iris (cont.)
  The Delaney Dynasty:
    This Fierce Splendor (Prequel)
    The Untamed Years:
      In sequence:
        Wild Silver
        Satin Ice
    The Shamrock Trinity:
      York, The Renegade   (LS168)
    The Delaneys Of Killaroo:
      Matilda, The Adventuress
  Doubleday Loveswept:
    Golden Barbarian, The   <HR>&
  Loveswept Exclusive:
    One Touch Of Topaz
  Loveswept Golden Classic:
    Trustworthy Redhead, The <LS35>
    Lady And The Unicorn,The <LS29>
  Loveswept Silver Signature Ed.:
    Capture The Rainbow   <LS55>
    Touch The Horizon   <LS59>
  Loveswept:
     14 Stormy Vows   @
     17 Tempest At Sea   @%
     24 Reluctant Lark, The   #
     27 Bronzed Hawk, The   #
     29 Lady And The Unicorn, The
     31 Golden Valkyrie, The   &
     35 Trustworthy Redhead, The &
     40 Return To Santa Flores *
     44 No Red Roses   *
     55 Capture The Rainbow   &
     59 Touch The Horizon   &
     82 White Satin   +
     86 Blue Velvet   +<
    122 Summer Smile, A   &
    126 And The Desert Blooms   &
    148 Always   =&
    152 Everlasting   >
    168 York, The Renegade
    176 'Til The End Of Time   >
    187 Last Bridge Home   =@
    191 Across The
              River Of Yesterday ^<
    221 Spellbinder, The
    232 Star Light, Star Bright @%
    257 Man From Half Moon Bay %
    274 Blue Skies And
              Shining Promises
    280 Strong, Hot Winds
    342 Magnificent Folly   @

JOHNSON, Christine
Clinic   <CO>
_____

_____

JOHNSON, Ellen Argo   (Deceased)
                           (Ellen Argo)

JOHNSON, Gretchen w/ Sally NETZEL
                     (Suzanne Jenner)

JOHNSON, Iris   <CO>
Designs
_____

_____

JOHNSON, Janice Kay
   [Janice Kay Johnson Baczewski]
   Harlequin Regency Romance:
   Imperiled Heiress, The
   Harlequin Temptation:
   149 Night And Day
_____

_____

JOHNSON, Joyce
In The Night Cafe
_____

_____

JOHNSON, Mary
                    (M. J. Rodgers)

JOHNSON, Mary Ellen   <HR>
Lion And The Leopard, The
_____

_____

JOHNSON, Maud/Maude   (Deceased)
   For Love Of Two Men
   First Love From Silhouette: <YA>
      10 Please Love Me...Somebody
      33 You And Me
      59 Rainbow For Alison, A
   Wildfire: <YA>
      Christy's Choice
      Christy's Love
      Christy's Senior Year

JOHNSON, Maud (cont.)
   Dating Blues
   I'm Christy
   Kiss For Tomorrow, A
   Saturday Night Date
   Sixteen Can Be Sweet
_____

_____

JOHNSON, Maud B.
   Love Cherished Is Forever
   Tomorrow And Forever
_____

_____

JOHNSON, Natalie
   Caprice Romance: <YA>
      1 Jenny
_____

_____

JOHNSON, Norma/Norma Tadlock
        [Norma Kay Tadlock Johnson]
   Judy Sullivan Books:
      Inca Gold   <RS>
      Too Hot To Handle   <RS>
_____

_____

JOHNSON, Norma Kay Tadlock w/
        Janice Kay Johnson BACZEWSKI
                      (Kay Kirby)

JOHNSON, Renate
                 (Ellen Tanner Marsh)

JOHNSON, Susan/Susan M.   <HR>
        [Susan Marie Aho Johnson]
                     (Jill Barkin)
   Honey Bear (see Jill Barkin)
   Play, The   <YA>
   Russian Trilogy: &
      Seized By Love
      Lovestorm
      Sweet Love, Survive
   In sequence:
      Blaze
      Silver Flame

JOHNSON, Susan (cont.)
Harlequin Historical <Set#2>:
51 Golden Paradise &

JOHNSON, Walter Reed <HR>
In sequence:
Oakhurst
Mistress Of Oakhurst
Lion Of Oakhurst
Fires Of Oakhurst

JOHNSTON, Corinne <HO>
Texan Woman, The
Wild Gypsy Love

JOHNSTON, Joan
[Joan Mertens Johnson]
Colter's Wife
Sweetwater Seduction
Silhouette Desire:
424 Fit To Be Tied
489 Marriage By The Book
Sisters Of The Lone Star Trilogy:
Frontier Woman
Comanche Woman
Texas Woman
Tapestry: <HR>
57 Loving Defiance, A

JOHNSTON, Norma
(Nicole St. John)
Watcher In The Mist, The <RM>

JOHNSTON, Terry C.
In sequence: <HS>
Carry The Wind
Borderlords
One-Eyed Dream

JOHNSTON, Velda <GOT><RS>
(Veronica Jason)
Along A Dark Path
Deveron Hall
Etruscan Smile, The
Face In The Shadows, The
Fatal Affair
Fateful Summer, The
Frenchman, The
Girl On The Beach, The <MYS>
Hour Before Midnight, The
House Above Hollywood
House On Bostwick Square, The
House On The Left Bank
Howling In The Woods, A
I Came To A Castle
I Came To The Highlands
Late Mrs. Fonsell, The
Light In The Swamp, The
Man At Windmere, The
Masquerade In Venice
Mourning Trees, The
Other Karen, The
People From The Sea, The
People On The Hill, The
Phantom Cottage, The
Presence In An Empty Room, A
Room With Dark Mirrors, A
Silver Dolphin, The
Stone Maiden, The
Voice In The Night
White Pavilion, The

351

JOHNSTON, William
                         (Willa Jay)
                 (Heather Sinclair)
House On Corbett Street
King
Manipulator, The

JONES, Alexandra   <HR>
  Mandalay

JONES, Annabel   <RE>
  Radiant Dove, The

JONES, Beth Carlsey   <HR>
  Hall Of Sparrows

JONES, Deborah w/ Carol BURNS
             ·(Samantha Holder)

JONES, Diane McClure
            (Phoebe Matthews)

JONES, Douglas C.   <HO>
  Arrest Sitting Bull
  Winding Stair
  Creek Called Wounded Knee, A
  Hasford Family Series:
    Barefoot Brigade, The
    Elkhorn Tavern
    Roman
    Weedy Rough

JONES, Elinor   <HR>
  Lucetta
  Tamara

JONES, Jan
               (Caron Welles)

JONES, Kathy
  Heartfire Romance: <HR>
    Defiant Captive
    Golden Fire
    Sweet Obsession

JONES, Kit O'Brien   <GOT>
  To The Dark Tower Came

JONES, Marian
  SuperRomance:
    68 Bonds Of Enchantment

JONES, McClure
        (Diane McClure Jones)
  Fix-Up Service   <YA>
  First Love From Silhouette:
    23 When September Returns
   140 What I Know About Boys

JONES, Merle
  Woman's Estate

JONES, Mervyn   <HO><RE>
  Lord Richard's Passion
  Privacy
  Pursuit Of Happiness, The
  Twilight Of The Day

JONES, Minka
Harlequin Romance:
      Master Of Bucklands   HRS33

JORDAN, Deborah w/ Mary Johnston
DAVIS   (Rosemary Jordan)

JORDAN, Duncan   <HO>
1779, The Indian Wilderness

JONES, Nancy L.
                     [Nancy Holder]
Jessie's Song   <CO>

JORDAN, Gail
                          [Peggy Dern]
Love On The Run
Starlight:
      Gambling On Love

JONES, Peggy Loosemore
Love Dangerously

JORDAN, Hope
Avalon:
      Middlecliff Treasure

JONES-WOLF, Gloria
Heartfire Romance: <HR>
      Secret Rapture

JORDAN, Joanna
      [Debrah Morris w/ Pat Shaver]
SuperRomance:
      72 Never Say Farewell
The Avon Romance:
      Destiny's Dream
      Temptation's Darling

JORDAN, Alexis Hill
[Ruth Glick w/ Louise Titchener]
Candlelight Ecstasy:
      163 Brian's Captive
      195 Reluctant Merger
      250 Summer Wine
      291 Beginner's Luck
      316 Mistaken Image
      347 Hopelessly Devoted
      373 Summer Stars
      455 Stolen Passion

JORDAN, Laura
                        [Sandra Brown]
Hidden Fires   <HR>
Silken Web, The   <CO>

JORDAN, Anne   <HO>
Plains Woman, The

JORDAN, Maggie
                        (see Myra Rowe)

JORDAN, Nicole
                        [Anne Bushyhead]
JORDAN, Carrie   <RE>
Rivals For Love

Heartfire Romance: <HR>
      Desire And Deception
      Velvet Embrace

353

JORDAN, Nicole (cont.)
  Harlequin Historical <Set #2>:
  62 Moonwitch

JORDAN, Penny
                    [Penny Halsall]
  Silver
  Power Play   <RS>
  Harlequin Signature Edition:
  Love's Choices
  Stronger Than Yearning
  Harlequin Presents:
  471 Falcon's Prey
  477 Tiger Man
  484 Marriage Without Love
  489 Long Cold Winter
  508 Northern Sunset
  517 Blackmail
  519 Caged Tiger, The
  537 Daughter Of Hassan
  553 An Unbroken Marriage
  562 Bought With His Name
  569 Escape From Desire
  584 Flawed Marriage, The
  591 Phantom Marriage
  602 Rescue Operation
  609 Desire's Captive
  618 Sudden Engagement, A
  633 Passionate Protection
  641 Island Of The Dawn
  650 Savage Atonement
  655 Man-Hater
  667 Forgotten Passion
  706 Shadow Marriage
  713 Inward Storm, The
  728 Response
  738 Wanting
  746 Darker Side Of Desire
  755 Rules Of The Game
  761 Campaign For Loving
  770 What You Made Me
  785 Only One, The
  794 Friendship Barrier, The
  809 Six-Month Marriage, The
  818 Taken Over
  826 Time Fuse

JORDAN, Penny (cont.)
  833 You Owe Me
  850 Exorcism
  868 Permission To Love
  883 Injured Innocent
  897 Hard Man, The
  916 Fire With Fire
  931 Capable Of Feeling
  946 Desire Never Changes
  962 Man Possessed, A
  978 Desire For Revenge
  994 Research Into Marriage
  1000 Passionate Relationship
  1023 Too Short A Blessing
  1041 Reason For Marriage, A
  1057 Savage Adoration, A
  1075 Loving
  1089 Fight For Love
  1105 Substitute Lover
  1113 Levelling The Score
  1137 For One Night
  1153 An Expert Teacher
  1169 Force Of Feeling
  1180 Reason For Being, A
  1193 Potential Danger
  1201 Without Trust
  1216 Lovers Touch
  1243 Valentine's Night
  1265 Equal Opportunities
  1282 Beyond Compare
  1297 Free Spirit
  1314 Payment In Love
  1324 Rekindled Passion, A
  1339 Time For Trust

JORDAN, Rosemary
  [Mary Johnston Davis
                w/ Deborah Jordan]
  Love's Legacy

JOSCELYN, Archie L.
                    (Lynn Westland)

354

JOSEPH, Joan   <HR>
In Joy And In Sorrow
Love's Frantic Flight
Now Is The Hour
World For The Taking, A

_____

_____

JOSEPH, Marie
Lisa Logan
Maggie Craig

_____

_____

JOSEPH, Robert, M. D.
Mercy Hospital

_____

_____

JOSEPH, Robert F./R. F.   <HR>
                    (Robin Joseph)
Buccaneer, The
Diva, Kate's Way
Odile   <Saga>

_____

_____

JOSEPH, Robin   <HR>
                    [Robert F. Joseph]
Love's Fervent Fury

_____

_____

JOSEPH, Ronald S.   <HO>
French Kisses
Texas Trilogy: <HS>
  Kingdom, The
  Power, The
  Glory, The

_____

_____

JOURDAIN, Rose   <HO>
Those The Sun Has Loved

_____

_____

JOYCE, Brenda   <HR>
          [Brenda Joyce Dworman]
Conqueror, The
Darkest Heart, The
Lovers And Liars   <CO>
Bragg Family Series:
  The Avon Romance:
    Innocent Fire
    Firestorm
    Violet Fire
    Dark Fire

_____

_____

JOYCE, Deborah
[Joyce Porter w/ Deborah Bryson]
Harlequin Intrigue:
  37 Matter Of Time, A
SuperRomance:
  61 Questing Heart, A
Harlequin SuperRomance:
  108 Dream To Share, A
  125 Never Look Back
  142 Silver Horizons
Second Chance At Love:
  109 In The Arms Of A Stranger

_____

_____

JOYCE, Janet
     [Janet Bieber w/ Joyce Thies]
Conquer The Memories
Silhouette Desire:
  53 Winter Lady
  71 Man Of The House
  98 Man Of Glory
  116 Controlling Interest
  140 Run To Gold
  168 Rare Breed
  199 Out Of The Shadows
  259 Out Of This World
  313 Courting Trouble
Silhouette Romance:
  287 Permanent Fixture
Tapestry: <HR>
  11 Libertine Lady
  34 Fields Of Promise
  59 Secrets Of The Heart

355

JOYCE, Janet (cont.)
71 Glorious Destiny

JOYCE, Jenna Lee
[Janet Bieber w/ Joyce Thies]
Harlequin Temptation:
39 Wintersfield
59 Crossroads
81 One On One
110 Package Deal, A
134 Awake Unto Me

JOYCE, Julia   <RE>
[Julie Tetel Andresen]
Lord Laxton's Will

JOYCE, Marianne
Bewitched Desire   <RS>
Haunted Passion, A   <GOT>
Velvet Glove: <RS>
24 Edge Of Reckoning

JOYCE, Marie
[Virginia Deberry w/ Donna Grant]
Lovestruck:
Exposures

JOYCE, Rosemary
Dream Girls: <YA>
1 Anything To Win
2 Love Or Glory
3 Tarnished Victory
4 Bond Of Love
5 Too Close For Comfort
6 Up To No Good

JOYNER, Carolyn
(Carrie Hart)
(Jackie Merritt)

JUDSON, Jeanne
Alice Comes Home
All's Fair In Love
Barbara Ames, Private Secretary
Captive Maid, The
Carol Trent Air Stewardess
Doctor Mary
Haunted Summer
Helen Walks Alone
House Of Enchantment
Island Heirs, The
Janet Goes Abroad
Love Regained
Marcia And The Inca Gold
Meg's Choice
Only Girl, The
Other Love, The
Pledge Of Love, A
Prelude To Spring
Small Town Girl
Strange Case For Dr. Roland, A
Temple Of The Sun
Visiting Nurse
Walled Garden, The
Avalon:
Legacy Of Redfern, The
Treasure Of Wycliffe House
Candlelight:
21 John Keith, Intern

JULIAN, Jane   <HO>
Ellen Bray

JUON, Sarah   <CO>
Private Passion, A

JURCZYK, Mary Irene Donohue
(Irene Michaels)

JURIN-REID, Barbara
          (Leslie Reid)

JUSKEVICE, Mildred Havill
          (Antonio Blake)
          (Sarah James)

JUSTIN, Jennifer
          (Jennifer West)
  Silhouette Special Edition:
   90 Passion's Victory

KACHELMEIER, Glenda   <HR>
   [Glenda Sanders Kachelmeier]
               (Glenda Sanders)
               (Glenda Sands)
  Rose

KADISON, Ellis   <HR>
  Eighth Veil, The

KAHN, Evelyn
  Wayward Winds, The

KAHN, Mary
            (Miranda Cameron)
            (Amanda Troy)

KAIL, Robert
      (see Richard Hale Curtis)

KAISER, Janice
  Harlequin Intrigue:
    58 Black Pearl, The
  Harlequin SuperRomance:
   187 Harmony
   209 Lotus Moon
   224 Meant To Be
   242 Love Child
   256 Chances
   287 Stolen Moments
   403 Body And Soul
  Silhouette Desire:
   483 Rookie Princess, The
   503 Moon Shadow
  Silhouette Special Edition:
   466 Borrowed Time
   489 Lieutenant's Woman, The

KAKADE, Geeta M.
           (Geeta Kingsley)

KAKU, Louzana
           (Christina Dair)

KALIS, Murray   <YA>
  Love In Paris

KALMAN, Yvonne   <HR>
  Passion's Gold
  Summer Rain
  In sequence: <Saga>
    Greenstone
    Silver Shores
    Riversong

KALMES, Susan
  Silhouette Romance:
   564 Sweetheart Waltz, The
   721 Sassafras Street

KALPAKIAN, Laura   <HR>
  These Latter Days

KAMADA, Annelise
  Banner Red And Gold, A   <HS>
  Love So Bold, A   <HS>

KAMAROFF, Alex w/ Irene GOODMAN
           (Diana Morgan)

KAMIEN, Marcia Silverman w/
            Rose NOVAK
           (Marcia Rose)
  Music Of Love

KAMM, Dorinda   <GOT>
    Cliff's Head
    Devil's Doorstep
    Drearloch
    Kingsroads Legacy, The
    Marly Stones, The
    Secret Of The Marly Stones, The
    Shadow Game
    Winteredge Whispers, The

KANE, Carol J.   <HR>
    Blood And Sable

KANE, Gil w/ John JAKES   <HO>
    Excalibur

KANE, Julia
                (see Denise Robins)

KANE, Valerie
    Meteor Kismet:
        19   Sunday Drive

KANIN, Garson
    Cordelia?

KANTER, Marianne
    [Marianne Kanter w/
        Richard M. Lieberman]
        (see Brenda Leslie Segal)
    White Satin Nights

KANTOF, Albert
    Judith

KAPLAN, Barry Jay   <HO>
    That Wilder Woman

KARK, Nina Mary MaBey
                (Nina Bawden)

KARLOVA, Irina   <GOT>
    Dreadful Hollow

KARNI, Michaela w/ Sue BURRELL
                (Diana Burke)

KAROL, Alexander
    Sword Of Vengeance

KARR, Kathleen
    Serenade/Saga: <HR><Insp>
        9   Light Of My Heart
       16   From This Day Forward

KARR, Lee   <GOT>
                        [Leona Karr]
    Beware, My Love
    Castle Of Crushed Shamrocks
    Dark Cries Of Gray Oaks
    Mistress Of Moontide Manor
    Velvet Glove: <RS>
        23   Tangled Mesh

KARR, Leona   <CO><GOT><RS>
                        (Lee Karr)
    Beyond The Texas Rainbow
    Forbidden Treasure
    Illusions
    Obsession
    Heartfire Romance: <HR>
        Nightfire

359

KARR, Leona (cont.)
Harlequin Intrigue:
  120 Treasure Hunt   <DTR>
  144 Falcon's Cry

KARR, Phyllis Ann   <RE>
Coventry:
   35 My Lady Quixote
  138 Meadowsong
  178 Perola
  190 Elopement, The

KARRON, Kris
        [Carolyn Brimley Norris]
Rainbow Chase, The   <CO>

KARY, Elizabeth   <HR>
        [Karyn Whitmer-Gow]
From This Day Onward
Let No Man Divide
Love, Honor And Betray   <Saga>
Midnight Lace
KARY, Elizabeth N.
Second Chance At Love:
  285 Portrait Of A Lady

KASEY, Michelle   <RE>
        [Kathryn Seidick]
Difficult Disguise, A
Enterprising Lord Edward, The
Final Farce, A
Moonlight Masquerade
Trilogy:
  Beleaguered Lord Bourne, The
  Toplofty Lord Thorpe, The
  Ruthless Lord Rule, The

KASHNER, Rita
To The Tenth Generation

KASPER, Gayle
           (Susan Gayle)

KATA, Elizabeth
Patch Of Blue, A (Be Ready With
  Bells & Drums)   <YA>
Someone Will Conquer Them

KATKOV, Norman
With These Hands

KATZ, Carol
          (Penny Allison)
        (Rosalynn Carroll)
Harlequin SuperRomance:
  152 Then Came Laughter
Second Chance At Love:
  374 Fire And Ice

KATZ, Molly
        [Molly Simon Katz]
Candlelight Ecstasy:
  341 No Reservations
  383 Always Keep Him Laughing
  402 Heights Of Desire
  461 Best Bet Of His Life
  480 Worth His Weight In Gold
  506 Mischief-Maker
  531 When Sparks Fly

KAUFELT, David A.
American Tropic   <Saga>
Silver Rose
Wine And The Music, The

KAUFMAN, Bel
Love, Etc.

KAUFMAN, Charles
After The Dream

KAUFMAN, Pamela
In sequence: <HS>
  Shield Of Three Lions
  Banners Of Gold

KAUFMANN, Myron S.
Love Of Elspeth Baker

KAUKAS, Bevlyn Marshall
                  (Bevlyn Marshall)

KAVALER, Rebecca   <GOT>
Doubting Castle

KAVANAGH, Maria   <CO>
We Were Once Beautiful
  Butterflies

KAVANAUGH, Cynthia   <GOT>
                  [Dorothy Daniels]
Bride Of Lenore
Deception, The

KAVANAUGH, Ian
                  [Morris Hershman]
The O'Donnells: <HS>
  An Irish-American Saga
In sequence:
  From The Shamrock Shore
  Faithful And The Few
  Far From The Blessed Land
  Waltz On The Wind, A

KAVANAUGH, James
Coward For Them All, A

KAY, Catherine
  [Catherine Dees w/ Kay Croissant]
Legacy Of Passion
SuperRomance:
  45 Dawn Of Passion
  80 Interlude
Harlequin SuperRomance:
  127 Critic's Choice

KAY, Pat
                  [Trisha Alexander]

KAY, Susan   <HR>
Legacy

KAY, Tessa
Crosswinds Keepsake: <YA>
  17 My Funny Valentine
  40 Confessions Of Abby
        Winslade
First Love From Silhouette: <YA>
  106 French Summer, The
  179 Wild One, The
  232 Boy In White, The

KAYE, Barbara
　　　　　[Barbara Kaye Walker]
Harlequin American Romance:
　19　Call Of Eden
SuperRomance:
　46　Heart Divided, A
Harlequin SuperRomance:
　124　Come Spring
　161　Home At Last
　206　Southern Nights
　219　Just One Look
　257　Season For Roses, A
　270　By Special Request
　316　Right Place To Be, The
　332　Traditions
　379　Ramblin' Man
　　Hamilton House Trilogy:
　411　Choice Of A Lifetime
　433　Challenge Of A Lifetime
　449　Chance Of A Lifetime

KAYE, Joanne
　　　　　[Rachel Cosgrove Payes]
World Of High Fashion:　　<CO>
　1　Rags & Riches
　2　Love & Betrayal
　3　Fame & Fortune
　4　Satin & Stars
　5　Playing For Keeps
　6　To Love Again

KAYE, Judy
　　　　　[Judy Baer]
Harlequin Romance:
　3021　Letters Of Love

KAYE, M. M. (Mollie)　　<RM><HR>
　Far Pavilions
　Shadow Of The Moon
　Trade Winds
　Death In Berlin

KAYE M. M. (cont.)
　Death In Cyprus
　Death In Kashmir
　Death In Kenya
　Death In The Andamans
　Death In Zanzibar

KAZAN, Elia
　Acts Of Love
　Arrangement, The
　Assassins
　Kazan Reader, A
　Understudy, The
　In sequence:
　　America, America
　　Anatolian, The

KEANE, Lucy
　Harlequin Romance:
　　Innocent Pretences　HRS42
　　Mask Of Passion　　HRS75

KEARNY, Jillian　　　　<RE>
　　　　　[Ronald Joseph Goulart]
Warner Regency:
　4　Agent Of Love
　26　Love's Claimant

KEAST, Karen
　　　　　[Sandra Canfield]
From Silhouette Books:
　Birds, Bees And Babies
　Taylor's Ladies
Harlequin Historical <Set#2>:
　13　China Star
Second Chance At Love:
　225　Suddenly The Magic
　244　Notorious

KEAST, Karen (cont.)
294 Forbidden Dream
316 Dark Lightning
351 Tender Treason
365 Conquer The Night
Silhouette Special Edition:
435 Once Burned
469 One Lavender Evening
536 Tender Silence, A
614 Night Spice

KEATON, Corey
[Mary Frances Tate Engels w/
        Vickie Lewis Thompson]
Harlequin Temptation:
194 Nesting Instinct, The

KEEGAN, Mary Heathcott
                    (Mary Raymond)

KEEL, Charlene
Tavern House, The

KEENE, Carolyn
                [Sharon Wagner]
River Heights: <YA>
    1 Love Times Three
    2 Guilty Secrets
    3 Going Too Far
    4 Stolen Kisses
    5 Between The Lines
    6 Lessons In Love
    7 Cheating Hearts

KEENE, Sarah
                [Jane Atkins]
Harlequin Romance:
2698 Tender Season, A
2740 Air Of Enchantment
2828 Earthly Treasures

KEENE, Sarah (cont.)
Silhouette Special Edition:
14 Eye Of The Hurricane

KEENER, Joyce   <CO>
Limits Of Eden

KEILER, Barbara
                    (Judith Arnold)
                    (Ariel Berk)
                    (Thea Frederick)

KEITH, Judith
Choices   <CO>

KELLER, Barbara   <HR>
Captive Heart, The
In sequence:
    Exiled Heart, The
    Diamond Splei lor

KELLER, Kathy   <HR>
Homeward Heart, The
Love Too Proud, A

KELLER, Kirk   <RS>
Final Landscapes

KELLEY, Dorsey
                [Dorsey Adams]
Silhouette Romance:
714 Montana Heat

363

KELLEY, Leo P.
(see Lee Davis Willoughby <MOAS>)

KELLIER, Elizabeth   <RS>
Matravers Hall
Patient At Tonesburry Manor, The
Wayneston Hospital

KELLOGG, Marjorie
Like The Lion's Tooth
Tell Me That You Love Me,
  Junie Moon

KELLS, Susannah   <HR>
Aristocrats, The   <Saga>
Crowning Mercy, A
Fallen Angels, The

KELLY, Carla   <HR><RE>
Daughter Of Fortune
Marian's Christmas Wish
Miss Chartley's Guided Tour
Ms. McVinnie's London Season

KELLMAN, Ellen
              (Leonora Woodbury)

KELRICH, Victoria   <CO>
Charades
High Fashion
Scaffold, The
Sombody Else's Wife

KEMP, Shirley
· Harlequin Romance
    Flight From Love   HRS34
    Question Of Trust, A   HRS40

KENDALL, Julia
              [Julia Jay Kendall]
Portraits

KENDALL, Julia Jay   <CO>
              (Julia Kendall)
              (Katherine Kingsley)
Memento

KENDALL, Katherine
              [Katherine Applegate]
Harlequin Temptation:
  231 Midas Touch, The

KENDRICK, Jessalyn
Heartfire Romance: <HR>
  Tender Texas Touch

KENDYL, Sharice
To Share A Sunset

KENNEDY, Jr, Cody   <HO>
              [John Reese]
This Wild Land
Warrior Flame, The

KENNEDY, Kim   <YA>
Two by Two Romance:
  7 In-Between Love

KENNEDY, Lena
Autumn Alley
Kitty
Lizzie
Maggie

KENNEDY, M. L.   <YA>
Turning Points:
    2 Kerry's Dance
    7 Winner's Smile, A
Two-By-Two Romance:
    12 Here To Stay
Wildfire:
    Love Signs
    Ten Cupcake Romance

KENNEDY, Marilyn
Silhouette Desire:
    81 Opening Bid

KENNEDY, Nancy/Nancy M.   <GOT><RS>
              [Nancy MacDougall Kennedy]
Bright Passage
Brief Autumn
Cherished Heart, The
Heart In The Highlands
Joy In The Morning
Shadow On The Cliff
Summer Frost
Village Tale
Winter Reckoning
Candlelight:
    9   Tender Branch, The
    69 Grey-Eyed Stranger, The
    104 There's Always Tomorrow
    116 Shadow On The Snow   <MY>
    135 Lingering Shadows
    541 Secret Longings   <RO>

KENNEDY, Raymond
Columbine

KENNETT, Frances
Woman By Design, A   <Saga>

KENT, Amanda
                    [Betty L. Henrichs]
Second Chance At Love:
    111 Ardent Protector, The <RE>

KENT, Andrea
                    (see Bette McNicholas)

KENT, Deborah   <YA>
Talk To Me, My Love
Caprice Romance:
    36 Heartwaves
First Love From Silhouette:
    22 That Special Summer
Sweet Dreams:
    47 Te Amo Means I Love You
    77 Ten-Speed Summer
Sweet Dreams Special:
    4 Taking The Lead
Turning Points:
    10 Honey And Spice
Wildfire:
    Cindy

KENT, Fortune   <GOT><RS>
                    [John Toombs]
House At Canterbury, The
House Of Masques
Isle Of The Seventh Sentry
Opal Legacy   <BGS:#10>

KENT, Jean
                    [Jean Salter Kent]
                    (Kathryn Kent)
Second Chance At Love:
    321 On Cloud Nine

KENT, Jean (cont.)
399 Night Moves
Silhouette Special Edition:
237 Love's Advocate
268 Memories Of The Heart

KENT, Katherine
[Joan Dial]
Dream Tide   <CO>
Druid's Retreat   <RS>
Midnight Tango   <CO>
Waters Of Eden
Judy Sullivan Books:
  Tawny Rose   <HR>

KENT, Kathryn
[Jean Kent]
Rapture Romance:
  28 Precious Possession
  52 Silk And Steel
  63 Reluctant Surrender
  77 Orchid Of Love
  90 An Affair Of Interest
  97 Love And Lilacs

KENT, Pamela
[Ida Pollock]
Harlequin Classic:
  62 City Of Palms   (791)
  98 Sweet Barbary   (829)
 125 Desert Doorway   (909)
 152 Moon Over Africa   (983)
Harlequin Romance:
 791 City Of Palms
 804 Bladon's Rock
 829 Sweet Barbary
 909 Desert Doorway
 943 Enemy Lover
 983 Moon Over Africa
1005 Gideon Faber's Chance
1035 Star Creek

KENT, Pamela (cont.)
1061 Meet Me In Istanbul
1091 Cuckoo In The Night
1134 Man Who Came Back, The
1234 Desert Gold
1274 Man From The Sea
1384 Beloved Enemies
1798 Nile Dust

KENYON, Bruce
                    (Meredith Leigh)
                    (Daisy Vivian)

KENYON, Cory
[Mary Frances Tate Engels
        w/ Vicki Lewis Thompson]
Candlelight Ecstasy:
 407 Sheer Delight
 422 Fortune Hunter
 457 Ruffled Feathers
 496 Quintessential Woman, The&
 507 Fancy Footwork   &

KENYON, F. W.   <HO>
Duke's Mistress, The
That Spanish Woman

KENYON, Joanna
[Janet Kotselas Clarke]
Silhouette Intimate Moments:
  32 Dangerous Paradise

KEOGH, Theodora
Double Door, The
Fascinator, The
Gemini
Meg

KEOGH, Theodora (cont.)
Mistress, The
My Name Is Rose
Street Music
Tatooed Heart

KEPPEL, Charlotte   <GOT>
                    [Ursula Torday]
I Could Be Good To You
Loving Sands, Deadly Sands
My Name Is Clary Brown

KER, Madeleine
Harlequin Presents:
  642 Aquamarine
  656 Virtuous Lady
  672 Pacific Aphrodite
  699 Winged Lion, The
  739 Working Relationships
  778 Out Of The Darkness
  795 Fire Of The Gods
  884 Danger Zone
  947 Impact
  1090 Frazer's Law
  1114 Wilder Shores Of Love, The
  1138 Judgement
  1161 Takeover
  1185 Stormy Attraction
  1249 Tuscan Encounter
  1274 Special Arrangement, A
Harlequin Romance:
  2595 Voyage Of The Mistral
  2636 Street Of The
        Fountain, The
  2709 Ice Princess
  2716 Hostage
  3017 Troublemaker
  3063 Passion's Far Shore
  3094 Duel Of Passion

KERIGAN, Florence (cont.)
Hearts In Jeopardy

KERIGAN, Florence (cont.)
Passion Under The Falmboyante, The
Romance Of The Moss Agate
Avalon:
  Headline, Romance!
Candlelight:
  77 Runaway From Romance

KERNS, Frances Casey   <HR>
Cold, Wild Wind, A
Cana And Wine
Edges Of Love, The
Errand, The
Savage
Stinsons, The
This Land Is Mine
Winter Heart, The

KERR, Katharine   <RF>
Trilogy:
  Daggerspell
  Darkspell

KERR, M. E.   <YA>
Him She Loves
I Stay Near You   <Saga>

KERR, Robert   <HR>
Dark Lady, The
In sequence:
  Stuart Legacy, The
  Black Pearls, The

KERRIGAN, Kate Lowe
Another World

367

KETCHAM, Helen
          (Meg Haviland)

KETTER, Pam
        [Pamela Browning]
  Caprice Romance: <YA>
    19 Wish For Tomorrow
    37 Stardust Summer
  First Love From Silhouette: <YA>
    36 One On One

KETTLE, Jocelyn   <HO>
  Athelsons, The
  Gift Of Onyx, A
  Memorial To The Duchess

KEVERN, Barbara   <GOT><RS>
  Dark Eden
  Darkness Falling
  Devil's Vineyard, The
  Key, The

KEVERN, Mary w/ Nancy AUSTIN
        (Miranda North)

KEYES, Frances Parkinson
  All Flags Flying
  All That Glitters
  Also The Hills
  Blue Camellia
  Came A Cavalier
  Career Of David Noble, The
  Chess Players, The
  Crescent Carnival
  Dinner At Antoines
  Explorer, The
  Fielding's Folly
  Great Tradition, The
  Heritage, The
  Honor Bright
  I, The King
  Joy Street

KEYES, Frances Parkinson (cont.)
  Lady Blanche Farm
  Madame Castel's Lodger
  Old Gray Homestead, The
  Once On Esplanade
  Parts Unknown
  Queen Anne's Lace
  Restless Lady And Other Stories
  River Road, The
  Roses In December
  Royal Box, The
  Safe Bridge, The
  Senator Marlowe's Daughter
  Silver Seas And Golden Cities
  Sylvia Cary
  Station Wagon In Spain
  Steamboat Gothic
  Three Ways Of Love
  Tongues Of Fire
  Victorine

KEYWORTH, Anne   <RE>
  Spring Bride

KICHLINE, Linda
        (Carin Rafferty)
        (Allyson Ryan)

KIDD, Elisabeth   <RE>
        [Linda Triegel]
  For Love Of Celia
  Hero For Antonia, A
  Lady Lu
  LadyShip, The
  My Lord Guardian
  Sweet Secrets
  The Avon Romance:
    Dancer's Land, The   <HR>

KIDD, Flora
  Harlequin Presents:
    212 Dangerous Pretense
    216 Jungle Of Desire

KIDD, Flora (cont.)
240 Night Of The Yellow Moon
261 Sweet Torment
276 Castle Of Temptation
304 Marriage In Mexico
309 Passionate Encounter
327 Together Again
333 Tangled Shadows
344 Stay Through The Night
370 Arranged Marriage, The
379 Silken Bond, The
400 Wife By Contract
434 Beyond Control
447 Personal Affair
464 Passionate Stranger
485 Bride For A Captain
495 Meeting At Midnight
520 Makebelieve Marriage
554 Between Pride And Passion
577 Tempted To Love
592 Dark Seduction
643 Tropical Tempest
657 Dangerous Encounter
682 Passionate Pursuit
729 Desperate Desire
756 Open Marriage, The
771 Flight To Passion
834 Secret Pleasure, A
848 Arrogant Lover, The
970 Passionate Choice
995 Married Lovers, The
1024 Masquerade Marriage
1058 Beloved Deceiver
1091 When Lovers Meet
1154 Loving Gamble, The
Harlequin Romance:
1058 Nurse At Rowanbank
1122 Whistle And I'll Come
1191 Love Alters Not
1265 Strange As A Dream
1471 When Birds Do Sing
1503 My Heart Remembers
1540 Dazzle On The Sea, The
1573 Love Is Fire
1602 Remedy For Love
1640 If Love Be Love
1663 Cave Of The
     White Rose, The
1684 Taming Of Lisa, The

KIDD, Flora (cont.)
1732 Beyond The Sunset
1774 Legend Of The Swans, The
1796 Gallant's Fancy
1833 Paper Marriage, The
1865 Stranger In The Glen
1907 Enchantment In Blue
1977 Dance Of Courtship, The
1999 Summer Wife, The
2056 Black Knight, The
2146 To Play With Fire
2228 Bargain Bride, The

KIDD, Jacqueline
Flame In A High Wind

KIDDER, Jane w/ Charla CHIN
                    (Charlotte Simms)

KIDWELL, Catherine
Dear Stranger
Woman I Am, The

KIEHL, Claire w/ Susan PHILLIPS
                    (Justine Cole)

KIHLSTROM, April   <RE>
An Improper Companion
Captain Rogue
Charming Imposter
Choice Of Cousins, A
Counterfeit Betrothal, The
Miss Redmond's Folly
Mysterious Governess, The
Nabob's Widow, The
Scandelous Bequest, A
Scholar's Daughter, The
Twice Bethrothed
Wary Spinster, The
Avalon:
    My Love Betrayed

KIHLSTROM, April (cont.)
Paris Summer
Trondelaine Castle

KILCHENSTEIN, Mary I.
(Jean Faure)
(Mary Kirk)

KILCHENSTEIN, Mary I. w/
Nancy Linda RICHARDS-AKERS
(Mary Alice Kirk)

KILLORAN, Geraldine   <GOT>
Stones Of
Strendleigh, The   <CGS:#4>
Willough Haven   <CGS:#23>

KILMER, Wendela
(Karen van der Zee)
(Mona van Wieren)

KIMBERLY, Gail   <CO>
Goodbye Is Just The Beginning

KIMBRO, Jean
[John M. Kimbro]
Twilight Return - Cancer   <ZGS>

KIMBRO, John M.
(Kym Allyson)
(Ann Ashton)
(Charlotte Bramwell)
(Jean Kimbro)
(Katheryn Kimbrough)
Night Of Tears

KIMBROUGH, Coleen
[Kay Porterfield]
Harlequin Temptation:
30   Swept Off Her Feet

KIMBROUGH, Katheryn   <GOT><RS>
[John M. Kimbro]
Broken Sphinx, The
Children Of Houndstooth, The
Heiress Of Wolfskill, The
House On Windswept Ridge, The
Phantom Flame Of Wind House, The
Shadow Over Pheasant Heath, The
Shriek In The Midnight Tower, A
Specter Of Dolphin Cove, The
Thanesworth House
Three Sisters Of Briarwick, The
Twisted Cameo, The
Unseen Torment
Saga Of The Phenwick Women:
    1   Augusta, The First
    2   Jane, The Courageous
    3   Margaret, The Faithful
    4   Patricia, The Beautiful
    5   Rachel, The Possessed
    6   Susannah, The Righteous
    7   Rebecca, The Mysterious
    8   Joanne, The Unpredictable
    9   Olivia, The Tormented
   10   Harriet, The Haunted
   11   Nancy, The Daring
   12   Marcia, The Innocent
   13   Kate, The Curious
   14   Ilene, The Superstitious
   15   Millijoy, The Determined
   16   Barbara, The Valiant
   17   Ruth, The Unsuspecting
   18   Ophelia, The Anxious
   19   Dorothy, The Terrified
   20   Ann, The Gentle
   21   Nellie, The Obvious
   22   Isabelle, The Frantic
   23   Evelyn, The Ambitious
   24   Louise, The Restless
   25   Polly, The Worried
   26   Yvonne, The Confident

KING, Dianne (cont.)
  Harlequin SuperRomance:
    182 Believe In Magic:
  Harlequin Temptation:
    10 Friend Of The Heart
    68 Essence Of Summer

KING, Elnora w/ Pamela Dianne
  WALLACE   (Dianne King)

KING, Josie
                [Jo Germany]
  Silhouette Romance:
    228 Dance At Your Wedding

KING, Louise   <GOT>
  Rochemer Hag, The

KING, Natalie
  Badge Of Courage
  Desire And Dawn
  Faint Echo
  Flowers By Wanda
  Listening Heart, The
  Magic Mirror, The
  Morning Glory
  Orphan Heart, The
  Wedding Bouquet
  Candlelight:
    15 Bravely To Dream

KING, Peggy E.
          (see Velma S. Daniels)

KING, Randall   <HO>
          [William Krasner]
  Francis Parkman: <AES:#9>
    Dakota Legend

KING, Stephanie
  Marble Virgins, The

KING, Tabitha
  Caretakers

KING, Valerie   <RE>
          [Valerie Bosna]
  Daring Wager, A
  Fanciful Heiress, The
  Reluctant Bride
  Rogue's Masquerade

KINGSBURY, Dawn
  First Love From Silhouette: <YA>
    93 South Of The Border
    150 Heartbreak Of
          Haltom High, The
    200 Only Make Believe

KINGSBURY, Myra   <GOT>
  Beware The Bog
  Island Of Fog

KINGSLEY, Bettina   <GOT><RS>
  Black Angel, The
  Blind Chance
  Captive
  Darwich Castle
  House On The Drive, The
  Mistress Of Destiny
  Stages Of Terror

KINGSLEY, Geeta
                    [Geeta M. Kakade]
   Silhouette Romance:
   726 Faith, Hope, And Love
   775 Project Valentine

KINGSLEY, Johanna   <CO>
                    [Donna Meyer]
   Faces
   Scents
   Treasures

KINGSLEY, Kate
   Harlequin Historical <Set #2>
   72 Ransom Of The Heart

KINGSLEY, Katherine   <RE>
                    [Julia Jay Kendall]
   Dishonorable Proposal
   Natural Attachment, A
   In sequence:
      Wild Rose
      Honor's Way

KINGSLEY, Mary   <RE>
                    [Mary Kruger]
   Sabrina

KINGSTON, Beryl   <HR>
   Time To Love, A

KINGSTON, Kate
   Harlequin Romance:
   2981 Alien Moonlight

KINGSTON, Kate (cont.)
   Bitter Inheritance   HRS14
   Yesterday's Fires   HRS58

KINGSTON, Meredith
             [Meredith Babeaux Brucker]
   Second Chance At Love:
     2 Winter Love Song
    10 Aloha, Yesterday
    24 Passion's Games
    72 Mixed Doubles
   126 Longing Unveiled

KINGSTON, Roberta
   MacFadden Romance:
   124 Above The Clouds
   210 Love Storm

KINSALE, Laura
                    [Amanda Moor Jay]
   Prince Of Midnight, The
   Sieze The Fire
   The Avon Romance:
      Hidden Heart, The   <HR>
      Midsummer Moon
      Uncertain Magic

KIRBY, Jean
   Olympic Duty

KIRBY, Kay
   [Janice Kay Baczewski
            w/ Norma Kay Johnson]
   Adventures In Love:
    25 Summertime Love
    31 Autumn Beginning

KIRBY, Penny
English Miss, The

KIRBY, Rowan
Harlequin Romance:
  2675 Silent Stream
  2758 Hunger
  2776 Power Point
  2829 Contrasts
  2847 Fusion
  2873 Shadow Fall
  2907 Harmonies
  2960 Only My Dreams

KIRBY, Susan/Susan E.
  Avalon:
    Blizzard Of The Heart
    Chasing A Dream
    Lessons Of The Heart
    Love's Welcome Home
    Maple Princess, The
    Reach For Heaven
  Everlasting Love: <Insp>
    2 Love, Special Delivery
    4 Perfect Harmony
  Serenade/Serenata: <Insp>
    30 Heart Aflame
  Silhouette Inspirations:
    24 One Whispering Voice

KIRK, Alexandra
              [Sherryl Woods]
  Circle Of Love:
    18 Sand Castles
    26 Images Of Love

KIRK, Margaret P.
              [Margaret Prasniewski]
  Always A Stranger

KIRK, Margaret P. (cont.)
  Gypsy   <Saga>

KIRK, Mariel
  Harlequin Romance:
    2786 Prisoner Of Shadow
          Mountain

KIRK, Mary
              [Mary I. Kilchenstein]
  Silhouette Special Edition:
    524 Phoenix Rising
    628 Miracles

KIRK, Mary Alice
  [Nancy Linda Richards-Akers
          w/ Mary I. Kilchenstein]
  Silhouette Desire:
    387 In Your Wildest Dreams
  Silhouette Special Edition:
    462 Promises

KIRK, Risa
              [Janis Flores]
  Harlequin SuperRomance:
    200 Beyond Compare
    238 Tempting Fate
    273 Dreams To Mend
    300 Without A Doubt
    361 Playing With Fire
    408 Trade Secrets
    441 Send No Regrets

KIRK, Russell   <GOT>
  Lord Of The Hollow Dark
  Lost Lake
  Old House Of Fear

KIRK, Russell (cont.)
Princess Of All Lands, A

KIRKBRIDE, Ronald
Jordan Saga, The   <HS>

KIRKLAND, Elithe Hamilton   <HO>
Divine Average
Love Is A Wild Assault

KIRKLAND, Rainy
Heartfire Romance: <HR>
Passion's Golden Bounty

KIRSCH, Robert R.
                 (Robert Bancroft)

KISTLER, Julie
Harlequin American Romance:
   158 Van Renn Legacy, The
   Wentworth Sisters Trilogy:
   207   Christmas In July
   236   Wildflower
   266   Always A Bridesmaid
   329   Best Wishes   <RMM>

KISTLER, Mary   <GOT>
                    (Jean Reece)
   Jarrah Tree, The
   Night Of The Tiger, The
   Stranger At My Door, A
   Harlequin Gothic Romance:
      Mirage On The Amazon

KITT, Sandra
Harlequin American Romance:
   43   Rites Of Spring
   86   Adam And Eva
   97   Perfect Combination
   112 Only With The Heart
   148 With Open Arms
   280 An Innocent Man
   327 Way Home, The
Starlight Romance:
   All Good Things

KITZMILLER, Virginia
Dreams To Shatter

KJELLBERG, Pauline A.
                 (Jacqueline Fleury)

KLEEB, Pamela M.
Harlequin SuperRomance:
   148 Genuine Article, The

KLEIHAUER, Lois
Don't Ever Leave Me

KLEIN, Elinor w/ Dora LANDEY
                  (see Dora Landey)
   Dazzle   <CO>

KLEIN, Norma   <YA>(Deceased)
   It's OK If You Don't Love Me
   Love Is One Of The Choices
   Family Secrets

KLEINSASSER-TESTERMAN, Lois
                     (Cait Logan)
                     (Cait London)

375

KLEINSCHMIDT, Dianne M. w/
                Sandra SMITH-WARE
                (Gabrielle DuPre)

KLEINSCHMIT, Sandra
                (Sandra James)
  Loveswept:
    72 Probable Cause
  Silhouette Desire:
    255 Heaven On Earth
    297 Love Undercover
    412 An Irresistible Force

KLEM, Kaye Wilson
                (Cathleen Carleton)
  Defiant Desire, The
  East Of Jamaica
  Mirrors   <CO>
  Reckless Fires

KLETZING, Karen
  Serenade/Saga: <HR><Insp>
    3 Ina

KLEVIN, Jill Ross   <YA>
  Wildfire:
    Best Of Friends, The
    Summer Of The
      Sky-Blue Bikini, The
    That's My Girl

KLEYPAS, Lisa   <HR>
  Give Me Tonight   <T-T>
  Love, Come To Me
  In sequence:
    Where Passion Leads
    Forever My Love

KLOEPFER, Marguerite
  Bently, Passion's Daughter
  But Where Is Love
  Heart And The Scarab

KNAPP, Daniel   <HO>
  California Woman

KNIGHT, Alanna   <GOT><RS>
                (Margaret Hope)
  Black Duchess, The
  Castle Clodha
  Castle Of Foxes
  Estella
  Lament For Lost Lovers
  Legend Of The Loch
  Outward Angel, The
  October Witch, The
  White Rose, The
  Wicked Wynsleys, The

KNIGHT, Alicia
                [Lucretia Wright]
  Harlequin Intrigue:
    33 Crescent Carnival
  Silhouette Desire:
    146 Eternal Flame

KNIGHT, Allison
                [Martha Kreiger]
  Heartfire Romance: <HR>
    Captive Innocent
    Satin Seduction
    Sea-Spun Ecstasy
    Willow Embrace

KNOLL, Anne   <GOT>
Stolen Bride Of Glengarra Castle

KNOLL, Patricia
        [Patricia Forsythe Knoll]
Harlequin Romance:
    2902 Gypsy Enchantment
    2961 Always A Bridesmaid
    3002 Send In The Clown

KNOLL, Patricia Forsythe w/ Barbara
    WILLIAMS   (Charlotte Nichols)

KNOTT, William C.
    Texan, The   <HS>

KNOWLES, Mable Winnifred
                      (Wynne May)

KNYE, Cassandra   <GOT>
    Castle And The Key, The
    House That Fear Built, The
    Steps To The Grotto

KOEHLER, Margaret Hudson
                    (Maggi Charles)
                    (Meg Hudson)

KOEN, Karleen   <HR>
    Through A Glass Darkly

KOENIG, Laird
    Sea Wife, The   <CO>

KNIGHT, Barbara
    Woodsedge   <RS>

KNIGHT, Bud
                  (see Stanley Levine)

KNIGHT, Doris   <RS>
    Nurse By Night
    Nurse On Terror Island

KNIGHT, Joan Giezey w/ Mary KUCZKIR
                       (Iris Summers)

KNIGHT, Kathleen Moore   <GOT>
    Robineau Look, The

KNIGHT, Nancy   <HR>
                 [Nancy C. Knight]
    Twice Promised   <AAS>

KNIGHT, Sali
                   [Tina Serafini]
    Starlit Surrender
    For Honor's Lady

KOLACZYK, Anne Mikita
                    (Anne Benson)
                    (Anne Hillary)

KOLACZYK, Anne w/ Ed KOLACZYK
    [Anne Mikita Kolaczyk w/
                 Edward Kolaczyk]
                 (Adrienne Edwards)
                 (Andrea Edwards)
                 (see Kathryn Jessup)
    Loveswept:
        89 Captain Wonder

KOLACZYK, Anne w/Ed KOLACZYK(cont.)
125 Oranges In The Snow
131 Butler And His Lady, The
184 Sultry Nights

KONINGSBERGER, Hans
American Romance
I Know What I'm Doing
Walk With Love And Death, A

KOONTZ, Dean R.
(Leigh Nichols)

KOPPEL, Lillian w/ Shelley KOPPEL
(Lillian Shelley)

KORBEL, Kathleen
[Eileen Dreyer]
(see Silhouette Summer Sizzlers)
Silhouette Desire:
286 Playing The Game
389 Prince Of A Guy, A   &
455 Princess And The Pea, The&
582 Hotshot   <MMS>
Silhouette Intimate Moments:
163 Stranger's Smile, A
191 Worth Any Risk
222 Edge Of The World
276 Perchance To Dream   @
309 Ice Cream Man, The
351 Lightning Strikes   @

KOSNER, A   <GOT>
My Sister Ophelia

KOUMALATS, Jodi
(Jodi Thomas)

KOVACS, Katherine Coffaro
(Katherine Coffaro)

KOVAK, Teri Shapiro   (Deceased)
(Tess Holloway)
(Tess Oliver)

KOVATS, Nancy   <HR>
Passion's Gold

KRAFT-MACOY, Lia
To Love And Honor

KRAHN, Betina
(see Avon Christmas Romance)
In sequence:
Caught In The Act

KRAHN, Betina M.   <HR>
Hidden Fires
Love's Brazen Fire
Midnight Magic
Passion's Ransom
Passion's Storm
Passion's Treasure
Rapture's Ransom
Heartfire Romance: <HR>
Rebel Passion

KRAMER, Kathryn   <HR>
[Kathryn Lynn Kramer]
(Katherine Vickery)
Desire's Masquerade
Destiny And Desire
Flame From The Sea
Highland Bride
Love's Blazing Ecstasy
Siren Song
Under Gypsy Skies
In sequence:
Desire's Deception

KROKOSZ, Emily
          (Emily Carmichael)

KROPP, Lloyd
  Drift, The

_____

_____

KRUEGER, Elizabeth
  Silhouette Romance:
  774 Saving Grace, A

_____

_____

KRUGER, Answald
          (see Maria Matray)

KRUGER, Mary
          (Mary Kingsley)

KUCZKIR, Mary
          (Jean Michaels)

KUCZKIR, Mary w/ Roberta ANDERSON
          (Fern Michaels)

KUCZKIR, Mary w/ Joan Giezey KNIGHT
          (Iris Summers)

KUETHER, Edith Lyman
          (Margaret Malcolm)

KUHLIN, Suzanne J.
          (Jennifer Mikels)

KUHN, Phyllis
  Candlelight:
  628 Dazzled By Diamonds <RO>

_____

_____

KURLAND, Michael Joseph
          (Jennifer Plum)

KURR, Maureen <HR>
  Deceptive Heart
  Northward The Heart
  Sword Of The Heart

_____

_____

KUTZ, Cynthia Van Hazinga
          (Cynthia Van Hazinga)

KWOCK, Laureen
          (Clarice Peters)
  Candlelight Regency:
  680 Miss Claringdon's
      Condition

_____

_____

KYLE, Elisabeth <RS>
  Love Is For The Living
  Mally Lee (The Second Mally Lee)
  Mirror Dance
  Scent Of Danger, The

_____

_____

KYLE, Marlaine [Jean Hager]
  Candlelight:
  692 Suitable Marriage, A <RE>
  705 Game Of Hearts, A <RE>

_____

_____

KYLE, Susan
          [Susan Spaeth Kyle]
  Diamond Spur
  Night Fever
  Lovestruck:
    Fire Brand

_____

_____

KYLE, Susan S.
          [Susan Spaeth Kyle]
  Morcai Battalion, The <SF>

_____

_____

KYLE, Susan Spaeth
          [Susan Eloise Spaeth Kyle]
          (Diana Blayne)
          (Katy Currie)
          (Susan Kyle)
          (Susan S. Kyle)
          (Diana Palmer)

L

La BARRE, Harriet   <RS>
Stranger In Vienna

382

LAMB, Nancy
    End Of Summer, The

LAMBERT, Carla
    Delta Queen

LAMBERT, Elizabeth
              (Penelope Williamson)
    The Avon Romance:
      Wings Of Desire

LAMBERT, Willa
              [William J. Lambert III]
    SuperRomance:
       2 Love's Emerald Flame
      23 From This Beloved Hour
      59 Love's Golden Spell

LAMBERT, William J. III
              (Willa Lambert)

LAMBOT, Isobel   <GOT>
    Taste Of Murder

LAMBRIGHT, Jeanie w/ Carolyn HAKE
              (Kate Denton)

LAMMERT, Charlotte   <GOT>
    Mistress Of Falcon Court

LAMON, Mrs. Sydney J.
              (Martha Albrand)

LAMP, C. O.
    Distant Love, Lasting Love
    Gentle Tigress

LAMPI, Kathlyn
    Crosswinds: <YA>
      15 Lighten Up, Jennifer

LAMPITT, Dinah
    To Sleep No More   <RS>

LANCASTER, Bruce   (Deceased)<HO>
    Big Knives, The
    Blind Journey
    Bride Of A Thousand Cedars
    Bright To The Wanderer
    For Us The Living
    Guns Of Burgoyne
    Guns On The Forest
    Night March
    No Bugles Tonight
    Phantom Fortress
    Roll Shenandoah
    Scarlet Patch, The
    Secret Road, The
    Trumpet To Arms
    Venture In The East

LANCASTER, Joan
              [Marlene J. Anderson]
    Summer Eyes
    Second Chance At Love:
      257 Promise Me Rainbows

LANCASTER, Lisa   <HR>
              [Elizabeth Young Lane]
    Capture The Wind

LANCASTER, Lydia   <HR>
              [Eloise Meaker]
    After Tomorrow
    Always The Dream
    Desire And Dreams Of Glory

384

LANCASTER, Lydia (cont.)
Heaven's Horizon
Her Heart's Honor
Love's Hidden Glory
Passion And Proud Hearts
Stolen Rapture
Temptation, The
To Those Who Dare
Tapestry: <HR>
    63 Arms Of A Stranger, The
    92 False Paradise

LANCASTER, Sheila   <HR>
                [Sheila Holland]
Dark Sweet Wanton
Mistress Of Fortune

LANCE, Leslie   <GOT><RS>
            [Charles John Swatridge]
Bride Of Emersham
House In The Woods, The

LANCOUR, Gene   <HR>
              [Gene Louis Fisher]
Lerios Mecca, The
Sword For The Empire
Carlisle Series: In sequence:<HS>
    Candle In The Wind, A
    Fortune's Tide
    Southern Wind, A

LANCOUR, Jeanne
              [Gene Louis Fisher]
Age Of Chivalry: <HS>
    1 Storm And The Sword, The
    2 Armour And The Veil, The
    3 Mace And The Plume, The

LANDERS, Lynda Stowe
Avalon:
    Season To Remember, A

LANDEY, Dora w/ Elinor KLEIN
                (see Elinor Klein)
Sonya   <Saga>

LANDIS, J. D.
Starfire: <YA>
    Love's Detective

LANDIS, Jill Marie   <HR>
Wild Flower
Sunflower   &
Rose   &

LANDON, Jeanne
              [Jill Marie Landis]
NOTE: Jeanne Landon is pen name
        for Jill Marie Landis
        which has not been used.

LANDON, Nancy
              [Nancy Berland]
Harlequin SuperRomance:
    358 Midnight Blue
    424 Soundwaves

LANDRESS, Elee
        [Jacqueline Elee Pennington]
Promise Romance: <Insp>
    9 Windsong
   20 Love's Design
   32 Destination Unknown

LANG, Angela
Priceless Passion, The

LANG, Eve
                    [Ruth Ryan Langan]
Dawnstar Romance:
  Cross His Heart

LANG, Frances   <HR>
          [Winifred Langford Mantle]
Marquis' Marriage, The
Masquerade:
  12 Stranger At The Gate

LANG, Grace
                    [Lea Floren]
Nedra
Shining Mountains
Springboard To Love
Avalon:
  Love A Hostage

LANG, Heather
                    [Darlene Baker]
Harlequin American Romance:
  31 Thorn In My Side

LANG, Maud
Moon Tree, The
Summer Station

LANG, Miriam
                    (Margot Leslie)

LANGAN, Ruth
                    [Ruth Ryan Langan]
          (see HQ Christmas Stories)
Harlequin Historical <Set#2>:
  10 Mistress Of The Seas
  31 Texas Heart
  In sequence:
  41   Highland Barbarian
  65   Highland Heather
Silhouette Romance:
  121 Just Like Yesterday
  224 Hidden Isle
  303 No Gentle Love
  317 Eden Of Temptation
  371 This Time Forever
  407 Family Secrets
  458 Mysteries Of The Heart
  492 Proper Miss Porter, The
Silhouette Special Edition:
  119 Beloved Gambler
  218 To Love A Dreamer
  266 Star-Crossed
  354 Whims Of Fate

LANGAN, Ruth Ryan   <HR>
                    (Eve Lang)
                    (Ruth Langan)
Captive Of Desire
Destiny's Daughter
Heart's Secrets, The
Passage West
Tapestry: <HR>
  55 Nevada Nights
  78 September's Dream

LANG-CARLIN, Alexandra   <HR>
Dark Destiny
Wings Of Love

LANGE, Emma   <RE>
  Brighton Intrigue, The
  Cost Of Honor, The
  False Fiancee, The
  Reforming Of Lord Roth, The
  Scottish Rebel, The
  Unwavering Miss Winslow, The

LANGER, Maryn
                [Maryn Langer Smith]
  Serenade/Saga: <HR><Insp>
    19 Wait For The Sun
    25 Moon For A Candle
    28 Divide The Joy

LANGFORD, Sandra
                    (Olivia Sinclair)
  The Avon Romance:
    Midnight's Lady

LANGLEY, Tania
                [Tilly Armstrong]
  Coventry:
    45 Dawn   <HR>

LANGTRY, Ellen
                [Nancy Elliott]
  Silhouette Desire:
    66 Fierce Gentleness, The

LANIGAN, Catherine
                    (Joan Wilder)
  All Or Nothing   <CO>
  Bound By Love
  Sins Of Omission   <Saga>
  Web Of Deceit   <CO>
  Admit Desire

LANSBURY, Carol   <GOT>
  Ringarra

LANSDALE, Nina   <RS>
                [Marilyn Meeske Sorel]
  White Island, The

LANSING, Jessica
                      [David Ritz]
  In The Name Of Love   <CO>

LANTZ, Fran
                [Francess Lin Lantz]
  Swept Away: <YA>
    2 Woodstock Magic
    4 Star Struck
    8 All Shook Up

LANTZ, Francess Lin
                      (Fran Lantz)
  Caprice Romance: <YA>
    12 Love Song For Becky, A
    28 Surfer Girl
    40 Rock 'n' Roll Romance
    46 Senior Blues

LaPIETRA, Mary
  Serenade/Serenata: <Insp>
    21 Disguise Of Love, The

La POINT, Diane   <GOT>
  Picture Of Death, A   <CGS:#12>
  Flames Over The Castle <CGS:#6>
  Gold Of Karinthy, The

LARA, Jan   <RS>
    [Michael Thomas Hinkemeyer]
Soulcatcher

_____

_____

LARKIN, Elinor
                [Diane Lefer]
Candlelight:
    618 Twice Bought
         Bride, The   <RE>
    655 Love's Tempest   <RE>

_____

_____

LARKIN, Rochelle
    [Rochelle Richter Larkin]
Angels Never Sleep
Bed Of Roses   <CO>
Crystal Heart, The   <CO>
Glitterball
Golden Days, Silver Nights
Hail, Columbia
Kitty
Only Perfect
Civil War Trilogy: <HR>
    Harvest Of Desire
    Mistress Of Desire
    Torches Of Desire

_____

_____

LAROSA, Linda J.   <HR>
Winter Of The Heart

_____

_____

LARSON, Shirley
    [Shirley Roberta Cox Larson]
                (Shirley Hart)
Season Of Loving   <HR>
Harlequin SuperRomance:
    232 See Only Me
    368 Honor Bound
Harlequin Temptation:
    64   Where The Heart Is
    99   Face In The Crowd, A
    145 Laughter In The Rain

LARSON, Shirley (cont.)
    178 Wit And Wisdom
    214 Building On Dreams
    314 Just Jake
Now And Forever:
    4   Tempting Liza
Silhouette Desire:
    131 To Touch The Fire
Silhouette Romance:
    369 Slice Of Paradise, A

_____

_____

LARSON, Susan w/ Barbara MICHELS
                (Suzanne Michelle)

LARUE, Brandy
Second Chance At Love:
    97   Ecstasy Reclaimed

_____

_____

LASKIN, Pamela L.
Sweet Dreams: <YA>
    173 Music From The Heart

_____

_____

La SPINA, Greye   <GOT>
Shadow Of Evil

_____

_____

LATHAM, Robin
                (Cassandra Bishop)
                (Robin Lynn)

LA TOURRETTE, Jacqueline <GOT><HR>
                [Jacqueline Gibeson]
An Ancient Rage
Cruel Heart, A
Incense Tree, The
Joseph Stone, The
Madonna Creek Witch, The
Patarran
Pompeii Splendor, The
Wild Harp, The

_____

_____

LATOW, Roberta   <CO>
  Cheyney Fox
  Three Rivers
  Tidal Wave

LAURENCE, Anne
             [Sally Pfisterer]
  Harlequin SuperRomance:
  394 Always Say Yes

LAURENCE, Berthe   <CO>
  Moments

LAURENCE, Josephine
  Hearts Do Not Break
  Ring Of Truth, The

LAURENCE, Margaret
  Diviners, The
  Fire-Dwellers, The
  Jest Of God, A
  New Wind In A Dry Land
  Stone Angel, The
  This Side Of Jordan

LAURIE, Jessica   <GOT>
  Mistress Of Harrowgate, The

LAURIN, Alison T.
  When Love Is There

LAVEN, Marti
    [J.C. Marti Laven O'Laimhin]
  Harlequin Intrigue:
  22 Matter Of Revenge, A

LAVENDER, Gwyn
  Harlequin Romance:
  1830 Falcon On The Mountain

LAVENDER, William   <HR>
  Chinaberry
  Flight Of The Seabird
  Stone Hill
  Hargrave Journal Trilogy: <HS>
    Children Of The River
    Journey To Quiet Waters
    Fields Above The Sea, The

LAW, Carol Russel   <HO>
  Overture To Love

LAW, Elizabeth   <RE>
            [Maureen Peters]
  Double Deception
  Regency Morning
  Scent Of Lilac, A
  Simon And Sparrow Series:
    Sealed Knot, The

LAWRENCE, Allison
              [Judy Bryer]
  Candlelight:
  702 Highland Lover   <TUD>

LAWRENCE, Amy
                [Joyce Schenk]
Andrea
Blues For Cassandra
Caprice Romance: <YA>
  15 Color It Love
  73 Madly In Love

LAWRENCE, D. H.
Escaped Cock, The
Fox, The
John Thomas And Lady Jane
  (second version of
  "Lady Chatterley's Lover")
Lady Chatterley's Lover
Man Who Died, The
Merry-Go-Round, The
Plumed Serpent
Saint Mawr
Sons & Lovers
Virgin And The Gypsy, The
Women In Love

LAWRENCE, Fred   <HO>
                [Fred Feldman]
Jed Smith: Freedom River
                        <AES:#1>
Joseph Walker: Frontier Sheriff
                        <AES:#14>

LAWRENCE, Hilda   <GOT>
Pavilion, The

LAWRENCE, Irene
Candlelight:
  535 Love Is Like That   <RO>

LAWRENCE, James   <HR>
In sequence:
  Rebel Hawke
  Rebel Agent

LAWRENCE, Juliet
Circle Of Love:
  8 Reluctant Dawn

LAWRENCE, Kathleen
(see Lee Davis Willoughby <WWWW>)

LAWRENCE, Kathy   <HR>
[Kathleen Kelly Martin
        w/ L. Jay Martin]
The Avon Romance:
  Tin Angel

LAWRENCE, Lynn
                [Sherry Garland]
Second Chance At Love:
  85 Familiar Touch, The
  157 Deep In The Heart

LAWRENCE, Margery   <GOT>
Bride Of Darkness

LAWRENCE, Mary Margaret   <RS>
Seven Thunders

LAWRENCE, Nancy   <RE>
                [Nancy Starts]
Delightful Deception

LAWRENCE, Sarah
An Island Called Paradise

_____

_____

LAWRENCE, Susannah   <GOT>
   [Lorie Hartman w/ Jan Hartman]
   Daughters Of Music, The

_____

_____

LAWRENCE, Terry
               [Mary Terese Lawrence]
   Loveswept:
      288 Where There's Smoke
             There's Fire
      399 Outsider, The
      416 Wanted: The Perfect Man
      441 Unfinished Passion
   Silhouette Desire:
      465 Cabin Fever
      526 Before Dawn

_____

_____

LAWSON, JoNell   (Deceased)
   Roses Are For The Rich

_____

_____

LAWTON, Lynna   <HR>
   Glory's Mistress
   Under Crimson Sails

_____

_____

LAYE, Patricia   <RE>
   Touch Of Venus

LAYE, Patricia S.   <RS>
   Perilous Castle, The

_____

_____

LAYMON, Richard
   (see Lee Davis Willoughby <MOAS>)

LAYNE, Laura
   Nurse June's Dilema

_____

_____

LAYTON, Andrea   <HR>
                    [Iris Bancroft]
   Love's Gentle Fugitive
   Midnight Fires
   Rebel's Passion
   So Wild A Rapture

_____

_____

LAYTON, Edith   <HR><RE>
                    [Edith Felber]
      (see A Regency Christmas)
   Abandoned Bride, The
   Crimson Crown, The
   False Angel
   Fireflower, The
   Indian Maiden, The
   Lady Of Spirit
   Lord Of Dishonor
   Mysterious Heir, The
   Red Jack's Daughter
   In sequence:
      Duke's Wager, The
      Disdainful Marquis, The
   Love Trilogy:
      Love In Disguise
      Game Of Love, The
      Surrender To Love

_____

_____

LAZARUS, Marguerite
                    (Anna Gilbert)

LAZIER, Audrey
   Avalon:
      Cinderella Summer

_____

_____

LAZLO, Kate
   Forever After

_____

_____

LEA, Constance
Nurse In New York   <M&B>

_____

LEABO, Karen
Silhouette Desire:
629 Close Quarters
Silhouette Romance:
648 Roses Have Thorns
692 Ten Days In Paradise
707 Domestic Bliss
731 Full Bloom
764 Smart Stuff

_____

LEADER, Evelyn Barbara Blackburn
           (Barbara Blackburn)

LEAHY, Syrell Rogovin
Book Of Ruth, A
Circle Of Love
Love Affair
Only Yesterday
In sequence: <Saga>
Family Ties
Family Truths

_____

LEAR, Caty
Silhouette Romance:
493 Pursued By Love

_____

LEATHER AND LACE: <L&L>   <HR>
1 Lavender Blossoms, The
                  Dorothy Dixon
2 Trembling Heart, The
                  Dorothy Dixon
3 Belle Of The Rio Grande
                  Dorothy Dixon
4 Flame Of The West
                  Dorothy Dixon

LEATHER AND LACE (cont.)
5 Cimarron Rose
                  Dorothy Dixon
6 Honeysuckle Love
              Carolyn T. Armstrong
7 Diamond Queen
                  Dorothy Dixon
8 Texas Wildflower
                    Tammie Lee
                  [Tom Townsend]
9 Yellowstone Jewel
                  Dorothy Dixon

_____

LECLAIR, Day
                [Day Totton Smith]
Harlequin Romance:
3028 Jinxed

_____

LeCOCQ, Tracy
                  (Marilyn Tracy)
LE COMPTE, Jane
                  (Jane Ashford)
Moon Passage

_____

LEDERER, Mira   <CO>
Tell Me No Lies

_____

LEDERER, Paul Joseph   <HO>
Indian Heritage Series:
1 Manitou's Daughter
2 Shawnee Dawn
3 Seminole Skies
4 Cheyenne Dreams

_____

LEE, Amanda
 [Ruth Glick w/ Eileen Buckholtz]
 Silhouette Desire:
  173 Love In Good Measure
  192 More Than Promises
            (only Ruth GLICK)
  267 Logical Choice
  347 Great Expectations
  425 Place In Your Heart, A
 Silhouette Romance:
  651 Silver Creek Challenge

 Silhouette Special Edition:

  165 End Of Illusion

LEE, Andrea   <HR>
 Lady Cavaliers, The

LEE, Bayonne
                        (Joy Wu)

LEE, C. Y.
 Cripple Mah And The New Order
 Flower Drum Song, The
 Land Of The Golden Mountain, The
 Lover's Point
 Madam Goldenflower

LEE, Devon
         [Robert Warren Pohle Jr.]
 MacFadden Romance:

  44 Dark Intrigue

LEE, Doris
 Silhouette Romance:
  351 Alesandro's Gift
  383 Reluctant Bride
 Silhouette Special Edition:

  131 Fire In The Soul, A

LEE, Edna/Edna L.   <GOT>
 Queen Bee, The
 Web Of Days, The

LEE, Elizabeth
 Way Of Passion, The

LEE, Ellen
 Rendezvous With Love

LEE, Elsie   <GOT><HR><RE><RS>
                    (Elsie Cromwell)
                     (Jane Gordon)
 An Eligible Connection
 Barrow Sinister
 Blood Red Oscar
 Clouds Over Vellanti
 Curse Of Carranca, The
 Dark Moon, Lost Lady
 Diplomatic Lover, The
 Doctor's Office
 Drifting Sands, The
 Fulfillment
 Mansion Of Golden Windows
 Masque Of Red Death
 Mistress Of Mount Fair
 Mystery Castle
 Nabob's Widow, The
 Passions Of Medora Graeme, The
 Pryor Betrothal
 Roommates
 Satan's Coast
 Season Of Evil
 Second Romance
 Second Season
 Silence Is Golden
 Sinister Abbey
 Spy At The Villa Miranda, The
 Star Of Danger
 Wicked Guardian, The
 Wingarden

LEE, Jennifer
Promise Me Tomorrow

LEE, Maureen
Lila

LEE, Joyce
Candlelight:
  564 Best Laid Schemes, The\<RE>
  671 Oh, What A Tangled Web\<RE>
  700 Joy Forever, A   \<RE>
  715 Perchance To Dream   \<RE>

LEE, Rachel
Silhouette Intimate Moments:
  370 An Officer And A
       Gentleman

LEE, Sandra
              [Sandra Lee Smith]
Harlequin Temptation:
  196 Over The Rainbow

LEE, Katherine
MacFadden Romance:
  159 Emerald Morning
  174 Worlds Apart
  190 Written In The Stars
  222 Crystal Web, The

LEE, Tammie
              [Tom Townsend]
Texas Wildflower   \<L&L:#8>

LEE, Linda
              (Hope Goodwin)
How To Write And Sell Romance
Novels   \<NF>

LEE, Tessa
Spanish Interlude

LEE, Lucy
        [Charlene Joy Talbot]
SuperRomance:
  10 Heart's Fury
  44 Rite Of Love, The
  93 Heart's Paradise

LEECH, Audrey   \<GOT>\<RS>
Pawn Of Evil
Terror Of Stormcastle, The
Witches Of Omen, The

LEEDS, Wendy
Cameo

LEE, Lydia
            (Rose Marie Lima)
Impetuous Pandora, The
Magnificent Mirabelle, The\<RE-IN>
Silhouette Romance:
  642 Valentino's Pleasure
  784 Thank Your
         Lucky Stars \<WITS>

LEEKLEY, John
Blue And The Gray, The

LEES, Hannah
Woman Doctor

LEES, Marguerite
                    [Margaret Baumann]
Harlequin Romance:
   756 Ward Hostess
   769 Nursing Auxiliary
   795 Back Room Girl
   881 Don't Marry A Doctor
  1205 Sun And The Sea, The
  1235 Love As It Flies
  1264 Secret Star
  1303 Still Waters
  2034 Green Folly

Le FANU, J. Sheridan   <GOT><RS>
Le FANU, Sheridan
   Carmilla & The Haunted Baronet
   Diabolical Genius
   House By The Churchyard
   Uncle Silas
   Wylder's Hand

LEFER, Diane
                    (Elinor Larkin)

LEFFLAND, Ella
   Love Out Of Season

Le GRAND, Sybil
                    [Kaa Byington]
Second Chance At Love:
   148 Silken Tremors

LEHMAN, Yvonne
   Cherish Romance: <Insp>
      8 Taken By Storm

LEHMAN, Yvonne (cont.)
   Serenade/Serenata: <Insp>
     10 Smoky Mountain Sunrise
     23 More Than A Summer's Love

LEHR, Helene   <HR>
                    (Helene Sinclair)
   Princess Of Hanover
   The Avon Romance:
      In sequence:
         Gallant Passion, A
         Capture The Dream

LEIGH, Ana   <HR>
                    [Anna Lee Baier]
   Love's Long Journey
   Paradise Redeemed
   Sweet Enemy Mine
   Kirkland Chronicles:
      In sequence:
         These Hallowed Hills
         Question Of Honor, A
         Oh, Promised Destiny
         Kindled Flame, A

LEIGH, Catherine
                    [Catherine Lee Donich w/
                     Linda Sherwood Wolthausen
   Harlequin Romance:
      3075 Place For The Heart

LEIGH, Cynthia   <HR>
   Silken Tiger

LEIGH, Elizabeth   <HR>
   [Caroline Bourne w/Debbie Hancock]
   Creole Caress

LEIGH, Jackie
                              [Deborah Smith]
  Second Chance At Love:
    372 Proud Surrender
    386 Cupid's Verdict
    394 No Holds Barred
    414 Sweet Talkin' Man, A   &
    421 Young At Heart
    428 Angel On My Shoulder   &

_____

_____

LEIGH, Lori
                              [Lori Carlton]
  The Avon Romance:
    On The Winds Of Love

_____

_____

LEIGH, Meredith   <RE>
                              [Bruce Kenyon]
  An Elegant Education
  Lady Of Qualities

_____

_____

LEIGH, Micah
  [D. Evelyn Hoyle Gee w/
            Emma Frances Merritt]
  Texas Dreams   <CO>

_____

_____

LEIGH, Petra   <HR>
                              [Peter Ling]
  In sequence:
    Garnet
    Coral
    Rosewood

_____

_____

LEIGH, Roberta
                        (Rozella Lake)
                        (Roumelia Lane)
                        (Rachel Lindsay)
                        (Janey Scott-Eng)

LEIGH, Roberta (cont.)
  Facts Of Love
  Flower In The Desert
  Love In Store
  Love Match
  Night Of Love
  Savage Aristocrat, The
  Harlequin Presents:
    64   Beloved Ballerina
    68   And Then Came Love
    76   Heart Of The Lion
    109 Temporary Wife
    127 Man In A Million
    161 To Buy A Bride
    169 Cupboard Love
    175 Man Without A Heart
    182 Unwilling Bridegroom
    193 Too Young To Love
    204 Girl For A Millionaire
    233 Not A Marrying Man
    461 Confirmed Bachelor
    819 No Time For Marriage
    954 Maid To Measure
   1026 Racy Affair, A
   1043 Too Bad To Be True
   1066 An Impossible Man To Love
   1092 No Man's Mistress
   1115 Storm Cloud Marriage
   1217 Not Without Love
   1275 Man On The Make
   1298 Most Unsuitable Wife, A
  Harlequin Romance:
   1196 Dark Inheritance
   1269 Pretence
   1424 Vengeful Heart, The
   1696 My Heart's A Dancer
   1715 In Name Only
   1783 Cinderella In Mink
   1800 Shade Of The Palms

_____

_____

LEIGH, Robin   <HR>
                        [Robin Lee Hatcher]
  The Avon Romance:
    Rugged Splendor

_____

_____

LEIGH, Susannah   \<HR>
   Cheyenne Star   \<Saga>
   Dark Labyrinth
   Fleur de Lys
   Glynda
   Moonwind
   Silver Swan, The
   Wine Of The Dreamers
   Winter Fire
   Yesterday's Tears

LEIGH, Veronica   \<GOT>
   Boris Story, The
   Cat Of Nine Tales, The
   Dark Seed, Dark Flower
   Heston House Horror

LEIMAS, Brooke
   Intruder, The
   Summer Visitors, The

LEMBERGER, LeAnn
            (Leigh Michaels)

LEMERY, Alysse
          [Alysse Rasmussen]
   Harlequin American Romance:
    46   Twilight Dawn
    98   Wishing Star
   199   Winter's End

LeMON, Lynn   \<HR>
          [Lynnette L. Wert]
   Sunrise Temptation
   This Rebel Hunger

LENARD, Yvone
   Shantal

L'ENGLE, Madeleine
      [Madeleine L'Engle Franklin]
   Circle Of Quiet, A
   Ring Of Endless Light, A
   Small Rain, The
   Summer Of The Great-Grandmother
   Winter's Love, A
   In sequence: \<RS>
    Love Letters, The
    Other Side Of The Sun, The
   Young Love: \<YA>
    And Both Were Young
    Camilla

LENNOX, Jacquelyn
          [Deborah Smith]
   Silhouette Desire:
   429   Force Of Habit

LENNOX, Susan
   Candlelight:
    12   Adventure In Jamaica

LENOIR, Cathie
   Serenade/Serenata: \<Insp>
    29   Born To Be One

LENORE, Lisa
          [Craig Howard Broude]
   SuperRomance:
    18   Dance Of Desire
    39   Love's Hour Of Danger

LENOTRE, Teresa
Mystique:
  21 Strange Encounter

LERNER, Carrole
Promise Romance: <Insp>
  23 Imperfect Stranger

LENZ, Jeanne R.
Caprice Romance: <YA>
  24 Do You Really Love Me?

LEONARD, Constance   <RS>
Hostage In Illyria
Other Maritha, The
Shadow Of A Ghost
Steps To Nowhere

LEONARD, Phyllis/Phyllis G.
                     <GOT><HR>
                  [Isabel Ortega]
Beloved Stranger
Mariposa
Phantom Of The Sacred Well
Prey Of The Eagle
Tarnished Angel
Warrior's Woman

LEONE, Adele
                  (Charlotte Austen)

LEONE, Laura
                  [Laura Resnick]
Silhouette Desire:
  478 One Sultry Summer
  507 Wilder Name, A
  531 Ulterior Motives
  560 Guilty Secrets
  610 Upon A Midnight Clear
  632 Celestial Bodies
Silhouette Special Edition:
  608 Woman's Work, A

LEROE, Ellen
Have A Heart, Cupid Delaney <YA>
First Love From Silhouette: <YA>
  87 Enter Laughing
  123 Give And Take
Two Hearts: <YA>
  Confessions Of A
  Teenage TV Addict

LeROY, Irene
                     [Sally Svee]
Silhouette Intimate Moments:
  235 Nothing To Hide

LESKO, Ruth
                  (Blanche Garland)

LESLIE, Alice
Torch:
  Stormy Obsession

LESLIE, Doris   <HO><HR>(Deceased)
                [Doris Fergusson-Hannay]
Desert Queen, The
Great Corinthian, The
King's Traitor, The
Perfect Wife, The
Peridot Flight
Polonaise
Rebel Princess, The
Sceptre And The Rose, The
That Enchantress
This For Caroline
Toast To Lady Mary, A
Wreath For Arabella

LESLIE, Joann
         (Darla Benton)
         (Jessica Dare)

LESLIE, Lynn
  [Sherill Bodine w/ Elaine Sima]
  Harlequin Intrigue:
  129 Street Of Dreams
  Harlequin SuperRomance:
  472 End Of Innocence

LESLIE, Margot
        [Miriam Lang]
  Second Chance At Love:
  156 Lovestruck

LESLIE, Miriam
       [W. E. Daniel Ross]
  Cavanaugh Keep

LESLIE, Rochelle   <HR>
        [Graham Diamond]
  Tears Of Passion, Tears Of Shame

LESLIE, Susan
         (Ashley Allyn)
         (Evelyn Grey)
  An Unfinished Tapestry

LESOING, Jan   <HR>
  Destiny's Interlude
  Forever Yesterday

LESTER, Samantha
        [Lester Roper]
  Candlelight:
  250 Lady Rothchild, The   <RE>
  521 Love's Captive   <RE>
  612 Duke's Ward, The   <RE>
  637 Brash American, The <RE>

LESTER, Teri   <GOT>
  Dawn Of Love, The
  Everything But Love
  Episode In Rome
  Island Mystery
  Quija Board
  Tania

L'ESTRANGE, Anne
        [Rosemary Ellerbeck]
  Return To Wuthering Heights

LETTON, Jennette   <GOT><RS>
  Allegra's Child
  Cragsmoor
  Don't Cry, Little Sister
  Haunting Of Cliffside, The
  Hilltop
  Incident At Hendon
  Robsart Affair, The

Le VARRE, Deborah   <HR>
      [Deborah M. Varlinsky]
  Captive Mistress

LEWIS, Coleen
  Avalon:
    Nurse At Lookout Rock
    Tracy Sterling, M. D.

LEWIS, Paul   <HO>
                    [Noel B. Gerson]
  Gentle Fury, The   <HofFS>

LEWIS, Deborah   <GOT>
                  [Charles L. Grant]
  Eve Of The Hound, The
  Kirkwood Fires
  Voices Out Of Time
  Wind At Winter's End, The

LEWTY, Marjorie
  Harlequin Premiere Edition:
    21 Million Stars, The
  Harlequin Presents:
    140 Fire In The Diamond, The
    875 Acapulco Moonlight
    932 Villa In The Sun
  Harlequin Romance:
    953 Alex Rayner, Dental Nurse
   1146 Imperfect Secretary, The
   1183 Never Call It Loving
   1203 Lucky One, The
   1297 Dental Nurse At Denley's
   1489 Town Nurse-Country Nurse
   1725 Extraordinary Engagement
   1759 Rest Is Magic, The
   1819 All Made Of Wishes
   1914 Flowers In Stony Places
   2075 To Catch A Butterfly
   2144 Time And The Loving, The
   2196 Short Engagement, The
   2282 Very Special Man, A
   2331 Certain Smile, A
   2382 Prisoner In Paradise
   2421 Love Is A Dangerous Game
   2450 Beyond The Lagoon
   2498 Girl Bewitched, A
   2546 Makeshift Marriage
   2579 One Who Kisses
   2587 Dangerous Male
   2650 Riviera Romance
   2678 Lover's Knot
   2746 Lake In Kyoto, A
   2848 In Love With The Man
   2985 Bittersweet Honeymoon
         Honeymoon Island   HRS 6
         Falling In Love Again HRS32
         Kiss Is Still A Kiss,A HRS60
         Man-Trap   HRS73

LEWIS, Hilda   <HO>(Deceased)
            [Hilda Winifred Lewis]
  Harlot Queen
  I Am Mary Tudor
  Witch And The Priest

LEWIS, Kathryn,
  Avalon:
    Capitol Kisses

LEWIS, Mary Christianna Milne
                  (Christianna Brand)

LEWIS, Maynah   <GOT>
  Give Me This Day
  Long Hot Days, The
  Make Way For Tomorrow
  No Place For Love
  Pride Of Innocence, The
  Symphony For Two Players
  Unforgiven, The   <CGS:#24>

LEY, Alice Chetwynd   <RE>
   [Alice Chetwyn Humphrey Ley]
An Advantageous Marriage
At Dark Of The Moon
Beau And The Bluestocking, The
Beloved Diana
Conformable Wife, A
Courting Of Joanna, The
Georgian Rake, The
Guinea Stamp, The
Intrepid Miss Haydon, The
Jewelled Snuff Box, The
Letters For A Spy
Master And The Maiden
Regency Scandal, A
Season At Brighton, A
Sentimental Spy, The
Tenant Of Chesdene Manor
In sequence:
   Clandestine Betrothal, The
   Toast Of The Town, The
In sequence:
   Reputation Dies, A
   Fatal Assignation, A

LIBBY, Patricia
Hollywood Nurse
Winged Victory For Nurse Kerry

LICHTE, Prudence Bingham
   [Prudence Jane Bingham Lichte]
              (Henrietta Houston)
              (Prudence Martin)

LIDE, Mary
   Isobelle
   Tregaran

LIDE, Mary (cont.)
   In sequence: <HS>
   Ann Of Cambray
   Gifts Of The Queen
   Royal Quest, A

LIEBERMAN, Ricard M.
              (see Marianne Kanter)

LIEDERMAN, Judith   <HR>
   Pleasure Dome, The   <Saga>

LIGHT, Caroline
              [Lucetta L. Hynnes]
   Starlight Romance:
   Gift In Secret, A
   Minor Royalty

LIMA, Rose Marie
              [Lydia Lee]
   Promise Romance:
   28 Homeless Heart

LINARES, Luisa-Maria
   Mystique:
   27 Web Of Fear
   44 Fatal Legacy

LINCOLN, Lillian   <RE>
              [Barbara Hazard]
   Bellwood Treasure, The
   Change Of Heart, A
   Fine Feathers

LIND, Pamela
                    [Saranne Hoover]
  Silhouette Desire:
    30 Past Forgetting
    51 Shadow Of The Mountain
  Silhouette Special Edition:
    197 Echoes Of The Past

LINDEN, Catherine
  Baron's Woman, The   <HR>
  Close Associates
  Diamonds In The Night
  Her Master's Pleasure   <RE>
  Highland Rose   <HR>
  Kiss...But Never Tell   <RS>
  Lover's Moon
  Wakefield's Passion

LINDEN, Monica
  Chiara

LINDLEY, Erica   <RS>
                    [Aileen Quigley]
  Belladonna
  Brackenroyd Inheritance, The
  Devil In Crystal, The
  Harvest Of Destiny

LINDLEY, Meredith
            [Meredith Babeaux Brucker]
  Silhouette Romance:
    116 Against The Wind

LINDON, Deanna
                    [Dana Rae Pugh]
  Second Chance At Love:
    469 Air Dancer

LINDOP, Audrey Erskine   <GOT>
  I Start Counting
  Journey Into Stone
  Self-Appointed Saint, The
  Sight Unseen
  Way To The Lantern

LINDQUIST, Marie
  Texas Promises Trilogy: <YA>
    1 Dreams At Dawn
    2 Untamed Heart
    3 Hidden Longings

LINDSAY, Devon   <HR>
                    [Cynthia Wright]
  Crimson Intrigue

LINDSAY, Josephine   <GOT>
  Shadow Of The House

LINDSAY, Perry
                    [Peggy Dern]
  Desire Under The Rose

LINDSAY, Rachael
                    [Roberta Leigh]
  Harlequin Classic:
    148 Heart Of A Rose   (888)
  Harlequin Presents:
    45 Price Of Love, The
    48 Business Affair
    53 Mask Of Gold
    60 Castle In The Trees
    73 Food For Love
    80 Innocent Deception
    85 Love In Disguise

LINDSAY, Rachael (cont.)
104 Affair In Venice
117 Prince For Sale
164 Secretary Wife
172 Roman Affair
176 Tinsel Star
184 Man To Tame, A
188 Marquis Takes A Wife, The
201 Forbidden Love
217 Prescription For Love
220 Brazilian Affair
228 Forgotten Marriage
241 Love And Dr. Forrest
249 Unwanted Wife
257 Rough Diamond Lover
265 An Affair To Forget
274 Man Out Of Reach
280 Designing Man
315 My Sister's Keeper
346 Widening Stream, The
359 Man Of Ice
375 Rent A Wife
381 Love And No Marriage
413 Wife For A Year
467 Untouched Wife
555 Substitute Wife
Harlequin Romance:
888 Heart Of A Rose
1014 House Of Lorraine
1039 Taming Of Laura, The
1614 Love And Lucy Granger
1648 Moonlight And Magic
1667 Question Of Marriage, A
1742 Alien Corn
1763 Cage Of Gold

LINDSEY, Betina   <HR>
Waltz With The Lady
Swan Bride, The

LINDSEY, Dawn   <RE>
     [Cherylle Lindsey Dimick]
Daughter Of Fortune
Duchess Of Vidal, The

LINDSEY, Dawn (cont.)
Dunraven's Folly
Great Lady Tony, The
Nonpareil, The
Notorious Lady
Proper Proposal, A
Talisman, The
Victory Summer

LINDSEY, Johanna   <HR><RE>
Captive Bride
Defy Not The Heart
Gentle Feuding, A
Gentle Rogue
Glorious Angel
Heart Of Thunder
Heart So Wild, A
Paradise Wild
Pirate's Love, A
Secret Fire
Silver Angel
So Speaks The Heart
Tender Is The Storm
Warrior's Woman   <RF>
When Love Awaits
In sequence:
   Love Only Once
   Tender Rebel
In sequence:
   Fires Of Winter
   Hearts Aflame
In sequence:
   Brave The Wild Wind
   Savage Thunder

LING, Peter
                    (Petra Leigh)

LININGTON, Elizabeth
                    (Dell Shannon)

LINK, Gail   <HR>
Wolf's Embrace

405

LINSLEY, Judith w/ Ellen RIENSTRA
                    (Marie Beaumont)
                    (Elinor Lynley)

LINZ, Cathie
          [Cathie Linz Baumgardner]
   Candlelight Ecstasy:
      52 Remembrance Of Love
     157 Wildfire
     178 Summer's Embrace, A
     203 Charming Strategy, A
     242 Private Account
     266 Winner Takes All
     313 Pride And Joy
     330 Glimpse Of Paradise, A
     364 Tender Guardian
     394 Lover And Deceiver
     482 Handful Of Trouble, A
   Candlelight Supreme:
     130 Continental Lover
   Silhouette Desire:
     408 Change Of Heart
     443 Friend In Need, A
     484 As Good As Gold
     519 Adam's Way
     575 Smiles
     616 Handyman

_____

_____

LIPPENCOTT, Dorothy
   MacFadden Romance:
      27 Storm Affair, The

_____

_____

LIPTON, Dean   <HR>
   Bluegrass Frontier

_____

_____

LIPTON, JAMES
   Mirrors   <CO>

_____

_____

LISLE, Mary
                    (Marylyle Rogers)

LISTON, Robert
                    (Elizabeth Bright)

LITCHMAN, Frank
                    (Ursula Nightingale)

LITTLE, Paul H.   (Deceased)
                    (Marie de Jourlet)
                    (Leigh Franklin James)
                    (Paula Little)
                    (Paula Minton)

LITTLE, Paula
                    [Paul H. Little]
   Love Conquers All
   Love In Style
   One True Love

_____

_____

LITTON, Pamela
   Harlequin Historical <Set #2>
      69 Stardust And Whirlwinds

_____

_____

LIVIANT, Curt
   Yemenite Girl, The

_____

_____

LIVINGSTON, Alice
   MacFadden Romance:
       1 Sweet Deception
      45 Stars Above, The
      67 Shadow Of Love, The
      74 Time Of Tenderness

_____

_____

LIVINGSTON, Georgette
                    (Diane Crawford)
   SuperRomance:
      92 Serengeti Sunrise

_____

_____

LIVINGSTON, Nancy   <HS>
    Far Side Of The Hill, The

LLEWELLYN, Caroline   <RS>
    [Caroline Llewellyn Champlin]
    Masks Of Rome, The

LLEWELLYN, Richard   <HR>
    How Green Was My Valley
    Night Of Bright Stars, A
    Tell Me Now & Again

LLOYD, ADRIEN   <HO>
                    (see Rebecca Drury)
    Fever On The Wind

LLOYD, Frances
    Silhouette Romance:
    200 Savage Moon
    319 Desert Rose
    425 Wild Horizons
    473 Castaways, The
    497 Tomorrow's Dawn
    549 Touched By Magic
    569 Takeover Man, The
    624 Lord Of The Glen

LLOYD, Marta
                    [Marta Buckholder]
    Torchlite:
    Lion's Shadow, The
    Winds Of Love, The

LLOYD, Stephanie   <RS>
    Graveswood

LLOYD, Sylvia
    Down East Nurse
    Heart Must Learn, The
    Weddings By Gwen

LLYWELYN, Morgan   <HO>
    Bard
    Grania
    Isles Of The Blest, The   <RF>
    Red Branch
    In sequence:
      Horse Goddess, The
      Lion Of Ireland
      Wind From Hastings, The

LOBDELL, Helen
    Terror In The Mountains

LOCKE, Douglas   <GOT>
    Death Lives In The Mansion
    Drawstring, The

LOCKWOOD, Elinor
    Miranda

LOCKWOOD, Ethel
    Hopeless Love
    House In The Hollow

LOCKWOOD, Edith (cont.)
Island By The Keys
Miracle On The Mountain
Mistress Of The Manor
Sands Of Destiny
Starlight On The Bayou
Wayward Love
Witness To The Wedding

LODGE, Elizabeth   <HR>
Cassandra

LODI, Maria
Charlotte Morel Trilogy:
  Charlotte Morel
  Charlotte Morel: The Dream
  Charlotte Morel: The Siege

LOFTS, Norah   (Deceased)
                    <GOT><HO><RS>
              [Norah Robinson Lofts]
                   (Juliet Astley)
                    (Peter Curtis)
Afternoon Of An Autocrat
Bless This House
Blossom Like The Rose
Bride Of Moat House
Brittle Glass, The
Calf For Venus, A
Checkmate
Colin Lowrie
Crown of Aloes
Concubine, The
Day Of The Butterfly
Deadly Gift, The
Eleanor The Queen
Eternal France (w/Margery WEINER)
Gad's Hall
Golden Fleece, The
Haunting Of Gad's Hall, The   <SN>
Hauntings
Hauntings: Is Anybody There?

LOFTS, Norah (cont.)
Heaven In Your Hand
Here Was A Man
Hester Roon
I Met A Gypsy
Jassy
King's Pleasure, The
Lady Living Alone
Letty
Little Wax Doll, The
Lonely Furrow, The
Lost Queen, The
Lovers All Untrue
Lute Player, The
Madselin
Maude Reed Tale, The
Nethergate
Old Priory, The
Out Of The Dark
Out Of This Nettle
Pargetters
Requiem For Idols
Rose For Virtue, A
Scent Of Cloves
Silver Nutmeg
To See A Fine Lady
Uneasy Paradise
Wayside Tavern, A
White Hell Of Pity   <SN>
Winter Harvest
You're Best Alone   <SN>
House Trilogy:
  Town House, The
  House At Old Vine, The
  House At Sunset, The
In sequence:
  Knight's Acre
  Homecoming, The

LOGAN, Cait
        [Lois Kleinsasser-Testerman]
Tame The Fury   <HR>
Second Chance At Love:
  325 Lady On The Line   &
  370 Rugged Glory
  419 Gambler's Lady
  432 Lady's Choice, A

LONDON, Laura (cont.)
    263 Moonlight Mist
    565 Love's A Stage
    644 Gypsy Heiress, The

LONGFELLOW, Pamela
    China Blues

LONDON, Victoria   <HR>
    Destiny's Desire
    Ecstasy's Embers
    Passion's Pirate
    Seductive Scoundrel

LONGFORD, Lindsay
                        [Jimmie L. Morel]
    Silhouette Romance:
    696 Jake's Child

LONG, Gabrielle Margaret (Deceased)
                    (Marjorie Bowen)
                    (Margaret Campbell)
                    (Joseph Shearing)

LONGRIGG, Roger Erskine
                        (Megan Barker)

LONGSTREET, Stephen
    Ambassador
    Bank, The
    Beach House

LONG, Lyda Belknap   <GOT><RS>
    Crucible Of Evil
    Fire Of The Witches
    House Of The Deadly Nightshade
    Legacy Of Evil
    Lemoyne Heritage, The
    Shape Of Fear, The
    To The Dark Tower
    Witch Tree, The

    Burning Man
    Delilah's Fortune
    Few Painted Feathers
    Divorce, The
    Geisha
    Kingston Fortune, The   <HS>
    Lion At Morning
    Masts To Spear The Stars
    Pembroke Colors, The
    Promoters, The
    She Walks In Beauty
    Stormwatch
    Straw Boss
    Strike The Bell Boldly
    In sequence:
        All Or Nothing
        Our Fathers House
    Pedlocks: <HS>
        God And Sarah Pedlock
        Pedlock And Sons
        Pedlock At Law
        Pedlock Inheritance
        Pedlock Saint, Pedlock Sinner
        Pedlocks In Love, The
        Pedlocks, The

LONG, William Stuart   <HO>
                [Vivian Stuart Mann]
    Australian Series:
        1   Exiles, The
        2   Settlers, The
        3   Traitors, The
        4   Explorers, The
        5   Adventurers, The
        6   Colonists, The
        7   Gold Seekers, The
        8   Gallant, The
        9   Empire Builders, The
        10 Seafarers, The
        11 Nationalists, The
        12 Imperialists, The

LONGSTREET, Stephen (cont.)
  Trilogy:
    Dream Seekers, The
    Wheel Of Fortune, The
    Golden Touch, The

LOOK, Jane H.
                        (Lee Damon)

LOOMIS, Stanley   <HO>(Deceased)
  Fatal Friendship, The
  Paris In The Terror

LOPEZ, Dee w/ Norma WILLIAMS
                        (Dee Norman)

LORAINE, Philip   <RS>
  Day Of The Arrow
  Dead Men Of Sestos, The
  Mafia Kiss
  Nightmare In Dublin
  Photographs Have Been
    Sent To Your Wife
  Voices In An Empty Room
  Wrong Man In The Mirror

LORD, Alexandra
  [Paticia A. Williams w/
          Catherine Seibert]
  Candlelight:
    643 Harmless Ruse, A   <RE>

LORD, Bette Bao
  Eighth Moon
  Spring Moon

LORD, Graham   <RS>
  Spider And The Fly, The

LORD, Jeanne Day
  Breed Apart, A

LORD, Moira
                        [Miriam Lynch]
  Calendar Of Sinners
  Nightingale Park

LORD, Shirley
              [Shirley Lord Anderson]
  Golden Hill   <Saga>
  One Of My Very Best Friends

LORD, Vivian   <HR>
              [Pat Wallace Strother]
  Once More The Sun
  Summer Kingdom
  Traitor In My Arms
  Unyielding Fire   <Saga>
  Voyagers, The

LORDAHL, Jo Ann   <GOT>
  Those Subtle Weeds

LOREL, Claire
                      [Daphne de Jong]
  Coventry:
    130 Lord Brandsley's Bride<RE>
    160 Miss Miranda's Marriage
                                <RE>

LORENA
  Mystique:
    42 Identity Unknown

LORIN, Amii
                          [Joan M. Hohl]
Come Home to Love (original by
  Paula Roberts)
Candlelight:
  592 Morning Rose,
          Evening Savage   <RO>
Candlelight Ecstasy:
    1 Tawny Gold Man, The
    7 Game Is Played, The
  11 Morgan Wade's Woman   &
  22 Breeze Off The Ocean   @
  50 Snowbound Weekend
  99 Gambler's Love
 391 Power And Seduction
Candlelight Ecstasy Supreme:
  32 While The Fire Rages   @
 113 Night Striker   &
Harlequin Romance:
2662 Candleglow

_____

_____

LORING, Anne   <GOT>
Mark Of Satan

_____

_____

LORING, Emilie
   1 For All Your Life
   2 What Then Is Love
   3 I Take This Man
   4 My Dearest Love
   5 Look To The Stars
   6 Behind The Cloud
   7 Shadow Of Suspicion, The
   8 With This Ring
   9 Beyond The Sound Of Guns
  10 How Can The Heart Forget
  11 To Love And To Honor
  12 Love Came Laughing By
  13 I Hear Adventure Calling
  14 Throw Wide The Door
  15 Beckoning Trails
  16 Bright Skies
  17 There Is Always Love
  18 Stars In Your Eyes
  19 Keepers Of The Faith
  20 Where Beauty Dwells

LORING, Emilie (cont.)
  21 Follow Your Heart
  22 Rainbow At Dusk
  23 When Hearts Are Light Again
  24 Today Is Yours
  25 Across The Years
  26 Candle In Her Heart, A
  27 We Ride The Gale!
  28 It's A Great World
  29 Give Me One Summer
  30 High Of Heart
  31 Uncharted Seas
  32 With Banners
  33 As Long As I Live
  34 Forever And A Day
  35 Lighted Windows
  36 Hilltops Clear
  37 Fair Tomorrow
  38 Gay Courage
  39 Swift Water
  40 Solitary Horseman, The
  41 Certain Crossroad, A
  42 Trail Of Conflict, A
  43 Spring Always Comes
  44 Here Comes The Sun!
  45 Key To Many Doors, A
  46 In Times Like These
  47 Love With Honor
  48 No Time For Love
  49 Forsaking All Others
  50 Shining Years, The
Other:
  Siamese Twin Mystery
  For All Your Love

_____

_____

LORING, Jenny
                    [Martha Sans]
SuperRomance:
  74 Stranger's Kiss, A
Harlequin SuperRomance:
 129 Right Woman, The
 202 Scenes From A Balcony
 280 Whole Truth, The
 388 Interlude

_____

_____

LORING, Lynn
Avalon:
  Snow Kisses

LORRAINE, Anne
                              [Jane Alan]
Harlequin Romance:
  750 Nurse About The Place, A
  786 Ring For The Doctor, A
  849 Nurse For Mr. Henderson, A
  867 Elusive Lady
  891 Hospital World Of Susan
       Wray, The

LORRAINE, Marian   <RE>
            [Marian Lorraine Horton]
Mischievous Spinster, The
Candlelight:
  589 Ardent Suitor, The   <RE>
  639 Enterprising Minx, The<RE>

LORRIMER, Claire   <HR><RS>
            [Patricia Denise Robins]
Frost In The Sun
Relentless Storm
Secret Of Quarry House, The
Shadow Falls, The
Voice In The Dark, A
In sequence:
  Chatelaine, The
  Wilderling, The
Trilogy:
  Mavreen
  Tamarisk
  Chantal

LOTTMAN, Eileen   <GOT><HO>
After The Wind
Brahmins, The

LOTTMAN, Eileen (cont.)
Doctor's Hospital #1:
  One Of Our Own
Greek Tycoon, The
Hemlock Tree, The
Orphan, The
Summersea

LOUIS, Jacqueline
            [Jacqueline Hacsi]
SuperRomance:
  84 Love's Stormy Heights

LOUIS, Pat
                        [Dorothy Francis]
SuperRomance:
  14 Treasure Of The Heart

LOVAN, Thea
                        [Christine King]
Silhouette Desire:
  28 Passionate Journey
Silhouette Romance:
  281 Tender Passion, A
  326 Story Well Told, A
  361 Blue Sea Of August, The

LOVELACE, Jane   <RE>
                        [Dixie McKeone]
Eccentric Lady
Rolissa   <RE><RS>

LOVELL, Marc   <RS>
                        [Mark McShane]
Blind Hypnotist, The
Dreams In A Haunted House
Fog Sinister

LOVELL, Marc (cont.)
Guardian Specter, The
Memory Of Megan

LOVESMITH, Janet   <RS>
                    [Paul Fairman]
Inherit The Shadows
Legacy Of Fear
Lock, The

LOW, Dorothy Mackie   <GOT>
              [Lois Dorothea Low]
                       (Zoe Cass)
                     (Lois Paxton)
Isle For A Stranger
To Burgundy And Back

LOWE, Charlotte
                      (Annabella)
Lord Of The River

LOWE, Marjorie G.   <GOT>
          [Marjorie Griffiths Lowe]
Sudden Lady, The

LOWE, Susan L.
          [Susan Claire Leach Lowe]
                 (Andrea Davidson)
                 (Elise Randolph)

LOWELL, Anne Hunter
                      [Jan Boies]
Sorority Girls: <YA>
   1 Getting In
   2 Nowhere To Run
   3 Starting Over

LOWELL, Anne Hunter (cont.)
   4 Dangerous Secrets
   5 Settling The Score
   6 Winner Take All
   7 Change Of Heart, A
   8 Mistaken Identity
   9 Risking It All
  10 Rumors
  11 Breaker, The
  12 Holding On

LOWELL, Elizabeth
          [Ann Elizabeth Maxwell]
Tell Me No Lies   <RS>
Harlequin Historical <Set#2>:
  38 Reckless Love   @
Silhouette Classic:
   7 Danvers Touch, The   (IM18)
  17 Summer Games   (IM57)
Silhouette Desire:
  77 Summer Thunder
 265 Fire Of Spring, The
 319 Too Hot To Handle
 355 Love Song For A Raven   &
 415 Fever
 462 Dark Fire
 546 Fire And Rain   <MMS>@
      Western Lovers Trilogy:
 624   Outlaw   <MMS>
 625   Granite Man
 631   Warrior
Silhouette Intimate Moments:
  18 Danvers Touch, The
  34 Lover In The Rough
  57 Summer Games
  72 Forget Me Not
  81 Woman Without Lies, A   &
  97 Traveling Man
 109 Valley Of The Sun
 128 Sequel
 141 Fires Of Eden
 178 Sweet Wind, Wild Wind
 256 Chain Lightning

LOWELL, J. R.
Daughter Of Darkness

LOWERY, Lynn
                [Mona Lynn Lowery Hahn]
Larissa
Lorelei
Loveswept
Sweet Rush Of Passion
In sequence:
  Moonflower
  Starflower

LOWERY, Marilyn M.
                (Philippa Castle)

LOWING, Anne
                [Christine Geach]
Gossamer Thread, The
Melyonen
Napoleon Ring, The
Shadow On The Wind

LOWRY, Harold
                (Leigh Greenwood)

LOWRY, Nan
                [Ruth MacLeod]
Crystal Manning, Maternity Nurse

LOY, Diana
                [Rhoda Cohen]
After All

LOZANO, Wendy
She Who Was King
Sweet Abandon

LUCAS, Mayo
                [Mary M. Lucas]
The Avon Romance: <HR>
  Camelot Jones
  Matters Of The Heart

LUCKIE, L. F.   <HR>
Beware The Horse

LUEDTKE, Julie
Avalon:
  Dare To Love
  Therapy Of Love

LUELLEN, Valentina
                [Judith Polley]
Harlequin Historical <Set#1>:
   2 Passionate Pirate, The
   8 Where The Heart Leads
Masquerade:
   6 Francesca
   9 Madelon
  17 Gambler's Prize
  31 Pride Of MacDonalds, A
  34 Countess, The
  53 Marie Elena
  69 Castle Of The Mist
  84 Moon Shadow
Mills & Boon:
  Black Ravenswood
  Devil Of Talland
  Elusive Flame Of Love
  Lord Of Darkness
  Mistress Of Tanglewood
  Moonflower, The
  Moonshadow
  Passionate Pirate, The
  Prince Of Deception
  Silver Salamander
  Valley Of Tears, The
  Where The Heart Leads

LUELLEN, Valentina (cont.)
    Wild Wind In The Heather
    Other:
        Children Of The Devil
                (reprint "Francesca")
        King's Cavalier
        Slightly Scarlet
        (reprint "The Gambler's Prize")

LUKE, Mary/Mary M.   <HO>
    Catherine The Queen
    Crown For Elizabeth
    Ivy Crown, The   <RS><Saga>
    Nonsuch Lure, The   <RS>

LUPTON, Mary
    Avalon:
        Dangerous Kisses
        Fantasy At Midnight
        Fear To Love
        House Of Vengeance   <GOT>
        Night Glow   <GOT>

LUSTBERG, Jean Anne
                (Jean Anne Bartlett)

LUTYENS, Mary
                (Esther Wyndham)

LUTZ, Norma Jean
    First Love From Silhouette: <YA>
        167 Blossom Into Love

LYKKEN, Laurie
    Sweet Dreams: <YA>
        132 Winner Takes All
        144 Priceless Love
        153 Perfect Catch, The
        170 Rock 'N' Roll Sweetheart

LYLE, Elizabeth   <RE>
    Cassy
    Claire

LYLE-SMYTHE, Alan
                (Alan Caillou)

LYNCH, Frances   <GOT>
                [David Guy Compton]
    Candle At Midnight
    Dangerous Magic, A
    Fine And Handsome Captain, The
    In The House Of Dark Music
    Stranger At The Wedding
    Twice Ten Thousand Miles

LYNCH, Marilyn/Marilyn D.
    Lady Of Longing
    Nightmare's Morning
    Where Love Was Lost

LYNCH, Miriam   <GOT><RE><RS>
                (Dolores Craig)
                (Moira Lord)
                (Claire Vincent)
    Amber Twilight
    An Echo Of Weeping
    Bells Of Widows Bay
    Blacktower
    Brides Of Lucifer, The
    Creighton's Castle
    Daughters Of Cain
    Deadly Rose, The
    Devil's Mirror, The
    Doomsday Bells, The
    Flowering Green
    From Secret Places
    Garden Of Satan
    Graymists
    Hate Thy Neighbor
    House Of Yesteryear

416

LYNCH, Miriam (cont.)
Journey Into Twilight
Lonely Toys, The
Mark Of The Rope, The
Moon Of Darkness
Night Of The Moonrose
Nightmare Dance, The
Nightmare's Morning
Pale Hand Of Danger
Road To Midnight, The
Scalpel Of Honor
Secret Of Lucifer's Island, The
Silken Web, The
Spellbound
Twilight For Taurus   <BZG>
Unwilling Rebel
Where Evil Waits
Where Shadows Lie
Witches Of Windlake, The
Witch's Holiday
Witch's Song
Candlelight:
  45 Doctor Garrett's Girl
  201 Winter In A Dark Land
Coventry:
  29 Regency Rose, A
  72 Regency Ball
  150 Fair Impostor

LYNCH, W. Ware
Island Promise

LYNDELL, Catherine
                    [Margaret Ball]
Ariane
Border Fires
Journey To Desire
Stolen Dreams
Tapestry Of Pride
Tapestry: <HR>
  31 Alliance Of Love
  43 Masquerade
  58 Captive Hearts
  68 Vows Of Desire

LYNDON, Amy
[Richard Francis Radford, Jr.]
MacFadden Romance:
  146 One White Rose
  168 Opal Moon
  171 Tournament Of Love

LYNDON, Diana   <RE>
                    [Diana Antonio]
Cotillion Regency:
  3 Her Heart's Desire
  6 My Lord, My Love
  9 Country Rose, The

LYNLEY, Elinor   <HR>
[Judith Linsley w/ Ellen Rienstra]
Song Of The Bayou

LYNN, Ann
[Karen Paradiso w/ Nancy Harlow]
Heartfire Romance: <HR>
  Slave Of My Heart

LYNN, Anne
Stardom For Sandra

LYNN, Barbara
              [Charles R. MacKinnon]
Candlelight:
  230 Tender Longing's   <RO>

417

LYNN, Karen
    [Lynn Taylor w/ Karen Maxfield]
    Starlight Romance:
        Double Masquerade
        Dual Destiny
        Midsummer Moon
        Rake, The   <RE>
        Scottish Marriage, The

_____

_____

LYNN, Leslie   <RE>
    [Sherrill Bodine w/ Elaine Sima]
    Rake's Redemption, The
    Scandal's Child

_____

_____

LYNN, Margaret   <GOT><RS>
                       [Gladys Battye]
    Light In The Window, A
    To See A Stranger
    Whisper Of Darkness

_____

LYNN, Mary
    [Mary Elizabeth Nelson Lynn]
                       (Angel Milan)

LYNN, Robin
                       [Robin Latham]
    Second Chance At Love:
        209 Dreams Of Gold And Amber

_____

_____

LYNN, Tressa
    Avalon:
        Search For Tiger Moon

_____

_____

LYNN, Virginia   <HR>
                     (Virigina Brown)
    Doubleday Loveswept:
        River's Dream
        Cutter's Woman

_____

_____

LYNNE, Deborah
    Harlequin Regency Romance:
        Gentlemen's Agreement, A

_____

LYNNE, Suzanna
    Harlequin Presents:
        88 Red Feather Love
    Harlequin Romance:
        2007 Beloved Viking

_____

_____

LYNSON, Jane   <RE>
                        [Lynne Smith]
    Captain Rakehell

_____

_____

LYON, Dana   <RS>
    Trusting Victim, The

_____

_____

LYONS, Delphine C.   <GOT>
    Depths Of Yesterday, The
    Flower Of Evil
    House Of Four Widows
    Phantom At Lost Lake
    Valley Of The Shadows

_____

LYONS, Genevieve
Last Inheritor, The   <HS>

LYONS, Jacqueline
                      (Veronica Flynn)

LYONS, Leila   <HO>
                      [James Conaway]
Bridge To Tomorrow
Pillars Of Heaven
Star Quality   <CO>

LYONS, Maggie   <HR>
Bayou Passions
Heirs Of Rebellion
In sequence:
  Flame Of Savannah
  Flame Of Charleston

LYONS, Mary
Harlequin Presents:
  625 Passionate Escape, the
  673 Caribbean Confusion
  701 Desire In The Desert
  714 Spanish Serenade
  763 Dangerous Stunt
  779 Love's Tangled Web
  796 Mended Engagement
        (M&B: No Other Love)
  828 Eclipse Of The Heart
  908 Passionate Deception
  938 Escape From The Harem
 1002 Hay Fever
 1144 Stranger At Winterfloods
 1171 Hurricane!
 1276 Love In A Spin
 1346 No Surrender

LYONS, Pam
Heartlines: <YA>
   7 Tug of Love
   8 Danny's Girl
   9 Boy Called Simon, A
  10 Love Around The Corner

LYONS, Ruth   <CO>
Love Has Two Faces
Love Is Not Enough

MAAS, Donald
           (Stephanie St. Clair)

MacALLISTER, Heather
           (Heather Allison)

MACALUSO, Pamela
  Meteor Kismet:
    24 Remember My Love

MACARDLE, Dorothy   <GOT>
      [Dorothy Callan Macardle]
  Dark Enchantment
  Unforeseen, The
  Uninvited, The

MacBAIN, Carol
  Sweet Dreams: <YA>
    116 Heartbreak Hill
    136 Stand By For Love

MacBRIDE, Kate
  Love's Tormented Flame

MacCARTHY, Dorothy   <HR>
  Rapture's Reign

MacCULLOGH-WEIR, Nancie
  Jade   <CO>

MacDONALD, Elisabeth
          (Sabrina Ryan)
  Always Tomorrow   <Saga>
  House At Gray Eagle, The
  Watch For The Morning   <HR>
  In sequence: <HS>
    Falling Star
    Wyoming Star
  Candlelight Supreme:
    137 Fire In Her Eyes, The
  Harlequin Temptation:
    18 Love Me Again

MacDONALD, George   <Insp><GOT>
  Baronet's Song, The
  Curate's Awakening, The
  Lady's Confession, The
  Maidens's Bequest, The
  Musician's Quest, The
  Princess And The Goblin, The
  Shepherd's Castle, The
  Tutor's First Love, The
  In sequence:
    Fisherman's Lady, The
    Marquis' Secret, The

MACDONALD, Malcolm   <HR>
    [Malcolm John Ross-Macdonald]
          (Malcolm Ross)
  For They Shall Inherit   <Saga>
  Goldeneye
  Honour And Obey
  Notorious Woman, A
  On A Far Wild Shore
  Silver Highways, The   <Saga>
  Tessa d'Arblay
  Stevenson Family Saga: <HS>
    In sequence:
      World From Rough Stones, The
      Rich Are With You Always, The
      Sons Of Fortune
      Abigail

MacDONALD, Roslyn
               [Louise Clark]
Silhouette Special Edition:
  261 Second Generation
  293 Transer Of Loyalties
  583 An Independent Lady

MacDONALD, Sue
Barefoot Nurse
Charge Sister At Rangiatea
Doctor In Pinafores
Prescription For A Doctor
Woman Or Surgeon

MacDONALD, Zillah K.
Nurse Fairchild's Decision

MacDONNELL, Megan
           [Serita Stevens]
Dream Forever, A   <YA>

MacDOUGALL, Ruth Doan
Flowers Of The Forrest, The

MACE, Gertrude
Avalon:
  Elusive Memory
  Follow Your Dreams
  Mysterious Orchid, The

MacGREGOR, Miriam
Harlequin Romance:
  2710 Boss Of Brightlands
  2733 Spring At Sevenoaks

MacGREGOR, Miriam (cont.)
  2794 Call Of The Mountain
  2823 Winter At Whitecliffs
  2849 Stairway To Destiny
  2890 Autumn At Aubrey's
  2931 Rider Of The Hills
  2996 Lord Of The Lodge
  3022 Riddell Of Rivermoon
  3060 Man Of The House
  3083 Carville's Castle
  Malvern Man, The   HRS4

MacINNES, Helen   (Deceased)
           [Helen Highet]
              <GOT><RS>
Above Suspicion
Agent In Place
Assignment In Brittany
Assignment: Suspense
Cloak Of Darkness
Decision At Delphi
Double Image, The
Friends And Lovers
Hidden Target, The
Home Is The Hunter
Horizon
I And My True Love
Message From Malaga
Neither Five Nor Three
North From Rome
Pray For A Brave Heart
Prelude To Terror
Rest And Be Thankful
Ride A Pale Horse
Salzburg Connection, The
Snare Of The Hunter, The
Triple Threat
Venetian Affair, The
While Still We Live

MacIVER, Sharon   <HR>
        [Sharon J. Ihle]
Dakota Dream

MACK, Amanda
                                    [Jean Adelson]
  Candlelight:
    631 Makeshift Mistress   <RE>

MACK, Dorothy   <RE>
                           [Dorothy McKittrick]
  An Unconventional Courtship
  Blackmailed Bridegroom, The
  General's Granddaughter, The
  Last Waltz, The
  Luckless Elopement, The
  Prior Attachment, A
  Reluctant Heart, The
  Steadfast Heart, The
  Unlikely Chaperone, The
  Candlelight Regency:
    221 Raven Sisters, The
    225 Substitute Bride, The
    253 Impossible Ward, The
    602 Companion In Joy, A
    666 Belle Of Bath, The

MACK, Elsie
  Echanted Highway, The
  Avalon:
    Magic Is Fragile
  Candlelight:
    75 Deborah

MacKEEVER, Maggie   <HR><RE>
                              [Gail Clark]
  Banbury Tale, A
  Caprice
  El Dorado
  French Leave
  Lady Sherry And The Highwayman
  Lord Fairchild's Daughter
  Notorious Lady, A
  Our Tabby
  Outlaw Love
  Sweet Vixen

MacKEEVER, Maggie (cont.)
  Coventry:
    13 Lady Bliss
    27 An Eligible Connection
    55 Misses Millikin, The
    79 Fair Fatality   <RE>
    121 Jessabelle   <RE>
    169 Lady Sweetbriar   <RE>
    174 Lady In The Straw
    189 Strange Bedfellows

MacKENDRICK, Louise
                           [Freida Thomsen]
  Glory Seeker, The
  Natchez
  Passion For Honor, A
  Passion's Thief

MacKENZIE, Maura
  SuperRomance:
    6 Sweet Seduction
    76 Mirror Of The Heart

MacKENZIE, Tina w/ Jean HARVEY w/
  Laura BENNETT   (Justine Harlowe)

MacKENZIE, Trix
  Enchantment

MACKESY, Leonora
                           (Dorothy Rivers)
                           (Leonora Starr)

MACKEY, Mary
  Kindness Of Strangers, The   <CO>
  Grand Passion, A   <Saga>

MACKIE, Mary
                (Mary Christopher)
                (Susan Stevens)
Circle Of Love:
  17 Pamela

MACKIN, Jeanne
Frenchwoman, The

MACKINNON, Charles/Charles R. <HO>
    [Charles Roy Mackinnon]
              (Vivian Donald)
              (Barbara Lynn)
           (Charles Stuart)
    (Charles Stuart-Vernon)
                  (I. Torr)
         (Vivian Stuart **)
** (DO NOT confuse this pseudonym
    with that of another author)
Castlemore
Farthingale's Folly
Happy Hostage, The
Matriarch, The
Mereford Tapestry   <Saga>

MACKINTOSH, May   <GOT><RS>
Appointment In Andulusia
Assignment In Andorra
Balloon Girl
Dark Paradise
Highland Fling
Roman Adventure

MACKLEM, Francesca
Tomorrow & Forever

MacLEAN, Jan
    [Jill MacLean w/ Anne MacLean]
Harlequin Presents:
  529 An Island Loving
Harlequin Romance:
  2210 To Begin Again
  2287 Bitter Home Coming
  2295 Early Summer
  2348 White Fire
  2547 All Our Tomorrows

MacLEAN, Jill
                (Sandra Field)
                (Jocelyn Haley)

MACLEOD, Alison   <HR>
Muscovite, The

MacLEOD, Ellen Jane
    [Ellen Jane Anderson MacLeod]
Broken Melody, The
Stranger In The Glen

MacLEOD, Jean S.
    [Jean Sutherland MacLeod]
            (Catherine Airlie)
Harlequin Premiere Edition:
    3 Ruaig Inheritance, The
  22 Phantom Pipes, The
Harlequin Classic:
    7 Cameron Of Gare   (586)
  17 Way In The Dark, The (541)
  27 Dangerous Obsession (651)
  35 Silver Dragon, The (674)
  48 Chalet In The Sun,The(638)
  64 Stranger In
        Their Midst   (630)
  79 Black Cameron, The (797)
 116 Sugar Island   (853)
 155 Crane Castle   (966)
Harlequin Romance:
 797 Black Cameron, The

MADISON, Winifred
First Love From Silhouette: <YA>
   45 Touch Of Love
   64 Mix And Match
Wildfire: <YA>
   Dance With Me
   Sing About Us
   Suzy Who?

MADL, Linda <HR>
  Sweet Ransom
  Sunny

MAGALI
Mystique:
    1 Vanishing Bride
    7 Master Of Palomar, The
   10 In Search Of Sybil
   20 Moment Of Truth, The
   24 Loss Of Innocence
   56 Night Of The Storm
   68 Captive In Paradise
   71 Maze Of The Past
   83 Caught By Fate
   88 Deadly Pawn, The
  103 Question Of Guilt, A
  113 Love In Jeopardy
  126 Pact Of Love
  146 Tender Fate
  158 All That Glitters
  163 Healing Heart, The

MAGER, Marcia
  Woman Of New York <AWD>

MAGNER, Laura
           (Laura Parris)

MAGNER, Lee
    [Ellen Lee Magner Tatara]
Candlelight Ecstasy:
  398 Gambler's Game, The
  529 Beguiling Pretender
Candlelight Ecstasy Supreme:
   65 Tender Refuge
   86 Hidden Charms
  122 Torch Song
Candlelight Supreme:
  169 Night Of The Matador
Silhouette Intimate Moments:
  246 Mustang Man
  274 Master Of The Hunt, The &
  312 Mistress Of Foxgrove,The &
  Trilogy:
  326   Sutter's Wife
  356   Dragon's Lair, The
  382   Stolen Dreams

MAGUIRE, Anne
           [Penny Nearing]
Avalon:
  Nurse At Towpath Lodge
  Nurse In Las Palmas
  Pride Of Folly
  Run Before Midnight
  Strings To Love
  Substitute Nurse

MAI, Denyse
Mystique:
   59 Shadowed By Danger
  110 Invitation To Danger
  116 Ruins Of Love, The

MAITLAND, Margaret
    [Elizabeth Lorinda DuBreuil]
  Channings Of Everleigh, The

MAITLAND, Margaret (cont.)
East Side, West Side
Love's Golden Circle
Sacred And Profane
Tidewater
Unconquered, The

MAITLAND, Pamela
MacFadden Romance:
  60 My Life, My Love

MAJOR, Ann
      [Margaret Major Cleaves]
(see Silhouette Christmas Stories)
Silhouette Classic:
  13 Seize The Moment   (IM54)
Silhouette Desire:
  16 Dream Come True
  35 Meant To Be
  99 Love Me Again
 151 Wrong Man, The
 198 Golden Man
 229 Beyond Love
 301 In Every Stranger's Face
 331 What This Passion Means
     Children Of Destiny Series:
 445 Passion's Child
 451 Destiny's Child
 457 Night Child
 535 Wilderness Child   <MMS>
 564 Scandal's Child   <MMS>
Silhouette Intimate Moments:
  54 Seize The Moment
Silhouette Romance:
  90 Wild Lady
 150 Touch Of Fire, A
Silhouette Special Edition:
  83 Brand Of Diamonds
 229 Dazzle
 390 Fairy Tale Girl, The

MAKEPEACE, Joanna
    [Margaret Elizabeth York]
Temptation's Triumph

MAKRIS, Kathryn
First Love From Silhouette: <YA>
  98 One Of The Guys
 154 One In A Million
Heavenly Romance: <YA>
  Change In Monica, The
Sweet Dreams: <YA>
 106 Mission: Love
Two By Two Romance: <YA>
   4 Only A Dream Away
   9 Weekends For Us
Wildfire: <YA>
  Wrong Love, The

MALCOLM, Aleen   <HR>
Children Of The Mist
Devlyn Tremayne   <RM>
Kenlaren
Sinclair Trilogy:
  Taming, The
  Ride Out The Storm
  Daughters Of Cameron, The

MALCOLM, Anthea   <RE>
    [Tracy Grant w/ Joan Grant]
In sequence:
  Widow's Gambit, The
  Courting Of Phillipa, The
  Frivolous Pretence

MALCOLM, Jahnna N.
Hart & Soul: <YA>
  1 Kill The Storm
  2 Play Dead

MALCOLM, Jahnna N.
  3 Speak No Evil
  4 Get The Picture
  5 Too Hot To Handle

MALCOLM, Jane
                              (Jane Gentry)

MALCOLM, Margaret
              [Edith Lyman Kuether]
  Harlequin Classic:
   42 Until You Came   (596)
   46 Marriage Compromise   (592)
  Harlequin Romance:
  777 Scatterbrains -
         Student Nurse
  809 Send For Nurse Vincent
  923 Kit Cavendish -
         Private Nurse
  945 Doctor Sandy
  978 Dr. Gregory Misunderstands
 1002 Doctor For Diana, A
 1028 Master Of Normanhurst, The
 1054 My Tender Fury
 1084 Galleon House
 1098 Uncharted Ocean, The
 1120 Heart In Hand
 1140 Man In Homespun, The
 1164 Meadowsweet
 1199 Johnny Next Door
 1219 No Place Apart
 1255 Little Savage
 1287 Walled Garden, The
 1316 Can This Be Love?
 1340 House Of Yesterday, The
 1363 Star Dust
 1391 My Valiant Fledgling
 1419 So Enchanting An Enemy
 1447 Turning Tide, The
 1488 Head Of The House, The
 1516 Those Endearing
         Young Charms
 1539 Next Door To Romance
 1563 This Tangled Web
 1607 Not Less Than All

MALCOLM, Margaret (cont.)
 1635 Marriage By Agreement
 1664 Faithful Rebel, The
 1699 Sunshine On The Mountains
 1728 Lonely Road, The
 1746 Without Any Amazement
 1781 Cherish This Wayward Heart
 1805 Return To Blytheburn
 1828 Bright Particular Star, A
 1864 Dear Tyrant
 1934 Stranger Is My Love, A
 1971 Heartfire Glows, The
 2037 Flight To Fantasy
 2252 Summer's Lease

MALECKAR, Nicolette
  Lilac Tree, The   <CO>

MALEK, Doreen Owens
                          (Faye Morgan)
  Clash By Night
  First Love From Silhouette: <YA>
   71 That Certain Boy
   83 Where The Boys Are
  113 Season Of Mist
  146 Call Back Yesterday
  Lovestruck:
    Fair Game
  Silhouette Classic:
   31 Eden Tree, The   (IM88)
  Silhouette Desire:
   86 Native Season
  222 Reckless Moon
  240 Winter Meeting
  260 Desperado
  290 Firestorm
  343 Bright River
  450 Roughneck
  Silhouette Intimate Moments:
   88 Eden Tree, The
  105 Devil's Deception
  169 Montega's Mistress
  204 Danger Zone
  282 Marriage Of Convenience, A

MALEK, Doreen Owens (cont.)
  Silhouette Romance:
    363 Crystal Unicorn, The
  Silhouette Special Edition:
    154 Ruling Passion, A

MALLORY, Kathryn
  Silhouette Desire:
    6 Frenchman's Kiss, A
    40 Gentle Conquest
    58 One Night's Deception

MALES, Carolyn w/ Eileen BUCKHOLTZ,
  Ruth GLICK, and Louise TITCHENER
         (Alyssa Howard)

MALES, Carolyn w/ Louise TITCHENER
         (Clare Richards)
         (Clare Richmond)

MALKIND, Margaret
         (Kate Nevins)
  Candlelight Ecstasy Supreme:
    104 Lust For Danger, A
  Candlelight Supreme:
    186 One More Night For Love
  Loveswept:
    295 Late Night Rendezvous
  Silhouette Intimate Moments:
    227 Winds Of Fear

MALLASCH, Marion   <HR>
  Passion's Harvest

MALLETTE, Gertrude E.
  Probation Nurse (Into The Wind)

MALLORY, Fawne
  Love Trial, The

MALLORY, Kate   <RS>
  Sarton Kell

MALLOWAN, Mrs. Max
      (Agatha Christie-MY)
      (Mary Westmacott)

MALM, Dorothea   <GOT><RS>
  Claire
  On A Fated Night
  Pamela Foxe
  To The Castle

MALONE, Bev
  Torch:
    Fiery Encounter
    Haunting Melody
    Silent Partner
  Torchlite:
    Fair Exchange

MALONE, Lucy
  Two By Two Romance: <YA>
    6 Handle With Care

MALONE, Margaret Gay
  Love's Sweet Surrender

MALONE, Vicki
  Strangers By Day

430

MALTERRE, Elona   <HR>
  Celts, The
  Last Wolf Of Ireland, The
  Mistress Of The Eagles

MAN OF THE MONTH SERIES: <MMS>
Silhouette Desire:
  469 Reluctant Father
               Diana Palmer
  475 Gentleman Insists, The
               Joan Hohl
  481 Night Of The Hunter
               Jennifer Green
  487 Dangerous Kind Of Man, A
               Noami Horton
  493 Vengeance Is Mine
               Lucy Gordon
  499 Irresistible
               Annette Broadrick
  511 Mountain Man
               Joyce Thies
  517 Beginner's Luck
               Dixie Browning
  523 Branigan's Touch
               Leslie Davis Guccione
  529 Shiloh's Promise
               B. J. James
  535 Wilderness Child
               Ann Major
  546 Fire And Rain
               Elizabeth Lowell
  552 Loving Spirit, A
               Annette Broadrick
  558 Rule Breaker
               Barbara Boswell
  564 Scandal's Child
               Ann Major
  570 Kiss Me Kate
               Helen R. Myers
  576 Showdown
               Nancy Martin
  582 Hotshot
               Kathleen Korbel
  588 Twice In A Bluemoon
               Dixie Browning
  594 Loner, The
               Lass Small

MAN OF THE MONTH (cont.)
  600 Slow Dance
               Jennifer Green
  606 Hunter
               Diana Palmer
  612 Handsome Devil
               Joan Hohl
  618 Nelson's Brand
               Diana Palmer
  624 Outlaw
               Elizabeth Lowell
  630 McAllister's Lady
               Naomi Horton
  636 Drifter, The
               Joyce Thies
  642 Sweet On Jessie
               Jackie Merritt

MANDE, Elizabeth Erin   <GOT>
  Phantom Room
  Spirit Of Melissa Norgate, The
  Tower Of The Dark Light

MANDEL, Mary
  Harvest Of Love

MANDEL, Sally
       [Sally Elizabeth Mandel]
  Change Of Heart
  Lion Of Justice, The
  Portrait Of A Married Woman <CO>
  Quinn
  Time To Sing, A

MANDEVILLE, Francine
       (Francine Christopher)

MANDINGO/FALCONHURST SERIES
In Chronological Order:
    Mistress Of Falconhurst
    Drum
    Falconhurst Fancy
    Flight To Falconhurst
    Rogue Of Falconhurst
    Falconhurst Fugitive
    Mandingo
    Mandingo Master
    Mustee, The
    Miz Lucretia Of Falconhurst
    Taproots Of Falconhurst
    Scandal Of Falconhurst
    Heir To Falconhurst
    Master Of Falconhurst
(see Ashley CARTER,
    Lance HORNER and Kyle ONSTOTT)

MANGRUM, Valerie
                    (Patricia Ellis)

MANLEY, Edna Maye   <RE>
    Agatha
    Coventry:
        202 Final Season

MANLEY-TUCKER, Audrie   (Deceased)
    Door Without A Key
    Love Spreads Your Wings
    Memory Of Summer, A
    Aston Hall:
        110 Shetland Summer
    Harlequin Romance:
        Rain On A Summer Afternoon
                            HRS20

MANN, Margaret
    Harlequin Romance:
        1813 Destiny Decrees

MANN, Margaret Boyer
                    (Grace Pendleton)

MANN, Vivian Stuart   (Deceased)
                    (Barbara Allen)
                (William Stuart Long)
                    (Alex Stuart)
                    (Robyn Stuart)
                 (Vivian Stuart **)
** (Do Not Confuse This Pseudonym
    With That Of Another Author)

MANNERS, Alexandra   <GOT><HO><RS>
                        [Anne Rundle]
    Candles In The Wood
    Cardigan Square
    Singing Swans, The
    Stone Maiden, The
    Wilford's Daughter

MANNING, Bruce
                    (see Gwen Bristow)

MANNING, Jessica   <HR>
    Magnolia Landing   <Saga>

MANNING, Jo
                    [Irene Robinson]
    SuperRomance:
        15 Cherished Destiny

MANNING, Lisa
    Harlequin Romance:
        2818 Glass Madonna, The

MANNING, Marilyn
    First Love From Silhouette: <YA>
        48 Summer Illusion

MANNING, Marilyn (cont.)
  Silhouette Romance:
    206 An Adventure In Love

MANNING, Marsha
                    (Hettie Grimstead)
  Dance Of Summer
  Dreams Of The Sun
  Kisses For Three
  Lover Come Lonely
  Magic City, The
  Magic Of The Moon
  Proud Lover, The
  Smiling Moon, The
  Summer Song
  Sweet Friday
  To Catch A Dream
  Uninvited Wedding Guest
  Wedding Of The Year
  Yesterday's Love

MANNING, Mary Louise   <HR>
                    [Lou Cameron]
  This Fever In My Blood

MANNION, Michael   <CO>
  Colleen

MANSELL, Joanna
  Harlequin Presents:
    1116 Miracle Man
    1139 Lord And Master
    1156 Illusion Of Paradise
    1186 Third Kiss, The
    1218 Wild Justice
    1250 Night With a Stranger
    1291 Seduction Of Sara, The
    1331 Kiss By Candlelight, A

MANSELL, Joanna (cont.)
  Harlequin Romance:
    2836 Night Is Dark, The
    2866 Sleeping Tiger
    2894 Black Diamond

MANSFIELD, Elizabeth   <RE>
                [Paula Reibel Schwartz]
  Accidental Romance, The
  Bartered Bride, The
  Brilliant Mismatch, A
  Bluestocking
  Christmas Kiss, A
  Counterfeit Husband, The
  Duel Of Hearts
  Fifth Kiss, The
  Frost Fair, The
  Grand Deception, A
  Grand Passion, The
  Her Heart's Captain
  Her Man Of Affairs
  Lady Disguised, The
  Love Lessons
  Magnificent Masquerade
  Marriage Of Inconvenience, A
  My Lord Murderer
  Passing Fancies
  Phantom Lover, The
  Prior Engagement, A
  Regency Charade, A
  Regency Galatea
  Regency Match, A
  Regency Sting
  Regency Wager
  Reluctant Flirt, The
  Splendid Indiscretion, A
  Unexpected Holiday
  Very Dutiful Daughter, A

MANSFIELD, Helene   <HR>
  Contessa   <Saga>
  Some Women Dance

MANSFIELD, Libby
        [Paula Reibel Schwartz]
Candlelight:
    233 Unexpected Holiday   <RE>

MANTLE, W./Winnifred
        [Winifred Langford Mantle]
Chateau Holiday, The
Inconvenient Marriage, The
Penderal Puzzle, The
Question Of The Painted Cave, The

MARACOTTA, Lindsay   <RS>
Caribe
Sad-Eyed Ladies, The

MARAGAKIS, Helen C.
                    (Eleni Carr)
                    (Helen Carras)
                    (Helen Carter)

MARATH, Laurie
        [Suzanne Roberts]
Second Chance At Love:
    13 Wings Of Morning

MARAVEL, Gailanne
Sweet Dreams: <YA>
    27 Too Young For Love
    50 Lights, Camera, Love

MARCEAU, Adrienne
First Love From Silhouette: <YA>
    4 Serenade

MARCH, Jessica
Embrace The Fury
Illusions
Obsessions
Temptations

MARCH, Josie
First Love From Silhouette: <YA>
    34 Perfect Figure

MARCH, Lindsay   <RS>
These Cliffs Are Dangerous

MARCH, Stella
        [Marguerite Mooers Marshall]
Sapphire Romance: <Eng>
    Out Of The Shadows
    Sentimental Journey
    Wrong Doctor, The

MARCHANT, Catherine   <RS>
        [Catherine McMullen Cookson]
Fen Tiger, The
Heritage Of Folly
House Of Men
House Of The Fens
Iron Facade, The
Miss Martha Mary Crawford
Mist Of Memory, The
Slow Awakening, The

MARCHANT, Jessica
Harlequin Presents:
    1145 Journey To Discovery
Harlequin Romance:
    2986 Stranger's Glance, A

434

MARDON, Deirdre
                    [Allan Mardon]
  Harlequin American Romance:
     9 Canvas Of Passion
    33 Destiny's Sweet Errand
  Harlequin Intrigue:
     2 In For A Penny
    15 Reluctant Lover
    20 With Penalty And Interest
  Harlequin Temptation:
    15 Jealous Mistress, A
    31 Touch Of Madness, A

MARIE, Susan
  Starlight Romance:
    Never Bring Her Roses
    When The Spotlight Fades

MARIEL, Aimee   <RS>
  Secrets Not Shared

MARIEL, Anne
  Embrace My Scarlet Heart
  One Evening I Shall Return
  Rendezvous In Peking
  Tigress Of The Evening

MARINO, Susan   <GOT>
                   [Julie Ellis]
  Vendetta Castle

MARITANO, Adela
                    (Jane Converse)
                    (Adela Gale)
                    (Kay Martin)

MARK, Polly
  Avalon:
    Jungle Nurse
    Nurse At Seaview
    Nurse In Singapore
    Nurse Marla's Plan
    Nurse Molly's Search

MARKHAM, Patricia
                    [Patricia Carro]
  Candlelight Ecstasy:
    280 River Rapture

MARKS, Arlene
                    (Edwina Franklin)

MARKS, Joanna
                    [Joanna Darby]
  Silhouette Intimate Moments:
    315 Love Is A Long Shot

MARKSTEIN, George   <HR>
  Cooler, The
  Tara Kane

MARLETT, Melba   <GOT>
  Death Is In The Garden
  Escape While I Can

MARLISS, Deanna
                    (Diana Mars)
                    (Diana Moore)

MARLOW, Edwina   <GOT><RS>
                    [Tom E. Huff]
  Danger At Dahlkari
  Falconridge

MARLOW, Edwina (cont.)
Lady Of Lyon House, The
Master Of Phoenix Hall, The
Midnight At Mallyncourt
When Emmalyn Remembers

MARLOWE, Ann   <RS>
Thunder In The Kerk
Violet Harvest
Winnowing Winds, The

MARLOWE, Delphine   <HR>
                        [Ronald Singer]
Bonnaire

MARLOWE, Stephen
Deborah's Legacy   <HS>

MARLOWE, Tess
[Ruth Glick w/ Louise Titchener]
Silhouette Desire:
402 Indiscreet

MARNAY, Jane
Harlequin Romance:
955 Nurse With A Problem
969 Nurse Afloat
1006 Courageous Heart, The

MARR, Anne
            [Nell Marr Dean Ratzlaff]
Sweeter Than Wine

MARRINGTON, Pauline
Lindseys, The (The October Horse)

MARRIOT, Thomas   <HO>
Pagan Land, The

MARRS, Pauline D.
Coventry:
7 Second Season   <RE>

MARS, Diana
                    [Deanna Marliss]
Second Chance At Love:
95 Sweet Surrender
122 Sweet Abandon
182 Sweet Trespass
214 Sweet Splendor
234 Sweet Deception
279 Sweet Enchantment
367 Sweet Temptation

MARSH, Ellen Tanner   <HR>
                    [Renate Johnson]
If This Be Magic
In My Wildest Dreams
Reap The Savage Wind
Scarlet And Gold
Silk And Splendour
Tame The Wild Heart
In sequence: <Saga>
    Wrap Me In Splendour
    Sable

MARSH, Jean
                    [Evelyn Marshall]
Aston Hall:
116 Loving Partnership

436

MARSH, Joan
  Victim Of Love
  Candlelight:
    103 Prince Of Hearts

MARSH, John   <GOT>
                    (Grace Richmond)
                    (Lilian Woodward)
  Monk's Hollow

MARSH, Lillian   <RE>
                    [Ruby Frankel]
  Second Chance At Love:
    51 Love's Masquerade
    99 Forgotten Bride, The

MARSH, Rebecca
            [William Arthur Neubauer]
  Always In Her Heart
  Assistant Angel
  Backhand To Love
  But Love Remains
  Footsteps To Romance
  Girl For Him, The
  Girl In Love
  Hill Top House
  Home For Mary, A
  Lady Detective
  Library Lady
  Million Dollar Nurse
  Mystery In Nevada
  No Time For Love
  Nurse Annette
  Nurse Ann's Emergency
  Nurse Of Ward B
  Office Nurse
  Quiet Corner, The
  Recovery Room Nurse
  Redwood Valley Romance
  Remembered Heritage
  Somebody's Sweetheart
  Summer In Vermont

MARSH, Rebecca (cont.)
  Tiger In Her Heart
  Trial By Love
  Unofficial Engagement
  Walks Of Dreams, The
  Way Of The Heart, The
  When Love Wakes
  Willow Tree, The
  Sharon Romance:
    Maverick Heart

MARSH, Valerie
  Harlequin Presents:
    820 Dark Obsession
  Harlequin Romance:
    2676 Echo Of Betrayal

MARSHACK, Laddie
  Crowd Of Lovers, A   <Saga>

MARSHALL, Andrea
                    [Karen Crawford]
  First Love From Silhouette: <YA>
    99 Written In The Stars
    107 Handle With Care
    151 Against The Odds

MARSHALL, Beverley
  Orchids For Heather

MARSHALL, Bevlyn
            [Bevlyn Marshall Kaukas]
  Silhouette Special Edition:
    407 Lonely At The Top
    441 Pride Of His Life, The
    506 Grady's Lady
    544 Radio Daze

MARSHALL, Bevlyn (cont.)
562 Goddess Of Joy
598 Treasure Deep
665 Thunderbolt

MARSHALL, Catherine   <Insp>
Christy
Julie

MARSHALL, Edison   (Deceased)<HR>
American Captain
Benjamin Blake
Caravan To Xanader
Castle In The Swamp
Conqueror
Cortez And Marina
Earth Giant
Gentleman, The
Great Smith, The
Gypsy Sixpence
Infinite Woman, The
Lost Colony
Lost Land, The (Dian Of The
  Lost Land)
Pagan King, The
Princess Sophia
Rogue Gentleman (Bengal Tiger)
Upstart, The
Viking, The
West With The Vikings
Yankee Pasha

MARSHALL, Evelyn
                        (Jean Marsh)

MARSHALL, Jacqueline
               [Deborah Austin]
Harlequin Intrigue:
54 Drastic Measures

MARSHALL, Joanne   <GOT><RS>
                      [Anne Rundle]
Flower Of Silence
Follow A Shadow
Wild Boar Wood
Candlelight:
569 Peacock Bed, The   <IN>

MARSHALL, Marguerite Mooers
                     (Stella March)
Her Soul To keep
Nurse With Wings
Path To Peace, The
Ward Nurse
Wilderness Nurse

MARSHALL, Marilyn
Adventures In Love:
  Turquoise Talisman, The

MARSHALL, Robert
                  (Claire Clairmont)

MARTEL, Aimee
           [Aimee Salcedo Thurlo]
Silhouette Desire:
136 Fires Within, The
249 Hero At Large

MARTEN, Jacqueline   <GOT>
          [Jacqueline Stern Marten]
Chateau Chaumond
Dream Walker
Kiss Me, Catriona
Let The Crags Comb Out Her
  Dainty Hair
Promise Me Forever   <CO>
Constitution Trilogy:
  To Pluck A Rose
  Glory In The Flower
  In The Long Green Grass

MARTEN, Jacqueline (cont.)
  New Age Trilogy: <T-T>
    Forevermore
    Bryarly
  Tapestry: <HR>
    26 English Rose
    37 Irish Rose
    47 French Rose
    61 An Unforgotten Love
    79 Loving Longest

MARTIN, Caroline
  Masquerade:
    57 Captain Black
    80 Man With A Falcon

MARTIN, DeAnn   <GOT>
  Nightmare House
  Nightmare Island

MARTIN, Don   <HR>
  Great Silver Bonanza, The

MARTIN, Ethel Bowyer   <GOT>
  Nightmare House

MARTIN, Evelyn
  Avalon:
    Love's Sweet Survey

MARTIN, Ione
  Silhouette Romance:
    260 Goldenrain Tree, The

MARTIN, Judy Wells
                    (Jeanette Ernest)
                    (Andra Erskine)

MARTIN, Kat   <HR>
            [Kathleen Kelly Martin]
  Captain's Bride, The
  Dueling Hearts
  Magnificent Passage

MARTIN, Kathleen Kelly w/ L. Jay
  MARTIN   (Kathy Lawrence)

MARTIN, Kay
            [Adela Maritano]
  Vanessa

MARTIN, Liz
  Rage To Live, A   <CO>

MARTIN, Marcia
  Southern Nights

MARTIN, Marian   <RS>
  Tiara Romance:
    Dangerous Stranger
  Harlequin Gothic Romance:
    Ravens Of Rockhurst, The

MARTIN, Mary   <HR>
  Caress Of Silk
  Outlaw's Caress
  Pirate's Conquest
  Rebel Pleasure

MARTIN, Monica
                    [Ingrid Betz]
 Harlequin Romance:
 2908 Buttercup Dream, The

MARTIN, Nancy
                    (Elissa Curry)
 Harlequin SuperRomance:
 133 Flight Into Sunshine
 170 Beyond The Dream
 197 An Unexpected Pleasure
 221 Nightcap
 305 Sable And Secrets
 Silhouette Classic:
  29 Black Diamonds   (IM60)
 Silhouette Desire:
 461 Hit Man
 522 Living Legend, A
 The Fletchers:
 576 Showdown   <MMS>
 590 Ready, Willing And Abel
 608 Looking For Trouble
 Silhouette Intimate Moments:
  60 Black Diamond

MARTIN, Pam
 First Love From Silhouette: <YA>
  43 Knight To Remember

MARTIN, Patricia
 Tiara Romance:
  Meadowlark Calling, A

MARTIN, Prudence
            [Prudence Bingham Lichte]
 Passion's Persuasion   <RE>
 Wager On Love   <RE>
 Candlelight:
  710 Counterfeit Courtship   <RE>

MARTIN, Prudence (cont.)
 Candlelight Ecstasy:
  93 Strange Elation, A
 119 Heart's Shadow
 137 Love Song
 148 Moonlight Rapture
 168 Champagne Flight
 234 Better Fate, A
 279 Sinner And Saint
 Candlelight Ecstasy Supreme:
   4 Lovers And Pretenders
  12 No Strings Attached
  55 Moonstruck

MARTIN, Rhona
 Gallow's Wedding

MARTIN, Valerie
 Alexandra
 Love
 Set In Motion

MARTIN, Vicky
            [Victoria Caroline Story]
 Obey The Moon
 Wildfire: <YA>
  Boy Next Door, The

MARTIN, Wendy
                    [Teri Martini]
 Avalon:
  Love's Journey
  Island Magic

MARTIN, William
 Back Bay   <HS>
 Rising Of The Moon, The   <HO>

MARTINI, Teri
(Alison King)
(Wendy Martin)
(Therese Martini)
Avalon:
Two Hearts Adrift

MARTINI, Therese   <HR>
[Teri Martini]
Arrundel Touch, The
Dreams To Give
Love's Lost Melody
To Love And Beyond

MARTON, Sandra
[Sandra Myles]
Harlequin Presents:
 988 Game Of Deceit, A
1027 Out Of The Shadows
1067 Intimate Strangers
1082 Lovescenes
1121 Heart Of The Hawk
1155 Flood Of Sweet Fire, A
1194 Deal With The Devil
1219 Cherish The Flame
1244 Eye Of The Storm
1277 Fly Like An Eagle
1308 From This Day Forward
1347 Night Fires

MARVAL, Helen
Mystique:
131 At Devil's Bridge

MARVIN, Susan   <GOT>
[Julie Ellis]
Chalet Bougy-Villars
Chateau In The Shadows
Secret Of The Chateau Laval

MARVIN, Susan (cont.)
Summer Of Fear
Where Is Holly Carleton?

MASCOTT, Holly Anne
Cherish The Dream

MASCOTT, Trina   <RS>
Wife Who Ran Away, The

MASON, Amelia
MacFadden Romance:
203 Love's Bright Promise

MASON, Connie
Beyond The Horizon   <WWP>
Bold Land, Bold Love
Caress And Conquer
Desert Ecstasy
For Honor's Sake
My Lady Vixen
Promised Splendor
Tempt The Devil '
Tender Fury
Wild Is My Heart

MASON, Hilary
[Barbara Roddick]
Morisco

MASON, Lois
Masquerade:
49 Abigail's Quest

MASON, Paule   <GOT>
   Man In The Garden, The

MASSEY, Charlotte
   Bride Of Invercoe
   Polmarran Towers

MASON, F. van Wyck   (Deceased)
                       <HR><RS>
   [Francis van Wyck Mason]
   Barbarians, The
   Blue Hurricane
   Captain Judas
   Captain Nemesis
   China Sea Murders, The
   Cutlass Empire
   Dardanelles Derelict
   Deadly Orbit Mission
   End Of Track
   Golden Admiral
   Gracious Lily Affair, The
   Harpoon In Eden
   Himalayan Assignment
   Log Cabin Noble
   Lysander
   Multimillion-Dollar Murders, The
   Our Valiant Few
   Rascal's Heaven
   Return Of The Eagles
   Saigon Singer
   Sea Venture, The
   Secret Mission To Bangkok
   Silver Leopard
   Sulu Sea Murders, The
   Trouble In Burma
   Trumpets Sound No More
   Two Tickets For Tangier
   Wild Drums Beat
   Wild Horizon
   Young Titan, The
   American Revolution:
     Eagle In The Sky
     Proud New Flags
     Rivers Of Glory
     Stars On The Sea
     Three Harbors

MASSEY, Erika
   Career For Carol, A
   My Love To Give
   Wish For Celia, A

MASSEY, Jessica
                 [Alison Hart]
   Candlelight Ecstasy:
   218 Stormy Surrender

MASSIE, Sonja   <HR>
   Carousel
   Silhouette Special Edition:
   384 Legacy Of The Wolf

MASSMAN, Patti
               (see Pamela Beck)

MASTERS, John   <HO>(Deceased)
   Bhowani Jucntion
   Coromandel
   Deceivers, The
   Far, Far The Mountain Peak
   Himalayan Concerto, The
   Lotus And The Wind, The
   Nightrunners Of Bengal
   Thunder At Sunset
   Rock, The:
     A Novel About Gibraltar
   Loss Of Eden Trilogy:
     Now God Be Thanked
     Heart Of War

MATHEWS, Pat w/ Denise HRIMAK
                    (Denise Mathews)

MATHIEU, Marilyn
  Second Chance At Love:
    16 Passion's Flight

MATHIS, Clara   <GOT>
  Hendon Inheritance, The
  To Wed A Stranger

MATLOCK, Curtiss Ann
  (see Silhouette Christmas Stories)
  Harlequin Historical <Set#2>:
    37 Forever Rose, The   &
  Silhouette Romance:
   422 Crosswinds
   482 For Each Tomorrow
   605 Good Vibrations
  Silhouette Special Edition:
   275 Time And A Season, A
   333 Lindsey's Rainbow
   384 Time To Keep, A
   426 Last Chance Cafe
   454 Wellspring
   589 Intimate Circle   &
   601 Love Finds Yancey Cordell&
   668 Heaven In Texas

MATRANGA, Frances Carfi
  Land Of Shadows
  Candlelight:
   503 Summer Magic   <RO>
   526 Destiny In Rome   <RO>

MATRAY, Maria w/ Answald KRUGER
  Liaison, The

MATTHEWMAN, Phyllis
  Harlequin Romance:
   825 Make Up Your Mind, Nurse
  1231 Imitation Marriage

MATTHEWS, Bay
                    [Penny Richards]
  (see Silhouette Christmas Stories)
  Silhouette Special Edition:
   298 Bittersweet Sacrifice
   347 Roses And Regrets
   391 Some Warm Hunger
   420 Lessons In Loving
   464 Amarillo By Morning
   613 Laughter On The Wind
   648 Sweet Lies, Satin Sighs

MATTHEWS, Carolyn Seabaugh
                    (Carolyn Seabaugh)

MATTHEWS, Clayton   <HO>
              [Clayton Hartley Matthews]
  Big Score, The
  Bounty Hunt At Ballaret
  Dallas   <HofCS>
  Harvesters, The
  Las Vegas   w/Arthur MOORE<HofCS>
  New Orleans   <HofCS>
  Power Seekers, The
  Proud Castles, The   <CO>
  Rage Of Desire
  Moraghan Trilogy: <Saga>
    Birthright, The
    Disinherited, The
    Redeemers, The

MATTHEWS, Laura   <RE>
                    [Elizabeth Rotter]
  Alicia
       (orign. by Elizabeth Walker)
  Ardent Lady Amelia, The
  Emotional Ties   <CO>
  Holiday In Bath (Reprint WR#24)

MATTHEWS, Laura (cont.)
  Lord Clayborne's Fancy
    (Reprint WR#20)
  Lord Greywell's Dilemma
  Miss Ryder's Memoirs
  Proud Viscount, The
  Very Proper Widow, A
  Warner Regency:
     9 Seventh Suitor, The
    15 Aim Of A Lady, The
    20 Lord Clayborne's Fancy
    22 Baronet's Wife, The
    24 Holiday In Bath

MATTHEWS, Patricia   <HR>
  [Patricia Anne Ernest Matthews]
                (Laura Wiley-OCC)
  Dancer Of Dreams
  Death Of Love, The
  Dreaming Tree, The
  Embers Of Dawn
  Enchanted
  Flames Of Glory
  Gambler In Love
  Love, Forever More
  Love's Avenging Heart
  Love's Bold Journey
  Love's Daring Dream
  Love's Golden Destiny
  Love's Magic Moment
  Love's Many Faces (Poems)
  Love's Pagan Heart
  Love's Raging Tide
  Love's Sweet Agony
  Love's Wildest Promise
  Mirrors   <RS>
  Night Visitor, The
  Oasis
  Sapphire
  Tame The Restless Heart
  Thursday And The Lady
  Tides Of Love

MATTHEWS, Patricia w/
              Clayton MATTHEWS
                 (Patty Brisco)
  Empire
  Midnight Lavender   <RM>
  Midnight Whispers   <RS>

MATTHEWS, Phoebe
              [Diane McClure Jones]
  Boy On The Cover, The   <YA>
  Honeymoon House
  Candlelight:
    682 Unsuitable Lovers, The<RE>

MATTINGLY, Joan
  Rose And The Sword, The

MATTSSON, Gunnar
  Princess,The

MAX, Barbara
              [Justine Valenti]
  Candlelight:
    641 Love Island   <RO>
    673 Whispers Of Love   <RO>

MAXAM, Mia
              [Ethel Maxam Crews]
  Silhouette Romance:
    205 Race The Tide
    236 Lost In Love
    324 Loyal Opposition
    450 Something Sentimental
    513 On Restless Wings

MAXFIELD, Karen w/ Lynn TAYLOR
(Karen Lynn)

MAXWELL, A. E.   <HR>
[Ann Elizabeth Maxwell
w/ Evan Maxwell]
Another Day In Paradise
Gatsby's Vineyard
Golden Empire
Just Enough Light To Kill   <RM>
Redwood Empire

MAXWELL, Ann Elizabeth
(Elizabeth Lowell)

MAXWELL, Colin   <HS>
In sequence:
Sun Rises, The
Sun In Splendor, The

MAXWELL, Emily   <RE>
[Linda J. Schwab]
Wicked Count, The

MAXWELL, Helen K.   <RS>
Girl In A Mask, The
Leave It To Amanda
Livingston Heirs, The

MAXWELL, Kathleen
[Kathryn Grant]
Scarlet Ribbons: <HR>
Devil's Heart, The
Winter Masquerade

MAXWELL, Patricia   <GOT><RS>
[Patricia Ponder Maxwell]
(Jennifer Blake)
(Maxine Patrick)
(Patricia Ponder)
Bewitching Grace
Bride Of A Stranger
Court Of The Thorn Tree, The
Dark Masquerade
Night Of The Candles
Notorious Angel, The
Secret Of Mirror House
Stranger At Plantation Inn
Sweet Piracy

MAXWELL, Patricia w/ Carol
ALBRITTON   (Elizabeth Trehearne)

MAXWELL, Vicky
[Anne Worboys]
Other Side Of Summer, The

MAY, Clara
Mystique:
145 Forbidden Love

MAY, Helen
[Eileen Jackson]
Sea-Raven's Bride
Masquerade:
55 Duel Of Love
85 Chance Of Love

MAY, Isabel Stewart
Lindy Haynes, M. D.

MAY, Janis Susan
Heritage Of Shadows   <RS>
Lacey   <RE>
Candlelight:
  556 Where Shadows Linger   <IN>
  625 Avengin Maid, The   <RE>
Judy Sullivan Books:
  Devil Of Dragon House, The   <RS>
  Family Of Strangers   <HR>

MAY, Marjory
                        (Dinah Dean)

MAY, Wynne
        [Mabel Winnifred Knowles]
Harlequin Romance:
  1158 Valley Of Aloes, The
  1310 Tawny Are The Leaves
  1343 Tamboti Moon
  1691 Bowl Of Stars, A
  1794 Pink Sands
  1875 Plume Of Dust, A
  2100 Plantation Of Vines, A
  2286 Scarf Of Flame, A
  2321 Island Of Cyclones
  2532 Peacock In The Jungle
  2548 Wayside Flower
        Flaunting Cactus, A   HRS16
        Tomorrow's Sun   HRS48
        Diamonds And Daisies   HRS56
        Filagree Of Fancy   HRS79

MAYBURY, Anne   <GOT><RS>
                        [Anne Buxton]
  Brides Of Bellenmore, The
  Dark Star
  Falcon's Shadow
  Green Fire
  House Of Fand, The
  I Am Gabriella!
  Jessamy Court
  Jeweled Daughter, The
  Midnight Dancers, The
  Minerva Stone, The
  Monkshood

MAYBURY, Anne (cont.)
  Moonlit Door, The
  Night My Enemy, The
  Pavilion At Monkshood, The
  Radiance
  Ride A White Dolphin
  Roseheath
  Shadow Of A Stranger
  Someone Waiting
  Stay Until Tomorrow
  Terracotta Palace, The
  Winds Of Night, The
  Walk In The Paradise Garden
  Whisper In The Dark

MAYER, Judy
First Love From Silhouette: <YA>
  236 King For Queen

MAYER, Suzanne
              [Linda Susan Meier]
Harlequin Intrigue:
  139 In For Life

MAYERSON, Evelyn Wilde
  Princess In Amber   <HO>

MAYFIELD, Anne
                [Kathy Ptacek]
Second Chance At Love:
  81 Wayward Widow, The   <RE>

MAYFIELD, Jack
                [Parley J. Cooper]
  Appraiser, The
  Loving Strangers

448

MAYFIELD, Jack (cont.)
Magnate, The

_____

_____

MAYFIELD, Serena   <GOT><RS>
Lonely Terror, The
Stranger In The House

_____

_____

MAYHEW, Elizabeth
                      [Joan E. Bear]
Felicia
In The Path Of Eagles
My Son Charles
Queen Of Naples, The

_____

_____

MAYHEW, Margaret   <GOT>
Cry Of The Owl, The
Master Of Aysgarth, The
Railway King, The
Regency Charade   <RE>

_____

MAYLEAS, Davidyne Saxon   <CO>
By Appointment Only
Man Of Property, A   <Saga>
Woman Who Had Everything, The

_____

_____

MAYO, Margaret
                  [Margaret Mary Mayo]
Harlequin Premiere Edition:
   11 Pirate Lover
   32 Unwilling Wife, The
Harlequin Presents:
  963 Passionate Vengeance
 1045 Savage Affair
 1108 Painful Loving, A
 1187 Prisoner Of The Mind
Harlequin Romance:
 1980 Destiny Paradise

MAYO, Margaret (cont.)
 1996 Shades Of Autumn
 2028 Perilous Waters
 2051 Land Of Ice And Fire
 2086 Rainbow Magic
 2118 Sea Gypsy
 2280 Afraid Of Love
 2327 Stormy Affair
 2360 Valley Of The Hawk
 2385 Burning Desire
 2439 Taste Of Paradise, A
 2474 Divided Loyalties
 2557 Dangerous Journey
 2602 Return A Stranger
 2795 Impulsive Challenge
 2805 At Daggers Drawn
 2937 Feelings
 2955 Unexpected Inheritance
 3003 Bittersweet Pursuit
 3029 Conflict
        Marriage Game, The   HRS 2
        Mutual Attraction   HRS81

_____

_____

MAZER, Harry   <YA>
I love You, Stupid
Hey, Kid! Does She Love Me?

_____

McALLISTER, Amanda   <RS>
(publishers pseudonym for
            writers in this series)
Pretty Enough To Kill
            [Dorothy Dowdell]
Waiting For Caroline
            [Eloise Meaker]
No Need For Fear
Trust No One At All
Look Over Your Shoulder
            [Eloise Meaker]
Death Comes To The Party
Terror In The Sunlight
            [Jean Hager]

_____

_____

McALLISTER, Anne
                    [Barbara Schenck]
Harlequin American Romance:
  89 Starstruck
      Quicksilver Series: &
  108   Quicksilver Season
  132   Chance Of Rainbows, A
  186   Body And Soul
  202 Dream Chasers
  234 Marry Sunshine   &
  275 Gifts Of The Spirit   &
  309 Saving Grace   <GCT>
  341 Imagine
  387 I Thee Wed
Harlequin Presents:
  844 Lightning Storm
  1060 To Tame A Wolf
  1099 Marriage Trap, The
  1257 Once A Hero
Harlequin Romance:
  2721 Dare To Trust

_____

_____

McANDREW, Cass
                    [Mary Ann Taylor]
Second Chance At Love:
  411 Primitive Glory

_____

_____

McANENY, Marjorie
Pageant Romance:
  Summer Love Match

_____

_____

McAVOY, Elaine Anne
Serenade/Serenata: <Insp>
  12 Irresistable Love

_____

_____

McBAIN, Laurie   <HR>
                    [Laurie Lee McBain]
Devil's Desire

McBAIN, Laurie (cont.)
  Tears Of Gold
  When The Splendor Falls
  Wild Bells To The Wild Sky
  In sequence:
    Moonstruck Madness
    Chance The Winds Of Fortune
    Dark Before The Rising Sun

_____

_____

McBRIDE, Harper
                    [Judith Weaver]
Candlelight Ecstasy:
  10 Gentleman In Paradise
  175 Tender Torment

_____

_____

McCAFFREE, Sharon
  [Sharon McCaffree Shallenberger]
Harlequin American Romance:
  4 Now And Forever
  87 Misplaced Destiny
  110 Secret Longing's
Harlequin Temptation:
  36 One Bright Morning
SuperRomance:
  85 Passport To Passion

_____

_____

McCAFFREY, Anne   <RS>
  Kilternan Legacy, The
  Lady, The
  Mark Of Merlin, The
  Ring Of Fear
  Ship Who Sang
  Stitch In Snow
  Year Of The Lucy, The

_____

_____

McCAIG, Edith w/ Robert McCAIG
                    (Edith Engren)

McCALL, Kathleen   <HR>
                    [Kathleen Drymon]
  Heartfire Romance:
    Ivory Rose
    Windswept Heart

McCALL, Virginia Nielsen
                    (Virginia Nielsen)

McCALLUM, Kristy
  Harlequin Romance:
    Independent Lady   HRS46

McCARRICK, Marsha
  MacFadden Romance:
    Almost Eden

McCARRY, Charles
  Bride Of The Wildernes   <Saga>

McCARTHY, Candace
  Embrace Me Sweet Stranger
  Candlelight Ecstasy:
    409 Together In The Night

McCARTHY, Gary   <HR>
  Colorado, The   <RWS:#3>
  Silver Winds
  Transcontinental
  Winds Of Gold
  In sequence:
    Wind River
    Powder River

McCARTHY, Jane
  Dark Deception, The
  Nurse April's Dilemma
  Roses In The Snow
  Sinister Tapestry, The
  Avalon:
    All That Glitters
    Listen To The Skylark
    Nurse Of Thorne Grotto
  Candlelight:
    114 Carlotta's Castle

McCARTHY, Susanne
  Harlequin Presents:
    979   Long Way From Heaven, A
    1036 Don't Ask For Tomorrow
    1123 Too Much To Lose
    1146 Caught In A Dream
    1299 Love Is For The Lucky
    1348 Trial By Love

McCARTNEY, Brenna   <HR>
  Passion's Blossom
  Rebel Bride

McCARTY, Betsy   <HR>
  Silhouette Romance:
    332 Golden Rose, The
  The Avon Romance:
    Passionate Flower, A

McCLARY, Jane Mcilvaine
  Portion For Foxes, A

McCLELLAND, Diane Margaret
                    (Diane Pierson)

McCOY, Cathlyn
                              [Fran Baker]
   Silhouette Desire:
    132 On Love's Own Terms

_____

_____

McCOY, Susan Hatton   <HR>
   Frontier Wife, A

_____

_____

McCRAE, Elizabeth
   House Of The Whispering Winds
   Intrusion, The
   Sudden Darkness, A
   Well-Furnished Life, A

_____

McCUE, Noelle Berry
                         (Nicole Monet)
   Candlelight Ecstasy:
      5 Only The Present
      8 Oceans Of Regrets
     88 Forever Eden
    484 Once More With Passion
    524 Winter's Flame
   Loveswept:
      3 Joining Stone, The
     11 Beloved Intruder
     50 In Search Of Joy
   Silhouette Desire:
    510 Magic Touch
    572 Look Beyond The Dream

_____

_____

McCULLOCH, Sara
                              [Jean Ure]
   Coventry:
     96 Not Quite A Lady

_____

_____

McCULLOUGH, Coleen
      [Coleen McCullough-Robinson]
   An Indecent Obsession
   Creed For The Third Millennium
   First Man In Rome, The
   Ladies Of Missalonghi, The
   Thorn Birds, The
   Tim

_____

_____

McCULLOUGH, Helen   <HR>
   Time To Love, A

_____

_____

McCULLOUGH, Karen G.
   Avalon:
      Night Prowlers, The

_____

_____

McDaniel, Jan
   Gifts Of Spring, The
   Avalon:
      This Fragile Heart
      Angels In The Sand
      Distant Dream, A
      October Magic
      One Step From Wonderland

_____

_____

McDANIEL, Lurlene
   Serenade/Serenata: <Insp>
     13 Eternal Flame
     20 Hold Fast The Dream
     33 Love's Full Circle

_____

_____

McDONALD, Coleen
   MacFadden Romance:
     72 Other Side Of Love, The

_____

_____

453

McDONALD, Eva   <RE>
[Eva Rose McDonald]
French Mademoiselle, The
Lady Caroline's Folly
Lost Lady, The
Runaway Countess, The
White Petticoat, The
Wicked Squire, The

McDONALD, Kay L.   <HO>
[Kay Laureen McDonald]
Trilogy:
Journey On The Wind (The
Brightwood Expedition)
Vision Of The Eagle
Vision Is Fulfilled, The

McDONNELL, Margie
[Margie Pritchard McDonnell]
(Margie Michaels)
Loveswept:
72 Conflict Of Interest
212 Banish The Dragons
258 Conflict Of Interest
273 Land Of Enchantment, The

McDONNELL, Virginia/Virginia B.
[Virginia Bleecker McDonnell]
(Virginia Barclay)
Annapolis Nurse
Nurse With The Silver Skates, The
Storm Over Garnet
West Point Nurse

McDOWELL, Donna
Silhouette Desire:
204 September Winds
Silhouette Romance:
451 Swept Away

McELFRESH, Adeline
[Elizabeth Adeline McElfresh]
(Jennifer Blair)
(Jane Scott)
(Elizabeth Wesley)
Ann And The Hoosier Doctor
Calling Dr. Jane
Charlotte Wade
Doctor Jane
Doctor Jane Comes Home
Homecoming
Jill Nolan, R. N.
Magic Of Dr. Farrar, The
New Nurse At Dorn Memorial
Nightcall
Nurse Anne
Nurse Kathy
Nurse Nolan's Private Duty
Shattered Halo
Two Loves Of Nurse Ellen, The
Candlelight:
34 Nurse For Mercy's Mission
36 Kay Manion, M. D.
40 Nurse In Yucatan
50 Wings For Nurse Bennett
51 Ann Kenyon, Surgeon
63 Flight Nurse
66 Ellen Randolph, R. N.
68 Doctor For Blue Hollow
Silhouette Romance:
618 If Dreams Were Wild Horses
750 Sycamore Point
762 Crane's Mountain

McELHANEY, Carole
Silhouette Special Edition:
332 Slice Of Heaven, A
581 Perfect Clown, The

McELWAIN, Dean
(Shana Clermont)

454

McEVOY, Marjorie   <GOT><RS>
                 (Marjorie Harte)
Brazilian Stardust
Castle Doom
Echoes From The Past
Greenfell Legacy, The
Hermitage Bell, The
No Castle Of Dreams
Peril At Polvellyn
Queen Of Spades, The
Ravensmount
Who Walks By Moonlight?
Wych Stone, The
Starlight Romance:
  Black Pearl, The
  Calabrian Summer
  Camelot Country
  Sleeping Tiger, The
  Star Of Randevi
  Temple Bells

McFATHER, Nelle   <GOT><HR><RS>
Dark Refuge
Ecstasy's Captive
Entangled
Lovespell
Mistress Of Shades
Red Jaguar, The
Woman Alive
Whispering Island
Dark Desire Romance:
  Thunder Heights

McGAURAN, Joanna
               (Joanna Gilpin)
               (Jan McGowan)
             (Christa Merlin)
Pageant Romance:
  That Shining Aura

McGEE, Emilie Richards
              (Emilie Richards)

McGERR, Patricia   <GOT><RS>
Dangerous Landing
Daughter Of Darkness
Fatal In My Fashion
For Richer, For Poorer, Til
  Death
Legacy Of Danger
Murder Is Absurd
Pick Your Victim
Stranger With My Face

McGILL, Joyce
Crosswinds Keepsake: <YA>
  26 Love Song
First Love From Silhouette: <YA>
 122 Lovetalk
 144 Country Boy
 160 Other Langley Girl, The
 184 Here We Go Again
 202 Soap Opera
 223 Diamond In The Rough
Silhouette Intimate Moments:
 347 Through The Looking Glass
 368 Loving Touch, The

McGIVENY, Maura
Harlequin Presents:
 674 Grand Illusion, A
 723 Promises To Keep
 803 Almost A Bride
Harlequin Romance:
2511 Duquesa By Default
2679 Megan's Folly
2781 Right Time, The

McGLAMRY, Beverly   <HR>
     (Kate Cameron**)
**(DO NOT confuse this pseudonym
   with that of another author)
In sequence:
   Family Bible
   Goodly Heritage

McGONGLE, Cheryl
      (Carly Bishop)

McGORIAN, Gladys
     [Gladys M. Dressler]
Prince Regent's Silver Bell   <RE>
Judy Sullivan Books:
   Gown By Fortuny   <CO>

McGOWAN, Jan   <HR>
     [Joanna McGauran]
Flame In The Night
Heart Of The Storm
Winds Of Enchantment
Tapestry: <HR>
   50   Silversea
   75   Golden Lily, The

McGRATH, Kay
Seeds Of Singing, The

McGRATH, Laura
Harlequin Romance:
   2588   Mayan Magic

McGRAW, Terri
Silhouette Romance:
   439   Hero In Blue
   476   Eyes Of A Stranger, The

McGUIRE, Jenny
    [Nancy Morgan w/ Kate Fleming]
Harlequin Temptation:
   232   Christmas Wishes

McHUGH, Frances/Frances Y.   <RS>
Bluethorne
Emerald Mountain
Hyacinth Spell, The
Ghost Wore Black, The
Love Like An Arrow
Masqueraders, The
Missing Grandfather, The
Root Of Evil, The
Shadow Over Mount Sharon
Vow For Love
Window On The Seine

McINNES, Graham   (Deceased)
Lost Island
Road To Gundagai

McINTYRE, Hope
    [Ruth Barsten Tucker]
Silhouette Desire:
   160   Moon On East Mountain

McKAY, Rena
     [Lorena McCourtney]
Silhouette Inspirations:
   31   Top Of The Moon
Silhouette Romance:
   36   Bridal Trap
   92   Desert Devil
   239   Valley Of Broken Hearts
   291   Singing Stone, The
   347   Golden Echo
   713   Just You And Me

McLEAN, Joyce   <HR>
  Scatter The Tempest
  Shower Of Stars

McLEAY, Alison
  Passage Home

McLINN, Patricia
            [Patricia McLaughlin]
  Silhouette Special Edition:
  587 Hoops
  641 New World, A

McMAHAN, Ian
      (see Richard Hale Curtis)
  (see Lee Davis Willoughby - MOAS)

McMAHON, Barbara
  Harlequin Romance:
  2643 Come Into The Sun
  2777 Bluebells On The Hill
  2895 Winter Stranger, Summer
         Lover

McMAHON, Kay   <HR>
            (Catherine Emm)
  Bandits Brazen Kiss
  Dara's Desire
  Defy The Thunder
  Pirate's Lady, The
  River Rapture
  Tender Lies
  Wild Rapture
  Yankee's Lady
  Remington Story Order:
    Passion's Slave
    Defiant Spitfire
    Virginia Vixen
    Ecstasy's Conquest

McMAHON, Kay (cont.)
  Remington Story Order (cont.)
    Love's Desperate Deceit

McMASTER, Mary
  Aston Hall:
  113 To Him Who Waits

McMICKLE, Barbara   <GOT>
  Secret Of The Weeping Monk, The

McMILLAN, Maxine
  Silhouette Romance:
  378 Race For The Roses

McMULLEN, Katie
            [Catherine Cookson]
  Heritage Of Folly
  House Of Men

McNAMARA, Lena Brooke   <RS>
  Pilgrim's End

McNAUGHT, Ann Boyce
             (Ann Gilmour)

McNAUGHT, Judith   <HR>
  Almost Heaven   &
  Double Standards (HQT#16)
  Kingdom Of Dreams, A
    (Prequel to "Whitney, My Love")
  Once And Always
  Something Wonderful   &
  Tender Triumph (SR#86)
  Whitney, My Love

MEADOWS, Alicia (cont.)
Woman Of Boston, A   <AWD>
Finding Mr. Right:
  Opposites Attract

MEADOWS, Rose
Bouquet Of Brides, A
Farewell To Love (Eng: The Show
  Must Go On)
Imperial Pawn, The
Queen's Consent, The
Royal Mistress
To Be My Wedded Wife

MEAKER, Eloise
              (Lydia Benson Clark)
                 (Valancy Hunter)
              (Lydia Lancaster)
      (see Amanda McAllister)

MEDEIROS, Teresa   <HR>
Lady Of Conquest
Shadows And Lace

MEEKS, Dianne
MacFadden Romance:
  214 Heart That Waits, A
  221 Tell Me True

MEIER, Linda Susan
                 (Suzanne Mayer)
                  (Susan Meier)

MEIER, Susan
            [Linda Susan Meier]
Silhouette Desire:
  567 Take The Risk

MELLINGS, Rose
Sapphire Romance:
  Side Of The Angels, The

MELLOWS, Joan   <HR><RE>
Different Face, A
Family Affair, A
Friends At Knoll House
Harriet
Coventry:
  61 Letty Barlow

MELVILLE, Anne
    [Margaret E. Newman Potter]
Lorimer Family Saga:
  Alexa
  Blaize
  Family Fortunes
  Lorimer Line, The

MELVILLE, Jennie   <GOT><RS>
    [Gwendeline Williams Butler]
Dragon's Eye
Hunter In The Shadows
Ironwood
New Kind Of Killer
Nun's Castle
Raven's Forge
Tarot's Tower

MENDONCA, Susan
    [Susan Mendonca Smith]
Sweet Dreams: <YA>
  11 Problem With Love, The
Wildfire: <YA>
  Once Upon A Kiss

MENZEL, Lois/Lois J.   <RE>
   At Dagger's Drawn
   Reckless Wager, A
   Ruled By Passion

MERCER, Charles   <HO>
      [Charles Edward Mercer]
   Castle On The River, The
   Enough Good Men
   Minister
   Murray Hill
   Promise Morning
   Rachael Cade
   Watch Tide

MERCER, June
   Clearing Mists, The   <ENG>

MERCER, Peggy
   Velvet Glove: <RS>
      13 Strangers In Eden

MEREDITH, Marcia
   Mirabeau Plantation

MEREDITH, Marilyn
   Trail To Glory   <Saga>

MEREDITH, Nicolete
         [Nicolete Meredith Stack]
   Milestone Summer

MERIWETHER, Kate
                [Patricia Ahearn]
   Silhouette Special Edition:
       89 Sweet Adversity
      144 Courting Game, The
      179 Strictly Business
      369 Honorable Intentions
      513 Small-Town Secrets
      622 Petticoat Lawyer

MERKT, Frankie
                     (Ann Richards)

MERLIN, Christa
                [Joanna McGauran]
   Second Chance At Love:
      199 Kisses Incognito
      253 Forever Eden
      295 Love With A Proper
                Stranger
      328 Snowflame
      420 Accent On Desire

MERLIN, Christina   <RS>
                [Constance Heaven]
   Spy Concerto, The
   Sword Of Mithras   <ENG>

MERLIN, Jan   <HR>
   Brocade

MERRELL, Barbara   <GOT>
   Sigh Of Death

MERRILL, Jean   <RE>
            [Jean Fairbanks Merrill]
   Girl From The Diadem, The

462

MERRILL, Jean (cont.)
Coventry:
  85 Seraphina   <EDW>

MERTES, Jack   <HR>
Empress Of Desire

MERRIT, Elizabeth
Silhouette Desire:
  178 Till We Meet Again

MERTZ, Barbara Gross
              (Barbara Michaels)
              (Elizabeth Peters)

MERRITT, Emma   <HR>
        [Emma Frances Merritt]
           (Emma Bennett)
Autumn's Fury
Comanche Bride
Emerald Ecstasy
Lone Star Lovesong
Masque Of Jade
        (see also Deana James)
Restless Flames
Satin Secret
Sweet, Wild Love
Harlequin American Romance:
  276 Wish Upon A Star
  337 Return To Summer   <RMMS>

MERWIN, Lucy
McFadden Romance:
    8 Blue Skies, White Sand
   11 Island Of Dreams
   57 Image Of Love, The
   79 Dangerous Romance
  100 Autumn Gold
  158 Summer Song

MERWIN, Marjorie   <GOT>
And Thereby Hangs

MERRITT, Emma w/ Evelyn GEE
[Emma Frances Merritt w/
        D. Evelyn Hoyle Gee]
         (Micah Leigh)

MESSMANN, Jon
               (Colleen Moore)
           (Claudette Nicole)
            (Claudia Nicole)
           (Pamela Windsor)

MESTA, Emily
            (Valerie Giscard)
SuperRomance:
   34 Fugitive Heart
   73 Forbidden Destiny

MERRITT, Jackie
        [Carolyn Joyner]
Silhouette Desire:
  466 Big Sky Country
  551 Heartbreak Hotel
  566 Babe In The Woods
  587 Maggie's Man
  605 Ramblin' Man
  622 Maverick Heart

  642 Sweet On Jessie   <MMS>

METTLER, George
      [George Barry Mettler]
Tower Hill   <CO>

METZGER, Barbara   <RE>
An Early Engagement
Bething's Folly

METZGER, Barbara (cont.)
Cupboard Kisses
Earl And The Heiress, The
My Lady Innkeeper
Rake's Ransom

METZLER, Jack
Super Saga: <Insp>
    Tachechana

MEYER, Donna
                    (Megan Daniel)
                    (Johanna Kingsley)

MEYER, Karl   <HO>
(see Lee Davis Willoughby - MOAS)
Cherokee Mission   <AIS:#7>

MEYERS, Julie
            [Judy Blackwell Myers]
Harlequin Temptation:
    258 Face To Face
Harlequin SuperRomance:
    396 In The Cards

MEYLER, Zena
Flowers For The Fallen

MEYNELL, Laurence
            [Laurence Walter Meynell]
Burlington Square
Death By Arrangement
Fortunate Miss East, The
Great Men Of Stafford Ship
Thirteen Trumpeters
Virgin Luck

MEYRICK, Polly
Masquerade:
    18 Damask Rose, The
    74 Reluctant Match, The

MICHAEL, Judith   <CO>
    [Judith Barnard w/ Michael Fain]
Deceptions
Inheritance
Possessions
Private Affairs
Ruling Passion, A

MICHAEL, Marie
    [Marie Rydzynski Ferrarella]
Loveswept:
    9 December 32nd...And Always
    37 Irresistible Forces
    156 No Way To Treat A Lover

MICHAELJOHN,   <GOT>
Deathbed Of Roses   <CGS:#26>

MICHAELS, Alison
Love Is The Beginning

MICHAELS, Anne   <RE>
An Amicable Arrangement

MICHAELS, Barbara <GOT><M-GOT><RS>
            [Barbara Gross Mertz]
Ammie, Come Home
Be Buried In The Rain
Black Rainbow
Crying Child, The

MICHAELS, Barbara (cont.)
Dark On The Other Side, The
Grey Beginning, The
Greygallows
Here I Stay   <OCC>
House Of Many Shadows
Into The Darkness
Master Of Blacktower, The
Mystery On The Moors
Patriot's Dream
Prince Of Darkness
Sea King's Daughter, The
Search The Shadows
Shattered Silk
Smoke And Mirrors
Someone In The House
Wait For What Will Come
Walker In Shadows, The   <SN>
Wings Of The Falcon
Witch
Wizard's Daughter, The

_____

_____

MICHAELS, Cheri
Dawn Of Love: <YA>
    2 Wild Prairie Sky
    5 Defiant Dreams

_____

_____

MICHAELS, Elizabeth
              [Jeanne M. Stanton]
Harlequin Regency Romance:
   17 Tollin's Daughter

_____

_____

MICHAELS, Elizabeth Ann   <HR>
Destiny's Will

_____

_____

MICHAELS, Fern
[Roberta Anderson w/ Mary Kuczkir]
Cinders To Satin

MICHAELS, Fern (cont.)
Delta Ladies, The
Panda Bear Is Critical   <SN>
Pride And Passion
Tender Warrior
To Taste The Wine
Valentina
Vixen In Velvet
Wild Honey
Without Warning   <SN>
Coleman Trilogy: <CO><Saga>
    Texas Rich
    Texas Heat
    Texas Fury
In sequence: <HR>
    Captive Passions
    Captive Embraces
    Captive Splendors
    Captive Innocence
Love & Life:
    All She Can Be
    Free Spirit
Silhouette Romance:
    15 Sea Gypsy
    32 Golden Lasso
    61 Whisper My Name
    87 Beyond Tomorrow
   114 Paint Me Rainbows
   146 Nightstar

_____

_____

MICHAELS, Fern
                 [Mary Kuczkir]
In sequence:
    Sins Of Omission
    Sins Of The Flesh

_____

_____

MICHAELS, Fran
Sweet Dreams: <YA>
   120 Mr. Wonderful
   134 Past Perfect

_____

_____

MICHAELS, Irene
    [Irene Donohue Jurczyk]
    Frenchman's Mistress

_____

_____

MICHAELS, Jan
    [Jan Milella]
    Harlequin Intrigue:
    32 Pursuit In The Wilderness
    71 Only Witness, The
    89 Red Dog Run
    96 Into The Night

_____

MICHAELS, Kasey   <RE>
    [Kathryn Seidick]
    Anonymous Miss Addams, The
    Dubious Miss Dalrymple, The
    Mischievous Miss Murphy, The
    Playful Lady Penelope, The
    Questioning Miss Quinton, The
    Rambunctious Lady Royston, The
    Savage Miss Saxon, The
    Tenacious Miss Tamerlane, The
    In sequence:
      Belligerent Miss Boynton, The
      Lurid Lady Lockport, The
    Silhouette Romance:
    331 Maggie's Miscellany
    542 Compliments Of The Groom
    572 Popcorn And Kisses
    616 To Marry At Christmas
    701 His Chariot Awaits
    743 Romeo In The Rain

_____

_____

MICHAELS, Kristin
    Enchanted Journey
    Enchanted Twilight
    Magic Side Of The Moon, The
    Song Of The Heart
    Special Kind Of Love, A
    Voyage To Love
        [Jeanne Williams]
    Design For Love

MICHAELS, Kristen (cont.)
    Love's Pilgrimage
        [Martha Corson]
    Heartsong
    Shadow Of Love
        [Gwen Choate]
    Forecast For Love
        [Sue Long Tucker]
    Adventures In Love:
    5 To Begin With Love
    7 Make-Believe Love
        [Jeanne Williams]
    26 Love On Course
        [Martha Corson]

_____

_____

MICHAELS, Leigh
    [LeAnn Lemberger]
    Harlequin Presents:
    702 Kiss Yesterday Goodbye
    811 Deadline For Love
    835 Dreams To Keep
    876 Touch Not My Heart
    900 Leaving Home
    1004 Grand Hotel, The
    1028 Brittany's Castle
    1049 Carlisle Pride
    1068 Rebel With A Cause
    1107 Close Collaboration
    1147 New Desire, A
    1162 Exclusively Yours
    1245 Once And For Always
    1266 With No Reservations
    Harlequin Romance:
    2657 On September Hill
    2734 Wednesday's Child
    2748 Come Next Summer
    2806 Capture A Shadow
    2830 O'Hara's Legacy
    2879 Sell Me A Dream
    2951 Strictly Business
    2987 Just a Normal Marriage
    2997 Shades Of Yesterday
    3010 No Place Like Home
    3023 Let Me Count the Ways
    3070 Matter Of Principal, A

MICHAELS, Leigh (cont.)
3086 An Imperfect Love

MICHAELS, Lorna
        [Thelma Zirkelbach]
Harlequin SuperRomance:
412 Blessing In Disguise

MICHAELS, Lynn
        [Lynne Smith]
Harlequin Temptation:
304 Remembrance
Velvet Glove: <RS>
  8 Like A Lover
 15 Tainted Gold
 20 Lover's Gift, A

MICHAELS, Margie
        [Margie McDonnell]
Harlequin Temptation:
 12 Untamed Desire
Second Chance At Love:
 15 Beloved Pirate
 61 Mirage

MICHAELS, Susan   <RE>
An Infamous Fiasco

MICHEL, Freda   <HO><RE>
Counter-Parry
Price Of Vengeance, The
Quest For Lord Quayle
Subterfuge
Coventry:
 11 Machiavellian
    Marquess, The
 53 Curious Proposal, A

MICHEL, Freda (cont.)
 80 Requiem For A Rake   <RE>
124 Lady Valiant   <RE>
Coventry Classic:
Machiavellian Marquess, The

MICHELLE, Suzanne
[Barbara Michels w/ Susan Larson]
Silhouette Desire:
 29 Enchanted Desert
 47 Silver Promises
 57 No Place For A Woman
 76 Stormy Serenade
 87 Recipe For Love
106 Fancy Free
128 Political Passions
152 Sweetheart Of A Deal
170 Forbidden Melody
189 Starstruck Lovers

MICHELS, Barbara w/ Susan LARSON
       (Suzanne Michelle)

MICKLES, Linda
MacFadden Romance:
227 Return With A Whisper
235 River Of Rain

MIDDLETON, Jan
Learn To Say Goodbye

MIDGLEY, Amy w/ Janet O'DANIEL
       (Amanda Clark)

MIKELS, Jennifer
       [Suzanne J. Kuhlin]
Silhouette Romance:
462 Lady Of The West
487 Maverick

MIKELS, Jennifer (cont.)
   511 Perfect Partners
   551 Bewitching Hour, The
Silhouette Special Edition:
   66 Sporting Affair, A
   124 Whirlwind
   478 Remember The Daffodils
   521 Double Indentity
   574 Stargazer
   623 Freedom's Just Another
        Word

MIKLOWITZ, Gloria D.
Caprice Romance: <YA>
   5 Before Love
   16 Carrie Loves Superman
Young Love Romance: <YA>
   Day The Senior Class Got
   Married, The

MILAN, Angel
                    [Mary Lynn]
Silhouette Desire:
   34 Snow Spirit
   64 Sonatina
   96 SummerSon
   118 Out Of Bounds
   153 Danielle's Doll
   214 Sugarfire
   226 Anna's Child
   285 Knock Anytime
Silhouette Special Edition:
   39 Autumn Harvest
   200 Sea Of Dreams

MILBURN, Cynthia
Sharon Contemporary Teens:
   Spin A Dream

MILBURN, Ellen   <GOT>
   Wings Of Darkness

MILELLA, Jan   (Deceased)
                        (Jan Mathews)
                        (Jan Michaels)
Silhouette Intimate Moments:
   175 Night Heat
   269 Once Forgotten

MILES, Cassie
                    [Kay Bergstrom]
Critic's Choice
Harlequin Historical Romance:
   13 Sweet Mary Anne
Harlequin Intrigue:
   122 Hide And Seek   <DTR>
   150 Handle With Care
Harlequin Temptation:
   26 Tongue-Tied
   61 Acts Of Magic
   104 It's Only Natural
   170 Seems Like Old Times
   235 Monkey Business
   305 Under Lock And Key
Meteor Kismet:
   10 Full Steam
Second Chance At Love:
   333 No Place For A Lady
To Have And To Hold:
   35 Fortune's Smile

MILES, Cynthia
MacFadden Romance:
   262 With This Ring

MILES, Deborah
Harlequin Historical <Set#1>:
   13 Sweet Mary Anne

MILES, Dorien K.   <GOT>
  Avalon:
    Terror Of Heartbreak House
  _____

  _____

MILES, Rosalind
  Return To Eden   <CO>
  _____

  _____

MILFORD, Nancy
  Zelda
  _____

  _____

MILIUS, John
  Wind And The Lion, The
  _____

  _____

MILLAR, Margaret   <GOT><RS>
             [Margaret Sturm Millar]
  Birds And The Beast Were There
  Devil Loves Me
  Do Evil In Return
  Fire Will Freeze
  Iron Gates, The
  Listening Walls, The
  Murder Of Miranda, The
  Wives And Lovers
  _____

  _____

MILLER, Ann   <CO>
                     (Anne London)
                    (Leslie Morgan)
  Guilty Pleasures
  Notorious
  Wild Nights
  Lovestruck:
    Star Struck
  _____

  _____

MILLER, Brooke
          [Victor Brooke Miller]
  American Dynasty Trilogy: <HS>
    Macauleys, The
    Carricks, The
    Sterns, The
  _____

  _____

MILLER, Caroline
  Lamb In His Bosom
  _____

MILLER, Cissie
             [Stanlee Miller Coy]
  Coventry:
    200 Tish
  Starlight Romance:
    Tish
  _____

  _____

MILLER, Dallas
  Passage West   <HS>
  _____

  _____

MILLER, Hugh
  In sequence:
    District Nurse, The
    Snow On The Wind
  _____

  _____

MILLER, Lanora   <GOT>
             [Lanora Welzenbach]
  Devil's Due, The   <CGS:#9>
  House On Wolf Trail, The
  Quickthorn
  _____

  _____

MILLER, Linda Lael
  Lauralee
  My Darling Melissa   @

469

MILLER, Linda Leal (cont.)
Wanton Angel
In sequence:
  Moonfire
  Angelfire
Orphan Train Trilogy:
  Lily And The Major
Silhouette Desire:
  438 Used-To-Be-Lovers
  480 Only Forever
  516 Just Kate
  547 Daring Moves
  568 Mixed Messages
  589 Escape From Cabriz
  607 Glory, Glory
Silhouette Intimate Moments:
  59 Snowflakes On The Sea
  87 Part Of The Bargain
Silhouette Special Edition:
  277 State Secrets
  324 Ragged Rainbows
Tapestry: <HR>
  22 Fletcher's Woman   &
  30 Desire And Destiny
  44 Banner O'Brien   @&
  51 Willow
  69 Corbin's Fancy   @
  80 Memory's Embrace   @

MILLER, Marcia   <GOT>
                          [Marc Baker]
Broken Dream
Dark Journey
Deadly Crescent, The
Dear Kate...
Designed By Stacey
False Love
Fashion Game, The
Heart's Song
Jealous Yesterdays
Jonah Book, The
Love Betrayed
Love Is Blind
Nurse Kris's Trust
Nurse Of The High Sierras
Roving Heart, The
Secret Love

MILLER, Marcia
Stand-In For Romance
Tender Heart, The
To Marry For Love
Waiting Heart, The
Avalon:
  Deadly Pursuit
  Nightmare In Brown
  Nurse In Peril
  Sleeping Heart, The
  Spotlight On Romance
  Stage Mother
  Woman In The Window
Candlelight:
  18 Spotlight For Megan

MILLER, Maurine
Caprice Romance: <YA>
  22 Two Loves For Tina

MILLER, Merle
Day In Late September, A

MILLER, Sandy   <YA>
                       [Sandra Miller]
Freddie The Thirteenth
Smart Girl
Two Loves For Jennie
Heart To Heart: <YA>
  This Song Is For You
Magic Moments: <YA>
  3 Lynn's Challenge
  11 Tale Of Two Turkeys, A

MILLER, Sigmund
                    (Stephanie Blackwood)

MILLER, Theresa   <HO>
Remnants Of Glory

MILLER, Valerie
                        (Hilary Cole)

MILLER, Victor   <HO>
        [Victor Brooke Miller]
  Glory Sharers, The
  Windborn   <Saga>

MILLER, Victor Brooke
                        (Brooke Miller)
                        (Victor Miller)

MILLER, W. Maureen   <HO>
  French, The   <IMS>

MILLHISER, Marlys   <RS>
        [Marlys Joy Millhiser]
  Michael's Wife
  Mirror, The
  Nella Waits
  Willing Hostage

MILLS, Anita   <RE>
        (see A Regency Christmas)
  Devil's Match   &
  Duel Of Hearts
  Duke's Double, The
  Follow The Heart
  Newmarket Match
  Scandal Bound   &
  In Sequence: <HR>
    Lady Of Fire
    Fire And Steel
    Hearts Of Fire

MILLS, Carla J.   <HR>
  Three Rivers

MILLS, Catherine
  Second Chance At Love:
    34 Lured Into Dawn

MILLS, Diana
  Reapers Of The Wind   <Saga>

MILLS, Robert E.   <HR>
  Daughters Of Conquest
  Thunder Ridge

MILNE, Rosaleen   <RE>
  Borrowed Plumes
  Cotillion Regency:
    5 Major's Lady, The

MIMS, Emily
                        (Emily Elliott)

MINAHAN, John
  Almost Summer
  Dream Collector
  Jeremy
  Nine-Thirty-Fifty-Five
  Passing Strange

MINER, Jane Claypool
                        (Veronica Ladd)
  Sunfire: <HR><YA>
     5 Joanna
    15 Roxanne
    18 Veronica
    22 Corey
    27 Margaret
    31 Jennie
  Wildfire: <YA>
    Senior Dreams Can Come True

MINER, Jane Claypool (cont.)
  Senior Class

_____

_____

MINER, Mae
  Avalon:
    Terror In The Timberland
    Danger In The Amazon

_____

MINGER, Elda
  Heartfire Romance: <HR>
    Velvet Fire
  Harlequin American Romance:
    12   Untamed Heart
    95   Another Chance At Heaven
    106 Touched By Love
    117 Seize The Fire
    133 Bachelor Mother
    162 Billion-Dollar Baby
    229 Nothing In Common
    314 Wedding Of The Year
    338 Spike Is Missing

_____

MINGER, Miriam   <HR>
  Twin Passions
  The Avon Romance:
    Captive Rose, A
    Hint Of Rapture, A
    Stolen Splendor

_____

MINTON, Paula   <GOT><RS>
                    [Paul H. Little]
  Dark Of Memory, The
  Engraved In Evil
  Fog Hides The Fury
  Girl From Nowhere, The
  Hand Of The Imposter
  Loom Of Terror, The
  Orphan Of The Shadows
  Portrait Of Terror

MINTON, Paula (cont.)
  Secret Melody
  Shadow Of A Witch
  Mask Of Medusa, The
  Thunder Over The Reefs

_____

_____

MIRELES, Sandra
  Candlelight:
    687 Lady Nell   <RE>

_____

_____

MITCHELL, Allison
                [William E. Butterworth]
  In sequence: <HS>
    Wild Harvest
    Wild Heritage

_____

_____

MITCHELL, Ann
  Sapphire Romance: <ENG>
    Amberly Cure, The

_____

_____

MITCHELL, Erica
  Tapestry: <HR>
    32   Jade Moon
    70   Bright Desire

_____

_____

MITCHELL, Kerry
  Doctor's Challenge
  Doctor's Decision, The
  Security Surgeon

_____

_____

MITCHELL, Margaret   <HR>
  Gone With The Wind

_____

_____

MITCHELL, Paige
                    [Judith S. Ginnes]
  Wild Seed   <Saga>
_____

_____

MITCHELL, Ruth Comfort
  Legend Of Susan Dane, The
_____

_____

MITCHELL, Sara T.
  Serenade/Serenata: <Insp>
    22 Through A Glass Darkly
    37 Song In The Night, A
_____

_____

MITFORD, Nancy   (Deceased)
  Blessing, The
  Christmas Pudding
  Don't Tell Alfred
  Frederick The Great
  Highland Fling
  Love In A Cold Climate
  Pigeon Pie
  Pursuit Of Love, The
  Voltaire In Love
  Wigs On The Green
_____

_____

MITTERMEYER, Helen
[Helen Hayton Monteith Mittermeyer]
                    (Ann Cristy)
                 (Hayton Monteith)
                  (Danielle Paul)
  Brief Encounter   <CO>
  Diamond Fire
  Loveswept:
     2 Surrender
    15 Brief Delight
    57 Unexpected Sunrise
    67 Vortex
   121 Tempest
   210 Kismet

MITTERMEYER, Helen (cont.)
  Men Of Fire Trilogy:
   269   Ablaze
   310   Blue Flame
   341   White Heat
  Men Of Ice Trilogy:
   371   Quick Silver
   396   Black Frost
   425   Frozen Idol
   The Mask
  Now And Forever:
     2 Golden Touch
_____

_____

MO, Timothy   <HO>
  An Insular Possession
_____

_____

MOCKLER, Gretchen   <RS>
  Roanleigh
_____

_____

MODARRESSI, Anne Tyler
                    (Anne Tyler)

MODEAN, Mary
                    [Modean Moon]
  Second Chance At Love:
   400 In Name Only
   452 All The Flowers
   463 Heart Song
_____

_____

MODROVICH, Kathleen Creighton
                 (Kathleen Carrol)
              (Kathleen Creighton)

MOFFETT, Paula
                 (Vanessa Richards)

MOLTKE-HANSEN, David
                    (Peter Hensen)

MONARCH, Diane J. A.
  (Jeanne Abbott)
  (Jennie Abbott)

MONDEZ, Dorothea
  Foolish Heart
  Love Rides A Dark Horse

MONET, Nicole
  [Noelle Berry McCue]
  Silhouette Desire:
    2 Love's Silver Web
   39 Shadow Of Betrayal
   62 Passionate Silence
  133 Love And Old Lace
  177 Casey's Shadow
  228 Rand Emory's Widow
  266 Sandcastle Man, The
  405 Stand By Me
  473 Twilight Over Eden
  Silhouette Romance:
  615 Guardian Angel

MONEYHUN, George
  Mill Girls, The

MONIGLE, Martha
  Doll Castle, The

MONSARRAT, Nicholas <GOT>(Deceased)
  Castle Garac
  Cruel Sea

MONSELL, Helen A. (Deceased)
  Nabby Comes To Lowell

MONSIGNY, Jacqueline <HR>
  Floris
  Floris And The Belle Of Louisiana
  Floris, My Love
  Floris, The Horseman Of St.
    Petersburg

MONSON, Christine <HR>
  Flame Run Wild, A
  Golden Nights
  Rangoon
  Stormfire
  Surrender The Night <Saga>
  This Fiery Splendor

MONTAGUE, Jeanne <GOT>
  [Jeanne Betty Frances Yarde]
  Castle Of The Winds, The
  Clock Tower, The
  Diamond Heart <HR>
  Midnight Moon
  Passion Flame <HR>

MONTAGUE, Lisa
  [Sandra Dawn Shulman]
  Masquerade:
   24 Lady Of Darkness
   37 Emperor's Jewel, the
   89 Fortune's Folly

MONTCLAIR EMERALDS QUARTET <MEQ>
  Harlequin Temptation:
  217 Impulse
        Vicki Lewis Thompson
  218 Fulfillment
        Barbara Delinsky
  219 Joy
        Jayne Ann Krentz

MONTCLAIR EMERALDS QUARTET (cont.)
220 Trust
                Rita Clay Estrada

MONTEE, Kristy w/ Daniel NORMAN
                (Kristy Daniels)

MONTEITH, Hayton
           [Helen Mittermeyer]
Candlelight Ecstasy:
  62 To Love A Stranger
  80 Relentless Love
  95 Jinx Lady
 210 Lover's Knot
Candlelight Ecstasy Supreme:
  47 Pilgrim's Soul
  74 Lotus Blossom
 117 Desert Princess
Candlelight Supreme:
 143 Endless Obsession
 164 Silver Love
 178 Sapphire Heart

MONTEREY, Elizabeth
           [Victor J. Banis]
Westward Love, A

MONTGOMERY, Bettina   <CO>
           [Edythe Cudlipp]
Familiar Strangers

MONTGOMERY, Marianne   <HR>
           [D. H. Allen]
Passionate Pretender, The

MONTGOMERY, Mary
Somebody Knew

MONTROSE, Sarah   <RE>
           [Valerie Bosna]
Golden Heiress, The

MONTUPET, Janine
Lacemaker

MOON, Alicia
Caprice Romance: <YA>
  76 Long Distance Romance

MOON, Modean
           (Mary Modean)
Harlequin American Romance:
  77 Dare To Dream
 113 Hiding Places
 146 An Uncommon Hero
 271 Simple Words

MOONEY, Mary Alice
MacFadden Romance:
 258 Silent Tears

MOORE, Anne   <HR>
Golden Rogue, The
Passion's Glory
Tapestry: <HR>
  56 Tangled Vows

MOORE, Arthur   <HO>
          (Aurora Moore)
Burning Sky, The
Honolulu   <HofCS>
Kid From Rincon
Las Vegas   <HofCS>

MOORE, Arthur (cont.)
  Look Down, Look Down
  Lovers In The Sun
  Miami   <HofCS>
  Night Riders
  Raiders, The
  Ravagers, The   <Saga>
  Rivals, The
  Storm Trail
  Track Of The Killer
  California Saga: In sequence:
    Sword And The Cross, The
    Flame And The Dagger, The
    Viper And The Hawk, The
  Mississippi Saga: In sequence:
    River Of Fortune: The Passion
    River Of Fortune: The Pagans
    River Of Fortune: The Proud
  Tolliver Saga: In sequence:
    The Tempest
    The Turmoil
    The Triumph
    The Tapestry

MOORE, Aurora   <HR>
                         [Arthur Moore]
  Strong Americans: In sequence
    Savage Heart
    Secret Heart
    Raging Heart

MOORE, Colleen
                       [Jon Messmann]
  Candlelight:
    690 Bold Venture   <RE>

MOORE, Diana
                     [Deanna Marliss]
  Torch:
    Blossoms In The Wind
  Torchlite:
    Unfinished Business

MOORE, Dorinne   <GOT><RS>
  Bride Of The Dark Castle
  Castle Hohenfels
  Caverns Of Falkenhorst, The
  Flight From Eden Key
  Legend Of Monk's Court, The
  Masquerade At Monfalcone
  Miranda's Curse

MOORE, Edith
  Avalon:
    Girl Called Sam, A

MOORE, Emily
  MacFadden Romance:
    196 Golden Destiny

MOORE, Eula w/ Miriam MOORE
                       (Miriam Morton)

MOORE, Frances Sarah
  Blue Locket
  Fair Is My Love
  Hidden Boundary
  Legacy Of Love
  Storm, The

MOORE, Gwyneth
                   [Patricia Bannister]
  Harlequin Regency Romance:
    16 Men Were Deceivers Ever
    27 Dirty Frog, The

MOORE, Isabel
  That Summer In Connecticut

MOORE, Mary
Harlequin Premiere Edition:
    33 Hills Of Amethyst
Harlequin Romance:
    1315 Where The Kowhai Blooms
    1557 Along The Ribbonwood Track
    1578 Rata Flowers Are Red
    1712 Matai Valley Magic
    2349 Man Of The High Country
    2512 Run Before The Wind
    2606 Springs Of Love
    2686 Lake Haupiri Moon
    2927 Golden Touch, A

MOORE, Miriam w/ Eula MOORE
                    (Miriam Morton)

MOORE, Patti
                    [Margaret Daley]
Second Chance At Love:
    25 Gift Of Orchids

MOORE, Paula   <HR>
                [Robert Vaughan]
Hearts Divided   <MOAS:#5>
Love Pirate, The
Nothing But Roses   <CO>
Perfect Couple, The   <CO>
Savage Rapture
This Golden Rapture
Dark Desire Romance: <RS>
    Forbidden Rapture
    Hostage Of Desire

MOORE, Rayanne
Harlequin American Romance:
    8 Thin White Line
    65 Images On Silver

MOORE, Sandra Crockett
Private Woods

MOORE, Susan   <HO>
In sequence:
    Paths Of Fortune
    World Too Wide, A

MOORE, Teresa   <HR>
Swords & Camellias

MOORHOUSE, Catherine   <RE>
[Dorothea Jensen w/
            Catherine R. Allen]
In sequence:
    Adriana
    Louisa
    Dorothea

MORAY, Ann
Dawn Falcon
Rising Of The Lark, The

MORAY, Helga
                    (Helene Moreau)
Dark Fury
Flaming Hills, The
Harvest Burns, The
I, Roxana
Roxana And Alexander
Savage Earth, The
Son For Roxana, A
Tempest Lily, The
Tisa
Trenfell Castle
Untamed

MOREAU, Helene
                  [Helga Moray]
Roxana

MOREL, Jimmie L.
                (Lindsay Longford)

MORELAND, Peggy
           [Peggy Bozeman Morse]
Silhouette Desire:
  515 Little Bit Country, A
  598 Run For The Roses

MORELLA, Jane   <GOT>
Dark Memories

MOREN, Sally
                (Jane Morgan)

MORGAN, Alice
      [Alice Anne Heckler Morgan]
Candlelight Ecstasy:
  48 Masquerade Of Love   &
  54 Sands Of Malibu, The   @
  67 Impetuous Surrogate   @
Candlelight Ecstasy Supreme:
  35 Man In Control   @
  80 Stolen Idyll   &
Candlelight Supreme:
 177 Bedroom Magic   &@
Harlequin American Romance:
  35 Branded Heart
  68 Deception For Desire

MORGAN, Alyssa
            [Edith Delatush]
Candlelight:
 629 Beckoning Heart, The <RO>

MORGAN, Alyssa (cont.)
Candlelight Ecstasy:
  58 White Water Love
 191 No Other Love

MORGAN, Arlene
      [Lauran Bosworth Paine]
Aston Hall:
 106 Starfire

MORGAN, Carole
Heirlooms

MORGAN, Cary
Forests Of The Night
Spoils Of Eden, The

MORGAN, Diana
    [Alex Kamaroff w/ Irene Goodman]
Moments To Share   <CO>
Paradise Found
Trade Secrets   <CO>
Rapture Romance:
   9 Crystal Dreams
  20 Emerald Dreams
  43 Amber Dreams
  72 Lady In Flight
  86 Ocean Fire
  95 Hidden Fires
Second Chance At Love:
 286 Anything Goes
 309 Two In A Huddle
 329 Bringing Up Baby
 354 Pocketful Of Miracles
 377 To Catch A Thief
 403 Wedding Belle, The
 444 Stranger Than Fiction
 453 Blonds Perfer Gentlemen
 476 Worlds Apart

MORGAN, Diana (cont.)
  Silhouette Romance:
    293 Behind Closed Doors

_____

_____

MORGAN, Faye
                    [Doreen Owens Malek]
  Second Chance At Love:
    104 Trial By Fire

_____

_____

MORGAN, Jane
                    [Sally Moren]
  Caroline
  Lord Courtney's Lady
  Louis

_____

_____

MORGAN, Kristin
  Silhouette Romance:
    787 Love Child

_____

_____

MORGAN, Leslie
                    [Ann Miller]
  Rapture Romance:
    18 Silken Webs
    34 Against All Odds

_____

_____

MORGAN, Marley
  Silhouette Desire:
    340 Just Joe   &
    459 No Holds Barred   &

_____

_____

MORGAN, Marybeth   <GOT>
  Darkness At Bromley Hall <CGS#15>

_____

_____

MORGAN, Meredith
  Emerald Destiny

_____

_____

MORGAN, Michaela   <HR>
                    [Gloria Vitanza Basile]
  Madelaina
  Zanzara

_____

_____

MORGAN, Nancy
  First Love From Silhouette: <YA>
    163 Blue Ribbon Summer

_____

_____

MORGAN, Nancy w/ Kate FLEMING
                    (Jenny McGuire)

MORGAN, Patricia   <RS>
  Destiny's Child

_____

_____

MORGAN, Raye
                    [Helen Conrad]
  Silhouette Desire:
    52   Embers Of The Sun
    101 Summer Wind
    141 Crystal Blue Horizon
    393 Lucky Streak, A
    434 Husband For Hire   &
    543 Too many Babies
    562 Ladies' Man   &
    623 In A marrying Mood
  Silhouette Romance:
    427 Roses Never Fade

_____

_____

MORGAN, Stanley
  Dark Side Of Destiny, The
  Laura Fitzgerald

_____

_____

479

MORGAN, Virginia   <HR>
    Tame The Rising Tide

MORLAND, Catherine   <GOT>
    Castle Black
    Hawksmoor Heritage, The
    Legacy Of Winterwyck, The

MORLAND, Lynnette
                [Karen O'Connell]
    Silhouette Romance:
    339 Occupational Hazard
    399 Camera Shy
    432 Irish Eyes
    443 Magic City
    483 No Questions Asked
    548 Mid-Air

MORLEY, Adele
    Home In His Heart, A

MORRIS, Debrah w/ Pat SHAVER
                (Pepper Adams)
                (Joanna Jordan)
                (JoAnn Stacey)
                (Dianne Thomas)

MORRIS, Elizabeth
                [Jean M. Favors]
    Harlequin American Romance:
    178 This Day Forward
    221 Touch Of Moonshine, A
    Harlequin Intrigue:
    125 Teaspoon Of Murder

MORRIS, Hilda Mitchell
    Time Of Grace

MORRIS, Ira J.
    Fortune Hunter, The
    Troika Belle, The

MORRIS, Janet   <HO>
    I, The Sun

MORRIS, Kathleen
        [Mary Hanford Brannum Bringle]
    An Elegant Affair   <CO>
    Mara

MORRIS, Suzanne
    Galveston
    Keeping Secrets
    Wives And Mistresses   <Saga>

MORRIS, Terry
    Wildfire: <YA>
    Just Sixteen

MORRISON, Jo
                [Jo Lee Stafford]
    Harlequin Temptation:
    312 Always

MORRISON, Nan
    Tell Me, River
    Web Of Gold
    Avalon:
        Katherine Tree, The
    Candlelight:
    5 Faces Of Love, The

MORRISON, Roberta <GOT>
[Jean Francis Webb III]
Tree Of Evil

MORROW, Victoria <HR>
Jenny's Dream
Beneath A Pale Moon

MORSE, Ann Head
(Ann Head)

MORSE, Nancy <HR>
[Nancy Lupo Morse]
(Danielle Fleming)
Race Against Love
Silver Lady
This Tender Prize
Silhouette Intimate Moments:
  181 Sacred Places
  210 Run Wild, Run Free

MORSE, Peggy Bozeman
(Peggy Moreland)

MORSI, Pamela
Doubleday Loveswept:
  Heaven Sent

MORTIMER, Carole
Harlequin Signature Edition:
  Gypsy
  Just One Night(Eng: Witchchild)
  Merlyn's Magic
Harlequin Presents:
  294 Passionate Winter, The
  323 Tempted By Desire
  340 Savage Interlude
  352 Tempestuous Flame, The

MORTIMER, Carole (cont.)
  365 Deceit Of A Pagan
  377 Fear Of Love
  383 Yesterday's Scars
  388 Engaged To Jarrod Stone
  406 Brand Of Possession
  418 Flame Of Desire, The
  423 Living Together
  430 Devil Lover
  437 Ice In His Veins
  443 First Love, Last Love
  452 Satan's Master
  473 Freedom To Love
  479 Point Of No Return
  502 Only Lover
  510 Love's Duel
  518 Burning Obsession
  522 Red Rose For Love
  531 Shadowed Stranger
  539 Forgotten Lover
  547 Forbidden Surrender
  556 Elusive Lover
  564 Passion From The Past
  571 Perfect Partner
  579 Golden Fever
  587 Hidden Love
  594 Love's Only Deception
  603 Captive Loving
  611 Fantasy Girl
  619 Heaven Here On Earth
  627 Lifelong Affair
  636 Love Unspoken
  645 Undying Love
  651 Subtle Revenge
  659 Pagan Enchantment
  669 Trust In Summer Madness
  675 Failed Marriage, The
  684 Sensual Encounter
  716 Everlasting Love
  724 Hard To Get
  740 Lost Love, A
  757 Untamed
  773 An Unwilling Desire
  780 Past Revenge, A
  786 Passionate Lover, The
  797 Tempestuous Affair
  804 Cherish Tomorrow
  812 No Risk Affair, A
  829 Lovers In The Afternoon
  852 Devil's Price, The
  860 Lady Surrender

MORTIMER, Carole (cont.)
877   Knight's Possession
892   Darkness Into Light
909   No Longer A Dream
923   Wade Dynasty, The
939   Glass Slippers And
        Unicorns
955   Hawk's Prey
989   Velvet Promise
1005 Rogue And A Pirate, A
1019 After The Loving
1037 Tangled Hearts
1050 Taggart's Woman
1069 Secret Passion
1083 Wish For The Moon
1100 Uncertain Destiny
1117 One Chance At Love   &#
1131 To Love Again   &
1227 Loving Gift, The   #
1258 Elusive As The Unicorn
1325 Christmas Affair, A   #

MORTIMER, June
Angel In Abbey Road

MORTMAN, Doris
Circles   <CO>
First Born   <CS>
Rightfully Mine

MORTON, Joyce   <GOT>
Avalon:
    Edge Of Fear
    Speak No Evil

MORTON, Miriam
    [Miriam Moore w/ Eula Moore]
First Love From Silhouette: <YA>
152   On The Road Again

MORTON, Miriam (cont.)
168   Birds Of Passage
180   All At Sea
207   Shadows On The Mountain
220   Mind Over Matter
228   Kiss Of The Cobra
235   Nights On The Bayou

MORTON, Patricia   <GOT>
                    [Morton J. Golding]
Destiny's Child
Gathering Of Moondust, A
Province Of Darkness, The

MORTON, Tommye Ring
                    (Thomasina Ring)

MOSCO, Maisie
Trilogy:
    From The Bitter Land
    Scattered Seed, The
    Glittering Harvest
Plantaine Trilogy: <Saga>
    Between Two Worlds
    Worlds To Win
    Price Of Fame, The

MOSER, Alma
                    (Alison Gray)

MOSLER, Blanche Y.
Horror At The Hacienda
Marie Warren, Night Nurse

MOSS, Jan
The Avon Romance:
    Onyx Flame

MOTLEY, Annette
  My Lady's Crusade
  Sins Of The Lion, The

_____

MOULTON, Nancy   <HR>
  The Avon Romance:
    Crosswinds
    Defiant Heart
    Tempest Of The Heart
  In sequence:
    Defiant Destiny
    Dark Desires

_____

MOUNTJOY, Roberta Jean
                     [Jerry Sohl]
  In sequence: <HS>
    Night Wind
    Black Thunder

_____

MOWERY, Betty Chezum   <GOT>
  Avalon:
    Clock Without Hands, The
    Echoing Heart, The
    Fragrance Of Lilies
    Voice Of Terror
    Wailing Terror, The

_____

MOYER, Florence   <HR>
  Changing Winds
  Golden Fury   <WOW:#4>

_____

MUELHBAUER, Pamela
                     (Pamela Bauer)

MUGAN, Monica
  Errant Knight, The
  Flight Of The Jenny Bird, The

MUGAN, Monica (cont.)
  Seas And The Gallows, The
  Smuggler's Wench, The

_____

MUIR, Jean   <GOT>(Deceased)
  Smiling Medusa, The
  Stranger, Tread Lightly

_____

MUIR, Lucy
                     [Lucile Moore]
  Harlequin Regency Romance:
    18 Imprudent Wager, The
    33 Sussex Summer
    43 Highland Rivalry

_____

MUIR, Marie
                     (Monica Blake)

MULHOLLAND, Judith
                     (Judith Duncan)

MULLALLY, Frederick   <RS>
  Assassins, The

_____

MULLAN, Celina Rios
                     (Ana Lisa de Leon)
                     (Marisa de Zavala)
                     (Rachel Scott)

MULLEN, Dore   <HR>
                     [Dorothy Mullen]
  All We Know Of Heaven
  Far Side Of Destiny, The
  Shanghai Bridge   <Saga>

_____

MULVEY, William w/ Richard FEHR
                     (Sharon Steele)

MULVIHILL, Rochelle A.
           (Rochelle Wayne)

MUNN, Vella
            (Dawn Flindt)
Avalon:
  Moonlight And Memories
  Whispers From Yesterday
Harlequin American Romance:
  42 Summer Season
  72 River Rapture
  96 Hearts Reward, The
 115 Wanderlust
 164 Black Magic
 184 Wild And Free
 264 Firedance
 308 White Moon
 332 Memory Lane
Harlequin Intrigue:
  6 Touch A Wild Heart

MUNRO, Mary
        [Doris Kathleen Howe]
Aston Hall:
 118 This Girl Of Mine

MUNSON, Sheryl McDanel
Meteor Kismet:
  13 Siege Of The Heart

MURDOCH, Anna
Family Business
In Her Own Image

MURDOCH, Iris   <RS>
An Accidental Man
An Unofficial Rose
Black Prince, The

MURDOCH, Iris (cont.)
Book And The Brotherhood, The
Bruno's Dream
Fairly Honorable Defeat, A
Flight From The Enchanter, The
Henry And Cato
Italian Girl, The
Nice And The Good, The
Sacred And Profane Love
  Machine, The
Sandcastle, The
Sea, The Sea, The
Severed Head, A
Under The Net
Unicorn, The   <GOT>
Word Child, A

MURPHY, James F. Jr.
Mill, The

MURPHY, Lynne
          (Georgina Gentry)

MURPHY, Tom   <RS>
      [Thomas Basil Murphy, Jr.]
Aspen Incident
Auction
Ballet
Lily Cigar
Sky High

MURRAY, Annabel
           [Marie Murray]
Harlequin Presents:
 933 Land Of Thunder
 972 Fantasy Woman
1029 No Strings Attached
1076 Gift Beyond Price
1148 Promise Kept, A
1188 Question Of Love, A
1228 Don't Ask Why
1259 Black Lion Of Skiapelos &
1283 Island Turmoil   &

MURRAY, Annabel (cont.)
    1340 Let Fate Decide
    Harlequin Romance:
    2549 Roots Of Heaven
    2558 Keegan's Kingdom
    2596 Chrysanthemum
          And The Sword, The
    2612 Villa Of Vengeance
    2625 Dear Green Isle
    2717 Cotswold Lion, The
    2782 Plumed Serpent, The
    2819 Wild For To Hold
    2843 Ring Of Claddagh
    2932 Heart's Treasure
    2952 Colour The Sky Red
    2974 Sympathetic Strangers
          Untamed Sanctuary   HRS 8
          Eagle Of Solamenza,The HRS67

MURRAY, Beatrice   <GOT>
                [Richard Posner]
    Dark Sonata, The

MURRAY, Caitlin
                [Patricia Ahearn]
    Candlelight Ecstasy Supreme:
    115 Risking It All

MURRAY, E. P.   <HR>
    Firecloud
    Savage Sunrise
    Savage River   <WOW:#3>
    Savage Whisper

MURRAY, Earl
    High Freedom   <HS>

MURRAY, Edna
                [Donald Sydney Rowland]
    Nurse In Danger

MURRAY, Frances   <HR>
                [Rosemary Frances Booth]
    Brave Kingdom
    Burning Lamp, The
    Castaway
    Dear Colleague, The
    Heroine's Sister, The
    Red Rowan Berry

MURRAY, Helen
    Doctor Of The Isles
    Island Of Desire
    To Love Again
    Tiara Romance:
        African Love Song
        Prescription For Love

MURRAY, Joan
    Ride To Romance

MURRAY, Julia
    Masquerade:
        11 Notorious Lady May, The
        32 Wed For A Wager
        43 Rosamund
        66 Perfect Match, A

MURRAY, Marie
                (Annabel Murray)

MURRAY, Maysie Greig
                (Maysie Greig)

MYERS, Eve
Harlequin Romance:
    Blissful Reality   HRS18

MYERS, Harriet Kathryn
            [Harry Whittington]
Small Town Nurse

MYERS, Helen R.
Silhouette Desire:
    370 Partners For Life
    454 Smooth Operator
    471 That Fontaine Woman
    506 Pirate O'Keefe, The   &
    570 Kiss Me Kate   <MMS>&
    599 After You   &
Silhouette Romance:
    557 Donovan's Mermaid
    643 Someone To Watch Over Me
    677 Confidentially Yours
    737 Invitation To A Wedding
    776 Fine Arrangement, A

MYERS, Judy Blackwell
                (Judith Blackwell)
                (Julie Meyers)

MYERS, Katherine   <HR>
The Avon Romance:
    Dark Soldier
    Ribbons Of Silver

MYERS, M. Ruth/Mary Ruth
    An Officer And A Lady
    Captain's Pleasure
    Costly Pleasures
    Friday's Daughter
    Journey To Cuzco, A
    Touch Of Magic, A   <RM>

MYERS, M. Ruth/Mary Ruth (cont.)
    Love & Life:
        Insights
        Private Matter, A

MYERS, Peggy A.
                (Ann Williams)

MYERS, Virginia   <HR>
    Californio!
    Lady Of Means, A
    Ramona's Daughter
    This Land I Hold
    Candlelight:
        507 Winds Of Love, The   <RO>
        606 Come November   <RO>
    Harlequin SuperRomance:
        105 Sunlight On Sand

MYERS, Virginia w/ Stella CAMERON
                (Jane Worth Abbott)

MYLES, Frances
MacFadden Romance:
    176 Shadow Of The Andes

MYLES, Sabrina
                [Lois A. Walker]
    Candlelight Ecstasy:
        25 Freedom To Love

MYLES, Sandra
                (Sandra Marton)

MYRUS, Joyce   <HR>
    Angel's Ecstasy
    Beyond Surrender
    Island Enchantress
    Sweet Fierce Fires
    Tender Torment

NAGY, Gloria   <CO>
  Virgin Kisses

NAISMITH, Marion   <RS>
  Handful Of Miracles, A
  Most Eloquent Music
  Phillipa
  Prelude To Darkness
  Rainbow Chasers, The

  •

NAPIER, Mary
  Budapest Risk, The

NAPIER, Melissa   <GOT>
  Castle Of Dark Evil
  Child Of Satan
  Haunted Woman, The
  House Of Rising Water

  Mermaid Of Dark Mountain

  Posession Of Elizabeth Calder,The

NAPIER, Priscilla

  Imperial Winds   <HS>

NAPIER, Susan
  Harlequin Presents:
    885 Sweet As My Revenge
    924 Counterfeit Secretary
    940 Lonely Season, The
    1051 True Enchanter

NAPIER, Susan (cont.)
    1093 Reasons Of The Heart
    1211 Another Time
    1252 Love Conspiracy, The
    1284 Bewitching Compulsion, A
    1332 Fortune's Mistress
  Harlequin Romance:
    2711 Love In The Valley
    2723 Sweet Vixen

NASH, Anne   <RS>
  Prize Of Fear

NASH, Jean
              (Jean Sutherland)
  Golden Reckoning
  Sand Castles
  Last Of The Lattimers: <HR>
    In sequence:
      Silver Web, The
      Golden Thread, The
  The Avon Romance:
    Forever, My Love
    Surrender The Heart

NASH, Noreen   <HR>
      [Norabelle Roth Siegel]
  By Love Fulfilled

NASH, Petra
  Harlequin Regency Romance:
    36 Lady Harriet's Harvest

NATHAN, Robert
  Portrait Of Jennie
  Stonecliff

NATION, Allan
           (see Carolyn Thornton)

NAU, Erika
  Angel In The Rigging

_____

_____

NAUGHTON, Lee
  Harlequin Romance:
  2236 Sand Through My Fingers

_____

_____

NAUMAN, Eileen
           (Beth Brookes)
           (Lindsay McKenna)
  Harlequin Temptation:
    51 Touch The Heavens
    Travis Family Trilogy:
    (cont. from Lindsay McKenna)
    76 Dare To Love
    101 Right Touch, The
  Lovestruck:
    Beginnings
    Night Flight
  The Avon Romance:
    Hostage Heart

_____

_____

NEAL, Hilary
          [Olive Marion Norton]
  Harlequin Romance:
    812 Factory Nurse
    931 Charge Nurse
    1034 Nurse Meg's Decision

_____

_____

NEALE, Linda   <HR>
  Briar Rose, The

_____

_____

NEELS, Betty
  Harlequin Premiere Edition:
    35 Heaven Round The Corner
  Harlequin Romance:
    1361 Sister Peters In Amsterdam
    1385 Nurse In Holland
    1409 Blow Hot, Blow Cold
    1441 Nurse Harriet Goes To
          Holland
    1465 Damsel In Green
    1498 Fate Is Remarkable
    1529 Tulips For Augusta
    1569 Tangle Autumn
    1593 Wish With The Candles
    1625 Victory For Victoria
    1641 5th Day Of Christmas, The
    1666 Saturday's Child
    1689 Cassandra By Chance
    1705 Three For A Wedding
    1737 Winter Of Change
    1761 Stars Through The Mist
    1777 Enchanting Samantha
    1801 Uncertain Summer
    1817 Gemel Ring, The
    1841 Magic Of Living, The
    1857 Cruise To A Wedding
    1881 End Of The Rainbow, The
    1905 Tabitha In Moonlight
    1921 Heaven Is Gentle
    1937 Henrietta's Own Castle
    1954 Star Looks Down, A
    1970 Cobweb Morning
    1987 Moon For Lavinia, The
    2009 Esmeralda
    2025 Roses For Christmas
    2041 Edge Of Winter, The
    2063 Gem Of A Girl, A
    2080 Small Slice Of Summer, A
    2095 Matter Of Chance, A
    2110 Hasty Marriage, The
    2127 Grasp A Nettle
    2137 Pineapple Girl
    2153 Little Dragon, The
    2169 Britannia All At Sea
    2202 Philomena's Miracle
    2226 Never While The
          Grass Grows
    2250 Ring In A Teacup
    2275 Sun And Candlelight
    2301 Promise Of Happiness, The
    2314 Midnight Sun's Magic

NEIL, Barbara
                [Barbara Sherrod]
Someone Wonderful
Harlequin Regency Romance:
   21 Lessons For A Lady
   30 Celebrated Miss
       Neville, The
   41 Lucy's Scoundrel

NEIL, Joanna
Harlequin Romance:
   Reckless Loving, A   HRS82

NEILAN, Sarah
An Air Of Glory
Braganza Pursuit, The
Paradise

NEILL, Robert
Devil's Door
Golden Days, The
Lillibullero
Rebel Heiress

NEILSON, Eric
Haakon Series:
   Golden Ax, The
   Viking Revenge, The
   Haakoms Iron Hand
   War God, The

NEILSON, Marguerite
              [Julia Tompkins]
Bride Of Alderburn, The
Dark Path, The

NEL, Stella Frances
Harlequin Romance:
   1559 Singing Bird, A
   1708 Golden Harvest
   1743 Destiny Is A Flower

NELSON, Judith   <RE>
Beau Guest
Julianna
Kidnap Confusion
Lady's Choice
Merry Chase, The
Patience Is A Virtue

NELSON, Louella
Harlequin American Romance:
   In sequence:
   214   Mail-Order Mate
   379   Emerald Fortune
SuperRomance:
   96 Sentinel At Dawn
Harlequin SuperRomance:
   128 Freedom's Fortune

NELSON, Marguerite
              [Lee Floren]
Air Stewardess
Dr. Gail's Dilemma
Far Are The Hills
Hollywood Nurse
Nancy's Dude Ranch
Wait For The Day

NELSON, Mildred
Island, The

NELSON, Peter
  Crosswinds: <YA>
    7 Sylvia Smith-Smith

_____

_____

NELSON, Valerie K.
  Harlequin Romance:
    764 Nurse Ann Wood
    793 Starched Cap, The
    818 Second Year, The
    834 Nurse Annabel
    852 Fair Stranger, The
    890 Two Sisters
    940 Substitute Nurse
    961 Nurse Jane And Cousin Paul
    1590 Girl From
           Over The Sea, The

_____

_____

NEMETH, Linell Evanston
                    (Linell Anston)

NEMSER, Cindy
  Eve's Delight   <CO>

_____

_____

NERI, Penelope   <HR>
  Bold, Breathless Nights
  Crimson Angel
  Desert Captive
  Forever And Beyond   <THR>
  Hearts Enchanted
  Jasmine Paradise
  Midnight Captive
  Sea Jewel
  Silver Rose
  In sequence:
    Passion's Betrayal
    Loving Lies
  In sequence:
    Passion's Rapture
    Beloved Scoundrel

_____

_____

NETZEL, Sally w/ Gretchen JOHNSON
                    (Suzanne Jenner)

NEUBAUER, William Arthur
                    (Christine Bennett)
                    (Joan Garrison)
                    (Jan Hathaway)
                    (Rebecca Marsh)
                    (Norma Newcomb)
  Assignment: Romance
  Blue Waters
  Bride To Love, A
  Duel Of Hearts
  Girl Of Big Mountain
  Golden Heel, The
  High-Country Dreamer, The
  Love Remains
  Old Covered Bridge
  Police Nurse
  River Song
  Roses For Carol
  Summer Of The Shore
  Sweetheart Of The Air
  This Darkling Love
  Trouble In Ward J
  Wing Of The Blue Air
  Sharon Romance:
    Beckoning Star

_____

_____

NEUKRUG, Linda
                    (Jill Castle)

NEVILLE, Anne
                    [Jane Viney]
  Circle Of Love:
    1 Gold In Her Hair
    10 Voices Of Loving
    16 Innocent Deception

_____

_____

NEVILLE, Katherine
  Eight, The

_____

_____

NEVIN, David
Dream West   <HS>

_____

_____

NEVINS, Kate
                    [Margaret Malkind]
Second Chance At Love:
    90 Forbidden Rapture
   162 Midsummer Magic
   191 Spellbound
   215 Breakfast With Tiffany
   267 Venetian Sunrise
To Have And To Hold:
    47 Memory And Desire

_____

_____

NEWCOMB, Kerry   <HO><HR>
In The Season Of The Sun   <HO>
Morning Star
Sacred Is The Wind
Scalpdancers

_____

_____

NEWCOMB, Kerry w/ Frank SCHAEFER
                    (Shana Carrol)
                    (Peter Gentry)
                    (Christina Savage)

NEWCOMB, Norma
            [William Arthur Neubauer]
Angel Of The Hills
Bend In The River, A
Boss Lady
Change Of Heart, A
Forest Creek
Girl And The Eagle, The
Girl Of Big Mountain
Green Bench, The
Happiness Inn
Jade Shamrock, The
Large Land, The
Love Comes First
Love Comes Riding
Memo Of The Heart

NEWCOMB, Norma (cont.)
Nurse To Marry, A
Questing Heart, A
Singing Heart, A
Sparkles In The Water
Special Kind Of Love, A
This Darkling Love
This Love To Hold
Woman's Place, A
Sharon Romance:
   Bright Stars
   Eve's Hour

_____

_____

NEWMAN, Holly   <RE>
Grand Gesture, A   &
Heart's Companion, The
Honor's Players   &@
Waylaid Heart, The   @
American Regency Romance:
   Gentleman's Trade

_____

_____

NEWMAN, Mona
            [Mona Alice Jean Newman]
Aston Hall:
   101 Night Of A Thousand Stars

_____

_____

NEWMAN, Mona Alice Jean
                   (Mona Newman)
                   (Jean Stewart)

NEWMAN, Robert
Enchanter, The

_____

_____

NICHOLAS, Simone
Love Scenes: <YA>
     1 Face The Music
     2 Stage Fright
     3 Star Crowd

_____

_____

493

NICHOLS, Aeleta   <GOT>
  Third Child, The

_____

_____

NICHOLS, Carolyn w/ Stanlee
  Miller COY
                    (Iona Charles)

NICHOLS, Charlotte
  [Patricia Forsythe Knoll
            w/ Barbara Williams]
  Silhouette Inspirations:
    18 For The Love Of Mike
  Silhouette Romance:
    403 Eye Of The Beholder

_____

_____

NICHOLS, Leigh   <RS>
                    [Dean Koontz]
  Eyes Of Darkness, The
  House Of Thunder, The
  Key To Midnight, The

_____

_____

NICHOLS, Pamela
  Escape To Romance (Mexican
    Interlude)

_____

_____

NICHOLS, Ruth   <HR>
  Burning Of The Rose, The

_____

_____

NICHOLS, Sarah   <GOT>
                      [Lee Hays]
  Amy Marsh In Copenhagen
  Amy Marsh In London
  Amy Marsh, Star Nurse
  Amy Marsh, TV Nurse
  Clouded Moon, The
  Grave's Company
  House Of Rancour

NICHOLS, Sarah (cont.)
  Moon Dancers, The
  Rosemary For Remembrance
  Satan's Spring
  Serpents Tooth
  Sunless Day, The
  That Dark Inn
  Very Dead Of Winter, The
  Widows Walk
  Wyndham Saga:
    1 Silsby
    2 Rachael
    3 Fleur
    4 Valerie
    5 Nell
    6 Tracey
    7 Charity
    8 Elspeth

_____

NICHOLS, Suzanne
                  [Marlys Stapelbroek]
  Harlequin SuperRomance:
    392 Rings Of Gold
    458 Lady's Choice

_____

NICHOLSON, Christina   <HR>
                  [Christopher Nicole]
  Power And The Passion, The
  Queen Of Paris, The
  Savage Sands, The

_____

_____

NICHOLSON, Peggy
  Harlequin Presents:
    732 Darling Jade, The
    741 Run So Far
    764 Dolphins For Luck
  Harlequin Romance:
    3009 Tender Offer
    3100 Burning Dreams
  Harlequin SuperRomance:
    193 Soft Lies, Summer Light

NICHOLSON, Peggy
  237 Child's Play
  290 Light Fantastic, The

NICKELS, Meryl
              [Martha Unickel]
  Heartfire Romance: <HR>
  Love's Lying Eyes

NICKSON, Hilda
  Kiss For Elaine, A
  Harlequin Romance:
    776 Her Foolish Heart
    794 Surgeon's Return
    820 World Of Nurse Mitchel,The
    836 He Whom I Love
    882 For Love Of A Surgeon
    986 Surgeon At Witteringham
  1050 Nurse Adele
  1210 Friend Of The Family, A
  1279 Gather Then The Rose
  1323 Moonlight On The Water
  1360 This Desirable Residence
  1437 To My Dear Niece
  1484 On A May Morning
  1556 No Enemy
  1647 Sweet Spring, The
  1718 Lord Of The Forest
  2859 Voyage Of Discovery
        So Tempting An Offer HRS35

NICKSON, Jeanne   <HR>
  Tears Of The Moon

NICOLAYSEN, Bruce   <HR>
  New York Series: In sequence:
    From Distant Shores
    On Maiden Lane

NICOLAYSEN, Bruce (cont.)
    Beekman Place
    Pirate Of Grammercy Park, The
    Gracie Square

NICOLE, Christopher   <HR>
            (Daniel Adams)
            (Leslie Arlen)
            (Robin Cade)
            (Peter Grange)
            (Mark Logan)
            (Simon McKay)
     (Christina Nicholson)
            (Alison York)
  Crimson Pagoda, The
  Darknoon
  Face Of Evil, The
  Heroes
  Longest Pleasure, The
  Lord Of The Golden Fan
  Off White
  Operation Destruct
  Operation Neptune
  Ratoon
  Scarlet Princess, The
  Secret Memoirs Of Lord Byron, The
  Self-Lovers, The
  Shadows In The Jungle
  Thunder And The Shouting, The
  White Boy
  In sequence:
    Black Majesty
    Wild Harvest
  Amyot Series:
    Amyot's Cay
    Blood Amyot
    Amyot Crime, The
  Carribbean Saga: In sequence:
    Caribee
    Devil's Own, The
    Mistress Of Darkness
    Black Dawn
    Sunset
  Haggard Chronicles: In sequence:
    Haggard
    Inheritors, The

NIGHTINGALE, Ursula (cont.)
  Deviltower

_____

NILAND, D'Arcy   (Deceased)
  Dead Men Running
  Woman From The Country

_____

_____

NILE, Dorothea   <RS>
                [Michael Avallone]
  Mistress Of Farrondale
  Terror At Deepcliff
  Third Shadow, The

_____

_____

NIXON, Joan Lowery
  Sweet Dreams: <YA>
    24 Trouble With Charlie, The

_____

_____

NOBILE, Jeanette
  Sweet Dreams: <YA>
    15 Thinking Of You
    37 Portrait Of Love

_____

_____

NOBISSO, Josephine
                    (Nadja Bride)
                    (Nuria Wood)

NOBLE, Frances   <HR>
  Destiny's Daughter

_____

_____

NOBLE, Hollister   <HR>
  Winds Of Love, The

_____

_____

NOEL, Angela
  Sapphire Romance: <ENG>
    Promise Me

_____

NOEL, Denise
  Mystique:
     2 House Of Secrets
     6 Love's Rebel
    12 Bitter Honey
    25 Two Faces Of Love
    36 Affair Of Hearts
    43 To Love Again
    47 Traitor's Mask
    57 Prisoner Of The Past
    70 Blind Obsession
    78 Treacherous Mission
    81 Night Intruder
    87 Death Of A Stranger
   121 Bitter Hostage
   142 Secret Love
   157 Season Of Anguish

_____

_____

NOGA, Helen
  Ayisha

_____

NOLAN, Frederick   <HR>
  Blind Duty   <Saga>
  Carver's Kingdom
  Promise Of Glory, A
  White Night's, Red Dawn   <Saga>

_____

NOLAN, Jenny
                    [Mary Jo Young]
  Second Chance At Love:
    31 Summer Lace

_____

_____

NOLLET, Lois S.
(Diana Delmore)
(Lois Stewart)

NOONE, Edwina   <GOT>
[Michael Avallone]
Cloisonne Vase, The
Corridor Of Whispers
Dark Cypress
Daughter Of Darkness
Heirloom Of Tragedy
SeaCliffe
Second Secret, The
Victorian Crown, The
Craghold Chronicles:
  Craghold Legacy, The
  Craghold Curse, The
  Craghold Creatures, The
  Craghold Crypt, The
Dark Desire Romance: <RS>
  Tender Loving Fear

NORBERG, Marcia K.
(M. K. Kauffman)

NORBY, Lisa
Heart To Heart: <YA>
  Friendly Rivals
  Waiting In The Wings
Turning Points: <YA>
  1 Friends Forever
Two By Two Romance: <YA>
  10 Just The Way You Are

NORCROSS, Lisabet   <HR><RE>
[Arthur M. Gladstone]
Dandy's Dilemma, The
Heiress To Love
Lady And The Rogue, The
Masquerade Of Love
My Lady Scapegrace
Reluctant Heiress

NORE, Rochelde
Rebel In Love

NORMAN, Daniel w/ Kristy MONTEE
(Kristy Daniels)

NORMAN, David   <HO>
Frontier Rakers: In sequence:
  Frontier Rakers, The
  Forty-Niners, The
  Gold Fever
  Silver City
  Montana Pass
  Santa Fe Dream   <Saga>

NORMAN, Dee
[Norma Williams w/ Dee Lopez]
Silhouette Special Edition:
  417 White Nights

NORMAN, Elizabeth   <RS>
Castle Cloud
If The Reaper Ride
Silver Jewels And Jade
Sleep My Love

NORMAN, Hilary   <CS>
Chateau Ella

NORMAN, Nicole   <HR>
[Edythe Cudlipp]
Firebird, The
Heather Song

NORMAN, Yvonne
　　　　　[Norma Yvonne Seely]
Treasure Of Seacliff Manor
Avalon:
　Leaves On The Wind　　　　<GOT>

NORRELL, Marjorie
　　　　　[Marjorie Ellison]
Harlequin Romance:
　759　No Regrets
　819　Nurse Saxon's Patient
　883　Nurse Trudie Is Engaged
　906　Nurse Molly
　930　There's Always Someone
　946　Phantom Rival
　962　Nurse Madeline Of Eden
　　　　Grove
　993　Send For Nurse Alison
1009　Nurse At Fairchilds
1042　Promise The Doctor
1057　Lesley Bowen, M.D.
1073　Torpington Annexe, The
1097　Thank You, Nurse Conway
1129　My Friend, Doctor John
1177　Marriage Of Doctor Royle
1241　Nurse Barlow's Jinx
1273　If They Could Only Forget
1329　Unexpected Millstone, The
1353　Nurse Lavinia's Mistake
1377　Sister Darling
1410　More Than Kind
1433　Pursuit Of Doctor Lloyd
1457　Nurse Kelsey Abroad
1513　Change Of Duty
1545　Pride's Banner
1577　Dr. Maitland's Secretary

NORRIS, Carol
　　　　　[Carolyn Brimley Norris]
Feast Of Passions, A
Breath Of Paradise, A
Candlelight Ecstasy:
　246　Secrets For Sharing

NORRIS, Carol (cont.)
　311　Lost Letters
　340　Hideaway

NORRIS, Carolyn Brimley　　<GOT>
　　　　　　　　　　　(Kris Karron)
　　　　　　　　　　　(Carol Norris)
Island Of Silence
Signs Unseen, Sounds Unheard

NORRIS, Kathleen　　　<GOT><RS>
　　　　　[Kathleen Thompson Norris]
American Flaggs, The
An Apple For Eve
Angel In The House
Barberry Bush
Beauty And The Beast
Beauty's Daughter
Beloved Woman, The
Bread Into Roses
Burned Fingers
Butterfly
Callahans And The Murphys, The
Certain People Of Importance
Come Back To Me, Beloved
Corner Of Heaven
Dina Cashman
Family Gathering
Foolish Virgin, The
Gabrielle
Hands Full Of Living
Harriet And The Piper
Heartbroken Melody
Heart Of Rachael, The
High Holiday
Hildegarde
Josselyn's Wife
Little Ships
Love Calls The Tune
Love Of Julie Borel, The
Lost Sunrise
Lucky Lawrences, The
Lucretia Lombard
Maiden Voyage

NORRIS, Kathleen (cont.)
  Manhatten Love Song
  Margaret Yorke
  Martie The Unconquered
  Mink Coat
  Miss Harriet Townshend
  Mother, A Story
  My Best Girl
  Mystery House
  Over At The Crowleys'
  Passion Flower
  Poor, Dear Margaret Kirby
  Red Silence
  Rich Mrs. Burgoyne, The
  Rose Of The World
  Runaway, The
  Sacrifice Years, The
  Sea Gull, The
  Second-Hand Wife
  Secret Marriage
  Secret Of The Marshbanks, The
  Secrets Of Hillyard House, The
  Shadow Marriage
  Shining Windows
  Sisters
  Storm House
  Story Of Julia Page
  Three Men And Diana
  Through A Glass Darkly
  Treasure And Uneducating Mary,The
  Treehaven
  Undertow
  Venables, The
  Walls Of Gold
  Wife For Sale
  Woman In Love
  World Is Like That, The
  You Can't Have Everything
  Younger Sister

  _____

  _____

NORRIS, Maureen
                [Edythe Cudlipp]
  Second Chance At Love:
    165 Starry Eyed
    205 Seaswept

  _____

  _____

NORTH, Jessica   <RS>
                [Robert Somerlott]
  River Rising
  High Valley, The
  Legend Of The 13th Pilgrim, The
  Mask Of The Jaguar

  _____

  _____

NORTH, Miranda
                [Nancy Austin w/
                   Mary Kevern]
  Heartfire Romance: <HR>
    Desert Slave
    Forever Paradise

  _____

  _____

NORTH, Rachel   <HR>
  Flower Of Love

  _____

  _____

NORTH, Sara   <RS>
  (publishers pseudonym for
              writers in this series)
  Evil Side Of Eden
                [Jean Hager]
  Jasmine For My Grave
                [Barbara Bonham]
  Message For Julie, A
  Shadow Of The Tamaracks
                [Jean Hager]

  _____

  _____

NORTHAN, Irene   <RE>
  Phyllida   <GEO>
  Harlequin Regency Romance:
    42 Marriage Brokers, The

  _____

  _____

NORTON, Andre   <RS>
                [Alice Mary Norton]
  Caroline   w/ Enid CUSHING

500

NORTON, Andre (cont.)
  Follow The Drum
  Huon Of The Horn
  Iron Butterflies
  Ralstone Luck, The
  Snow Shadow
  Stand And Deliver
  Velvet Shadows
  White Jade Fox, The

NORTON, Bess
              [Olive M. Norton]
  Harlequin Classic:
    89 Nurse Is Born, A   (710)

NORTON, Olive M.   (Deceased)
  [Olive Marion Claydon Norton]
              (Hilary Neal)
              (Bess Norton)
              (Kate Norway)

NORWAY, Kate
              [Olive M. Norton]
  Harlequin Classic:
    25 Nurse Elliot's Diary (525)
  Harlequin Romance:
    1449 Dedication Jones
    1505 Paper Halo

NOSSACK, Hans Erick   (Deceased)
  Wait For November

NOTTINGHAM, Poppy   \<GOT\>\<RS\>
              [Patti Dunaway]
  Cry Of The Cat
  Hatred's Web
  Shadow Of A Cat   \<CGS:#3\>

NOTTINGHAM, Poppy (cont.)
  Wasted Pride
  Without A Grave   \<CGS:#8\>

NOVA, Craig
  Congressman's Daughter, The

NOVAK, Rose w/ Marcia Silverman
  KAMIEN
              (Marcia Rose)

NOWELS, Conrad
  Wildfire: \<YA\>
    That Other Girl

NOYES, Patricia Ann
  MacFadden Romance:
    16 Continental Dreams

NUCCIO, Marsha L.
              (M. L. Gamble)

NUELLE, Helen/Helen S.   \<GOT\>
        [Helen Shearman Nuelle]
  Evil Lives Here
  Haunting Of Bally Moran, The
  Sins Of The Past
  Candlelight:
    194 Shadows Of Amanda
    237 Surrender To Love   \<RO\>
    540 Long Enchantment, The \<RO\>
    605 Danger In Loving, The \<RE\>
    642 Treacherous Heart, The\<RO\>

NUNN, Rebecca
Candlelight Ecstasy Supreme:
    38 Another Day Of Loving
First Love From Silhouette: <YA>
    191 Wheels

_____

_____

NYE, Cassandra   <RS>
Requiem For Mignon
Steps To The Grotto

_____

_____

NYE, Valerie
Second Chance At Love:
    23 Crystal Fire

_____

_____

OAKSON, Pat C. w/ Leslie BISHOP
                    (Robin Tolivar)

OATES, Joyce Carol
  Angel Of Light
  Bellefleur
  Bloodmoor Romance
  Mysteries Of Winterthurn
  Solstice   <CO>
  You Must Remember This

O'BANYON, Constance   <HR>
                    [Evelyn Gee]
  Cheyenne Sunrise
  Dakota Dreams
  Enchanted Ecstasy
  Estasy's Promise
  Golden Paradise
  Lavender Lies
  Moontide Embrace
  Pirate's Princess
  Rebel Temptress
  September Moon
  Velvet Chains
  In sequence:
    Savage Desire
    Savage Splendor
  Savage Seasons Series:
    In sequence:
      Savage Autumn
      Savage Winter
      Savage Spring
      Savage Summer

OBERLIN, Diana   <HR>
  Affair At Highland Terrace

O'BRIAN, Eve
                    [Judith E. Bryer
                     w/ Arnie Heller]
  Candlelight Ecstasy:
    503 Mystery At Midnight

O'BRIAN, Gayle   <HR>
  Reckless Rapture

O'BRIEN, Edna
  Ausust Is A Wicked Month
  Casualties Of Peace
  Country Girls, The
  Girl With Green Eyes
  Girls In Their Married Bliss
  I Hardly Knew You
  Lonely Girls, The
  Love Object, The
  Mother Ireland
  Night
  Pagan Place
  Rose In The Heart, A
  Some Irish Loving: A Selection
  Country Girls Trilogy: Inclueds:
    The Country Girl
    The Lonely Girls
    Girls In Their Married Bliss

O'BRIEN, Kathleen
                    [Kathleen Pynn]
  Harlequin Presents:
    1011 Sunswept Summer
    1189 White Midnight
    1267 Dreams On Fire

O'BRIEN, Saliee   <GOT><HR>
                    [Frankie-Lee Janas]
  Beelfontaine

O'BRIEN, Saliee (cont.)
  Black Ivory
  Blood West
  Bride Of Gaylord Hall, The
  Captain's Woman
  Cayo
  Farewell The Stranger
  Heiress To Evil (Sunset)
  Night Of The Scorpion   <BZG>
  Shadow Of The Caravan
  So Wild The Dream
  Too Swift The Tide
  In sequence:
    Bayou
    Cajun
    Creole

O'BRYAN, Sofi
  Roman Candles   <CO>
  Candlelight:
    180 Secret Of The Priory, The

O'CARAGH, Mary
  Silhouette Romance:
    445 Mirage

O'CONNELL, Karen
                  (Lynnette Morland)

O'CONNOR, Megan
  Candlelight:
    563 Pippa   <RE>

O'CORK, Shannon
  In sequence: <RM>
    Turning Point
    Ice Fall

O'DANIEL Janet w/ Amy MIDGLEY
                  (Amanda Clark)

O'DAY-FLANNERY, Constance   <RF>
  This Time, Forever
  Time-Kept Promises
  The Travel Trilogy:
    Timeless Passion
    Timeswept Lovers
    Time-Kissed Destiny

O'DELL, Amanda
  Heartfire Romance: <HR>
    Kentucky Fire
    Wanton Surrender

O'DONNELL, Jan
  Wildfire: <YA>
    Funny Girl Like Me, A

O'DONNELL, Kate
                  [Nancy Garcia]
  The Avon Romance:
    Defy The Wind

O'DONNELL, Lillian   <GOT><RS>
          [Lillian Udvardy O'Donnell]
  Aftershock
  Dive Into Darkness
  Falling Star
  Leisure Dying
  Murder Under The Sun
  Sleeping Beauty, The
  Tachi' Tree, The

504

O'DONOGHUE, Maureen   \<HR\>
  Jedder's Land
  Wild Honey Time
  Winner   \<Saga\>
_____

_____

O'FAOLAIN, Julia
  Irish Signorina, The
  No Country For Young Men

_____

_____

O'FLAHERTY, Louise   \<HO\>\<RS\>
  Dreamers, The
  Gospel Swamp
  House Of The Lost Woman
  Innocents, The   \<Saga\>
  Tear In The Silk, A
  This Golden Land
  In sequence:
    Farthest Eden, The
    Poppies In The Wind

_____

_____

OGAN, George F. w/ Margaret E.
  Nettles OGAN   (Rosetta Stowe)

OGAN, Margaret Nettles   (Deceased)
  Candlelight:
    560 Ruthana   \<RO\>

_____

_____

OGILVIE, Charlot
  Love Song On A Chinese Flute

_____

_____

OGILVIE, Elisabeth   \<RS\>
    [Elisabeth May Ogilvie]
  An Answer In The Tide
  Bellwood
  Dancer In Yellow, A
  Dawning Of The Day, The
  Dreaming Swimmer, The

OGILVIE, Elisabeth (cont.)
  Ebbing Tide, The
  Face Of Innocence
  High Tide At Noon
  Image Of A Lover
  No Evil Angel
  Rowan Head
  Seasons Hereafter, The
  Silent Ones, The
  Storm Tide
  Strawberries In The Sea
  Theme For Reason, A
  There May Be Heaven
  Waters On A Starry Night
  Weep And Know Why
  When The Music Stopped   \<RM\>
  Where The Lost April's Are
  Witch Door, The
  Scottish Trilogy: \<HR\>
    Jennie About To Be
    World Of Jennie G., The
    Summer Of The Osprey, The
  Wildfire: \<YA\>
    Beautiful Girl
    My Summer Love
    Too Young To Know

_____

_____

OGILVIE, Gordon
  Jamie Reid
  Riddle Of Richard Pearse, The

_____

_____

O'GRADY, Leslie   \<HR\>
  Lady Jade
  Passion's Fortune
  Sapphire And Silk
  Second Sister, The   \<RS\>
  Seek The Wild Shore
  So Wild A Dream
  Wildwinds   \<GOT\>
  In sequence: \<RE\>
    Artist's Daughter
    Lord Raven's Widow

_____

_____

O'GRADY, Rohan   <GOT>
     [June O'Grady Skinner]
Bleak November
Curse Of The Montrolfes, The
Master Of Montrolfe Hall, The

_____

_____

O'GREEN, Jennifer
     [Jennifer Roberson]
Royal Captive   <HR>

_____

_____

O'HALLION, Sheila   <HR>
     [Sheila Rosalynd Allen]
American Princess
Kathleen
Masquerade Of Hearts
Tapestry: <HR>
  35 Fire And Innocence

_____

_____

O'HARA, Gerry
               (Michelle Christie)

O'HARA, Kate
Harlequin Romance:
  2560 Summerhaze

_____

_____

OKE, Janette   <Insp>
Praire Love Stories:
  Seasons Of The Heart Series:
    In sequence:
      Once Upon A Summer
      Winds Of Autumn, The
      Winter Is Not Forever
  Canadian West Series:
    In sequence:
      When Calls The Heart
      When Comes The Spring
      When Breaks The Dawn
      When Hope Springs New

OKE, Janette (cont.)
Love Comes Softly Series:
  In Sequence:
    Love Come Softly
    Love's Enduring Promise
    Love's Long Journey
    Love's Abiding Joy
    Love's Unending Legacy
    Love's Unfolding Dream
    Love's Takes Wing
    Love Finds A Home

_____

_____

O'LAIMHIN, J. C. Marti Laven
                  (Marti Laven)

OLDEN, Marc
     (see Terry Nelsen Bonner)
Dangerous Glamour, A

_____

OLDENBOURG, Zoe   <HO>
Awakened, The
Catherine The Great
Chains Of Love, The
Cities Of The Flesh
Destiny Of Fire
Heirs Of The Kingdom, The
World Is Not Enough, The

_____

_____

OLDFIELD, Elizabeth
Harlequin Presents:
  604 Dream Hero
  608 Second Time Around
  637 Florida Fever
  652 Beloved Stranger
  676 Take It Or Leave It
  685 Fighting Lady
  691 Submission
  742 Rough And Ready
  758 Too Far, Too Fast
  765 Ego Trap, The
  805 Dragon Man
  901 Sunstroke

OLDFIELD, Elizabeth (cont.)
```
 948  Bodycheck
 964  Bachelor In Paradise
1012  Beware Of Married Men
1030  Touch And Go
1077  Quicksands
1101  Living Dangerously
1132  Close Proximity
1212  Sparring Partners
1300  Rendezvous In Rio
1333  Price Of Passion, The
```

OLDSHAKER, Thelma   <CO>
Intimate Strangers
More Than This

OLEYAR, Rita Balkey
                        (Rita Balkey)

OLIPHANT, Eleana   <RS>
Haunting Of Lost Lake, The

OLIVER, Jan
            [Janece Oliver Hudson]
Candlelight Supreme:
  188 Perfect Love Test, The

OLIVER, Jane
[Helen Christina Easson
                    Evans Rees]
Alexander The Glorious
Flame Of Fire
Heart In The Highlands, A
Lion And The Rose, The
Lion Is Come, The
Sunset At Noon

OLIVER, Tess
            [Terry Shapiro Kovak]
Silhouette Romance:
  14 Red, Red Rose
  78 Double Or Nothing

OLMSTEAD, Lorena Ann   <RS>
Dorothea's Revenge
Faces Of Danger, The
Many Paths Of Love
Return To Peril
To Love A Stranger
Trouble In Paradise
Avalon:
  Dangerous Memory
  Journey To Adventure, A
  Strange Inheritance
  Tender Season, A
  Warning Of Danger
Candlelight: (also Avalon)
  145 Faithful Promise, The

OLSEN, Helen C.
Avalon:
  To Catch The Wind

OLTMANN, Vanessa
                        (Vanessa Grant)

O'MALLEY, Mary Dolling Sanders
                        (Ann Bridge)

O'MEARA, Walter   <GOT>
Castle Danger (Minnesota Gothic)

ORBACH, Frank
          (see Megan Hughes)

ORD, Irene
          (Kate Fairfax)

ORDE, Lewis   <HR>
  Heritage
  Lion's Way, The
  Rag Trade
  Tiger's Heart, The
  In sequence: <Saga>
    Eagles
    Proprietor's Daughter, The

O'REILLY, Jackson   <HO>
     [James O. Rigney, Jr.]
  Cheyenne Raiders   <AIS:#6>

ORFORD, Ellen   <GOT>
    [William Delligan]
  Bride Of Raven Island, The
  Maze, The
  Sutter House, The

ORMSBY, Patricia
  Masquerade:
    19 Joanna
    28 Set To Partners
    36 Heir Presumptive
    52 Elusive Marriage, The
    68 Lysander's Lady

ORR, Alice Harron
       (Elizabeth Allison)
        (Morgana Starr)
  Harlequin Intrigue:
    56 Sabotage

ORR, Helen   <GOT>
  Web Of Days   <CGS:#19>

ORR, Kathleen
         (Kathy Orr)
      (Catherine Spencer)

ORR, Kathy
        [Kathleen Orr]
  Candlelight Ecstasy:
    460 Seductive Deceiver
    486 Drifter's Revenge, The
    522 An Invitation To Love

ORR, Mary
        [Mary Orr Denham]
  Grass Widows
  Rich Girl, Poor Girl
  Tejera Secrets, The

ORR, Zelma
  Harlequin American Romance:
    7 Miracles Take Longer
    18 In The Eyes Of Love
    55 Love Is A Fairy Tale
    82 Measure Of Love
    94 Someone Else's Heart
    111 From This Day
    124 Where Fires Once Burned
  Harlequin Intrigue:
    12 Night Shadows

ORTEGA, Isabel
       (Phyllis Leonard)
      (Phyllis G. Leonard)

ORWIG, Sara
        (Daisy Logan)
  Family Fortunes
  Favors Of The Rich
  Flight To Paradise

OSBORNE, Louise   <GOT><RS>
  Keys Of Hell
  Rite Of The Damned
  Satan Stone, The
  Witches' Ladder, The

———————————————————

———————————————————

OSBORNE, Maggie   <HR>
       [Margaret Ellen Osborne]
       (Margaret St. George)
  Alexa
  Chase The Heart
  Portrait In Passion
  Salem's Daughter
  Yankee Princess
  Rapture Romance:
    66 Flight Of Fancy
  Scarlet Ribbons: <HR>
  Rage To Love

———————————————————

———————————————————

OSBURN, Jesse
       [Candice F. Ransom]
  First Love From Silhouette: <YA>
    130 Nightshade
    175 Blackbird Keep
    183 Marigold Beach

———————————————————

———————————————————

OSSANA, Susan w/ Kristine BURTON
       (Susanna Christie)

OSTRANDER, Kate   <GOT>
  Dance With A Ghost
  Ghosts Of Ballyduff, The
  Image Seller, The
  Love's Tender Tears   <CO>
  Ring Of Darkness
  Sea Tower, the
  Specter Of The Dunes, The

———————————————————

———————————————————

O'SULLIVAN, Ellen
  MacFadden Romance:
    2 Widow And The Wanderer,The

———————————————————

OTT, Patricia   <HR>
  Bitter Passion, Sweet Love

———————————————————

OUST, Gail
       (Elizabeth Turner)
OUTLAW-SHALLIT, Louise Lee
       (Juliet Ashby)
       (Lee Canaday)
OVERFIELD, Joan/Joan E.   <RE>
  Prodigal Spinster, The
  In sequence:
    Journals Of Lady X, The
    Her Ladyship's Man
  American Regency Romance:
    Cabinetmaker's Daughter, The
    Charleston Tangle

———————————————————

———————————————————

OVERHOLTZER, Merle C.
  Avalon:
    Nurse Loreen's Nightmare

———————————————————

———————————————————

OVSTEDAL, Barbara
       (Rosalind Laker)
       (Barbara Paul)**
  ** (DO NOT confuse this pseudonym
       with that of another author)

OWEN, Ann
  Silhouette Romance:
    41 Sands Of Time, The

OWEN, Wanda   <HR>
  Deceptive Desires
  Ecstasy's Fancy
  Kiss Of Fire
  Moonlit Splendor
  Reckless Ecstasy
  Savage Fury
  Summer Splendor
  Texas Captive
  Texas Wildfire
  In sequence:
    Captain's Vixen, The
    Rapture's Bounty
  In sequence:
    Golden Gypsy
    Golden Ecstasy

OWENS, Marrissa
  Silhouette Intimate Moments:
    95 Dangerous Charade

OXLEY, Gillian
                    (Kerry Vine)

PACE, Alison
  Avalon:
    Sweet Deception
    That Touch Of Magic

PACE, DeWanna   <HR>
  So Close To The Flame
  Surrender Sweet Stranger

PACE, Laurel
              [Barbara M. Wojhoski]
  Harlequin American Romance:
    192 On Wings Of Love
    220 When Hearts Dream
    312 Island Magic
    370 May Wine, September Moon

PACE, Miriam   <HR>
  New Orleans Saga:
    1 New Orleans   <CofCWS>
    2 Delta Desire   <CofCWS>

PACKER, Joy   (Deceased)<GOT>
              [Joy Petersen Packer]
  Home From Sea
  Man In The Mews, The
  Moon By Night, The
  Valley Of The Vines

PACOTTI, Pamela   <GOT><RS>
  Lost Heiress Of Merriott Manor

PACOTTI, Pamela (cont.)
  Legacy Of Secrets
  Winds Of Desire

PADE, Victoria
  Harlequin Historical <Set#2>:
    53 Doubletree, The
  The Avon Romance:
    Ladylight
    Passion's Torment
    Reckless Yearning
    When Love Remains
  Silhouette Special Edition:
    402 Breaking Every Rule
    473 Devine Decadence
    502 Shades And Shadows
    527 Shelter From The Storm
    558 Twice Shy
    600 Something Special
    629 Out On A Limb

PADGET, Meg   <GOT>
  House Of Strangers

PAGE, Betsy
              [Bettie Wilhite]
  Harlequin Presents:
    965 Arrangement, The
  Harlequin Romance:
    2627 Bonded Heart, The
    2704 Dark-Night Encounter
          (M&B: Dark-Night Stranger)
    2730 Wyomian, The

PAGE, Vicki   <GOT>
              [Ruby Avey]
  House Of Harron, The

PAIGE, Laurie
[Olivia M. Hall]
Silhouette Desire:
123 Gypsy Enchantment
195 Journey To Desire
304 Misty Splendor
404 Golden Promise
Silhouette Romance:
296 South Of The Sun
333 Tangle Of Rainbows, A
364 Season Of Butterflies, A
382 Nothing Lost
398 Sea At Dawn, The
Homeward Bound:
727 Season For Homecoming, A
733 Home Fires Burning Bright
772 Man Fron The North
Country   <WITS>
Silhouette Special Edition:
170 Lover's Choice

PAIGE, Leslie   <GOT>
Dying Embers
House Possessed, A
Queen Of Hearts
She Walks In Shadow

PAINE, Lauran Bosworth
(Kathleen Bartlett)
(Beth Gorman)
(Arlene Morgan)
(Helen Sharp)
PAISLEY, Rebecca   <HR>
[Rebecca Boado Rosas]
The Avon Romance:
Barefoot Bride, The
Moonlight And Magic

PALA, Dolores
In Search Of Mihailo
Trumpet For A Walled City

PALENCIA, Elaine Fowler
(Laurel Blake)
Candlelight:
623 Heart On Holiday   <RO>

PALL, Ellen Jane
(Fiona Hill)

PALMER, Catherine
Burning Plains, The   <HR>
Wild Winds, The   <HR>
Silhouette Intimate Moments;
367 Land Of Enchantment

PALMER, Diana
[Susan Spaeth Kyle]
(see Silhouette Christmas Stories)
(see Silhouette Summer Sizzlers)
MacFadden Romance:
MacFadden Romances by this
author have been reprinted
as "Duets".
Duets:
1 Sweet Enemy   <McF179>
Love On Trial   <McF218>
2 Storm Over The Lake <McF139>
To Love And Cherish <McF256>
3 If Winter Comes   <McF>
Now And Forever   <McF127>
4 After The Music   <SR406>
Dream's End   <McF223>
5 Bound By A Promise <McF250>
Passion Flower   <SR328>
6 To Have And To Hold <McF150>
The Cowboy And The Lady
<SD12>
Silhouette Classic:
10 Heather's Song   (SE33)&
Silhouette Desire:
12 Cowboy And The Lady, The &
26 September Morning

514

PAPPANO, Marilyn
(see Silhouette Christmas Stories)
Silhouette Intimate Moments:
  182 Within Reach
  214 Lights Of Home, The
  233 Guilt By Association   &
  258 Cody Daniels' Return
  268 Room At The Inn
  294 Something Of Heaven   &
  310 Somebody's Baby
  338 Not Without Honor
  363 Safe Haven

PAQUIN, Ethel
Halequin Temptation:
  44 Summer Wine

PARADISE, Mary   <GOT>
                [Dorothy Eden]
Face Of An Angel
Marriage Chest, The
Shadow Of A Witch

PARADISO, Karen w/ Nancy HARLOW
                  (Ann Lynn)

PARENTEAU, Shirley
    [Shirley Laurolyn Parenteau]
Vulnerable   <CO>
Harlequin Historical <Set#2>:
  34 Hemlock Feathers
Love & Life:
  Hot Springs

PARETTI, Sandra   <HR>
Drums Of Winter, The
Fields Of Battle
Magic Ship, The
Maria Canossa

PARETTI, Sandra (cont.)
Rose And The Sword, The
Tenants Of The Earth
Wishing Tree, The

PARGETER, Edith
        [Edith Mary Pargeter]
              (Ellis Peters)
Brothers Of Gwynedd Quartet, The
Marriage Of Meggotta, The
Trilogy:
  Heaven Tree, The
  Green Branch
  Bloody Field, The

PARGETER, Margaret
Harlequin Presents:
  145 Stormy Rapture
  366 Savage Possession
  431 Dark Oasis, The
  453 Boomerang Bride
  503 Collision
  523 Loving Slave, The
  540 Not Far Enough
  548 Storm Cycle
  572 Prelude To A Song
  580 Substitute Bride
  588 Clouded Rapture
  595 Man From The Kimberleys
  620 Demetrious Line, The
  638 Caribbean Gold
  653 Chains Of Regret
  660 Storm In The Night
  788 Total Surrender
  813 Captive Of Fate
  821 Born Of The Wind
  845 Impasse
  861 Model Of Deception, A
Harlequin Romance:
  1899 Winds From The Sea
  1951 Ride A Black Horse
  1973 Kilted Stranger, The
  2022 Hold Me Captive
  2058 Blue Skies, Dark Waters

PARGETER, Margaret (cont.)
2112 Never Go Back
2140 Flamingo Moon
2168 Wild Inheritance
2183 Better To Forget
2193 Midnight Magic
2211 Jewelled Caftan, the
2227 Wild Rowan, The
2241 Man Called Cameron, A
2260 Marriage Impossible
2284 Only You
2296 Devil's Bride, The
2350 Autumn Song
2375 Kiss Of A Tyrant
2409 Dark Surrender
2416 Deception
2422 Captivity
2475 At First Glance
2613 Silver Flame, The

PARIS, Ann   <GOT>
                [Orania Papazoglou]
Arrowheart
Graven Image

PARK, Anne
Sweet Dreams: <YA>
   19 Love Song
   43 Tender Loving Care
   83 Love By The Book

PARK, Ruth
                [Rosina Ruth Park]
Swords And Crowns And
   Rings   <Saga>

PARKER, Beatrice   <GOT><RS>
                [Tom E. Huff]
Betrayal At Blackcrest
Come To Castlemoor

PARKER, Beatrice (cont.)
Jamintha
Stranger By The Lake
Wherever Lynn Goes

PARKER, Cynthia
SuperRomance:
   100 Tiger Eyes

PARKER, Karen Blair w/
        Mary Kathryn SCAMEHORN
                (Kathryn Blair)
                (Blair Cameron)

PARKER, Laura   <HO><HR>
                [Laura Castoro]
Jim Bridger: Mountain Man<AES:#3>
Kit Carson: Trapper King <AES:#6>
Rebellious Angels
Silks And Sabers
Wilder Love, A
Rose Trilogy:
   Rose Of the Mist
   Rose In Splendor, A
   Secret Rose, The
Finding Mr. Right:
   Until Love Is Enough
Silhouette Special Edition:
   137 Perfect Choice, The
   203 Dangerous Company
Tapestry: <HR>
   16 Emerald And Sapphire
   36 Moth And Flame

PARKER, Norah   <HR>
                [Eleanor Parker Hodgson]
Sweet Surrender
Wild Splendid Love
Heartfire Romance: <HR>
   Gyspy Lover

PARKER, Robert B.
       [Robert Brown Parker]
  Love & Glory

PARKHURST, Jane
  Isobel
  Southern Moon, The   <Saga>

PARKIN, Bernadette   <HR>
  Nate's Lady
  Sweet Barbarian

PARKINSON, Cornelia M. w/
          Sharon SALVATO
  [Cornelia McNary Parkinson w/
    Sharon Anne Zetler Salvato]
            (Day Taylor)

PARMETT, Doris
  Loveswept:
    234 Stiff Competition   &
    267 Made For Each Other
    316 Diamond In The Rough &
    349 Sassy
    388 Heartthrob
    412 Off Limits
        Sweet Mischief

PARNELL, Andrea   <GOT>
  Dark Splendor
  Delilah's Flame
  Lovespell
  Whispers At Midnight
  Lovestruck:
    Wild Glory
  Silhouette Intimate Moments:
    250 Silver Swan, The

PARRIS, Laura
           [Laura Magner]
  Harlequin American Romance:
    60 High Valley Of The Sun

PARRISH, Barney
  Big Night At Mrs. Maria's
  Closed Circle, The

PARRISH, Laura
        [Elizabeth Graham]
  Avalon:
    Love's Gentle Season
    Love's Quiet Corner

PARRISH, Patt
        [Patt Bucheister]
  Circle Of Love:
    24 Sheltered Haven, The
    33 His Fierce Angel
  Dawnstar Romance:
    Gift To Cherish, A
  Harlequin Temptation:
    85 Lifetime Affair
  Judy Sullivan Books:
    Escape The Past

PARTAIN, Floydene
  Caribbean Chronicles:
    1 Crying In The Wilderness

PARV, Valerie
  Harlequin Presents:
    1229 Man Without A Past
    1260 Tasmanian Devil
  Harlequin Romance:
    2589 Tall Dark Stranger

PASCOE, Irene
                    [Irene M. Pascoe]
                    (Andrea Haley)
Harlequin Gothic Romance:
Lord Of High Cliff Manor
Shadow Over Bright Star

PASTERNAK, Boris   (Deceased)
    Doctor Zhizago   <HO>

_____

_____

PASTOREK, Alba Marie
    Avalon:
        Fashioned For Love

_____

PATRICK, Ann
    Metor Kismet:
        17   Opening Act

_____

_____

PATRICK, DeAnn
        [Dorothy Corcoran w/
              Mary Ann Slojkowski]
    Tapestry: <HR>
        Kindred Spirit
        18   Montana Brides

_____

_____

PATRICK, Lynn
        [Patricia Pinianski
                w/ Linda Sweeney]
    Candlelight Ecstasy:
        276   Perfect Affair, The
        334   More Than A Dream
        390   Mistletoe Magic
        428   Just A Lot More To Love
    Candlelight Ecstasy Supreme:
        87   Double Or Nothing
    Candlelight Supreme:
        142   Mystery In The Moonlight
        168   Gentleman Farmer, The
        180   Mermaid's Touch, The
    Harlequin SuperRomance:
        343   Good Vibrations
        421   Marriage Project, The
        461   Cheek To Cheek

_____

_____

PATRICK, Maxine
              [Patricia Maxwell]
    April Of Enchantment
    Bayou Bride
    Captive Kisses
    Snowbound Heart
    Adventures In Love:
        8   Abducted Heart, The
        12 Love At Sea

_____

PATTEN, Darlene
    Silhouette Romance:
        570   Half-Dozen Reasons, A

_____

PATTERSON, Betty Ann
                      (Vickie York)

PATTERSON, Morgan
    Harlequin Romance:
        2667   Darker Fire

_____

PATTERSON, Sarah
    Distant Summer, The

_____

PATTISON, Nancy
                      (Nan Asquith)
                      (Susan Broome)

PATTISON, Olive Ruth
                      (Ruth Abbey)

PATTON, Oliver B.   <HO>
              [Oliver Beirne Patton]
    Hollow Mountains, The
    Mojave Design, The
    My Heart Turns Back
    Western Wind

_____

_____

PATTON, Sarah
          (Genevieve English)

PAUL, Barbara   <RS>
          [Barbara Ovstedal]
Devil's Fire, Love's Revenge
Frenchwoman, The
Seventeenth Stair, The
To Love A Stranger

PAUL, Barbara
An Exercise For Madmen
Bibblings
Fourth Wall, The
Pillars Of Salt
Under The Canopy

PAUL, Charlotte
          [Charlotte Paul Reese]
Child Is Missing, A
Gold Mountain
Hear My Heart Speak
Image, The
Phoenix Island
Seattle   <HS>
Wild Valley

PAUL, Danielle
          [Helen Mittermeyer]
Harlequin Temptation:
13 Chameleon

PAUL, Paula/Paula G.   <RS>
Dateline: Danger!
Wail Of La Llorona, the
Avalon:
  Inn Of The Clowns

PAUL, Paula (cont.)
Harlequin Intrigue:
47 Silent Partner
67 Night Of The Jaguar

PAUL, Phyllis   <GOT>
Echo Of Guilt
Twice Lost

PAUL, Wynne
Sapphire Romance:
  Room With A View

PAULEY, Barbara Anne   <GOT>
Blood Kin
Voices Long Hushed

PAULOS, Sheila
Candlelight Ecstasy:
  75 Champagne And Red Roses
  108 Wild Roses
  189 Love's Madness
  230 Heaven's Embrace
  261 Give And Take
  307 Off Limits
  344 Till Morning's Light
  370 So Much To Give
  416 With Every Kiss

PAULSON, Tim
Success Story   <CO>

PAVLIK, Evelyn Marie w/ Jane Fay
     HONG   (Adora Sheridan)

PAXTON, Jean   <RE>
      [Martha Jean Powers]
  American Regency Romance:
      Divided Loyalty

PAXTON, Lois   <GOT>
      [Lois Dorothea Low]
  Man Who Died Twice, The
  Quiet Sound Of Fear, The
  Who Goes There?

PAYES, Rachel Cosgrove
      [Rachel Ruth Cosgrove Payes]
              (Rachel Cosgrove)
                 (Joanne Kaye)
          <GOT><HR><RE><RS>
  Black Swan, The
  Bride Of Fury
  Coach To Hell, The
  Devil's Court
  Forbidden Island
  House Of Tarot
  Malverne Hall
  Moment Of Desire
  Peace Corps Nurse
  Sapphire Legacy, The
  Satan's Mistress
  Silent Place, The
  Seven Sisters Regency:
      1 Love's Charade
      2 Love's Renegade
      3 Love's Promenade
      4 Love's Serenade
      5 Love's Escapade
  Avalon:
      Death Sleeps Lightly
      Memoirs Of Murder
  Harlequin Regency Romance:
      Lady Alicia's Secret
  Starlight Romance:
      Emeralds And Jade

PAYNE, Charlotte
                    [Charles O'Neal]
  Bitter Promise
  Glitterati, The   <CO>
  Lord Of The River

PAYNE, Oliver   <HO>
  Northwest Territory Series:
      In sequence:
          Warpath
          Conquest
          Defiance
          Rebellion
          Conflict
          Triumph
          Betrayal
          Honor

PAYNE, Rachel Ann   <GOT>
  Ghostwind

PAYNE, Tiffany
  Silhouette Romance:
      283 Stirring's Of The Heart

PEAKE, Lilian
  Harlequin Presents:
      113 Man Of Granite
      120 Till The End Of Time
      136 Sun Of Summer, The
      150 Tender Night, The
      157 Distant Dream, The
      166 Familiar Stranger
      186 Bitter Loving, A
      190 This Man Her Enemy
      198 No Friend Of Mine
      206 Little Imposter, The

PEARSON, John (cont.)
  Love Is Most Mad And Moonly
  Magic Doors
  Sun's Birthday, The
  To Be Nobody Else

_____

PEARSON, Michael   <HO>
  Store, The
  Keys Of The City, The

_____

PEART, Jane   <GOT><RS>
  Night Of The Darkest Moon
  Vintage Evil
  Candlelight:
    568 Spanish Masquerade   <RO>
    653 Portrait In Shadows   <RO>
  Heavenly Romance: <YA>
    It's Your Move, Lori
  Promise Romance: <Insp>
    4 Love Takes Flight
   11 Sign Of The Carousel
   15 Scent Of Heather, A
   25 Autumn Encore
  Serenade/Saga: <HR><Insp>
    8 Yankee Bride
   14 Rebel Bride
   18 Valiant Bride
   36 Ransomed Bride

_____

_____

PECK, Maggie
                [Marjorie Price]
  Second Chance At Love:
    151 Moonlight On The Bay

_____

_____

PECK, Nancy B.
  Second Chance

_____

PECK, Richard
  Amanda/Miranda   <HR>
  Close Enough To Touch
  New York Time   <CO>
  Representing Super Doll
  This Family Of Women   <Saga>
  Those Summer Girls I Never Met
  Through A Brief Darkness

_____

_____

PEDERSON, Gloria
  Nighthawk's Embrace

_____

PEDERSON, Rachael Field
                (Rachael Field)

PEISER, Maria Lilli
                (Lilli Palmer)

PELFREY, Judy
                (Judith Daniels)
                (Rhett Daniels)

PELL, Sylvia
  Shadow Of The Sun, The
  Sun Princess, The

_____

_____

PELLA, Judith
                (see Michael R. Phillips)

PELLICANE, Patricia   <HR>
  Creole Captive
  Deceptions Of The Heart
  Desire's Rebel
  Ecstasy's Treasure
  Embers Of Desire
  Frontier Temptress
  This Wild Heart
  Tapestry: <HR>
    42 Charity's Pride
    62 Whispers In The Wind
    85 Sweet Revenge

_____

_____

PELTON, Sonya T.   <HR>
  Awake Savage Heart
  Bittersweet Bondage
  Captive Chains
  Dakota Flame
  Love, Hear My Heart
  Passion's Paradise
  Phantom Love
  Tiger Rose
  Wild Island Sands
  Windswept Passion
  In sequence:
    Texas Tigress
    Captive Caress
  In sequence:
    Forbidden Dawn
    Twilight Temptress

PELTONEN, Carla w/ Molly SWANTON
  [Carla Friedenberg Peltonen
          w/ Molly Butler Swanton]
                  (Lynn Erickson)

PEMBERTON, Margaret   <CO><HR><RS>
  Flower Garden, The
  Goddess (Eng: Silver Shadows,
    Golden Dreams)
  Guilty Secret, The
  Multitude Of Sins, A
  Never Leave Me
  Rendezvous With Danger
  Shadows Over Silver Sands
  Some Distant Shore
  Masquerade:
    73 Lion Of Languedoc

PEMBERTON, Nan   <RE>
                    [Nina Pykare]
  Cotillion Regency:
    4 Love's Delusion

PENCE, Joanne
  Silhouette Intimate Moments:
    219 Armed And Dangerous

PENDER, Laura
  Harlequin Intrigue:
    62   Taste Of Treason
    70   Hit And Run
    91   Traitor's Dispatch
    108 Sky Pirate
    142 Deja Vu

PENDLETON, Chris
  Too Soon Tomorrow

PENDLETON, Grace
                 [Margaret Boyer Mann]
  Silhouette Special Edition:
    579 Heartstrings

PENMAN, Sharon Kay   <HR>
  Falls The Shadow
  Here Be Dragons
  Sunne In Splendour, The

PENNINGTON, Jacqueline Elee
                  (Elee Landress)

PENNY, Julie
  Narcissa   <Saga>

PEPLOE, Dorothy Emily Stevenson
                        (Deceased)
                 (D. E. Stevenson)

526

PERCY, Karen
                              [Karen Pershing]
    Harlequin Temptation:
    260 Home Stretch, The

_____

_____

PEREZ-VENERO, Mirna
                              (Mirna Pierce)

PERKINS, Barbara
    Harlequin Romance:
    1374 Fortune's Lead
    1402 Dear Doctor Marcus
    1521 My Sisters And Me

_____

_____

PERKINS, Deborah
                              (Samantha Grey)

PERLBERG, Deborah
    Cliff House

_____

_____

PERRICHE, Marlene
    Avalon:
        Bride Of Windemere, The
        Carribbean Love Song
        Heart Triumphant, A
        Mansion Of Peril

_____

_____

PERRY, Michalann   <HR>
                              (Megan Blythe)
    Defiant Splendor
    Fortune's Choice
    Lakota Trilogy:
        Untamed Surrender
        Captive Surrender
        Savage Rogue
    Love's Windswept Embrace

    Rapture's Deception

_____

_____

PERSHALL, Mary   <HR>
                              (Susan Shelley)
    Gold Coast   <CO>&
    In sequence: <Saga>
        Behold The Dream   &
        Forever The Dream   &
    Rose Quartet: <Saga>
        Shield Of Roses, A
        Dawn Of The White Rose
        Triumph Of Roses, A
        Roses Of Glory

_____

_____

PERSHING, Karen
                              (Karen Percy)
                              (Kerry Price)
    Harlequin American Romance:
    168 Opposites Attract

_____

_____

PERSHING, Marie
                    [Perle Henriksen Schultz]
    Candlelight:
    531 First A Dream   <RO>
    553 Maybe Tomorrow   <RO>
    Starlight Romance:
        Handful Of Stars

_____

_____

PETERS, Anne
                              [Anne Hansen]
    Silhouette Desire:
    497 Like Wildfire
    739 Through Thick And Thin

_____

_____

PETERS, Clarice   <RE>
                              [Laureen Kwock]
    False Betrothal, The
    Rosalind
    Roxanne
    Samantha
    Thea

PETERS, Clarice (cont.)
Harlequin Regency Romance:
   Contrary Lovers
  2 Marquis And The Miss, The
 11 Vanessa
 23 Prescott's Lady

PETERS, Elizabeth   <GOT><RS>
       [Barbara Gross Mertz]
Copenhagen Connection, The
Dead Sea Cipher, The
Devil-May-Care
Her Cousin John
Jackal's Head, The
Legend In Green Velvet
Love Talker, The   <SN>
Naked Once More
Night Of Four Hundred Rabbits,The
Scroll Of Wadi Qumran, The
Summer Of The Dragon
In sequence:
  Crocodile On The Sandbank
  Curse Of The Pharaohs, The
  Mummy Case, The
  Lion In The Valley
Jacqueline Kirby Series:
  Seventh Sinner, The
  Murders Of Richard III, The
  Die For Love
Victoria Bliss/John Smythe Ser.
  Borrower The Night
  Camelot Caper, The
  Street Of The Five Moons
  Silhouette In Scarlet

PETERS, Ellis   <GOT><RS><HO>
       [Edith Pargeter]
City Of Gold And Shadows
Death And The Joyful Woman
Fifth Chronicle Of
  Brother Cadfael, The
Grass-Widow's Tale, The
Horn Of Roland, The

PETERS, Ellis (cont.)
House Of Green Turf, The
Knocker On Death's Door, The
Leper Of St. Giles, The
Mourning Raga
Never Pick Up Hitch-Hikers
Piper On The Mountain, The
Rainbow's End
Virgin In The Ice, A

PETERS, Jennifer
Promise Broken, A

PETERS, Louise
MacFadden Romance:
 173 Dreams Never Die

PETERS, Maureen   <HO>
      (Veronica Black)
      (Catherine Darby)
      (Elizabeth Law)
Destiny's Lady
Enigma Of The Brontes
Henry The Eighth & His Six Wives
Princess Of Desire
Queen Who Never Was, The
Virgin Queen, The

PETERS, Natasha
      [Anastasia Cleaver]
Darkness Into Light
Enticers, The
Immortals, The
Splendid Torment
Wild Nights
In sequence:
  Savage Surrender
  Dangerous Obsession

PETERS, Sue
                    (Angela Carson)
  Harlequin Romance:
  1850 Storm Within, The
  1874 Design For Destiny
  1916 Wheels Of Conflict
  1959 Deep Furrows
  1975 Clouded Waters
  2030 One Special Rose
  2104 Portrait Of Paradise
  2156 Lure Of The Falcon
  2204 Entrance To The Harbour
  2351 Shadow Of An Eagle
  2368 Claws Of A Wildcat
  2410 Marriage In Haste
  2423 Tug Of War
  2471 Dangerous Rapture
  2501 Man Of Teak
  2583 Lightning Strikes Twice
  2812 Never Touch A Tiger
  2892 Entrance To Eden
  2915 Capture A Nightingale
  2938 One-Woman Man
  3018 Unwilling Woman

PETERS, Valerina
  Competition For Alan, The

PETERSON, Christmas
  [Jon Peterson w/ Joyce Christmas]
  Hidden Assets

PETERSON, Laura
  Promise Of The Heart

PETITCLERC, Dennel Bart
  Rage Of Honor
  (see Peter Bart)

PETKUS, Peggy Murphy
  Millionaire's Row

PETRATUR, Joyce
                    (Joyce Verrette)

PETRI, David
  Curtain Of Night, The

PETRIE, Glen   <HR>
  Branch Bearers, The
  Marianne

PETRON, Angela
  Prelude To Happiness

PETTY, Elizabeth
  Beloved Stranger
  Love Of Sister Nichole, The <M&B>

PFISTERER, Sally
                    (Anne Laurence)

PHILLIPS, Barbara
  Spitfire

PHILLIPS, Dorothy
                    [Dorothy Garlock]
  Nicki
  Candlelight Ecstasy:
    71 Marriage To A Stranger
   411 Sing Softly To Me
   458 She Wanted Red Velvet

PHILLIPS, Erin
First Love From Silhouette: <YA>
96 Research For Romance

_____

_____

PHILLIPS, Jean   <GOT>
Greenwood
Hermit's Island
House Of Darkness

_____

_____

PHILLIPS, Jill M.   <HO>
[Jill Meta Phillips]
Rain Maiden, The

_____

_____

PHILLIPS, Johanna
[Dorothy Garlock]
Second Chance At Love:
20 Gentle Torment
30 Amber-Eyed Man
43 Strange Posession
88 Passion's Song
125 Hidden Dreams

_____

_____

PHILLIPS, Laura
Meteor Kismet:
22 Never Let Go

_____

_____

PHILLIPS, Lyn
[James Scafidel]
Dark Desire Romance: <RS>
If The Flesh Be Willing

_____

_____

PHILLIPS, Michael R. w/Judith PELLA
Heather Hills Of Stonewycke
Lady Of Stonewycke, The

_____

_____

PHILLIPS, Pat
[Patricia Phillips]
Avalon: <RS>
Invitation To Danger
Lady Of The Moor
Love Waits At Penrhyn
Mediterranean Adventure

_____

_____

PHILLIPS, Patricia   <HR>
[Patricia Sonia Powell Phillips]
(Pat Phillips)
(Sonia Phillips)
Anise
Captive Flame
Flame Of Love
Jenny
Love's Defiant Prisoner
Marie Fleur   <RE>
More Precious Than Gold
My Soul With Thine
Rose And The Flame, The
Royal Captive
Touch Me With Fire

_____

_____

PHILLIPS, Sonia   <HO>
[Patricia Phillips]
Beatrice
Girl In The Yellow Dress
Venetian Spring

_____

_____

PHILLIPS, Susan
Promise Romance:
21 Honorable Intentions   <Insp>
Serenade/Serenata: <Insp>
35 Lessons Of Love, The
Silhouette Romance:
470 Sheer Honesty

_____

_____

530

PHILLIPS, Susan   <HR>
    [Susan Leslie Phillips]
Rapture's Legacy   <AAS>
_____

_____

PHILLIPS, Susan w/ Claire KIEHL
                    (Justine Cole)

PHILLIPS, Susan Elizabeth
    Fancy Pants
    Glitter Baby
    Risen Glory   <HR>
_____

_____

PHILLIPSON, Sandra
    McFadden Romance:
        11 Moonlight Interlude
        17 Enchanted Twilight
        46 Time To Dream, A
        51 Turn Back The Dawn
        87 Heiress And The
            Highlander, The
       105 Wish And A Promise, A
       130 First And Only Love
       143 Castaway Heart, The
       185 In The Arms Of Love
       212 Where Love May Lead
       228 Fountain Of Love, The
       236 Capture The Dream
       236 Wild Roses Red Wine
       261 Gypsy Heart
_____

_____

PIANKA, Phyllis/Phyllis Taylor
    [Phyllis Fay Taylor Pianka]
                    (Winter Ames)
    Sharon Garrison, Clinic Nurse
    Avalon:
        Nurse Of The Island
    Candlelight: <RE>
       517 Golden Pirate, The <RO>
       543 Sleeping Heiress, The
       627 Paisley Butterfly,The
       696 Heather Wild

PIANKA, Phyllis (cont.)
    Harlequin Intrigue:
        16 Midsummer Madness
    Harlequin Regency Romance:
            Dame Fortune's Fancy
            Midnight Folly
         3 Tart Shoppe, The
        34 Calico Countess, The
        48 Lark's Nest, The
_____

_____

PICANO, Felice   <RS>
    Eyes
    House Of Cards
    Late In The Season
    Lure, The
    Mesmerist, The
    Smart As The Devil
_____

_____

PICKART, Joan Elliot
                    (Robin Elliott)
    Lovestruck:
        Family Secrets   <CO>
    Doubleday Loveswept:
        Bonnie Blue, The
    Loveswept:
        61 Breaking All The Rules
        74 Charade
        80 Finishing Touch, The
        85 All The Tomorrows
        90 Look For The Sea Gulls
        94 Waiting For Prince
            Charming
        99 Fascination
       105 Shadowless Day, The
       110 Sunlight's Promise   &
       114 Rainbow's Angel   &
       116 Midnight Ryder
       138 Eagle Catcher, The
       146 Journey's End
       153 Mister Lonelyhearts
       162 Secrets of Autumn
       166 Listen For The Drummer
       179 Kaleidoscope
       190 Wild Poppies

PICKER, Rita
                    (Martina Sultan)

PIEPER, Kathleen
  Avalon:
    Hidden Heritage
    Kiss For Samantha, A
    Summer Kisses
    To Know Love

PIERCE, Georgia w/ Linda CHESNUTT
                    (Lindsey Hanks)

PIERCE, Mirna   <HR>
                [Mirna Perez-Venero]
    Panama Flame
    Panama Glory

PIERCE, Noel   <RS>
    Messenger From Munich
    Praetorius Point

PIERCE, Richard   <GOT>
             [Richard Austin Pierce]
    Kiss My Aztec
    Other Side Of Hate, The
    Run, Traitor Run
    Tremble Of A Hand

PIERCY, Marge
    Fly Away Home
    Gone To Soldiers
    Summer People

PIERLAIN, Nell
    Mystique:
      125 Cruel Triumph

PILCHER, Rosamunde
                     (Jane Fraser)
    Another View
    Carousel, The
    Day Of The Storm, The
    Empty House, The
    End Of Summer, The
    On My Own
    Secret To Tell, A

PILCHER, Rosamunde (cont.)
  September   &

PILCHER, Rosamunde (cont.)
- September &
- Shell Seekers, The   `<Saga>`&
- Sleeping Tiger
- Snow In April
- Under Gemini
- Voices In Summer
- Wild Mountain Thyme

PINCHOT, Ann
                 [Ann Kramer Pinchot]
- An Independent Heart
- Certain Rich Girls
- Doctors And Wives
- Love Will Find Me
- Luck Of The Linscotts, The
- Man Chasers, The
- Once More With Feeling
- Rival To My Heart
- Vanessa

PINDRUS, Nancy Elaine   `<HS>`
- Love To Match These Mountains, A

PINES, Nancy
- Sweet Dreams: `<YA>`
    55   Spotlight On Love

PINIANSKI, Patricia
               (RoseAnne McKenna)
               (Patricia Rosemoor)

PINIANSKI, Patricia w/Linda SWEENEY
               (Lynn Patrick)

PIPKIN, Denice
               (Denice Greenlea)

PITT, Jane
- Heartlines: `<YA>`
    2   Secret Hearts

PITTINGER, Virginia   `<GOT>`
- Wait Until Midnight

PLAGAKIS, Jim
               (Christy Dore)

PLAGEMANN, Bentz   `<GOT>`
- Boxwood Maze, The
- Wolfe's Cloister

PLAIDY, Jean   `<HO>`
         [Eleanor Burford Hibbert]
- General Historical Novels:
  Beyond The Blue Mountains
  Daughter Of Satan
  Defenders Of The Faith
  Goldsmith's Wife, The
  Scarlet Cloak, The
- Stories Of Victorian England:
  It Began In Vauxhall Gardens
  Lilith
- Tudor Novels:
  Katharine Of Aragon:
    Katharine, The Virgin Widow
    Shadow Of The Pomegranate,The
    King's Secret Matter
  Murder Most Royal
  St. Thomas's Eve
  Sixth Wife, The
  Thistle And The Rose
  Mary, Queen Of France
  Spanish Bridegroom, The
  Gay Lord Robert
- Ferdinand And Isabella Trilogy:
  Castle For Isabella
  Spain For The Sovereigns
  Daughter Of Spain

PLAIDY, Jean (cont.)
  French Revolution Trilogy:
    Louis The Well-Beloved
    Road To Compiegne, The
    Flaunting, Extravagent Queen
  Georgian Saga:
    Princess Of Celle, The
    Queen In Waiting
    Caroline The Queen
    Prince And The Quakeress, The
    Third George, The
    Perdita's Prince
    Sweet Lass Of Richmond Hill
    Indiscretions Of The Queen
    Regent's Daughter, The
    Goddess Of The Green Room
    Victoria In The Wings
  Henri Of Navarre:
    Evergreen Gallant
  Lucrezia Borgia Series:
    Madonna Of The Seven Hills
    Light On Lucrezia
  Mary Queen Of Scots Series:
    Royal Road To Fotheringay
    Captive Queen Of Scots, The
  Medici Trilogy:
    Madame Serpent
    Italian Woman, The
    Queen Jezebel
  Norman Trilogy:
    Bastard King, The
    Lion Of Justice, The
    Passionate Enemies, The
  Plantagenet Saga:
    Plantagenet Prelude, The
    Revolt Of The Eaglets, The
    Heart Of The Lion, The
    Prince Of Darkness, The
    Battle Of The Queens, The
    Queen From Provence, The
    Hammer Of The Scots
    Follies Of The King, The
    Vow On The Heron, The
    Passage To Pontefract
    Star Of Lancaster, The
    Epitaph For Three Women
    Red Rose Of Anjou
    Sun In Splendor, The
    Edward Longshanks
    Uneasy Lies The Head

PLAIDY, Jean (cont.)
  Queen Victoria Series:
    Captive Of Kensington Palace
    Queen And Lord M, The
    Queen's Husband, The
    Widow Of Windsor, The
  Queen Of England Series:
    Myself My Enemy
    Queen Of The Realm
    Victoria, Victorious
    Lady In The Tower, The
    Courts Of Love, The
    In The Shadow Of The Crown
    Queen's Secret, The
  Stuart Saga:
    Murder In The Tower, The
    Charles II:
      Wandering Prince, The
      Health Unto His Majesty, A
      Here Lies Our Sovereign Lord
    The Last Of The Stuarts:
      Three Crowns, The
      Haunted Sisters, The
      Queen's Favorites, The
  Non-Fiction:
    Fair Devil Of Scotland, The
    Triptych Of Poisoners, A
    The Spanish Inquisition:
      Rise Of The Spanish
        Inquisition
      Growth Of The Spanish
        Inquisition
      End Of The Spanish
        Inquisition
  Juvenile:
    Young Elizabeth, The
    Meg Roper, Daughter Of Sir
      Thomas More
    Young Mary Queen Of Scots, The

———————————————

———————————————

PLAIN, Belva   <HR>
  Blessings
  Crescent City
  Eden Burning
  Random Winds

PLAIN, Belva (cont.)
Werner Family Saga:
In Sequence:
Evergreen
Golden Cup, The
Tapestry
Harvest

PLOWDEN, Judith
Afterglow   <CO>

PLUM, Jennifer   <GOT>
[Michael Joseph Kurland]
Secret Of Benjamin Square, The

PLUMMER, Clare
[Clare Emsley Plummer]
Cruel Enchantment
Destroying Limelight, The
Destroying Passion, The

POGONY, Jean Coulter
(Catherine Coulter)

POHLE, Robert Warren Jr.
(Devon Lee)

POLCOVAR, Jane
Sweet Dreams: <YA>
82 Hey, Good Looking

POLK, Dora   <GOT>
[Dora Beale Polk]
House On The Black Moor, The

POLLACHEK, Ellin Ronnee   <CO>
Seasons

POLLAND, Madeleine A.
[Madeleine Angela Cahill Polland]
All Their Kingdoms
Children Of The Red King
Diedre
Heart Speaks Many Ways, The
Little Spot Of Bother, The
No Price Too High   <GOT>
Package To Spain
Sabrina
Shattered Summer
Thicker Then Water   <GOT>
To Tell My People

POLLEY, Judith   <HR>
[Judith Anne Polley]
Passion's Prisoner
Serpent And The Dove, The

POLLEY, Judith Anne
(Judith Hagar)
(Helen Kent-Eng)
(Valentina Luellen)
(Judith Stewart)

POLLOCK, Ida
(Susan Barrie)
(Jean Beaufort)
(Rose Burghley)
(Anita Charles)
(Pamela Kent)
(Barbara Rowen)
(Mary Whistler)

POLLOCK, Rosemary
Harlequin Romance:
1294 Breadth Of Heaven, The
1379 Touch Of Starlight, A
1542 Mountains Of Spring, The
1675 Song Above The Clouds
2067 Summer Comes Slowly
2219 Tiger In Darkness
2315 White Hibiscus
2486 Sun And Catriona, The

POLLOWITZ, Melinda
[Melinda Kilborn Pollowitz]
Sweet Dreams: <YA>
4 Princess Amy
34 Country Girl

PONDER, Patricia
[Patricia Maxwell]
Haven Of Fear
Murder For Charity

POOLE, Helen Lee   <HO>
Whitewater Dynasty: In sequence:
Hudson!
Ohio!
Cumberland!
Wabash!, The
Mississippi, The
Missouri, The

POORE, Dawn Aldredge   <HR>
Sweet Deceit

POPE, Pamela
Harlequin Presents:
525 Magnolia Siege, The
628 Eden's Law

POPE, Pamela (cont.)
Harlequin Romance:
2573 Candleberry Tree, The

POPKIN, Zelda   (Deceased)
[Zelda F. Popkin]
Dear Once
Death Of Innocence
Herman Had Two Daughters

PORTER, Donald   <HO>
[Donald Clayton Porter]
Apache War Cry   <AIS:#8>
Sioux Arrows   <AIS:#9>
Kiowa Fires   <AIS:#11>

PORTER, Donald Clayton   <HO>
(Donald Porter)
Day Of The Animals
Colonization Of America:
White Indian Series:
In sequence:
White Indian
Renegade, The
War Chief
Sachem, The
Renno
Tomahawk
War Cry
Ambush
Seneca
Cherokee
Choctaw
Seminole
War Drums
Apache
Spirit Knife
Manitou
Seneca Warrior
Father Of Waters
Fallen Timbers
Sachem's Son

PORTER, Donald Clayton (cont.)
Pony Express &
Winning The West Trilogy: &
   1 Rio Grande
   2 Fort Laramie
   3 Union Pacific

_____

_____

PORTER, John D.
Yesterday's Storm

_____

_____

PORTER, Joyce
Harlequin Intrigue:
   66 No Easy Answers
  127 Kaleidoscope

_____

_____

PORTER, Joyce w/ Deborah BRYSON
              (Deborah Joyce)

PORTER, Madeline w/ Shannon HARPER
       (Elizabeth Habersham)
         (Madeline Harper)
            (Anna James)

PORTER, Margaret
Starlight Romance:
  Heiress Of Ardara

_____

_____

PORTER, Margaret Evans   <RE>
Irish Autumn
Road To Ruin

_____

_____

PORTER, Nina   <RE>
    [Nina Coombs Pykare]
Design For Love
Heart In Flight, A
Miss Dudley's Dilemma

_____

_____

PORTERFIELD, Kay
         (Coleen Kimbrough)

PORTERFIELD, Marie
MacFadden Romance:
   83 This Love To Share
   91 Polynesian Song
 104 East Of Tomorrow
 109 Evensong
 114 Desert Lies Waiting, The
 123 Farewell To Yesterday
 138 Winding Path, The
 169 Blue Ridge Ballad
 172 Desert Flower
 193 Love Of Her Own
 211 Kiss For Luck, A
 237 Blue Twilight
 238 With This Ring
 238 As Long As We Love

_____

_____

POSNER, Richard
        (Beatrice Murray)

POST, Mary Brinker
Annie Jordan
Matt Regan's Lady

_____

_____

POTTER, Allison
MacFadden Romance:
   84 Springtime Heart, The
   94 Scarlet Blossoms
   97 Fallen Petals
 110 Silent Trees, The
 122 Midnight Sun
 137 Home To Stay
 177 Summer Winds
 237 Lady In Waiting
 259 When September Comes

_____

_____

POTTER, Jacqueline
        (Jane Ireland)

POZZESSERE, Heather Graham
        [Heather Elizabeth
         Graham Pozzessere]
         (Shannon Drake)
         (Heather Graham)
        (see HQ Christmas Stories)
Harlequin Historical <Set#2>:
  Slater Bros Trilogy:
    9   Dark Stranger
   19   Rides A Hero
   33   Apache Summer
   66   Forbidden Fire
Silhouette Classic:
   35   Night Moves   <IM118>
Silhouette Intimate Moments:
  118   Night Moves
  132   Di Medici Bride, The
  145   Double Entendre
  165   Game Of Love, The
  174   Matter Of Circumstance, A
  192   Bride Of The Tiger   &
  205   All In The Family
  220   King Of The Castle
  225   Strangers In Paradise
  248   Angel Of Mercy   &
  260   This Rough Magic
  265   Lucia In Love
  293   Borrowed Angel   &
  328   Perilous Eden, A
  340   Forever My Love
  352   Wedding Bell Blues

PRATE, Kit
          [Dorothy Howell]
Defiant Echantress
Wild Texas Winds
Woman Of Chicago, A   <AWD>

PRATT, Elizabeth Stuart
       (Elizabeth Stuart)

PREBLE, Amanda
      [Christine B. Tayntor]
Candlelight:
  647   Half-Heart   <RO>

PRENTICE, Wendy
Harlequin Presents:
 1342 Conditional Surrender

PRENTISS, Charlotte
Love's Savage Embrace

PRESSLEY, Hilda
Harlequin Petite:
    3 Journey To Love
Harlequin Romance:
  751 Night Superintendent
  788 Gentle Surgeon, The
  900 There Came A Surgeon
  932 Nurse's Dilemma
  987 Senior Staff Nurse
 1233 Love Of Her Own, A
 1295 Suddenly, It Was Spring
 1327 More Than Gold
 1389 Man Of The Forest
 1429 Man In Possession, The
 1469 To The Highest Bidder
 1509 Summer To Remember, A
 1565 Harbinger Of Spring
 1601 Newcomer, The
 1821 When Winter Has Gone
Other:
  New Registrar   <M&B>

PRESTIE, Taylor Caldwell (Deceased)
       (Taylor Caldwell)

PRESTON, Fayrene
                    (Jaelyn Conlee)
The Delaney Dynasty
The Untamed Years:
    In sequence:
        Copper Fire
        Silken Thunder
The Shanrock Trinity:
    Burke, The Kingpin   (LS#169)
The Delaneys Of Killaroo:
    Sydney, The Temptress
Loveswept
    4   Silver Miracles
    21 Seduction Of Jason, The   &
    34 For The Love Of Sami   &
    45 That Old Feeling
    98 Mississippi Blues
    107 Rachel's Confession
    133 Mysterious   &
    140 Fire In The Rain
    169 Burke, The Kingpin
    181 Robin and Her Merry People
    199 Allure
    244 Sapphire Lightning   @
    284 Emerald Sunshine   @
    Pearls Of Sharah Trilogy:
    306   Alexandra's Story
    318   Raine's Story
    330   Leah's Story
    347 Amethyst Mist
    353 Witching Time, The
    SwanSea Place Quartet:
    383   Legacy, The
    407   Deceit
    419   Promise, The
    437   Jeopardy
Loveswept Golden Classic:
    For The Love Of Sami   <LS34>
    That Old Feeling   <LS45>
Note:
    @ Also "Satin And Steel"
      SCAL #71 by Jaelyn Conlee

_____

_____

PRESTON, Ivy
        [Ivy Alice Kinross Preston]
Fleeting Breath, A

PRESTON, Ivy (cont.)
Interrupted Journey
Romance In Glenmore Street

_____

_____

PREWIT-PARKER, Jolene   <HR>
Bahama Rapture
Homecoming
Lovers And Deceivers
Rapture's Raging Storm
Reckless Abandon
Sweet Paradise
Velvet Glove: <RS>
    10 Forbidden Dreams

_____

_____

PRICE, Ashland   <HR>
                        [Janice Carlson]
Enemy In My Arms
Heartfire Romance:
    Brenton Family Saga:
        Autumn Angel
        Cajun Caress
        Captive Conquest

_____

_____

PRICE, Dianne   <GOT>
Proud Captive   <HR>
Savage Spirits Of Seahedge
    Manor, The
Shadowtide

_____

_____

PRICE, Eugenia   <HO>
Don Juan McQueen
Margaret's Story
Maria
Woman To Woman
Share My Pleasant Stones
St. Simons Trilogy:
    Beloved Invader, The
    New Moon Rising
    Lighthouse

PRICE, Eugenia (cont.)
The Savannah Quartet:
Savannah
To See Your Face Again
Before The Darkness Falls
Stranger In Savannah

PRICE, Kerry
[Karen Pershing]
Second Chance At Love:
347 Frenchman's Kiss
389 Dash Of Spice, A
415 Touch Of Midnight

PRICE, Linda
Dare To Dream

PRICE, Marjorie
(Maggie Peck)
(Margot Prince)
Heartfire Romance: <HR>
Desire's Dawning
Emerald Embrace
Renegade Heart

PRIDDY, Fran
Promise Romance: <Insp>
19 Bridge To Love

PRIESTLEY, Lee
Avalon:
Sound Of Always
Tour To Romance

PRIME, Joan C.
Avalon:
Love's Way

PRINCE, Margot
[Marjorie Price]
Candlelight Ecstasy:
206 Man Who Came To Stay, The
264 Run To Rapture

PRINCE MICHAEL Of Greece   <HR>
Sultana

PRITCHETT, Ariadne   <RS>
Ghosts Of Kings
Karamour
Legacy Of Evil
Malpas Legacy, The
Mill Reef Hall

PROCTOR, Carol   <RE>
An Unlikely Guardian
Drawing Masters Dilemma, The

PROCTOR, Kate
Harlequin Presents:
1195 Sweet Captivity
1253 Wild Enchantment
1292 Reckless Heart
Harlequin Romance:
Raindance   HRS26

PROFFIT, Nicholas
Gardens Of Stone   <CO>

PUTNEY, Mary Jo (cont.)
  Would-Be Widow, The   &
  Uncommon Vows

PUYEAR-ALERDING, Kathleen
                    (Kathy Alerding)

PYATT, Rosina
                    (Anne Beaumont)
  An Unquestionable Lady
  To Chase A Dream
  To Chase A Moonbeam
  Harlequin Historical <Set#1>:
    12 Marquess And Miss
        Yorke, The
  Harlequin Regency Romance:
    To Catch An Earl
  Sapphire Romance: <ENG>
    Wish Me Happy

PYKARE, Nina/Nina Coombs
          [Nina Ann Coombs Pykare]
                    (Ann Coombs)
                    (Nina Coombs)
                    (Nan Pemberton)
                    (Nina Porter)
                    (Nora Powers)
                    (Regina Towers)
  Lost Duchess Of
        Greyden Castle, The <GOT>
  Candlelight Regency's:
    501 Scandalous Season, The
    509 Love's Promise
    548 Love In Disguise
    554 Man Of Her Choosing, A
    581 Dazzled Heart, The
    594 Lady Incognita
    610 Love's Folly
    645 Innocent Heart, The

PYKARE, Nina (cont.)
    675 Love Plays A Part
    716 Matter Of Honor, A
  Candlelight Ecstasy:
    65 Heritage Of The Heart

PYM, Barbara   (Deceased)
  No Fond Return Of Love

PYNN, Kathleen
                    (Kathleen O'Brien)

QUENTIN, Dorothy   <RS>
Prisoner In The Square, The
Wedding At Blue Lake
What's News Of Kitty?
Harlequin Romance:
 1596 Inn By The Lake, The
 1724 Wedding At Blue River

QUICK, Amanda   <HR>
             [Jayne Ann Krentz]
Seduction
Surrender
Scandal

QUICK, Barbara
Northern Edge

QUIGLEY, Aileen
          (Aileen Armitage)
            (Ruth Fabian)
          (Erica Lindley)

QUIGLEY, John   <HR>
King's Royal
Queen's Royal

QUILLER-COUCH, Arthur
      (see Daphne duMaurier)

QUIN-HARKIN, Janet   <YA>
Caprice Romance:
  35 Tommy Loves Tina
  53 Winner Take All
Heartbreak Cafe: <YA>
   1 No Experience Required
   2 Main Attraction
   3 At Your Service
   4 Catch Of The Day
   5 Love To Go
   6 Just Deserts
Sugar And Spice: <YA>
   1 Two Girls, One Boy
   2 Trading Places
   3 Last Dance, The
   4 Dear Cousin
   5 Nothing In Common
   6 Flip Side
   7 Tug Of War
   8 Surf's Up
   9 Double Take
  10 Make Me A Star
  11 Big Sister
  12 Out In The Cold
  13 Blind Date
  14 It's My Turn
  15 Home Sweet Home
  16 Dream Come True
  17 Campus Cousins
  18 Roadtrip
  19 One Step Too Far
  20 Having A Ball
Sweet Dreams:
   6 California Girl
  10 Love Match
  18 Ten-Boy Summer
  32 Daydreamer
  53 Ghost Of A Chance
  61 Exchange Of Hearts
  65 Two Of Us, The
  68 Lovebirds
  89 101 Ways To Meet Mr. Right
  92 Kiss And Tell
  93 Great Boy Chase, The
 100 Follow That Boy
 127 My Best Enemy

QUIN-HARKIN, Janet (cont.)
On Our Own: <YA>
    Sweet Dreams Miniseries:
      1 Graduates, The
      2 Trouble With Toni, The
      3 Out Of Love
      4 Old Friends, New Friends
      5 Growing Pains
    Sweet Dreams Special: <YA>
      1 My Special Love
      5 Never Say Goodbye
Wildfire: <YA>
    Write Every Day

QUINN, Alison
    Harlequin Gothic Romance:
      Fourth Letter, The
      Satyr Ring, The

QUINN, Christina
    Tender Price, A

QUINN, Colleen
          [Colleen Quinn Bosler]
    Heartfire Romance: <HR>
      Colorado Flame
      Daring Desire
      Golden Splendor
      Outlaw's Angel
      Twilight Ecstasy

QUINN, Elizabeth
          [Elizabeth Quinn Barnard]
    Alliances   <Saga>
    Any Day Now

QUINN, Lisa
    First Love From Silhouette: <YA>
      30 Boy To Dream About, A

QUINN, Sally
    Regrets Only   <CO>

QUINN, Samantha
                   [Mareen Bullinger]
    Second Chance At Love:
      362 Forever Kate   &
      393 Country Dreaming
      429 Rules Of The Heart   &
    Silhouette Special Edition:
      551 Promise Made, A

QUOIREZ, Francoise
                   (Francoise Sagan)

RABE, Sheila   <RE-IN>
  Light-Fingered Lady, The
  Faint Heart
_____

_____

RADCLIFF, Ann
  Mystries Of Udolpho
_____

RADCLIFFE, Janette   <HR><RE>
            [Janet Louise Roberts]
  American Baroness
  Court Of The Flowering Peach
  Heart Awakens, The
  Hidden Fires
  Lovers And Liars (formerly 'Ship
    Of Hate' by Rebecca Danton)
  Stormy Surrender
  Vienna Dreams
  Candlelight:
    128 Blue-Eyed Gypsy, The <RE>
    174 Moonlight Gondola, The
    185 Gentleman Pirate, The
    190 White Jasmine
    198 Lord Stephen's Lady
    204 Azure Castle, The
    206 Topaz Charm, The
    212 Scarlet Secrets
    216 Gift Of Violets, A   <RE>
_____

_____

RADFORD, Richard Francis, Jr.
                (Amy Lyndon)

RAE, Catherine M.
  Julia's Story
  Sarah Cobb
_____

_____

RAE, Doris
  Awake To The Dawn
  Echo Of Romance
  Flame Of The Forest
_____

_____*_____

RAE, Hugh Crawford w/ Peggie
  COGHLAN   (Jessica Stirling)

RAE, Judie
  Boyfriend Blues
  Caprice Romance: <YA>
    43 Prescription For Love
    55 Third Time Lucky
_____

RAE, Lona   <HR>
  Down River
_____

RAE, Patricia   <MED>
                [Patricia Walls]
  Charge Nurse
  Emergency Nurse
  Hospital Nurse
  Maternity Nurse
  Storm Tide   <HR>
  Student Nurse   <CO>
  To Suffer In Silence
  Trauma Nurse
  Ways Of The Wind   <RW>
_____

RAEF, Laura/Laura C.   <GOT>
        [Laura Gladys Cauble Raef]
  Nurse In Fashion
  Nurse Jan And The Legacy
  Symphony In The Sky
  Avalon:
    Dangerous Designs
    Dr. Terri's Project
    Miracle At Seaside

RAEF, Laura (cont.)
Moonlight Kisses
Target For Terror
Waikiki Nurse

RAESCHILD, Sheila   <HR>
(see Terry Nelsen Bonner)
Earthstones   <Saga>
Trolley Song

RAFFAT, Donne   <HO>
Caspian Circle, The

RAFFEL, Elizabeth
Candlelight Ecstasy:
180 Lost Without Love

RAFFEL, Elizabeth And Burton
In sequence: <HR>
Founder's Fury
Founder's Fortune

RAFFERTY, Carin
[Linda Kichline]
Harlequin American Romance:
320 Full Circle
359 Change Of Seasons, A
Harlequin Temptation:
281 I Do, Again
319 My Fair Baby

RAGEN, Naomi
Jepthe's Daughter

RAGOSTA, Millie J.   <RS>
[Millie Jane Ragosta]
(Melanie Randolph)
House Of The Evil Winds
House On Curtin Street, The
King John's Treasure
Lighthouse, The
Lorena Veiled
Taverna In Terrazzo
Witness To Treason
Coventry:
203 Gerait's Daughter
Starlight Romance:
Dream Weaver, The
Druid's Enchantment
Gerait's Daughter
Sing Me A Love Song
Winter Rose, The

RAINBOW, Elizabeth   <GOT>
Wall Of Night

RAINONE, Christopher
(Violet Hawthorne)

RAINTREE, Lee   <RS>
[Connie Leslie Sellers, Jr.]
Bed Of Strangers w/Anthony WILSON
Dallas
This Promised Earth   <CO>

RAINVILLE, Rita
(see Silhouette Christmas Stories)
Silhouette Desire:
495 Touch Of Class, A
639 Paid In Full
Silhouette Romance:
313 Challenge The Devil
346 McCade's Woman
370 Lady Moonlight
400 Written On The Wind
418 Perfect Touch, The

RAINVILLE, Rita (cont.)
    448 Glorious Quest, The
    478 Family Affair   &
    502 It Takes A Thief   &
    535 Gentle Persuasion
    556 Never Love A Cowboy
    598 Valley Of Rainbows
    663 No Way To Treat A Lady
    706 Never On Sundae
    746 One Moment Of Magic

RAMIN, Terese
                    [Terey Daly Ramin]
    Silhouette Intimate Moments:
    279 Water From The Moon
    Silhouette Special Edition:

    656 Accompanying Alice

RAMIREZ, Alice
                    (Serena Alexander)
                    (Candice Arkham)

RAMSEY, Eileen Ainsworth   <RE>
    Mysterious Marquis, The

RAND, Suzanne
                        [Debra Brand]
    Sweet Dreams: <YA>
      3 Laurie's Song
      7 Green Eyes
     17 Ask Annie
     49 Too Much To Lose
     57 On Her Own
     62 Just Like The Movies
     76 Three Cheers For Love
     85 Boy She Left Behind, The

RANDALL, Christine   <GOT><RS>
    Black Candle, The
    Curse Of Deepwater, The

RANDAL, Christine (cont.)
    Mallory Grange
    Secret Of Tarn-End House, The
    Weeping Tower, The
    Whisper Of Fear
    Woman Possessed, A

RANDALL, Diana   <HR>
                    [W.E. Daniel Ross]
    Dragon Lover

RANDALL, Florence E.   <RS>
                [Florence Engel Randall]
    Place Of Sapphires, The

RANDALL, Lindsay   <HR>
                    [Susan M. Anderson]
    Desire's Storm
    Silversword
    Two Hearts Too Wild
    Heartfire Romance: <HR>
      Fortune's Desire
      Jade Temptation

RANDALL, Rona   <GOT><RE><RS>
                [Rona Randall Shambrook]
    Arrogant Duke, The
    Broken Tapestry
    Curtain Call   <HR>
    Dragonmede
    Eagle At The Gate, The
    Girl Called Ann, A
    Glenrannoch
    God Of Mars
    Hotel DeLuxe
    Journey To Love
    Knight's Keep
    Ladies Of Hanover Square, The
    Leap In The Dark
    Lyonhurst

548

RANDAL, Rona (cont.)
 Mating Dance, The
 Midnight Walker
 Mountain Of Fear
 Nurse Stacy Comes Aboard
 Potter's Niece, The
 Seven Days From Midnight
 Shadows On The Sand
 Silver Cord, The
 Time Remembered, Time Lost
 Walk Into My Parlor
 Watchman's Stone
 Willow Herb, The
 Witching Hour, The

RANDALL, Virginia
 Follow Your Heart

RANDOLPH, Elise
                    [Susan L. Lowe]
 Candlelight Ecstasy:
   60 Love, Yesterday And
         Forever
   73 Spark Of Fire In The Night
  143 Passionate Appeal
  415 Hands Off The Lady
 Candlelight Ecstasy Supreme:
   19 Shadow Games

RANDOLPH, Ellen   <RE>
 Rushden Legacy, The

RANDOLPH, Ellen
                  [W. E. Daniel Ross]
 Nurse Of The North Woods
 Secret Of Gray Towers
 Avalon:
   Nurse Martha's Wish

RANDOLPH, Melanie
                  [Millie J. Ragosta]
 To Have And To Hold:
    9 Heart Full Of Rainbows

RANGEL, Doris
 Harlequin Presents:
  878 Legacy

RANSOM, Candice/Candice F.
                    [Jesse Osburn]
 Chrystal Falls: <YA>
    2 Breaking The Rules
 Crosswinds: <YA>
   12 Kaleidoscope
 First Love From Silhouette: <YA>
  225 Cat's Cradle
 Sunfire: <HR><YA>
   Amanda
   Susannah
   Kathleen
   Emily
   17 Sabrina
   19 Nicole
 Windswept: <RS>
   Silvery Past, The

RANSOM, Dana
                    [Nancy Gideon]
 Heartfire Romance:
   Liar's Promise
   Love's Glorious Gamble
   Rebel Vixen
   Wild, Savage Love
   In sequence:
     Pirate's Captive, The
     Alexandra's Ecstasy

RANSOM, Katherine
    [Mary Fanning Sederquest]
  Rapture Romance:
    37 O'Hara's Woman
    65 Wish On A Star

RAVENLOCK, Constance
           [June E. Casey]
  Candlelight:
    676 Rendezvous At Gramercy<RE>

RASCOVICH, Mark   (Deceased)
  Bedford Incident
  Falkenhorst

RAWLINGS, Cynthia
  McFadden Romance:
    48 Tiara
    48 Moonchild

RASLEY, Alicia Todd
          (Elizabeth Todd)
          (Michelle Venet)

RAWLINGS, Ellen   <RE>
  Serious Pursuit, A

RASMUSSEN, Alysse
    [Alysse Suzanne Rasmussen]
          (Alysse Lemery)
  Candlelight Ecstasy:
    221 Night In The Forest, A

RAWLINGS, Louisa   <HR>
        [Sylvia Baumgarten]
  Dreams So Fleeting
  Forever Wild
  Stolen Spring
  Harlequin Historical <Set#2>:
    60 Stranger In My Arms
  Lovestruck:
    Promise Of Summer

RATHER, Deborah Arlene Roper
          (Arlene James)

RATHJEN, Carl Henry
          (Charlotte Russell)

RAY, Jane
  Harlequin Romance:
    1013 Mary Into Mair

RATZLAFF, Nell Marr Dean
          (Ann Marr)
          (Nell Marr Dean)
          (Virginia Roberts)

RAU, Deborah
  Super Saga: <Insp>
    Dearest Anna

RAY, Karen w/ D. H. GAZDAK
          (Anne Bernadette)

RAYE, Linda
          [Linda Turner]
  Second Chance At Love:
    222 Made In Heaven
    344 All The Right Moves
    416 Hart's Desire   &
    437 Temptress   &

RAU, Margaret
  Starlight Romance:
    Hoyden Bride, The

RAYES, Rachel   <GOT>
  Devil's Court
  Forbidden Island

RAYMOND, Ernest   (Deceased)
  Gentle Greaves
  Georgian Love Story, A
  Mountain Farm, The
  Old June Weather, The
  We, The Accused

RAYMOND, James
               [James Scafidel]
  Lewis & Clark: Northwest
    Glory   <AES:#2>

RAYMOND, Mary   <GOT><RS>
         [Mary Heathcott Keegan]
  Divided House, The
  Long Journey Home, The
  Surety For A Stranger
  That Summer

RAYNER, Claire   <GOT>
       [Claire Berenice Rayner]
  Charing Cross
  Covent Garden
  Enduring Years, The
  House On The Fen, The
  Trafalgar Square
  Performers Series: In sequence:
    Gower Street
    Haymarket, The
    Paddington Green
    Soho Square
    Bedford Row

RAYNES, Jean
  Blood Carnelian
  Legacy Of The Wolf   <VIC>

READ, Lorna
           (Caroline Standish)

READING, Margot w/ R. J. MINNEY
  Love In Chains   <HR>

REAVIN, Sara
  Elise

REAVIS, Cheryl
           (Cinda Richards)
  Promise Me A Rainbow
  Silhouette Special Edition:
    487   Crime Of The Heart, A
    627   Patrick Gallegher's Widow

REBUTH, Jeanette
  Cinnamon Gardens, The

RECEVEUR, Betty Layman   <HR>
  Oh, Kentucky
  Sable Flanagan
  In sequence:
    Molly Gallagher
    Carrie Kingston

REDD, Joanne
           (Lauren Wilde)
  Apache Bride
  Border Bride
  Chasing A Dream

REDD, Joanne (cont.)
  Desert Bride
  To Love An Eagle

REED, Anne
  Second Chance At Love:
  83 Starlit Seduction

REDDOCK, Jennifer   <GOT><RS>
  Chair For Death, A
  Legacy Of Mendoubia
  Night OF The Hellebore

REED, Jackson
                [George Jackson Eder]
  Raptures Of Love, The

REDISH, Jane
  Sweet Dreams: <YA>
  115 Promise Me Love

REED, Miriam
  Starlight Romance:
  Summer Song

REDMAYNE, Ann
  No Room For Love

REEP, Diana
  [Diana Reep w/ Emily Ann Allen]
  Silhouette Romance:
  601 Blakemore Touch, The

REECE, Colleen L.
  Avalon:
  Alpine Meadows Nurse
  Ballad For Nurse Lark
  Come Home, Nurse Jenny
  Everlasting Melody
  Heritage Of Nurse O'Hara
  In Search Of Twilight
  Nurse Autumn's Secret Love
  Nurse Camilla's Love
  Nurse Julie's Sacrifice
  Nurse Of The Crossroads
  Yellowstone Park Nurse

REES, Barbara
  [Barbara Elizabeth Rees]
  Harriet Dark: Bramwell Bronte's
  Lost Novel

REES, Eleanor
  Harlequin Presents:
  1285 Seal Wife, The
  Harlequin Romance:
  Love's Destiny   HRS57

REECE, Jean
                [Mary Kistler]
  Harlequin Regency Romance:
  Primrose Path, The
  10 Devil's Dare, The

REES, Helen Christina Easson Evans
                (Deceased)(Jane Oliver)

REES, Joan   <GOT>
  Bride In Blue, The

552

REESE, Charlotte Paul
                    (Charlotte Paul)

REESE, John
                    (Cody Kennedy, Jr.)

REEVE, Elaine
  Masquerade:
    64 Lady In The Lion's Den

_____

_____

REEVES, Fionnuala   <RS>
  Deadly Inheritance

_____

_____

REGAN, Dian Curtis   <YA>
  I've Got Your Number

_____

_____

A REGENCY CHRISTMAS (1989)
  Old Acquaintances
                    Gayle Buck
  The Duke's Progress
                    Edith Layton
  The Kissing Bough
                    Patricia Rice
  A Gift Of Fortune
                    Anita Mills
  The Star Of Bethlehem
                    Mary Balogh

_____

A REGENCY CHRISTMAS (1990)
  Star Of Bethleham,The
                    Mary Balogh
  Duke's Progress, The
                    Edith Layton
  Gift Of Fortune, A
                    Anita Mills
  Kissing Bough, The
                    Patricia Rice
  Old Acquaintances
                    Gayle Buck

_____

_____

REIBEL, Paula
        [Paula Reibel Schwartz]
  Morning Moon, A

_____

_____

REID, Charles Stuart w/ Charles R.
  MACKINNON   (Charles Stuart)

REID, Grace
                    [Grace Green]
  Candlelight Ecstasy:
    493 Black Lace

_____

_____

REID, Henrietta
  Harlequin Romance:
    1094 My Dark Rapparee
    1126 Man Of The Islands
    1206 Substitute For Love
    1247 Laird Of Storr
    1292 Falcon's Keep
    1317 Beloved Sparrow
    1380 Reluctant Masquerade
    1430 Hunter's Moon
    1460 Black Delaney, The
    1495 Rival Sisters
    1528 Made Marriage, The
    1575 Sister Of The Bride
    1621 Garth Of Tregillis
    1720 Intruder At Windgates
    1764 Bird Of Prey
    1851 Dragon Island
    1902 Man At The Helm, The
    1953 Love's Puppet
    2001 Greek Bridal
    2049 Tartan Ribbon, The
    2113 Push The Past Behind
    2345 Paradise Plantation
    2442 Lord Of The Isles
    2524 New Boss At Birchfields

_____

_____

REID, Leslie
       [Barbara Jurin-Reid]
American Regency Romance:
  Letter Of Intent
Harlequin Regency Romance:
  Grand Style, The

REID, Margaret Ann   <CO>
(publishers pseudonym for
      writers in this series)
Charleston Saga:
  Charleston
  White Lies
      [Sally Schoeneweiss]
  Blue Bloods
  Golden Touch, The

REID, Mary
  Everlasting Love: <Insp>
    5 Legend Of Love
  Serenade/Serenata: <Insp>
    32 Karaleen

REID, Michelle
Harlequin Presents:
  1140 Question Of Pride, A
Harlequin Romance:
  2994 Eye Of Heaven

REILLY, Helen   <RS>
  Canvas Dagger, The
  Certain Sleep
  Compartment K
  Day She Died, The
  Dead Man Control
  Death Demands An Audience
  Ding Dong Bell
  Follow Me
  Line Up, The

REILLY, Helen (cont.)
  Mr. Smith's Hat
  Murder In Shinbone Alley
  Murder In The Mews
  Not Me, Inspector
  Opening Door, The

REINGOLD, Carmel B.
        (Alexandra Ellis)

REISNER, M.
  Emily Fair

REISNER, Mary   <GOT><RS>
  Bride Of Death
  Death Hall
  Four Witnesses
  House Of Cobwebs
  Mirror Of Delusion
  Shadows On The Wall

REISSER, Anne N.
  Candlelight Ecstasy:
    20 Face Of Love, The
    24 Captive Love, The
    33 Deceptive Love
    51 All's Fair
    76 Come Love, Call My Name
    81 By Love Betrayed
  Loveswept:
    28 Love, Catch A Wild Bird

REIT, Ann   <YA>
  First Time, The
  Wildfire: <YA>
    Yours Truly, Love, Janie

RELLAS, Dorothy
  Harlequin Intrigue:
    44 Hidden Motives

REMARQUE, Erich Maria   (Deceased)
  Black Obelisk
  Bobby Deerfield
  Drei Kameraden
  Full Circle
  Night In Lisbon, The
  Shadows In Paradise
  Three Comrades
  Time To Love And A Time To Die

RENAULT, Mary
              [Mary Challans]
  Kind Are Her Answers
  Middle Mist
  Nature Of Alexander, The
  North Face
  Promise Of Love
  Return To Night
  Alexander The Great Trilogy:
    Fire From Heaven
    Persian Boy, The
    Funeral Games

RENIER, Elizabeth   <HR><RE>
        [Betty Doreen Flook Baker]
  Blade Of Justice
  By Sun And Candlelight
  Generous Vine, The
  House Of Granite
  House Of Water, The
  If This Be Love
  Landscape Of The Heart   <VIC>
  Love Divided, A
  Moving Dream, The   <VIC>
  Prelude To Love
  Ravenstor
  Renshawe Inheritance, The

RENIER, Elizabeth (cont.)
  Singing In The Woods, A
  Spanish Doll, The
  Time For Rejoicing, A
  Tomorrow Comes The Sun
  Valley Of Nightingales
  Valley Of Secrets
  Woman From The Sea

RENO, James
  In sequence: <HS>
    Texas Anthem
    Texas Kings

RENO, Marie R.   <HO>
              [Marie Roth Reno]
  Final Proof
  When The Music Changed

RENSEL, Anne Marron
  Broken Tryst
  New Dreams For Old

RENWICK, Gloria
  Candlelight Ecstasy:
    69 Strictly Business

RESNICK, Laura
                    (Laura Leone)

REITKE, Marian Pope
                    (Anne Devon)
                    (Marian Devon)
  Georgiana   <RE>
  Highland Rapture   <HR>

REVESZ, Etta
 Empire   <CO>
 Miss Fancy

REYNARD, Carol w/ Shirl HENKE
                        (Shirl Henke)

REYNOLDS, Anne
                        [Ann Steinke]
 Sailboat Summer
 Magic Moments: <YA>
   7 Jeff's New Girl

REYNOLDS, Bonnie Jones
 Confetti Man, The
 Truth About Unicorns, The

REYNOLDS, Catherine
 Harlequin Regency Romance:
   47 Thoroughly Compromised
       Bride, The
   56 An Unlikely Alliance

REYNOLDS, Elizabeth
                        [Ann Steinke]
 Silhouette Romance:
   158 An Ocean Of Love
 Sweet Dreams: <YA>
   105 Perfect Boy, The
   111 Stolen Kisses

REYNOLDS, Maureen   <HR>
 One Golden Hour
 Wild Nights, Silver Dreams

REYNOLDS, Maxine   <GOT>
 House In The Kasbah, The

RHEE, Dena
                        [Deana Brauer]
 MacFadden Romance:
   92 If Ever We Meet
   96 Lessons Of Love
 Candlelight:
   694 An Immodest Proposal <RE>

RHOADES, Sandra K.
 Harlequin Presents:
   917 Risky Business, A
   956 Bitter Legacy
   1021 Shadows In The Limelight
   1214 Yesterday's Embers
 Harlequin Romance:
   3030 Foolish Deceiver

RHODES, Evan H.
 American Palace Series: <HS>
   Bless This House
   Forged In Fury
   Valiant Hearts
   Distant Dream, A

RHODES, J. H.   <GOT>
 Avalon:
   Clouds Over Stormcrest
   Crying Winds, The
   Danger At Darkoaks
   Dangerous Summer
   Evil At Sunfire
   Fear In The Night
   Fear Island
   Legacy Of Greenbrier
   Menace In The Fog
   Night Of The Half-Moon

RHODES, J. H. (cont.)
    Shadow Over Hawkhaven
    Summer Mysteries
    Watcher Of Windcliff, The

RHYNE, Julia A.
                        (Lucy Hamilton)

RICE, Bebe Faas
    Crosswinds Keepsake: <YA>
        27 Boy Crazy
        30 Spring Break

RICE, Linda w/ Stella CAMERON
                        (Alicia Brandon)

RICE, Linda w/ Walter RICE
                        (Linda Walters)

RICE, Molly
    Harlequin SuperRomance:
        440 Where The River Runs

RICE, Pat/Patricia   <HR>
        (see A Regency Christmas)
    Cheyenne's Lady
    Indigo Moon   <RE>
    Lady Sorceress
    Lord Rogue
    Love Betrayed
    Love Forever After
    Love's First Surrender
    Moon Dreams
    Moonlight Mistress
    Silver Enchantress

RICE, Walter w/ Linda RICE
                        (Linda Walters)

RICH, Harriet   <GOT>
                        [Margaret Richley]
    Candlelight:
        179 Bride Of Belvale

RICH, Kathleen   <GOT><RS>
    Deadly Rose, The
    Lucifer Mask, The

RICH, Meredith   <CO>
    Bare Essence
    Bijoux
    Little Sins
    Virginia Clay

RICHARD, Susan   <GOT><RS>
                        [Julie M. Ellis]
    Ashley Hall
    Chateau Saxony
    Intruder At Maison Benedict
    Poles, The   <IMS>
    Secret Of Chateau Kendell, The
    Terror At Nelson Woods

RICHARDS, Ann
                        [Frankie Merkt]
    Sweet Dreams: <YA>
        152 Cross-Country Match

RICHARDS, Celia Gardner   <HR>
    Jade Ecstasy

RICHARDS, Cinda
                        [Cheryl Reavis]
    Second Chance At Love:
        237 This Side Of Paradise

RICHARDS, Penny
                    (Bay Matthews)
    Harlequin SuperRomance:
    323 Unforgettable
    350 Eden   <CCS>
_____

_____

RICHARDS, Penny w/ Sandra CANFIELD
                    (Sandi Shane)

RICHARDS, Serena   <HR><RE>
                    [Susan Coppula]
    Masquerade
    Rendezvous

_____

_____

RICHARDS, Stephanie
    Rapture Romance:
    5 Chesapeake Autumn

_____

_____

RICHARDS, Tad
            (see Richard Hale Curtis)
            (see Lee Davis Willoughby)

RICHARDS, Vanessa
                    [Paula Moffett]
    Candlelight Ecstasy:
    487 Bittersweet Torment

_____

_____

RICHARDS-AKERS, Nancy   <RE>
    Lilac Garden, The
    Mayfair Season, The
    American Regency Romance:
        Philadelphia Folly   &
        Season Abroad, A   &

_____

_____

RICHARDS-AKERS, Nancy Linda w/
            Mary I. KILCHENSTEIN
                    (Mary Alice Kirk)

RICHARDSON, Alaina
                    (Alaina Hawthorne)

RICHARDSON, D. C.
    All That Heaven Allows   <Saga>

_____

_____

RICHARDSON, Evelyn   <RE>
                [Cynthia Whealler]
    Education Of Lady Frances, The
    Miss Creswell's London Triumph

_____

_____

RICHARDSON, Henry V. M.   <HR>
    In sequence:
        Skarra
        Lady Of Skarra, The

_____

RICHARDSON, Hope
    MacFadden Romance:
        21 Love Match
        65 Dear Stranger

_____

_____

RICHARDSON, Kay
    Amberwood
    Love's Turning Point
    Stonehaven
    Women Of La Dina
    Avalon:
        Briarwood Summer
        Come To Greenleaves
        Heart Surrendered, A
        No Time For Love

_____

_____

RICHARDSON, Mozelle   <GOT><RS>
            [Mozelle Groner Richardson]
    Candle In The Wind, A
    Curse Of Kalispoint, The

RICHARDSON, Mozelle (cont.)
Daughter Of The Sacred Mountain
Masks Of Thespis, The
Portrait Of Fear
Song Of India, The

RICHARDSON, Susan
Loveswept:
186 Fiddlin' Fool
205 Slow Simmer, A
240 Cajun Nights

RICHESON, Cena Golder
(Cyndi Richards)

RICHEY, Cynthia   <RE>
Love's Masquerade

RICHLEY, Margaret
(Harriet Rich)

RICHMOND, Clare
[Carolyn Males w/ Louise Titchener]
Harlequin American Romance:
174 Runaway Heart
215 Bride's Inn
352 Pirate's Legacy

RICHMOND, Emma
Harlequin Presents:
1203 Take Away The Pride
1230 Unwilling Heart
1317 Heart In Hiding
Harlequin Romance:
Suspicious Heart   HRS66
Gentle Trap, The   HRS80

RICHMOND, Grace
[John Marsh]
Run Away From Love

RICHTER, Conrad   (Deceased)<HO>
[Conrad Michael Richter]
The Awakening Land Trilogy:
Trees, The
Fields, The
Town, The

RICKETT, Frances
Doctors' Affairs

RICKS, Patricia W. B.
(Patricia Wynn)

RICO, Don   <RS>
Lorelei
Last Of The Breed, The

RIEFE, A. R.
[Alan Riefe]
Fortunes West Series: <HS>
In sequence:
Tucson
Cheyenne
San Francisco
Salt Lake City

RIEFE, Alan   <HR>
(A. R. Riefe)
(Barbara Riefe)
Fire In The Wind, A

RIEFE, Barbara   <HR>
                [Alan Riefe]
  Auldearn House
  Barringer House
  Rowleston
  Wild Fire
  Woman Of Dreams, A
  Dandridge Trilogy:
    This Ravaged Heart
    Far Beyond Desire
    Fire And Flesh
  In sequence:
    Wicked Fire
    This Proud Love
  In sequence:
    Tempt Not This Flesh
    So Wicked The Heart
    Black Fire
  Shackleford Legacy: In sequence:
    Olivia
    Julia
    Lucretia

RIEFFE, Rebecca
  Turning Points: <YA>
    9 Somebody's Girl

RIENSTRA, Ellen w/ Judith LINSLEY
               (Marie Beaumont)
               (Elionor Lynley)

RIFE, Ellouise A.   <GOT>
  Broken Promise
  House At Stonehaven, The
  House At Windridge, The

RIGDON, Charles   <CO>
  Caramour Woman, The
  Diosa
  Hamptons, The
  Last Ball, The
  Sun Lovers, The

RIGGS, Paula Detmer
  Silhouette Desire:
    633 Rough Passage
  Silhouette Intimate Moments:
    183 Beautiful Dreamer
    226 Fantasy Man
    251 Suspicious Minds
    283 Desperate Measures
    303 Full Circle
    314 Tender Offer
    344 Lasting Promise, A
    364 Forgotten Dream

RIGNEY, Jr., James O.
              (Reagan O'Neal)
              (Jackson O'Reilly)

RIGSBY, Howard   <GOT><RS>
  Calliope Reef
  For An Island Lost
  For Charlie In The Morning
  In a Carmel Sea
  Lone Gun, The
  Thee And Me
  Tulip Tree, The

RIKER, Leigh   <CO>
  Acts Of Passion
  Heartsong

RILEY, Barbara   <CO>
  Guilty Parties
  Heart Forgives, The

RILEY, Eugenia   <HR>
    [Eugenia Riley Essenmacher]
  Angel Flame
  Ecstasy's Triumph
  Laura's Love

RILEY, Eugenia (cont.)
  Mississippi Madness
  Sweet Reckoning
  Harlequin Temptation:
    292 Love Nest
    324 Perfect Mate, The
  Loveswept:
    102 Remember Me, Love
    135 Stubborn Cinderella
    174 Where The Heart Is
  Pageant Romance:
    Night It Rained, The

RILEY, Judith Merkle   <HR>
  Vision Of Light, A

RILEY, Sandra   <HR>
  Captain's Ladies, The

RILEY, Stella
                  (Juliet Blyth)

RIMMER, Christine
  Harlequin Temptation:
    154 Road Home, The
  Silhouette Desire:
    418 Turning Back
    458 Call It Fate
    602 Temporary Temptress
    640 Hard Luck Lady

RIMMER, Robert/Robert H.
          [Robert Henry Rimmer]
  Adventures In Loving
  Come Live My Life
  Gold Lovers
  Love Me Tomorrow
  That Girl From Boston

RIMMER, Robert (cont.)
  Thursday, My Love
  You And I, Searching For Tomorrow

RINEHART, Mary Roberts   (Deceased)
                                <RS>
  After House, The
  Alibi For Isabel
  Album, The
  Bat, The
  Breaking Point, The
  Case Of Jennie Bryce, The   <MY>
  Circular Staircase, The
  Confession, The
  Dangerous Days
  Doctor, The
  Door, The
  Episode Of The Wandering
    Knife,   <MY>
  Frightened Wife, The
  Great Mistake, The
  Haunted Lady
  Lost Ecstasy
  Man In Lower Ten, The   <MY>
  Married People
  Miss Pinkerton
  Mystery Library - Vol. III   <MY>
  Red Lamp, The   <MY>
  Sight Unseen
  State vs. Elinor Morton, The
  Strange Adventure, The
  Street Of Seven Stars, The
  Swimming Pool, The
  Wall, The
  Window Of The White Cat, The
  Yellow Room, The

RINEHOLD, Connie
          [Constance Vader Rinehold]
  Harlequin American Romance:
    380 Veil Of Tears
  Harlequin SuperRomance:
    374 Silken Threads

562

RING, Thomasina   <HR>
          [Tommye Ring Morton]
Time-Spun Rapture

_____

_____

RINGER, Vivian
Secretary, The

_____

_____

RINZLER, Carol Eisen
Girl Who Got All The Breaks, The

_____

_____

RIPLEY, Alexandra   <HR>
          [Alexandra Braid Ripley]
Caril
New Orleans Legacy
Time Returns, The
Who's That Lady In The
     President's Bed?
In sequence: <Saga>
     Charleston
     On Leaving Charleston

_____

_____

RIPY, Margaret
          [Margaret Daley]
Silhouette Romance:
    71 Second Chance On Love, A
   170 Treasure Of Love, A
Silhouette Special Edition:
    28 Flaming Tree, The
    76 Tomorrow's Memory
   114 Rainy Day Dreams
   134 Matter Of Pride, A
   164 Firebird
   189 Feathers In The Wind
   209 Promise Her Tomorrow
   351 Wildcatter's Promise

_____

_____

RISEDEN, Elizabeth I.   <HR>
Frontier Dynasty

_____

_____

RISING, Clara   <HO>
In The Season Of The Wild Rose

_____

_____

RISKU, Cillay   <GOT>
White Midnight

_____

_____

RITTER, Margaret   <RS>
Caroline, Caroline
Burning Woman, The
Lady In The Tower, The
Women In The Wind   <HR><Saga>

_____

_____

RITZ, David
               (Jessica Lansing)
               (Ester Elizabeth Pearl)

RIVERS, Dorothy
               [Leonora Mackesy]
Harlequin Classic:
   168 There Will Come A
        Stranger   (1135)
Harlequin Romance:
  1088 Spanish Moonlight
  1110 Labour Of Love
  1135 There Will Come A Stranger
  1163 Love In The Wilderness
  1198 Happy Ever After
  1260 We Live In Secret
  1304 Sharlie For Short

_____

_____

RIVERS, Francine   <HR>
          [Francine Sandra Rivers]
Fire In The Heart, A
Kathleen
Not So Wild A Dream

RIVERS, Francine (cont.)
  Outlaw's Embrace
  Rebel In His Arms
  Sycamore Hill
  Sarina
  This Golden Valley
  Second Chance At Love:
    142 Hearts Divided
    208 Heart In Hiding
    250 Pagan Heart

RIVERS, Georgina
  MacFadden Romance:
    201 Andalusian Interlude

RIVERS, Kendall
  Adventures In Love:
    33 Master Of Hearts

RIVERS WEST SERIES: <RWS>   <HO>
  1 Yellowstone, The
                      Winfred Blevins
  2 Smoky Hill, The
                      Don Coldsmith
  3 Colorado, The
                      Gary McCarthy
  4 Powder River
                      Winfred Blevins

ROARK, Garland
  Hellfire Jackson w/Charles THOMAS
  Slant Of The Wild Wind
  Wake Of The Red Witch, The
  Wreck Of The Running Gale

ROBARCHEK, Peg
                      (Katheryn Brett)
                      (Peg Sutherland)

ROBARDS, Karen   <HR>
  Amanda Rose
  Dark Of The Moon
  Dark Torment
  Desire In The Sun
  Forbidden Love
  Green Eyes
  Loving Julia
  Morning Song
  Night Magic   <CO>
  To Love A Man   <CO>
  Wild Orchids
  Tiger's Eye
  In sequence:
    Island Flame
    Sea Fire

ROBB, Christine
  Twilight's Key

ROBB, JoAnn
                      [JoAnn Ross]
  Dangerous Passion, A
  High Stakes Affair
  Promises To Keep
  Rapture Romance:
    29   Stardust And Diamonds
    49   Dreamlover
    61   Sterling Deceptions
    70   Secure Arrangement, A
    81   Tender Betrayal
    93   Touch The Sun
   100   Wolfe's Prey

ROBB, Sandra
  Silhouette Romance:
    43 Surrender In Paradise

ROBBE, Michele
                    [Lucy Seaman]
  Candlelight Ecstasy:
    357 Walking On Air

_____

_____

ROBBINS, Andrea   <HR>
                    [Peter Albano]
  Fires Of Oakheath, The

_____

_____

ROBBINS, JoAnn
                    [JoAnn Ross]
  Silhouette Desire:
    94 Winning Season

_____

_____

ROBBINS, Kay
                    [Kay Hooper]
  Second Chance At Love:
    73 Return Engagement
   110 Taken By Storm
   130 Elusive Dawn
   155 Kissed By Magic
   190 Moonlight Rhapsody
   262 Eye Of The Beholder
   322 Belonging To Taylor
   378 On Her Doorstep

_____

_____

ROBBINS, Serena
  SuperRomance:
    35 Isle Of Rapture

_____

_____

ROBERSON, Jennifer
                  (Jennifer O'Green)
  Judy Sullivan Books:
    Smoketree   <RS>

_____

_____

ROBERTS, Ann Victoria
  Louisa Elliot

_____

_____

ROBERTS, Casey
  Harlequin SuperRomance:
    429 Homecoming

_____

_____

ROBERTS, Doreen
  Silhouette Intimate Moments:
    215 Gambler's Gold   &
    239 Willing Accomplice
    266 Forbidden Jade   &
    295 Threat Of Exposure
    319 Desert Heat
    379 In The Line Of Duty
  Silhouette Romance:
    765 Home For The Holidays

_____

_____

ROBERTS, Irene
            [Irene Williamson Roberts]
  Golden Rain
  Harlequin Historical <Set#1>:
    14 Moonpearl

_____

_____

ROBERTS, Jacqueline
  MacFadden Romance:
    58 Road To Love, The

_____

_____

ROBERTS, Janet Louise   (Deceased)
                    (Louise Bronte)
                    (Rebecca Danton)
                    (Janette Radcliffe)
                    <GOT><RE><RS>
  Black Horse Tavern
  Black Pearls
  Castlereagh
  Curse Of Kenton, The

ROBERTS, Janice Louise (cont.)
Dark Rose
Devil's Own, The
Dorstein Icon, The
Flamenco Rose
Flower Of Love
Forget-Me-Not
Golden Lotus
Her Demon Lover
Island Of Desire
Isle Of The Dolphins
Jade Vendetta
Jewels Of Terror, The
Lord Satan
Love Song
Ravenswood
Rivertown
Scarlet Poppies
Sign Of The Golden Goose, The
Silver Jasmine
This Shining Splendor
Weeping Lady, The
Wilderness Inn
Candlelight:
  98 Marriage Of
     Inconvenience, A   <RE>
 105 My Lady Mischief   <RE>
 111 Dancing Doll, The   <RE>
 117 Golden Thistle, The   <RE>
 125 La Casa Dorado
 132 Cardross Luck, The   <RE>
 153 First Waltz, The   <RE>
REPRINTS:
 239 Dancing Doll, The   (C# 111)
 240 My Lady Mischief   (C# 105)
 245 La Casa Dorado   (C# 125)
 246 Golden Thistle   (C# 117)
 247 First Waltz, The   (C# 153)
 248 Cardross Luck,The   (C# 132)

_____

_____

ROBERTS, Jennifer
              [Jennie Zaldivar]
Tender Fugitive

_____

_____

ROBERTS, Leigh
              [Lora Roberts Smith]
Harlequin SuperRomance:
 390 Piece Of Cake, A
Harlequin Temptation:
  20 Love's Circuits   &
  55 Siren Song
  97 Head Over Heels
 147 Birds Of A Feather   &
 186 Wishing Pool, The
SuperRomance:
  81 Moonlight Splendor

_____

_____

ROBERTS, Lisa
              [Robert Harry Turner]
Dream To Share, A

_____

_____

ROBERTS, Nora
              [Eleanor Robertson]
   (see HQ Christmas Stories)
(see Silhouette Christmas Stories)
(see Silhouette Summer Sizzlers)
Hot Ice
Promise Me Tomorrow
Public Secrets
Sweet Revenge
In sequence:
   Sacred Sins
   Brazen Virtues
Harlequin Historical <Set#2>:
   4 Rebellion   @
  21 Lawless   +
Harlequin Intrigue:
  19 Night Moves
Silhouette Classic:
   3 This Magic Moment   (IM25)
  24 Heart's Victory, The(SE59)
Silhouette Intimate Moments:
   2 Once More With Feeling
  12 Tonight And Always
  25 This Magic Moment
  33 Endings And Beginnings >>
  49 Matter Of Choice, A
  70 Rules Of The Game

ROBERTS, Paula
                              [Joan M. Hohl]
Come Home To Love

ROBERTS, Phyllis
Harlequin Temptation:
213 Man Like David, A

ROBERTS, Rinalda   <GOT>
                         [Edythe Cudlipp]
Four Marys, The

ROBERTS, Suzanne
                          (Laurie Marath)
Celebrity Suite Nurse
Co-Ed In White
Cross Country Nurse
Emergency Nurse
Gracie
Heart Comes First, The
Hearts Measure, The
Hootenanny Nurse
Hope Farrell, Crusading Nurse
Katie Jones Goes To Washington

ROBERTS, Suzanne (cont.)
Lovliest Librarian, The
Prize For Nurse Darci, A
Rangeland Nurse
Sisters In White
To Kill A House
Two Dr. Barlowes, The
Vietnam Nurse
Avalon:
   Danger In Paradise   \<GOT\>
Candlelight:
  11 Summer Love
  55 Nurse Penny
 134 Holly Andrews,
      Nurse In Alaska
 163 House Of Cain
 168 Terror At Tansey Hill
 236 Precious Moments
 249 The Searching Heart   \<RO\>
 525 Love's Sweet Illusion \<RO\>
 547 Farewell To Alexandria\<RO\>
 590 Love In The Wilds   \<RO\>
Promise Romance: \<Insp\>
  17 Morning's Song
  22 Angel's Tears
  31 Skylark

ROBERTS, Virginia
     [Nell Marr Dean Ratzlaff]
Beauty By Diane
Nurse Kay
Studio Nurse

ROBERTS, Willo Davis   \<GOT\>\<RS\>
          (Joanne Holden)
Bacca's Child
Cape Of Black Sands
Dangerous Legacy
Dark Rose
Destiny's Women
Devil Boy
Evil Children
Face Of Danger, The
Gates Of Montrain, The

ROBERTS, Willo Davis (cont.)
Ghost Of Harrel, The
Gods In Green, The
House In Fern Canyon, The
House Of Imposters
Inherit The Darkness
Invitation To Evil
Jaubert Ring, The
Keating's Landing   \<HR\>
King's Pawn
Madawaska   \<HR\>
Nurses, The
Nurse At Mystery Villa
Nurse In Danger
Nurse Kay's Conquest
Once A Nurse
Rangeland Nurse
Return To Darkness
Search For Willie, The
Shadow Of A Past Love
Shroud Of Fog
Sing A Dark Song
Sinister Gardens
Tarot Spell, The
Terror Trap, The
To Share A Dream
View From The Cherry Tree, The
Waiting Darkness, The
Watchers, The
White Jade
Black Pearl Series:
  1 Dark Dowry, The
  2 Cade Curse, The
  3 Stuart Stain, The
  4 Devil's Double, The
  5 Radkin Revenge, The
  6 Hellfire Heritage, The
  7 Macomber Menace, The
  8 Gresham Ghost, The
In sequence: \<HS\>
  Gallant Spirit, The
  Days Of Valor
Sunfire: \<YA\>\<HR\>
  Elizabeth
  Caroline
  Victoria
Tapestry: \<HR\>
  86 My Rebel, My Love

ROBERTSON, Carol
  First Love From Silhouette: <YA>
    52 Summer To Remember, A

_____

_____

ROBERTSON, Eleanor
                         (Nora Roberts)

ROBERTSON, Janet
  Journey Home   <Saga>

_____

_____

ROBERTSON, Susan Emrick
                    (Susan Haynesworth)

ROBIN, Liliane
  Mystique:
    13 Sisters At War
    19 Cruise Of The Sphinx
    29 Spell Of The Antilles
    33 Letter From A Stranger
    49 No Turning Back
    54 Stalked By Fear
    60 Summer Of Deceit
    74 Gamble With Death
    86 Fury On The Pampas
    92 Night Of The Scorpion
    96 Snare, The
    114 Dangerous Fascination
    119 Chasm Of Fear
    132 Love's Captive
    144 Search For Yesterday

_____

_____

ROBINS, Denise
        [Denise Naomi Klein Robins]
                      (Ashley French)
                      (Harriet Gray)
                      (Julia Kane)
                    (Francesca Wright)
  All For You
  And All Because
  Bitter Core, The
  Bittersweet

ROBINS, Denise (cont.)
  Breaking Point, The
  Bride Of Revenge
  Could I Forget?
  Crash, The
  Dance In The Dust
  Dark Secret Love
  Desert Rapture
  Dust Of Dreams
  Enchanted Island
  Escape To Love
  Family Holiday
  Fauna
  Feast Is Finished, The
  First Long Kiss, The
  Give Me Back My Heart
  Gold For The Gay Masters
  Heart Of Paris
  Heavy Clay
  I Should Have Known
  Island Of Flowers
  I, Too, Have Loved
  Khamsin
  Kiss Of Youth
  Long Shadow, The
  Life And Love
  Love Is Enough
  Love Like Ours
  Love Me No More
  Love, Volumes I - X
  Meet Me In Monte Carlo
  Moment Of Love
  Moment Of Truth
  More Than Love
  My Lady Destiny
  My True Love
  Never Look Back
  Nightingale's Song
  Noble One
  Once Is Enough
  Only My Dreams
  Other Side Of Love, The
  Put Back The Clock
  Restless Heart, The
  Seagulls Cry, The
  Second Marriage
  Set The Stars Alight

ROBINS-CLARK, Patricia Denise
                    (Claire Lorrimer)

ROBINSON, Barbara   <YA>
Temporary Times, Temporary Places

_____

_____

ROBINSON, Constance
Promise Romance: <Insp>
    14 Song In My Heart, A

_____

_____

ROBINSON, Henry Morton
Water Of Life   <Saga>

_____

_____

ROBINSON, Irene
                    (Jo Manning)

ROBINSON, Jeanne
Avalon:
    Kerry Diamonds
    Quest For Black Gold
    That Special Summer

_____

_____

ROBINSON, John   <HO>
Chinese, The   <IMS>

_____

_____

ROBINSON, Kathleen
    [Chaille Howard Payne Robinson]
Designed By Suzanne
Runaway Heart
When Debbie Dared
When Sara Smiled

_____

_____

ROBINSON, Margaret A.
Courting Emma Howe

_____

_____

ROBINSON, Patricia Colbert
                    (Daria Macomber)

ROBINSON, Suzanne   <HR>
    [Lynda Suzanne Robinson]
Heart Of The Falcon

_____

_____

ROBISON, Nancy
    [Nancy Louise Robison]
Heavenly Romance: <YA>
    Laughter In The Rain
    Love: Lost And Found

_____

_____

ROBSON, Lucia St. Clair   <HO>
Light A Distant Fire
Ride The Wind
Walk In My Soul

_____

_____

ROBY, Mary Linn   <GOT><RE><RS>
                    (Valerie Bradstreet)
                    (Pamela D'Arcy)
                    (Georgia Grey)
                    (Pauline Pryor)
                    (Elizabeth Welles)
                    (Mary Wilson)
Afraid Of The Dark
All Your Lovely Words Are Spoken
And Die Remembering
Broken Key, The
Christobel
Dig A Narrow Grave
Fortune's Smile
Heritage Of Strangers, A
Herrick Inheritance, The
Hidden Book, The
House At Kilgallen, The
House Of Destiny
I Should Have Known
If She Should Die
In The Dead Of Night
Lie Quiet In Your Grave

ROBY, Mary Linn (cont.)
 Love's Willful Call
 Marsh House
 My Lady's Mask
 Passing Fancy
 Pennies On Her Eyes
 Reap The Whirlwind
 Shadow Over Grove House
 Silent Walls, The
 Some Die In Their Beds
 Speak No Evil Of The Dead
 That Fatal Touch
 This Land Turns Evil Slowly
 To Love Again
 Tower Room, The
 Trapped
 Treasure Chest
 White Peacock, The
 When The Witch Is Dead
 Candlelight:
  555 Passing Fancy   <RE>

ROCHE, Ben
 Legend Of Shame

ROCHLIN, Harriette
 So Far Away

ROCK, Philip
 Flickers
 Greville Family Trilogy: <HS>
  Passing Bells, The
  Circles Of Time
  Future Arrived, A

ROCKER, Judy S. w/ Doris S. ENGLISH
             (Anna Lloyd Staton)

ROCKY MOUNTAIN MAGIC SERIES <RMMS>
 Harlequin American Romance:
  329 Best Wishes
                     Julie Kistler
  333 Sight Unseen
                     Kathy Clark
  337 Return To Summer
                     Emma Merritt

RODDICK, Barbara
                     (Hilary Mason)

RODDY, Lee
 Love's Far Horizon

RODGERS, M. J.
                     [Mary Johnson]
 Harlequin Intrigue:
  102 For Love Or Money
  128 Taste Of Death, A
  140 Blood Stone
  157 Dead Ringer

RODING, Frances
 Harlequin Presents:
  1052 Open To Influence
  1163 Man Of Stone
  1190 Different Dream, A
  1213 Law Unto Himself, A
  1293 Gentle Deception
 Harlequin Romance:
  2901 Some Sort Of Spell

ROFFMAN, Jan   <GOT><RS>
                [Margaret Summerton]
 Ashes In An Urn
 Bad Conscience, A
 Daze Of Fears
 Death Of A Fox
 Grave Of Green Water

ROFFMAN, Jan   <GOT><RS>
  Mask Of Words
  One Wreath With Love
  Reflection Of Evil, The
  Walk In The Dark
  Why Someone Had To Die
  With Murder In Mind

_____

_____

ROFFMAN, Sara
              [Morris Hershman]
  Family Round

_____

_____

ROFHEART, Martha   <HO>
  Alexandrian, The
  Fortune Made His Sword
  Glendower Country
  Lionheart
  My Name Is Sappho
  Savage Brood, The

_____

_____

ROGAN, Barbara
  Changing States

_____

_____

ROGERS, Eleanor Woods
              (Eleanor Woods)

ROGERS, Elizabeth J.
              (Rebecca Swan)

ROGERS, Evelyn
  Heartfire Romance: <HR>
    Midnight Sins
    Texas Kiss
    Wanton Slave

_____

_____

ROGERS, Evelyn w/ Kathryn
  DAVENPORT   (Keller Graves)

ROGERS, Gayle
              [Gayle Rogers Brown]
  Nakoa's Woman

_____

_____

ROGERS, Lee   <HR>
  All These Splendid Sins

_____

_____

ROGERS, Robert Lee
              (Jean Barrett)
              (Lee Rogers)

ROGERS, Marylyle   <HR>
              [Mary Lisle]
  Dragon's Fire, The
  Heart Trilogy:
    Wary Hearts
    Hidden Hearts
    Proud Hearts
  Tapestry: <HR>
    72 Enchanted Desire
    81 Minstrel's Song, A

_____

_____

ROGERS, Patricia
              (Patricia Welles)
              (Rachel Welles)

ROGERS, Rosemary   <HR>
  Crowd Pleasers, The   <CO>
  Insiders, The   <CO>
  Love Play   <CO>
  Surrender To Love
  Wanton, The
  Wicked Loving Lies
  Wildest Heart, The
  In sequence:
    Sweet Savage Love
    Dark Fires
    Lost Love, Last Love
    Bound By Desire

_____

_____

ROGERS, Samuel   <GOT>
  Don't Look Behind You
  Dusk At The Grove

ROLLINS, Helen
  MacFadden Romance:
    75 High Tide Of Love

ROHR, Paula M.
              (Faye Summers)

ROIPHE, Anne
      [Anne Richardson Roiphe]
  Long Division
  Torch Song

ROLOFSON, Kristine
  Harlequin Temptation:
   179 One Of The Family
   259 Stuck On You
   290 Bound For Bliss
   323 Somebody's Hero

ROLAND, Michelle
      [Rose Marie Ferris]
  Second Chance At Love:
   54 Venus Rising
  102 Beloved Stranger

ROMAINE, Dallas   <GOT>
            [Nora Gibbs]
  Malicious Madonna
  Shadow Of Evil

ROLAND, Paula   <RE>
  Faro's Lady
  Rogue's Bride, The

ROMBERG, Nina
              (Jane Archer)

ROME, Margaret
  Harlequin Presents:
   58 Man Of Fire
   62 Marriage Of Caroline
        Lindsay, The
  101 Palace Of The Hawk
  118 Bartered Bride, The
  128 Cove Of Promises
  158 Adam's Rib
  438 Second-Best Bride
  532 Castle Of The Fountains
  Harlequin Romance:
 1307 Chance To Win, A
 1611 Chateau Of Flowers
 1645 Bride Of The Rif
 1676 Girl At Eagle's Mount, The
 1701 Bird Of Paradis
 1776 Island Of Pearls, The
 1939 Girl At Danes' Dyke, The
 1957 Valley Of Paradise
 2052 Bride Of Zarco
 2096 Thistle And The Rose, The
 2152 Lion In Venice
 2235 Son Of Adam

ROLEINE, Roberta
  Mystique:
    8 Terror At Golden Sands
   31 Time Of Illusion
   34 Fated To Love
   38 Deadly Triangle
   41 Kiss Of Vengeance
   45 Secret At Jester Moor
   52 Flight Into Peril
   55 Sealed Fountain, The
   67 Storm Over Ibiza

ROLLINS, Anita Best
  Avalon:
    Disses Where Eagles Fly

ROME, Margaret (cont.)
2264 Isle Of Calypso
2332 Champagne Spring
2369 Marriage By Capture
2428 Wild Man, The
2445 Miss High And Mighty
2464 Castle In Spain
2487 King Of Kielder
2513 Valley Of Gentians
2553 Rapture Of The Deep
2561 Lord Of The Land
2584 Bay Of Angels
2615 Castle Of The Line
2694 Bride By Contract
2759 Pagan Gold
Masquerade:
25 Maid Of The Border

RONNING, Pamela
                    (Pamela Jerrold)

ROOT, Pat   <RS>
Devil Of The Stairs, The
Evil Became Them

ROPER, Lester
                    (Samantha Lester)
Love's Captive

ROPER, Susan Bonthron
                    (Susan Brand)

ROSAS, Rebecca Boado
                    (Rebecca Paisley)

ROSCOE, Janet
Troubled Summer, The

ROSE, Jennifer
                         [Nancy Weber]
Second Chance At Love:
4 Out Of A Dream
35 Shamrock Season
86 Twilight Embrace
278 Suddenly That Summer
To Have And To Hold:
2 Taste Of Heaven, A
11 Keys To The Heart
27 Kisses Sweeter Than Wine
46 Pennies From Heaven

ROSE, Louise Blecher
Launching Of Barbara
Fabrikant, The

ROSE, Marcia   <CO>
[Marcia Silverman Kamien
                w/ Rose Novak]
Admissions   <MED>
All For The Love Of Daddy   &
Choices
Connections
House Of Her Own, A
Music Of Love
Prince Of Ice
Second Chances
Songs My Father Taught Me   &
Summertimes

ROSE, Marilyn
                    [Marilyn Gaddis Rose]
Forbidden Flame

ROSEMEYER, Nita
Bamboo And The Heather, The

575

ROSEMOOR, Patricia
    [Patricia Pinianski]
Harlequin Intrigue:
  38 Double Images
  55 Dangerous Illusions
  74 Death Spiral
  81 Crimson Holiday
  95 Ambushed
 113 Do Unto Others
 121 Ticket To Nowhere
 161 Pushed To The Limit
Harlequin SuperRomance:
 301 Against All Odds
 334 Working It Out
Torchlite:
    Tender Spirit

ROSENSTOCK, Janet   \<CO\>
          (~ee Dennis Adair)
  China Nights

ROSS, Ann B.   \<RS\>
  Murder Stroke, The

ROSS, Caroline
  Miss Nobody

ROSS, Carolyn
  Sweet Dreams: \<YA\>
    97 Dancing In The Dark

ROSS, Clarissa   \<GOT\>\<HR\>\<RS\>
      [W. E. Daniel Ross]
  Beloved Scoundrel
  Beware The Kindly Stranger
  Cavanaugh Keep
  Casablanca Intrigue
  China Shadow

ROSS, Clarissa (cont.)
  Corridors Of Fear
  Dancing Years, The
  Dark Harbor Haunting
  Denver's Lady
  Drifthaven
  Durrell Towers
  Eternal Desire
  Evil Of Dark Harbor
  Face In The Pond
  Fan The Wanton Flame
  Flame Of Love
  Gemini In Darkness
  Ghost Of Dark Harbor
  Ghosts Of Grantmeer
  Glimpse Into Terror
  Haunting Of Villa Gabriel, The
  Hearse For Dark Harbor, A
  Istanbul Nights
  It Comes By Night
  Jade Princess
  Jennifer By Moonlight
  Kashmiri Passions
  Let Your Heart Answer
  Love To Cherish, A
  Masquerade
  Mists Of Dark Harbor
  Moscow Mists
  Of A Red Rose
  Only Make-Believe   \<CO\>
  Out Of The Fog
  Phantom Of Dark Harbor
  Phantom Of Glencourt, The
  Room Without A Key, The
  Satan Whispers
  Scandalous Affair, A
  Secret Of The Pale Lover
  Shadow On Capricorn, A
  Shadow On The Garden
  So Perilous, My Love
  Spectral Mist
  Summer Of The Shaman
  Tangier Nights
  Terror At Dark Harbor
  Venetian Moon
  Voice From The Grave
  Whisper Of Danger
  Whispers In The Night
  Wine Of Passion

ROSS, Dan   <GOT>
        [W. E. Daniel Ross]
Behind Locked Shutters
Cliffhaven
Dark Is My Shadow
Dark Is My Memory
Dark Villa Of Capri
Fogbound
Murder At City Hall
Mystery Of Fury Castle
Pride Of Nurse Edna, The
Secret Of Mallet Castle
Third Spectre
Whispering Gallery

ROSS, Dana   <GOT>
        [W. E. Daniel Ross]
Demon Of The Darkness
Figure In The Shadows
Haunting Of Clifton Court, The
Lodge Sinister
Night Of The Dead
Raven And The Phantom, The
This Shrouded Night

ROSS, Dana Fuller   <HO>
        [Noel B. Gerson]
Yankee
Yankee Rogue
The Holts: American Dynasty
    Oregon Legacy
    Oklahoma Pride
    Carolina Courage
Wagons West Series: In sequence:
    Independence
    Nebraska!
    Wyoming!
    Oregon!
    Texas!
    California!
    Colorado!
    Nevada!
    Washington!
    Montana!

ROSS, Dana Fuller (cont.)
    Dakota!
    Utah!
    Idaho!
    Missouri!
    Mississippi!
    Louisiana!
    Tennessee!
    Illinois!
    Wisconsin!
    Kentucky!
    Arizona!
    New Mexico!
    Oklahoma!
    Celebration!

ROSS, Erin
        [Shirley Bennett Tallman]
Silhouette Desire:
    18   Second Harvest
    89   Time For Tomorrow
    114 Fragrant Harbor
    137 Tide's End
    155 Odds Against
    171 Child Of My Heart
    217 Roses For Remembrance
    280 Willing Spirit
    383 Carnival Madness
Silhouette Special Edition:
    107 Flower Of The Orient

ROSS, JoAnn
                        (JoAnn Robb)
                        (JoAnn Robbins)
Secret Sins
Harlequin Intrigue:
    27   Risky Pleasure   #
    36   Bait And Switch
Harlequin Temptation:
    42   Stormy Courtship
    67   Love Thy Neighbor
    77   Duskfire   #
    96   Without Precedent
    115 Hero At Heart, A

ROSS, Marilyn (cont.)
Temple Of Darkness - Pisces <ZGS>
Terror At Marbury Hall
Widows Of Westwood, The
Witch Of Bralhaven, The
Tread Softly, Nurse Scott
Witches' Cove
Dark Shadow Series:
1 Dark Shadows
2 Victoria Winters
3 Strangers At Collins House
4 Mystery Of Collinwood, The
5 Curse Of Collinwood, The
6 Barnabas Collins
7 Secret Of
  Barnabas Collins, The
8 Demon Of
  Barnabas Collins, The
9 Foe Of
  Barnabas Collins, The
10 Phantom And
  Barnabas Collins, The
11 Barnabas Collins
  vs. The Warlock
12 Peril Of
  Barnabas Collins, The
Barnabas Collins -
And The Gypsy Witch
And The Mysterious Ghost
And The Quentin's Demon
In A Funny Vein
Barnabas, Quentin -
And Dr. Jekyll's Son
And The Avenging Ghost
And The Body Snatchers
And The Crystal Coffin
And The Frightened Bride
And The Grave Robbers
And The Haunted Cave
And The Hidden Tomb
And The Mad Magician
And The Magic Potion
And The Mummy's Curse
And The Nightmare Assassin
And The Sea Ghost
And The Serpent
And The Scorpio Curse
And The Vampire Beauty
And The Witch's Curse

ROSS, Marilyn (cont.)
Harlequin Gothic Romance:
Castle Malice
Shadows Over Briarcliff
Jeremy Quentin Series:
1 Vampire Contessa, The
Stewarts Of Stormhaven Series:
1 Curse Of Black Charlie, The
2 Cellars Of The Dead
3 Waiting In The Shadows
4 Death's Dark Music
5 Cauldron Of Evil
6 This Evil Village
7 Phantom Of The Snow
8 Mask Of Evil
9 This Frightened Lady
10 Twice Dead, The
11 Awake To Terror
12 Dead Of Winter

_____

_____

ROSS, Phyliss
Headline Nurse
Priscilla White, TV Secretary
Sybil Larson, Hospital Nurse

_____

_____

ROSS, Susan
                [Susan Rau Jamison]
Heart

_____

_____

ROSS, W. E. Daniel
    [William Edward Daniel Ross]
                (Leslie Ames)
                (Marilyn Carter)
                (Rose Dana)
                (Ruth Dorset)
                (Ann Gilmer)
                (Diana Randall)
                (Ellen Randolph)
                (Clarissa Ross)
                (Dan Ross)

ROSS, W. E. Daniel (cont.)
(Dana Ross)
(Marilyn Ross)
(W. E. D. Ross)
(Jane Rossiter)
(Rose Williams)

ROSS, W. E. D.   <GOT><RS>
[W. E. Daniel Ross]
Alice In Love
Beauty Doctor's Nurse
Dark Mansion
Ghost Of Oaklands, The
Haunted Garden, The
House On Mount Vernon Street, The
Love Is Forever
Music Room, The
Nightway Alley
One Louisburg Square
Personal Secretary
Promise Of Love, A
Reunion In Renfrew
Rothhaven
Sable In The Rain
Summer Star
Summer's End
Twilight Web, The
Whispering Gallery, The
Witch Of Goblin Acres
Yesteryear Phantom, The
Avalon:
Christopher's Mansion
Dark Lane
Flight To Romance
Ghostly Jewels, The
Hospital Crisis
House On Lime Street
Let Your Heart Answer
Magic Of Love
Midhaven
Nurse Ann's Secret
Nurse At The Ritz
Nurse Grace's Dilemma
Nurse Janice's Dream
Onstage For Love
Phantom In Red
Phantom Of Edgewater Hall

ROSS, W. E. D. (cont.)
Queen's Stairway, The
Rehearsal For Love
Return To Barton
This Dark Lane
This Uncertain Love
Candlelight:
62 Christopher's Mansion
139 Mansion On The Moors

ROSSE, Susanna   <HO>
[Vivian Connolly]
Dance On The Tightrope
To Love As Eagles

ROSSEN, Steven
Naked Angel

ROSSETTA, Jean
Avalon:
Love In The Fast Lane
Perilous Promises
Game Of Love, The

ROSSITER, Clare   <HR>
Anne Of Summer Ho
Galliard's Hay
Lady For The Lacey's
Three Seasons At Askrigg
White Rose, The

ROSSITER, Jane
[W. E. Daniel Ross]
Backstage Nurse
Love Is A Riddle
To Know And To Love

ROSSITER, Phyllis
Avalon:
O The Scent Of Danger

ROSSNER, Judith   <CO>
        [Judith Perelman Rossner]
August
Any Minute I Can Split
Attachments
Emmeline
Looking For Mr. Goodbar
Nine Months In The Life Of
  An Old Maid
To The Precipice

ROSZEL, Renee
                    [Renee Wilson]
Harlequin American Romance:
   10 Hostage Heart
  129 Another Man's Treasure
Harlequin Temptation:
  246 Another Heaven
  279 Legendary Lover
  334 Valentine's Knight
Silhouette Desire:
   90 Wild Flight
Silhouette Special Edition:
  207 Wind Shadow
  313 Nobody's Fool   <ATS>

ROTCHSTEIN, Janice
                    (see Alan Ebert)

ROTH, Jillian
                    [Linda King Ladd]
Rapture Romance:
   55 Bittersweet Temptation
   71 On Wings Of Desire
   96 Broken Promises

ROTH, Pamela
                    [Pamela Toth]
Harlequin Temptation:
  254 Too Many Weddings

ROTHCHILD, Lee
Love Has No Boundries

ROTHWEILER, Joanne Metro w/
                    Paul ROTHWEILER
(see Lee Davis Willoughby <MOAS>)

ROTHWEILER, Paul
        [Paul Roger Rothweiler]
        (see Jonathan Scofield)
Westward Rails Series:
   1 Railroad Kind
   2 Fortune's Mistress
   3 Empire Builder
   4 Troubled Empire

ROTHWELL, Una
Harlequin Romance:
  2165 Long Way To Go, A

ROTTER, Elizabeth
     [Elizabeth Neff Walker Rotter]
                    (Laura Matthews)
                    (Elizabeth Walker)
                    (Elizabeth Neff Walker)
Seasons Of Love
Finding Mr. Right:
  Paper Tiger

ROUGIER, Georgette   (Deceased)
                    (Georgette Heyer)

ROUVEROL, Jean   <RS>
        [Jean Rouverol Butler]
    Storm Wind Rising

ROWAN, Barbara
                    [Ida Pollock]
    Harlequin Classic:
        95 Flower For A Bride   (845)
        132 Mountain Of Dreams   (902)
    Harlequin Romance:
        799 Love Is For Ever
        845 Flower For A Bride
        902 Mountain Of Dreams
        1554 Keys Of The Castle, The

ROWAN, Deirdre   <RS>
                    [Jeanne Williams]
    Dragon's Mount
    Ravensgate
    Shadow Of The Volcano
    Silver Wood
    Time Of The Burning Mask

ROWE, Jack
    Brandywine   <Saga>

ROWE, Melanie
                    [Pamela Browning]
    Silhouette Romance:
        133 Sands Of Xanadu
    Silhouette Special Edition:
        129 Sea Of Gold

ROWE, Myra   <HR>
    Cajun Rose   w/ Maggie JORDAN
    Cypress Moon

    Louisiana Lady
    Pair Of Hearts   &

ROWE, Myra (cont.)
    River Temptress
    Splendid Yearning, A
    Treasure's Golden Dream   &
    Wild Embrace

ROWLAND, Donald Sydney
                    (Vera Craig)
                    (Edna Murray)
ROWLAND, Susannah   <HR>
    Coral Winds

ROYAL, Rosamond
                    [Jeanne Hines]
    Rapture

ROYALL, Vanessa   <HR>
        [Michael Thomas Hinkemeyer]
    Come Faith, Come Fire
    Firebrand's Woman
    Passionate And The Proud, The
    In sequence:
        Flames Of Desire
        Fires Of Delight
    In sequence:
        Wild Wind Westward
        Seize The Dawn

RUARK, Robert   (Deceased)
        [Robert Chester Ruark]
    Honey Badger
    Horn Of The Hunter
    Old Man And The Boy
    Poor No More
    Something Of Value
    Uhuru

RUBENS, Bernice
  Birds Of Paradise   <CO>
  Brothers   <Saga>
  Favours
  I Sent A Letter To My Love
  Ponsonby Post, The
  Spring Sonata

RUBIN, Susan
  Crosswinds: <YA>
    27 Black Orchid, The
  First Love From Silhouette: <YA>
    214 Walk With Danger

RUDEEN, Anne
  American Royal
  Grey Ghyll
  Summerblood

RUDEEN, Anne w/ Louisa RUDEEN
                   (Leigh Ellis)

RUDICK, Marilynne
  Harlequin Temptation:
    128 Fixing To Stay
    308 Glory Days

RUE, Rosina F.
                   (Nicole Hart)

RUFF, Bonnie B.
  Avalon:
    Heart Of The Matter, The

RUGG, Leslie w/ Gilda FELDMAN
                (Louisa Gillette)

RUNDLE, Anne   <RS>
             (Marianne Lamont)
          (Alexandra Manners)
            (Joanne Marshall)
  Amberwood
  Heronbrook

RUNYON, Jr., Charles
  Gypsy King

RUPPERCHT, Olivia
  Loveswept:
    428 Bad Boy Of New Orleans

RUSH, Ann
  Mine To Cherish

RUSHING, Jane Gilmore
  Mary Dove

RUSSELL, Agnes   <GOT>
  Larksong At Dawn

RUSSELL, Amanda   <HR>
         [Ellen "Bette" Feldman]
  Woman Once Loved, A

RUSSELL, Charlotte   <GOT>
         [Carl Henry Rathjen]
  Dark Music

RUSSELL, Sybil
(Janet Gray)

RUTHERFORD, Pat w/ June HAYDON
(Taria Hayford)

RUTLAND, Eva
Harlequin Regency Romance:
  1 Matched Pair
  20 Vicar's Daughter, The
  28 Enterprising Lady
  45 Willfull Lady, The
Harlequin Romance:
  2897 To Love Them All
  2944 At First Sight
  3064 No Accounting For Love

RUUTH, Marianne   <GOT><RS>
Game Of Shadows
Journey Into Fear
Look To The Blue Horse
Outbreak
Question Of Love, A
Tapestry Of Terror   <CGS:#7>

RYAN, Allyson
                    [Linda Kichline]
Silhouette Special Edition:
  398 Love Can Make It Better
  460 Moon And sun

RYAN, Courtney
                    [Tonia Wood]
Second Chance At Love:
  308 For Love Of Mike
  352 Best Of Strangers   &
  383 Lady Incognito
  408 Temporary Angel
  438 Cody's Gypsy   &

RYAN, Courtney (cont.)
  451 Never Say Never
  462 Absolute Beginners
  468 Ten To Midnight
  474 Sugar & Cinnamon

RYAN, George
(see Lee Davis Willoughby <MOAS>)

RYAN, Jeanette Miles   <YA>
Reckless

RYAN, Jenna
                    [Jacqueline Goff]
Harlequin Intrigue:
  88 Cast In W~x
  99 Suspended Animation
  118 Cloak And Dagger
  138 Carnival
  145 Southern Cross

RYAN, Katherine   <CO>
Risks

RYAN, Nan   <HR>
                [Nancy Henderson Ryan]
Cloudcastle
Desert Storm
Midnight Affair
Outlaw's Kiss
Savage Heat
Silken Bondage
Stardust
Sun God
Wayward Lady
Silhouette Desire:
  351 Love In The Air

584

RYAN, Nancy Henderson   <HR>
                           (Nan Ryan)
    Kathleen's Surrender

_____

_____

RYAN, Oneta
    F⁺rst Love From Silhouette: <YA>
        13 Sometime My Love
        19 Tomorrow's Wish
        26 Time For Us, A
        63 New Beginning, A
        72 Love And Honors

_____

_____

RYAN, Rachel
                        [Sandra B ơ n]
    Candlelight Ecstasy:
        21 Love's Encore
        29 Love Beyond Reason
        49 Eloquent Silence
        59 Treasure Worth Seeking, A
       151 Prime Time

_____

_____

RYAN, Sabrina
                [Elisabeth Macdonald]
    Candlelight Supreme:
       137 Fire In Her Eyes, The

_____

_____

RYAN, Tom   <HO>
    Savage, The

_____

_____

RYDER, Pamela
    Dakin Field   <Saga>

_____

_____

585

SAAL, Jocelyn
  Sweet Dreams: <YA>
    14 Dance Of Love
    28 Trusting Hearts
    38 Running Mates
    46 On Thin Ice

SABATINI, Rafael
  Black Swan, The
  Fortunes Of Captain Blood, The
  Master-At-Arms
  Mistress Wilding
  Scaramouche
  Scaramouche The King-Maker
  Sea Hawk, The
  Sword Of Islam, The
  Tavern Knight, The

SABBAGH, Pierre w/ Antoine
  GARAZIANI   <HR>
  Fanina

SACHS, Judith
                    (Petra Diamond)
SACHS, Marilyn   <YA>
             [Marilyn Stickle Sachs]
  Fourteen
  Hello...Wrong Number

SACKETT, Susan   <HR>
                   [Susan Stern]
  The Avon Romance:
    Passion's Gold
  Heartfire Romance: <HR>
    Emerald Angel

SACKETT, Susan (cont.)
  Island Captive
  Lawless Ecstasy
  Passion's Golden Fire

SACKVILLE-WEST, Vita   (Deceased)
  [Victoria Mary Sackville-West]
  Challenge
  Edwardians, The

SAFFORD, Leslie A.
             (Caroline Campbell)

SAGAN, Francoise
             [Francoise Quoirez]
  Bonjour Tristesse
  Certain Smile, A
  La Chamade
  Scars On The Soul
  Silken Eyes
  Sunlight On Cold Water
  Unmade Bed, The
  Wonderful Clouds, The

SAGER, Esther
  Chasing Rainbows
  Only 'Til Dawn
  Moment To Moment

SAINT-LAMBERT, Patrick
  Mystique:
    89 Wheel Of Fate

ST. CLAIR, Elizabeth   <GOT><RS>
                   [Susan Cohen]
  DeWitt Manor
  Jeweled Secret, The

ST. GEORGE, Margaret
          [Maggie Osborne]
Harlequin American Romance:
  142 Winter Magic
  159 Castles And Fairy Tales
  203 Heart Club, The
  231 Where There's Smoke...
  272 Hearts Desire
  323 Dear Santa   <CIFK>
  345 American Pie   <COAR>
Harlequin Intrigue:
  133 Jigsaw

ST. JAMES, Emma
MacFadden Romance:
  102 Days Of Blue And Gold

ST. JAMES, Ian
Killing Anniversary, The   <Saga>

ST. JAMES, Jessica
  [Linda Varner w/ Charlotte Hoy]
Silhouette Special Edition:
  561 Perfect Lover, The
  603 Showdown At Sin Creek
  631 Country Christmas, A

ST. JAMES, Scotney
  [Linda Varner Palmer
          w/ Charlotte Hoy]
Northern Fire, Northern Star
Heartfire Romance: <HR>
  By Honor Bound
  Defiant Bride

ST. JOHN, Andrea
          [Donald M. Howard]
Candlelight Ecstasy:
  372 Never Love A Cowboy
  399 At Long Last Love
Candlelight Supreme:
  167 Perfect Exchange, The

ST. JOHN, Gail   <GOT>
          [Irving A. Greenfield]
Dunsan House

ST. JOHN, Genevieve   <GOT><RS>
Dark Watch, The
Daughter Of Evil
Death In The Desert
Ghost Of Channing House, The
Invisible Trap, The
Night Of Evil
Secret Of Dresden Farm, The
Secret Of Kensington Manor, The
Shadow On Spanish Swamp, The
Sinister Voice, The
Strangers In The Night

ST. JOHN, Lisa
          [Annette Sanford]
Rapture Romance:
  16 Gossamer Magic
  60 Starfire

ST. JOHN, Nesta
Floodgates Of Love

ST. JOHN, Nicole   <RS>
          [Norma Johnston]
  Guinevera's Gift
  Medici Ring, The
  Wychwood

_____

_____

ST. JOHN, Sally
  Harlequin Romance:
          Study In Love   HRS68

_____

_____

ST. PIERRE, Lisann   <HR>
          [Lisa A. Verge]
  The Avon Romance:
    Defiant Angel

_____

_____

ST. PIERRE, Stephanie
  Sweet Dreams: <YA>
    165 Brush With Love, A
    172 Sun Kissed

_____

_____

ST. THOMAS, Robin   <CO>
          [Tom Bade w/ Robin Stevenson]
  Appearances
  Fortune's Sisters
  Lovers' Masquerade
  Places

_____

_____

SAKOL, Jeannie
  Flora Sweet
  Hot Thirty
  I Was Never The Princess
  Maiden Voyage
  Mothers And Lovers   <CO>
  New Year's Eve
  Promise Me Romance

_____

_____

SALEMO, Nan F. w/ Rosamond M.
                VANDERBURGER <HO>
  Shaman's Daughter

_____

_____

SALERNO, Ann
                    (Ann Hurley)
  Harlequin SuperRomance:
    195 Rain Of Flowers
  Harlequin Temptation:
    58 Fires Of Night

_____

_____

SALERNO, Jeanette
  Princessa

_____

_____

SALISBURY, Carola   <RS>
          [Carola Isobel Julien Salisbury]
  Count Vronsky's Daughter
  Dark Inheritance
  Dolphin Summer
  Pride Of The Trevallions, The
  Shadowed Spring, The
  Winter Bride, The

_____

_____

SALLIS, Susan
  Summer Visitors   <Saga>
  Troubled Waters

_____

_____

SALOFF-ASTAKHOFF, N. I.
  A Hearth Romance:
    19 Judith

_____

_____

SALTER, Elizabeth   (Deceased)<GOT>
Daisy Bates
Death In A Mist
Once Upon A Tombstone
There Was A Witness
Will To Survive

SALVATO, Sharon/Sharon Anne<HR><RS>
[Sharon Anne Zetler Salvato]
Bitter Eden
Briarcliff Manor
Donovan's Daughter
Meredith Legacy, The
Scarborough House
Manning Family Saga:
In sequence:
Fires Of July, The
Drums Of December, The

SALVATO, Sharon w/ Cornelia M.
PARKINSON
[Sharon Anne Zetler Salvato w/
Cornelia McNary Parkinson]
(Day Taylor)

SAMUEL, Barbara
(Ruth Wind)

SAMUELS, Gertrude
Adam's Daughter
Of David And Eva: A Love Story
Mottell: A Partisan Odyssey
Run Shelly Run

SAND, George
Marianne

SANDERS, Dennis
Heart Of The Land   <Saga>

SANDERS, Dorothy Lucie
(Lucy Walker)

SANDERS, Glenda
[Glenda Sanders Kachelmeier]
Harlequin Temptation:
234 Gypsy
257 Daddy Darling
277 All-American Male, The
300 Island Nights
316 Dark Secrets
329 Doctor, Darling

SANDERS, Leonard   <HO>
Light On The Mountain
In sequence: <HS>
Fort Worth
Texas Noon

SANDERS, Lia
[Angela Jackson w/Sandra Jackson]
Candlelight Ecstasy:
41 Tender Mending, The

SANDERS, Madelyn
Harlequin Intrigue:
158 Under Venice

SANDERS, Shirley/Shirley F.
Avalon:
Search For Enchantment
Promise Romance: <Insp>
6 Song Of Tannehill

590

SANDERSON, Jill
                    [Helen Beaumont]
  Sapphire Romance: <ENG>
    Leaping Flame, The
    Never Forget Me

_____

_____

SANDERSON, Nora
  Harlequin Romance:
    752 Ordeal Of Nurse Thompson
    762 Hospital In New Zealand
    787 Two Faces Of Nurse Roberts
    865 Partner For Doctor Philip
    937 Case For Nurse Sheridan

_____

_____

SANDIFER, Linda P.   <HR>
                [Linda Prophet Sandifer]
  The Avon Romance:
    Heart Of The Hunter
    In sequence:
      Tyler's Woman
      Pride's Passion

_____

_____

SANDS, Glenda
      [Glenda Sanders Kachelmeier]
  Silhouette Romance:
    337 Mockingbird Suite, The
    389 Taste Of Romance, A
    409 Heart Shift
    434 Tall, Dark And Handsome
    447 Amended Dreams
    477 Hero On Hold
    496 Logan's Woman
    514 Things We Do For Love, The
    538 Treadmills And Pinwheels
    565 Man Of Her Dreams, The
    602 Home Again

_____

_____

SANDS, JoAnn
  Avaolon:
    Reluctant Bride, The
    Shadows From The Past

_____

_____

SANDS, Leslie
  MacFadden Romance:
    32   If This Be Love

_____

SANDS, Marche
  Odds On Love

_____

SANDSTROM, Eve K.
                    (Elizabeth Storm)

SANDYS, Elspeth
      [Elspeth Sandilands Purchase]
  Burning Dawn, The

_____

_____

SANFORD, Annette
            [Annette Schorre-Sanford]
                    (Mary Carroll)
                    (Meg Dominique)
                    (Lisa St. John)
                    (Anne Shore)
                    (Anne Starr)

SANFORD, Teddi w/ Mickie
  SILVERSTEIN
    Number One Sunset Blvd   <CO>

_____

_____

SANFORD, Ursula   <GOT>
  Poisoned Anemones, The

_____

_____

SANS, Martha

                    (Jenny Loring)
                    (Lee Sawyer)

SANTINI, Rosemarie
All My Children Series:
  I   Tara & Philip
  II   Erica
  III Lovers, The

SANTMYER, Helen Hooven (Deceased)
...And Ladies Of The Club
Farewell Summer
Fierce Dispute, The
Herbs And Apples
Ohio Town

SANTORE, Sue
Silhouette Romance:
  480 Man For Sylvia, A

SANTORI, Helen
               (Helen Erskine)
First Kiss: <YA>
  4 Perfect Couple, The

SARABANDE, William
Wolves Of The Dawn   <HS>
First Americans:
  Beyond The Sea Of Ice
  Forbidden Land, The
  Into The Corridor Of Storms

SARGENT, Elizabeth
Woman In Love, A

SARGENT, Joan
         [Sarah Lucille Jenkins]
Cruise Nurse
Head In The Clouds
My Love An Alter
Portrait With Love
Rainbow's End

SARGENT, Katherine   <HR>
Cajun Lover
Lovespell
Outcasts From Eden
Rose And The Sword, The
Triumph Of Andrea, The

SARGENT, Lynda   <HO>
Judith Duchesne

SARK, Sylvia
Masquerade:
  7 Sophie And The Prince

SATRAN, Pamela
       [Pamela Redmond Satran]
Finding Mr. Right:
  Balancing Act

SATTLER, Veronica   <HR>
Bargain, The
Christie's Rapture
Dangerous Longing, A
Jesse's Lady
Promise Of Fire

SAUCIER, Donna
          [Donna Schomberg]
Harlequin SuperRomance:
  109 Amethyst Fire

SAUNDERS, Anne
          [Margaret Alred]
Aston Hall:
  . 119 Dancing In The Shadows
Circle Of Love:
    9 Heather Is Windblown, The
   21 Circles Of Fate

SAUNDERS, Diana   <HR>
          [Virginia Coffman]
Passion Of Letty Fox, The
Tana MaGuire

SAUNDERS, Irene   <RE>
  Colonel's Campaign, The
  Gambler's Daughter, The
  Invincible Viscount, The
  Impetuous Twin, The
  Laces For A Lady
  Lady Lucinde's Locket
  Lucky Lady, A
  Reluctant Bride, The
  Willful Widow, The

SAUNDERS, Jean   <HR>
          [Jean Innes Saunders]
Scarlet Rebel
  (prequel to "Golden Destiny")
Silhouette Romance:
  149 Kissing Time, The
  216 Love's Sweet Music
  243 Language Of Love, The
  261 Taste The Wine
  289 Partners In Love

SAUNDERS, Jean (cont.)
Tapestry: <HR>
   88 Golden Destiny

SAUNDERS, Jean Innes
              (Jean Innes)
              (Jean Saunders)
              (Rowena Summers)

SAUNDERS, Jeraldine   <HR>
  Love Boats, The
  Signs Of Love   <Astro>
  In Sequence:
    Frisco Lady
    Frisco Fortune, The

SAUNDERS, Laura
Candlelight:
  120 Never To Be Alone
  149 Strange Exile   <RO>

SAUNDERS, Rubie
          [Rubie Agnes Saunders]
  Marilyn Morgan: Cruise Nurse
  Marilyn Morgan: R. N.
  Nurse Morgan's Triumph

SAVAGE, Christina   <HR>
  [Frank Schaefer w/ Kerry Newcomb]
  Dawn Wind
  Hearts Of Fire   <Saga>
  Love's Wildest Fires
  Tempest

SAVAGE, Elizabeth
          [Elizabeth Fitzgerald Savage]
  Willowwood

SAVAGE, Mary   <GOT>
Coach Draws Near, The

SAXON, Antonia
Silhouette Special Edition:
88 Paradiso
141 Above The Moon

SAVARY, Marie   <GOT>
Black Velvet Secrets

SAXON, Davidyne Mayleas
Darling, No Regrets   <CO>

SAVITZ, Harriet May
Summer's End   <YA>

SAXON, Judith   <HS>
All My Fortunes

SAVOY, Suzanne
                [Susan Stern]
More Than Forever

SAXON, William
For Love Or Honor   <CO>
Majestic Dreams

SAWYER, Lee
                [Martha Sans]
Silhouette Romance:
156 Time Remembered

SAYER, Shannon
Avalon:
Orchids For Hilary
Summer Of Pearls

SAWYER, Meryl   <CO>
                [Martha Sawyer Unickel]
Blind Chance

SAYLER, Mary Harwell   <Insp>
Candle
Serenade/Saga: <HR>
13 Hand Me Down The Dawn
23 Beyond The Smoky Curtain

SAWYER, Nancy Buckingham w/ John
SAWYER   (Christina Abbey)
              (Nancy Buckingham)
              (Nancy John)
              (Hilary London)

SCAFIDEL, James
                (Lyn Phillips)
                (James Raymond)
        (see Amanda Jean Jarrett)
        (see Jonathan Scofield)
(see Lee Davis Willoughby <MOAS>)

SAXE, Coral Smith   <HR>
Silver And Sapphire

594

SCAMEHORN, Mary Kathryn w/ Karen
Blair PARKER
                        (Kathryn Blair)
                        (Blair Cameron)

SCANTLIN, Bea
                        (Ruth Stewart)

SCARIANO, Margaret M.
  Caprice Romance: <YA>
    27 Too Young To Know
  Harlequin Gothic Romance:
    Island Of Mystery

_____

_____

SCHAAL, Elizabeth w/ Elaine F.
  CICHANTH   (Elizabeth Shelley)

SCHAEFER, Frank w/ Kerry NEWCOMB
                        (Shana Carrol)
                        (Peter Gentry)
                      (Christina Savage)

SCHAEFFER, Susan Fromberg   <CO>
  Anya
  Buffalo Afternoon
  Injured Party, The
  Love
  Madness Of A Seduced Woman, The
  Mainland
  Time In Its Flight

_____

_____

SCHAFER, Rosemary   <RS>
  Last Of The Whitcombes, The
_____

_____

SCHARF, Marian F. w/Carol I. WAGNER
                        (Malissa Carroll)
                        (Marisa Carroll)

SCHATTNER, E.
                        (Emma Church)
                      (Elizabeth Graham)

SCHEIRMAN, Marian w/ Marie
  FLASSCHOEN   (Lucinda Day)

SCHELLENBERG, Helene Chambers
  Beth Adams, Private Duty Nurse
  Breath Of Life
  Nurse In Research
  Candlelight:
    4 Nurse's Journey

_____

_____

SCHENCK, Anita Allen
                        (Anita Allen)

SCHENCK, Barbara
                        (Anne McAllister)

SCHENK, Joyce
                        (Amy Lawrence)
                        (Jo Stewart)
  Avalon:
    Caves Of Darkness   <GOT>

_____

_____

SCHERE, Monroe
                        (Abigail Winter)

SCHERE, Monroe w/ Jean K. SCHERE
                        (Jessica Howard)

SCHIFF, Harriet Sarnoff
  Well Spring   <CO>

_____

_____

SCHIMEK, Gale Malone
                        (Joleen Daniels)

SCHMIDT, Anna
                        (Anne Shorr)
  Silhouette Desire:
    381 Give And Take

_____

_____

SCHNEIDER, Meg
Choose Your Own Adventure: <YA>
  Confidentially Yours
Two Hearts: <YA>
  Two In A Crowd
Young Love: <YA>
  Romance Can You Survive It?

SCHNEIDER, Rosemary
Harlequin Presents:
  925 Best Laid Plans

SCHODER, Judith w/ Sharon Sigmond
  SHEBAR   (Lacey Shay)

SCHOMBERG, Donna
          (Donna Saucier)

SCHOONOVER, Lawrence (Deceased)<HO>
  [Lawrence Lovell Schoonover]
  Burnished Blade, The   <HR>
  Chancellor, The
  Gentle Infidel, The
  Golden Exile, The
  Key To Gold
  Queen's Cross, The
  Prisoner Of Tordesillas, The
  Revolutionary, The
  Spider King, The
  To Love A Queen

SCHOONOVER, Shirley
  Mountain Of Winter
  Season Of Hard Desires, A
  Winter Dream

SCHREINER, JR., Samuel A.   <HO>
  [Samuel Agnew Schreiner, Jr.]
  Angelica
  Pleasant Places

SCHREINER, JR., Samuel A. (cont.)
  Possessors And The Possessed, The
  Thine Is The Glory
  Van Alens, The

SCHREMPP, Elizabeth K.
          (Katherine Court)

SCHUBERT, John D.   <RS>
  Devil At Castelnero, The
  Keep, The

SCHULER, Candace
          (Jeanette Darwin)
          (Candace Spencer)
  Harlequin Temptation:
    28 Desire's Child
  102 Designing Woman
  129 For The Love Of Mike
  183 Home Fires
  205 Soul Mates
  250 Almost Paradise
  261 Sophisticated Lady
  281 Wildcat
  331 Easy Lovin'

SCHULTE, Elaine L.   <Insp>
  [Elaine Louise Schulte]
  Echoes Of Love
  Serenade/Saga: <HR>
    35 Westward My Love
    37 Dreams Of Gold
  Serenade/Serenata:
    1 On Wings Of Love

SCHULTZ, Duane   <HO>
  [Duane Phillip Schultz]
  Sabers In The Wind

SCHULTZ, Janet
                 (Tracy Sinclair)
                 (Jan Stuart)

SCHULTZ, Marion
          [Marion C. Schultz]
          (Marion Clarke)
Make Believe Boyfriend, The   <YA>
Mysterious Summer   <RS>
Sunfire Romance: <YA><HR>
  Caroline

SCHULTZ, Mary
            (Leandra Logan)
Sweet Dreams: <YA>
  131 Hand-Me-Down Heart
  151 Fortunes Of Love

SCHULTZ, Pearle Henriksen
           (Marie Pershing)

SCHULZE, Dallas
           (Dallas Hamlin)
Harlequin American Romance:
  154 MacKenzie's Lady
  185 Stormwalker
  235 Tell Me A Story
  263 Lost And Found
  291 Together Always
  302 Morning After, The
  317 Of Dreams And Magic
  349 Saturday's Child   <COAR>
  368 Summer To Come Home, A
Now And Forever:
    4 So Much Love
Silhouette Intimate Moments:
  170 Moment To Moment
  247 Donovan's Promise   &
  318 Vow, The   &

SCHULZE, Hertha
         (Kate Wellington)
Harlequin Temptation:
  222 Twice A Miracle
Loveswept:
  120 Before And After
  196 Solid Gold Prospect

SCHURFRANZ, Vivian
  Sunfire Romance: <YA><HR>
    Cassie
    Danielle
    Laura
    Megan
   20 Julie
   21 Rachel
   23 Heather
   25 Merrie
   28 Josie
   30 Renee

SCHWAB, Linda J.
         (Emily Maxwell)

SCHWARTZ, Anne Powers   (Deceased)
         (Anne Powers)

SCHWARTZ, Elroy
Tulsa Gold   <HS>

SCHWARTZ, Paula Reibel
     (Elizabeth Mansfield)
       (Libby Mansfield)
        (Paula Reibel)

SCHWARTZ, Sheila   <YA>
    [Sheila Ruth Schwartz]
Solid Gold Circle, The
Sorority

SCHWARTZ, Shelia (cont.)
Crosswinds: <YA>
  9 Bigger Is Better
Crosswinds Keepsake: <YA>
  20 Most Popular Girl, The
Wildfire: <YA>
  One Day You'll Go

SCHWEITZER, Gertrude   <GOT>
Ledge, The
Stand Before Kings   <Saga>

SCOFIELD, Carin
Silhouette Romance:
  122 Winterfire
  249 Silverwood

SCOFIELD, Jonathan   <HO>
(publishers pseudonym for
            writers in this series)
Freedom Fighters Series:
  1 Tomahawks And Long Rifles
              [Daniel Streib]
  2 Muskets Of '76
              [George Granger]
  3 King's Cannon, The
              [Paul Rothweiler]
  4 Guns At Twilight
              [John Van Zwienen]
  5 Bullets On The Border
              [Evan Heyman]
  6 Storm In The South
              [John Toombs]
  7 Turning Of The Tide, The
              [Barry Myers]
  8 Frontier War, The
              [Stephen Winsten]
  9 Shellfire On The Bay
              [Daniel Streib]
  10 Volunteers For Glory
              [Daniel Streib]
  11 Bayonets In No-Man's Land
              [Len Levinson]

SCOFIELD, Jonathan (cont.)
  12 Armageddon In The West
              [Lou Cameron]
  13 Pacific Hellfire
              [James Busbee, Jr.]
  14 Far Shores Of Danger
              [James Scafidel]
  15 Junglefire
              [Robert Vaughan]

SCOPPETTONE, Sandra
Starfire: <YA>
  Long Time Between Kisses

SCOTLAND, Jay
              [John Jakes]
  Arena

SCOTT, Adrienne
              [Laurie Williams]
Tapestry: <HR>
  52 Pride And Promises

SCOTT, Alexandra
Harlequin Romance:
  2506 Love Me Again
  2514 This Side Of Heaven
  2554 Catch A Star
  2585 Love Comes Stealing
  2604 Borrowed Girl
  2663 Storm Warning
  2769 Wildfire
  2868 An Old Affair

SCOTT, Alison
World Full Of Secrets, A

SCOTT, Amanda   <RE>
            [Lynne Scott-Drennan]
An Affair Of Honor
Battling Bluestocking, The
Border Bride
Dauntless Miss Wingrave, The
Fugitive Heiress, The
Indomitable Miss Harris, The
Kidnapped Bride, The
Lady Brittany's Choice   &
Lady Escapade
Lady Hawk's Folly
Lady Lyford's Secret
Lady Meriel's Duty
Lord Abberley's Nemesis
Lord Grayfalcons Reward
Madcap Marchioness, The
Mistress Of The Hunt
Ravenwood's Lady   &

_____

_____

SCOTT, Annjeanette   <GOT>
            [Scott Wright]
Castle For The Left Hand

_____

_____

SCOTT, Antonia
Falcon's Island

_____

_____

SCOTT, Araby   <HR>
            [Barbara Brouse]
Heart Of The Flame
Wild Sweet Witch

_____

_____

SCOTT, Ariana   <CO>
Fleeting Images
Indiscretions

_____

_____

SCOTT, Celia
Harlequin Romance:
   2568 Seeds Of April
   2638 Starfire
   2735 Where The Gods Dwell
   2831 Talent For Loving, A
   2945 Catch A Dream
   2998 Love On A String
   3040 Rumor Has It
   3087 Give Me Your Answer Do

_____

_____

SCOTT, Deborah   <RS>
Deathbed Of Roses

_____

_____

SCOTT, DeLoras
                     (Lisa Scott)
Harlequin Historical <Set#2>:
   12 Bittersweet
   40 Fire And Ice
   52 Miss And The Maverick, The

_____

_____

SCOTT, Elizabeth A.
Rim Of The Tub, The

_____

_____

SCOTT, Fela Dawson
The Avon Romance:
   Shadow Of Desire   <HR>

_____

_____

SCOTT, Isobel
Circle Of Love:
   27 Wild Sweetness, A

_____

_____

599

SCOTT, Jane
                    [Adeline McElfresh]
Nurse For Rebel's Run, The
Candlelight:
    74 New Love For Cynthia, A

SCOTT, Janey
                    [Roberta Leigh]
Mills & Boon:
    Melody Of Love
    Memory Of Love
    Time To Love, A
    (same as HQ467 by Rachel Lindsay)

SCOTT, Joanna
    Silhouette Intimate Moments:
    86 In All Honesty
    Silhouette Romance:
    50 Dusky Rose
    68 Marriage Bargain, The
    117 Manhattan Masquerade
    169 Lover Come Back
    187 Moonlit Magic
    Silhouette Special Edition:
        Perfect Passion, A <PROM>
    26 Flight Of Swallows, A
    136 Exclusively Yours
    186 Corporate Policy

SCOTT, Marianne deJay   <GOT>
    Drumbuie House
    Van Dyne Collection, The

SCOTT, Melissa
                    [Janet Thies]
    Silhouette Desire:
    147 Territorial Rights

SCOTT, Michael William
    Rakehell Dynasty: <HS>
    1 Rakehell Dynasty
    2 China Bride
    3 Orient Affair
    4 Mission To Cathay

SCOTT, Rachel
                    [Celina Mullan]
    Velvet Glove: <RS>
    6 In The Dead Of The Night
    22 Stalk A Stranger

SCOTT, Samantha
                    [Nancy Hermann]
    Candlelight Ecstasy:
    64 Sweet Healing Passion
    147 Love's Unveiling
    204 After The Loving
    Candlelight Ecstasy Supreme:
    22 All In Good Time

SCOTT, Theresa   <HR>
    Bride Of Desire
    In sequence:
        Savage Betrayal
        Savage Revenge

SCOTT, Valerie X.
                [Donald Sydney Rowland]
    Surrogate Wife

SCRIMGEOUR, G. J.   <HO>
                [Gary James Scrimgeour]
    Woman Of Her Times, A

SEABAUGH, Carolyn
    [Carolyn Seabaugh Matthews]
Silhouette Romance:
    468 Butterfly Autumn
Silhouette Special Edition:
    580 Lean On Me
    634 Cicada Summer

SEALE, Sara
    [Mrs. A. D. L. MacPherson]
Harlequin Classic:
    18   Wintersbride, The   (560)
    30   Gentle Prisoner, The   (645)
    61   Then She Fled Me   (781)
    66   Forbidden Island   (719)
    73   Orphan Bride   (657)
    90   Youngest
         Bridesmaid, The   (816)
    93   Only Charity, The   (692)
    105 Dark Stranger, The   (870)
    114 Child Friday   (896)
    122 Charity Child   (991)
    137 This Merry Bond   (583)
    146 Maggy   (469)
    169 Castle Cloud   (1096)
Harlequin Presents:
    97   To Catch A Unicorn
    137 Silver Sky, The
Harlequin Romance:
    781 Then She Fled Me
    816 Youngest Bridesmaid, The
    838 Dear Dragon
    870 Dark Stranger, The
    896 Child Friday
    918 These Delights
    949 Third Uncle, The
    973 Time Of Grace
    991 Charity Child
    1021 Folly To Be Wise
    1045 Green Girl
    1072 Young Amanda, The
    1096 Cloud Castle
    1114 Trevallion
    1144 Truant Bride, The
    1174 English Tutor, The

SEALE, Sara (cont.)
    1197 Penny Plain
    1218 Beggars May Sing
    1263 Lordly One, The
    1293 I Know My Love
    1324 Queen Of Hearts, The
    1347 Truant Spirit, The
    1392 That Young Person
    1524 Dear Professor
    1597 Unknown Mr. Brown, The
    1988 My Heart's Desire

SEAMAN, Lucy
                        (Michele Robbe)

SEARIGHT, Ellen
                        [Doris Stuart]
    Candlelight:
    566 Golden Interlude   <RO>

SEARLE, Judith
    Lovelife

SEARLE, Julia
    Harlequin Romance:
         Carousel Waltz   HRS36

SEARS, Jane L.
    Song Of The River
    Surfboard Summer

SEARS, Ruth McCarthy
    Cruise Of The Golden Poppy
    Dr. Toni's Miracle
    Friday's Child

SEELEY, Mabel   \<GOT>
  Beckoning Door, The
  Chuckling Fingers, The
  Crying Sisters, The
  Listening House, The
  Whistling Shadow, The
  Woman Of Property

SEELY, Norma
              [Norma Yvonne Seely]
              (Yvonne Norman)
  Starlight Romance:
    Depths Of Love, The
    Dream Chaser
    Love In The Wind
    Silver Lining

SEGAL, Brenda Lesley   \<HR>
  Aliya: A Love Story   \<CO>
            w/ Marianne KANTER
  If I Forget Thee
  Tenth Measure, The

SEGAL, Erich
             [Erich Wolf Segal]
  Man, Woman And Child
  In sequence:
    Love Story
    Oliver's Story

SEGAL, Harriet
  Shadow Mountain   \<Saga>
  Hillman Saga: In sequence:
    Susquehanna   \<HS>
    Catch The Wind   \<CO>

SEGER, Maura
             (Jenny Bates)
        (Maeve Fitzgerald)
         (Sara Jennings)
        (Anne MacNeill)
      (Laurel Winslow)
(see Silhouette Christmas Stories)
  Before The Wind   \<HR>
  Empire Of The Heart   \<HR>
  Into The Storm   \<HR>
  Calvert Trilogy: \<HR>
    Sarah
    Elizabeth
    Catherine
  In sequence:
    Eye Of The Storm
    Echo Of Thunder
    Edge Of Dawn
  Series: What If...:   \<HR>
    Fortune's Tide
    Perchance To Dream
  Harlequin SuperRomance:
    181 Spring Frost, Summer Fire
  Harlequin Temptation:
    69 Undercover
  Now And Forever:
    3 Summer Heat
  Silhouette Desire:
    282 Cajun Summer
    295 Treasure Hunt
  Silhouette Intimate Moments:
    61 Silver Zephyr   &
    96 Golden Chimera   &
    108 Comes A Stranger
    137 Shadows Of The Heart
    149 Quest Of The Eagle
    162 Dark Of The Moon
    176 Happily Ever After
    194 Legacy
    209 Sea Gate   &
    224 Day And Night
    236 Conflict Of Interest
    253 Unforgettable
    280 Change Of Plans
    342 Painted Lady
  Silhouette Special Edition:
    135 Gift Beyond Price, A

Tapestry: <HR>
In sequence:
    Defiant Love
13 Rebellious Love
20 Forbidden Love
23 Flame On The Sun

SEIBERT, Catherine w/ Patricia A.
WILLIAMS   (Alexandra Lord)

SEIDEL, Kathleen Gilles
Don't Forget To Smile
Maybe This Time
Harlequin American Romance:
    2 Same Last Name, The
   17 Risk Worth Taking, A
   57 Mirrors And Mistakes
   80 When Love Isn't Enough
Harlequin American Romance
    Premier Edition:
    After All These Years

SEIDICK, Kathryn
        [Kathryn Amelia Seidick]
        (Michelle Kasey)
        (Kasey Michaels)

SEIFERT, Elizabeth
        [Elizabeth Gasparotti]
Army Doctor
Bachelor Doctor
Bright Banners
Bright Coin, The
Bright Scalpel
Call For Dr. Barton, A
Certain Doctor French, A
Challenge For Doctor Mays
Doctor At The Crossroads
Doctor Comes To Bayard
Doctor Disagrees, The
Doctor Ellison's Decision
Doctor For Blue Jay Cove, A

Doctor In Judgement
Doctor In Love
Doctor In The Family, A
Doctor Jeremy's Wife
Doctor Makes A Choice, The
Doctor Of Mercy
Doctor On Trial
Doctor Samaritan
Doctor Scott: Surgeon On Call
Doctor Takes A Wife, The
Doctor Tuck
Doctor With A Mission
Doctor Woodward's Ambition
Doctor's Affair, The
Doctor's Bride, The
Doctor's Confession, The
Doctor's Daughter, The
Doctor's Desperate Hour, The
Doctor's Destiny
Doctor's Husband, The
Doctor's Kingdom
Doctors On Eden Place, The
Doctor's Private Life, The
Doctor's Promise, The
Doctor's Reputation, The
Doctor's Second Love, The
Doctor's Strange Secret, The
Doctor's Two Lives, The
Doctors Were Brothers, The
Dusty Spring
For Love Of A Doctor
Four Doctors, Four Wives
Girl Intern
Glass And The Trumpet, The
Great Day, A
Hegerty, M. D.
Hillbilly Doctor
Homecoming
Hometown Doctor
Honor Of Dr. Skelton, The
Hospital Zone
Katie's Young Doctor
Legacy For A Doctor
Love Calls The Doctor
Lucinda Marries The Doctor
Marriage For Three

SEIFERT, Elizabeth (cont.)
Miss Doctor
New Doctor, The
Old Doc
Orchard Hill
Ordeal Of Three Doctors
Pay The Doctor
Problems Of Doctor A, The
Rebel Doctor
Rival Doctors, The
So Young, So Fair
Story Of Andrea Fields, The
Strange Loyalty Of Dr. Carlisle
Substitute Doctor
Surgeons In Charge
Take Three Doctors
Thus Doctor Mallory
To Wed A Doctor
Two Doctors And A Girl
Two Doctors, Two Loves
Two Faces Of Dr. Collier, The
When Doctors Marry
Young Doctor Galahad

SEIGEL, Benjamin
This Healing Passion

SEILAZ, Aileen   <GOT>
Veil Of Silence, The

SELDEN, Bernice
Heavenly Romance: <YA>
Music In My Heart

SELDEN, Neil
                    [Neil Roy Selden]
Caprice Romance: <YA>
38 Last Kiss In April

SELIG, Elaine Booth   <RS>
Demon Summer
Mariner's End
Scorpion Summer

SELINKO, Anne Marie
Desiree

SELLERS, Alexandra
Candlelight:
674 Indifferent Heart,The <RO>
Harlequin Temptation:
6 Forever Kind, The
Silhouette Intimate Moments:
73 Real Man, The
110 Male Chauvinist, The
154 Old Flame, The
348 Best Of Friends, The
SuperRomance:
13 Captive Of Desire
42 Fire In The Wind
87 Season Of Storm

SELLERS, Catherine
         [Catherine Rhodes Sellers]
Meteor Kismet
1 Always

SELLERS, Con   <HR>
         [Connie Leslie Sellers, Jr.]
Keepers Of The House
Last Flower
Marilee
Sweet Caroline

SELLERS, Connie Leslie, Jr.
                    (Lee Raintree)
                    (Con Sellers)

605

SELLERS, Lorraine
  Silhouette Intimate Moments:
    15 Shadow Dance

SELLERS, Mary
  Cry Of The Cat, The
  House On Black Bayou, The

SETTLE, Mary Lee
  Celebration   <HO>
  Fight Night On A Sweet Saturday
  Prides Promise
  Beulah Quintet: <HS>
    1 O Beulah Land
    2 Blood Tie
    3 Know Nothing
    4 Scapegoat, The
    5 Killing Ground, The

SERAFINI, Tina
              (Sali Knight)

SETON, Anya
          [Anya Seton Chase]
  Avalon
  Devil Water
  Dragonwyck
  Foxfire
  Green Darkness
  Hearth And Eagle, The
  Katherine
  Mistletoe & Sword, The
  My Theodosia
  Smouldering Fires
  Turquoise, The
  Winthrop Woman, The

SETON, Cynthia Propper   (Deceased)
  Fine Romance, A
  Glorious Third, A
  Half-Sisters, The
  Mother Of The Graduate
  Privite Life, A
  Sea Change Of Angela Lewes, The

SETTE, Frank
  Legend

SEUBERUSH, Hertha
  Candle In The Wind

SEVERSON, K. D.
            (Robin Gideon)

SEYMOUR, Arabella   <HR>
  Dangerous Deceptions
  Passion In The Blood, A

SEYMOUR, Janette   <HR>
  Emmie's Love
  Reckless Lady   <CO>
  In sequence:
    Purity's Passion
    Purity's Ecstasy
    Purity's Shame

SEYMOUR, Miranda   <HO>
        [Miranda Sinclair]
  Count Manfred
  Daughter Of Shadows
  Goddess, The
  Medea

SHAHEEN, Leigh
                    (Leigh Haskell)
                    (Harriet L. Hudson)
                    (Valerie Zayne)

SHAKARJIAN, Victoria
                    (Veronica Gregory)

SHALLENBERGER, Sharon McCaffree
                    (Sharon McCaffree)

SHAMBROOK, Rona Randall
                    (Rona Randall)
                    (Virginia Standage)

SHANDS, Sondra   <HR>
  Time Of Passion

SHANE, Marsena
  Tender Love:
    Sweet Dreams, Lady Moon

SHANE, Sandi
    [Sandra Canfield w/
                    Penny Richards]
  Silhouette Classic:
    33 No Perfect Season   (IM91)
  Silhouette Intimate Moments:
    91 No Perfect Season
  Silhouette Special Edition:
    257 Sweet Burning

SHANKMAN, Sarah
  Keeping Secrets

SHANN, Renee   (Deceased)
  Cloud Over The Sun
  Detour To Destiny
  Forecast For Love
  Girl In A Trap

SHANN, Renee (cont.)
  Girl Like Marilyn, A
  Green Willows
  Harmony Of Hearts
  Hasty Marriage, The
  Man Of Her Dreams
  Never Again
  Nurse In Paris
  Right Man For Julie
  Set Love In Order
  Summer To Decide, A
  Tread Softly In Love

SHANNON, Bess
                    [Allyn Thompson]
  Harlequin Temptation:
    298 Going, Going, Gone!

SHANNON, Colleen   <HR>
                    [Colleen Jeske]
  Hawk's Lady, The
  Midnight Rider
  Tender Devil, The
  Wild Heart Tamed

SHANNON, Dell
                    [Elizabeth Linington]
  Dispossessed, The
  Scalpel And The Sword, The   <HS>

SHANNON, Doris   <GOT><RS>
  Beyond The Shining Mountains
  Cain's Daughter
  Hawthorn Hill
  Lodestar Legacy, The
  Punishment, The
  Seekers, The
  Twenty-Two Hallowfield
  Whispering Ruins, The

SHANNON, Evelyn
    [Maureen Crane Wartski]
  Harlequin Temptation:
   84 Two For The Road

SHANNON, Kathleen
             (Shannon Waverly)

SHARMAT, Marjorie   <YA>
    [Marjorie Weinman Sharmat]
  How To Meet A Gorgeous Guy
  Young Love Romance: <YA>
  How To Have A Gorgeous Wedding

SHARP, Helen
    [Lauran Bosworth Paine]
  Love Is A New World

SHARPE, Alice
  Avalon:
    Garland Of Love, A
    Just One More Secret
    Storybook Love, A
    Vanishing Bridegroom, The

SHARPE, Susan
  Softsell
  Sonata
  Ten Miles From Tomorrow

SHAVER, Pat w/ Debrah MORRIS
           (Pepper Adams)
           (JoAnna Jordan)
           (JoAnn Stacey)
           (Dianne Thomas)

SHAW, Catherine
  Harlequin Romance:
  2465 Chateau Of Dreams

SHAW, Eunice
  Clouded Legacy

SHAW, Heather
  MacFadden Romance:
  113 Cape Flower
  129 Beyond This Bright Horizon
  136 Spanish Sun And Wine
  175 Mexican Moon
  194 Meeting At Midnight
  243 Fields Of Love

SHAW, Linda   <HR>
    [Linda Louise McCullough Shaw]
  Ballad In Blue
  Innocent Deception, An   <CO>
  Satin Vixen, The
  Songbird
  Silhouette Classic:
    6 December's Wine   (SE6>
  Silhouette Intimate Moments:
   78 Sweet Rush Of April, The
  324 Case Dismissed
  360 One Sweet Sin
  Silhouette Special Edition:
   19 December's Wine
   43 All She Ever Wanted
   67 After The Rain
   97 Way Of The Willow
  121 Thistle In The Spring, A
  151 Lovesong And You, A
  224 One Pale, Fawn Glove
  276 Kisses Don't Count
  325 Something About Summer
  367 Fire At Dawn
  403 Santiago Heat
  450 Disarray

SHAW, Linda (cont.)
    492 Thunder High
    540 Love This Stranger

SHAW, Susan
    Caprice Romance: <YA>
        25 Bicycle Built For Two, A
        59 Two Of A Kind

SHAY, Lacey
    [Sharon Sigmond Shebar
                    w/ Judith Schoder]
    Serenade Romance:
        Loving Enemy

SHEARING, Joseph   <GOT>
            [Gabrielle Margaret Long]
    Abode Of Love, The
    Aunt Beardie
    Blanche Fury(w/Margaret CAMPBELL)
    Crime Of Laura Sarelle, The
    Golden Violet, The
    Moss Rose
    Spectral Bride, The
    Spider In The Cup, The
    Strange Case Of Lucile Clery
    To Bed At Noon

SHEARS, J. A   <HO>
    Fire In The Sky

SHEARS, Judith   <HO>
    Russians, The   <IMS>

SHEARS, Judith w/ Bill HOTCHKISS
    Pawnee Medicine   <AIS:#14>
    Shoshone Thunder   <AIS:#12>

SHEBAR, Sharon Sigmond w/ Judith
    SCHODER   (Lacey Shay)

SHEEHAN, Nancy
    Avalon:
        Summer Of Secrets
        Harvest Of Love

SHELBOURNE, Cecily
    Stage Of Love

SHELBY, Graham   <HR>
    The Cannaway saga: In sequence:
        Cannaways, The
        Cannaway Concern, The

SHELBY, Philip
    This Far From Paradise

SHELDON, Mary
    I'll Dream Of Darkness

SHELDON, Sidney
    Bloodline
    If Tomorrow Comes
    Master Of The Game
    Naked Face, The
    Rage Of Angels
    Sands Of Time, The

SHELDON, Sidney (cont.)

Stranger In The Mirror, A
Windmills Of The Gods
In sequence:
  Other Side Of Midnight, The
  Memories Of Midnight

_____

_____

SHELL, Peggy
Avalon:
  Dr. Lindsey's Strategy

_____

_____

SHELLABARGER, Samuel   <HO>
King's Cavalier, The

_____

_____

SHELLEY, Elizabeth
[Elizabeth Schaal w/
        Elaine F. Cichantk]
Caravan Of Desire

_____

_____

SHELLEY, Lillian
[Shelley Koppel w/ Lillian Koppel]
Starlight Romance:
  Belle Of Bath, The
  Secret Heiress, The   <RE>

_____

_____

SHELLEY, Susan
                [Mary Pershall]
Love's Enchantment

_____

_____

SHENKIN, Elizabeth   <GOT>
Secret Heart, The

_____

_____

SHEPARD, Fern   <RS>
An Old-Fashioned Love

SHEPARD, Fern (cont.)
Believe In Love
Courtroom Nurse
Meter Maid
Nurse's Longing, A
Psychiatric Nurse
Rejected Love
Sacrifice For Love
Walk In A Spring Rain,

_____

_____

SHEPHERD, L. P.   <GOT>
Cape House

_____

_____

SHEPHERD, Perdita
                [Mary Lee Grisanti]
Mornings In Heaven   <CO>
Promise In The Wind, A   <HR>

_____

_____

SHEPPARD, Mary
Humming Precipice, The
Strangers In The Sun

_____

_____

SHERBURNE, Zoa   <GOT><RS>
                [Zoa Morin Sherburne]
Girl In The Shadows   <CGS:#20>
Jennifer
Leslie
Too Bad About The Haines Girl

_____

_____

SHERIDAN, Adora   <RS>
        [E. M. Pavlik w/ J. F. Hong]
Season, The
Signet Ring, The

_____

_____

SHERIDAN, Ainslie
  Trophies   <CO>

SHERIDAN, Anne-Marie   <RS>
  Far-Off Rhapsody, The
  Summoned To Darkness

SHERIDAN, Jane   <HR>
  Damaris
  Love At Sunset
  My Lady Hoyden

SHERMAN, Jory
  Santa Fe Trail: <HR>
    1 Eagles Of Destiny

SHERRILL, Dorothy
  Captain From Nantucket

SHERRILL, Suzanne
                    [Sherryl Woods]
  Candlelight Ecstasy:
    46 Restoring Love
    209 Desirable Compromise

SHERROD, Barbara   <RE>
                    (Barbara Neil)
  Lady Devine
  Mary Ashe

SHERWOOD, Deborah
  Candlelight Supreme:
    141 Winds Of A Secret Desire
    166 Lovers And Liars
    185 Gypsy Love

SHERWOOD, Valerie   <HR>
                    [Jeanne Hines]
  Born To Love   <Saga>
  Lisbon   <HS>
  Lovely Lying Lips
  These Golden Pleasures
  This Loving Torment
  To Love A Rogue
  In sequence:
    This Towering Passion
    Her Shining Splendor
  Quartet:
    Bold Breathless Love
    Rash Reckless Love
    Wild Willful Love
    Rich Radiant Love
  Trilogy:
    Lovesong
    Windsong
    Nightsong

SHEWMAKE, Georgia M.   <GOT><RS>
  Avalon:
    Balcony Of Evil
    Beckoning Moon
    Curse Of The Rebellars, The
    Ghosts Of Yesterday
    Lake Of Shadows
    Love's Strange Mysteries
    Love's Sweet Victory
    Peril Of The Dunes
    Ridge Of Fear
    Shadow Of Dolores, The
    Thicket Of Terror

SHIELDS, Dinah
    (Jane Clare)
Harlequin Intrigue:
 29 Just Before Dawn

SHIFFMAN, Janis Laden
    (Janis Laden)

SHIMER, Ruth   <GOT>
Correspondent, The

SHIPLETT, June Lund   <HR>
Beloved Traitor
Hold Back The Sun
Lady Wildcat
In sequence: <RF>
 Journey To Yesterday
 Return To Yesterday
Wind Series: In sequence:
 Raging Winds Of Heaven, The
 Reap The Bitter Winds
 Wild Storms Of Heaven, The
 Defy The Savage Winds
 Thunder In The Wind
 Wild Winds Calling
 Winds Of Betrayal
 Gathering Of The Winds, The

SHIPMAN, Natalie
Once Upon A Summer
Sister Of The Bride
Candlelight:
 129 Follow Your Heart

SHIVELLEY, Angela   <GOT>
Dread Of Night

SHNAYERSON, Michael
    (Michael Behan)

SHOCK, Marianne
Loveswept:
 69 Queen's Defense, The
 101 Worthy Opponents
 127 Storm's Thunder
 172 Inherited
Silhouette Special Edition:
 412 Run Away Home

SHOEBRIDGE, Marjorie <HR>
Bride Of The Saracen Stone
Destiny's Desire
Ranleigh Court   <VIC>
Reluctant Rapture
Wreath Of Orchids, A <VIC>
Lovestruck:
 To Love A Stranger

SHOESMITH, Kathleen A.<GOT><RE><RS>
   [Kathleen Anne Shoesmith]
Belltower
Cloud Over Calderwood
Highwayman's Daughter, The
Jack O'Lantern
Mallory's Luck
Reluctant Puritan
Tides Of Tremannion, The

SHOOK, Sheila
Silhouette Inspirations:
 14 Question Of Trust, A

SHORE, Anne   <RO>
    [Annette Sanford]
Candlelight:
 241 Heart's Horizons, The
 243 Whispers Of The Heart

SHORE, Anne (cont.)
256 Winter Kisses, Summer Love
261 Promise By Moonlight
558 Tender Is The Touch
608 Searching Heart, The
668 Valley Of The Butterflies
697 Faraway Land, The

SHORE, Edwina
Harlequin Presents:
1172 Just Another Married Man
Harlequin Romance:
2753 Will To Love, A
2798 Last Barrier, The
2946 Not-So-Perfect Marriage, A
2962 Storm Clouds Gathering

SHORE, Francine
        [Maureen Crane Wartski]
Rapture Romance:
11 Flower Of Desire
22 Golden Maiden, The
36 Love's Gilded Mask
51 Lover In The Wings
75 Lover's Run

SHORE, Jane
Avalon:
Cinderella Game, The
This Time, For Always

SHORE, Juliet
        [Jan Haye]
Harlequin Classic:
4 Doctor Memsahib   (531)
Harlequin Romance:
757 Palm-Thatched
        Hospital, The
876 Serenade For Doctor Bray
929 Hospital Of Bamboo

SHORE, Juliet (cont.)
1017 Attached To
        Doctor Marchmont
1185 When Doctors Meet
1256 Pink Jacaranda, The
1299 Listening Palms, The
1617 Tree Of Promise

SHORR, Anne
        [Anna Schmidt]
Harlequin Temptation:
132 For All Time

SHREVE, Anita
Eden Close

SHUB, Joyce   <RS>
Moscow By Nightmare

SHULER, Linda Lay
She Who Remembers   <HS>

SHULMAN, Sandra   <GOT><RS>
        [Sandra Dawn Shulman]
        (Lisa Montague)
Brides Of Devil's Leap, The
Castlecliffe
Daughters Of Astaroth, The
Florentine, The
Lady Of Arlac, The
Menacing Darkness, The
Nightmare
Prisoner Of Garve, The
Temptress, The

SHURA, Mary Francis
        [Mary Francis Craig]
Shop On Threnody Street, The
Sunfire Romance: <HR><YA>
  Jessica
  Marilee
  24 Gabrielle
  29 Diana
  32 Darcy

_____

_____

SHYER, Marlene Fanta
Weekend   <CO>

_____

_____

SIBSON, Caroline
Chosen One, The

_____

_____

SIDDON, Barbara
[Sally Siddon w/ Barbara Bradford]
Pageant Romance:
  Deceive Me, Darling

_____

_____

SIDDON, Sally w/ Barbara BRADFORD
                (Sally Bradford)
                (Barbara Siddon)

SIEGEL, Norabelle Roth
                (Noreen Nash)

SIEGENTHAL, Deborah
                (Deborah Simmons)

SIERRA, Patricia   <YA>
One-Way Romance

_____

_____

SIGHTLER, Verna Wolters
Wait For Me

SIGHTLER, Verna Wolters (cont.)
Avalon:
  Reach For The Stars

_____

_____

SILHOUETTE CHRISTMAS STORIES:
1986 - (4 story volume)
  Home For Christmas
                Nora Roberts
  Let It Snow
                Debbie Macomber
  Under The Mistletoe
                Tracy Sinclair
  Starbright
                Maura Seger

_____

1987 - (4 story volume)
  Henry The Ninth
                Dixie Browning
  Season Of Miracles
                Ginna Gray
  Bluebird Winter
                Linda Howard
  The Humbug Man
                Diana Palmer

_____

1988 - (4 story volume)
  The Twelfth Moon
                Kathleen Eagle
  Eight Nights
                Brooke Hastings
  Christmas Magic
                Annette Broadrick
  Miracle On I-40
                Curtis Ann Matlock

_____

1989 - (4 story volume)
  The Greatest Gift
                Marilyn Pappano
  The Voice Of The Turtles
                Lass Small
  A Christmas For Carole
                Bay Matthews
  Silent Night
                Brittany Young

_____

SILHOUETTE CHRISTMAS STORIES(cont.)

1990 - (4 story volume)
Santa's Special Miracle
                 Ann Major
Lights Out!
                 Rita Rainville
Always And Forever
                 Lindsay McKenna
Mysterious Gift, The
                 Kathleen Crieghton

SILHOUETTE SUMMER SIZZLERS:
1988 - (3 story volume)
Fiesta
                 Barbara Faith
The Image Of A Girl
                 Billie Green
Grand Illusion
                 Joan Hohl

1989 - (3 story volume)
Impulse
                 Nora Roberts
Ravished
                 Parris Afton Bonds
The Road To Manderlay
                 Kathleen Korbel

1990 - (3 story volume)
Miss Greenhorn
                 Diana Palmer
A Bridge To Dreams
                 Sherryl Woods
Easy Come...
                 Patricia Coughlin

SILVER, Warren A.
Green Rose, The

SILVERLOCK, Anne
                 [Louise Titchener]
Candlelight Ecstasy:
  284 Casanova's Master
  331 With Each Caress
  426 Fantasy Lover
Candlelight Ecstasy Supreme:
   81 Aphrodite's Promise
  103 An Invincible Love
Candlelight Supreme:
  152 In The Heat Of The Sun

SILVERSTEIN, Mel w/
                Karen SILVERSTEIN
Side Effects   <CO>

SILVERSTEIN, Mickie
               (see Teddi Sanford)

SILVERWOOD, Jane
                [Louise Titchener]
Harlequin SuperRomance:
  282 Tender Trap, The
  314 Beyond Mere Words
  375 Handle With Care
   Byrnside:
  434   High Stakes
  438   Dark Waters
  442   Bright Secrets
Harlequin Temptation:
   46 Voyage Of The Heart
   93 Slow Melt
  117 Permanent Arrangement, A

SIMA, Elaine w/ Sherrill BODINE
 (Lynn Leslie)
 (Leslie Lynn)

SIMART, Helena
 Mystique:
 32 Dark Shadow Of Love
 35 Cruel Masquerade
 40 Dangerous Pretense
 109 Till Proven Guilty
 136 Duel Of Happiness

SIMBAL, Joanne
 Sweet Dreams: <YA>
 146 Gifts From The Heart

SIMMONS, Deborah
 [Deborah Siegenthal]
 The Avon Romance:
 Heart's Masquerade

SIMMONS, Mary Kay <GOT><RS>
 [Mary Kay Simmons Freed]
 Cameron Hill
 Captain's House, The
 Clock Face, The
 Dark Holiday
 Diamonds Of Alcazar, The
 Fire In The Blood, A
 Flight From Riversedge
 Girl With The Key, The
 Gypsy Grove, The
 Haggard's Cove
 Hermitage, The
 Kill Cross, The
 Megan
 Saracen Gardens, The
 Smuggler's Gate
 Willow Pond, The
 With Rapture Bound
 Year Of The Rooster, The

SIMMONS, Suzanne
 [Suzanne Simmons Guntrum]
 MacFadden Romance:
 116 Summer Storm
 134 Winter Wine
 140 Dream Weaver
 140 From This Day Forward
 166 Velvet Morning
 204 Touch The Wind
 Candlelight Ecstasy:
 12 Tempestuous Lovers, The
 44 Never As Strangers
 98 As Night Follows Day

SIMMONS, Trana Mae
   (see Carolyn Chase)

SIMMS, Charlotte
 [Charla Chin w/ Jane Kidder]
 The Avon Romance:
 Silver Caress

SIMMS, Suzanne
 [Suzanne Simmons Guntrum]
 Silhouette Desire:
 9 Moment In Time
 17 Of Passion Born
 43 Wild, Sweet Magic, A
 61 All The Night Long
 79 So Sweet A Madness
 109 Only This Night
 150 Dream Within A Dream
 258 Nothing Ventured
 299 Moment Of Truth

SIMON, Jean
 First Love From Silhouette: <YA>
 203 Playing House

SIMON, JoAnn
              (JoAnna Campbell)
  Beloved Captain   <T-T>
  Hold Fast To Love
  Sojourn
  In sequence:
    Love Once In Passing
    Love Once Again

SIMON, Laura   <HR>
  Taste Of Heaven, A
  Until I Return

SIMONS, Renee
  Silhouette Intimate Moments:
    187 Colton's Folly

SIMONSON, Sheila   <RE>
      (see A Regency Valentine)
  Cousinly Connection, A
  Story Order:
    Bar Sinister, The
    Lady Elizabeth's Comet
    Love And Folly

SIMPSON, Carla   <HR>
  Always, My Love   <T-T>
  Desire's Flame
  Memory And Desire   <HR-Reic>
  Passion's Splendor
  Silken Surrender
  Silver Mistress

SIMPSON, Carla w/ Pamela WALLACE
           (Pamela Simpson)

SIMPSON, Judith w/ June HAYDON
           (Roz Denny)
          (Rosalind Foxx)
          (Sara Logan)

SIMPSON, Pamela
  [Pamela Wallace w/Carla Simpson]
  Partners In Time   <T-T>

SIMPSON, Rosemary
  Dreams And Shadows

SIMS, Lavonne
  Court Of Sighs

SINCLAIR, Alberta
         [Theresa Grazia]
  Harlequin Regency Romance:
    Hint Of Scandal, A
    5 Cousin Nancy

SINCLAIR, Brooke
         [Kandius Brooks]
  Meteor Kismet:
    2 No Hiding Place

SINCLAIR, Cynthia   <HR>
      [Maureen Crane Wartski]
  Fair As A Rose
  Tapestry:
    27 Winter Blossom
    48 Promise Of Paradise
    65 Beloved Enemy
    73 Journey To Love
    77 Loving Enchantment, A

SINCLAIR, Heather
          [William Johnston]
For The Love Of A Stranger
Follow The Heart
Adventures In Love:
  16 Remembered Kiss, The

SINCLAIR, Rebecca
          [Patricia F. Viall]
Heartfire: <HR>
  California Caress
  Passion's Wild Delight
  Praire Angel

SINCLAIR, Helene   <HR>
          [Helene Lehr]
Bayou Fox, The
Stranger In My Heart   <Saga>
Twilight Of Innocence

SINCLAIR, Brooke
Meteor Kismet:
  No Hiding Place

SINCLAIR, James   <HO>
          [Reginald Thomas Staples]
Canis The Warrior
Warrior Queen

SINCLAIR, Tracy
          [Janet Schultz]
(see Silhouette Christmas Stories)
Silhouette Classic:
  18 Never Give Your Heart(SE12)
Silhouette Romance:
   39 Paradise Island
  123 Holiday In Jamaica
  174 Flight To Romance
  244 Stars In Her Eyes
  345 Catch A Rising Star
  459 Love Is Forever
Silhouette Special Edition:
   12 Never Give Your Heart
   34 Mixed Blessing
   52 Designed For Love
   68 Castles In The Air
  105 Fair Exchange
  140 Winter Of Love
  153 Tangled Web
  183 Harvest Is Love, The
  208 Pride's Folly
  232 Intrigue In Venice
  249 Love So Tender, A
  287 Dream Girl
  309 Preview Of Paradise
  355 Forgive And Forget
  386 Mandrego
  421 No Room For Doubt
  453 More Precious Than Jewels
  481 Champagne For Breakfast
  493 Proof Positive
  512 Sky High
  531 King Of Hearts
  565 Miss Robinson Crusoe

SINCLAIR, Katherine   <HR>
          [Joan Dial]
Different Eden, A
Far Horizons
Visions Of Tomorrow   <Saga>

SINCLAIR, Miranda
          (Miranda Seymour)

SINCLAIR, Olga   <GOT>
Bittersweet Summer
Never Fall In Love
Night Of The Black Tower
Candlelight:
  94 Man At The Manor, The

SINCLAIR, Olivia
          [Sandra Langford]
Ecstasy's Torment

SINCLAIR, Tracy (cont.)
584 Willing Partners
605 Golden Adventure
619 Girl Most Likely To, The
672 Change Of Place, A

_____

_____

SINCLAIRE, Francesca
Second Chance At Love:
143 Splendid Obsession, A

_____

_____

SINGER, Brett
Petting Zoo, The

_____

_____

SINGER, June Flaum   <CO>
Debutantes, The
Markoff Woman, The   <Saga>
Movie Set, The
President's Women, The
Star Dreams
Till The End Of Time

_____

_____

SINGER, Ronald
                    (Margaret Hunter)
                    (Delphine Marlowe)

SINGER, Sally M.
                    (Amelia Jamison)
Giver Of Song   <CO>

_____

_____

SIPHERD, Ray
Courtship Of Peggy McCoy, The

_____

_____

SISSON, Rosemary Anne
Manion's Of America, The

_____

_____

SIZER, Mona
                    (Deana James)

SKELTON, C. L.
            [C. Lister Skelton]
Hardacre   <HS>
Regiment Quartet: <HS>
    Maclarens, The
    Regiment, The
    Imperial War, The
    Beloved Soldiers

_____

_____

SKILLERN, Christine
Silhouette Special Edition:
71 Moonstruck

_____

_____

SKIMIN, Bob
Gray Victory   <HS>

_____

_____

SKINNER, Gloria Dale   <HR>
Lovestruck
    Passion's Choice

_____

_____

SKINNER, June O'Grady
                    (Rohan O'Grady)

SKYE, Christina   <HR>
            [Roberta Stalberg]
Defiant Captive

_____

_____

SKYE, Lauren   <HO>
Of Love And Longing

_____

_____

SLACK, Claudia
Hired, The
Moon In Eclipse, The
Outrageous Fortune
Web Of Enchantment

SLATER, Elizabeth

Love's Last Chance
Sapphire Romance:
  Man Of Honour, A

SLATTERY, Sheila
             (Roseanne Williams)

SLAUGHTER, Frank G.
 Air Surgeon
 Apalachee Gold
 Battle Surgeon
 Buccaneer Surgeon
 Code Five
 Countdown
 Curse Of Jezebel, The
 Darien Venture
 David: Warrior King
 Daybreak
 Deadly Lady Of Madagascar, The
 Devil's Gambit
 Devil's Harvest
 Divine Mistress
 Doctor's Daughters
 Doctor's Wives
 East Side General
 Epidemic!
 Flight From Natchez
 Fort Everglades
 Galileans, The
 God's Warrior
 Golden Isle, The
 Golden Ones, The
 Healer, The
 In A Dark Garden
 Land And The Promise, The

SLAUGHTER, Frank G. (cont.)
 Lorena
 Map Maker, The
 No Greater Love
 Passionate Rebel, The
 Pilgrims In Paradise
 Plague Ship, The
 Purple Quest, The
 Road To Bithynia, The
 Sangaree
 Savage Place, A
 Scarlet Cord, The
 Shadow Of Evil
 Sins Of Herod, The
 Song Of Ruth, The
 Spencer Blade, M. D.
 Stonewall Brigade, The
 Storm Haven
 Stubborn Heart, The
 Surgeon, U.S.A.
 Surgeon's Choice
 Sword And Scalpel
 That None Should Die
 Thorn Of Arimathea, The
 Touch Of Glory, A
 Tomorrow's Miracle
 Warrior, The
 Women In White

SLAUGHTER, Pamela   <RS>
 Ravished

SLAWSON, Judith
 Legal Affairs   <CO>

SLEAR, Genevieve   <RS>
 Golden Bauble, The
 Candlelight:
  520 Perilous
      Homecoming, The <IN>

SLIDE, Dorothy
  Harlequin Romance:
  1381 Music On The Wind
  1598 Star In A Dark Sky

_____

_____

SLOAN, Barbara
  Promises

_____

_____

SLOANE, Sara
                    [Ursula Bloom]
  Heaven Lies Ahead

_____

_____

SLOJKOWSKI, Mary Ann
                (Mary Ann Hammond)

SLOJKOWSKI, Mary Ann w/ Dorothy
  CORCORAN   (DeAnn Patrick)

SMALL, Bertrice   <HR>
            [Bertrice Williams Small]
  Adora
  Beloved
  Blaze Wyndham
  Enchantress Mine
  Spitfire, The
  Unconquered
  The Leslie Women:
    Kadin, The
    Love Wild And Fair
  The O'Mally Series: Story Order:
    Skye O'Malley
    All The Sweet Tomorrows
    Love For All Time, A
    This Heart Of Mine
    Lost Love Found

_____

_____

SMALL, Lass
                    (Cally Hughes)
  (see Silhouette Christmas Stories)
  Candlelight Ecstasy:
    192 Dedicated Man, The
  Harlequin Temptation:
     54 Collaboration
    197 Marry Me Not
  Silhouette Desire:
    241 Tangled Web
    322 To Meet Again
    341 Stolen Day
    356 Possibles
    373 Intrusive Man
    397 To Love Again
    413 Blindman's Bluff   &
    Lambert Sisters Series: &
    437 Goldilocks And The Behr
    453 Hide And Seek
    491 Red Rover
    505 Odd Man Out   <MMS>
    534 Tagged
    548 Contact
    569 Wrong Address, Right Place
    578 Not Easy
    594 Loner, The   <MMS>
    613 Four Dollars
         And Fifty-One Cents
    638 No Trespassing Allowed
  Silhouette Romance:
    444 An Irritating Man
    521 Snow Bird

_____

_____

SMILEY, Virginia K.
            [Virginia Kester Smiley]
                    (Tess Ewing)
  Haven For Jenny, A
  Long Road Home, The
  Nurse For The Civic Center
  Nurse For The Grand Canyon
  Nurse Karen's Summer Of Fear
  Nurse Kate's Mercy Flight
  Return To Love
  Under Purple Skies
  Avalon:
    Cove Of Fear, The
    Liza Hunt, Pediatric Nurse
    Love Rides The Rapids

SMILEY, Virginia K. (cont.)
Libby Williams –
Nurse Practitioner
Nurse For Morgan Acres
Nurse Of The Grand Canyon
Sugar Bush Nurse
Candlelight:
  86 High Country Nurse
  90 Guest At Gladehaven
 108 Mansion Of Mystery
First Love From Silhouette: <YA>
 124 Sugarbush Spring
Sweet Dreams: <YA>
 123 Love In The Wings
 160 Blue Ribbon Romance
Velvet Glove: <RS>
  11 Tender Betrayal

SMITH, Alana
         [Ruth Alana Smith]
Silhouette Desire:
  10 Whenever I Love You

SMITH, Barbara Cameron
         (Barbara Cameron)

SMITH, Barbara Dawson <HR>
    (see Avon Christmas Romance)
Fletcher Trilogy:
  Defiant Embrace
  Defiant Surrender
Silhouette Special Edition:
 246 No Regrets
The Avon Romance:
  Dreamspinner
  Silver Splendor
  Stolen Heart

SMITH, Betty   (Deceased)
    [Betty Wehner Smith]
Joy In The Morning

SMITH, Betty (cont.)
Maggie Now
Tomorrow Will Be Better
Tree Grows In Brooklyn, A

SMITH, Bobbi <HR>
    [Roberta F. Smith Walton]
Arizona Caress
Arizona Temptress
Captive Pride
Desert Heart
Forbidden Fires
Island Fire
Pirate's Promise
Sweet Silken Bondage
Texas Splendor
Wanton Splendor
In sequence:
  Rapture's Rage
  Rapture's Tempest

SMITH, Carol Sturm
Only A Dream
Love & Life:
  Emily's Place
  Renewal
  Right Time, The
  Partners

SMITH, Christine
Harlequin Intrigue:
  72 Murder Most Strange

SMITH, Clare Breton
Doctor's Problem, The <M&B>

SMITH, Dana Warren
                [A. L. Brown]
Silhouette Special Edition:
  563 High Stakes

SMITH, Day Totton
              (Day Leclaire)

SMITH, Deborah
            (Jackie Leigh)
        (Jacquelyn Lennox)
Beloved Woman,The   <HR>
Miracle   <CO>
Doubleday Loveswept:
  Silver Fox
    And The Red Hot Dove <TMC>
Loveswept:
  245 Jed's Sweet Revenge
  255 Hold On Tight   &
  278 California Royale
  290 Caught By Surprise   @%&
  308 Never Let Go   @&
      Cherokee Trilogy: #
  326   Sundance And The
          Princess   @%
  338   Tempting The Wolf
  350   Kat's Tale
  356 Hot Touch
  376 Sara's Surprise   &@
  395 Legends
  411 Honey And Smoke
      Follow The Sun <DNS><TMC>#

SMITH, Doris E.
Harlequin Premiere Edition:
  23 Back O' The Moon
Harlequin Romance:
 1341 Fire Is For Sharing
 1427 To Sing Me Home
 1454 Seven Of Magpies
 1599 Dear Deceiver
 1690 One And Only, The
 1922 Cotswold Honey
 1992 Smuggled Love

SMITH, Doris E. (cont.)
 2071 Wild Heart

SMITH, Elaine C.
              (Kami Lane)
Candlelight:
  688 Love's Brightest Hour <RO>

SMITH, F. E.   <GOT>
            [David Farrell]
Dark Cliffs
Lydia Trendennis

SMITH, Florence Margaret
          (Stevie Smith)

SMITH, Frank w/ Ware Torrey BUDLONG
          (Jennifer Hale)

SMITH, George
  [George Everard Kidder Smith]
          (Diana Summers)
The American Freedom Series: <HS>
  1 Devil's Breed, The
  2 Rogues, The
  3 Fire Brands, The

SMITH, Harriet
Two Against The World

SMITH, Joan   <GOT><HR><RE>
          (Jennie Gallant)
Babe
Bath Belles
Country Flirt

SMITH, Joan (cont.)
Country Wooing, A
Cousin Cecilia
Dame Durden's Daughter
Destiny's Dream
Drury Lane Darling
Ecsapade
Emerald Hazard
Flowers Of Eden
Hermit's Daughter, The
Imprudent Lady
La Comtesse
Lace For Milady
Lady Madeline's Folly
Larcenous Lady
Letters To A Lady
Love Bade Me Welcome
Love's Harbinger
Love's Way
Lover's Quarrels
Lovers' Vows
Madcap Miss
Memoirs Of A Hoyden
Merry Month Of May, The
Prelude To Love
Romantic Rebel
Royal Scamp, The
Silken Secrets
Silver Water, Golden Sand
Strange Capers
Sweet And Twenty
Talk Of The Town
True Lady
Waltzing Widow, The
Whisper On The Wind, A
Winter Wedding
In sequence:
  Midnight Masquerade
  Royal Revels
  Devious Duchess, The
Coventry:
  10 Aunt Sophie's Diamonds
  22 Babe
  47 Endure My Heart
  69 Rose Trelawney
  93 Aurora
  105 Perdita
  111 Lace For Milady
  123 Valerie
  141 Blue Diamond, The

SMITH, Joan (cont.)
  159 Delsie
  182 Reprise
  195 Wiles Of A Stranger
Coventry Classic:
  An Affair Of The Heart
  Aunt Sophie's Diamonds
Dawnstar Romance:
  Strictly Business
Silhouette Romance:
  234 Next Year's Blonde
  255 Caprice
  269 From Now On
  288 Chance Of A Lifetime
  302 Best Of Enemies
  315 Trouble In Paradise
  325 Future Perfect
  343 Tender Takeover
  354 Yielding Art, The
  430 Infamous Madam X, The
  452 Where There's A Will
  546 Dear Corrie
  562 If You Love Me
  591 By Hook Or By Crook
  617 After The Storm
  635 Maybe Next Time
  656 It Takes Two
  669 Thrill Of The Chase
  711 Sealed With A Kiss
  755 Her Nest Egg
  795 Her Lucky Break

SMITH, Julia Cleaver
Morning Glory

SMITH, Kenn   <HR>
               (Robin Leigh Smith)
Flower Of Gold
River Of The Wind

SMITH, Lady Eleanor   <GOT>
Caravan
Dark And Splendid Passion
Magic Lantern
Romany

SMITH, Naomi G.   <GOT>
Buried Remembrance   <CGS:#22>

SMITH, Lois
                (Cleo Chadwick)

SMITH, Lora Roberts
                (Leigh Roberts)

SMITH, Patrick D.
                [Patrick David Smith]
Land Remembered, A   <HS>

SMITH, Lynne
                (Paula Christopher)
                (Jane Lynson)
                (Lynn Michaels)

SMITH, Richard Rein
                (Diana Tower)

SMITH, Robin Leigh   <HR>
                [Kenn Smith]
Passage To Glory

SMITH, Marcine
  Silhouette Desire:
   364 Never A Stranger
  Silhouette Romance:
   589 Murphy's Law
   659 Waltz With The Flowers
   683 Perfect Wife, The
   716 Just Neighbors
   767 Two Of Us, The

SMITH, Ruth Alana
                (Eileen Bryan)
                (Alana Smith)
  Harlequin SuperRomance:
   158 Wild Rose, The
   208 For Richer, Or Poorer
   265 After Midnight
   311 Second Time Around, The
   356 Spellbound
   400 Gentleman's Honor, A
   456 Soulbound

SMITH, Marion
                [Marion Smith Collins]
  Harlequin Romance:
  2598 Beachcomber, The

SMITH, Nancy Carolyn   <GOT>
To Dwell In Shadows

SMITH, Sally Tyree   <GOT>
  Avalon:
     House On Stone Quarry
     Incident At Caprock
     Never Leave Shadow Wood
     Return To Terror
     Secret Of Harpen's Landing, The
     Visitor At Merville House, The

SMITH, Nancy T.   <GOT>
                [Nancy Taylor Smith]
                (Amber Fitzgerald)
Golden Fig, The   <CGS:#1>

SMITH, Sandra Lee
                    (Sandra Lee)
    Lovestruck:
        Dream Song
        Love's Miracles

_____

_____

SMITH, Steve
                    (Jane Fleming)

SMITH, Stevie
            [Florence Margaret Smith]
    Trilogy:
        Over The Frontier
        Notes On Yellow Paper
        Holiday, The

_____

_____

SMITH, Susan Mendonca
                    (Susan Mendonca)

SMITH, Veronica   <GOT>
    Bride Of Fairchild Abbey, The
    Crystal Web
    Thunder Castle

_____

_____

SMITH, Wilbur
    Cry Wolf
    Courtneys, The (1-volume)   <HS>
    Dark Of The Sun, The
    Delta Decision, The
    Diamond Hunters, The
    Eagle In The Sky
    Eye Of The Tiger, The
    Gold Mine
    Hungry As The Sea
    Roar Of Thunder, The
    Shout At The Devil
    Sunbird, The
    When The Lion Feeds
    The Ballantine Novels:
        Flight Of The Falcon

SMITH, Wilbur
    Men Of Men
    Angels Weep, The
    Leopard Hunts In Darkness, The
    The Courtney Novels: <HS>
        When The Lion Feeds
        Sound Of Thunder, The
        Sparrow Falls, A
        Burning Shore, The
        Power Of The Sword, The
        Rage

_____

_____

SMITH, William J.   <GOT>
                    (Stephanie Hall)
    Queen Of Coins

_____

_____

SMITH, Wynne   <RE-IN>
    Rushmoreland Rubies, The

_____

_____

SMITH-WARE, Sandra w/
            Dianne M. KLEINSCHMIDT
                    (Gabrielle DuPre)

SNODGRASS, Melinda
                    (Melinda Harris)
                    (Melinda McKenzie)
    High Stakes   <CO>
    Queen's Gambit Declined   <HF>
    Santa Fe

_____

_____

SNOW, Ashley
            [Maryhelen Clague]
    Heartfire Romance: <HR>
        Dangerous Desire
        Rapture's Splendor
        Yankee Mistress

_____

_____

SNOW, Dorothea J.
          [Dorothea Johnston Snow]
  Avalon:
    By Love Bewitched
    Garden Of Love
    Golden Summer
    Love's Dream Remembered
    Love's Wonderous Ways
    Secret Of The Silver Bird

_____

_____

SNOW, Leo
  Southern Dreams
    And Trojan Women   <Saga>

_____

_____

SNOW, Lucy
          [Rosemary Aubert]
  SuperRomance:
    83 Song Of Eden
  Harlequin SuperRomance:
    115 Red Bird In Winter, A
    155 Garden Of Lions

_____

_____

SOHL, Jerry
          (Roberta Jean Mountjoy)

SOLOMON, Ruth Freeman   <HR>
  Ultimate Triumph
  In sequence: <HS>
    Eagle And The Dove, The
    Candlesticks And The Cross, The
    Two Lives, Two Lands

_____

_____

SOLOW, Martin
  Second Love

_____

_____

SOMAN, Florence Jane
  Gloria Barney
  Picture Of Success

_____

_____

SOMERLOTT, Robert
                    (Jessica North)

SOMERS, Suzanne   <GOT>
          [Dorothy Daniels]
  House On Thunder Hill, The
  Mist Of Mourning, The
  Nurse For Doctor Keith
  Romany Curse
  Shadow Of A Man
  Tidemill
  Touch Me
  Touch Me Again
  Until Death
  Avalon:
    House Of Eve
    Image Of Truth

_____

_____

SOMERSET, Rose
  Highwayman's Lady, The

_____

_____

SOMMARS, Colette
  Distant Heaven, A

_____

_____

SOMMER, Scott   <CO>
  Last Resort
  Nearing's Grace

_____

_____

SOMMERFIELD, Sylvie F.   <HR>
  Autumn Dove
  Betray Not My Passion

SOMMERS, Justine (cont.)
Kiss Remembered, A
So Wild, So Wonderful
Surrender To Love

SOMMERS, Lilah
MacFadden Romance:
  240 Heart's Desire
  247 Twenty/Love
  254 Velvet Rose, The

SOMMERSET, Judith
MacFadden Romance:
  148 Island In The Sun
  161 Wish Upon A Star

SOREL, Marilyn Meeske
               (Nina Lansdale)

SORENSON, Jody
Caprice Romance: <YA>
  58 To Take Your Heart Away

SORRELS, Roy
              (Anna McClure)

SORTORE, Nancy
Border Gentry   <HS>

SOULE, Maris
Harlequin Temptation:
     First Impressions <PROM>
  24 No Room For Love
  50 Lost And Found
 112 Sounds Like Love
 148 Winning Combination, A
 206 Best Of Everything, The

SOULE, Maris (cont.)
 225 Law Of Nature, The
 242 Storybook Hero

SOUTH, Barbara
          (Barbara Stephens)
Silhouette Romance:
 111 Wayward Lover

SOUTH, Grace
             [Gail Clark]
Coventry:
 126 Merrie

SOUTH, Pamela
Daughter Of The Sand

SPARK, Natalie
Harlequin Romance:
 2633 Once More With Feeling
 2799 One Life At A Time

SPARROW, Laura
         (Jocelyn Griffin)
          (Laura Halford)

SPEARE, Elizabeth George <RS>
Witch At Blackbird Pond, The
Calico Captive

SPEARMAN, Stephanie
Maid Of Honor   <RE-IN>

SPEARS, Helen
Avalon:
  Aloha Kisses

SPEAS, Jan Cox
  Bride Of The MacHugh
  Growing Season, The
  My Lord Monleigh
  My Love, My Enemy

SPECTOR, Debra
  Sweet Dreams: <YA>
    12 Night Of The Prom
    31 Too Close For Comfort
    39 First Love
    51 Magic Moments
    81 Secret Admirer
   101 Wrong For Each Other

SPECTOR, Robert D.   <GOT>
         [Robert Donald Spector]
  Candle And The Tower, The

SPEER, Flora/Flora M.
  By Honor Bound
  In sequence:
    Castle Of Dreams
    Castle Of The Heart
  Destiny's Lovers
  Much Ado About Love
  Venus Rising

SPEICHER, Helen Ross Smith w/
           Kathryn Kilby BORLAND
           (Alice Abbott)

SPELLMAN, Cathy Cash
  An Excess Of Love   <Saga>
  Paint The Wind
  So Many Partings

SPENCER, Anne
  MacFadden Romance:
    24 Midnight Jewel
    61 Sweet Surrender

SPENCER, Candace
           [Candace L. Schuler]
  Silhouette Desire:
    581 Between Friends

SPENCER, Catherine
           [Kathleen Orr]
  Harlequin American Romance:
    296 Fires Of Summer
  Harlequin Presents:
    910 Lasting Kind Of Love, A

SPENCER, Cheryl   <GOT>
           [Cheryl Lynn Purviance]
  The Avon Romance:
    Fortune's Bride

SPENCER, LaVyrle   <CO><HR>
           [LaVyrle Joy Kulick Spencer]
  Bitter Sweet
  Endearment, The
  Fulfillment, The
  Gamble, The
  Heart Speaks, A (SCAL #76 & #100)
  Hellion, The   (HQS#130)
  Hummingbird
  Morning Glory
  Separate Beds

SPENCER, LaVyrle (cont.)
Spring Fancy   (HQT#1)
Sweet Memories
Twice Loved
Vows
Years
Harlequin SuperRomance:
130 Hellion, The
Harlequin Temptation:
1 Spring Fancy
Second Chance At Love:
76 Forsaking All Others
100 Promise To Cherish, A

SPENCER, Scott
Endless Love
Last Night At The
Brain Thieves Ball
Preservation Hall
Waking The Dead .   <CO>

SPENSER, Emily
[Charlotte Elkins]
Harlequin Romance:
2668 Chateau Villon
2681 Where The Wind Blows Free
2813 Unlikely Lovers
2898 Where Eagles Soar

SPENSER, Emma Jane
Harlequin Temptation:
248 Novel Approach, A
273 That Holiday Feeling
327 Two Can Play

336 Detente

SPICER, Dorothy   <GOT>
[Dorothy Gladys Spicer]
Crystal Ball, The
Eye Of The Cat

SPICER, Dorothy (cont.)
Humming Top, The
Tower Room, The
Witch's Web, The
Avalon:
Desert Adventure

SPINDLER, Erica
Loveswept:
423 Rhyme Or Reason
Wishing Moon
Silhouette Desire:
442 Heaven Sent
482 Chances Are
538 Read Between The Lines

SPRING, Marianna   <HR>
Wildfire Woman

SPRINGER, Lacey
Silhouette Inspirations:
7 Wealth Of Love, A
25 Winter Rose
30 Fair Lady
Silhouette Romance:
402 Kindred Hearts
419 Silent Song, A

SPROUSE, Gene
Avalon:
Mystery Of Spindle Key
Secret Of The Satin Doll, The

STABLES, Mira   <HR><RE>
Byram Succession, The
Honey-Pot
Lissa

STAFFORD, Lee (cont.)
  Masquerade:
    40 Fountains Of Paradise

STAHL, Norman
  Towers   <Saga>

STAINFORTH, Diana
  Mara's Way (HB: Bird Of Paradise)
  Scandalous Desires

STALBERG, Roberta
                    (Christina Skye)

STAMFORD, Sarah   <RE>
  Candlelight:
    619 Magnificent Duchess, The

STANCLIFFE, Elaine
                    (Elisa Stone)

STANDAGE, Virginia   <HR>
            [Rona Randall Shambrook]
  Golden Rebel

STANDARD, Patti
            [Patti Standard-Cronk]
  Silhouette Romance:
    636 Pretty As A Picture

STANDISH, Caroline   <HR>
            [Lorna Read]
  Sweet Temptation

STANFIELD, Ann   <RE>
            [Virginia Coffman]
  Doxy Masque, The
  Royal Summer
  Coventry:
    128 Golden Marguerite, The

STANFILL, Francesca
  Shadows And Light   <CO>

STANFORD, Mary Lee
  Candlelight:
    584 Touched By Fire   <RO>

STANFORD, Sondra
            [Sondra Williams Stanford]
  Harlequin Romance:
    2208 Stranger's Kiss, A
    2354 Bellefleur
  Silhouette Classic:
    22 Silver Mist   (SE7)
  Silhouette Romance:
     6 Golden Tide
    25 Shadow Of Love
    35 Storm's End
    46 No Trespassing
    58 Long Winter's Night
    88 And Then Came Dawn
   100 Yesterday's Shadow
   112 Whisper Wind
   131 Tarnished Vows
   530 Stolen Trust
   586 Heart Of Gold
   646 Proud Beloved
  Silhouette Special Edition:
     7 Silver Mist
    37 Magnolia Moon
    55 Sun Lover
    91 Love's Gentle Chains
   161 Heart Knows Best, The
   187 For All Time

STARR, Kate
               [Joyce Dingwell]
Harlequin Classic:
   65 Nurse Most Likely,The(679)
  117 Ship's Doctor   (828)
  142 Enchanted Trap, The (951)
Harlequin Romance:
 828 Ship's Doctor
 951 Enchanted Trap, The
1076 Bells In The Wind
1105 Wrong Doctor John
1130 Dalton's Daughter
1166 Dolan Of Sugar Hills
1200 Satin For The Bride

STARR, Leonora
             [Leonora Mackesy]
Harlequin Romance:
1147 Fantails
1236 Jemima

STARR, Martha
             [Martha Gordon]
Harlequin American Romance:
  84 From Twilight To Sunrise
Harlequin Intrigue:
  11 Bitter Fruit

STARR, Morgana
           [Alice Harron Orr]
Satin Swan Romance:
  Nothing Short Of A Miracle

STARTS, Nancy
          (Nancy Lawrence)

STATHAM, Frances P.
  Bright Sun, Dark Moon <CGS:#18>

STATHAM, Frances Patton <HR>
  Flame Of New Orleans
  In sequence:
    Jasmine Moon
    Daughters Of The Summer Storm
  In sequence: <HS>
    Roswell Women, The
    Roswell Legacy, The
  The Phoenix Quartet: <HS>
    Phoenix Rising
    From Love's Ashes
    On Wings Of Fire
    To Face The Sun

STATON, Anna Lloyd
        [Judy S. Rocker w/
             Doris E. English]
  Promise Romance: <Insp>
    2 Challenged Heart, The

STAUB, Molly Arost   <HR>
  Pirate's Passion

STEARN, Jess
         (see Taylor Caldwell)

STEEBER, Sharon   <HO>
  Jews, The   <IMS>

STEEL, Danielle
         [Danielle Steel Traina]
  Changes
  Crossings
  Daddy
  Family Album
  Fine Things
  Full Circle
  Going Home
  Kaleidoscope

STEELE, Marianne
MacFadden Romance:
  202 Midnight Magic

STEELE, Sharon
  [William Mulvey w/ Richard Fehr]
  Dangerous Woman, A

STEELMAN, Robert
        [Robert James Steelman]
  Blood And Dust

STEEN, Sandy
  Silhouette Intimate Moments:
  155 Sweet Reason
  202 Past Perfect
  375 Simple Truth, The
  Silhouette Special Edition:
  638 Vanquish The Night

STEIN, Toby   <CO>
  All The Time There Is
  Only The Best

STEINER, Barbara
        [Barbara Annette Steiner]
  Caprice Romance: <YA>
   21 Hat Full Of Love, A
  First Love From Silhouette: <YA>
  118 See You In July
  Sweet Dreams: <YA>
  107 If You Love Me
  Wildfire: <YA>
  Searching Heart, The
  Secret Love

STEINER, Irene Hunter
  Gentle Intruder, The

STEINER, Merilee
  Swept Away: <YA>
   7 Pirate Moon

STEINKE, Anne
  [Anne Elizabeth Reynolds Steinke]
              (Anne Reynolds)
          (Elizabeth Reynolds)
             (Anne Williams)
  Finding Mr. Right:
  Woman In Flight

STEPHENS, Barbara
           (Barbara South)
  Starlight Romance:
  Toast To Love, A

STEPHENS, Blythe
         [Sharon Wagner]
  Silhouette Romance:
  786 Gift Of MIschief
  Silhouette Special Edition:
  554 Rainbow Days

STEPHENS, Casey   <GOT>
         [Sharon Wagner]
  Porterfield Legacy, The
  Shadows Of Fieldcrest Manor, The

STEPHENS, Cleo M.
  Born With A Mask
  Duel Of Hearts, The
  Girl Of The Ozarks
  Royal Feather, The
  Stormy Tide
  Third Passenger, The
  Avalon:
    Island Adventure
    Mexican Mantilla, The

STEPHENS, Jeanne
                         [Jean Hager]
  Harlequin Historical <Set#2>:
   18 Wild Horizons
  Silhouette Classic:
   16 Splendored Sky, The (SE84)
  Silhouette Desire:
  504 Sharing California
  Silhouette Imtimate Moments:
   14 Reckless Surrender
   38 Memories
  127 Whispers On The Wind
  161 Haunted Season, The
  200 Mistress Of Cliff House
  259 Dangerous Choices
  308 At Risk
  353 Hiding Places
  Silhouette Romance:
   22 Mexican Nights
   80 Wonder And Wild Desire
  189 Sweet Jasmine
  531 Broken Dreams
  Silhouette Special Edition:
   30 Bride In Barbados
   47 Pride's Possession
   84 Splendored Sky, The
  108 No Other Love
  217 Mandy's Song
  252 Coming Home
  295 This Long Winter Past<ATS>
  308 Few Shining Hours, A
  372 Return To Eden
  431 Neptune Summer

STEPHENS, Jennifer
  Silver Rose, The

STEPHENS, Kay
  Silhouette Romance:
  300 Felstead Collection, The

STEPHENS, Sharon
                     [Candace Camp]
  Tapestry: <HR>
    Black Earl, The

STEPHENS, Vivian
  Starlight Romance:
    Final Summer

STEPHENSON, Maureen   <GOT>
  House On The Heath, The
  House On Wath Moor, The

STERN, Susan
                   (Susan Sackett)
                   (Suzanne Savoy)
  Desert Nights Jane   <HR>

STERN, Tracy   <CO>
  Longings
  This I Promise You

STEVENS, Amanda
          [Marilyn Medlock Amann]
  Silhouette Intimate Moments:
  159 Killing Moon

STEVENS, Amanda (cont.)
   199 Dreaming, The

STEVENS, Ann Gilmer
   Traveling With Sara

STEVENS, Blaine
                [Harry Whittington]
   Embrace The Wind
   Island Of Kings   <HS>
   Outlanders, The

STEVENS, Diane   <GOT>
   Labyrinth

STEVENS, Janice
   [Janice Kay Johnson Baczewski]
   Magic Moments: <YA>
    10 Test Of Love
    13 Dream Summer
   Sweet Dreams: <YA>
   104 Playing For Keeps

STEVENS, Kimberly
   Love's Deception

STEVENS, Linda
   [Stephen G. Hamilton w/
          Melinda Hobaugh-Hamilton]
   Harlequin Intrigue:
   130 Shadowplay
   156 One Step Ahead

STEVENS, Lucile Vernon
   Heart Everlasting
   Search Through The Mist
   Wise Heart, A
   Avalon:
      Crape Myrtle Tree, The
      Death Wore Gold Shoes
      Dowry Of Diamonds
      Green Shadows
      Home To Cypresswood
      Joni Of Storm Hill
      Of Dreams And Danger
      Phantom Rubies
      Red Tower, The
      Redbird Affair, The

STEVENS, Lynsey
         [Lynnette Desley Howard]
   Harlequin Presents:
   497 Ryan's Return   &
   606 Man Of Vengeance
   654 Forbidden Wine
   692 Starting Over
   774 Lingering Embers
   996 Leave Yesterday Behind
   Harlequin Romance:
  2488 Play Our Song Again
  2495 Race For Revenge
  2507 Tropical Knight   &
  2574 Closest Place To Heaven
  2608 Ashby Affair, The
  2706 Terebori's Gold
  2988 But Never Love

STEVENS, R. T.
         [Reginal Thomas Staples]
   In My Enemy's Arms
   My Enemy, My Love
   Summer Day Is Done, The
   Woman Of Texas, A

STEVENS, Serita/Serita Deborah <HR>
[Serita Deborah Mendelson Stevens]
(Shira Stevens)
(Megan MacDonnell)
Bloodstone Inheritance, The <RS>
Daughters Of Desire
Lightning & Fire
Shrieking Shadows
Of Penporth Island, The <GOT>
This Bitter Ecstasy
First Love From Silhouette: <YA>
190 Gathering Storm, A
Tapestry: <HR>
25 Tame The Wild Heart
Torchlite:
Spanish Heartland

STEVENS, Shira <HR>
[Serita Stevens]
Deceptive Desires

STEVENS, Susan
[Mary Mackie]
Silhouette Romance:
230 Ivory Innocence

STEVENSON, Anne <RS>
[Anne Katharine Stevenson]
Coil Of Serpents
Enough Of Green
French Inheritance, The
Game Of Statues, A
Masks Of Treason
Relative Stranger, A

STEVENSON, D. E. (Deceased)
[Dorothy Emily Peploe]
Alister & Co.
Amberwell

STEVENSON, D. E. (cont.)
Anna And Her Daughters
Baker's Daughter, The
Bel Lamington
Blue Sapphire, The
Celia's House
Crooked Adam
Enchanted Isle, The
English Air, The
Five Windows
Fletchers End
Four Graces, The
Gerald And Elizabeth
Golden Days
Green Money
House Of The Deer, The
House On The Cliff, The
Kate Hardy
Katherine Wentworth
Listening Valley
Marriage Of Katherine, The
Miss Buncle
Miss Buncle's Book
Miss Buncle Married
Mrs. Tim Carries On
Mrs. Tim Christie
Mrs. Tim Flies Home
Mrs. Tim Gets A Job
Mrs. Tim Of The Regiment
Musgraves, The
Rochester's Wife
Sarah Morris Remembers
Sarah's Cottage
Story Of Rosabelle Shaw, The
Smouldering Fire
Spring Magic
Still Glides The Stream
Summerhills
Tall Stranger, The
Two Mrs Abbotts, The
World In Spell, A
Young Clementina, The
Young Mrs Savage
Dering Family Trilogy:
Vittoria Cottage
Music In The Hills
Shoulder The Sky

STEVENSON, Florence   <GOT><HR><RS>
               (Zandra Colt)
               (Lucia Curzon)
               (Zabrina Faire)
           (Ellen Fitzgerald)
           (Pamela Frazier)
Bianca   w/Patricia Hagan MURRAY
Curse Of The Concullens, The
Dark Encounter
Dark Odyssey
Darkness On The Stairs, A
Feast Of Eggshells, A   <SN>
Golden Galatea, The
House Of Luxor, The
Ides Of November, The
Julie
Kilmeny In The Dark Woods
Mistress Of Devil's Manor
Moonlight Variations
Ophelia
Shadow On The House, A
Witch's Crossing
Kitty Telefair Gothic Series:
  In sequence:
    Witching Hour, The
    Where Satan Dwells
    Altar Of Evil
    Sorcerer Of The Castle
    Silent Watcher, The
    Horror From The Tombs, The

STEVENSON, Janet   <HR>
Weep No More

STEVENSON, Robin w/ Tom BADE
          (Robin St. Thomas)
Switchback

STEWARD, Ada
              [Ada Sumner]
Silhouette Special Edition:
 227 This Cherished Land
 289 Love's Haunting
      Refrain   <ATS>
 319 Misty Morning,
      Magic Nights   <ATS>
 343 Walk In Paradise, A
 604 Galahad's Bride

STEWARDSON, Dawn
Harlequin Intrigue:
  80 Peril In Paradise
  90 No Rhyme Or Reason
Harlequin SuperRomance:
 329 Vanishing Act
 355 Deep Secrets
 383 Blue Moon
 405 Prize Passage   &
 409 Heartbeat   &
 432 Full House
 477 Prime Time

STEWART, Edward
Ariana
Ballarina
For Richer, For Poorer

STEWART, Fred Mustard   <HR><RS>
Century
Ellis Island
Glitter And The Gold, The   <HS>
Lady Darlington
Mannings, The
Rage Against Heaven, A
Six Weeks
Star Child
Titan, The   <HS>

STEWART, Isobel
Aston Hall:
103 Time In September
Masquerade:
78 Stranger In The Glen

STEWART, Jean
[Mona Alice Jean Newman]
Where Love Could Not Follow

STEWART, Jo   <YA>
[Joyce Schenk]
Andrea
Magic Moments: <YA>
1 Love Vote, The
8 Love Contest, The

STEWART, Judith
[Judith Anne Polley]
Masquerade:
13 Laird's French Bride, The

STEWART, Kathryn,
Silhouette Intimate Moments:
372 Dangerous Bargain, A

STEWART, Leigh
MacFadden Romance:
163 Les Mots D'Amour
197 On The Wings Of Love
234 Sweet Sorrow

STEWART, Lois   <GOT><RE>
[Lois S. Nollet]
Dark Rendezvous At Dungariff
Romantic Masquerade

STEWART, Lucy Phillips
Destiny's Bride   <RS>
Candlelight: <RE>
232 Captive Bride, The
251 Bride Of Chance
512 Bride Of Torquay
530 Bride Of A Stranger
Burning Fires Of Passion

STEWART, Mary   <RS>
[Mary Florence Elinor Stewart]
Airs Above The Ground
Gabriel Hounds, The
Ivy Tree, The
Madam, Will You Talk?
Moon-Spinners, The
My Brother Michael
Nine Coaches Waiting
Snow Fire
This Rough Magic
Thornyhold
Thunder On The Right
Touch Not The Cat
Walk In Wolf Wood, A   <SN>
Wildfire At Midnight
Merlin Novels:
Crystal Cave, The
Hollow HIlls, The
Last Enchantment, The
Wicked Day, The

STEWART, Ramona
Seasons Of The Heart   <CO>

STEWART, Ruth
                        [Bea Scantlin]
  Silhouette Desire:
    42 Ask Me No Secrets

STEWART, Sally
  Harlequin Romance:
    2862 Love Upon The Wind

STEWART, Savannah
  Friends And Fortunes

STEWART, Walter
                        (Mary Elgin)

STILES, Deidre
  Dangerford
  Rakehell
  Tara
  That Collison Woman

STINE, R. L.
  Crosswinds: <YA>
    21 Broken Date

STINE, Whitney
                [Whitney Ward Stine]
                (Constance F. Peale)
  Jewel Of The Klondike   <Saga>
  Liberty   <Saga>
  Stardust   <Saga>
  In sequence:
    First Daughter, The
    Vision Of Destiny
  Oklahomans Series:
    1 The Oklahomans

STINE, Whitney (cont.)
    2 The Oklahomans:
          The Second Generation
    3 The Oklahomans:
          The Third Generation
    4 Survivors, The

STIRLING, Elaine K.
  Harlequin Intrigue:
    28   Unsuspected Conduct
    35   Midnight Obsession
    53   Foul Play
    85   Chain Letter
    126 Sleepwalker
  Harlequin SuperRomance:
    261 This Time For Us
    345 More Than A Feeling   &
    385 Cross Tides   &
  Harlequin Temptation:
    139 Almost Heaven
    332 Different Worlds

STIRLING, Jessica
  [Peggie Coghlan w/
              Hugh Crauford Rae]
  Dresden Finch, The
  Stalker Trilogy:
    Strathmore
    Call Home The Heart
    Dark Pasture, The
  Beckman Family Trilogy:
    Drums Of Time, The
    Blue Evening Gone, The
    Gates Of Midnight, The
  Trilogy:
    Treasures On Earth
    Creature Comforts
    Hearts Of Gold
  Glasgow Saga: Trilogy:
    Good Provider, The
    Asking Price, The
    Wise Child, The

STIRLING, Jocelyn   <HR>
  Promises To Keep   <Saga>
  Venture To Love

STONE, Fay
  Challenge For Nurse Laurel

STOCKENBERG, Antoinette
         (Antoinette Hale)
         (Antoinette Hardy)
  Challenge And The Glory,The<Saga>

STONE, Gillian   <HR>
  Land Of Golden Mountains   <Saga>

STONE, Grace Zaring   <GOT>
  Dear Deadly Cora

STOCKHALM, Marjorie
  Man From The Vineyards

STONE, Harriet   <GOT>
  Heiress Of Bayou Vache

STOKER, Bram   (Deceased)<GOT><RS>
                  [Abraham Stoker]
  Dracula
  Dracula's Guest
  Garden Of Evil, The
  Lady Of The Shroud, The
  Lair Of The White Worm

STONE, Irving
  Adversary In The House
  Agony And The Ecstasy, The
  Greek Treasure, The
  Immortal Wife
  Love Is Eternal
  Lust For Life
  Men To Match The Mountains
  Origin, The
  Passionate Journey, The
  Passions Of The Mind
  President's Lady, The
  They Also Ran
  Those Who Love

STONE, Andy
  Song Of The Kingdom

STONE, Elisa
              [Elaine Stancliffe]
  Rapture Romance:
    31 Shared Love, A

STONE, Karen
                    (Karen Young)

STONE, Elna   <GOT><RS>
  Dark Masquerade
  Ghost At The Wedding
  Secret Of The Willows
  Visions Of Esmaree
  Whisper Of Fear

STONE, Katherine
  Bel Air
  Carlton Club, The
  Roommates
  Twins

STONE, Leslie   <CO>
  Siren Song

STONE, Natalie
  [Sally Goldenbaum w/
                  Adrienne Staff]
  Candlelight Ecstasy:
    198 Double Play
    235 Blue Ridge Autumn
    288' Summer Fling
    322 Sky Gypsy
    360 Words From The Heart
    445 With A Little Love

STONE, Patti
  Beyond The Storm   <GOT>
  Calling Nurse Linda
  Nina Grant, Pediatric Nurse

STONE, Sharon
  Second Chance At Love:
    114 Moonlight Persuasion

STOREY, Victoria Carolyn
             (Vicky Martin)

STORM, Elizabeth
          [Eve K. Sandstrom]
  Harlequin Intrigue:
    93 Firing Line

STORM, Wendy
  Caprice Romance: <YA>
    20 Boy Next Door, The

STOWE, Rosetta   <HR>
  [George F. Ogan w/
        Margaret E. Nettles Ogan]
  Cannons And Roses
  Outlaw Heart, The

STOYENOFF, Norma Davis
  Avalon:
    Love's Magic Melody
    Where Love Waits
    One Night To Remember

STRASSER, Heidi
          [Ilse Dallmayr]
  Pageant Romance:
    Love's Memories

STRATTON, Rebecca
          (Lucy Gillen)
  Harlequin Presents:
    106 Yellow Moon
    121 Warm Wind Of Farik, The
  Harlequin Romance:
   1748 Golden Madonna, The
   1770 Fairwinds
   1799 Bride Of Romano, The
   1816 Castles In Spain
   1839 Run From The Wind
   1858 Island Of Darkness
   1883 Autumn Concerto
   1898 Firebird
   1913 Flight Of The Hawk, The
   1942 Fire And The Fury, The
   1955 Moon Tide
   1976 Goddess Of Mavisu, The
   1991 Isle Of The Golden Drum
   2006 Proud Stranger
   2018 Chateau d'Armor
   2036 Road To Gafsa, The
   2050 Gemini Child

STROTHER, Patricia
    [Pat Wallace Strother]
Constant Star, The   <Saga>
Golden Windows   <Saga>
Grand Design
Silvermore

STRUTT, Shiela
Harlequin Premiere Edition:
  36 No Yesterdays
Harlequin Romance:
  2447 On The Edge Of Love
  2496 Stamp Of Possession
  2562 Flight Of The Golden Hawk
  2699 Emperor Stone
  2754 He Was The Stranger

STUART, Alex
    [Vivian Stuart Mann]
On Her Majesty's Orders
Harlequin Classic:
  2 Queen's Counsel   (506)
  11 Return To Love   (527)
  34 Cruise For
      Cinderella, A   (669)
  40 Island For Sale   (614)
  56 Last Of The
      Logans, The   (705)
Harlequin Romance:
  810 Piper Of Laide, The
  1060 Huntsman's Folly
  1086 Gay Cavalier
  1112 Castle In The Mist

STUART, Anne
    [Anne Kristine Stuart-Ohlrogge]
Barrett's Hill
Houseparty, The   <RE>
Seen And Not Heard   <RM>

STUART, Anne (cont.)
Maggie Bennett Trilogy: <RM>
  Escape Out Of Darkness
  Darkness Before The Dawn
  At The Edge Of The Sun
Candlelight:
  504 Cameron's Landing <IN>
  523 Demonwood   <IN>
  557 Demon Count, The   <IN>
  561 Demon Count's Daughter<IN>
  649 Lord Satan's Bride <IN>
  711 Spinster And The Rake <RE>
Candlelight Ecstasy Supreme:
  84 Against The Wind
Harlequin American Romance:
  30 Chain Of Love
  39 Heart's Ease
  52 Museum Piece
  93 Housebound
  126 Rocky Road
  177 Bewitching Hour
  213 Blue Sage
  246 Partners In Crime
  260 Cry For The Moon   <YTS>
  311 Glass Houses
  326 Crazy Like A Fox
  346 Rancho Diablo
  361 Angel's Wings   <COAR>
  374 Lazarus Rising
Harlequin American Romance
Premier Edition:
  Banish Misfortune
Harlequin Intrigue:
  5 Tangled Lies
  9 Catspaw   &
  59 Hand In Glove
  103 Catspaw II   &
Silhouette Intimate Moments:
  321 Special Gifts

STUART, Becky
    [Stuart Buchan]
Crosswinds Keepsake: <YA>
  25 Last Summer, The
First Love From Silhouette: <YA>
  70 More Than Friends

STUART, Becky (cont.)
    81 Mockingbird, The
    97 Land's End
    112 Once In California
    136 Shadow Knows, The
    157 Journey's End
    173 Someone Else
    189 Ghost Ship
    199 Famous Last Words

STUART, Casey   <HR>
         [Ann Elizabeth Bullard]
    Beloved Pirate
    Midnight Thunder
    Moonlight Angel
    Passion's Dream
    Passion's Flame
    Passion's Prisoner
    Velvet Deception
    Waves Of Passion

STUART, Charles   <RS>
    [Charles R. Mackinnon w/
              Charles Stuart Reid]
    Cupids And Coronets
    Happy Hostess, The
    Lady Ambassador, The*
    Love Royal*
    *(see Vivian Donald)

STUART, Dee   <HR>
                   [Doris Stuart]
    Freedom's Flame
    Golden Interlude   <CO>
    Scarlet Lily, The
    Wings Of Morning
    Candlelight: <RE>
      686 Innocent Adultress, The
    Judy Sullivan Books:
      Christina   <RS>

STUART, Dee (cont.)
    Silhouette Special Edition:
    353 Out Of A Dream
    671 Moon Pool, The

STUART, Doris
                     (Joan Darling)
                      (Dee Stuart)
                   (Ellen Searight)

STUART, Elizabeth   <HR>
                 [Elizabeth Beach]
    Heartstorm   <Saga>
    Where Love Dwells

STUART, Elizabeth   <GOT>
          [Elizabeth Stuart Pratt]
    Shaking Shadow, The

STUART, Florence
                    (see Peggy Gaddis)
    Afraid To Love Again
    Believe In Miracles
    Be Sure It's Love
    Happiness Hill
    Honeymoon House
    Hope Wears White
    Mountain Sweetheart
    Necklace, The
    New Nurse, The
    No Greater Love
    Nurse And The Crystal Ball
    Nurse And The Orderly, The
    Nurse Under Fire
    Nurse's Nightmare, A
    Research Nurse
    "Right" Kind Of Man, The
    Runaway Nurse
    Spring Love
    Strange Triangle
    Wall Of Love
    Sharon Romance:
      I Love You Ruby Compton

STUART, Jan
                    [Janet Schultz]
Candlelight Ecstasy:
  255 Risk Worth Taking
  324 Encore Of Desire
  453 No Greater Love

STUART, Jessica   <HR>
Moonsong Chronicles: In sequence:
  Moonsong Chronicles
  Daughters Of Moonsong
  Sins Of Moonsong, The
  Shadows Of Moonsong, The
  Winds Of Moonsong

STUART, Penelope
                    (Penelope Wisdom)

STUART, Robyn
                    [Vivian Stuart Mann]
Masquerade:
  82 Buccaneer's Lady

STUART, Sandra Lee
Grand Cru   <HS>

STUART, Sheila
            [Mary Gladys Steel Baker]
Harlequin Premiere Edition:
  36 No Yesterday

STUART, Sherry
MacFadden Romance:
  232 Something Borrowed,
          Something Blue
  246 Song Of Winds

STUART, Sherry (cont.)
  264 More Than A Feeling
  266 Amber Glow

STUART, Vivian
                    [Vivian Stuart Mann]
Harlequin Classic:
  77 Pilgrim Heart

STUART, Vivian
                [Charles R. Mackinnon]
Darkness Of Love, The
Darnley's Bride
New Mrs Aldrich, The   <GOT>

STUART-OHLROGGE, Anne Kristine
                    (Anne Stuart)

STUBBS, Jean   <HR>
An Unknown Welshman
Case Of Kitty Ogilvie, The
Dear Laura
Eleanor Duse
Golden Crucible, The
My Grand Enemy
Painted Face, The
Howarth Saga: In sequence: <HS>
  By Our Beginnings
  An Imperfect Joy
  Vivian Inheritance, The

SUBOND, Valerie   <GOT>
            [Valerie Merle Spanner Grayland]
Heights Of Havenrest, The
House Over Hell Valley, The
Avalon:
  House At Haunted Inlet

SUITER, Sheary
Caprice Romance: <YA>
  72 Right Kind Of Guy, The
  83 Boy Crazy

_____

_____

SULLIVAN, Jo
Harlequin Romance:
  2544 Suspicion

_____

_____

SULTAN, Martina
                         [Rita Picker]
Second Chance At Love:
  376 When Lightning Strikes

_____

_____

SUMMERS, ASHLEY
                         [Faye Ashley]
Silhouette Desire:
   36 Fires Of Memory
   95 Marrying Kind, The
  In sequence:
  291   Juliet
  374   Heart's Delight
  509   Eternally Eve
Silhouette Romance:
  197 Season Of Enchantment
  223 Private Eden, A

_____

_____

SUMMERS, Diana   <HR>
                       [George Smith]
Drumbeat Of Desire
Louisiana
Love's Wicked Ways
Rebel's Pleasure, A
Wild Is The Heart
In sequence:
  Fallen Angel
  Emperor's Lady, The

_____

_____

SUMMERS, Essie
Harlequin Classic:
   33 No Roses In June   (668)
   52 House Of The
          Shining Tide   (724)
   60 Lark In The Meadow, The
   67 Come Blossom-Time,
          My Love   (742)
   75 Heatherleigh   (774)
   84 Where No Roads Go   (784)
   97 Bachelors Galore   (886)
  100 Time And
          The Place, The   (822)
  109 Moon Over The Alps   (862)
Harlequin Romance:
  774 Heatherleigh
  784 Where No Roads Go
  802 South To Forget
  822 Time And The Place, The
  847 Smoke And The Fire, The
  862 Moon Over The Alps
  886 Bachelors Galore
  910 Master Of Tawhai, The
  933 Bride In Flight
  957 No Legacy For Lindsay
  982 No Orchids By Request
 1015 Sweet Are The Ways
 1055 Heir To Windrush Hill
 1093 His Serene Miss Smith
 1119 Postscript To Yesterday
 1156 Place Called Paradise, A
 1283 Rosalind Comes Home
 1326 Meet On My Ground
 1348 Revolt--And Virginia
 1375 Kindled Fire, The
 1416 Summer In December
 1445 Bay Of The
          Nightingales, The
 1502 Return To Dragonshill
 1535 House On Gregor's Brae,The
 1564 South Island Stowaway
 1702 Touch Of Magic, A
 1731 Forbidden Valley, The
 1854 Through All The Years
 1884 Gold Of Noon, The
 1917 Anna Of Strathallan
 2000 Not By Appointment
 2021 Beyond The Foothills
 2068 Goblin Hill
 2133 Adair Of Starlight Peaks

SUMMERS, Essie (cont.)
2148 Spring In September
2239 Lake Of The Kingfisher,The
2281 My Lady Of The Fuchaias
2322 One More River To Cross
2453 Tender Leaves, The
2525 Daughter Of
      The Misty Gorges
2590 Mountain For Luenda, A
2622 Lamp For Jonathan, A
2645 Season Of Forgetfulness
2688 Winter In July
2766 To Bring You Joy
2801 Autumn In April
2883 High-Country Governess

SUMMERS, Faye   <HR>
         [Paula M. Rohr]
Stormspell

SUMMERS, Iris   <HR>
[Mary Kuczkir w/
      Joan Giezey Knight]
Whitefire

SUMMERS, Jessica   <CO>
Unfair Advantage

SUMMERS, Judith
Journeys

SUMMERS, Rowena
      [Jean Innes Saunders]
Clay Country
Killigrew Clay

SUMMERS, Rowena (cont.)
Savage Moon, The

SUMMERS, True
         [Hope Campbell]
Poppy

SUMMERSKILL, Shirley
Harlequin Romance:
  763 Surgical Affair, A

SUMMERTON, Margaret <GOT><RS>
         (Jan Roffman)
Dark And Secret Place, A
Ghost Flowers, The
Memory Of Darkness, A
Nightingale At Noon
Quin's Hide
Quin's House
Ring Of Mischief
Saffron Summer, The
Sand Rose, The
Sea House
Sweetcrab

SUMMERVILLE, Margaret   <RE>
[Pamela Wilson w/ Barbara Wilson]
Cotton Caliph, The
Duke's Disappearance, The
Highland Lady
Knave's Gambit
Rogue's Masquerade   <GEO>
Scandal's Daughter
Town Tangle
Viscount's Lady, The
Wicked Wager, The
Candlelight:
  571 Sensible Cecily   <RE>

SUMMERVILLE, Margaret (cont.)
  580 Infamous Isabelle   <RE>
  714 Lord Wicked Wolf   <RE>

_____

_____

SUMNER, Ada
                          (Ada Steward)

SUMNER, Richard
       [Richard William Sumner]
  Nell Gwynne Trilogy:
    Mistress Of The Boards
    Mistress Of The Streets
    Mistress Of The King

_____

_____

SUN, Annalise
  Golden Mountain, The   <HR>

_____

_____

SUNSHINE, Linda
  Silhouette Desire:
    23 Constant Stranger

_____

_____

SUNSHINE, Madeline   <YA>
  Summer Of The Rising Stars

_____

_____

SUSANN, Jacqueline   (Deceased)
  Dolores
  Every Night Josephine
  Love Machine, The
  Once Is Not Enough
  Valley Of The Dolls, The
  Yargo

_____

_____

SUSON, Marlene   <RE>
  An Infamous Bargain

SUSON, Marlene (cont.)
  Desire's Command   <HR>
  Duke's Revenge, The
  Errant Earl, The
  Lady Caro
  Notorious Marquess
  Reluctant Heiress, The

_____

_____

SUTCLIFFE, Katherine   <HR>
     (see Avon Christmas Romance)
  Fire In The Heart
  Heart Possessed, A   <RS>
  Love's Illusion
  Shadow Play
  The Avon Romance:
    Desire And Surrender   &
    Renegade Love   &
    Windstorm   <GOT>

_____

_____

SUTHERLAND, Jean
                          [Jean Nash]
  Ties That Bind

_____

_____

SUTHERLAND, Peg
                      [Peg Robarchek]
  Harlequin SuperRomance:
    398 Behind Every Cloud
    428 Along For The Ride

_____

_____

SUTHERLAND, Sarah
  Memories

_____

_____

SUTTON, Judy
  Shadows From Njara

_____

_____

SUYIN, Han
                    [Suyin Han]
  And The Rain My Drink
  Enchantress, The
  Many Splendored Thing, A
  Mountain Is Young, The
  Till Morning Comes

SVEE, Sally
                    (Irene LeRoy)

SWAN, Rebecca
             [Elizabeth J. Rogers]
  Silhouette Special Edition:
    281 Love's Perfect Island
    393 Chase The Wind

SWAN, Rose
  Hidden Spring, The   <ENG>

SWANN, Francis   <GOT>
  Brass Key, The
  Royal Street
  You'll Hang My Love
                    w/ Lucille EMERICK

SWANN, Lois
  In sequence:
    Mist Of Manittoo, The
    Torn Covenants

SWANTON, Molly Butler w/ Carla
  Friedenberg PELTONEN
                    (Lynn Erickson)

SWATRIDGE, Charles John w/
    Irene Maude Mossop SWATRIDGE
                    (Theresa Charles)

SWATRIDGE, Irene Maud Mossop
                    (Fay Chandos)
                    (Jan Tempest)

SWAZEY, Lisa
  First Love From Silhouette: <YA>
    212 Ask Me No Questions
    215 Falling For You

SWEENEY, Linda w/Patricia PINIANSKI
                    (Lynn Patrick)

SWEENEY, Veronica Geoghegan
  Emancipist, The   <HS>

SWINDELLS, Madge   <HS>
  Corsican Woman, The
  Song Of The Wind
  Summer Harvest

SWINFORD, Katherine
  Second Chance At Love:
    41 Primitive Splendor

SWINNERTON, Frank   (Deceased)
          [Frank Arthur Swinnerton]
  Rosalind Passes   <RS>
  Tigress In The Village, A

SYDNEY, Diana
    Pleasures   <CO>
_____

_____

SYRIL, Binnie
        [Binnie Syril Braunstein]
    Harlequin Temptation:
        247 Color Of Love, The
        276 Out Of The Darkness
_____

_____

SZOLD, Barbara
    Moment Caught In Time, A
    Nora's Innocents
    Promises
_____

_____

TAHOURDIN, Jill
Harlequin Classic:
   9 Summer Lightning   (615)
 170 Sound Of Gutars,The (1092)
Harlequin Romance:
         Hummingbird Island <PROM>
 1092 Sound Of Guitars, The
 1106 Welcome To Paradise
 1276 Steeple Ridge

TALBOT, Charlene Joy
                    (Elizabeth Alden)
                    (Lucy Lee)

TALBOT, Katherine   <RE>
             [Katherine Ashton]
  Lady Molly (Reprint-Warner)
  Philippa (Reprint-Warner#3)
  Warner Regency:
         Lady Molly
   3 Philippa
  14 Theodosia
  28 Tiffany's True Love

TALBOT, Michael   <HO>
  To The Ends Of The Earth

TALIAS, Angela Dunton
                    (Angela Alexie)

TALLMAN, Shirley Bennett
                    (Erin Ross)

TALMAGE, Anne   <GOT>
             [Talmage Powell]
  Dark Over Acadia

TANNAHILL, Reay
  Passing Glory
  In sequence: <HS>
    World, The Flesh,
    And The Devil, The
    Dark And Distant Shore, A

TANNER, Janet
  Emerald Valley, The
  Oriental Hotel
  Women And War

TANNER, Susan   <HR>
  Highland Captive

TAPSELL, R. F.   <HO>
             [Robert Frederick Tapsell]
  Year Of The Horsetails, The

TARLING, Moyra
  Silhouette Romance:
    541 Tender Trail, A
    679 Kiss And A Promise, A
    763 Just In Time For Christmas

TATARA, Ellen Lee Magner
                    (Lee Magner)

TATTERSALL, Jill   <RS>
             [Honor Jill Tattersall]
  Chanters Chase
  Damnation Reef
  Dark At Noon
  Lady Ingram's Room
  Lyonesse Abbey
  Midsummer Masque
  Shadows Of Castle Fosse, The

TATTERSALL, Jill (cont.)
   Summer Cloud, A
   Wild Hunt, The
   Witches Of All Saints, The

TAVARE, Gwendoline
   MacFadden Romance:
   165 Southwest Song

TAX, Meredith
   Rivington Street

TAYLOR, Abra
                   [Barbara Brouse]
   Hold Back The Night
   Harlequin Presents:
   342 Lost Mountain
   Harlequin Temptation:
   23 Summer Surrender
   Silhouette Special Editon:
   73 Season Of Seduction
   103 Wild Is The Heart
   127 Woman Of Daring, A
   157 Forbidden Summer
   192 Sea Spell
   SuperRomance:
   1 End Of Innocence
   5 Cloud Over Paradise
   12 Taste Of Eden, A
   21 River Of Desire
   38 Rage To Possess, A

TAYLOR, Allison
   McFadden Romance:
   36 Winter White

TAYLOR, Beatrice   <RS>
   Journey Into Danger
   Shadow And The Star, The   <ENG>

TAYLOR, Day   <HR>
   [Sharon Salvato w/
               Cornelia M. Parkinson]
   In sequence:
   Magnificent Dream, The
   Sands Of Gold
   In sequence:
   Black Swan, The
   Moss Rose

TAYLOR, Dorothy E.
   The Avon Romance:
   Fleur de Lis   <HR>

TAYLOR, Elizabeth   (Deceased)
   Blaming
   Sleeping Beauty, The
   Wedding Group, The

TAYLOR, Elizabeth Tebbetts   <RS>
   Challoners Of Bristol, The
   Harlequin House
   Tarifa   <HR>

TAYLOR, Georgia Elizabeth <GOT><RS>
   Death Of Jason Darby, The
   Infidel, The

TAYLOR, Janelle   <HR>
          [Janelle Williams Taylor]
   Destiny's Temptress

TAYLOR, Janelle (cont.)
  First Love, Wild Love
  Follow The Wind
  Fortune's Flames
  Golden Torment
  Kiss Of The Night Wind
  Love Me With Fury
  Moondust And Madness   <RF>
  Passions Wild And Free
  Savage Conquest
  Sweet Savage Heart
  Whispered Kisses
  In sequence:
    Wild Is My Love
    Wild, Sweet Promise
  Ecstasy Saga: In sequence:
    Savage Ecstasy
    Defiant Ecstasy
    Forbidden Ecstasy
    Brazen Ecstasy
    Tender Ecstasy
    Stolen Ecstasy
    Bittersweet Ecstasy
  Harlequin American Romance:
    54 Valley Of Fire

TAYLOR, Jayne
                [Jayne Ann Krentz]
  Whirlwind Courtship

TAYLOR, Jennifer
  Harlequin Presents:
    1173 Final Score
    1326 Magical Touch, A
    1349 Tender Pursuit
  Harlequin Romance:
        Unexpected Challenge HRS50
        Lease On Love   HRS72

TAYLOR, Laura
  Honorbound
  Silhouette Desire:
    407 Troubled Waters

TAYLOR, Laura (cont.)
  501 Wildflower
  586 Jade's Passion

TAYLOR, Lucy
  Avenue Of Dreams

TAYLOR, Lynn w/ Karen MAXFIELD
                   (Karen Lynn)

TAYLOR, Mary Ann   <GOT>
                   (Kate Bowe)
                   (Cass McAndrew)
  Aloha To Love
  Apointment In Verona
  Bittersweet Love
  Capture My Heart
  Capture My Love
  Hawaiian Interlude
  Portrait Of A Dead Lady
  Romance In The Headlines
  Serpent Heart, The
  Adventures In Love:
    4 Bon Voyage, My Darling
  Pageant Romance:
    My Enemy, My Love

TAYLOR, Salley Ann
  MacFadden Romance:
    71 Legacy Of Love

TAYLOR, Susan
                [Mary Cummins]
  Girl Of The Sea

TAYNTOR, Christine B.
                   (Amanda Preble)

657

TEER, Barbara
    (Barbara Allister)

TEGLER, Leta
  The Avon Romance:
    Wild Splendor
    Gabrielle

_____

_____

TELFAIR, David   <HO>
  Duchess Polly

_____

TELFER, Dariel
  Caretakers, The
  Corrupters
  Guilty Ones

_____

_____

TELLER, Lee Stewart   <HO>
  Centennial Ball

_____

_____

TEMPEST, Jan
  [Irene Maude Mossop Swatridge]
  House Of The Pines   <GOT>
  Harlequin Romance:
    775 That Nice Nurse Nevin
    963 Nurse Willow's Ward
    994 Jubilee Hospital

_____

_____

TEMPEST, Sarah
  Winter Of Fear, A

_____

_____

TEMPLE, Sarah
                  [Cheryl Arguile]
  Silhouette Special Edition:
    593 Kindred Spirits

_____

_____

TEMPLETON, Janet
                  [Morris Hershman]
  Coventry:
    205 Lover's Knot
  Starlight Romance:
    Lady Fortune
    Love Is The Winner
    Lover's Knot
    Reluctant Heiress, The
    Scapegrace, The
    Suitor To Spare, A
    Virtuous Vixen, The

_____

TEMTE, Myrna
                  (Molly Thomas)
  Silhouette Special Edition:
    483 Wendy Wyoming
    572 Powder River Reunion
    643 Last Good Man Alive, The

_____

TERASAKI, Gwen
  Bridge To The Sun

_____

TERRILL, Dana
  Silhouette Romance:
    181 Man Of Velvet

_____

TERRITO, Mary Jo
                  (Kate Belmont)
                  (Kathryn Belmont)
                  (Gwen Fairfax)
  Harlequin SuperRomance:
    190 Two To Tango
  Harlequin Temptation:
     52 Just Friends
    111 Catch A Rising Star
    121 Vital Ingredient, The
    142 No Passing Fancy
    180 Before And After

_____

_____

658

TERRY, Beverly
                    [Beverly T. Haaf]
  Silhouette Romance:
    414 Before The Loving
    607 Love Bandit, The
    685 Thief Of Hearts

TERRY, Carolyn
  King Of Diamonds   <Saga>

TERRY, Judith
  Version And Diversion (A tale of
    a character from Jane Austen's
    "Mansfield Park")

TERRY , Margaret
  Avalon:
    Last Of April, The
    Love For Tomorrow

TESSLER, Stephanie Gordon
  Caprice Romance: <YA>
    49 Wanted: A Little Love
    57 I Double Love You

TESSLER, Stephanie Gordon w/
                    Judith ENDERLE
                (Jeffie Ross Gordon)
  Bayshore Medical Center
    Series: <YA>
    Andrea Whitman: Pediatrics
    Monica Ross: Maternity
    Elizabeth Jones: Emergency
    Gabriella Ortiz: Crisis
      Center Hot Line

TETEL, Julie   <HR>
              [Julie Tetel Andresen]
  For Love Of Lord Roland
  Viking's Bride, The
  Lovestruck:
    Swept Away
    Tangled Dreams
    And Heaven, Too

TEW, Marzee King
  Avalon:
    Country Style Romance
    Fireside Love
    Love's Tender Promise
    Pearl Of Great Price

THACKER, Cathy
              [Cathy Gillen Thacker]
  Second Chance At Love:
    153 Intimate Scoundrels

THACKER, Cathy Gillen
                    (Cathy Gillen)
                    (Cathy Thacker)
  Harlequin American Romance:
    37   Touch Of Fire
    75   Promise Me Today
    102 Heart's Journey
    134 Reach For The Stars
    143 Family To Cherish, A
    156 Heaven Shared
    166 Devlin Dare, The
    187 Rogue's Bargain
    233 Guardian Angel
    247 Family Affair
    262 Natural Touch
    277 Perfect Match
    Birth Order Trilogy:
    307 One Man's Folly
    318 Lifetime Guarantee
    334 Meant To Be

THACKER, Cathy Gillen (cont.)
    367 It's Only Tempoary
    388 Father Of The Bride
Harlequin Intrigue:
    94 Fatal Amusement
    104 Dream Spinners
    137 Slalom To Terror
Harlequin Temptation:
    47 Embrace Me, Love
    82 Private Passion, A
Velvet Glove: <RS>
    5 Wildfire Trace, The

THACKER, Shelly
    [Shelly Thacker Meinhardt]
The Avon Romance:
    Falcon On The Wind

THANE, Elswyth   <HO>
Bound To Happen
Cloth Of Gold
Echo Answers
From This Day Forward
His Elizabeth
Homing
Kissing Kin
Letter To A Stranger
Light Heart, The
Lost General, The
Melody
Mount Vernon: The Legacy
Queen's Folly
Remember Today
Riders Of The Wind
Tryst
Tudor Wench
Washington's Lady
Williamsburg Saga: In sequence:
    Dawn's Early Light
    Yankee Stranger
    Ever After

THATCHER, Julia   <GOT>
    [Donald Ronald Bensen]
Home To The Night   <ZGS>
Inherit The Mirage   <ZGS>
Mask Of Love
Nightgleams   <ZGS>
Tempest At Summer's End   <ZGS>
Tower In The Sea

THATCHER, Phyllis
    (Catherine Hardcastle)

THAYER, Geraldine
    [Dorothy Daniels]
Candlelight:
    128 Dark Rider, The

THESMAN, Jean
Caprice Romance: <YA>
    47 New Kid In Town
    69 Two Letters For Jenny
    77 Secret Love, A

THIAN, Valerie
Harlequin Romance:
    1515 O Kiss Me, Kate

THIELS, Kathryn
    [Kathryn Maxine Gorsha Thiels]
Silhouette Intimate Moments:
    51 Alternate Arrangements
Silhouette Special Edition:
    10 Texas Rose
    234 An Acquired Taste

THIELS, Kathryn Gorsha   <HR>
  Savage Fancy

THIES, Joyce
              [Joyce Ann Scott Thies]
                   (Melissa Scott)
  Call Down The Moon   <HR>
  Silhouette Desire:
    348 Spellbound
    359 False Pretenses
    378 Primrose Path, The
      Tales Of The Rising Moon:
        In sequence:
    432   Moon Of The Raven
    444   Reach For The Moon
    456   Gypsy Moon
    511 Mountain Man   <MMS>
    563 King Of The Mountain
    636 Drifter, The   <MMS>

THIES, Joyce w/ Janet BIEBER
  [Joyce Ann Scott Thies w/
       Janet Lynn Parker Bieber]
                   (Janet Joyce)
                   (Jenna Lee Joyce)

THIMBLETHORPE, J. S.
                   (Sylvia Thorpe)

THIRKELL, Angela   (Deceased)
        [Angela Margaret Thirkell]
  August Folly
  High Rising
  Love At All Ages
  Never Too Late
  Pomfret Towers
  "Barsetshire" Romance Series:
    1 Brandons, The
    2 Before Lunch
    3 Cheerfulness Breaks In
    4 Northbridge Rectory
    5 Marling Hall
    6 Wild Strawberries

THIRKELL, Angela (cont.)
    7 Headmistress, The
    8 Miss Bunting
    9 Peace Breaks Out
   10 Private Enterprise
   11 Love Among The Ruins
   12 Duke's Daughter, The
   13 Old Bank House, The
   14 County Chronicle
   15 Happy Return
   16 Jutland Cottage
   17 What Did It Mean?
   18 Enter Sir Robert

THOENE, Bodie   <HO>
  In sequence:
    Gates Of Zion, The

THOM, James Alexander   <HO>
  Follow The River
  From Sea To Shining Sea   <HR>
  Long Knife
  Panther In The Sky

THOMAS, Alan
  First Love From Silhouette: <YA>
   195 Roar Of The Crowd, The

THOMAS, Bree
                   [Susannah Howe]
  Rapture Romance:
    42 Love's Journey Home

THOMAS, Charles
                   (see Garland Roark)

THOMAS, Dianne
    [Debrah Morris w/ Pat Shaver]
Second Chance At Love:
    364 Heaven Can Wait
    460 Overnight Sensation
    464 Out Of The Blue

THOMAS, Elizabeth Marshall
Raindeer Moon   <HO>

THOMAS, Jason
Haute   <CO>

THOMAS, Jodi   <HR>
    [Jodi Koumalats]
Beneath The Texas Sky
Northern Star

THOMAS, Leslie
Silhouette Special Edition:
    53 Goddess Of The Moon

THOMAS, Martha Lou   <RE>
    [Martha Lou Manson Thomas]
Lady True's Gate
Waltz With A Stranger
War Hero's Wife, The

THOMAS, Michele Y.   <GOT>
Crystal Shadows
Heath Hallows
House At Thunder Cove, The

THOMAS, Molly
                    [Myrna Temte]
Second Chance At Love:
    360 Rebel Heart

THOMAS, P. J.   <HR>
Passion's Child

THOMAS, Patricia
MacFadden Romance:
    131 Snow Maiden
    152 Touch Of Heaven, A
    183 Pocketful Of Wishes

THOMAS, Roberta
Avalon:
    Return To Paradise Cove

THOMAS, Rosie
Bad Girls Good Women
Follies
Sunrise
Strangers
White Dove, The   <Saga>
Woman Of Our Time, A
The Avon Romance:
    Love's Choice

THOMAS, Victoria
Starlight Romance:
    Ginger's Wish

THOMPSON, Alfie
                    (Val Daniels)

662

THOMPSON, Aline
    [Aline Beeson Thompson]
  Pleasure Class, The

THOMPSON, Allyn
              (Bess Shannon)

THOMPSON, Ann
  House Of Strange Music

THOMPSON, Ann Lorraine
  Cry For Love, A
  Hands Of Fate
  Love, The Sorcerer

THOMPSON, Anne Armstrong   <RS>
  Man Caine, The
  Message From Absalom, A
  Romanov Ransom, The
  Swiss Legacy, The

THOMPSON, Arthur
  Starned, The

THOMPSON, Christene
  MacFadden Romance:
    160 Chateau Of Love
    184 Sunshower
    209 Candles In The Rain

THOMPSON, Chris
  Torchlite:
    Whispers Of Desire

THOMPSON, E. V.   <HS>
  Cry Once Alone
  Republic
  Cornish Exile Saga: In sequence:
    Chase The Wind
    Harvest Of The Sun

THOMPSON, Estelle   <GOT>
  Hunter In The Dark
  Meadows Of Tallon
  Three Women In The House

THOMPSON, Joan
  [Joan Russell Phillips Thompson]
  Harbor Of The Heart
    (HB: Marblehead)
  Interesting Times   <Saga>
  Parker's Island
  Facing It

THOMPSON, Kate
  Great House

THOMPSON, Marcella
  Harlequin Romance:
    2802 Breaking Free
    2975 Bed, Breakfast & Bedlam
    3106 Of Rascals And Rainbows

THOMPSON, Marcella w/ Paula
  THOMPSON   (Pamela Thompson)

THOMPSON, Morton
  Cry And The Covenant, The
  Not As A Stranger

THOMPSON, Pamela
[Marcella Thompson w/
            Paula Thompson]
Harlequin American Romance:
  99 Wellspring, The
Harlequin Intrigue:
   7 Rainbow Ribbon

THOMPSON, Robert
                (see Rebecca Drury)

THOMPSON, Vicki Lewis
Harlequin SuperRomance:
  151 When Angels Dance
  211 Butterflies In The Sun
  269 Golden Girls
  326 Sparks
  389 Connections
Harlequin Temptation:
    9 Mingled Hearts
   25 Promise Me Sunshine
   92 An Impractical Passion
  113 Fix-It Man, The
  140 As Time Goes By
  155 Cupid's Caper
  192 Flip Side, The
  217 Impulse   <MEQ>
  240 Be Mine, Valentine
  256 Full Coverage
  278 'Tis The Season
  288 Forever Mine, Valentine

THOMPSON, Vicki Lewis w/
            Mary Frances Tate ENGELS
            (Corey Keaton)
            (Cory Kenyon)

THOMPSON, Victoria
          [Victoria Ellen Thompson]
Beloved Outcast
Bold Texas Embrace
Texas Blonde
Texas Treasure
Texas Vixen
Wild Texas Promise

THOMPSON, Victoria (cont.)
In sequence:
  Texas Triumph
  Angel Heart
The Avon Romance:
  Fortune's Lady
  Rogue's Lady
  Playing With Fire

THOMSEN, Frieda   <RS>
                (Louise MacKendrick)
  Second Lady Cameron, The

THOMSEN, Robert   <HR>
  Carriage Trade

THOMSON, Christine
MacFadden Romance:
  153 Passport To Love

THOMSON, D. H.
          [Daisy Hicks Thomson]
  Italian For Love, The

THOMSON, Daisy
          [Daisy Hicks Thomson]
In Love, In Vienna
Love At Leisure   <RS>
My Love
Nightingale For Love, A
Suddenly It Was Love
Time For Love, A
To Love And Be Wise
Thomson Series:
   1 Prelude To Love
   2 My Only Love
   3 Hello, My Love

THORNTON, Elizabeth (cont.)
  Scarlet Angel
  Virtuous Lady, A
  Worldly Widow, The

THORNTON, Helene   <HR>
  Cathay
  Family O'Rourke, The
  Journey To Desire
  Mistress From Martinique
  Scarlet Ribbons: <HR>
    Passionate Exile

THORNTON, Jane Foster
  Electric High Romance: <YA>
    1 Breakaway
    2 Close Harmony
    3 Heartbreaker

THORPE, Kay
  Harlequin Presents:
    81 Iron Man, The
    93 Opportune Marriage
   237 Lord Of La Pampa
   242 Caribbean Encounter
   299 Bitter Alliance
   311 Man From Tripoli, The
   336 This Side Of Paradise
   360 Dividing Line, The
   378 Chance Meeting
   394 No Passing Fancy
   425 Floodtide
   455 Copper Lake
   491 Temporary Marriage
   534 New Owner, The
   573 Man Of Means, A
   597 Master Of Morley
   646 Land Of The Incas, The
   678 Never Trust A Stranger
   710 Inheritance, The

THORPE, Kay (cont.)
   789 No Gentle Persuasion
   822 Double Deception
   853 South Seas Affair
   902 Dangerous Moonlight
   941 Win Or Lose
   973 Jungle Island
  1084 Time Out Of Mind
  1141 Land Of Illusion
  1204 Tokyo Tryst
  1261 Skin Deep
  1301 Steel Tiger
  Harlequin Romance:
  1237 Last Of The Mallorys, The
  1272 Devon Interlude
  1355 Rising Star
  1504 Curtain Call
  1583 Sawdust Season
  1609 Not Wanted On Voyage
  1661 Olive Island
  1756 An Apple In Eden
  1779 Man At Kambala, The
  1909 Shifting Sands, The
  1967 Sugar Cane Harvest
  1990 Royal Affair, The
  2046 Safari South
  2079 River Lord, The
  2109 Storm Passage
  2151 Timber Boss
  2232 Wilderness Trail, The
  2234 Full Circle
  Other:
    Man In A Box   <M&B>

THORPE, Sylvia   <GEO><HR><RE>
              [J. S. Thimblethorpe]
  Beggar On Horseback
  Beloved Rebel
  Captain Gallant
  Changing Tide, The
  Fair Shine The Day
  Flash Of Scarlet, A
  Golden Panther, The
  Highwayman, The
  Mistress Of Astington
  No More A-Rowing

THORPE, Sylvia (cont.)
Reluctant Adventuress, The
Rogue's Covenant
Scandalous Lady Robin, The
Scapegrace, The
Scarlet Domino, The
Silver Nightingale, The
Spring Will Come Again
Strangers On The Moor   <GOT>
Sword And The Shadow, The
Sword Of Vengeance
Varleigh Medallion, The
Coventry:
    9 House At Bell Orchard, The
   32 Devil's Bondman
   48 Dark Enchantress
  119 Three Loves
Coventry Classic:
    Romantic Lady
    Tarrington Chase
_____

_____

THUM, Marcella   <HR><RS>
Abbey Court
Blazing Star
Fernwood
Margarite
Mystery At Cranes Landing
White Rose, The
Wild Laurel
In sequence:
    Jasmine
    Mistress Of Paradise
_____

_____

THURLO, Aimee
            [Aimee Salcedo Thurlo]
Candlelight Ecstasy:
  509 Ariel's Desire
Harlequin Intrigue:
  109 Expiration Date
  131 Black Mesa
  141 Suitable For Framing
  162 Strangers Who Linger

THURLO, Aimee (cont.)
Harlequin SuperRomance:
  312 Right Combination, The
_____

_____

THURLO, Aimee Salcedo
                    (Aimee Duvall)
                    (Aimee Martel)
                    (Aimee Thurlo)
THURSTON, Anne
Harlequin American Romance:
   53 Pink Beds, The
_____

_____

THURSTON, Carol
Current Affairs
_____

_____

TICHENOR, Vivian H.
                    (Vivian Harris)

TIDD, Diane
                    (Catherine Hart)

TIERNEY, Ariel
Second Chance At Love:
   74 Sultry Nights
  129 Conquering Embrace
_____

_____

TIERNEY, Pat   <GOT>
Encounter In Eden
Powers Of Lismara, The
_____

_____

TIMSON, Keith
                    (Danielle De Winters)

TIMMS, E. V.
Beckoning Shore, The
Challenge, The

TIMMS, E. V. (cont.)
Forever To Remain
Fury, The
Pathway To The Sun
Robina
Scarlet Frontier, The
Shining Harvest
They Came From The Sea
Valleys Beyond, The

TINTLE, Louise K.
Avalon:
Highway To Love
Remembered Kisses
Destination: Love

TITCHENER, Louise
(Anne Silverlock)
(Jane Silverwood)

TITCHENER, Louise w/ Ruth GLICK,
Eileen BUCKHOLTZ and Carolyn MALES
(Alyssa Howard)

TITCHENER, Louise w/ Ruth GLICK
(Alexis Hill)
(Alexis Hill Jordan)
(Tess Marlowe)

TITCHENER, Louise w/ Carolyn MALES
(Clare Richards)
(Clare Richmond)

TITLE, Elise
(Alison Tyler)
Harlequin American Romance:
377 Till The End Of Time <COAR>
Harlequin Intrigue:
97 Circle Of Deception
119 All Through The Night
149 Face In The Mirror, The
160 Shadow Of The Moon
Harlequin SuperRomance:
363 Out Of The Blue

TITLE, Elise (cont.)
476 Trouble In Eden
Harlequin Temptation:
203 Love Letters
223 Baby, It's You
266 Macnamara And Hall
282 Too Many Husbands
340 Making It

TITO, Patricia   <HR>
Passion's Triumph

TITUS, Coral Hoyle
(Coral Hoyle)

TOBIAS, Katherine   <GOT>
[Theodore Mark Gottfried]
Lady In The Lightning, The
Slave Of Passion

TOBIN, Lee Ann
(Erika Favor)

TODD, Elizabeth   <RE>
[Alicia Todd Rasley]
Earl's Intrigue, The

TOKSON, Elliott   <HR>
When Dragons Dance

TOLIVAR, Robin
[Pat C. Oakson w/ Leslie Bishop]
The Avon Romance: <HR>
In Love's Fury

TOMPKINS, Julia
     (Marguerite Neilson)

TONE, Teona   <RS>
  Lady On The Line

TONNER, Leslie
  Five Towers
  Love Song
  Nothing But The Best

TOOMBS, Jane   <HO>
      [Jane Jenke Toombs]
        (Diana Stuart)
    (see Rebecca Drury)
  (see Lee Davis Willoughby <MOAS>)
  Arapaho Spirit   <AIS#13>
  Chippewa Daughter   <AIS#4>
  Doctors And Lovers
  Scots, The   <Saga>
  Topaz For My Fair Lady,A <BGS#11>
  Tule Witch   <GOT>
  Dark Desire Romance:
    Shadowed Hearts
  Harlequin Gothic Romance:
    An Innocent Madness
    Restless Obsession
  Heartfire Romance: <HR>
    Creole Betrayal
    Midnight Whispers
    Riverboat Rogue
    Sunset Temptation
  Judy Sullivan Books:
    Heart Of Winter   <RS>

TOOMBS, John   <HO>
      (Fortune Kent)
      (Jocelyn Wilde)
    (see Richard Hale Curtis)
    (see Jonathan Scofield)
  (see Lee Davis Willoughby <MOAS>)
  (see Lee Davis Willoubhby <WWWW>)

TOOMBS, John (cont.)
  Flag
  Forty Niners, The   <MOAS:#4>
  Silverfire

TOPAZ, Jacqueline
        [Jackie D. Hyman]
  Second Chance At Love:
   249 Swept Away
   258 Rites Of Passion
   297 Lucky In Love
   336 Golden Girl
   435 Warm December, A
  To Have And To Hold:
   39 Deeper Than Desire

TOPPER, Suzanne   <RS>
  Pulse Points

TORDAY, Ursula
      (Paula Allardyce)
     (Charity Blackstock)
     (Charlotte Keppel)

TORR, I.
     [Charles R. Mackinnon]
  Allison Comes Home
  Haven Of Peace
  Love On A Holiday
  Love Finds The Way
  Sundown

TORTORA, Gloria
  Heavenly Romance: <YA>
    Candidate For Love

TOTH, Emily Jane   <HR>
Daughters Of New Orleans

TOTH, Pamela
                          (Pamela Roth)
Candlelight Ecstasy:
  442 Fever Pitch
Silhouette Romance:
  500 Kissing Games
  595 Ladybug Lady, The
Silhouette Special Edition:
  411 Thunderstruck
  515 Dark Angel
  624 Old Enough To Know Better

TOWER, Diana   <GOT>
        [Richard Rein Smith]
Dark Diamond   <BGS:#4>
Gleam Of Sapphire, A   <BGS:#9>
Prisoner Of Evil
Red Lion

TOWERS, Regina
                        [Nina Pykare]
Candlelight:
  593 Rake's Companion, The <RE>

TOWNLEY, Pamela
  Foxy Lady
  Image, The
  Nearest Of Kin
  Rogan's Moor
  Winter Jasmine
  Woman In The Wind   <Saga>

TOWNSEND, Tom
                          (Tammie Lee)
  (see Leather And Lace <L&L>)

TRACY, Don   <HR>(Deceased)
              [Donald Fiske Tracy]
  Big X, The
  Chesapeake Cavalier
  Corpse Can Sure
   Louse Up A Weekend, A
  Crimson Is The Eastern Shore
  Death Calling Collect
  Editor, The
  High, Wide And Ransom

TRACY, Marie D.
                          (Audra Adams)

TRACY, Marilyn
                       [Tracy LeCocq]
  Silhouette Intimate Moments:
    311 Magic In The Air
    362 Blue Ice

TRACY, Pat
  Silhouette Romance:
    654 His Kind Of Woman
    710 Tiger By The Tail

TRACY, Susan
  Silhouette Romance:
    159 Yesterday's Bride

TRAILL-HILL, James
  Hetty

TRANBARGER, Charlotte
  Avalon:
    Destiny's Love
    Love Beyond Yesterday

670

TRANBARGER, Charlotte (cont.)
    Rules Of The Heart

TRANTER, Nigel   <HO>
        [Nigel Godwin Tranter]
    Pegasus Books:
    2 Scotland
    Queen's Scotland Series:
      Eastern Countries, The
      Heartland, The
    Robert The Bruce Series:
    1 Steps To The Empty Throne, The
    2 Path Of The Hero King, The
    3 Price Of The King's Peace, The

TRAVIS, Neal   <CO>
    Castles
    Island
    Mansions
    Palaces
    Manhattan
    Wings

TRAYNOR, Page w/ Anthony TRAYNOR
                        (Page Anthony)

TREADWELL, Constance
    First Love From Silhouette: <YA>
    24 Dream Lover

TREE, Cornelia   <RS>
    Child Of The Night

TREHEARNE, Elizabeth
    [Patricia Maxwell w/
                    Carol Albritton]
    Storm At Midnight

TREIBICH, S. J.   <GOT><RS>
    Burwyck's Wander
    Haelstrom Manor

TREMAINE, Claire   <HR>
    Cavalier's Gold
    Sand Against The Wind

TREMAINE, Jennie
        [Marion Chesney Gibbons]
    Lady Anne's Deception   <RE>
    Maggie   <RS>
    Candlelight:
      527 Kitty   <ED>
      542 Daisy   <ED>
      562 Lucy   <RE>
      573 Polly   <RE>
      587 Molly   <RE>
      596 Ginny   <ED>
      660 Tilly   <RE>
      685 Susie   <ED>
      704 Poppy   <ED>
      709 Sally   <ED>

TREMBLAY II, Ernest A.
            (see Rebecca Drury)

TREMBLAY, E. A.   <HO>
    Italians, The   <IMS>

TREMONTE, Julia   <GOT>
    Devil's House, The

TRENCH, Caroline
    Harlequin Romance:
      850 Other Anne, The

671

TRENT, Brenda
        [Brenda Lee Eanes Wilson]
    Silhouette Desire:
     122 Without Regrets
    Silhouette Romance:
      56 Rising Star
      74 Winter Dreams
     110 Stranger's Wife, The
     161 Run From Heartache
     193 Runaway Wife
     245 Steal Love Away
     266 Hunter's Moon
     423 Bewitched By Love
     488 Better Man, A
     506 Hearts On Fire
     540 Cupid's Error
     563 Something Good
     620 Man Of Her Own, A
     638 Someone To Love
     667 Be My Baby
     715 Woman's Touch, A
     757 That Southern Man
     778 For Heaven's Sake
    Silhouette Special Edition:
      51 Stormy Affair

TRENT, Danielle
        [Dan Trent w/ Linda Trent]
    Harlequin SuperRomance:
     121 Winter Roses

TRENT, Lynda
        [Dan Trent w/ Linda Trent]
    Master's Touch, The
    Opal Fires
    Rosehaven
    Shining Nights   <HR>
    Summerfield   <HR>
    Yesterday's Roses   <HS>
    In sequence:
      Wyndfell
      Tryst, The

TRENT, Lynda (cont.)
    Harlequin Historical <Set#2>:
      59 Heaven's Embrace
      75 Black Hawk, The
    Harlequin SuperRomance:
     348 Gift Of Summer, The
     430 Words Of Love
    Harlequin Temptation:
     291 Another Rainbow
    Silhouette Desire:
     201 Enchantment, The
     223 Simple Pleasures
    Silhouette Intimate Moments:
      36 Designs
      68 Taking Chances
     134 Castles In The Sand
    Silhouette Special Edition:
     378 High Society
     409 Certain Smile, A
     443 Heat Lightning
     457 Beguiling Ways
     504 Like Strangers
     534 Repeat Performance
    Tapestry: <HR>
      In sequence:
      14 Embrace The Storm
      17 Embrace The Wind
      28 Willow Wind

TRESILLIAN, Richard   <HR>
    In sequence:
      Bondmaster, The
      Blood Of The Bondmaster
      Bondmaster Breed, The

TREVELYAN, Julia   <GOT><RS>
    Blackmoor
    Greythorne
    Landsend Terror, The
    Tower Room, The

TREVOR, June
        [June E. Casey]
  Silhouette Desire:
    88 Winged Victory
  Silhouette Intimate Moments:
    11 Until The End Of Time

TREVOR, Meriol   <RE>
      [Lucy Meriol Trevor]
  Fortunate Marriage, The
  Coventry:
    94 Wanton Fires, The
   161 Sun With A Face, The

TREVOR, William
      [William Trevor Cox]
  Fools Of Fortune

TRIGLIA, June
    [June Casey w/ Joan Triglia]
  Bound By Blood   <CS>

TRIEGEL, Linda Jeanette
        (Elisabeth Kidd)

TRINER, Jeanne
  Harlequin SuperRomance:
   267 By Any Other Name
   319 Make No Mistake

TRIVELPIECE, Laurel
  Trying Not To Love You   <YA>

TROKE, Molly
      (Hester Bourne)

TROLLOPE, Joanna   <HR>
  Eliza Stanhope
  Leaves From The Valley
  Parson Harding's Daughter
  Steps Of The Sun, The
  Taverner's Place, The   <HS>

TROUTMAN, Jackie
        (Jackie Dalton)

TROY, Amanda
         [Mary Kahn]
  Second Chance At Love:
    63 Double Deception   <RE>

TROY, Katherine   <RS>
       [Anne Buxton]
  Farramonde
  Roseheath

TROYAT, Henri   <HO>
  Baroness
  Tolstoy
  Seed And The Fruit Series: <HS>
    Amelie And Pierre
    Amelie In Love
    Elizabeth
    Tender And Violent Elizabeth
    Encounter, The

TUCCI, Tony
  Butterfly Secret, The

TUCKER,
  Aston Hall:
   110 Shetland Summer

TUCKER, Delaine
        [Deborah Elaine Camp]
  Serenade Romance:
    Tomorrow's Bride

TUCKER, Elaine
        [Deborah Elaine Camp]
  To Have And To Hold:
    4 They Said It Wouldn't Last
   12 Strange Bedfellows

TUCKER, Helen   <RE>
  Guilt Of August Fielding
  No Need Of Glory
  Reason For Rivalry, A
  Sound Of Summer Voices, The
  Strange And
   Ill-Starred Marriage, A
  Virgin Of Lontano, The
  Coventry:
    24 Mistress To The Regent, A
    54 An Infamous Attachment
    74 Halverton Scandal, The
   151 Wedding Day Deception, A
   168 Double Dealers, The
   206 Season Of Dishonor
  Tapestry: <HR>
    29 Ardent Vows
    38 Bound By Honor

TUCKER, James
  Stone Saga: <HS>
    1 Birth, The
    2 Journey, The

TUCKER, Joy
            (Kelly Street)

TUCKER, Rosemary
  Heavenly Romance: <YA>
    Call Me Allison

TUCKER, Ruth Barsten (Deceased)
           (Hope McIntyre)

TUNBERG, Karl And Terence <HR>
  Master Of Rosewood
  Quest Of Ben Hur, The

TURLAND, Eileen
  Desert Quest
  Rocking Stone, The

TURNBULL, Agnes Sligh (Deceased)
           <HO><RS>
  Bishop's Mantle, The
  Day Must Dawn, The
  Flowering, The
  Golden Journey
  Gown Of Glory, The
  King's Orchard, The
  Many A Green Isle
  Nightingale, The
  Remember The End
  Richlands, The
  Rolling Years, The
  Two Bishops, The
  Wedding Bargain, The
  Whistle And I'll Come To You
  Winds Of Love, The

TURNER, Barbara
        [Barbara Kay Turner]
  Silhouette Desire:
   281 Blond Chameleon, The
  Silhouette Romance:
   350 Cassie Come Home
   410 Catnip Man, The

TURNER, Barbara (cont.)
   465 Las Vegas Match
   490 Satin And White Lace
   608 True Bliss
   641 Sister Wolf

TURNER, Elizabeth   <HR>
                [Gail Oust]
Heart's Desire
Tapestry:
   90 Sweet Possession
The Avon Romance:
   Forbidden Fires

TURNER, Joan
Harlequin Romance:
   772 Chloe Wilde, Student Nurse

TURNER, Judy
Masquerade:
   50 Follow The Drum
   77 Gift For Pamela, A
   87 Sherida

TURNER, Linda
            [Linda Ray Turner]
            (Linda Raye)
Silhouette Desire:
   220 Glimpse Of Heaven, A
Silhouette Intimate Moments:
   238 Echo Of Thunder, The
   263 Crosscurrents
   298 An Unsuspecting Heart
   316 Flirting With Danger
   354 Moonlight And Lace
Silhouette Special Edition
   350 Shadows In The Night
SuperRomance:
   65 Persistent Flame, A

TURNER, Lynn
          [Mary Frances Watson]
Harlequin Intrigue:
   45 Mystery Train
Harlequin Presents:
   893 Forever
   1205 Impulsive Gamble
Harlequin SuperRomance:
   134 Lasting Gift, A
   203 Double Trouble
Harlequin Temptation:
   8 For Now, For Always
   56 Another Dawn
   75 Up In Arms
   107 Hook, Line And Sinker

TURNER, Robert Harry
          (Lisa Roberts)

TURNER, Sue Long
       (see Kristin Michaels)

TURNEY, C. Dell
Avalon:
   Killing Tree, The

TURNEY, Catherine
Byron's Daughter
Surrender The Seasons

TURTON, Godfrey   <HO>
      [Godfrey Edmund Turton]
My Lord Of Canterbury
Devil's Churchyard

TUTTLE, Anthony   <CO>
Another Love, Another Time
Songs From The Night Before

TWADDLE, Susan Bowden
          (Elizabeth Barron)
          (Susan Bowden)

TYLER, Alison
          [Elise Title]
  The Jennifer Heath Series: <RM>
    Chase The Wind
    Chase The Storm
    Chase The Sun
  Candlelight Ecstasy:
   227 Business Before Pleasure
   245 Too Good To Be True
   259 Tender Awakening
   272 Daring Alliance, A
   304 Pulling The Strings
   318 Matter Of Style, A
   369 Lost In Love
   380 Free And Easy
   433 Bitter With The Sweet, The
   447 Take-Charge Lady
   471 King Of Seduction
   490 Restless Yearning
   521 Pink Satin Lady
   526 Wild Surrender
  Candlelight Ecstasy Supreme:
    36 Playing It Safe
    54 Tamed Spirit
    68 Question Of Honor, A
    79 How Many Tomorrows?
    99 Glimmer Of Trust, A
   109 Perfect Charade
  Candlelight Supreme:
   149 Today And Always
   161 Runaway Lover
   174 Double Masquerade
   187 Tempting Angel

TYLER, Anne
         [Anne Tyler Modarressi]
  Celestial Navigation
  Clock Winder, The
  Dinner At The
    Homesick Restaurant
  Earthly Possessions
  If Morning Ever Comes

TYLER, Anne (cont.)
  Morgan's Passing
  Searching For Caleb
  Slipping-Down Life, A
  Tin Can Tree, The

TYLER, Antonia
         [Susan Whittlesey Wolf]
  Second Chance At Love:
   303 This Shining Hour

TYLER, Vicki
  Heart To Heart: <YA>
    Senior Year
    Someday Soon

TYLER-WHITTLE, Michael Sidney
         (Tyler Whittle)

UNDSET, Sigrid   (Deceased)
Kristin Lavransdatter Trilogy:
  In sequence: <Saga>
    Bridal Wreath, The
    Mistress Of Husaby, The
    Cross, The

UNICKEL, Martha Sawyer
                (Meryl Nickels)
                (Meryl Sawyer)

UNSWORTH, Mair   <RE>
  Bride Of Pontravon, The
  Came A Stranger
  Daughter Of My House
  Home To My Love
  House Of Shadows
  Sicilian Inheritance, The
  White Hart Of Penlinton, The
  Wild Winds

UPPER, Gloria
          (Gloria Douglas)

UPSHALL, Helen
         (Susannah Curtis)
  Surgeon, RN   <M&B>

UPSHAW, Helen   <RS>
  Return Of Jennifer, The

UPTON, Peter
Green Hill Far Away

URE, Jean
          (Sara McCulloch)
  Young Love Romance: <YA>
    See You Thursday
    What If They Saw Me Now?

VAIL, Linda
[Melinda Hobaugh-Hamilton w/
Stephen G. Hamilton]
Holiday Confections: <RS>
My Wicked Valentine
Star Spangled Lover
Unmasked Passion
Moonlight And Mistletoe
Candlelight Ecstasy:
160 Fool's Paradise
243 Best Things In Life, The
289 Amber Persuasion
319 Magic Touch
Candlelight Ecstasy Supreme:
75 Prized Possession
96 Choices And Chances
107 Night Shadow
118 Treasure For A Lifetime
Candlelight Supreme:
129 Shadows Of The Heart
144 My Darling Pretender
158 Shattered Secrets
171 Secret Arrangement, A
179 Loving Charade

VALCOUR, Vanessa
[James Conaway]
Second Chance At Love:
121 Play It By Heart

VALDES, Ivy
Chase A Dark Shadow
Cristina's Fántasy
Drury Affair, The
Gift From A Stranger
It Happened In Spain
Over My Shoulder

VALDES, Ivy (cont.)
Sheila's Dilemma
Sylvia's Daughter

VALE, Rena M. <GOT>
House On Raindrop Leap, The

VALENTI, Justine
(Barbara Max)
(Vanessa Victor)
Building Dreams
Lovemates
No One But You <CO>
Protege
Twin Connections

VALENTINE, Jo
[Charlotte Armstrong]
And Sometimes Death (Original
"Trouble In Thor" by Charlotte
Armstrong)

VALENTINE, Terri
Heartfire Romance: <HR>
Golden Lies
Master Of Her Heart <HF>
Sea Dream
Traitor's Kiss
Yankee's Caress

VALLEY, Lorraine
Silhouette Desire:
14 Blanket Of Stars

VANDERBURGH, Rosamond
          (see Nan Salemo)

VANDERGRIFF, Aola   <GOT><HR>
                            (Kit Brown)
  House Of The Dancing Dead, The
  Silk And Shadow
  Sisters Of Sorrow
  Red Wind Blowing   <Saga>
  "Daughters" series: In sequence:
    Daughters Of The South Wind
    Daughters Of The Wild Country
    Daughters Of The Far Islands
    Daughters Of The Opal Skies
    Daughters Of The Misty Isles
    Daughters Of The Shining City
    Daughters Of The Storm
    Daughters Of The Silver Screen
  Trilogy:
    Wyndspelle
    Bell Tower Of Wyndspelle
    Wyndspelle's Child
  In This Sweet Land Series:
    In sequence:
      Inga's Story:
        In This Sweet Land
      Jenny's Story: Devilwind
  NOTE: "Kristen's Story" was
        never published.

_____

_____

VANDERVELDE, Isabel   <HR>
  Lace

_____

van der ZEE, Karen
                [Wendela Kilmer]
  Harlequin Presents:
    433 Secret Sorrow, A
    544 Waiting
    694 One More Time
    708 Going Underground
    798 Staying Close
    830 Pelangi Haven
    950 Time For Another Dream
    982 Fancy Free

van der ZEE, Karen (cont.)
   1126 Shadows On Bali
   1158 Hot Pursuit
   1222 Brazilian Fire
   1350 Java Nights
  Harlequin Romance:
   2334 Sweet Not Always
   2406 Love Beyond Reason
   2652 Soul Ties

_____

_____

VAN EVERY, Dale   <HR>(Deceased)
  Bridal Journey, The
  Captive Witch, The
  Scarlet Feather, The
  Shining Mountains, The
  Trembling Earth, The
  Voyagers, The
  Westward The River
  Frontier People Of America
    Series:
      Ark Of Empire
      Company Of Heroes, A
      Disinherited
      Final Challenge
      Forth To The Wilderness

_____

_____

VAN EVERY FROST, Joan
  Kings Of The Sea
  Lisa
  Masque Of Chameleons, A
  This Fiery Promise

_____

_____

VAN HAZINGA, Cynthia   <GOT><HR>
           [Cynthia Van Hazinga Kutz]
  Balance Of Terror   <BZG>
  Farewell My South
  Georgians, The
  Ghost River Inn
  House On Gannet's Point
  Louisiana Lady
  Our Hearts Divided
  Tower Room, The

VAN HAZINGA, Cynthia (cont.)
White Columns
In sequence: <HS>
Our Sacred Honor
These United Colonies
Our Common Ties

VAN KIRK, Eileen
Harlequin Gothic Romance:
Standing Stones, The

VAN-LOON, Antonio
For Love And Honor
For Us The Living
Katherine
Sunshine And Shadow
Woman Of The Dawn
(HB: Sunshine And Shadow)

VAN-LOON, Antonio w/ Roni
FINKLESTEIN   (Janine French)

VAN NUYS, Joan
                   (Marianna Essex)
Beloved Enchantress
The Avon Romance:
Beloved Avenger

VAN SLYKE, Helen   (Deceased)
                        (Sharon Aston)
All Visitors Must Be Announced
Always Is Not Forever
Best People, The
Best Place To Be, The
Necessary Woman, A
No Love Lost
Public Smiles,
Private Tears (w/James ELWARD)
Rich And The Righteous, The
Santa Ana Wind, The

VAN SLYKE, Helen (cont.)
Sisters And Strangers
In sequence:
Heart Listens, The
Mixed Blessing, The

VAN STEENWYK, Elizabeth
Caprice Romance: <YA>
3 Dance With A Stranger
Heavenly Romance: <YA>
Face Of Love, The

---

van WIEREN, Mona
                      [Wendela Kilmer]
Silhouette Romance:
630 Rhapsody In Bloom

VAN ZWIENEN, John   <HO>
(see Lee Davis Willoughby <MOAS>)
China Clipper

VARLINSKY, Deborah M.
                    (Deborah Le Varre)

VARNER, Linda
                   [Linda Varner Palmer]
Silhouette Romance:
625 Heart Of The Matter
644 Heart Rustler
665 Luck Of The Irish, The
698 Honeymoon Hideaway
734 Better To Have Loved
780 House Becomes A Home, A

VASILOPOULOS, Freda
                       (Freda Vasilos)
                       (Tina Vasilos)

680

VASILOS, Freda .
                [Freda Vasilopoulos]
  Silhouette Desire:
    231 Moon Madness
  Silhouette Special Edition:
    286 Summer Wine

VASILOS, Tina
                [Freda Vasilopoulos]
  Harlequin Intrigue:
     68 Unwitting Accomplice
    101 Wolf's Prey
    132 Past Tense
  Harlequin SuperRomance:
    351 Echoes On The Wind
    467 Black Night,

                Amber Morning

VASQUES, Richard
  Another Land

VAUGHAN, Carter A.   <HO>
                [Noel B. Gerson]
  Branded Bride   <HofFS>
  Charlaton, The   <HofFS>
  Dragon Cove   <HofFS>
  Fortress Fury   <HofFS>
  Invincibles
  River Devils, The   <HofFS>
  Roanoke Warrior   <HofFS>
  Scoundrel's Brigade   <HofFS>
  Seneca Hostage, The   <HofFS>
  Silver Saber
  Wilderness, The   <HofFS>
  Yankee Brig, The   <HofFS>
  Yankee Rascals

VAUGHAN, Louise
  Lovequest

VAUGHAN, Robert   <HO>
                [Robert Richard Vaughan]
                (Paula Fairman)
                (Paula Moore)
                (see Jonathan Scofield)
                (see Lee Davis Willoughby)
  Power And The Pride, The   <Saga>
  Savages
  Texas Proud   <HS>
  War-Torn Series:
    Brave And The Lonely, The
    Masters And Martyrs
    Fallen And The Free, The
    Divine And The Damned, The

VAUGHAN, Vivian
                [Vivian Jane Arnold Vaughan]
  Silver Creek Stories:
    In sequence:
      Heartfire Romance:
        Heart's Desire
        Texas Twilight
        Runaway Passion
        Sweet Texas Nights
      Texas Gamble
      Texas Dawn

VAUGHN, Dona
  Chasing The Comet   <RS>
  Glitter Gang, The
  Royale   <CO>

VAUGHTER, Carolyn
  West Wind Wild

681

VAYLE, Valerie   <HR>
  [Janice Young Brooks w/
                Jean Brooks-Janowiak]
  In sequence:
    Lady Of Fire
    Seaflame
    Oriana

VAYLE, Valerie   <HR>
    [Jean Brooks-Janowiak]
  In sequence:
    Mistress Of The Night
    Nightfire

VENDRESHA, Vita   <CO>
  Ride The Eagle

VENET, Michelle
            [Alicia Todd Rasley]
  Candlelight:
    713 Reluctant Lady, The <RE>

VERGE, Lisa Ann
                (Lisann St. Pierre)
  Lovestruck:
    Blaze Of Passion
    Heart's Disguise, The
    My Loving Enemy

VERLAG, Franz Schneekluth
                (Utta Danella)

VERN, Sarah
  Woman Of Ice

VERNON, Dorothy
  Silhouette Desire:
    15 Sweet Bondage
  Silhouette Romance:
    11 Awaken The Heart
    59 Kissed By Moonlight
    109 Fire Under Snow
    233 Edge Of Paradise
    276 Paradise Found
    295 That Tender Feeling
    312 Wild And Wanton

VERNON, Kay R.   <GOT>
  Ardreys, The
  Dark Seas Of Maltern Manor, The
  Phantom Of Fonthill Park, The

VERNON, Marjorie
  Brief Golden Time
  Enchanted Villa, The
  Singing Birds Lie, The
  Aston Hall:
    111 Roses Out Of Reach

VERNON, Rosemary
  Caprice Romance: <YA>
    68 First Comes Love
    79 With All My Heart
  Sweet Dreams: <YA>
    2 Popularity Plan, The
    20 Popularity Summer
    33 Dear Amanda
    64 Love In The Fast Lane
    73 Language Of Love
    86 Questions Of Love

VERONESE, Gina
  Masquerade:
    27 Serpent's Tooth, The
    46 Marietta

VERONESE, Gina (cont.)
   61 House Of Satan

VERRETTE, Joyce   <HR>
             [Joyce Petratur]
   Fountain Of Fire
   Rebel's Love, A
   Sweet Wild Wind
   To Burn Again Brightly
   To Love And To Conquer
   In sequence:
     Dawn Of Desire
     Desert Fires
     Sunrise Of Splendor
     Winged Priestess

VERYAN, Patricia   <RE>
          [Paticia Bannister]
   Logic Of The Heart   <HR>
   Married Past Redemption
   Some Brief Folly
   Wagered Widow, The
   The Golden Chronicles Series:
     Cherished Enemy
     Dedicated Villain, The
     Journey To Enchantment
     Love Alters Not
     Practice To Deceive
     Tyrant, The
   Sanguinet Series: In sequence:
     Nanette
     Feather Castles
     Noblest Frailty, The
     Sanguinet's Crown
     Give All To Love
   Coventry:
    18 Lord And The Gypsy, The
    46 Love's Duet
   112 Mistress Of Willowvale

VIALL, Patricia F.
        (Rebecca Sinclair)

VICARY, Jean   <RS>
   Castle At Glencarris
   Ice Maiden, The   <GOT>
   Saverstall

VICKERY, Katherine   <HR>
            [Kathryn Kramer]
   Flame Across The Highlands
   Flame Of Desire
   Tame The Wild Wind
   Desire Of The Heart

VICTOR, Barbara
   Misplaced Lives

VICTOR, Cindy   <HR>
   Heart For The Hermit Kingdom, A
   Candlelight Ecstasy:
    326 More Precious Than Gold
   Harlequin Temptation:
    60 An Intimate Oasis
    138 Kindred Spirits
   Second Chance At Love:
    417 Family Affair, A

VICTOR, Cynthia   <CO>
[Cynthia Katz w/ Victoria Skurnick]
   Consequences

VICTOR, Kathleen   <HR>
   Captive Desire

VICTOR, Vanessa
          [Justine Valenti]
Silhouette Desire:
  70 Dinner For Two

VIDA, Nina   <RS>
Maximilian's Garden
Return To Darkness

VIENS, Carol
              (Carol Daniels)

VIERTEL, Joseph
Life Lines

VILE, Dolores Holliday
         (Dolores Holliday)

VILLARS, Elizabeth
      [Ellen "Bette" Feldman]
Adam's Daughter
Lipstick On His Collar   <CO>
Normandie Affair, The
One Night In Newport
Rich Girl, The
Very Best People, The
Wars Of The Heart

VILLIERS, Margot   <GOT>
Serpent Of Lilith, The

VILLOT, Rhondi
Sweet Dreams: <YA>
  25 Her Secret Self

VINCENT, Claire   <GOT>
          [Miriam Lynch]
Believing In Giants
Garden Of Satan
Unholy Spell (Spellbound)

VINCENT, Joan
      [Joan C. Wesolowsky]
Candlelight: <RE>
  570 Thomasina
  586 Education Of Joanne, The
  595 Bond Of Honour, A
  604 Scheme Of Love, A
  632 Rescued By Love   <GEO>
  650 Curious Rogue, The <GEO>
  708 Audacious Miss, The

VINCENTNATHAN, Lynn
          (Sally DuBois)

VINE, Kerry
         [Gillian Oxley]
Silhouette Romance:
  264 Alpine Idyll

VINES-HAINES, Beverly
         (Becca Cassidy)
          (Jamie West)

VINET, Lynette   <HR>
Love's Golden Promise
Emerald Trilogy:
  Emerald Desire
  Emerald Enchantment
  Emerald Ecstasy
Heartfire Romance: <HR>
  Midnight Flame
  Pirate's Bride
  Savage Deception
  Wild Eden

VIVIAN, Daisy   <RE>
                    [Bruce Kenyon]
   Counterfeit Lady, The
   Fair Game
   Forrester Inheritance, The
   Marriage Of Inconvenience, A
   Return To Cheyne Spa
   In sequence:
     Rose White, Rose Red
     Wild Rose, Meg's Tale

VOELLER, Sydell
   Crosswinds Keepsake: <YA>
     14 Merry Christmas, Marcie

---

von FURSTENBERG, Betsy   <RS>
   Mirror, Mirror

---

von KREISLER, Kristin
   Bride And Groom:
     1   I Do, I Don't

VOSBEIN, Barbara
                    (Nikki Benjamin)

686

WAGNER, Sharon (cont.)
  Rapture Romance:
    26 Strangers Who Love

_____

_____

WAHL, Summit
  Birth Rights

_____

_____

WAHLSTROM, Carolyn
  Silhouette Inspirations:
    12 Sara's Story

_____

_____

WAINRIGHT, Christina
  Heavenly Romance: <YA>
    Designs On You
    Love Song

_____

_____

WAKE, Vivien Fiske   <GOT>
  Mists Of Ravensfall

_____

_____

WAKEFIELD, Maureen   <RE>
  Secret At Midwinter End
  Substitute Sweetheart
  Where Peacocks Cry
  Warner Regency:
    5 Accessory To Love

_____

_____

WAKELEY, Dorothy
    [Dorothy Lilley Wells Wakeley]
  Sweet Revenge
  In sequence:
    House In Holly Walk, The
    Mercy's Story

_____

_____

WALDEN, Luanne   <HR>
  Bittersweet Destiny
  Forbidden Flame
  Tides Of Ecstasy
  Tides Of Splendor
    American Regency Romance:
    Delicate Dilemma

_____

_____

WALDO, Ann Lee   <HS>
  Prairie
  Sacajawea

_____

_____

WALKER, Barbara Kaye
                    (Barbara Kaye)

WALKER, Constance   <GOT>
  Lost Roses Of Ganymede House
  Avalon:
    When The Heart Remembers
    Warm Winter Love
    One Perfect Springtime

_____

_____

WALKER, Elizabeth   <CO>
  Court, The
  Rowan's Mill
  Voyage

_____

_____

WALKER, Elizabeth   <RE>
                  [Elizabeth Rotter]
  Alicia
  Loving Seasons, The

_____

WALKER, Elizabeth Neff
                  [Elizabeth Rotter]
  Coventry:
    52 Nomad Harp, The
    78 Curious Courting, A   <RE>
    113 Lady Next Door, The
    142 In My Lady's Chamber   <RE>

688

WALKER, Elizabeth Neff (cont.)
Finding Mr. Right:
Paper Tiger
Silhouette Special Edition:
122 Antique Affair
176 That Other Woman
251 Paternity

WALKER, Irma
[Irma Ruth Roden Walker]
(Andrea Harris)
(Ruth Walker)
Country Love Song, City Lies <CO>
Lucifer Wine, The   <RS>
Murdock Legacy, The
In sequence: <HR>
Other Passions, Other Loves
Enduring Passion
Harlequin SuperRomance:
104 Sonata For My Love
147 Through Day And Night
163 Spangles
210 Games
247 Masks
339 Crystal Clear
417 Stormy Weather
Love & Life:
Her Decision
New Tomorrow, A
Next Step, The
Surrender

WALKER, Kate
Harlequin Presents:
1053 Broken Silence
1196 Chase The Dawn
1269 Leap In The Dark
Harlequin Romance:
2783 Game Of Hazard
2826 Rough Diamond
2910 Captive Lover
2920 Man Of Shadows
2957 Cinderella Trap, The
3078 Jester's Girl

WALKER, Kate (cont.)
3107 Golden Thief, The

WALKER, Linda   <RE>
My Lady's Deception

WALKER, Lois A./Lois Arvin   <RE>
(Candice Adams)
(Rebecca Ashley)
(Sabrina Myles)
An Elusive Love
Reckless Heart

WALKER, Lucy
[Dorothy Lucie Sanders]
1 Other Girl, The
2 Heaven Is Here
3 Distant Hills, The
4 Sweet And Faraway
5 Call Of The Pines, The
6 Come Home, Dear
7 Love In A Cloud
8 Follow Your Star
9 Home At Sundown
10 Reaching For The Stars
11 Man Called Masters, A
12 Stranger From The North, The
13 River Is Down, The
14 One Who Kisses, The
15 Man From Outback, The
16 Down In The Forest
17 Moonshiner, The
18 Wife To Order /
19 Ranger In The Hills, The
20 Shining River
21 Six For Heaven
22 Gone-Away Man, The
23 Kingdom Of The Heart
24 Loving Heart, The
25 Master Of Ransome
26 Joyday For Jodi
27 Bell Branch, The

WALLACE, Pamela Dianne w/
                    Elnora KING
                    (Dianne King)

WALLACE, Pamela Dianne w/ Carla
SIMPSON   (Pamela Simpson)

WALLACE, Pat
          [Pat Wallace Strother]
House Of Scorpio   <GOT><RF>
Wand And The Star, The <GOT><RF>
Silhouette Intimate Moments:
    4 Sweetheart Contract
   53 Objection Overruled
  100 Love Scene
  116 Star Rise
Silhouette Special Edition:
   56 Silver Fire
  104 My Loving Enemy
  145 Shining Hour

WALLACE, Sylvia   <CO>
Empress
Fountains, The

WALLACH, Susan
Sweet Dreams: <YA>
  117 Acting On Impulse

WALLER, Leslie   <HR>
Blood And Dreams

WALLERICH, Linda Hender
                    (Linda Benjamin)
                    (Jessica Douglas)

WALLMAN, Jeffrey M.   <HR>
          [Jeffrey Miner Wallman]
Blood And Passion
Clean Sweep

WALLMAN, Jeffery M. (cont.)
Judas Cross
Unconquered, The

WALLOTH, Wilhelm   <HO>
Octavia: Prisoner Of
  Passion   <GARS>

WALLS, Patricia Rae
                    (Patricia Rae)
                    (see Gina Delaney)

WALPOLE, Hugh   (Deceased)<GOT>
          [Hugh Seymour Walpole]
Cathedral
Portrait Of A Man With Red Hair
Herries Saga: In sequence: <HS>
  Rogue Herries
  Judith Paris
  Fortress, The
  Vanessa
  Bright Pavilions, The
  Katherine Christian

WALSH, Alida
Silhouette Special Edition:
  273 This Business Of Love

WALSH, Kelly
                    [V. P. Walsh]
Harlequin SuperRomance:
  248 Cherished Harbor
  286 Of Time And Tenderness
  336 Place For Us, A
  360 Private Affair, A
  415 Starlight, Star Bright
  445 Russian Nights
  480 Hand In Hand

WALSH, Maurice   <HO>
  Blackcock's Feather

WALSH, Patricia
          [Patricia Louise Walsh]
  Forever Sad The Heart

WALSH, Penelope
  Harlequin Classic:
    180 Sweet Brenda   (968)
  Harlequin Romance:
    968 Sweet Brenda
    1755 School My Heart

WALSH, Sheila   <RE>
  Arrogant Lord Alistair, The
  Bath Intrigue
  Diamond Waterfall, The
  Fine Silk Purse, A
  Golden Songbird, The
  Highly Respectable Marriage, A
  Incomparable Miss Brady, The
  Incorrigible Rake, The
  Lady Aurelia's Bequest
  Lord Gilmore's Bride
  Madalena
  Minerva's Marquess
  Notorious Nabob, The
  Pink Parasol, The
  Rose Domino, The
  Runaway Bride, The
  Sergeant Major's Daughter, The
  Wary Widow, The

WALTARI, Mika   <HO>(Deceased)
          [Mika Toimi Waltari]
  Egyptian, The
  Etruscan, The
  Roman, The
  Secret Of The Kingdom

WALTER, Dorothy Blake
                (Katherine Blake)

WALTERS, Jade
  Silhouette Romance:
    211 Greek Idyll

WALTERS, Janet Lane
  Avalon:
    Nurse Karen Comes Home

WALTERS, Linda
          [Linda Rice w/ Walter Rice]
  Harlequin Intrigue:
    60 Dragon's Eye
    82 Dead Reckoning

WALTON, Delsa
  Second Wedding

WALTON, Evangeline   <GOT-H>
  Cross And The Sword, The
  Witch House

WALTON, H. Dyke   <HO>
  Banished, The

WALTON, Kaye
  Harlequin SuperRomance:
    479 Over The Horizon

WALTON, Roberta F. Smith
                (Bobbie Smith)

692

WARADY, Phylis Ann   <RE>
  Scandal's Daughter

WARBURTON, Carol   <RS>
  Falcon's Haunt
  House Of Shadowed Roses, The

WARBY, Marjorie
  Bachelor Doctor
  Beloved Barbarian
  Girl In His Garden, The
  Gregory Girls, The
  Quiet House, The
  Sapphire Ring, The
  Aston Hall:
    104   To Love A Stranger
    112   Summer At Hope House

WARD, Dewey
  House In Paris, The
  Reception At High Tower
  Unsheltered, The

WARD, Jessica
  Passion's Dark Harvest

WARD, Kate
  Castle Dangerous

WARD, Lynda
  [Lynda Catherine Miller Ward]
        (Julia Jeffries)
  SuperRomance:
    3   Music Of Passion, The
   33   Touch Of Passion, The
   89   Sea Change, A

WARD, Lynda (cont.)
  Harlequin SuperRomance:
   119   Never Strangers
   162   Vows Forever
   218   Wildcat Summer
    Trilogy:
   317   Race The Sun
   321   Leap The Moon
   325   Touch The Stars
   402   Precious Things
  Harlequin Temptation:
   141   Love In Tandem

WARD, Rebecca   <RE>
  Fair Fortune
  Lady In Silver
  Lord Longshanks
  Promissory Note, The

WARDE, Joan
  Labor Of Love, A
  Tessa Jane

WARDLAW, Lee
  First Love From Silhouette: <YA>
   230   Alley Cat

WARD-THOMAS, Evelyn Bridget
          Patricia Stephens
           (Evelyn Anthony)

WARE, Ciji   <HR>
  Island Of The Swans

WARE, Joyce C.   <GOT>
  Lost Heiress Of Hawkscliffe, The

WARE, Judith   \<GOT>\<RS>
     [Ware Torrey Budlong]
  Faxon Secret, The
  Fear Place, The
  Quarry House
  Thorne House
  Touch Of Fear, A

WARNER, Lucille S.
     [Lucille Schulbert Warner]
  Wildfire: \<YA>
    Good-Bye, Pretty One
    Love Comes To Anne

WARREN, Andrea
  Sweet Dreams Special: \<YA>
    3 Searching For Love

WARREN, Beatrice
  Avalon:
    Hoodriver Nurse
    Nurse In Yosemite
    Nurse Monica's Legacy
    Nurse Onstage
    Nurse Paula's New Look
    Occupational Health Nurse

WARREN, Betsy
     [Elizabeth Avery Warren]
  Harlequin Romance:
  2770 Song Without Words

WARREN, Beverly C.   \<GOT>
  Bride Of Hatfield Castle
  Castle Of Shadows
  Lost Ladies Of The Windswept Moor
  Lost Wives Of Dunwick, The
  Sapphire Legacy

WARREN, Beverly C. (cont.)
  Starlight Romance:
    Invitation To A Waltz
    That Gentle Touch
    Stars Over Texas
    Wild Vines, The

WARREN, Joanna   \<HR>
  Conrad Chronicles:
    1 Bellemeade
    2 Dreamers, The
    3 Destined, The

WARREN, Linda
          (Frances West)

WARREN, Norma   \<HR>
  Trails West

WARREN, Pat
          (Patricia Cox)
  Silhouette Intimate Moments:
   288 Perfect Strangers
  Silhouette Romance:
   553 Season Of The Heart
  Silhouette Special Edition:
   375 With This Ring
   410 Final Verdict
   442 Look Homeward, Love
   458 Summer Shadows
   480 Evolution Of Adam, The
   514 Build Me A Dream
   548 Long Road Home, The
   582 Lyon And The Lamb, The
   610 My First Love, My Last
   632 Winter Wishes

WARREN, Paulette   \<GOT>\<RS>
          [Paul Fairman]
  Brooding Mansion
  Ghost At Ravenkill Manor

WARREN, Paulette (cont.)
  Golden Girl
  Hazard House
  Horror House
  Ravenkill
  Shadowed Staircase
  Some Reckoning Wraith
  Bitterhill Saga: In sequence:
    Storm Over Bitterhill
    Night Falls At Bitterhill
    Dark Shadows At Bitterhill
  Caliban: In sequence:
    Caliban's Castle
    Search In The Shadows

_____

_____

WARREN, Robert Penn
  Band Of Angels
  World Enough And Time

_____

_____

WARTSKI, Maureen
  Silken Tiger, The   <HR>

_____

_____

WARTSKI, Maureen Crane
      [Maureen Ann Crane Wartski]
                (Sharon Francis)
                (Evelyn Shannon)
                (Francine Shore)
                (Cynthia Sinclair)
  Boat To Nowhere, A
  Lake Is On Fire, The   <YA>
  Long Way From Home, A   <YA>
  My Brother Is Special

_____

_____

WASHINGTON, Elsie
                (Rosalind Welles)

WATERS, T. A   <GOT>
  Blackwood Cult, The
  Centerforce
  In The Halls Of Evil

WATERS, T. A. (cont.)
  Lost Victim, The
  Override
  Shrewsbury Horror, The

_____

_____

WATJEN, Carolyn L. T.
                (Caroline Stafford)

WATSON, Diane Masters
  Magazine

_____

_____

WATSON, Elaine
  Serenade/Saga: <HR><Insp>
    6 Anna's Rocking Chair
   24 To Dwell In The Land

_____

_____

WATSON, Julia   (Deceased)<HO>
                (Jane deVere - Eng)
                (Julia Fitzgerald)
                (Julia Hamilton)
  Lovechild, The
  Winter Of The Witch
  Gentian Trilogy:
    Mistress For The Valois, The
    King's Mistress, The
    Wolf And The Unicorn, The
  Other: <ENG>
    Medici Mistress
    Saffron At The
      Court Of Edward III
    Tudor Rose, The

_____

_____

WATSON, Marjorie
  Heir To Polventon

_____

_____

WATSON, Mary Frances
                (Lynn Turner)

WATT, Ruth McFetridge
  Avalon:
    And The Piper Played   <GOT>
    Love Makes A Difference
    Love Unveiled

  ────────────────────────────────

  ────────────────────────────────

WATT, Sebastian
                              [Geo. Wolk]
  Natchez Kingdom

  ────────────────────────────────

  ────────────────────────────────

WATTERS, Patricia
                        (Patricia Edwards)

WAUGH, Hillary   <GOT>
                    [Hillary Baldwin Waugh]
                    (Elissa Grandower)
  Bride For Hampton House, A
  Con Game
  Doctor On Trial
  Finish Me Off
  Madman At My Door
  Parrish For The Defense
  Prisoner's Plea
  Road Block
  Shadow Guest, The
  Thirty Manhattan East
  Young Prey, The

  ────────────────────────────────

  ────────────────────────────────

WAVERLY, Shannon
                      [Kathleen Shannon]
  Harlequin Romance:
    3072 Summer Kind Of Love, A

  ────────────────────────────────

  ────────────────────────────────

WAY, Isabel Stewart   <GOT>
  Bell, Book And Candleflame
  Calling Nurse Lorrie
  Fleur Macabre
  Fighting Dr. Diana
  House On Sky High Road, The
  Nurse Christy

  ────────────────────────────────

  ────────────────────────────────

WAY, Margaret
  Harlequin Presents:
      78 Man Like Daintree, A
      82 Copper Moon
      94 Bauhimia Junction
     102 Rainbow Bird, The
     134 Storm Flower
     154 Red Cliffs Of Malapara
     270 Ring Of Fire
     549 Broken Rhapsody
  Harlequin Romance:
    1446 Time Of The Jacaranda, The
    1470 King Country
    1500 Blaze Of Silk
    1530 Man From Bahl Bahla, The
    1571 Summer Magic
    1603 Ring Of Jade
    1687 Noonfire
    1766 Storm Over Mandargi
    1785 Love Theme, The
    1815 Wind River
    1840 Return To Belle Amber
    1863 McCabe's Kingdom
    1880 Sweet Sundown
    1889 Reeds Of Honey
    1974 Lesson In Loving, A
    2016 Flight Into Yesterday
    2060 Man On Half-Moon, The
    2074 Swans' Reach
    2111 One Way Ticket
    2132 Black Ingo
    2145 Portrait Of Jaime
    2174 Mutiny In Paradise
    2188 Wild Swan, The
    2203 Awakening Flame, The
    2258 Wake The Sleeping Tiger
    2265 Winds Of Heaven, The
    2276 White Magnolia
    2291 Valley Of The Moon
    2328 Blue Lotus
    2346 Butterfly
            And The Baron
    2357 Golden Puma, The
    2387 Lord Of The High Valley
    2400 Flamingo Park
    2429 Temple Of Fire
    2435 Shadow Dance
    2448 Season For Change, A
    2454 MacIvor Affair, The

WAY, Margaret (cont.)
```
2476  North Of Capricorn
2490  Home Of Morning Star
2537  Spellbound
2539  Silver Veil, The
2556  Hunter's Moon
2591  Girl At Colalt Creek, The
2609  House Of Memories
2634  Almost A Stranger
2639  No Alternative
2658  Place Called Rambulara, A
2700  Fallen Idol
2724  Eagle's Ridge
2784  Tiger's Cage, The
2820  Innocent In Eden
2832  Diamond Valley
2939  Morning Glory
2958  Devil Moon
2976  Mowana Magic
2999  Hungry Heart, The
3012  Rise Of An Eagle
```

WAYNAR, Chris   <GOT>
Fire On The Cliffs   <CGS:#10>

WAYNE, Rachel
Second Chance At Love:
```
136  Entwined Destinies
```

WAYNE, Rochelle   <HR>
            [Rochelle A. Mulvihill]
Ecstasy's Dawn
Elusive Enchantment
Loving Torment
Midnight Angel
Midnight Slave
Reckless Passion
Savage Abandon
Secret Ecstacy
Surrender To Ecstasy
Texas Ecstasy

WAYNE, Rochelle (cont.)
Wyoming Trilogy:
  Frontier Flame
  Savage Caress
  Untamed Heart

WEALE, Anne
                    (Andrea Blake)
All My Worldly Goods
Antigua Kiss
Flora
Summer's Awakening
Harlequin Classic:
```
  5  Castle In Corsica      (537)
 12  House Of Seven
       Fountains, The       (553)
 22  Winter Is Past         (582)
 39  Nurse Templar          (578)
 49  Never To Love          (644)
 80  Doctor's Daughter,The(716)
101  All I Ask              (830)
110  Until We Met           (855)
124  Hope For Tomorrow      (901)
133  Islands Of Summer      (948)
162  Christina
       Comes To Town        (981)
171  Terrace In The Sun    (1067)
```
Harlequin Presents:
```
 258  Now Or Never
 282  River Room, The
 312  Separate Bedrooms
 317  Stowaway
 395  First Officer, The
 408  Girl From The Sea, The
 444  Blue Days At Sea
 504  Passage To Paxos
 511  Touch Of The Devil, A
 541  Portrait Of Bethany
 565  Wedding Of The Year
 613  All That Heaven Allows
 622  Yesterday's Island
 670  Ecstasy
 846  Frangipani
1013  Girl In A Golden Bed
1061  Night Train
1085  Lost Lagoon
1133  Catalan Christmas
1270  Do You Remember Babylon?
```

WEALE, Anne (cont.)
Harlequin Romance:
767   Silver Dolphin, The
798   If This Is Love
830   All I Ask
855   Until We Met
879   Sweet To Remember
901   Hope For Tomorrow
914   Doctor In Malaya
948   Islands Of Summer
981   Christina Comes To Town
1007 Feast Of Sara, The
1027 Lonely Shore, The
1067 Terrace In The Sun
1123 Sea Waif, The
1224 South From Sounion
1271 Man In Command, The
1423 Sullivan's Reef
1512 That Man Simon
1629 Treasure For Life, A
1747 Fields Of Heaven, The
1848 Lord Of The Sierras
2411 Last Night
      At Paradise, The
2436 Rain Of Diamonds
2484 Bed Of Roses
2940 Neptune's Daughter
3108 Thai Silk

WEATHERBY, W. J.   <HR>
        [William John Weatherby]
Chariots Of Fire
Moondancers, The

WEAVER, Judith
                (Harper McBride)

WEAVER, Martha Ann
Love In The Lake District

WEBB, Jean Francis III   <GOT>
                (Roberta Morrison)
(see Lee Davis Willoughby <MOAS>)
Bride Of Cairngore, The
Carnavaron's Castle
Craigshaw Curse, The
Roses From A Haunted Garden
Somewhere Within This House

WEBB, Lilian
Marranos, The

WEBB, Lionel
                [Morris Hershman]
Flame And The Fury, The
Night Of The Dark Fires
Rogue Slave
Violater, The

WEBB, Mary
Precious Bane
Seven For A Secret

WEBB, Peggy
Loveswept:
106   Taming Maggie
112   Birds Of A Feather
137   Tarnished Armor
143   Donovan's Angel   @
157   Duplicity
170   Scamp Of Saltillo
178   Disturbing The Peace
192   Joy Bus, The   &
203   Summer Jazz   &
216   Private Lives
275   Sleepless Nights   @
301   Hallie's Destiny
328   Any Thursday   @

WEBB, Peggy (cont.)
   357 Higher Than Eagles   @
   381 Valley Of Fire
   402 Until Morning Comes
   439 Saturday Mornings
Silhouette Romance:
   645 When Joanna Smiles
   681 Gift For Tenderness, A
   712 Harvey's Missing
   735 Venus de Molly
   785 Tiger Lady

WEBER, Catherine   <HO>
Blackfoot Ambush   <AIS:#2>

WEBER, Nancy
           (Jennifer Rose)
Brokenhearted

WEBSTER, Jan
Collier's Row
Muckle Annie   <HR>
Saturday City

WEBSTER, Mary E.
Avalon:
  Love Storm
  Loves Dark Wilderness
  Swing Into Love

WEES, Frances Shelley   <GOT>
M'Lord, I Am Not Guilty
Where Is Jenny Now

WEGER, Jackie
Harlequin American Romance:
    5 Strong And Tender Thread,A
  48 Count The Roses
 289 Full House
 344 Best Behavior
 363 First Impressions
Harlequin SuperRomance:
 227 Beyond Fate
Harlequin Temptation:
    7 Cast A Golden Shadow
  29 Winter Song
  53 Beneath The Saffron Sky
  89 Wings Of Morning, The
 159 Way Of Destiny, The
 181 Eye Of The Beholder
 207 On A Wing And A Prayer

WEIGH, Iris
Tomorrow's Promise
Aston Hall:
 115 Someone To Love

WEINER, Margery
          (see Norah Lofts)

WEIR, Nancie MacCullough
Jade   <CO>

WEIR, Theresa
Amazon Lily
Silhouette Intimate Moments:
 339 Iguana Bay
Silhouette Romance:
 576 Forever Man, The
 650 Loving Jenny
 761 Pictures Of Emily

WEISER, Bruce   <HO>
  Chenevix Series:
    1 French Impostor, The
    2 Dispatch From Cadiz

WEISS, Herman
  Passion In The Wind
  Sound Of Dreams, The

WELD, Eloise
  Engagement
  Ring Of Gold

WELLER, Dorothy
                (Dorothy Ann Bernard)
                (Dorthea Hale)

WELLES, Alyssa
                [Nomi Berger]
  Scarlet Ribbons: <HR>
    Dragon Flower

WELLES, Caron
                [Jan Jones]
  Harlequin American Romance:
    13 Raven's Song

WELLES, Elisabeth
                [Mary Linn Roby]
  Waterview Manor

WELLES, Patricia
                [Patricia Rogers]
  Sara's Ghost

WELLES, Rachel   <HR>
                [Patricia Rogers]
  Fires In The East

WELLES, Rosalind
                [Elsie Washington]
  Candlelight:
    575 Entwined Destinies   <RO>

WELLINGTON, Kate
                [Hertha Schulze]
  To Have And To Hold:
    22 Delicate Balance, A

WELLS, Angela
                [Angela Bostwick]
  Harlequin Presents:
    1164 Love's Wrongs
    1181 Errant Daughter
  Harlequin Romance:
    2790 Sweet Poison
    2844 Moroccan Madness
    2903 Desperate Remedy
    2921 Fortune's Fool
    3006 Still Temptation
    3054 Rash Contract
          Rash Intruder   HRS74

WELLS, Elaine F./E. F.   <GOT>
  Legend Of Lostwithel, The
  Lords Of Castle Weirwyck, The
  Avalon:
    Run, Ellen, Run

WELLS, Elizabeth
  Where Love Is

WELLS, Lisa   <RS>
  Destiny's Star
  Magda

_____

_____

WELLS, Marian   <Insp>
  Wedding Dress
  Wishing Star, The
  With This Ring

_____

_____

WELLSLEY, Julie   <GOT><RS>
  Castle On The Mountain, The
  Climb The Dark Mountain
  Fateful Tide
  House Malign
  Stranger In A Dark Land
  Two Faces Of Fear
  Wine Of Vengeance, The

_____

_____

WELSH, Jeanette
  Harlequin Romance:
    1252 Last Rose Of Summer, The
    1362 Stranger By My Side

_____

_____

WELSH, Joan   <HR>
  Royal Lover

_____

_____

WENDT, Jo Ann   <HR>
  Beyond Surrender
  Beyond The Dawn
  Lovestruck:
    Beyond The Savage Sea
    Golden Dove, The

_____

_____

WENTWORTH, Julia
  MacFadden Romance:
    7 Light Of Love
   22 Debut Of Love
   30 Dark Of The Moon, The
  Other MacFadden:
    Mists Of Maunaloa, The

_____

_____

WENTWORTH, Sally
  Harlequin Presents:
   372 Candle In The Wind
   389 Set The Stars On Fire
   396 Betrayal In Bali
   414 Race Against Love
   426 Say Hello To Yesterday
   456 Summer Fire
   462 King Of Culla
   480 Judas Kiss, The
   512 Sea Master, The
   542 Semi-Detached Marriage
   557 Man For Hire
   581 Flying High
   614 Jilted
   629 Shattered Dreams
   662 Lion Rock, The
   686 Backfire
   733 Dark Awakening
   750 Viking Invader
   814 Wings Of Love, The
   837 Fatal Deception
   862 Hawk Of Venice, The
   926 Kissing Game, The
   974 Cage Of Ice
   997 Tiger In His Lair
  1046 Passionate Revenge
  1094 Dishonourable Intentions
  1109 Ultimatum
  1142 Mistaken Wedding
  1165 Satan's Island
  1197 Driving Force
  1220 Devil's Shadow, The
  1237 Strange Encounter
  1278 Wish On The Moon
  1309 Echoes Of The Past
  1334 Fire Island
  Harlequin Romance:
  2155 Island Masquerade
  2185 King Of The Castle
  2207 Conflict In Paradise

WENTWORTH, Sally (cont.)
  2254 Rightful Possession
  2262 Liberated Lady
  2310 Ice Maiden, The
  2361 Garden Of Thorns

WENTZIEN, Marion
  Avalon:
    Desert Shadows

WERLIN, Marvin and Mark MERLIN
  St. Clair Summer
  Shadow Play

WERNER, Hazeldell
  Golden Harvest   <Saga>

WERNER, Herma
                    (Roxanne Jarrett)

WERNER, Herma w/ Joyce GLEIT
                    (Eve Gladstone)

WERNER, Patricia   <GOT><HR><RS>
  Island Of Lost Rubies
  Prairie Fire
  Swirling Mists Of Cornwall, The
  Timbers And Gold Lace
  Will, The
  Harlequin Gothic Romance:
    Secret Of Orient Point
  Harlequin Intrigue:
    26 If Truth Be Known

WERNER, Vivian
  Passion's Splendid Wings

WERT, Lynette Lemon
                    (Lynn LeMon)

WESLEY, Caroline
  King's Castle

WESLEY, Elizabeth
              [Elizabeth A. McElfresh]
  Doctor Barbara
  Dr. Dorothy's Choice
  Nora Meade, M. D.
  Sharon James:
    Freelance Photographer
  Candlelight:
    78 Patient In 711, The

WESOLOWSKY, Joan C.
                    (Joan Vincent)

WEST, Anna
  Circle Of Love:
    7 Ring At The Ready, A

WEST, Cara
  Harlequin SuperRomance:
    259 Now There's Tomorrow
    299 There Is A Season
    410 Jenny Kissed Me
    471 Thy Heart In Mine

WEST, Christine
                    (Christine Baker)

WEST, Eugenia Lovett
  Ancestors Cry Out, The

WEST, Frances

               [Linda Warren]
Second Chance At Love:
   384 Softer Than Springtime
   441 Star Light, Star Bright
Silhouette Desire:
   496 Honky Tonk Angel
   604 White Heat

WEST, Jamie

               [Beverly Vines-Haines]
Dawnstar Romance:
  Flame In The Mountains, A

WEST, Jennifer

               [Jennifer Justin]
Silhouette Intimate Moments:
   10 Season Of Rainbows, A
   31 Star Spangled Days
   71 Edge Of Venus
   99 Main Chance
Silhouette Special Edition:
  262 Earth And Fire
  283 Return To Paradise
  339 Moments Of Glory
  366 Object Of Desire
  383 Come Pride, Come Passion
  404 Sometimes A Miracle
  432 Greek To Me
  476 Tender Is The Knight
  552 Last Stand
  594 Suddenly, Paradise

WEST, Jessamyn   (Deceased)<HR>
  Cress Delahanty
  Crimson Ramblers
   Of The World, Farewell
  Except For Me And Thee
  Friendly Persuasion, The
  Hide And Seek
  Leafy Rivers
  Love Is Not What You Think

WEST, Jessamyn (cont.)
  Love, Death, And
   The Ladies Drill Team
  Massacre At Fall Creek, The
  Matter Of Time, A
  South Of The Angels
  State Of Stony Lonesome, The
  To See The Dream
  Witch Diggers, The

WEST, Katrina
First Love From Silhouette: <YA>
  148 Meadow Wind
  158 Free Spirit
  211 Dash Of Pepper, A

WEST, Nicola
Harlequin Presents:
  589 Lucifer's Brand
  998 Unfinished Business
Harlequin Romance:
 2526 Devil's Gold
 2592 No Room In His Life
 2610 Wildtrack
 2640 Tyzak Inheritance, The
 2646 Carver's Bride
 2669 Tormented Rhapsody
 2718 Rooted Sorrow, A
 2760 Sky High
 2771 Comeback
 2884 Hidden Depths
 3089 Snow Demon
 3101 Woman's Place, A

      Another Eden   HRS22

WEST, Pat

               [Pat Wallace Strother]
Candlelight Ecstasy:
  475 Wife For Ransom, A
Candlelight Supreme:
  134 Under The Sign Of Scorpio

WEST, Sara Ann
Silhouette Desire:
44 Heart Over Mind

WEST, Tracy
Crosswinds: <YA>
23 Butterflies Of
Freedom, The
First Love From Silhouette: <YA>
28 Lesson In Love, A
194 Promises

WESTCOTT, Jan   <HO>
[Jan Vlachos Westcott]
Border Lord, The
Captain Barney
Captain For Elizabeth
Condottiere
Hepburn, The
Queen's Grace, The
Tower And The Drum, The
Walsingham Woman, The
White Rose, The
Woman Of Quality, A

WESTCOTT, Kathleen   <GOT>
[Christine Abrahamsen]
Bride Of Kilkerran

WESTFIELD, Ben   <CO>
Voyage Of Desire

WESTHAVEN, Margaret   <RE>
[Peggy M. Hansen]
City Heiress
Duke's Design, The
In For A Penny
Widow's Folly
Willful Wife, The

WESTHAVEN, Margaret (cont.)
Harlequin Regency Romance:
Miss Dalrymple's Virtue
6 False Impressions
22 Spanish Coin
35 Widow For Hire

WESTIN, Jeane   <HR>
[Jeanne Eddy Westin]
Love And Glory

WESTLAND, Lynn   <HR>
[Archie L. Joscelyn]
Seeds Of Fury

WESTMACOTT, Mary   <RS>
[Agatha Mary Clarissa Christie]
Absent In The Spring
Burden, The
Daughter's, A Daughter, A
Giant's Bread
Rose And The Yew Tree, The
Unfinished Portrait

WESTMINSTER, Aynn   <GOT>
Moon In Shadow

WESTON, Helen Gray
[Dorothy Daniels]
House Of False Faces
Mystic Manor

WESTON, Sophie
Harlequin Presents:
838 Executive Lady

704

WESTON, Sophie (cont.)
  870 Stranger's Touch, A
  918 Like Enemies
  942 Shadow Princess
  957 Yesterday's Mirror
  980 Beyond Ransom
 1014 Challenge
 1246 Matter Of Feeling, A
Harlequin Romance:
 1925 Beware The Huntsman
 2005 Goblin Court
 2129 Wife To Charles
 2218 Unexpected Hazard
 2362 An Undefended City

_____

_____

WESTWOOD, Gwen
Harlequin Romance:
 1333 Keeper Of The Heart
 1396 Bright Wilderness
 1463 Emerald Cuckoo, The
 1531 Castle Of The Unicorn
 1638 Pirate Of The Sun
 1716 Citadel Of Swallows
 1843 Sweet Roots And Honey
 1948 Ross Of Silver Ridge
 2013 Blossoming Gold
 2081 Bride Of Bonamour
 2363 Forgotten Bride
 2417 Lulu Moon
 2477 Dangerous To Love
 2586 Secondhand Bride
 2736 Wilderness Bride
 2796 Safari Heartbreak
 2885 Bitter Deception

_____

_____

WESTWOOD, Hillary
MacFadden Romance:
  217 Kisses And Lies
  245 Seasons For Love

_____

_____

WETHERELL, June   <GOT><HR><RS>
Cottage At Avalanche, The
Dark Wing, The

WETHERELL, June (cont.)
House Of Cabra, The
Isle Of Rapture
Her Stepfather's House
Legacy Of The Lost
Mahogany House, The
Maiden Of Glory Island   <BZG>
Night Of Secrets
Opal Street
Privateer's Woman, The
Reb
Tawny McShane
Thirteen Winston Street
Time For Desire, A
Touch Of The Witch, A
Tree Of Evil
Willoughby Manor
Candlelight:
  52 House By The Bay

_____

_____

WEYN, Suzanne
First Kiss: <YA>
  2 Love Song

_____

_____

WEYRICH, Becky Lee   <HR>
Captive Of Desire
Contents For Sale
Forever, For Love
Gypsy Moon
Hot Winds From Bombay
Image In A Golden Circle
Rainbow Hammock
Rapture's Slave
Scarlet Thread, The
Silver Tears
Summer Lightning
Tainted Lilies
Thistle And The Rose, The
Through Caverns Infinite
Loveswept:
 188 Detour To Euphoria

_____

_____

WHALEY, Frances
MacFadden Romance:
    53 Midnight Encounter
    86 Fountains Of Rome, The

WHARTON, Althea   <GOT>
White Ghost Of Fenwick Hall, The

WHEALLER, Cynthia
               (Evelyn Richardson)

WHEARLEY, Bob
                 (Fran Earley)

WHEAT, Carolyn
             (Corintha Bennett)

WHEELER, Richard S.
Where The River Runs

WHERLOCK, Julia   <HR>
Angel Dark, Angel Bright
Beloved, The
Fire Bride, The

WHINDHAM, Eleanor
MacFadden Romance:
    229 October Light

WHISENAND, Val
         [Valerie Whisenand]
           (Kasey Adams)
Silhouette Romance:
    655 Treasure Hunters
    695 Giveaway Girl

WHISTLER, Mary
               [Ida Pollock]
Harlequin Classic:
    181 Enchanted Autumn   (1151)
Harlequin Romance:
   1151 Enchanted Autumn
   1194 Sunshine Yellow
   1228 Young Nightingales, The
   1550 Pathway Of Roses
   1965 Escape To Happiness

WHITE, Alicen   <GOT>
Evil That Walks Invisible
Nor Spell, Nor Charm
Traitor Within, The
Watching Eye, The

WHITE, Charlotte
            (Marianne Cole)
            (Jennifer Dale)
Caprice Romance: <YA>
    42 Change Of Heart
    48 Hard Act To Follow, A
    61 Dream Come True, A
    80 Head Over Heels
Judy Sullivan Books:
    Impossible Love   <CO>
Sweet Dreams: <YA>
   109 No More Boys

WHITE, Ethel Lina   <GOT>(Deceased)
Fear Stalks The Village
Lady Vanishes, The
Man Who Was Not There, The
She Faded Into Air
Sinister Light
Spiral Staircase, The
Step In The Dark
Third Eye, The
Unseen, The
Wax
While She Sleeps!

WHITE, Jude Gilliam
(Jude Deveraux)

WHITE, Linda
MacFadden Romance:
  14 Love's Tender Path
Other MacFadden:
  Bermuda Sunset

_____

_____

WHITE, Patricia   <HR>
To Last A Lifetime

_____

_____

WHITE, Tiffany
                    [Anna Eberhardt]
Harlequin Temptation:
  274 Open Invitation
  318 Cheap Thrills

_____

_____

WHITED, Charles   <HR>
Spirit Of America: In sequence:
  Challenge
  Destiny
  Power

_____

_____

WHITEHEAD, Barbara   <RE>
          [Barbara Maude Whitehead]
Caretaker Wife, The
Ramillies
Coventry:
  148 Quicksilver Lady

_____

_____

WHITEHEAD, Jane   <GOT>
House On The Hill, The

_____

WHITFIELD, Martha   <GOT>
Bethnal Inheritance, The

_____

_____

WHITMER-GOW, Karen
                    (Karen Kary)
                    (Elizabeth N. Kary)

WHITMORE, Cilla
                    [Arthur M. Gladstone]
Candlelight: <RE>
  515 Manner Of A Lady
  537 His Lordship's Landlady
  613 Mansion For A Lady

_____

_____

WHITMORE, Loretta
MacFadden Romance:
  220 Moonlit Sea
  242 Moonlit Sea (reprint)

_____

_____

WHITNELL, Barbara
                    [Audrey Grace Hutton]
Cross Currents
Ring Of Bells   <Saga>
Song Of The Rainbird

_____

_____

WHITNEY, Amanda   <HR>
Lonely Is My Love

_____

_____

WHITNEY, Diana
                    [Diana Hinz]
Silhouette Romance:
  673 O'Brian's Daughter
  703 Liberated Man, A
  745 Scout's Honor
Silhouette Special Edition:
  508 Cast A Tall Shadow

WHITNEY, Phyllis A. (cont.)
    Secret Of The Stone Face
    Secret Of The Tiger's Eye, The
    Silver Inkwell, The
    Star For Ginny, A
    Step To The Music
    Vanishing Scarecrow
    Willow Hill
    Window For Julie, A

WHITTAKER, Charlotte Amalie
    Harlequin Gothic Romance:
    Terror At Westbourne

WHITTAL, Yvonne
    Harlequin Presents:
    318 Broken Link, The
    498 Lion Of La Roche, The
    550 Dance Of The Snake
    558 Bitter-Sweet Waters
    574 Late Harvest
    582 Web Of Silk
    590 Chains Of Gold
    598 Silver Falcon, The
    630 Dark Heritage
    726 Where Two Ways Meet
    782 Devil's Pawn, The
    790 Cape Of Misfortune
    894 Moment In Time, A
    958 Darker Side Of Loving, The
    1022 Sunset At Izilwane
    1038 Eldorado
    1118 There Is No Tomorrow
    1149 Too Long A Sacrifice
    Harlequin Romance:
    1915 East Of Barryvale
    2002 Slender Thread, The
    2077 Devil's Gateway
    2101 Where Seagulls Cry
    2128 Price Of Happiness
    2162 Handful Of Stardust
    2198 Scars Of Yesterday
    2243 Magic Of The Baobab
    2249 Love Is Eternal
    2304 Bitter Enchantment
    2358 Man From Amazibu Bay, The

WHITTAL, Yvonne (cont.)
    2412 Summer Of The Weeping Rain
    2430 Season Of Shadows
    2441 Light Within, The
    2478 Spotted Plume, The
    2538 House Of Mirrors
    2616 Ride The Wind
    2742 Wild Jasmine
    2922 Bid For Independence
         This One Night   HRS10
         Bridge To Nowhere   HRS64

WHITTENBURG, Karen
             [Karen Toller Whittenburg]
    Candlelight Ecstasy:
    216 Winds Of Heaven
    253 Golden Vows
    283 Ever A Song
    327 Distant Summer, A
    353 Nightsong
    382 That Special Smile
    423 Woman's Touch, A
    466 Magnificent Lover

WHITTENBURG, Karen Toller
                 (Karen Whittenburg)
    Harlequin American Romance:
    197 Summer Charade
    249 Matched Set
    294 Peppermint Kisses
    356 Happy Medium
    375 Day Dreamer
    Harlequin Temptation:
    303 Only Yesterday

WHITTINGTON, Harry
             [Harry Benjamin Whittington]
                     (Ashley Carter)
                  (Harriet Kathryn Myers)
                     (Blaine Stevens)
    Charro!

WHITTLE, Norah
In Search Of A Name

WHITTLE, Tyler   <HO>
[Michael Sidney Tyler-Whittle]
Bertie:
  Albert Edward, Prince Of Wales
  Edward King And Emperor
  Some Ancient Gentlemen
  Widow Of Windsor
Queen Victoria Trilogy:
  Albert's Victoria
  Young Victorian, The

WHITWORTH, Karen
McFadden Romance:
  12 Satin Promise, The
  12 Touch Of Velvet, A

WIATR, Linda Catherine
                    (Laurel Collins)

WIBBERLEY, Anna   <RE>
Time And Chance
Were This Wild Thing Wedded

WIBBERLEY, Mary
Harlequin Presents:
   89 Snow Of The Hills, The
  129 Man At La Valaise, The
  348 Savage Love
  390 Debt Of Dishonour
  419 Dream Of Thee, A
  432 Gold To Remember
  486 Devil's Causeway
  526 Law Of The Jungle
Harlequin Romance:
  1717 Black Niall
  1739 Beloved Enemy
  1775 Master Of Saramanca
  1790 Laird Of Gaela

WIBBERLEY, Mary
  1802 Benedict Man, The
  1827 Logan's Island
  1836 Kyle's Kingdom
  1879 Dark Viking
  1903 Country Of The Vine
  1924 Dark Isle, The
  1935 That Man Bryce
  1968 Wilderness Hut, The
  1994 Whispering Gate, The
  2031 Moon-Dancers, The
  2059 Silver Link, The
  2085 Dark Venturer
  2105 Wildcat Tamed
  2136 Daughter Of The Sun
  2147 Wild Goose
  2177 Lord Of The Island
  2221 Taming Of Tamsin, The
  2245 Witchwood
  2267 Love's Sweet Revenge
  2277 Dark Warrior, The
  2298 Runaway Marriage
  2316 With This Ring
  2340 Dangerous Man, A
  2364 Dangerous Marriage
  2388 Man Of Power
  2418 Fire And Steel
  2664 Golden Haven

WIDDEMER, Margaret   <HO>(Deceased)
Red Castle Woman, The
Red Cloak Flying

WIDDICOMBE, Susan
Empty Moon, The

WIDMER, Mary Lou   <HR>
Night Jasmine
In sequence:
  Lace Curtain
  Twin Oaks

710

WIETE, Robin LeAnne
  Fortune's Lady
  Rebel's Desire
  Freedom Angel

WIGGS, Susan   <HR>
                        (Susan Childress)
  Lily And The Leopard, The
  The Avon Romance:
    Briar Rose
    Moonshadow
    Wings Of Glory
  Heartfire Romance:
    Texas Wild Flower

WILBY, Jane
                        (Anne Hampson)
  Masquerade:
    1 Eleanor And The Marquis
    22 Man Of Consequence

WILCOX, Jessica
                        [Morris Hershman]
  This Wounded Passion

WILDE, Hilary
  Harlequin Romance:
    875 Doctor David Advises
    1011 Turquoise Sea, The
    1044 Paradise Island
    1077 Golden Valley, The
    1143 Journey To An Island
    1173 Red As A Rose
    1243 Isle Of Song, The
    1282 Shining Star, The
    1356 Man At Marralomeda, The
    1496 Blue Mountains Of Kabuta
    1546 Master Of Barracuda Isle

WILDE, Hilary (cont.)
    1591 Operation -
           In Search Of Love
    1624 Golden Maze, The
    1642 Fire Of Life, The
    1685 Impossible Dream, The
    1735 Temptations Of The Moon
    1768 Palace Of Gold, The
    1786 Sweeter Than Honey
    1824 Handful Of Dreams, A

WILDE, Jennifer   <HR>(Deceased)
                         [Tom E. Huff]
  Angel In Scarlet
  Dare To Love
  Once More, Miranda
  Slipper, The   <CO>
  They Call Her Dana
  In sequence:
    Love's Tender Fury
    Love Me, Marietta
    When Love Commands

WILDE, Jocelyn
                        [John Toombs]
  Bride Of The Baja
  Dark Desire Romance: <RS>
    Mists Of Passion
    Night Of Love And Peril
  Satin Swan Romance:
    Sweet Hawk Of Love

WILDE, Lauren   <HR>
                        [Joanne Redd]
  Captive Love
  Rapture's Revenge
  Nebraska Fire
  Rebel Heart
  Sweet Betrayal
  Tender Betrayal
  Texan's Lady, The

711

WILDER, Joan
       [Catherine Lanigan]
In sequence:
  Romancing The Stone
  Jewel Of The Nile, The
  NOTE: These are novelizations
    of the movies.

WILDER, Quinn
  Harlequin Romance:
  2772 That Man From Texas
  2886 To Tame A Wild Heart
  2904 Daughter Of The Stars
  3096 High Heaven
      MacNamara's Bride   HRS51

WILDING, Kay
       [Joan Wilson Hicks]
  Harlequin American Romance:
  340 Rainbow's End
  390 Stand By Me

WILDING, Lynne
  Silhouette Romance:
  793 Sheik, The

WILDMAN, Corinna
        (Corinna Cunliffe)

WILDMAN, Faye
       [Jillian Dagg]
  Silhouette Romance:
  29 Rain Lady
  48 Race For Love, A
  307 Fletcher Legacy, The
  Silhouette Special Edition:
  126 Lovesong

WILHITE, Bettie Marie
      (Elizabeth August)
      (Elizabeth Douglas)
      (Betsy Page)

WILKINS, Barbara
  Elements Of Chance

WILKINS, Gina
        (Gina Ferris)
  Harlequin Temptation:
    Hero Series:
  174 Hero In Disguise
  198 Hero For The Asking
  204 Hero By Nature
  212 Cause For Celebration
  245 Bright Idea, A
  262 Stroke Of Genius, A
  283 Could It Be Magic
  299 Changing The Rules
  309 After Hours
  337 Untaming Savage
  Pageant Romance:
  Partner For Life

WILKINSON, Frank
  Bygones

WILKINSON, Lee
  Harlequin Romance:
    Motive For Marriage HRS24

WILLARD, Barbara
  Mantlemass Chronicles: <HO><YA>
  Cold Wind Blowing, A
  Eldest Son, The
  Flight Of Swans, A
  Harrow And Harvest
  Iron Lily, The

WILLARD, Barbara (cont.)
    Lark And The Laurel, The
    Sprig Of Broom, The

WILLIAMS, Ann
                    [Peggy A. Myers]
    Silhouette Intimate Moments:
    302 Devil In Disguise
    335 Loving Lies
    358 Haunted By The Past
    384 What Lindsey Knew

WILLIAMS, Anne
                    [Anne Steinke]
    Circle Of Love:
    31 Rare Gem, The

WILLIAMS, Barbara w/
            Patricia Forsythe KNOLL
                (Charlotte Nichols)

WILLIAMS, Beryl
            [Beryl Williams Epstein]
    No Pattern For Love

WILLIAMS, Brad   <GOT>
    Stranger To Herself, A
    Tumulto

WILLIAMS, Bronwyn
    [Dixie Browning w/ Mary Williams]
    Harlequin Historical <Set#2>:
        Outer Bank Series:
        3   White Witch   &
        23   Dandelion
        47   Stormwalker   &

WILLIAMS, Bronwyn (cont.)
    67 Gideon's Fall

WILLIAMS, Claudette   <HR><RE>
                        (Melanie Davis)
    After The Storm
    Blades Of Passion
    Cassandra
    Cherry Ripe
    Cotillion For Mandy
    Desert Rose, English Moon
    Fire And Desire
    Heart Of Fancy
    Lacey (reprint Coventry #12)
    Lady Barbara
    Lady Bell
    Lady Madcap
    Lady Magic
    Lady Runaway
    Myriah
    Passion's Pride
    Sassy
    Silky
    Song Of Silkie
    Spring Gambit
    Sunday's Child
    In sequence:
        Lord Wildfire
        Regency Star
    Coventry:
        12 Lacey
        In sequence:
        41   Naughty Lady Ness
        63   Mary Sweet Mary
        99   Lady Brandy
        117   Hotspur And Taffeta
        135   Sweet Disorder
    Coventry Classic:
        Jewelene

WILLIAMS, Frances
                    [Frances Hardter]
    Silhouette Intimate Moments:
    223 Easy Target
    287 Night Secrets

WILLIAMS, Lynn (cont.)
   183 Walk A Dark Road

WILLIAMS, Margaret Wetherby
           (Margaret Erskine)

WILLIAMS, Mary   <HR>
           (Marianne Harvey)
   Stormswept
   In sequence:
     Gypsy Fires
     Gypsy Legacy

WILLIAMS, Mona   <GOT>
       [Mona Goodwyn Williams]
   Messenger, The

WILLIAMS, Norma
           (Wynn Norman)
           (Wynn Williams)

WILLIAMS, Norma w/ Dee LOPEZ
           (Dee Norman)

WILLIAMS, Patricia A. w/ Catherine
   SEIBERT   (Alexandra Lord]

WILLIAMS, Paula
         [Paula Darrington]
   Pageant Romance:
     Case For Love, A
     Lovesong

WILLIAMS, Rose   <RS>
       [W. E. Daniel Ross]
   Airport Nurse
   Bridge For Judith, A
   Nurse In Nassau

WILLIAMS, Roseanne
        [Sheila Slattery]
   Harlequin Temptation:
    237 How Sweet It Is!
    306 Magic Touch, The

WILLIAMS, Thomas
   Moon Pinnacle, The

WILLIAMS, Wright
   Fool For Love

WILLIAMS, Wynn
          [Norma Williams]
   Silhouette Romance:
    649 Starry Nights
    756 One Breathless Moment

WILLIAMSON, Amy
   Starlight, Starbright   <YA>

WILLIAMSON, C.N. w/ A.M.
   Adventure Of Princess Sylvia
   Car Of Destiny, The
   Guest Of Hercules, The
   Lady Betty Across The Sea
   Lightening Conductor, The
   My Friend The Chauffeur
   Night Of The Wedding, The
   Port Of Adventure, The
   Powers And Maxine, The
   Princess Virginia, The
   Silent Battle, The
   Winnie Childs Shop Girl

WILLIAMSON, Penelope   <HR>
        (Elizabeth Lambert)
The Avon Romance:
  Beloved Rogue
  Hearts Beguiled
  Wild Yearning, A

_____

_____

WILLMAN, Marianne   <HR>
        (Marianne Clark)
        (Sabina Clark)
Pieces Of Sky
Wildfire
Harlequin Historical <Set#2>:
  7 Vixen
 29 Rose Red, Rose White
 55 Tilly And The Tiger

_____

_____

WILLOCK, Ruth   <GOT>
I, Victoria Strange
Moonlight Trap, The
Night Of The Visitor
Street Of The Small Steps, The

_____

_____

WILLOUGHBY, Brenda
Serenade/Serenata: <Insp>
 39 Thetis Island

_____

_____

WILLOUGHBY, Lee Davis   <HO>
  (publishers pseudonym for
      writers in these series)
The Making Of The Cities <MOTC>:
 1 Cincinnati
 2 Baton Rouge
          [Jim Scafidel]

_____

Making Of America Series <MOAS>:
 1 Wilderness Seekers, The
          [Lou Cameron]

WILLOUGHBY, Lee Davis (cont.)
 2 Mountain Breed, The
          [Aaron Fletcher]
 3 Conestoga People, The
          [Jeanne Sommers]
          [Barry Myers]
 4 Forty Niners, The
          [John Toombs]
 5 Hearts Divided
          Paula Moore
          [Robert Vaughan]
 6 Builders, The
          Jeanne Sommers
          [Barry Myers]
 7 Land Rushers, The
          Elizabeth Zachary
 8 Wild And The Wayward, The
          Georgia Granger
          [George A. Granger]
 9 Texans, The
          [John Toombs]
10 Alaskans, The
          [Barry Myers]
11 Golden Staters, The
          [Charles Beardsley]
12 River People, The
          [Greg Hunt]
13 Land Grabbers, The
          [Barry Myers]
14 Ranchers, The
          [Robert Vaughan]
15 Homesteaders, The
          [Lou Cameron]
16 Frontier Healers, The
          [Aaron Fletcher]
17 Buffalo People, The
          [Barry Myers]
18 Far Islanders, The
          [Robert Vaughan]
19 Border Breed, The
          [John Toombs]
20 Boomers, The
          [Charles Beardsley]
21 Wildcatters, The
          [Walter Wager]
22 Gunfighters, The
          [Michael Avallone]
23 Cajuns, The
          [Jean Francis Webb]
24 Donner People, The
          [Barry Myers]

WILLOUGHBY, Lee Davis (cont.)
25 Creoles, The
                    [Jane Toombs]
26 Nightriders, The
                    [Mark Sufrin]
27 Sooners, The
                    [James Scafidel]
28 Express Riders, The
29 Vigilantes, The
                    [Ward Damio]
30 Soldiers Of Fortune, The
                    [George Ryan]
31 Wranglers, The
                    [Karl Meyer]
32 Baja People, The
                    [Charles Beardsley]
33 Yukon Breed, The
                    [Barry Myers]
34 Smugglers, The
                    [Richard Deming]
35 Voyageurs, The
                    [William L. DeAndrea]
36 Barbary Coasters, The
           [Joanne Metro Rothweiler
                 w/ Paul Rothweiler]
37 Whalers, The
                    [Michael Jahn]
38 Canadians, The
                    [Tad Richards]
39 Prophets People, The
                    [Leo P. Kelley]
40 Lawmen, The
                    [Richard Laymon]
41 Copper Kings, The
                    [Lou Cameron]
42 Caribbeans, The
                    [Walter Wager]
43 Trail Blazers, The
                    [Daniel Streib]
44 Gamblers, The
                    [Ian McMahan]
45 Robber Barons, The
                    [Barry Myers]
46 Assassins, The
                    [James Scafidel]
47 Bounty Hunters, The
                    [Richard Deming]
48 Texas Rangers, The
                    [John Toombs]

WILLOUGHBY, Lee Davis (cont.)
49 Outlaws, The
                    [Jane Toombs]
50 Fugitives, The
                    [John Van Zwienen]
51 Frontier Detectives, The
                    [Barry Myers]
52 Raiders, The
                    [Robert Vaughan]
53 Rough Riders, The
                    [Michael Avallone]
54 Warriors Of The Code
                    [Robert Vaughan]
55 Scarlet Sisters, The
                    [Barry Myers]
56 Sixgun Apostles, The
                    [Michael Avallone]

_____

WOMEN WHO WON THE WEST <WWWW>:
(Making Of America Series-Part 2)
1 Tempest Of Tombstone
                    [Tad Richards]
2 Dodge City Darling
                    [Stephen Winsten]
3 Duchess Of Denver
                    [Barry Myers]
4 Lost Lady Of Laramie
                    [Robert Vaughan]
5 Flame Of Virginia City
                    [John Toombs]
6 Angel Of Hangtown

7 Belle Of Fort Smith
                    [Lou Cameron]
8 Pricess Of Powder River
                    [Kathleen Lawrence]

_____

_____

WILLS, Ann Meredith
[Maralys Wills w/ Betty Jo Wills]
SuperRomance:
   62 Tempest And Tenderness
Harlequin SuperRomance:
   164 Mountain Spell

_____

_____

WILLS, Maralys
  Harlequin American Romance:
  198 Soar And Surrender
  Silhouette Special Edition:
  357 Match For Always, A

_____

_____

WILROY, Jan
  MacFadden Romance:
  118 My Heart Lies West

_____

_____

WILSON, Anthony
                    (see Lee Raintree)

WILSON, B. L.
          [Brenda Lee Eanes Wilson]
  Masseuse, The

_____

_____

WILSON, Barbara w/ Pamela Wilson
          (Margaret Summerville)

WILSON, Barbara Ker   <GOT>
  Quade Inheritance, The

_____

_____

WILSON, Brenda Lee Eanes
                    (Brenda Himrod)
                    (Megan Lane)
                    (Brenda Trent)
                    (B. L. Wilson)

WILSON, Carolyn   <GOT>
  Scent Of Violets

_____

_____

WILSON, Christine
                    [Christine Geach]
  Broken Vows
  Doubting Heart, The

_____

_____

WILSON, Ellen
                    (Laurel Evans)

WILSON, Fran
          [Frances Engle Wilson]
  Silhouette Romance:
    9 Where Mountains Wait
  138 Amber Wine
  237 Winter Promise
  251 After Autumn
  263 Souvenirs
  277 Together In Lisbon
  355 Clouds Against The Sun

_____

_____

WILSON, Frances Engle
                    (Fran Wilson)
  Avalon:
    Until Summer
    Candles In The Snow
    Dangerous Masquerade
    Yesterday's Secrets

_____

_____

WILSON, Jaye   <CO>
  Houston Heat

_____

_____

WILSON, Jeanne
  [Jeanne Patricia Pauline Wilson]
  Golden Harlot, The
  Mulatto
  Troubled Heritage
  Weep In The Sun

_____

_____

WILSON, Joyce   <HR>
                    (Sally James)
  Caresse
  Cressida
  Shadow Hill   <GOT>

_____

_____

WILSON, Mary   <GOT>
                [Mary Linn Roby]
  Changeling, The
  Wind Of Death

WILSON, Mary Anne
  Silhouette Intimate Moments:
    230 Hot-Blooded
    267 Home Fires
    292 Liar's Moon
    304 Straight From The Heart &
    336 Dream Chasers   &
    350 Brady's Law
    374 Child Of Mine

WILSON, Pamela w/ Barbara WILSON
            (Margaret Summerville)

WILSON, Patricia
  Harlequin Presents:
    934 Final Price, The
   1062 Lingering Melody, A
   1086 Ortiga Marriage, The
   1110 Moment Of Anger, A
   1125 Impossible Bargain
   1150 Beloved Intruder
   1174 Certain Affection, A
   1198 When The Gods Choose
   1221 Gathering Darkness, The
   1238 Temporary Bride
   1262 Guardian Angel
   1286 Dangerous Obsession
   1310 Secret Understanding, A
  Harlequin Romance:
   2856 Bride Of Diaz
   3102 Bond Of Destiny

WILSON, Renee Roszel
                (Renee Roszel)

WILSON, Rowena
  Candlelight:
    664 Man In A Million   <RO>
    683 Well Met By Moonlight <RO>

WILSON, Sandra   <RE>
                (Sandra Heath)
  Alice
  Cressida
  Lady Cicely, The
  Less Fortunate Then Fair
  Queen's Sister, The
  Wife Of The Kingmaker
  Woman Of Property, A
  Coventry:
    62 Jessica

WIMBERLY, Clara   <GOT>
  Emerald Tears
    Of Foxfire Manor, The
  Moonwatch

WIND, David
                [David M. Wind]
                (Monica Barrie)
                (Jenifer Dalton)
                (Marilyn Davids)
  Queen Of Knights   <HF>

WIND, Ruth
                [Barbara Samuel]
  Silhouette Special Edition:
    555 Strangers On A Train
    588 Summer's Freedom
    635 Light Of Day

WINSPEAR, Violet   (Deceased)
Harlequin Presents:
   5 Devil In A Silver Room
   6 Honey Is Bitter, The
   9 Wife Without Kisses
  12 Dragon Bay
  15 Little Nobody, The
  18 Kisses And The Wine, The
  21 Unwilling Bride, The
  24 Pilgrim's Castle
  27 House Of Strangers
  30 Bride Of Lucifer
  33 Forbidden Rapture
  36 Love's Prisoner
  39 Tawny Sands
  42 Strange Waif, The
  50 Glass Castle, The
  70 Chateau Of St. Avrell, The
  90 Noble Savage, The
  98 Girl At Goldenhawk, The
 114 Palace Of The Pomegranate
 122 Devil's Darling, The
 130 Dearest Demon
 138 Satan Took A Bride
 142 Darling Infidel
 146 Child Of Judas, The
 162 Sin Of Cynara, The
 174 Burning Sands, The
 178 Sun Tower, The
 214 Love In A Stranger's Arms
 222 Passionate Sinner, The
 226 Love Battle, A
 230 Time Of The Temptress
 238 Loved And The Feared, The
 246 Awakening Of Alice, The
 288 Valdez Marriage, The
 300 Desire Has No Mercy
 324 Sheik's Captive, The
 354 Love Is The Honey
 420 Girl Possessed, A
 450 Love's Agony
 492 No Man Of Her Own
 566 Man She Married, The
 718 By Love Bewitched
 734 Bride's Lace
 854 Sun Lord's Woman
1006 Silken Barbarity, A
Harlequin Romance:
 884 Nurse At Cap Flamingo

WINSPEAR, Violet (cont.)
 921 Desert Doctor
1008 Bride's Dilemma
1032 Beloved Tyrant
1080 Viking Stranger, The
1111 Tower Of The Captive, The
1208 Tender Is The Tyrant
1267 Court Of The Veils
1318 Palace Of The Peacocks
1344 Dangerous Delight, The
1399 Blue Jasmine
1434 Cazalet Bride, The
1472 Beloved Castaway
1514 Castle Of The Seven
      Lilacs, The
1555 Raintree Valley
1580 Black Douglas
1616 Pagan Island, The
1637 Silver Slave, The
1658 Dear Puritan
1680 Rapture Of The Desert
2682 Secret Fire
Harlequin Signature Edition:
  Honeymoon, The
  House Of Storms

_____

_____

WINSTEN, Stephen
        (see Jonathan Scofield)
  (see Lee Davis Willoughby <WWWW>)
  Whiskey Saga: In sequence: <HS>
  Moonshine County
  Cumberland Lightning
  Bluegrass Spirits

_____

_____

WINSTON, Betty   <HO>
  Africans, The   <IMS>

_____

_____

WINSTON, Daoma   <GOT><HR><RS>
  Adventuress, The
  Carnaby Curse, The
  Castle Of Closing Doors

WINSTON, Daoma (cont.)
  Death Watch, The
  Dennison Hill
  Devil's Daughter, The
  Devil's Princess, The
  Dream Killers, The
  Emerald Station
  Fall River Line, The   <Saga>
  Flight Of The Fallen Angel
  Gallows Way
  Golden Valley, The
  Haversham Legacy, The
  House Of Mirror Images
  Inheritance, The
  Kingdom's Castle
  Long And Living Shadow, The
  Lotteries, The
  Love Of Lucifer, The
  Mansion Of Smiling Masks
  Maybe This Time   <CO>
  Mayeroni Myth, The
  Mills Of The Gods
  Moderns, The
  Moorhaven
  Pity My Love
  Return, The
  Return To Elysium
  Secrets Of
    Cromwell Crossing, The
  Seminar In Evil
  Shadow Of An Unknown Woman
  Shadow On Mercer Mountain
  Sinister Stone
  Traficante Treasure, The
  Trap, The
  Unforgotten, The
  Vampire Curse, The
  Victim, The
  Visit After Dark, A
  Wakefield Witches, The ⁄
  Walk Around The Square

  _____

  _____

WINSTON, Donna
  MacFadden Romance:
    112 Whisper At Daybreak

  _____

  _____

WINTER, Abigail   <GOT>
                    [Monroe Schere]
  Olivia's Story
  Smiling Dragon, The
  Whispering Caverns

  _____

  _____

WINTER, Alice   <RS>
  Velvet Bubble, The

  _____

  _____

WINTER, Pat   <HR>
                 [Pat DeGraw Winter]
  Madoc
  River Of Destiny

  _____

  _____

WINTERS, Donna
  Promise Romance: <Insp>
    10 For The Love Of Roses
  Serenade/Saga: <HR><Insp>
    34 Elizabeth Of Saginaw Bay

  _____

  _____

WINTERS, Rebecca
                    [Rebecca Burton]
  Harlequin Romance:
    2953 Blind To Love
    3047 Fully Involved
    3090 Story Princess, The

  _____

  _____

WINTHROP, Caroline   <RS>
  Icons

  _____

  _____

WINTHROP, Wilma   <RS>
  Island Of The Accursed
  Tryst With Terror

  _____

  _____

WIRKNER, Linda
  Caprice Romance: <YA>
    67 Summer Romance

WISDOM, Linda
            [Linda Randall Wisdom]
  Silhouette Romance:
    49 Dancer In The Shadows
    95 Fourteen Karat Beauty
   132 Bright Tomorrow
   166 Dreams From The Past
   241 Snow Queen
  Silhouette Special Edition:
    27 Man With Doubts, A
    74 Unspoken Past
   160 Island Rogue
   190 Business As Usual
   220 World Of Their Own, A
  Torch:
    Forbidden Love

WISDOM, Linda Randall
          [Linda Jean Randall Wisdom]
                  (Linda Wisdom)
  Only Love
  Candlelight Ecstasy:
   196 Guardian Angel
   249 For Better Or For Worse
   321 Gentle Protector
   368 Birds Of A Feather
   397 Written In The Stars
   412 All A Man Could Want
  Candlelight Ecstasy Supreme:
    31 Caution: Man At Work
    58 Love Has Many Voices
   126 Love To Last Forever, A
  Candlelight Supreme:
   138 Splendor At Dawn
   151 Murphy's Charm
   173 Perilous Affair, A
  Harlequin American Romance:
   250 We Give Thanks
   284 Lady's Choice
   293 Appearances Are Deceiving
   310 Code Of Silence

WISDOM, Linda Randall (cont.)
   325 Sins Of The Past
   350 Man For Maggie, A
   372 O'Malley's Quest
   382 Voices In The Night

WISDOM, Penelope
                  [Penelope Stuart]
  Silhouette Desire:
   232 Starlight

WISE, Winifred
  Wildwood

WISELY, Charlotte
            [Charlotte Hastings]
  Rapture Romance:
     4 Welcome Intruder
    14 Love Has No Pride
    40 Passionate Enterprise

WISLER, G. C.
            [Gene Charles Wisler]
  Caprice Romance: <YA>
     7 Sunrise

WISSMANN, Ruth   <RS>
            [Ruth Leslie Wissmann]
  Celebration For Murder
  Claws Of The Cross, The
  Desert Of Darkness
  Dreamer Beware
  Shadow Of Shiela Ann, The
  To Hang A Witch

WITHERS, Julia   <GOT><RS>
  Echo In A Dark Wind
  Shuttered Room, The
  Won Ton Ton

WITTE, Glenna Finley
                  (Glenna Finley)

WITTON, Eileen
                  (Janice Bennett)
                  (Janice N. Bennett)
  American Regency Romance:
    Lady No More, A
    Racing Hearts

WITTON, Winifred
  Harlequin Regency Romance:
    46 Lady Elmira's Emerald
    55 Double Deception

WOHL, Burton
  All In The Family
  Amigos, The
  Casey's Shadow
  Cold Wind In August, A
  Rollercoaster
  Soldier In Paradise
  Ten Tola Bears, The
  That Certain Summer
  Network

WOJHOSKI, B.
            [Barbara M. Wojhoski]
  Harlequin Intrigue:
    112 Deception By Design

WOJHOSKI, Barbara M.
                  (Laurel Pace)
                  (B. Wojhoski)

WOLF, Bernice
  Candlelight:
    533 Ville-Marie   <IN>

WOLF, Joan   <HR><RE>
  American Duchess, The
  Counterfeit Marriage, The
  Difficult Truce, A
  Double Deception, A
  Fool's Masquerade
  Highland Sunset
  His Lordship's Mistress
  Kind Of Honor, A
  London Season, A
  Lord Richard's Daughter
  Margarita
  Rebel And The Rose, The
  Rebellious Ward, The
  Scottish Lord, The
  Wild Irish Rose
  Medieval Trilogy:
    Road To Avalon, The
    Born Of The Sun
    Edge Of Light, The
  Rapture Romance:
    8   Summer Storm
    19   Change Of Heart
    58   Beloved Stranger
    73   Affair Of The Heart
    89   Portrait Of A Love
    102 Fashionable Affair, A

WOLF, Susan Whittlesey
                  (Antonio Tyler)

WOLFE, Elizabeth   <GOT>
  Ice Castle

724

WOLFE, Lois
                    (Gillian Wyeth)

WOLFF, Ruth   <GOT>(Deceased)
  Abdication, The
  Crack In The Sidewalk, A   <YA>
  Hawthorne (I, Keturah)
  Space Between
  Trace Of Footprints

  _____

  _____

WOLFF, Victoria   <HR>
  Breakdown
  Fabulous City
  Spell Of Egypt

  _____

  _____

WOLFSON, Robert
          [Robert Joseph Wolfson]
  Dancers And Lovers

  _____

  _____

WOLFSON, Victor   <GOT>
  Cabral
  Lonely Steeple, The
  Midsummer Madness

  _____

  _____

WOLMAN, David
  Whispers On The Wind

  _____

  _____

WOLTHAUSEN, Linda Sherwood w/
          Catherine Lee DONICH
              (Catherine Leigh)

WOMACK, Burt
  This Savage Land

  _____

  _____

WOMAN'S DESTINY, A <AWD>   <HO>
  Woman Of San Francisco, A
                    Lynn Erickson
  Woman Of New Orleans, A
                    Rochel DeNorre
  Woman Of Boston, A
                    Alicia Medows
  Woman Of New York, A
                    Marcia Mager
  Woman Of Chicago, A
                    Kit Prate

  _____

  _____

WOMEN OF THE WEST <WOW>   <HO>
  1 Blue Fire
                    Emma Harrington
  2 Silver Eyes
                    Laurel Collins
  3 Savage River
                    E. P. Murray
  4 Golden Fury
                    Florence Moyer

  _____

  _____

WOMEN WEST TRILOGY   <WWT>
  Branigan Family:
    Promised Sunrise
                    Robin Lee Hatcher
    Beyond The Horizon
                    Connie Mason
    Thunder At Twilight
                    Hannah D. Howell

  _____

  _____

WOOD, Barbara
  Curse This House
  Domina   <MED>
  Green City In The Sun   <MS>
  Hounds And Jackals
  Magdalene Scrolls, The
  Soul Flame   <HS>
  Vital Signs   <MED>

  _____

  _____

WOOD, Deborah   <GOT>
  Mistress Of Soundcliff Manor

WOODHOUSE, Sarah
  India Widow
  Season Of Mists, A

WOOD, Nuria
                [Josephine Nobisso]
  Second Chance At Love:
    132 With No Regrets
  To Have And To Hold:
    7 Family Plan, The

WOODIWISS, Kathleen E.   <HR>
  Ashes In The Wind
  Come Love A Stranger
  Flame And The Flower, The
  Rose In Winter, A
  Shanna
  So Worthy My Love
  Wolf And The Dove, The

WOOD, Sara
  Harlequin Presents:
    981 Passion's Daughter
   1070 Pure Temptation
   1102 Wicked Invader
   1134 Savage Hunger
   1166 Count's Vendetta, The
   1182 Tender Persuasion
   1206 No Gentle Loving
   1302 Threat Of Possession
   1318 Love Not Dishonour
  Harlequin Romance:
   2814 Perfumes Of Arabia
   3066 Master Of Cashel

WOODLAND, Eva
                (Nicole De Lyn)
  MacFadden Romance:
    145 Love Like No Other

WOODLEY, Richard
  Zebulon Pike:
    Pioneer Destiny   <AES:#7>

WOOD, Tonya
                (Courtney Ryan)
  Loveswept:
    Sexiest Man Alive, The

WOODRUFF, Marian
                [Eileen Goudge]
  Sweet Dreams: <YA>
    26 This Must Be Magic
    35 Forbidden Love
    42 Perfect Match, The
    48 Dial L For Love
    63 Kiss Me, Creep

WOODBURY, Leonora   <RE>
                [Ellen Kelman]
  Game Of Hearts
  Runaway Countess, The

WOODRUM, Lon
  A Hearth Romance:
    20 Trumpets In The Morning

WOODCOCK, Maureen w/ Antoinette
  BRONSON   (Maureen Bronson)

WOODS, Eleanor
    [Eleanor Woods Rogers]
Candlelight Ecstasy:
  84 Love Has No Mercy
 128 Gentle Whisper, A
 141 Loving Exile
 174 Tempestuous Challenge
 199 Sensuous Persuasion
 224 Passionate Pursuit
 236 Beguiled By A Stranger
 251 No Love Lost
 270 High Stakes
 297 Forgotten Dreams
 325 Where Love May Lead
 358 Relentless Pursuit
 393 Evening The Score
 408 Mystery Lady
 472 Triple Threat
 508 Lover's Mystique, A
Candlelight Ecstasy Supreme:
  57 Hidden Maneuvers
  92 Just For The Asking
 121 Beyond A Doubt
Candlelight Supreme:
 132 Forbidden Refuge, A
 154 Breathless Temptation
 163 Texas Wildfire
 183 Reckless Encounter
Harlequin SuperRomance:
 307 Second Time Lucky
 395 Above Suspicion
MacFadden Romance:
 142 Afraid To Love
 144 Return To Love
 231 Echoes Of Love
Other MacFadden:
  If Not For You

WOODS, Margery
      (Rebecca Caine)
      (Margery Hilton)

WOODS, Sherryl
    [Sherryl Ann Woods]
      (Alexandra Kirk)
      (Suzanne Sherrill)
 (see Silhouette Summer Sizzlers)
Thrown For A Loss

WOODS, Sherryl (cont.)
  Lovestruck:
    In sequence: <RS>
    Reckless
    Body And Soul
    Stolen Moments
  Second Chance At Love:
 326 Kiss Away, A
 342 Prince Among Men, A
 375 All For Love
 398 Best Intentions
 412 Two's Company
 430 Prince Charming Replies
  Silhouette Desire:
 309 Not At Eight, Darling
 329 Yesterday's Love
 345 Come Fly With Me
 375 Gift Of Love, A
 431 Can't Say No
 472 Heartland
 521 One Touch Of Moondust
 601 Next Time...Forever
 620 Fever Pitch
  Silhouette Special Edition:
 425 Safe Harbor
 446 Never Let Go
 484 Edge Of Forever
 522 In Too Deep
 573 Mis Liz's Passion   &
 595 Tea And Destiny   &
 669 My Dearest Cal
  Velvet Glove: <RS>
  21 Jamaican Midnight

WOODWARD, Daphne
  Second Chance At Love:
  45 Intriguing Lady   <RE>

WOODWARD, Edward   <GOT>
  House Of Terror, The

WOODWARD, Jean
  Avalon:
    Brandy's Awakening
    Eyes Of Love
    Flowers Of Love
    Love's Inheritance
    Smile Of Love
    Summer At Whispering Hope
    That Tender Yearning
    Valley Of Romance

WOODWARD, Lilian
                    [John Marsh]
  In Another's Likeness

WOOLF, Victoria
                  [Sheila Holland]
  Harlequin Romance:
    2273 Sweet Compulsion

WOOLFOLK, William
  Beautiful Couple, The
  Hardcore
  Maggie
  My Name Is Morgan
  Overlords, The
  President's Doctor, The
  We Two

WOOLRICH, Cornell
  [Cornell George Hopley-Woolrich]
                  (George Hopley)
  Angels Of Darkness
  Bride Wore Black
  Night Has A Thousand Eyes
  Nightwebs

WORBOYS, Anne   <RS>
  [Annette Isobel Eyre Worboys]
                    (Annette Eyre)
                    (Vicky Maxwell)
  Aurora Rose   <HS>
  Barrancourt Destiny, The
  Bhunda Jewels, The
  Every Man A King
  High Hostage
  Lion Of Delos, The
  Rendezvous With Fear
  Run, Sara, Run
  Way Of The Tamarisk, The

WORLEY, Dorothy
  Brighter Dawn, A
  Cinderella Nurse
  Dr. Kilbourne Comes Home
  Girl Friday
  Heart Remembers, The
  Candlelight:
    48 High Road, The

WORTHINGTON, Avis   <HR>
  Bitter Honey
  Love, Sacred And Profane
  Love's Willing Servant

WORTHY, Judith   <M&B>
  Nurse With Wings
  Runaway Nurse

WOUK, Herman
  Inside Out
  Marjorie Morningstar
  Youngblood Hawk
  In sequence: <HS>
    Winds Of War, The
    War And Remembrance

WRAY, Evelyn   <GOT>
  Avalon:
    Horrow At Henning House
  _____

  _____

WRIGHT, Betty   <CO>
  Her Best Friend's Husband
  Man That She Married, The
  Memoirs Of A Doctor's Wife
  Memoirs Of A Married Woman

  _____

  _____

WRIGHT, Cynthia   <HR>
              [Cynthia Wright Hunt]
                 (Devon Lindsay)
  Brighter Than Gold
  In sequence:
    You And No Other
    Battle For Love, A
  Story Order:
    Silver Storm
    Caroline
    Touch The Sun
    Spring Fires
    Surrender The Stars

  _____

  _____

WRIGHT, Don
               [Donald K. Wright]
  Captives, The
  Woodsman, The

  _____

  _____

WRIGHT, Francesca
                 [Denise Robins]
  Loves Of Lucrezia, The
  She Devil

  _____

  _____

WRIGHT, Lucretia
                 (Alicia Knight)

WRIGHT, Patricia   <HR>
  [Mary Patricia Matthews Wright]
  Conflict On The Nile
  Heart Of The Storm
  Journey Into Fire
  Shadow Of The Rock
  Space Of The Heart, A
  Storms Of Fate
  In sequence: <HO><Epic>
    I Am England
    That Near And Distant Place

  _____

  _____

WRIGHT, Scott
               (Annjeanette Scott)
  Black Semesters
  Count Of Van Rheeden Castle, The

  _____

  _____

WRIGHT, Wendy
  Love Can Wait

  _____

  _____

WRITTEN IN THE STARS <WITS>
  Silhouette Romance:
    766 Undoing Of Justin Starbuck
                   Marie Ferrarella
    772 Man From The North Country
                      Laurie Paige
    778 For Heaven's Sake
                      Brenda Trent
    784 Thank Your Lucky Stars
                        Lydia Lee
    790 Man From Natchez, The
                   Elizabeth August

  _____

  _____

WUNSCH, Josephine   <YA>
  First Love From Silhouette:
    2   Girl In The Rough
    77   Free As A Bird
    139 Breaking Away
    182 Perfect 10, The

WUNSCH, Josephine   <YA>
  Crosswinds Keepsake:
    5 Lucky In Love
    42 Between Us
  Wildfire:
    Class Ring

WYATT, Stephanie
  Harlequin Presents:
    1054 This Man's Magic
    1254 Friday's Child

WYCKOFF, Julie
  Avalon:
    When Two Hearts Are One

WYDEN, Barbara
  Rich Wife, A   <HS>

WYETH, Gillian   <HR>
                    [Lois Wolfe]
  Dare I Love?

WYETH, Sharon Dennis
  Sweet Dreams: <YA>
    137 Rocky Romance

WYLAND, Amanda
  Passionate
  MacFadden Romance:
    33 Mountains Of The Moon
    50 Midnight Encounte

WYND, Oswald
                [Oswald Morris Wynd]
  Forty Days, The
  Ginger Tree, The
  Hawser Pirates

WYNDHAM, Esther
                    [Mary Lutyens]
  Harlequin Classic:
    82   Black Charles   (680)
    102 Above The Clouds   (846)
    111 Once You
           Have Found Him   (880)
    151 Tiger Hall   (936)
  Harlequin Romance:
    846   Above The Clouds
    880   Once You Have Found Him
    936   Tiger Hall
    1024 House Of Discontent, The
    1127 Blue Rose, The

WYNN, Patricia
                    [Patricia Ricks]
  Harlequin Regency Romance:
    Parson's Pleasure, The
    12 Sophie's Halloo
    24 Lord Tom
    38 Jack On The Box

WYNNE, Annabel
  Lady In Doubt, A   <VIC>

WYSOR, Bettie   <RS>
  Stranger's Eyes, A
  To Remember Tina

YATES, Judith
                              [Judith Yoder]
    Second Chance At Love:
        207 Tempting Magic, A
        236 Stars In Her Eyes

YALE, Diane   <GOT>
    Avalon:
        Dark Terror
        Deadly Manor
        Veiled Cliffs

YERBY, Frank   <HR>
                              [Frank Garvin Yerby]
    An Odor Of Sanctity
    Benton's Row
    Bride Of Liberty
YANKE, Phyllis   Captain Rebel
    April Has Cupid Wings (April   Dahomean, The
        Has Wings)   Darkness At Ingraham's Crest, A
                               Devil's Laughter, The
                               Devilseed
                               Fairoaks
                               Floodtide
YANSICK, Susan McGovern w/   Foxes Of Harrow, The
                Christine T. HEALY   Garfield Honor, The
                    (Erin Yorke)   Gillian
                               Girl From Storyville, The
YAPP, Kathleen   Goat Song
    Serenade/Saga: <HR><Insp>   Golden Hawk, The
        15 Speak Softly, Love   Griffins Way
    Silhouette Inspirations: Hail The Conquering Hero
        6 Fire In My Heart   Jarrett's Jade
        19 To Love And Cherish   Judas My Brother
                               McKenzie's Hundred
                               Old Gods Laugh, The
                               Pride's Castle
                               Rose For Ana Maria, A
YARBO, Chelsea Quinn   Saracen Blade, The
                (Vanessa Pryor)   Serpent And The Staff, The
    Crusader's Torch   <HF>   Speak Now
                               Tobias And The Angel
                               Treasure Of Pleasant Valley, The
                               Vixens, The
                               Voyage Unplanned, The
YARDE, Jeanne Betty Frances   Western   <Saga>
                (Joan Hunter)   Woman Called Fancy, A
              (Jeanne Montague)

YATES, Helen Eva
    Fire Orchid

YODER, Judith
                        (Judith Yates)
  Harlequin American Romance:
    228 September Glow

YORK, Alison   <HR>
                 [Christopher Nicole]
  Fire And The Rope, the
  Scented Sword, The
  Haggard
  Haggard Inheritance
  Harlequin Romance:
    2880 No Sad Song
    2970 That Dear Perfection
          Secret Truth, A   HRS52
    3042 Maxton Bequest, The
          Summer In Eden   HRS62

YORK, Amanda
                   [Joan Dial]
  Beloved Enemy
  Echoes Of Love
  Somewhere In The Whirlwind
  Silhouette Desire:
    205 Man's Best Friend
  Silhouette Intimate Moments:
    56 An Old Fashioned Love
    107 Stardust And Sand

YORK, Carol Beach
  Caprice Romance: <YA>
    52 Not Your Type
  Heart To Heart Romance: <YA>
    Likely Story, A
    Make A Wish
  Heavenly Romance: <YA>
    Candles In The Window

YORK, Charlotte
  Seven Oaks

YORK, Elizabeth   <GOT>
       [Margaret Elizabeth York]
  Medea Legend, The
  Rider On A Pale Horse

YORK, Georgia   <HR>
  Savage Conquest
  Savage Key
  Savannah Grey

YORK, Helen   <RS>
  Pennhaven
  Venetian Charade, A

YORK, Margaret Elizabeth
               (Margaret Abbey)
             (Joanna Makepeace)
               (Elizabeth York)

YORK, Pauline
           [Marcia Yvonne Howl]
  Harlequin Regency Romance:
    Torpid Duke, The

YORK, Rebecca
  [Ruth Glick w/ Eileen Buckholtz]
  Peregrine Connection Books: <RM>
    Talons Of The Falcon
    Flight Of The Raven
    In Search Of The Dove

YOUNG, Frederic
  Many Ingenious Lovely
    Things   <Saga>

YOUNG, Karen
                     [Karen Stone]
  Harlequin SuperRomance:
    341 All My Tomorrows
    371 Compelling Connection
  Silhouette Romance:
    212 Yesterday's Promise
    284 Irrestible Intruder
    380 Wilder Passion, A
    433 Darling Detective
    481 Forever Kind, The
    517 Maggie Mine
    575 Sarah's Choice

YOUNG, Marilyn
  Promise Romance: <Insp>
    5 Heart Of The Storm, The

YOUNG, Marsha   <RS>
  Chateau In Brittany, A

YOUNG, Mary Ann
  Candlelight:
    71 Key To The Past
    119 Shimmering Stones, The
    197 Dream Of Her Own, A
  Candlelight Ecstasy:
    16 Besieged By Love

YOUNG, Mary Jo
                     (Jenny Nolan)

YOUNG, Rena
  Harlequin Romance:
    2670 Catch A Falling Star

YOUNG, Sandra
                     (Brittany Young)

YOUNG, Selwyn Marie
  Silhouette Desire:
    369 Forever Mine

YOUNGBLOOD, Ila Dell   <HR>
  Bitter Promise

YOUNGBLOOD, Marilyn
  Cherish Romance:
    5 Heart Of The Storm, The
  First Love From Silhouette: <YA>
    76 Send In The Clowns
    86 Boy Next Door, The
    103 After Midnight
    109 Snap Judgement
    133 Manhatten Melody
    143 Hungarian Rhapsody
    162 Riding High

YOUNT, John
                   [John Alonzo Yount]
  Hardcastle

YUTANG, Lin
  Red Peony, The

ZACH, Cheryl
            [Cheryl Byrd Zach]
   First Love From Silhouette: <YA>
     104 Frog Princess, The
     131 Waiting For Amanda
     156 Fortune's Child
   Harlequin Temptation:
     19 Twice A Fool

ZACH, Cheryl Byrd
           (Jennifer Cole-YA)
           (Cheryl Zach)
   Harlequin Temptation:
     19 Twice A Fool

ZACHARY, Elizabeth   <HR>
   Blazing Vixen
   Dynasty Of Desire
   Land Rushers, The   <MOAS:#7>

ZACHARY, Hugh   <HO>
        (see Rebecca Drury)
   Bitter Victory
   Desert Battle
   Second Chance
   Sisters And Daughters
   Sierra Leone Series: <HS>
     1 Flight To Freedom
     2 Freedom's Passion
     3 Treasure Of Hope
     4 Freedom's Victory

ZACHARY, Hugh And Elizabeth   <CO>
   Of Love And Battle

ZAHN, Sara   <GOT>
   Avalon:
     Beckoning Ghost, The
     Nightmare At Greenwood Hall

ZALDIVAR, Jennie
        (Jennifer Roberts)

ZAROULIS, Nancy/Nancy L.
   Call The Darkness Light   <Saga>
   Certain Kinds Of Loving   <CO>
   Last Waltz, The   <Saga>
   Poe Papers: A Tale Of Passion

ZAVALA, Ann   <HR>
   Mormon Wives

ZAWADSKY, Patience   <GOT>
   Demon Of Raven's Cliff, The

ZAYNE, Valerie
        [Leigh Shaheen]
   Rapture Romance:
     79 Silver Dawn

ZEIG, Joan w/ Linda BURAK
      (Alicia Meadowes)

ZEIGER, Helane
   Caprice Romance: <YA>
     29 Love Byte
     54 Ski Bum

ZEITLIN, Marianne Langner
Mira's Passage

ZELDIS, Chayym
Forbidden Love, A   <Saga>

ZELLERBACH, Merla   <CO>
Cavett Manor
Love The Giver
Sugar
Wildes Of Nob Hill, The

ZIDE, Donna Comeaux   <HR>
Above The Wind And Fire
Promise Me Paradise
Savage In Silk
In sequence:
  Caress And Conquer
  Lost Splendor
Tapestry: <HR>
  83 Chelaine

ZIOBRO, Marie
Harlequin American Romance:
  59 Strange Bedfellows

ZIRKELBACH, Thelma
                    (Lorna Michaels)

ZODIAC GOTHIC SERIES <ZGS>:
Home To The Night-<Capricorn>
                    Julia Thatcher
Waiting Eyes, The-<Aquarius>
                    Evelyn Bond
Temple Of Darkness-<Pisces>
                    Marilyn Ross

ZODIAC GOTHIC SERIES (cont.)
Fear Stalks The Bayou-<Aries>
                    Juanita Coulson
Moormist-<Taurus>
                    Georgina Ferrand
Tempest At Summer's End-<Gemini>
                    Julia Thatcher
Twilight Return-<Cancer>
                    Jean Kimbro
Drums Of Darkness-<Leo>
                    Marion Z. Bradley
Cave Of The Moaning Wind-<Virgo>
                    Jean DeWeese
Inherit The Mirage-<Libra>
                    Julia Thatcher
Web Of Guilt-<Scorpio>
                    Jean DeWeese
Night Gleams-<Sagittarius>
                    Julia Thatcher

ZUCKERMAN, Suzanne
Heavenly Romance: <YA>
  Two Of A Kind

ZUMWALT, Eva   <GOT><HR><RE><RS>
Briarlea
Mansion Of Dark Mist
Masquerade Of Evil   <CGS:#21>
Sun Dust
Unforgiving, The
Yearning Years
Starlight Romance:
  Elusive Heart, The
  Love Sweet Charity
  When The Heart Remembers

ZWIENEN, John Van
                    (see Jonathan Scofield)

CAMFIELD ROMANCE
Berkley/Jove

1	The Poor Governess	45	An Angel Runs Away
2	Winged Victory	46	Forced To Marry
3	Lucky In Love	47	Bewildered In Berlin
4	Love And The Marquis	48	Wanted-A Wedding Ring
5	A Miracle In Music	49	The Earl Escapes
6	Light Of The Gods	50	Starlight Over Tunis
7	Bride To A Brigand	51	The Love Puzzle
8	Love Comes West	52	Love And Kisses
9	A Witch's Spell	53	Sapphires In Siam
10	Secrets	54	A Caretaker Of Love
11	The Storm Of Love	55	Secrets Of The Heart
12	Moonlight On The Sphinx	56	Riding In The Sky
13	White Lilac	57	Lovers In Lisbon
14	Revenge Of The Heart	58	Love Is Invincible
15	The Island Of Love	59	The Goddess Of Love
16	Theresa And A Tiger	60	An Adventure Of Love
17	Love is Heaven	61	The Herb For Happiness
18	Miracle For A Madonna	62	Only A Dream
19	A Very Unusual Wife	63	Saved By Love
20	The Peril And The Prince	64	Little Tongues Of Fire
21	Alone And Afraid	65	A Chieftain Finds Love
22	Temptation Of A Teacher	66	A Lovely Liar
23	Royal Punishment	67	The Perfume Of The Gods
24	The Devilish Deception	68	A Knight In Paris
25	Paradise Found	69	Revenge Is Sweet
26	Love Is A Gamble	70	The Passionate Princess
27	A Victory For Love	71	Solita And The Spies
28	Look With Love	72	The Perfect Pearl
29	Never Forget Love	73	Love Is A Maze
30	Helga In Hiding	74	A Circus For Love
31	Safe At Last	75	The Temple Of Love
32	Haunted	76	The Bargain Bride
33	Crowned With Love	77	The Haunted Heart
34	Escape	78	Real Love Or Fake
35	The Devil Defeated	79	Kiss From A Stranger
36	The Secret Of The Mosque	80	A Very Special Love
37	A Dream In Spain	81	The Necklace Of Love
38	The Love Trap	82	A Revolution Of Love
39	Listen To Love	83	The Marquis Wins
40	The Golden Cage	84	Love Is The Key
41	Love Casts Out Fear	85	Love At First Sight
42	A World Of Love	86	The Taming Of A Tigress
43	Dancing On A Rainbow	88	The Earl Rings A Belle
44	Love Joins The Clans		

OTHER BARBARA CARTLAND ROMANCE

BANTAM

Barbara Cartland's Library Of Love

1 The Sheik
   E. M. Hull
2 His Hour
   Elinor Glyn
3 The Knave Of Diamonds
   Ethel M. Dell
4 A Safety Match
   Ian Hay
5 The Hundredth Chance
   Ethel M. Dell
6 The Reason Why
   Elinor Glyn
7 The Way Of An Eagle
   Ethel M. Dell
8 The Vicissitudes
     Of Evangeline
   Elinor Glyn
9 The Bars Of Iron
   Ethel M. Dell
10 Man And Maid
   Elinor Glyn
11 The Sons Of The Sheik
   E. M. Hull
12 Six Days
   Elinor Glyn
13 Rainbow In The Spray
   Pamela Wynne
14 The Great Moment
   Elinor Glyn
15 Greatheart
   Ethel M. Dell
16 The Broad Highway
   Jeffery Farnol
17 The Sequence
   Elinor Glyn
18 Charles Rex
   Ethel M. Dell
19 Ashes Of Desire
20 The Price Of Things
   Elinor Glyn
21 Tetherstones
   Ethel M. Dell
22 The Amateur Gentleman
   Jeffrey Farnol
23 His Official Fiancee
   Berta Ruck

House Of Romance

Trio 1:

Cupids And Coronets
  Charles Stuart

Love Treasure Trove
  Julia Davis

The Hearts Own Sweet Music
  Georgina Ferrand

Trio 2:

Topaz
  Francis Hart

The Troubled Summer
  Janet Roscoe

A Girl Called Debbie
  Elizabeth Brennan

Ancient Wisdom Series:

1 The Forgotten City
2 The House Of Fulfillment
3 The Romance of Two Worlds
4 Black Light

Hardback:

I See The Miraculous
Love In The Clouds
Imperial Splendor

Other:

Captive Heart, The
Danger By The Nile
Elizabeth In Love
Fire Of Love
Love In The Dark
Horizons Of Love, The
Smuggled Heart, The